BOVIDS OF THE WORLD
Antelopes, Gazelles, Cattle, Goats, Sheep, and Relatives

José R. Castelló

Foreword by
Brent Huffman and Colin Groves

PRINCETON UNIVERSITY PRESS
PRINCETON AND OXFORD

Published by Princeton University Press,
41 William Street, Princeton, New Jersey 08540
In the United Kingdom: Princeton University Press, 6 Oxford Street,
Woodstock, Oxfordshire OX20 1TW
nathist.princeton.edu

ISBN 978-0-691-16717-6

British Library Cataloging-in-Publication Data is available

Production and design by José R. Castelló, Madrid, Spain.
Printed in China

10 9 8 7 6 5 4 3 2

CONTENTS

FOREWORD

I have been waiting for a book like *Bovids of the World* to be published since I was in seventh grade. In my science class that year, we were given the assignment of creating an identification key for 20 closely related animals. Having just completed a report on rumination, I naturally chose ruminants. ("Will you be able to find enough species for this assignment?" worried my teacher.) My childhood animal encyclopedia readily yielded 20 species, and although they were all interesting, the ones with horns immediately caught my eye. The horns, with their myriad ridges, curls, and twists, were like stunning pieces of art, the animals that possessed them simply beautiful. By the time I had finished the project, I was hooked. I began scouring my local library, searching for photos of these fabulous horned animals (or, scientifically speaking, the family Bovidae), but all I could find were scattered images. Even when I was in university, the specialized zoological library failed to yield an exclusive and all-encompassing guide to this family of hoofed mammals. So when José R. Castelló disclosed that he was embarking on a project to display every living species of the family Bovidae in a single volume, I was thrilled — and also apprehensive. Thrilled because such a volume would celebrate these species in a way that had never been accomplished before. And apprehensive because, although *Bovids of the World* has a simple concept, bringing it to fruition would be a massive undertaking.

For starters, Bovidae is the largest and most diverse group of hoofed mammals: it contains an astounding 279 species. (My science teacher needn't have been concerned.) These species show incredible variation in physical attributes, habitat preferences, physiology, and behavior but are all united by the presence of unbranched hollow horns. In no other ungulate family is there such a contrast in size between the largest and smallest species: the massive Asian Wild Water Buffalo (profiled on page 596) can weigh up to 1,200 kg at maturity, while the diminutive Royal Antelope (page 36) may weigh just 1.5 kg as an adult — that's nearly a thousand-fold difference! There is so much variation within the Bovidae that most people fail to recognize that it is, in fact, a unified group. Even our vocabulary lacks a popular term that reflects the commonalities. Instead, it fractures the Bovidae into disparate elements that prioritize the familiar (cattle, sheep, goats) and lump together the exotic ("antelope" is a broad term that even includes a non-Bovid, the North American pronghorn). This elusive vernacular, far from being a hindrance, is a demonstration of why works like *Bovids of the World* are needed: to highlight the common threads that link the diverse species of this family.

As the idea for this book was taking shape, its already immense scope doubled in size. Until this point, the classification of the Bovidae was well established. Its 140-odd accepted species had seen few changes in the previous half-century: a few subspecies had been elevated to full species, like the Serows (beginning on page 428), and in 1993 a surprising discovery in the forests of Vietnam added a brand new species (and genus!) to the list: the Saola (page 648). But the scientific community was unprepared for the entire family to receive a taxonomic overhaul in 2011. Using the Phylogenetic Species Concept, an evidence-based model for identifying species, Colin Groves and Peter Grubb reexamined the classification of ungulates without relying on previous assumptions. Their revision (*Ungulate Taxonomy*, Johns Hopkins University Press) put forth a startling theory: Bovidae contains twice as much species diversity as formerly thought. This revolutionary idea has been met with resistance, even though the Phylogenetic Species Concept is currently the most tenable method available for distinguishing species. Rather than accepting the status quo, Dr. Castelló embraced this latest taxonomic arrangement with its imposing additional workload. In doing so, he set out to produce an unprecedented guide to "new" Bovidae and thereby lend visual support to this updated taxonomy.

If this hurdle wasn't enough, I must confess that the goal of using photographs throughout this guide seemed an impossible challenge. The only other volume to visually depict the new Bovid taxonomy (*Handbook of the Mammals of the World*, Lynx Edicions, 2011) used illustrations. To find photographs of these same species would require significant research, a massive list of contributors, and more than a pinch of luck. Behind every image lies a photographer's investment of time, energy, and expertise. Photographing Aders's Duiker (page 260) in Zanzibar, for instance, was the culmination of months of planning, 2 weeks of traveling, 6 international plane flights, 20 hours in Duiker habitat, and 602 clicks of the shutter button. And that's just one species. It is a tribute to Dr. Castelló's tenacity that he has amassed so many contributing photographers and found consistent views for so many species. Their similarities and differences are emphasized by the removal of the background for each image, depicting them in the consistent manner of field-guide illustrations but with one key difference: with photographs, we get to share in the emotional thrill of observing not just a generic member of a species but an individual with all of its idiosyncrasies. There are some real photographic gems in these pages. For starters, check out the recently described Bangweulu Tsessebe (page 522), the Sudan Bohor Reedbuck (page 70) with its distinctive and unusual horns, and the fantastic variation in colors and markings between the 10 newly elevated Bushbuck species (beginning on page 578).

The beauty of this guide (its stunning images aside) is its simple concept and broad appeal. Readers who are passionate about mammal-watching can use this guide as a reference checklist to identify and keep track of their Bovid sightings. Photographers can look on the few picture-less species in this book as a challenge. (I already have a few ideas for where my next ungulate-finding trip could take me!) And those interested in classification and species identification will find this book an invaluable visual companion to the recent taxonomic changes. Regardless of why you have opened this guide, delving into it will leave you feeling not only informed but inspired by the beauty of the Bovidae just as I first was back in seventh grade. Outside of these pages, many Bovids are struggling for survival. Celebrating their diversity is a crucial step in developing a conservation ethic that ensures the living animals depicted in this vibrant volume do not fade away.

Brent Huffman
Author of ultimateungulate.com
Contributor to *Handbook of Mammals of the World, Volume 2: Hoofed Mammals*
Toronto, Canada

The family Bovidae is supremely important in human culture, because it contains almost all of our economically important domestic animals. Yet these animals are surprisingly poorly known — even the ancestors of the domestic ones are often disputed.

What to call them in popular language? Members of the closely related family Cervidae are called the deer; those of the somewhat less closely related family Suidae are called the pigs. But there is no really widespread popular name for the Bovidae — apart from "the Bovids," I have seen them called "hollow horned ruminants," which hardly whets the appetite. Many of them are dubbed "antelopes," but not all of them — Buffalo, for example, are not thought of as antelope, nor are wild sheep. And there is that North American ring-in, the Pronghorn, which is often popularly but incorrectly called "antelope," an important and very beautiful animal in its own right, but it is not a Bovid at all.

But the Bovidae comprises a truly beautiful and fascinating array of animals. Just look at the images in this book, painstakingly sought out and artfully arranged, as an obvious labor of love, by José R. Castelló: they are stunning, aren't they? Don't overlook these wonderful animals just because they lack a vernacular!

Most people who study mammals tend to concentrate on rats, or bats, or shrews, quite understandably because there are so many different species of them, but large mammals have often been rather neglected — the classification of the Bovidae commonly in use until very recently was derived, with just a little tweaking here and there over the next century, from a series of volumes published by Richard Lydekker and Gilbert Blaine between 1913 and 1915! My late friend and colleague Peter Grubb and I tried to rectify this situation in a slim volume published in 2011, and I must say the reaction among our colleagues was divided between enthusiastic endorsement and vociferous protest. One of the few who have actually thought about this, weaving his dextrous way through the problems of classification, is José R. Castelló, and the result is that, when you want to find out more about the little rock-living antelopes called Klipspringers, you won't find just a single page with an all-purpose Klipspringer on it, but you will find 11 pages, illustrating the rich variety of these delightful little creatures that live in different parts of Africa, how different they are from each other, and that you may see if you are lucky enough to take an African safari.

And you will find, on each page, descriptions of the habitat and behavior of each species, together with descriptions and range maps. Importantly, he says where he got his images from — but getting images was only the first step; it is what he has done with them that is the important thing.

After looking through this book, you will never think of Bovids in the same way again. You will realize not only how different a Gazelle is from an Oryx, but how different one species of Gazelle is from another, and you will never think of these beautiful animals in the same way again.

I congratulate Dr. Castelló for what he has done, and so will you.

Professor Colin Groves
Author of *Ungulate Taxonomy*, Johns Hopkins University Press
School of Archaeology & Anthropology, Australian National University
Australia

ACKNOWLEDGMENTS

First, I would like to thank my wife, **Beatriz**, who has been my companion during the years of work on this project. I could not have completed this book without her. I also thank my son Alejandro and my daughter Bea, for their support.

A special thanks to **Brent Huffman** for his expert and gracious assistance in preparing this book, and for sharing his vast knowledge of ungulates. Brent is a Canadian zoologist and author of one of the best online resources for ungulates: ultimateungulate.com. His contributions have appeared in several books. He is an avid wildlife photographer, and has traveled to numerous exotic locales in search of rare ungulate species.

Many thanks to **Colin Groves**, professor of biological anthropology at the Australian National University, for his gracious advice in the preparation of this manuscript. He is a major reference on the taxonomy of ungulates and other animals, and the author of *Ungulate Taxonomy* (2011, Johns Hopkins University Press).

A very special thanks goes also to my friend **Sergey Chichagov**, who has shared his profound knowledge of Bovids and hundreds of photographs with me. Sergey is a Latvian biologist, MSc in zoology, PhD, former employee at Riga Zoo, and a passionate photographer. He has visited and photographed many zoological institutions around the world, with the main objective of wildlife conservation. I would also like to thank **Alex Kantorovich**, curator of Hai Park Kiryat Motzkin, and ZIMS administrator at both Hai Park and Haifa Zoo in Israel, ISIS Eurasian Regional Association of Zoos and Aquariums regional coordinator, and the author of Zooinstitutes.com, a major online resource of zoological institutions. I also need to thank **Alex Meyer**, a devoted mammal photographer. He has photographed 901 unique mammal species at zoological institutions and national parks, and has traveled the globe to photograph endangered mammal species on 6 continents. Many thanks also to **Jonas Livet**, a French biologist, working full time as a consultant in zoology and zootechnics since 2011. He has visited over 1,000 zoological institutions around the world. His main expertise prevails in the field of the management and the development of modern zoos and in their role in the conservation of biodiversity. He created the website www.leszoosdanslemonde.com in 2001. Thank you also to **Pierre de Chabannes**, a photographer specializing in animal conservation and a former education material designer and lecturer. He has created www.photozoo.org, a website devoted to photography from animal parks, zoos, and breeding centers around Europe, Asia, and America. I need to further thank **Indigo Taylor**, zoologist, education volunteer at Los Angeles County Museum of Natural History, and volunteer animal keeper at Los Angeles Zoo and Botanical Gardens. Most of his knowledge about animals comes through years of proactive, continuous self-study in the fields of zoology and paleontology.

Finally, many thanks also to Andrey Kotkin, Nick Karpov, Arthur Ramos, Arturo Pardavila III, Tim Melling, Nick Hadad, Michelle Bender, Andrew Short, Ulrike Joerres, Klaus Rudloff, Johannes Pfleiderer, David Ellis, Arno Meintjes, Arjan Haverkamp, Jonas Van de Voorde, Ruslou Koorts, Gerrit De Vries, Scott Lamont, Heather Paul, Steve Garvie, Ignacio Yufera, Nico Smit, Kenneth K. Coe, Kevin Stalder, Ludwig Siege, Dominique Mignard, Jonathan Beilby, Ariadne Van Zandbergen, Heather Paul, Maxime Thué, Bernard Dupont, Nigel Voaden, Johan Bordonné, Kees Otte, Thomas Retterath and to all the great photographers for their enormous generosity in sharing their photographs; without them, this work would be impossible. I want also to acknowledge and thank Flickr and ZooChat, and their community of wildlife photographers.

RECOGNITION

The family Bovidae, which includes Antelopes, Cattle, Duikers, Gazelles, Goats, and Sheep, is the largest family within Artiodactyla and the most diverse family of ungulates, with more than 270 recent species. Their common characteristic is their unbranched, non-deciduous horns. Bovids are primarily Old World in their distribution, although a few species are found in North America. The name antelope is often used to describe many members of this family, but it is not a definable, taxonomically based term.

Shape, size, and color: Bovids encompass an extremely wide size range, from the minuscule Royal Antelope and the Dik-diks, weighing as little as 2 kg and standing 25 to 35 cm at the shoulder, to the Asian Wild Water Buffalo, which weighs as much as 1,200 kg, and the Gaur, which measures up to 220 cm at the shoulder. Body shape varies from relatively small, slender-limbed, and thin-necked species such as the Gazelles to the massive, stocky wild cattle (fig. 1). The forequarters may be larger than the hind, or the reverse, as in smaller species inhabiting dense tropical forests (e.g., Duikers). There is also a great variety in body coloration, although most species are some shade of brown. It can consist of a solid shade, or a patterned pelage. Antelopes that rely on concealment to avoid predators are cryptically colored. The stripes and blotches seen on the hides of Bushbuck, Bongo, and Kudu also function as camouflage by helping to disrupt the animals' outline. Sociable species that live in the open tend to have bold markings or a dark color which, along with conformation, help them to tell their own kind apart from all other species. The sexes may be differently colored, with males usually having the darker pelage (e.g., Sable Antelope). Frequently within species, there are also age-specific colorations.

Figure 1. Variety of size, weight, and body shape in Bovids: (1) Royal Antelope (*Neotragus pygmaeus*); (2) Kirk's Dik-dik (*Madoqua kirkii*); (3) Nubian Ibex (*Capra nubiana*); (4) Sable Antelope (*Hippotragus niger*); (5) Gaur (*Bos gaurus*). Sizes compared to an adult human.

Horns: One of the defining characteristics of the family Bovidae is the presence of unbranched horns (figs. 2 and 3). Horns are present in males of all Bovid species and in females of some genera, usually in large species. Horns in males are always thicker and more complex. The horns are permanently attached to the frontal bones of the skull, and are composed of a bone core covered with a keratin sheath which is never shed, with an air space separating these two layers. Horn size and shape vary greatly, often having a spiral, twisted, or fluted form. This unique horn structure is the only unambiguous morphological feature of Bovids that distinguishes them from other ruminants. *Tetracerus* is unique among wild Bovids in that males regularly bear four horns (two pairs); all other genera, with the exception of some domestic sheep, have only one pair. Horn growth in Bovids continues throughout the animal's life, and horn size and number of rings (not the annulations seen in some species) may be used for age determination (figs. 5 to 7), although size and quality of horns may be altered by several factors, such as food supply. Horns in young animals may seem quite odd compared with the final stage reached in the adult, and can sometimes resemble those of a very different species. Antlers (fig. 4.1), which are characteristic of the family Cervidae (deer), are not true horns: they are made of bone

Figure 2. Variety of horn shapes and sizes in Bovids: (1) Gemsbok (*Oryx gazella*); (2) Addax (*Addax nasomaculatus*); (3) Transcaspian Urial (*Ovis arkal*); (4) Kirk's Dik-dik (*Madoqua kirkii*); (5) Eastern White-bearded Wildebeest (*Connochaetes albojubatus*); (6) Common Eland (*Taurotragus oryx*); (7) Alpine Ibex (*Capra ibex*); (8) Northern Grant's Gazelle (*Nanger notata*); (9) Mountain Goat (*Oreamnos americanus*); (10) Red Hartebeest (*Alcelaphus caama*); (11) Ellipsen Waterbuck (*Kobus ellipsiprymnus*); (12) Four-horned Antelope (*Tetracerus quadricornis*); (13) Red-flanked Duiker (*Cephalophus rufilatus*); (14) Cape Buffalo (*Syncerus caffer*). Not to the same scale.

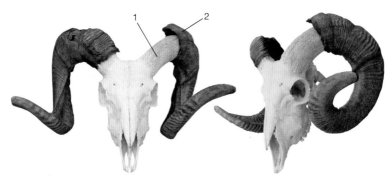

Figure 3. Horns: Horns are composed of a bony core (1) covered with a sheath of keratin (2). They are never branched, although they do vary in shape and size. Neither the sheath nor the core is ever shed, and in many species, the horns never stop growing. Horn cores begin as small bony growths under the skin, over the skull. Found only in Bovids. Photo credits: *Falln-Stock*.

Figure 4. Antlers (1)**:** Consist of bony outgrowths from the skull with no covering of keratin, usually large and branched, growing from an attachment point on the skull called a pedicel. While an antler is growing it is covered with highly vascular skin called velvet; once the antler has achieved its proper size, the velvet is lost and the antler's bone dies. Antlers shed after each mating season. Found only in Cervids. **Pronghorns** (2)**:** They differ from the horns of Bovids in two respects: they are branched, and, while the horns consist of a bony core and keratinous sheath, the sheaths are shed annually, while in Bovids, the sheaths are always permanent. Found only in the Pronghorn antelope. **Ossicones** (3)**:** Giraffes have a pair of short, unbranched, permanent bony processes that are covered with skin and hair, called ossicones. They derive from ossified cartilage, as true horn do, but they remain covered in skin and fur, rather than horn, while antlers are derived from bone tissue. Photo credits: *LaTaxidermia.com* and *Skulls Unlimited*.

without keratin, and are not permanent. Antlers will begin growing in the spring and will continue to grow until mating season, which is when they reach their full size. In late winter, the antlers are shed, and males may be without antlers for a few months until the cycle begins again. Antlers are branched and are only found on males (and female Caribou). Horns in the family Antilocapridae, with only a single extant species, the Pronghorn, are different from either true horns or antlers (fig. 4.2), but have characteristics of both: they are made of keratin growing on a bony core, like true horns, but they are shed annually; in addition, the horn sheath is branched in male Pronghorns, while true horns are always unbranched. Giraffes (family Giraffidae) have a pair of short, unbranched, permanent bony processes that are covered with skin and hair, called ossicones (fig. 4.3); they differ from horns in Bovids in that they do not project from the frontal bones, but lie over the sutures between the frontal and parietal bones. Rhinoceros horns differ from true horns because these horns have no core or sheath; they are made up of a multitude of epidermal cells and bundles of dermal papillae, extensions of the dermis, forming horny fibers similar to thick hair. A single horn is situated over the nasal bones;

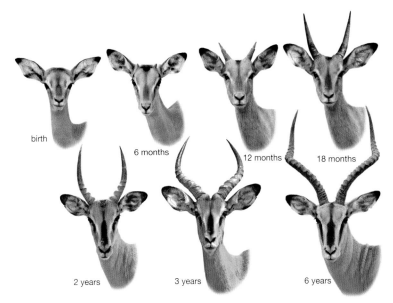

birth

6 months

12 months

18 months

2 years

3 years

6 years

Figure 5. Horn growth in male Black-faced Impala (*Aepyceros petersi*): Age can be estimated by rings on horns. Note that horns of young animals may seem quite odd compared with the final stage reached in the adult, and can sometimes resemble those of a very different species.

and in species that have two horns, the second horn lies over the frontal bones. Other ungulates may have tusks, which are elongated, continuously growing front teeth, that may protrude well beyond the mouth; they are most commonly canines, as with warthogs and pigs.

Hooves (fig. 8): Keratinous hooves sheathe the terminal bone of each toe. Hooves are modified toenails, and are composed of two structures: the unguis and the subunguis, which connect the unguis to the pad of the digit. Unlike claws and nails, hooves are the principal point of contact between the legs and the ground; as a result, ungulates are said to have unguligrade limbs. The tough unguis encircles the tip of the digit as a cylinder, enclosing the subunguis within it. Since the unguis is harder than the subunguis, it does not wear down as quickly, resulting in a firm leading edge to the hoof. Bovids walk on their hooves and have paraxonic feet, in which two well-developed digits, the third and fourth digits, bear the weight of the body. The second and fifth digits are either absent or, more often, small, forming the so-called lateral hooves, or dewclaws. The third and fourth metapodials, the only ones completely present, are fused into a single functional unit sometimes referred to as the cannon bone. Bovids walk primarily in diagonal couplets. They also trot, and larger forms can canter.

Skeletal System (figs. 9 and 10): The premaxillae exist as separate elements and often suture with nasals as well as with the maxillae. The orbits are fully ringed with bone, which generally is tubular. A single lacrimal canal is usually present in the orbits of the skull. There is no sagittal crest in the skull. Horns emerge above and behind the orbits, on the frontal bones. The interfrontal suture is obvious. An interparietal bone is present. The upper incisors are absent and the upper canines are either reduced or absent. Instead of upper incisors, Bovids have an area of tough, thickened tissue known as the dental pad, which provides a surface for gripping plant materials. The lower incisors project forward and are joined by modified canines that emulate the incisors. These modified incisors are followed by a long toothless gap known as a diastema. Bovids have a generalized dental formula of I 0/3, C 0/1, P 3/3, M 3/3 x 2 = 32. Age of Bovids may be determined by examination of the teeth. There are 7 cervical, 13 thoracic, 6 to 7 lumbar, 4 to 5 sacral, and 16 to 20 caudal vertebrae. Clavicles are absent. The scapulae are long, oblong in shape, with prominent cartilaginous dorsal margins. The ulna is fused with the radius and the fibula with the tibia. The navicular is fused to the cuboid in the tarsus. Metapodials III and IV are fused along the midline, and II and V are rudimentary. Phalanges III and IV are shortened. The phalanges are enclosed in hooves; in the case of the rudimentary phalanges of II and V, the distal ones are encased in small hooves.

Feeding and Digestive System: Most Bovids are herbivorous, except Duikers, which may be

11

birth   less than 1 year   2 years   3 years

4 years   5 years   6 years

Figure 6. Horn growth in male European Mouflon (*Ovis aries musimon*): Age can be estimated by rings on horns (but not the annulations seen in some species). Growth is slow in winter. Size increases up to 8 years. It must be noted that techniques that rely solely on horn size for estimation of age may be unreliable.

birth   4 months   8 months   12 months

18 months   2 years   adult

Figure 7. Horn growth in Blue Wildebeest (*Connochaetes taurinus*): Age can be estimated by horn shape and length, as there are no rings. Horns are present in both sexes, although those in females are thinner.

12

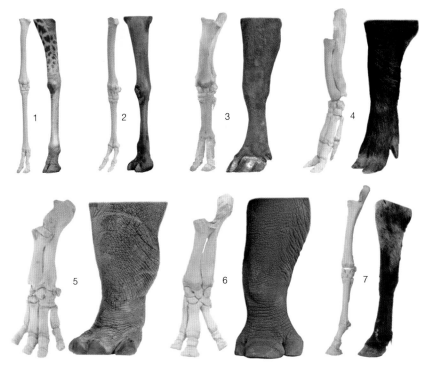

Figure 8. Hooves in Even-toed Ungulates (Artiodactyla): Weight is borne by the III and IV toes (paraxonic limb structure): (1) Family Giraffidae (*Giraffa camelopardalis*) without dewclaws; (2) Family Camelidae (*Camelus dromedarius*) with toenails instead of hooves; (3) Family Bovidae (*Syncerus caffer*); (4) Family Suidae (*Sus scrofa*) with four toes, although they walk only on the middle two digits; (5) Family Hippopotamidae (*Hippopotamus amphibius*) with pads instead of hooves and four toes, all of them used in walking. **Hooves in Odd-toed Ungulates (Perissodactyla):** Weight is mostly or entirely borne by the III toe, featuring an odd number of toes on the rear feet: (6) Family Rhinocerotidae (*Ceratotherium simum*) with three foot pads with nails; (7) Family Equidae (*Equus ferus*). Not to the same scale.

omnivorous. Bovids obtain their food by browsing or grazing, subsisting on plant material. Plants such as grasses and forbs are brought into the mouth by the lips and tongue, where they are severed by the lower incisors pressing against the hard cartilaginous pad of the upper palate, followed by a quick upward jerk of the head. Tougher plants such as shoots of shrubs are severed by the premolars and molars. Depending on diet, the incisors can be wide (spatulate) and relatively uniform in size, as in grazers, or narrower and often of various sizes, as in browsers. Ruminants' digestive system is characterized by functional and anatomical adaptations that allow them to unlock otherwise unavailable food energy in fibrous plant material, mainly in cellulose. This property gives them an advantage over non-ruminants. An important characteristic of ruminants' digestive system is the occurrence of microbial fermentation prior to gastric and intestinal digestion activity. Their unique digestive system integrates a large microbial population with the animal's own system in a symbiotic relationship. The microbial fermentation occurs mainly in the rumen, the first chamber of the four-compartment stomach, which consists also of the reticulum and omasum (act as filters), and the abomasum (the true enzymatic stomach).

Scent glands: Dense cluster of cells, generally flask shaped, derived from hair follicles. Their chemically complex secretions convey information about the individual's identity, sex, age, and social and reproductive status. The most common and important scent glands are the hoof or interdigital glands and the preorbital glands. The secretions of the hoof glands, exuding from the cleft between the hooves, leave a scent trace that helps antelopes follow one another. Preorbital glands are employed mainly for marking objects. Female Bovidae have either one or two pairs of functional mammae.

Sexual dimorphism: Most Bovids are sexually dimorphic. Adult males and females of a species

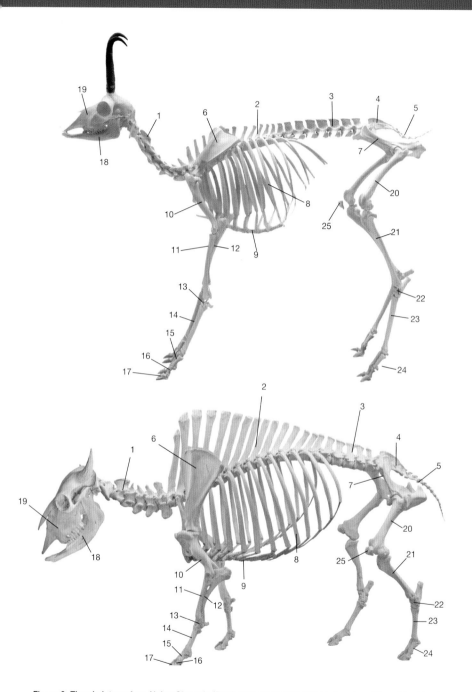

Figure 9. The skeleton of an Alpine Chamois (*Rupicapra rupicapra*) and an American Bison (*Bos bison*): (1) Cervical vertebrae; (2) dorsal vertebrae; (3) lumbar vertebrae; (4) sacrum; (5) coccygeal (caudal) vertebrae; (6) scapula; (7) ilium; (8) ribs; (9) sternum; (10) humerus; (11) radius; (12) ulna; (13) carpus; (14) metacarpus; (15) proximal phalanx; (16) middle phalanx; (17) distal phalanx; (18) mandible; (19) maxilla; (20) femur; (21) tibia; (22) tarsus; (23) metatarsus; (24) phalanges; (25) patella. Not to scale. Photo credits: Smithsonian.

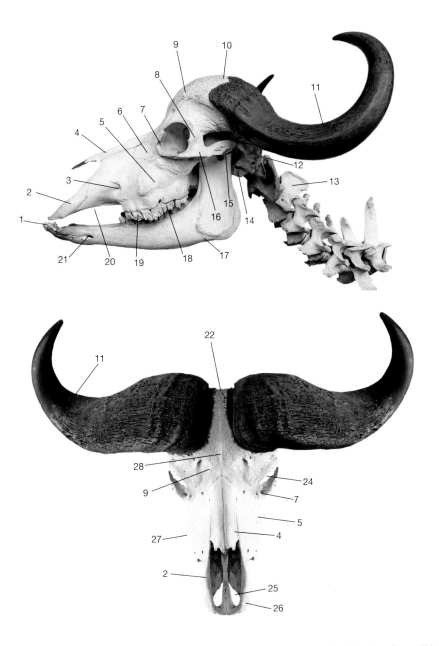

Figure 10. The skull of a Cape Buffalo (*Syncerus caffer*): (1) Lower incisors; (2) incisive bone (premaxilla); (3) infraorbital foramen; (4) nasal bone; (5) maxilla; (6) lacrimal bone; (7) fossa for lacrimal sac; (8) postorbital bar; (9) frontal bone; (10) cornual process; (11) horn; (12) occipital bone and condyle; (13) cervical vertebrae; (14) tympanic bulla; (15) condylar process of mandible; (16) zygomatic bone; (17) mandible; (18) molars; (19) premolars; (20) diastema; (21) mental foramen; (22) intercornual protuberance; (23) supraorbital foramen; (24) orbit; (25) palatine fissure; (26) body of incisive bone; (27) facial tuber; (28) sagittal crest. Photo credits: *Jebulon*, Muséum National d'Histoire Naturelle (Paris), *Boleslaw Kubica*.

Figure 11. Non-bovid Artiodactyls (from left to right): (1) Hippopotamidae (*Hippopotamus amphibius*), (2) Suidae (*Babyrousa celebensis*), (3) Tayassuidae (*Pecari tajacu*), (4) Cervidae (*Dama dama*), (5) Tragulidae (*Tragulus kanchil*), (6) Camelidae (*Camelus dromedarius*), (7) Giraffidae (*Giraffa camelopardalis*), and (8) Antilocapridae (*Antilocapra americana*). To the same scale. Photo credits: *Kol Tregaskes* (London Zoo), *Jeff Whitlock* (San Antonio Zoo), *Ken Trease, Samson, Dibrova.*

may differ in size, color, shape, or development of horns or scent glands. This is the result of male reproductive competition, which causes males to acquire physical and behavioral traits that enhance their ability to compete successfully with other males. The most striking sexually dimorphic characters in Bovids are size and development of horns. Bovids with polygynous reproductive systems, those that are diurnal, and open-habitat dwellers tend to present a greater sexual dimorphism. In monogamous systems, male sexual competition is minimal and consequently there is little dimorphism, and females may be slightly larger than males, as in Duikers and dwarf antelopes. Size dimorphism is much greater in Bovids of medium and large size, where males mature much later than females. Dimorphism is particularly well developed in Reduncini (Kob, Lechwe), Tragelaphini (Kudu, Eland), and Caprini (Ibexes and Goats). On the contrary, Alcelaphini (Hartebeest, Wildebeest) and Hippotragini (Oryxes, Roan Antelope) have little dimorphism. These species, though polygynous, share the tendency to form mixed herds containing adults of both sexes, and are usually under ecological pressure to integrate. Color dimorphism is less common than size or horn dimorphism, and in some Bovids adult males become much darker than adult females. Males also have better-developed scent glands than females.

TAXONOMY

The definition of a species and subspecies is subject to constant debate and revision by biologists, resulting in changes in the official lists of Bovid species. The taxonomy of the Bovidae stabilized after Ellerman in 1953, with little change by Ansell in 1972, and was based on the Morphological Species Concept, in which organisms are classified in the same species if they appear identical by

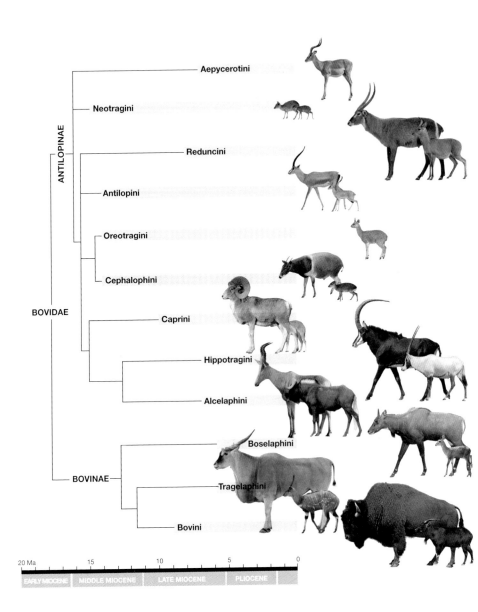

Figure 12. Systematic classification of the family Bovidae: Phylogenetic diagram charting the evolution of the major Bovid clades: the subfamily Antilopinae is very diverse, and its tribes are very distinct from one another, ranging from the smallest to medium and large-sized forms, usually smaller and more lightly built than many of the Bovinae; its horns are transversely ringed, and there are almost always prominent glands in front of the eye and in the forefeet. Most of them, except Cephalophini and Neotragini, live in open country or light cover. The subfamily Bovinae includes three well-distinguished tribes, with medium to very large species, usually heavily built and thick legged, with horns lightly or strongly spiraled, not ringed as in Antilopinae, and pelage with less contrast in color. They are usually adapted to heavy cover or deep forest. To the same scale. Modified from *Bibi, Bukhsianidze, Gentry, Geraads, Kostopoulos, and Vrba, 2009.*

17

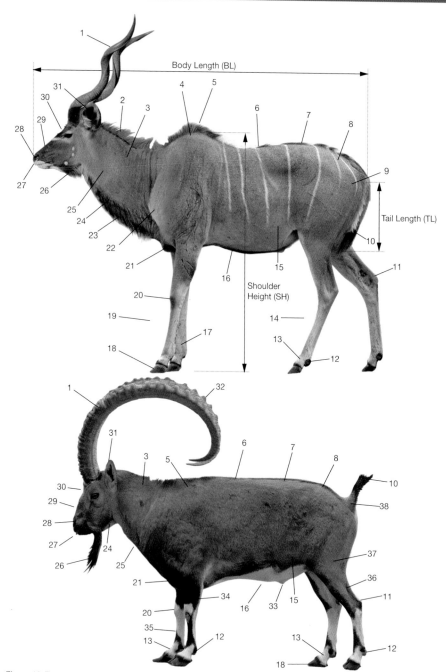

Figure 13. Topography of Zambezi Greater Kudu (*Tragelaphus strepsiceros*) and Sinai Ibex (*Capra nubiana*): (1) Horns; (2) nape mane; (3) neck; (4) top of shoulders; (5) withers; (6) chine; (7) loin; (8) rump; (9) buttock; (10) tail; (11) hock; (12) dewclaw; (13) pastern; (14) hind leg; (15) flank; (16) belly; (17) fetlock; (18) hoof; (19) foreleg; (20) knee; (21) brisket; (22) chest; (23) throat mane; (24) dewlap; (25) throat; (26) beard; (27) muzzle; (28) nostril; (29) bridge of the nose; (30) forehead; (31) ear; (32) horn rings; (33) sheath; (34) forearm; (35) cannon; (36) shank; (37) thigh; (38) tail head. Photo credit: *Gerrit De Vries* and *Sergey Chichagov*.

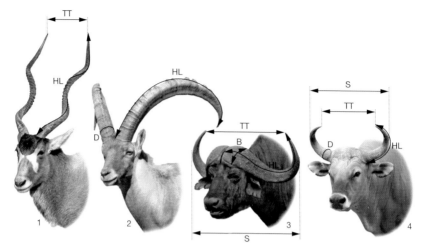

Figure 14. Horn measurements: HL: horn length, TT: tip to tip distance, D: horn diameter, S: horn spread, B: boss. For spiral horns (1), horn length (HL) is measured around the spiral, keeping the tape on top of the spiral ridge, starting at the lowest point at the front of the base and proceeding to the tip. For Ibexes (2), HL is measured from the lowest point in front to the tip. For Cape Buffalo (3), Wildebeest, and Muskox, HL is measured from the center of the boss to the tip following along the center of the horn surface. For European and Asian Wild Cattle (4), HL is measured from the lowest point on the underside along the outside curve to the tip. Horn diameter (D) is measured at right angles to the axis of the horn, usually at the base. Horn spread (S) is measured at the greatest distance between horns. Boss (B) is measured at the greatest width. Photo credits (1) *Alex Meyer,* San Antonio Zoo (USA), (2) *Alex Meyer,* Munich Zoo (Germany), (3) *Duncan Noakes,* (4) *Pierre de Chabannes,* Khao Kheow Open Zoo (Thailand). Not to the same scale.

morphological criteria, and on the Biological Species Concept, which defines a species as members of populations that interbreed in nature, but not neccesarily according to similarity of appearance. However, new evidence and shifting opinions have led to changes in this traditional classification. Groves and Grubb, applying the Phylogenetic Species Concept, in which a species is defined as the smallest population or group of populations displaying diagnostic, genetically based differences compared to other populations, revised the entire scope of hoofed mammals in 2011, and reclassified many subspecies of Bovids as full species. We have followed this approach in this book.

The application of the Phylogenetic Species Concept has increased the number of Bovid species so significantly that they may be perceived by some readers as surprising. This approach has brought to light a number of overlooked taxa, which may inadvertently have escaped deserving attention from scientists for decades through the 20th century, and which may face extinction in a matter of several years (e.g., *Hippotragus variani, Alcelaphus tora, Oreotragus porteousi, Ovis nigrimontana*). In addition, this approach emphasizes the conservation significance of ecosystems (e.g., Serengeti-Mara, Cape Region, Sudan Grasslands, Bangweulu-Upemba wetland complex).

Readers are encouraged to remain open to new findings and to be aware of the fact that taxonomy does not and probably for some time will not give definite answers with respect to Bovids. Even if some of our readers refuse the elevation of some subspecies into species, they are given the chance to see that the taxa actually represent different animals which should definitely not be forgotten.

CLASSIFICATION

Bovids belong to the taxonomic order Artiodactyla (fig. 11), also known as even-toed ungulates. This order includes nine families: Suidae (pigs), Tayassuidae (peccaries), Hippopotamidae (hippos), Camelidae (camels and llamas), Tragulidae (mouse deer), Giraffidae (giraffe and okapi), Antilocapridae (pronghorn), Cervidae (deer), and Bovidae. Close to 65% of the extant species of Artiodactyls are in the Bovidae. Suidae and Tayassuidae are distinguished from Bovidae by the absence of horns, the presence of four toes on each foot (although they walk only on the middle two digits), a simple stomach, and a compact body with an elongated head ending with a naked nasal disc. Hippopotamidae are stout, naked-skinned, amphibious Artiodactyls, possessing three-chambered

19

stomachs (pseudoruminants) and walking on four toes on each foot. Camelidae may be distinguished from Bovidae by the absence of horns and hooves (they have two-toed feet with toenails and soft foot pads), a different dentition (presence of upper incisors and upper canines), a three-chambered stomach, and a different musculature of the hind limbs. Tragulidae are small ungulates with no horns or antlers, four complete digits in all limbs, a three-chambered stomach, and tusk-like upper canines. Cervidae are recognized by the antlers, usually complexly branched, in males of most species. Female Cervids may be distinguished from Bovids by a combination of characters in the lacrimal bone; otherwise, they may look similar. Antilocapridae contains only one living species, the Pronghorn (*Antilocapra americana*); as in Bovidae, they have a four-chambered stomach, cloven hooves, a similar body shape to antelopes, a similar dental formula, and their horns resemble those of the Bovids, although they are branched and shed outside of the breeding season, and subsequently regrown. Giraffidae, which is composed of two genera: *Giraffa* (giraffes) and *Okapia* (okapi), may be recognized by the presence of ossicones instead of horns, the long limbs and neck, and a sloping body profile.

Systematic work on Bovids has been difficult, as it is one of the most troublesome groups of mammals to classify. Molecular studies have concluded the existence of a major division within the family Bovidae, with two main subfamilies: Antilopinae and Bovinae (fig. 12):

SUBFAMILY ANTILOPINAE: Includes nine tribes, which are very distinct from one another: Hippotragini, Alcelaphini, Reduncini, Cephalophini, Neotragini, Oreotragini, Aepycerotini, Antilopini, and Caprini. Horns in this subfamily are transversely ringed, and there are almost always prominent glands in front of the eye and in the forefeet.

Tribe Aepycerotinae: Consists of a single genus, the Impalas. Aepycerotinae is endemic to Africa. Impalas are sexually dimorphic, as only males possess horns.

Tribe Neotragini: Often referred to as dwarf antelopes, which are among the smallest ungulates, and includes only one genus: *Neotragus*. They are primarily forest-dwelling species, with a hare-like build, with long and slender legs, large eyes, and small muzzles. They have short, vertical, spike-like horns, found only in males, never in females. They have facial and inguinal glands; preorbital glands lack a surface fold of skin.

Tribe Reduncini: Includes Reedbucks, Lechwes, Kobs, Waterbucks, Rheboks, and relatives, primarily distributed throughout parts of Africa. Species in Reduncini are medium to large-sized grazers that often have strong ties to water. They also have long hair, and all species exhibit sexual dimorphism, as horns are only present in males.

Tribe Antilopini: Often referred to as true antelopes, includes small to medium-sized species, in native to open, arid environments in Africa and Eurasia, but occur in particularly high densities in East Africa. This tribe includes true Gazelles (genera *Eudorcas*, *Gazella*, and *Nanger*), *Procapra* (which appear to be as different from the Gazelles as they are from the dwarf antelopes), Saiga, and dwarf antelopes (*Dorcatragus*, *Madoqua*, *Ourebia*, and *Raphicerus*). There is little sexual dimorphism, and horns are generally present in both sexes. There are often striking markings on the face, flanks, and/or rump. Preorbital glands are well developed in most species.

Tribe Oreotragini: Represented by one living genus, the Klipspringers. They are small, stocky antelope, with females weighing more than and being slightly longer than males. Their hoof structure is unique because the last joints of the digits are rotated so they can walk on the tips of their hooves. Only the males have horns, except for one species.

Tribe Cephalophini: Consists of several species of Duiker. Duikers are highly specialized and are resident in the tropical forests of Africa. They are easily recognizable as they have the same basic body plan but differ significantly in size. Unlike in most Bovids, females are slightly larger than males. Also unlike most other Bovids, Duikers are primarily frugivorous.

Tribe Caprini: Consists of Goats, Sheep, Muskox, and relatives. Taxonomy of this tribe is complex and several classifications have been suggested. Most authors recognize four distinct groups: Sheep and Goats; Muskox and Takin; Serows, Gorals, and Chamois; and Tibetan Antelope. Caprini are especially adapted to montane and alpine environments, which explains why this is the only tribe that is more diverse in Eurasia than in Africa. In general, both genders have horns; however, horn morphology in many species is sexually dimorphic.

Tribe Hippotragini: This tribe consists primarily of large grazing antelopes with large horns: Oryxes, Addax, Sable, and Roan Antelopes. Hippotragini species are restricted to Africa and east-central Asia and are primarily grazers. Most species live in arid habitats and have an erect mane along the nape of the neck.

Tribe Alcelaphini: Includes Wildebeests, Hartebeests, Topis, Tsessebes, Blesbok, and relatives. All of the species in this tribe are nomadic grazers that are native to Africa. Most species are size-dimorphic, with males being larger than females, and both bearing double-curved (lyrate) horns.

SUBFAMILY BOVINAE: Includes three tribes: Bovini (cattle and Buffalo), Tragelaphini (spiral-horned antelopes), and Boselaphini (Nilgai, Four-horned Antelope). Sexual dimorphism is highly prevalent in this subfamily, with the males of some species weighing nearly twice as much as their female counterparts. Bovines have played an important role in the cultural evolution of humans, as numerous species within this subfamily have been domesticated for subsistence purposes.

Tribe Boselaphini: Includes only two species, both from India: Nilgai and Four-horned Antelope, which do not appear to be closely related. They are sexually dimorphic, and only males have short, smooth, conical horns. This tribe and the Saola are the only Bovinae that have facial glands.

Tribe Tragelaphini: A group of medium-sized to large antelopes, with spiral or twisted horns, white vertical stripes, and significant sexual dimorphism. Horns are found in the males of all species, while most females are hornless, except in the larger forms: Elands and Bongo.

Tribe Bovini: Includes three subtribes: Bovina (cattle and Bison), Bubalina (Buffalo), and Pseudoryina (only represented by the recently discovered Saola). They are usually large, massive, heavy-bodied animals, with short, thick legs, and smooth rather than annulated horns. There is significant sexual dimorphism, with males usually bigger than females. Horns are present in both sexes.

EVOLUTION AND FOSSIL RECORD (fig. 12)

Bovids are the most diverse ungulates, and their evolutionary history is similarly diverse. Evolution within this family is characterized by adaptive radiations, global migrations and mass extinctions, and today there are about 270 extant species of Bovids recognized. Until now, the impressive fossil record has revealed more than 300 extinct species or ancestors of modern species. However, the current knowledge on earliest Bovids is quite limited. Bovids diverged from Cervids and Giraffids in Eurasia, near the Oligocene/Miocene boundary approximately 23 Ma, due to the evolution of a more advanced ruminating digestive system, which allowed these species to exploit a different vegetation base. Cervids evolved in Eurasia from the early Miocene onward, taking to the cooler regions at higher latitudes, while Bovids, firmly established there by the middle Miocene, and were better adapted to warmer temperatures, facilitating their later migration into the African continent as the global climate warmed. *Eotragus*, a small gazelle-like animal with simple, straight horn cores, is considered the first true Bovid, and appeared more or less simultaneously in Europe and Asia at about 18 Ma. Living in woodland savannas, these early Bovids were moderately diverse, with only a few genera.

During the early Miocene, Bovids differentiated into two main lineages: Antilopinae and Bovinae. This divergence was related to a long period of continental separation, in which the Antilopinae would have evolved from Asian stock that migrated into Africa, where they initially specialized in drier habitats and were of a smaller size. Once in Africa they differentiated into tropical and arid types, some of which later returned to Asia and gave rise to the Caprini and to other specialized species. The Bovinae fossil record suggests a South Asian origin, from where they further radiated into Boselaphini, Bovini, and Tragelaphini. Tragelaphines migrated into Africa where they have been distinct for at least 15 million years. This explosive tribal radiation during the Middle Miocene, gave rise to the majority of extant Antilopinae and Bovinae tribes.

By the late Miocene, around 10 Ma, Bovids rapidly diversified, partly because many species became adapted to more open, grassland habitat, being able to move rapidly over the open plains, and having high-crowned teeth in order to cope with tough grasses. When the ice sheets advanced during the Plio-Pleistocene a number of Bovids became adapted for cold climates as well. Increased tolerance of cold climate also allowed a few Bovids to cross the Bering land bridge and invade the New World in the Pleistocene (e.g., Muskox, Bighorn Sheep, Mountain Goat). Bovids never reached South America until Europeans introduced domestic cattle and sheep, but Bison did reach as far south as El Salvador.

Aepycerotini first appeared in the late Miocene, and no significant difference between primitive and modern Impalas has been noted. Neotragines also retain many primitive features compared with other members of the Antilopinae, and they seem to have been one of the earliest branches to separate, more than 15 Ma. Reduncini probably diverged from Antilopini in the mid-Miocene, or both diverged from undifferentiated early Antilopinae, and they first appeared in the fossil record 7 Ma in Eurasia. Antilopini either originated 17 Ma in Africa, or still-unknown Eurasian ancestors migrated there at an early date; existing Asian and African lineages are distinctly different. Oreotragini are not related to other dwarf antelopes, but are distantly related to Duikers, from which they separated about 13 Ma. The Cephalophini fossil record is scarce, beginning approximately 6 Ma, although some records indicate that this tribe may have been present 12 Ma. Divergence times of most Duikers date to the Pleistocene, when the colder, drier temperatures during glacial maxima might have led to the isolation and subsequent diversification of tropical, forest-associated taxa. Caprini and their relatives Hippotragini and Alcelaphini are an extremely diversified group including several Bovid branches of probably different origin, which makes their supra-generic classification quite delicate. The origin of the tribe is dated back to the early-middle Miocene. Hippotragini, presently restricted to Africa, first appeared in the fossil record 6.5 Ma; they may have originated in Eurasia and then colonized Africa by crossing the Sahara Desert. Alcelaphini are a relatively recent evolutionary development, and the first fossils appear 5 Ma in Africa.

Boselaphini were a successful Eurasian group that appeared during the late Middle Miocene and strongly radiated and expanded during the Late Miocene from China to Europe and Africa; extant Nilgai and Four-horned Antelope are Miocene relicts and are most related to early Bovids. Bovini split off from a Boselaphine ancestral stock on the Indian subcontinent and then they expanded to Africa and Eurasia, invading North America too. Within this tribe, three divergent lineages have been identified: Bovina, Bubalina, and Pseudorygina, which may have diversified during the late Middle Miocene, approximately 13 Ma. Tragelaphini first appeared in the fossil record 6 Ma during the late Miocene.

Research is thus far showing Bovidae to be the most vastly diversified group of hoofed mammals as well as one of the most vastly diversified groups of herbivorious mammals to have inhabited the planet. Bovid fossils are of great use in the study of evolutionary biology and offer clues to patterns of adaptation and evolution.

HOW TO USE THIS BOOK (fig. 15)

The main purpose of this guide is to enable the observer to accurately identify all known species and subspecies of wild and feral Bovids from all over the world. Information is presented in the same format throughout, with maps showing geographic ranges, and photographs highlighting the specific identification criteria in each case. We have packed as much detail into this volume as possible, but also worked hard to keep it concise and efficient, so that it is not unwieldy in the field. All the information for a given species is displayed on two facing pages.

The overall structure of this guide is based on the taxonomic classification of the family Bovidae into tribes, and is organized to provide the maximum ease of use for its readers. To help the reader grasp the scientific arrangement, the pages for each tribe have a distinctive color on their top margin.

With very few exceptions, all the Bovids can be identified from field sightings by using the photographs and descriptions in this guide. Look through the color plates and determine what type of animal you saw. Turn to the text page for the species that most resembles your sighting and look at the distribution map. If the map is not shaded for your area, then return to the color plates and try another similar species or subspecies. Keep in mind that many species may vary slightly in color from one region to another and that not all color morphs can be illustrated in a guide. When you find a species that resembles your sighting and occurs in the correct geographic area, read the text to see if the description fits the habitat that you are in and any behavior you may have observed. Also check the Similar Species section for other possibilities.

Care should be taken when identifying juvenile animals or females as they may differ considerably from the adult males. Shape and development of horns can be especially misleading in the case of Bovids; the horns of young animals may seem quite odd compared with the final stage reached in the adult, and can sometimes resemble those of a very different species.

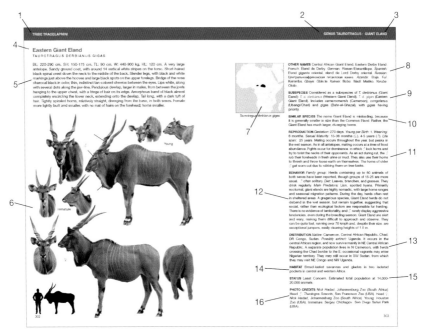

Figure 15. Understanding a page layout: (1) tribe; (2) genus; (3) common name; (4) common and scientific names; (5) measurements and description; (6) color plates and silhouette comparing size with a human figure; photographs of both sexes, young forms, and coat variations are usually included; features that are most important for identification are indicated by bars; (7) distribution map; (8) other names, including foreign and local names; (9) subspecies and taxonomy; (10) similar species or subspecies; (11) reproduction biology; (12) behavior; (13) distribution; (14) habitat; (15) conservation status, based on the IUCN Red List of Threatened Species, and estimated population; (16) photo credits.

ABBREVIATIONS

The following abbreviations, contractions, and symbols have been used in the book to make it simpler for the reader to access the information.

cm: centimeters	W: weight, west, western
g: grams	N: north, northern
kg: kilograms	NE: northeast, northeastern
m: meters	NW: northwest, northwestern
km: kilometers	S: south, southern
km²: square kilometers	SE: southeast, southwestern
ha: hectares	SW: southwest, southwestern
kmph: kilometers per hour	E: east, eastern
NP: National Park	♂: male, males
BL: body length	♀: female, females
TL: tail length	DR Congo: Democratic Republic of Congo
HL: horn length	Congo: Republic of Congo
Ma: million years ago	

Common Impala
AEPYCEROS MELAMPUS

BL: 125-160 cm (♂), 120-150 cm (♀). SH: 80-95 cm (♂), 75-90 cm (♀). TL: 30-45 cm. W: 45-80 kg (♂), 40-60 kg (♀). HL: 45-92 cm (♂). Short, glossy coat with a reddish saddle over a light tan torso. Undersides white, as are the rings around the eyes. Muzzle and chin lighter in color. Black markings on the ear tips and 3 black stripes on the rump: 2 on the flanks and 1 down the tail. Unique among the Bovidae, Impala possess metatarsal glands, which are strikingly marked with a tuft of black hair above the rear hooves. Lyre-shaped horns, only in males, S-shaped and slender, with strong ridges.

♀

Young

♂

Juvenile

Aepyceros melampus

OTHER NAMES Southern Impala. *French*: Impala, le pallah. *German*: Impala, Schwarzfersenantilope. *Spanish*: Impala. *Russian*: Южная импала. *Afrikaans*: Rooibok. *Kalenjin*: Chebotewerer. *Kikamba*: Ndarti. *Kisukuma*: Mhala. *Lozi*: Pala. *Luragoli*: Eswara. *Luganda*: Empala. *Lwo*: Nyakech. *Maasai*: Entarakwet. *Samburu*: Nkoperai. *Sepedi*: Phala. *Swahili*: Swala pala. *Swati*: Mpala. *Yei*: Umpala.

SUBSPECIES Monotypic. The name *A. melampus* formerly included *A. melampus* (Common Impala), and *A. petersi* (Black-faced Impala) as subspecies: these are elevated to full species here. Includes *johnstoni* (Malawi Impala), *katangaei* (Katangan Impala), *rendilis* (Kenyan Impala), and *suara* (Tanzanian Impala).

SIMILAR SPECIES Kob, but Common Impala is more lightly built, lighter colored, and with longer, less massive horns and a black stripe in the rump.

REPRODUCTION *Gestation*: 195-210 days. *Young per Birth*: 1. *Weaning*: 4-6 months. *Sexual Maturity*: 1 year (♂), 1.5 years (♀). *Life Span*: 15 years. Two birthing peaks occur, one in spring and one in autumn. After birth, kids lie concealed away from their mother, subsequently joining a "kindergarten" group with other animals of the same age.

BEHAVIOR *Family Group:* ♂ in herds of about 30, ♀ and young in herds of up to 200. *Diet*: Grasses, leaves, blossoms, fruit. *Main Predators:* Lion, leopard, Cape hunting dog, spotted hyena, crocodile, python. Active throughout the 24-hour day, alternating resting and grazing, and drinking at least once a day. Herds have a home range of about 2-6 km^2. About one-third of adult ♂ hold territories, which vary in size from 0.2 to 0.9 km^2. These territories are marked with urine and feces, and are defended against the intrusion of rival ♂. The owner of the territory attempts to control any ♀ herds which wander into it. Prodigious leaps are the most well-known feature of the Impala's movement. Executed seemingly without effort, these jumps may span over 9 m and may be 2.5 m high, often over bushes and even other Impala. Unlike many other plains grazers, they flee into dense vegetation rather than out into open grassland. During the breeding season, ♂ make a hoarse grunting sound.

DISTRIBUTION *Native*: Botswana, Kenya, Malawi, Mozambique, Rwanda, South Africa, Swaziland, Tanzania, Uganda, Zambia, Zimbabwe. *Introduced*: Gabon.

HABITAT Light open woodland and savanna. Prefers ecotones between open grassland and woodland; requires cover and surface water.

STATUS Least Concern. One of the most abundant antelopes, with about 25% of the population occurring in protected areas. The largest numbers occur in areas such as the Maasai Mara and Kajiado (Kenya), Serengeti, Ruaha, and Selous (Tanzania), Luangwa Valley (Zambia), Okavango (Botswana), Hwange, Sebungwe, and the Zambezi Valley (Zimbabwe), Kruger NP (South Africa) and on private farms and conservancies (South Africa, Zimbabwe, and Botswana).

PHOTO CREDITS ♂, ♀: *Arturo Pardavila III*, Samburu (Kenya). Head ♂: *Ludovic Hirlimann*, Nairobi (Kenya). Head ♀: *Dale LaFollete*, Selous (Tanzania). Young: *Louise Meintjes* and *Mike McWatts*, Pilanesberg (South Africa). Juvenile: *Achim Mittler*, South Luangwa NP (Zambia) and *Hannah Swithinbank*, Pilanesberg (South Africa). 25

Black-faced Impala
AEPYCEROS PETERSI

BL: 130-135 cm (♂), 125-130 cm (♀). SH: 97 cm (♂), 90 cm (♀). TL: 30-35 cm. W: 63 kg (♂), 50-52 kg (♀). HL: To 92 cm. General appearance like the Common Impala. Darker in color, purplish-black sheen. Tail longer and more bushy. Stripe extending through and in front of the eye is darker. In most individuals the face carries an indistinct, narrow, dark median stripe from the crown to the level of the eyes, which then broadens into a very dark, well demarcated blaze, down the muzzle. Undersides and rings around the eyes white. Muzzle and chin lighter in color. Tufts of dark hair above the rear hooves. Lyre-shaped ridged horns, found only in males, S-shaped and slender.

♀

Young

♂

♂
Juvenile

Aepyceros petersi

OTHER NAMES Angolan Impala. *French*: Impala à face noire. *German:* Schwarzfersenimpala. *Spanish:* Impala de cara negra. *Russian:* Ангольская, или чернолицая импала. *Afrikaans*: Swartneusrooibok. *Zulu*: Impala enobuso obunyama. *Sepedi*: Phala ya sefahlego se seso. *Setswana*: Phala. *Swati*: Imphala. *Xitsonga:* Mhala.

SUBSPECIES Monotypic. Formerly considered a subspecies of *A. melampus* (Impala).

SIMILAR SPECIES Similar to the Common Impala, but color is less reddish and more purplish, and it has a well-defined blackish blaze on the middle of the face below the eyes, more black on the tip of the ears, and a longer bushy tail. Some Common Impala, notably in the Transvaal in South Africa, may exhibit facial blazes of varying extent and blackness that are similar to those of the Black-faced Impala.

REPRODUCTION *Gestation*: 195-210 days. *Young per Birth*: 1. *Weaning:* 4-6 months. *Sexual Maturity*: 1 year (♀), 1.5 years (♂). *Life Span:* 15 years. ♀ conceive during a brief rut in June-early July and give birth in late December to mid-January.

BEHAVIOR *Family Group:* Small herds of 3-15 animals, rarely more than 20 in daytime, but resting groups at night may be larger. *Diet*: Browsers and grazers, consuming flowers, leaves, and shoots and the fruit, bark, and leaves of shrubs such as the small sour plum. They often compete for food with goats. *Main Predators*: Lion, leopard, Cape hunting dog, spotted hyena, crocodile, python. During and just after the breeding season the herds aggregate into larger herds which then split into smaller ones once the lambs have been born. Dominant ♂ establish territories in habitat occupied by ♀ herds, but appear not to monopolize access to water. ♂ create even larger latrines than those of the Common Impala, and many other mammal species will defecate on the latrines. Like Common Impala, they forage mainly by day, but also at night. They tend to move into more open habitat to lie down at night. Prodigious leaps are the most well-known feature of the Impala's movement. Executed seemingly without effort, these jumps may span over 9 m and may be 2.5 m high, often over bushes and even other Impala. Unlike many other plains grazers, the Impala flees into dense vegetation rather than out into open grassland.

DISTRIBUTION Native: Angola, Namibia. Found only in SW Angola and NW Namibia and its range does not naturally overlap with that of the Common Impala.

HABITAT Dense riverine vegetation, but also found in more moderate vegetation near water holes.

STATUS Vulnerable. In the 1970s 310 individuals were transferred to Etosha NP for better protection, and the number is steadily increasing. However, the current population is still fewer than 1,000. Their continued existence is being threatened by goats with which they have to compete throughout most of their range for food and water.

PHOTO CREDITS ♀: *Martha de Jong-Lantink*, Etosha (Namibia). ♂: Etosha (Namibia). Head ♀: *Stuart-Lee*, Etosha (Namibia). Head ♂: *Ian Yule,* Etosha (Namibia). Young: *Matthew Goulding,* Caprivi Strip (Namibia). Juvenile: *Jonathan Rubb*, Etosha (Namibia) and *Sergey Chichagov*, Lisbon Zoo (Portugal).

Coastal Suni
NEOTRAGUS MOSCHATUS

BL: 57-62 cm. SH: 33-35 cm. TL: 8-13 cm. W: 4.5 kg. HL: 6.5-13.3 cm (♂). A very small antelope, with long and slender legs, a typically compact stance, and a disproportionately broad head and short neck. Slightly smaller than the Livingstone's Suni, with a lighter, duller coloration. General coat color is reddish brown, with the back darker than the flanks and legs. Underparts, including the chin, throat, and insides of the legs, are white. Lighter ring around the eye. Facial glands are enormous, especially in males. Pink-lined ears. The legs are ringed with a black band just above the hooves. Black-colored horns, found only in males, ridged for most of their length, slanting back in line with the face. Female similar to male but without horns.

Neotragus moschatus

OTHER NAMES Zanzibar Suni. *French*: Suni de Zanzibar. *German*: Moschusböckchen, Suni. *Spanish*: Suni de Zanzibar. *Russian*: Восточноафриканский суни. *Swahili*: Paa mwekundu. *Zulu*: Inhlengane.

SUBSPECIES Monotypic. The name *N. moschatus* (Suni) formerly included *N. moschatus* (Coastal Suni), *N. kirchenpaueri* (Mountain Suni), and *N. livingstonianus* (Livingstone's Suni) as subspecies; these are all elevated to full species here. Includes *deserticola* (Kenya, from Maji ya Chumvi in desert of the Coast Province, from the Tana River S to Tanzanian border), *moschatus*, and *zanzibaricus* (Zanzibar Island), with *moschatus* having priority. There is little evidence to support a separation of the Zanzibar Suni from the mainland populations in Kenya and Tanzania.

SIMILAR SPECIES Much smaller than Sharpe's Grysbok. Blue Duiker is similar in size and appearance, but is generally darker in color, horns are not ringed for most of their length, facial scent gland is curved, and the tail moves up and down, not from side to side. Mountain Suni has a darker coloration, and is more speckled. Livingstone's Suni is slightly larger.

REPRODUCTION *Gestation*: About 180 days. *Young per Birth*: 1. *Weaning*: 2 months. *Sexual Maturity*: 1-1.5 years. *Life Span*: 10 years.

BEHAVIOR *Family Group*: Pairs or small groups of a single ♂ and a few ♀. *Diet:* Leaves, fungi, fruits, and flowers; although they prefer to live near a water source, they can survive long periods of time without water. *Main Predators:* All predators the size of the Suni and up, including cats, birds of prey, and snakes. Very shy and secretive, active only in the evenings or at night. Much of the day is spent sleeping in sheltered and shaded areas, and they are known to freeze in order to blend in with their surroundings when attempting to avoid detection by predators. ♂ are territorial and mark their space with dung piles and secretions from their preorbital glands. They usually allow one mate and other ♀ to share their territory.

DISTRIBUTION *Native*: Kenya, Malawi, Mozambique, Tanzania. Found in coastal Kenya and Tanzania (Maji ya Chumvi, Mombasa Island, Sokoke Forest, Takaungu), Zanzibar (including Chwaka and Dimani), Chapani Islet, Boydu Island, Rufiji River delta, Sambala, Kilwa, Lindi, Liwale, Ukami, Mafia Island, Mbulu and Iringa districts, inland from Kilwa, Mikindani, Morogoro, S to Mozambique (from N of the Zambezi), and S Malawi.

HABITAT Dry woodland with thickets and underbrush, coastal forest and thickets, and riparian scrub and dry scrub along drainage areas.

STATUS Least Concern. Considered as Endangered in Zanzibar and the other nearby islands. Threatened mainly by habitat destruction and excessive hunting.

PHOTO CREDITS ♂: *Pat Meyer*, San Diego Zoo (USA). Head ♀: *James Stejskal*. ♀ and head ♂: *Olivier Lejade*, Mnemba Island (Tanzania).

Mountain Suni
NEOTRAGUS KIRCHENPAUERI

BL: 57-62 cm. SH: 33-35 cm. TL: 8-13 cm. W: 4.5 kg. HL: 6.5-13.3 cm (♂). Slightly smaller than the Livingstone's Suni. Coloration dark, dull brown, speckled dorsally with brown buff, shading to dull sandy along the white belly patch, and warmer sandy on the lower neck. Tail not contrasted with the body, colored like the back, darkening toward the tip, white below. Legs light sandy brown. Pasterns and digits dark brown. Ears gray to brown. Dark brown to black streak on the muzzle. Lighter ring around the eye. Facial glands are enormous, especially in males. Black-colored horns, found only in males, ridged for most of their length, slanting back in line with the face. Female similar to male but without horns.

♂

♀

Neotragus kirchenpaueri

OTHER NAMES East African Suni, Mount Meru Suni. *French*: Suni de Kirchenpauer. *German*: Kirchenpauer-Moschusböckchen. *Spanish*: Suni de Kirchenpauer, suni de montaña. *Russian*: Горный суни. *Swahili*: Paa mwekundu. *Zulu*: Inhlengane.

SUBSPECIES Monotypic. Formerly considered a subspecies of *N. moschatus* (Suni). Includes *akeleyi* (central Kenya), and *kirchenpaueri* (SE Kenya and Tanzania including Mafia Island), with *kirchenpaueri* having priority.

SIMILAR SPECIES Much smaller than Sharpe's Grysbok. Blue Duiker is similar in size and appearance, but is generally darker in color, horns are not ringed for most of their length, facial scent gland is curved, and the tail moves up and down, not from side to side. Coastal Suni is much lighter in color and less strongly speckled. Livingstone's Suni is slightly larger and not obviously speckled.

REPRODUCTION *Gestation*: About 180 days. *Young per Birth*: 1. *Weaning*: 2 months. *Sexual Maturity*: 1-1.5 years. *Life Span*: 10 years. Most births occur from November to March. Slightly darker than adults, the young are kept hidden for several weeks, only emerging to suckle.

BEHAVIOR *Family Group:* Pairs or small groups of a single ♂ and a few ♀. *Diet:* Browsers, feeding on both fresh and fallen leaves as well as fallen and growing fruits of trees and shrubs. Probably independent of drinking water and can obtain all necessary moisture from the food that they eat. *Main Predators:* All predators the size of the Suni and up, including cats, birds of prey, and snakes. Primarily active during the evening and night, sleeping the rest of the day in a shady, sheltered area. These shy antelope have excellent camouflage, which they use to their advantage. When danger starts to approach, the Suni freezes, remaining hidden until the threat is nearly on top of it, at which point it leaps up and dodges around bushes and shrubs, quickly vanishing into the undergrowth. ♂ defend territories of about 3 ha, scent marking the boundaries with preorbital gland secretions. On the peripheries of each defended area may be individual or communal dung piles. Each ♂ generally associates with a single ♀, even if several others share his territory. Weak barking and sharp whistling have been reported.

DISTRIBUTION *Native*: Kenya, Malawi, Tanzania. Confined to the highlands of Kenya E of the Gregory Rift Valley, in N Tanzania (Aberdares Escarpment, Mount Kenya, Kikuyo and Langata, Mount Kilimanjaro, Mount Meru, Ngorongoro, Magamba, and the Olmoti and Empakaai craters), highlands of Malawi.

HABITAT Dry woodland with thickets and underbrush, coastal forest and thickets, and riparian scrub and dry scrub along drainage areas.

STATUS Least Concern. Total population estimate of 365,000 animals, over 100,000 on the Tanzania mainland.

PHOTO CREDITS ♂: *Lo Fion*, Mount Kenya Safari Club Wildlife Sanctuary (Kenya). Head ♂: *Stephen Mallison*, Mount Kenya Game Ranch (Kenya). ♀: *Bill Gozansky*, Aberdares NP (Kenya). Head ♀: *Nick Fraser*, Mount Kenya Safari Club Wildlife Sanctuary (Kenya).

Livingstone's Suni
NEOTRAGUS LIVINGSTONIANUS

BL: 57-62 cm. SH: 35-38 cm. TL: 8-13 cm. W: 4.5-6.8 kg. HL: 6.5-13.3 cm (♂). Larger subspecies, with longer and thicker horns. Coat color is brown or rufous fawn with minimal speckling. Flanks shading to buffy, with some contrast between the dorsum and the haunches. Underparts, including the chin, throat, and insides of the legs, are white. Back, neck, muzzle, and top of the head are darker. Lighter ring around the eye. Facial glands are enormous, especially in males. Pink-lined ears give the appearance of being almost transparent. Long and slender legs. Tail dark above, white below. Legs with a black band just above the hooves. Black-colored horns, found only in males, ridged for most of their length, slanting back in line with the face. Female slightly larger than male, without horns.

Neotragus livingstonianus
livingstonianus

Neotragus livingstonianus
zuluensis

OTHER NAMES Livingstone's Antelope. *French*: Antilope musquée, suni de Livingstone. *German*: Livingstone-Moschusböckchen. *Spanish*: Suni de Livingston. *Russian*: Суни Ливингстона. *Afrikaans*: Soenie. *Swahili*: Paa kusi. *Zulu*: Inhlengane.

SUBSPECIES Two subspecies are recognized: *N. l. livingstonianus*: S Malawi, central Mozambique S of the Zambezi River, and N Zimbabwe; *N. l. zuluensis*: S Mozambique and NE South Africa. Formerly considered a subspecies of *N. moschatus* (Suni).

SIMILAR SPECIES Larger, with thicker and longer horns, and much browner than East African Suni, with greater contrast between the dorsum and the haunches. Much smaller than Sharpe's Grysbok. Blue Duiker is similar in size and appearance, but is generally darker in color, horns are not ringed for most of their length, facial scent gland is curved, and the tail moves up and down, not from side to side.

REPRODUCTION *Gestation*: About 180 days. *Young per Birth*: 1. *Weaning*: 2 months. *Sexual Maturity*: 1-1.5 years. *Life Span*: 10 years. Most births occur from November to March. Newborns are hidden in thick bush and mothers return to suckle and groom them. Newborns are slightly darker than adults.

BEHAVIOR *Family Group*: Single adult ♂ or ♀, but sometimes adult pairs; occasionally adult ♀ with young, or a pair plus young. *Diet:* Browsers, feeding on both fresh and fallen leaves as well as fallen and growing fruits of trees and shrubs. Probably independent of drinking water and can obtain all necessary moisture from the food that they eat. *Main Predators:* All predators the size of the Suni and up, including cats, birds of prey, and snakes. Active at any time, mainly in the early morning and late afternoon, lies up in thickets during the hottest part of the day. Shy and wary; freezes if disturbed, then jumps away. Both sexes are territorial: ♂ territories overlap those of ♀. Territories cover 1-4 ha in good habitat and are larger in poor habitat. Scent marks of gland in front of the eyes are deposited on stems and twigs. Glands between the hooves mark pathways as it walks. Both sexes urinate and defecate in communal middens; if a strange Suni defecates on a midden, the territorial ♂ overmarks the deposit.

DISTRIBUTION *Native*: Malawi, Mozambique, South Africa, Swaziland, Zimbabwe. Found in South Africa, in Zululand N of the Hluhluwe River, and in NW Northern Province. Also in SE and NE Zimbabwe, most of Mozambique, S Malawi. They probably also occur in Swaziland.

HABITAT Dry closed woodland, bushland, and thicket on sand or clay soils. Scrub and bush along rivers and drainage lines. Independent of water. The preferred habitat is dense woody vegetation, with a high stem density in the shrub layer, and sparse ground cover.

STATUS Least Concern. The total number in KwaZulu-Natal is probably fewer than 1,000. The largest population of about 500 is in Tembe Elephant Park. Other protected areas which contain Sunis are Mkhuze, False Bay Park, and Ndumo. Considered as Endangered in South Africa (South African Red Data). Poaching with snares is the major cause of death.

PHOTO CREDITS ♂: *Dewi Edwards*, Tembe Elephant Park (South Africa). Head ♂: *AfriPics.com*, Tembe Elephant Park (South Africa). ♀: *Warwick Tarboton*, Caia Area (Mozambique). 33

Pygmy Antelope
NEOTRAGUS BATESI

BL: 50-57 cm. SH: 24-33 cm. TL: 4.5-8 cm. W: 2-3 kg. HL: 2-5.5 cm (♂). A very small antelope, extremely slender legged, with a short muzzle, large eyes, and moderately small ears. Coat is a glossy dark chestnut on the back, becoming lighter toward the flanks. Tail is dark brown. The only distinctive details are the black and white markings on the base of the ears, and the broad white band down the chin and throat. Chest, belly, inner parts of upper legs, front fetlocks white. Young may have a cream spot above the eye. Preorbital glands large, especially in males, round and not invaginated. Only males have smooth, brown or fawn horns, ringed at the base, that extend back over the head on the same plane as the face. Females are a little larger and heavier than males, without horns.

34

Neotragus batesi batesi

Neotragus batesi harrisoni

OTHER NAMES Bates's Pygmy Antelope, Dwarf Antelope. *French*: Antilope de Bates. *German*: Batesböckchen. *Spanish*: Antilope pigmeo de Bates, antílope enano. *Russian*: Антилопа Бейтса (антилопа-крошка). *Bila*: Ambilû. *Duala*: Jedu, Iseru. *Ewondo-Beti*: Odzoé.

SUBSPECIES Two subspecies are recognized: *N. b. batesi* (Cameroon Pygmy Antelope): Patchily distributed between Niger River and Zaire/Shanga River. *N. b. harrisoni* (Zaire Pygmy Antelope, Harrison Pygmy Antelope): NE DR Congo, W Uganda; more intense coloring, with dark areas darker and light areas lighter, and has white fetlocks and a small white spot above the front hoof; some authors consider it a separate species.

SIMILAR SPECIES Royal Antelope is smaller, the tail color is different, and there are no rings at the base of horns. It has recently been discovered that the Royal Antelope is not closely related to the other species in the genus, and the genus must be split up. Blue Duiker may be distinguished by its larger size, the curved profile of the head, the general shape of the body, and the presence of a crest between the tiny horns.

REPRODUCTION *Gestation*: 180 days. *Young per Birth:* 1. *Weaning*: 2 months. *Sexual Maturity*: 16 months (♀), 8-18 months (♂). Life Span: Up to 10 years. Pygmy Antelope apparently mates throughout the year, but peaks of mating activity occur in the late dry and early wet seasons.

BEHAVIOR *Family Group*: Most often solitary. *Diet*: Leaves, buds, shoots, fungi, and limited amounts of grasses and herbs. They also eat human food crops, such as peanuts, in areas where humans have intruded into their natural habitats. Pygmy Antelopes have a typical home range of 2 to 4 ha. ♂ are territorial, marking their territory with scent that is produced in the preorbital glands. ♀ are not as territorial as the ♂ and are sometimes found in small groups. ♂ emit a nasal call when seeking ♀, and both sexes often make a short, raspy bark when fleeing.

DISTRIBUTION *Native*: Cameroon, Congo, DR Congo, Equatorial Guinea, Gabon, Nigeria, Uganda. Pygmy Antelope are found in three disjunct regions: SE Nigeria, E of the Niger River to the Cross River; S and SE Cameroon (S of the Sanaga River) to SW Central African Republic (W of the Sangha River), Gabon, and NW and SW Congo; and NE DR Congo, N and E of the Congo-Lualaba, extending marginally into SW Uganda.

HABITAT An inhabitant of moist lowland forest, this species prefers dense, low undergrowth along rivers, tree falls within mature forests, areas regenerating after logging or cultivation, roadsides, village gardens and plantations.

STATUS Least Concern. Estimated total population of 219,000 animals in 1999.

PHOTO CREDITS Based on photos from *Bruce Davidson*, Epulu, Ituri Rainforest Reserve (DR Congo) and *Jim Shockey* (Cameroon).

Royal Antelope
NEOTRAGUS PYGMAEUS

BL: 40-50 cm. SH: 25 cm. TL: 5-8 cm. W: 1.5-3 kg. HL: To 3.8 cm (♂). A very small antelope, one of the smallest living ungulates, the size of a rabbit. Legs long and slender; hind legs much longer than front legs, giving the body a crouched appearance. Soft coat reddish brown in color; underparts, including chin and inside legs, white, but there is a brown band which crosses the chest and breaks up the white underside. White tuft at the end of the thin tail. No distinctive facial markings. Round, dark brown eyes are large and preorbital glands are present. Muzzle is petite and the large rhinarium is gray pink in color. Rounded ears translucent, with the inner surface being flesh colored. No tuft of hair on the forehead. Males grow a very small pair of black-colored cone-like horns, inclined backward in the plane of the face. Females similar to males, but without horns.

Young

♂

♀

Neotragus pygmaeus

OTHER NAMES *French*: Antilope royale, antilope pygmée. *German*: Kleinstböckchen. *Spanish:* Antílope enano, antílope real. *Russian*: Карликовая антилопа. *Twi*: Adowa. *Dyula*: Sagbene. *Igbo*: Ene.

SUBSPECIES Monotypic. Includes *perpusillus* (Guinea), *regia* (Senegal), *spiniger* (W coast of Africa) and *spinigera* (coast of Guinea). It has recently been discovered that the Royal Antelope is not closely related to the other species in the genus, and the genus must be split up.

SIMILAR SPECIES Pygmy Antelope is very similar, but is found only in central Africa, has small black and white markings on the ears, and tends to be slightly larger and darker in color. Mouse deer (*Tragulus*) from Asia are similar in size and form, but have very conspicuous white stripes on the throat.

REPRODUCTION *Gestation*: Unknown (probably 210 days). *Young per Birth*: 1. *Weaning*: 2 months. *Sexual Maturity*: After 1 year. *Life Span:* 10 years. In the wild, Royal Antelope are thought to give birth in November and December. Babies are extremely fragile and weigh less than 300 grams.

BEHAVIOR *Family Group*: Likely solitary or in monogamous pairs. *Diet*: Leaves and shoots, as well as flowers, fruit, and fungi; grass is rarely touched. *Main Predators*: Most predators found within its range, including birds of prey and large snakes. The Royal Antelope is a very shy species that is difficult to study. This species is most active around dawn and dusk, and may also be active at night. They inhabit very small territories (about 100 m²) which are marked with piles of dung. When a threat approaches, Royal Antelope will first crouch and slink into cover in the hope of going undetected. They will take flight only when the threat is very close, zipping through the undergrowth or using strong leaps to clear obstacles. While walking, the legs are lifted high and placed carefully, and the tail is constantly flicked. The powerful hind legs provide excellent propulsion, and fleeing animals disappear rapidly into undergrowth. They are reported to leap as far as 2.8 m, and as high as 55 cm from a standing start.

DISTRIBUTION *Native*: Côte d'Ivoire, Ghana, Guinea, Liberia, Sierra Leone. From SW Guinea, Sierra Leone, Liberia, SE Guinea, Côte d'Ivoire, to the Volta River, Ghana. Records from the forests east of the Volta River in NE Ghana remain questionable. There have been observations of the tracks of Royal Antelopes in Comoé NP in NE Côte d'Ivoire.

HABITAT Forested areas with dense undergrowth, and can be found in pockets of forest along roads and in farmland.

STATUS Least Concern. It was estimated that the total population of Royal Antelope numbered 62,000 in 1999, but this is thought to be an underestimate.

PHOTO CREDITS ♀: *Harry Kouwen* (Ghana). ♂ and head: *Alex Meyer,* San Diego Zoo (USA). Head ♂: *Dennis Chanter,* Freetown (Sierra Leone). Young: *Amy*, San Diego Zoo (USA).

Ellipsen Waterbuck
KOBUS ELLIPSIPRYMNUS

BL: 180-220 cm. SH: 100-136 cm. TL: 33-45 cm. W: 250-275 kg (♂), 160-180 kg (♀). HL: 79-92 cm (♂). Large and robust antelope. Shaggy, coarse coat is reddish brown to grizzled gray in color, darkening with age. Hair on the neck is especially long and forms a rough mane. Facial markings composed of a white muzzle, lighter eyebrows, and insides of the ears. Cream-colored bib on the throat. Large white halo surrounding the base of the tail on the rump (no other antelope has such a marking). Body is heavyset, strong legs are black in color, with a white ring above the hooves. Heavily ridged horns found only in males, sweeping in an arc backward and upward, with the tips pointing forward. Females similar to males, slightly smaller and without horns, and white markings tend to be less conspicuous than in males.

♀

♂
Juvenile

♂
Young

♂

Kobus ellipsiprymnus

OTHER NAMES Common Waterbuck, Ringed Waterbuck. *French*: Cobe à croissant, aussi appelé waterbuck. *German*: Ellipsen-Wasserbock. *Spanish*: Antílope acuático oriental, kob acuático oriental. *Russian*: Обыкновенный, или кольцехвостый водяной козёл. *Afrikaans*: Waterbok, kringgat. *Swahili*: Kuru. *Ndebele*: Isidumuka. *Zulu*: Isiphiva. *Sepedi*: Phitlwa, tomoga, tumuga, sekwele. *Sesotho*: Phitlwa. *Setswana*: Letimoga, motumoga, tumoga. *Shona*: Dhumukwa. *Swati*: Phiva, isiphiva, liphiva. *Xitonga*: Mhitlwa, phiva. *Lozi*: Ngunduma. *Damara*: Gampiris.

SUBSPECIES Monotypic. The name *K. ellipsiprymnus* formerly included *K. ellipsiprymnus* (Ellipsen Waterbuck), and *K. defassa* (Defassa Waterbuck) as subspecies: these are all elevated to full species here. Hybridization occurs in regions of sympatry. Includes *ellipsiprymnus* (S Africa), *kondensis* (S Tanzania), *pallidus* (Webi Shebeli drainage in Ethiopia, and Juba and Webi Shebeli drainages in Somalia), and *thikae* (S and E Kenya and NE Tanzania).

SIMILAR SPECIES Defassa Waterbuck is slightly smaller, with a longer tail, and the area within the circle on the rump is covered with white hair, creating a rump patch.

REPRODUCTION *Gestation*: 255-270 days. *Young per Birth*: 1, rarely 2. *Weaning*: 6-7 months. *Sexual Maturity*: 12-14 months (♀), 14-18 months (♂). *Life Span*: 18 years. Reproduction occurs throughout the year, although in South Africa, births tend to occur in December-June. After birth, the young lie concealed and away from their mothers for at least 2 weeks. After joining the herd, the young follow their mother, who raises her tail as a "follow me" signal, emphasized by the white rump ring.

BEHAVIOR *Family Group*: ♂, ♀, and mixed groups of up to 30 animals. *Diet*: Grasses, reeds, leaves. *Main Predators*: Lion, leopard, hyena, Cape hunting dog. Good swimmer and flees into water if pursued, although it does not actually like going into water. At 7-9 months, ♂ are driven from their maternal family and join up with a bachelor herd. These groups have a distinct social hierarchy based on size and strength, and contests are frequent. Around 6-7 years, ♂ become territorial, staking out areas of 60-250 ha and defending them against mature rivals with posturing and fights. These territories are maintained throughout the year, and a ♂ is generally overthrown before he reaches 10 years of age. Only about 5-10% of mature ♂ are territorial at the same time. ♀ groups wander over a home range of 200-600 ha, which may be kept for up to 8 years and encompasses several ♂ territories. Population densities in Uganda vary from 0.15 to 17.8 animals per km².

DISTRIBUTION *Native*: Botswana, Kenya, Malawi, Mozambique, Namibia, Somalia, South Africa, Swaziland, Tanzania, Zambia. *Regionally Extinct*: Ethiopia. Its distribution is separated from that of the Defassa Waterbuck by the Muchinga Escarpment in Zambia.

HABITAT Areas close to water in savanna grasslands, gallery forests, and riverine woodlands.

STATUS Least Concern. Estimated population of 105,000, with more than 50% in protected areas and 13% on private land.

PHOTO CREDITS ♂: *Ken Zaremba*, Moremi (Botswana). Head ♂: *Eric Isselee* (Tanzania). Head ♀: *Gerrit De Vries* (South Africa). ♀: *Arthur Ramos*, Lion Country Safari (USA). Young: *Sue Adlard* and *Nadja Späth*, Kruger (South Africa). Juvenile: *Derek Keats*, Borakalo (South Africa).

Defassa Waterbuck

KOBUS DEFASSA

BL: 175-235 cm. SH: 120-136 cm. TL: 33-40 cm. W: 198-262 kg (♂), 161-214 kg (♀). HL: 75-84 cm (♂). Large and robust antelope. In the western part of their range, coat is short and thin, and color is gray without any bright rufous tinge. In the eastern part, coat is long and shaggy and a bright reddish-brown color. Underparts and inner surfaces of legs vary from white to dusky brown. Rump is entirely white, and does not extend above the base of the tail. Legs dark, and a narrow white band is present above the hooves. Forehead bright rufous, and a brownish-black blaze extends along the bridge of the nose from the eyes to the nose. White superciliary stripes, markings around the nose and lips, and a bib on the upper throat, as in Ellipsen Waterbuck. Ears short and rounded; the inside of ears white. Horns extend backward from the forehead and then curve upward. Females smaller than males, without horns.

♀

Juvenile

♂

Young

♂

40

Kobus defassa

OTHER NAMES Sing-sing Waterbuck. *French*: Cobe defassa, antilope sing-sing. *German*: Defassa-Wasserbock. *Spanish*: Kob acuático septentrional. *Russian*: Восточноафриканская дефасса.

SUBSPECIES Monotypic. Formerly considered a subspecies of *K. ellipsiprymnus*. Hybridization may occur with *K. ellipsiprymnus*. Includes *adolfifriderici*, *annectens*, *crawshayi* (Crawshay Defassa Waterbuck), *defassa*, *harnieri*, *penricei* (Angolan Defassa Waterbuck), *tschadensis*, *tjaderi*, *ugandae* (Uganda Defassa Waterbuck) and *unctuosus* (Sing-sing Waterbuck), with *defassa* having priority.

REPRODUCTION *Gestation*: 272-287 days. *Young per Birth*: 1, rarely 2. *Weaning*: 6-7 months. *Sexual Maturity*: 12-14 months (♀), 14-18 months (♂). *Life Span*: 23 years. Reproduction occurs throughout the year. Peaks in birth rates are generally correlated with rainy seasons. A ♂ courts an estrous ♀ by following her while champing his lips; if the ♀ stops and urinates, the ♂ lets the urine flow over his nose and mouth, then performs flehmen by curling the lips distinctively. Mounting is presaged by gentle kicks of the forelegs directed between the hind legs to the abdomen of the ♀. After birth, the young lie concealed and away from their mothers for at least 2 weeks. They disperse from their mothers by 11 months and join a bachelor group.

BEHAVIOR *Family Group:* ♂, ♀, and mixed groups of up to 30 animals. *Diet:* Coarse grasses seldom eaten by other grazing animals, occasionally leaves from certain trees and bushes. *Main Predators:* Lion, leopard, hyena, Cape hunting dog. Active throughout the day and night. During daylight hours, there are peaks in activity in the morning and evening; resting increases with higher solar radiation. Sedentary and territorial. Daily movements rarely exceed 1 km. ♀ live in small maternal groups; associations are temporary, and no long-lasting social bonds have been observed. ♀ group size is smallest (3-6 individuals) during rains; during dry seasons associations may number up to 25 animals. ♀ groups wander over a home range of 200-600 ha, which may be kept for up to 8 years and encompass several ♂ territories. Mature ♂ are territorial, although in high-density populations only a few of them are able to maintain a territory. They may have an alliance with 1-3 other adult ♂. Fights between resident and intruding ♂ may be vigorous. Old ♂ often remain solitary. Unlike ♀ groups, bachelor herds are stable, with a hierarchy based on size.

DISTRIBUTION *Native*: Angola, Benin, Burkina Faso, Burundi, Cameroon, Central African Republic, Chad, Congo, DR Congo, Côte d'Ivoire, Eritrea, Ethiopia, Gabon, Ghana, Guinea, Guinea-Bissau, Kenya, Malawi, Mali, Namibia, Niger, Nigeria, Rwanda, Senegal, Sierra Leone, Somalia, Sudan, Tanzania, Togo, Uganda, Zambia.

HABITAT Scrub, savanna, and woodlands near water. Adult ♀ show greater use of open forest compared to adult ♂, which primarily inhabit open grassland.

STATUS Least Concern. Estimated population of 95,000, with about 60% in protected areas.

PHOTO CREDITS ♂: *Sara Hemcc*, Mweya (Uganda). Head ♂: *Sam D'Cruz*, Murchison Falls (Uganda). ♀: *Natividad Castillo Gonzalez*, Kidepo Valley (Uganda). Young: *Sven Tilemann* and *Rob Williams* (Kenya). Juvenile: *Joachim Niemeie* and *Isidro Vila Verde* (Kenya).

Buffon's Kob

KOBUS KOB

BL: 160-180 cm. SH: 90-100 cm (♂), 82-92 cm (♀). TL: 10-15 cm. W: 60 kg (♂), 45 kg (♀). HL: 48-65 cm (♂). Coat is smooth, shiny, and short. Color is golden brown to orange, with the underparts and inner surfaces of the legs bright white. Outer surfaces of the legs are the same color as the body, with a vertical black stripe on the front of all 4 limbs, and a white band is present above the hooves. White-colored facial markings include conspicuous eye rings, insides of ears, and throat and upper neck. Bushy tail is white underneath and terminates with a black tip. Lyre-shaped horns, strongly ringed, found only in males. Females similar to males, but smaller, and without horns.

♀

♂

Juvenile

♂

Young

Kobus kob

OTHER NAMES Senegal Kob, Western Kob. *French*: Cobe de Buffon. *German:* Senegal-Grasantilope. *Spanish*: Cobo de Buffon. *Russian*: Западный болотный козёл, или болотный козёл Бюффона.

SUBSPECIES Monotypic. The name *K. kob* formerly included *K. kob* (Buffon's Kob), *K. thomasi* (Uganda Kob), *K. loderi* (Loder's Kob), and *K. leucotis* (White-eared Kob) as subspecies: these are all elevated to full species here.

SIMILAR SPECIES White-eared Kob ♂ is almost black brown in color. Uganda Kob is larger, with a rich dark rufous color and has larger horns. Loder's Kob is very similar to Buffon's Kob, with sorter horns, and may have speckling of black hairs throughout the coat.

REPRODUCTION *Gestation*: 240 days. *Young per Birth*: 1. *Weaning:* 6-7 months. *Sexual Maturity*: 13 months (♀), 18 months (♂). *Life Span:* 7 years in the wild. They may breed throughout the year, although a peak in matings is seen in February-March. Births are concentrated at the start of the dry season. Lekking is now uncommon due to low population density. Breeding ♂ are territorial; ♀ pass freely through territories. ♂ follow estrous ♀ with their neck stretched forward and head low. Ritualized foreleg kicks (laufschlag) are a prelude to mounting. Juvenile ♂ are forced from their natal herds at 8 months of age.

BEHAVIOR *Family Group:* From solitary to large herds of 100 or more. *Diet:* Grasses; occasionally browse on young leaves of woody plants; drink daily and may consume mineral-rich soils. *Main Predators:* Lion, leopard, cheetah, hyena, Cape hunting dog. Active during the day and night, although activity levels are higher during the day. The largest groups are observed during the dry season (December-March), when they travel to drinking sites, and at the beginning of the rainy season (April-July), when they emerge onto open grasslands. Herds are very flexible and are mainly composed of ♀. ♂ are more solitary and often territorial. Young ♂ associate in bachelor herds. Fights are generally rare.

DISTRIBUTION *Native*: Benin, Burkina Faso, Côte d'Ivoire, Ghana, Guinea, Guinea-Bissau, Mali, Niger, Nigeria, Senegal, Togo. *Regionally Extinct*: Gambia, Sierra Leone, Mauritania.

HABITAT Open savannas and alluvial plains, inhabiting grasslands closely associated with lakes and rivers. It is rarely found more than a few km away from a permanent water source, particularly during the dry season.

STATUS Vulnerable. Population has declined over the past generations, primarily as a result of hunting. They are already extinct in Gambia, Sierra Leone, and possibly S Mauritania, and rare in several other West African countries. Total population is likely 40,000-75,000, the majority restricted to protected areas.

PHOTO CREDITS ♂: *Randy Siebert*, Mole NP (Ghana). ♀, head and juvenile: *Jonas Van de Voorde*, Pendjari NP (Benin).

Loder's Kob

KOBUS LODERI

BL: 160-180 cm. SH: 90-100 cm (♂), 82-92 cm (♀). TL: 10-15 cm. W: 60 kg (♂), 45 kg (♀). HL: 48-53 cm (♂). Very similar to the Buffon's Kob. The color is tawny to reddish brown in both sexes, with the underparts and inner surfaces of the legs bright white. Some individuals may have speckling of black hairs throughout the coat. Outer surfaces of the legs are the same color as the body, with a vertical black stripe on the front of all four limbs. Neck and face are paler than the rest of the body. White-colored facial markings include inconspicuous eye rings, the insides of ears, and throat and upper neck. Bushy tail is white underneath and terminates with a black tip. Lyre-shaped horns, strongly ringed, found only in males, tend to be shorter than in the Buffon's Kob. Males are larger and have prominent muscle definition, especially on the neck, and are more richly colored. Females are hornless.

♀

♂

44

Kobus loderi

OTHER NAMES Cameroon Kob. *French*: Cobe de Loder. *German*: Kamerun-Grasantilope. *Spanish*: Cobo de Loder. *Russian*: Камерунский болотный козёл.

SUBSPECIES Monotypic. Formerly considered a subspecies of *K. kob* (Kob). Some authors consider *loderi* an invalid species, including it under *thomasi* or *kob*.

REPRODUCTION *Gestation*: 9 months. *Young per Birth*: 1. *Weaning:* 3 months. *Sexual Maturity*: 12-16 months. *Life Span:* 11 years. Breeding occurs throughout the year, although a peak occurs during the dry season (February-March). Courtship often involves a parallel walk in pairs. Prior to giving birth, a ♀ isolates herself and seeks out dense brush. After birth, the young lie concealed for about 1 week; after 1-2 weeks they follow their mothers.

BEHAVIOR *Family Group:* Maternal and bachelor herds with 5-25 animals. *Diet:* Grasses. *Main Predators:* Lion, leopard, cheetah, hyena, Cape hunting dog. They tend to concentrate around water sources. Herds with more than 25 individuals are rarely seen nowadays. ♂ are usually solitary, especially during the breeding season when they become territorial and exclude other ♂ from their vicinity. Territories are delineated with urine, feces, and scent marks along the boundaries. ♂ will also stand on raised areas to advertise their presence. Immature and old ♂ form bachelor herds. They are most active in the morning and late afternoon. Population densities are low, usually 1-12 animals per km^2.

DISTRIBUTION *Native*: Cameroon, Central African Republic, Chad, DR Congo, Nigeria, Sudan.

HABITAT Well-watered areas, like floodplains. It is rarely found more than 10 km from a permanent source of water.

STATUS Vulnerable. Population is estimated at 30,000 individuals, with most large populations surviving in protected areas.

PHOTO CREDITS *Tore Berg* and *Michael Lorentz*, Zakouma NP (Chad).

45

Uganda Kob
KOBUS THOMASI

BL: 125-180 cm. SH: 70-105 cm. TL: 10-15 cm. W: 50-120 kg (♂), 60-77 kg (♀). HL: 50-69 cm (♂). The largest of the Kob species. Smooth, shiny coat is reddish brown, often with golden tones, with the underparts bright white. White-colored facial markings include conspicuous complete eye rings, chin and muzzle, insides of ears, and throat and upper neck. The outer sides of the legs have a vertical black stripe running down the length, while the insides are white in color. Bushy tail is white underneath and terminates with a black tip. A white bib is situated on the upper throat, particularly well defined in adult males. Males are 50% larger than females, and have distinctly muscular necks. The S-shaped horns, strongly ringed, found only in males, bend sharply backward, then curve up. Female similar to the male, but smaller, less richly colored, and without horns.

♀

Young

♂

♂

Juvenile

Kobus thomasi

OTHER NAMES Thomas's Kob. *French*: Cobe de Thomas. *German*: Uganda-Grasantilope. *Spanish*: Cobo de Uganda. *Russian*: Угандский болотный козёл. *Basari*: Endyay. *Gbaya*: Kòdé, kò, dè, pénya. *Manza*: Kò'dé. *Sango*: Tagba. *Shaba*: Sebula, sunnu. *Zande*: Tagba.

SUBSPECIES Monotypic. Formerly considered a subspecies of *K. kob* (Kob). Includes *alurae* (NW Uganda, S Sudan, and N DR Congo), *neumanni* (W Uganda and NE DR Congo), and *thomasi* (E Uganda, and formerly in W Kenya), with *thomasi* having priority.

SIMILAR SPECIES Largest subspecies. Leg markings deeper black than in the Buffon's and Loder's Kobs. White areas of the throat and face more extensive and distinct than in the Buffon's and Loder's Kobs, but less so than in the White-eared.

REPRODUCTION *Gestation*: 225-270 days. *Young per Birth*: 1. *Weaning:* 6-7 months. *Sexual Maturity*: 13 months (♀), 18 months (♂). *Life Span:* 17 years. While births may occur throughout the year, in drought-prone areas there is a peak at the end of the rains (September-December). After birth, the young lie concealed for about 6 weeks, after which they follow their mothers.

BEHAVIOR *Family Group:* Mixed groups of 30-50 individuals; in areas of high density up to 60-1,000 individuals. *Diet:* Selective grazer, preferentially foraging on short green grasses. *Main Predators:* Lion, leopard, cheetah, hyena, Cape hunting dog. Most active in the morning and late afternoon. The social system is loose, and long-term associations are rare. Herds are often temporary. The largest herds are most frequent during the wet season, when they congregate on short-grass pastures. Adult ♂ are territorial, although the size of their defended ranges varies depending on the habitat and population density. Leks are normally 200 m in diameter, with 12-15 (rarely over 200) approximately circular individual territories which measure 15-30 m across. The resident ♂ does not physically mark his area; rather he patrols its boundaries. Vocal and visual advertisements, such as whistling calls and strutting with head high and ears lowered, signify the occupancy of a territory. Serious fights occur whenever other ♂ try to displace a territory holder, and are highly attractive to ♀. The length of time a ♂ may hold his territory varies from days to months. Population densities vary from 8 to 50 animals per km² depending on the habitat.

DISTRIBUTION *Native*: DR Congo, Sudan, Uganda. *Regionally Extinct*: Kenya, Tanzania.

HABITAT Well-watered areas, like floodplains.

STATUS Least Concern. Estimated population is 40,000-100,000 individuals. Most common in Murchison Falls NP, Queen Elizabeth NP, and the Toro-Semliki area (Uganda).

PHOTO CREDITS ♂: *Dov Murik*, Kabarega NP, Nwoya (Uganda). Head ♂: *Scott Lamont*, Queen Elizabeth NP (Uganda). Head ♀ and young: *Martha de Jong-Lantink*, Queen Elizabeth NP (Uganda). ♀: *Stefano Madama,* Queen Elizabeth NP, Ishasha sector (Uganda). Juvenile: *Simon Whitaker*, Queen Elizabeth NP (Uganda) and *Walter Callens*, Murchison Falls (Uganda).

White-eared Kob

KOBUS LEUCOTIS

BL: 160-180 cm. SH: 82-100 cm. TL: 10-15 cm. W: 55-82 kg (♂), 40 kg (♀). HL: 55 cm (♂). Coloration shows extreme sexual dimorphism: males black sometimes with brown-black overtones, insides of ears extremely light, white eye rings sit heavily against the rest of the coat, white underparts; the outer surfaces of the legs are black, except for a white band just above the hooves, and the inside surfaces are white. Intermediate colors are seen as males mature. Females and young males chestnut red with white undersides and dark markings on the front of the forelimbs. Males significantly heavier than females. Lyre-shaped horns, strongly ringed, found only in males, emerging almost vertically, curving backward and then upward at the tips.

♀

♂
Juvenile

♂

Kobus leucotis

OTHER NAMES *French*: Cobe à orelles blanches. *German*: Weissohr-Moorantilope. *Spanish*: Cobo orejiblanco. *Russian*: Белоухий болотный козёл.

SUBSPECIES Monotypic. Formerly considered a subspecies of *K. kob* (Kob).

SIMILAR SPECIES It has the most distinctive appearance of any Kob. Larger in body and horns than Buffon's and Loder's Kobs, but about the same size as Uganda Kob. The darkest-colored ♂ are found on the East Bank of the White Nile, but those with the longest horns are from the West Bank. Nile Lechwe is larger, with a much shaggier coat, and a distinctive white shoulder patch.

REPRODUCTION *Gestation*: 240 days. *Young per Birth*: 1. *Weaning*: 6 months. *Sexual Maturity*: 12 months (♀), 18 months (♂). *Life Span:* 16 years. Breeding is spread between January and April, with births coinciding with the late wet season, from September to December. During the mating season, ♂ cluster together on small territories within traditional breeding grounds (leks). ♂ tend to court individual ♀ and actively try to prevent them from dispersing to neighboring ♂. Neonates are tucked away in tall grass and thickets for several weeks.

BEHAVIOR *Family Group:* Maternal and bachelor herds with 5-40 animals. Groups over 1,000 are known. *Diet:* Grasses; leaves and stems of short stoloniferous grasses are consumed year-round. *Main Predators:* Lion, leopard, cheetah, hyena, Cape hunting dog. Active both day and night, usually with a rest during the hottest parts of the day. During the dry season, this activity pattern becomes particularly pronounced; individuals will feed in swampy meadows at night and move into wooded areas during midday. ♀ are usually more active than ♂, likely due to the increased energy requirements associated with pregnancy and lactation. Its migrations represent the second largest migratory ungulate population in Africa after the Serengeti White-bearded Wildebeest. Migratory movements are driven by the availability of water. Very large herds, containing at least 700,000 animals of both sexes and all ages, travel 150-200 km between dry and wet season ranges. Territoriality among ♂ is only seen during the dry season, when lek territories are occupied. Twenty to 65 ♂ each defend a small territory within a lek, usually found withing a rough circle only 150-200 m in diameter. Leks are usually located near prime feeding areas so as to attract ♀. Levels of aggression are high, particularly at the start of the breeding season. Population densities vary from 5 to 20 animals per km^2; however, localized densities in excess of 1,000 animals per km^2 may be found in areas near water during the dry season.

DISTRIBUTION *Native*: Ethiopia, Sudan, Uganda. Found in SE Sudan and W Ethiopia, and occasionally seen in N Uganda.

HABITAT Open grassland with scattered wooded areas. It is found farther from permanent swamps than the sympatric Nile Lechwe, but it is rarely found more than 10 km from surface water.

STATUS Least Concern. An aerial survey in 2007 produced a population estimate for part of S Sudan of 753,000 animals.

PHOTO CREDITS *Dr. Ludwig Siege*, Gambella NP (Ethiopia). Head ♂: *Cherie Enawgaw Beyene*, EWCA/GCITF 2013, Gambella NP (Ethiopia).

Southern Puku
KOBUS VARDONII VARDONII

BL: 126-142 cm. SH: 77-83 cm. TL: 28-32 cm. W: 67-91 kg (♂), 48-78 kg (♀). HL: 45-53 cm (♂). Coarse coat uniformly golden brown in color, with underparts, including underside of the tail, being slightly paler. Forehead area generally darker than the body, while there are inconspicuous off-white areas around eyes and lips. Around the edge of ears is a fine black rim. No black markings on the front of the legs. Heavy body with a level back; legs are somewhat shorter than those of others in the genus *Kobus* and without any markings. Territorial males develop heavy neck musculature, while non-territorial males have thinner necks. Strongly ringed horns, found only in males, less lyrate than those of the Kob. Female similar to male, but with a brownish crown and without horns.

♀

Young

♂

♂
Juvenile

Kobus vardonii vardonii

OTHER NAMES Vardon's Kob, Yellow-footed Waterbuck. *French:* Puku. *German:* Gelnfuss-Moorantelope. *Spanish:* Pucú. *Russian:* Южный пуку. *Afrikaans:* Poekoe. *Bambara:* Sòn. *Banda-Linda:* Tagba. *Basari:* Endyay. *Chibisa:* Seulya. *Lozi:* Mitunya. *Manza:* Kòdè. *Shaba:* Sebula, sunna. *Setswana:* Phuku. *Wolof:* Mbadde. *Zande:* Tagba.

SUBSPECIES Considered as a subspecies of *K. vardonii* (Puku): *K. v. vardonii* (Southern Puku), *K. v. senganus* (Senga Puku, Senga Kob). Considered monospecific by some authors. Some authors propose that the Puku might be a subspecies of the Kob (*K. kob*) rather than a distinct species.

SIMILAR SPECIES Differs from the Kob by the absence of black markings on legs, shorter horns, longer and rougher coat, and the practical or complete absence of white hoof bands. Lechwe has longer and more divergent horns, and black markings on the legs.

REPRODUCTION *Gestation:* 240 days. *Young per Birth:* 1. *Weaning:* 6 months. *Sexual Maturity:* 12-14 months. *Life Span:* 17 years. Breeding occurs year-round, with a peak from May to September. During courtship, a ♂ follows an estrous ♀ with his head stretched forward and low; copulation is preceded by ritualized laufschlag in which the ♂ lifts a front leg between a ♀'s hind legs and taps her abdomen; copulation lasts less than 5 seconds. Neonates remain hidden in dense vegetation for a few weeks; young show a poorly developed following response, and if startled often flee away from their mothers. Young ♂ disperse from their mothers before 1 year of age, whereas a young ♀ may remain loosely associated with her dam into adulthood.

BEHAVIOR *Family Group:* Small maternal groups of 6-20 animals, adult ♂ solitary or in bachelor groups. *Diet:* Grasses. *Main Predators:* Lion, leopard, hyena, Cape hunting dog. Feeding activity is generally limited to the early mornings and late afternoons, although this period may extend long after dark. More adaptable in terms of habitat requirements than the Kob, and will inhabit areas of open woodland if conditions are suitable. During the rainy season, populations spread out on higher ground, descending to the margins of watercourses during the dry season. At this time, smaller groups may join together to form parties of 50 or more animals. When alarmed, it emits a shrill, repeated whistle. Solitary ♂ hold territories throughout the year, and each attempts to induce a herd of ♀ to remain on his patch of ground for as long as possible. These territories are spaced out over a considerable distance, and no lekking behavior, as seen in Kob, has been recorded.

DISTRIBUTION *Native:* Angola, Botswana, Namibia, Zambia. Found in SE Angola, SW Zambia, N Botswana, NE Namibia (Caprivi Strip), but it has been eliminated from large parts of its former range and reduced to fragmented, isolated populations, though some of these are still numerous. Large numbers now occur only in Zambia. Populations still occur in NE Botswana on the Chobe River floodplain.

HABITAT Floodplain grasslands near water in central S Africa.

STATUS Near Threatened.

PHOTO CREDITS ♂: *Andy Lowe*, Kafue (Zambia). Head ♂: *Kevin Stalder,* Chobe (Botswana). ♀: *Edward Schonsett* and *Margaret Elman*, Kafue (Zambia). Juvenile: *Nico Smit* and *Graham Bugg,* Kafue (Zambia). Young: *Philip J. Bergan*, Kafue (Zambia). 51

Senga Puku
KOBUS VARDONII SENGANUS

BL: 126-146 cm. SH: 73-83 cm. TL: 26-30 cm. W: 67-91 kg (♂), 48-78 kg (♀). HL: 41-55 cm (♂). Midsized antelope. Shaggy coat uniformly tan to golden brown in color, darker than in Southern Puku, with underparts, including underside of the tail, being slightly paler. Forehead area generally darker than the body, while there are inconspicuous off-white areas around eyes and lips. Around the edge of ears is a fine black rim. Chin and throat are paler. No black markings on the legs. Heavy body with a level back; legs are somewhat shorter than those of others in the genus *Kobus* and without any markings. Territorial males develop heavy neck musculature and black streaks on the lower neck, while non-territorial males have thinner necks. Strongly ringed horns, found only in males. Female similar to male, but with a brownish crown and without horns.

♀

Young

♂

Juvenile

♂

Kobus vardonii senganus

OTHER NAMES Northern Puku, Senga Kob. *French*: Puku. *German*: Gelnfuss-Moorantelope. *Spanish*: Pucú. *Russian*: Сенгский пуку. *Swahili*: Sheshe.

SUBSPECIES Considered as a subspecies of *K. vardonii* (Puku): *K. v. vardonii* (Southern Puku): SE Angola, SW Zambia, N Botswana, NE Namibia (Caprivi Strip); *K. v. senganus* (Senga Puku, Senga Kob). Considered monospecific by some authors.

SIMILAR SPECIES Smaller and darker colored, especially on head, than Southern Puku, with the black of ear tips occupying fully one-third the length of backs of ears, instead of being restricted to summits; otherwise, very similar. Female Bohor Reedbuck and Southern Common Reedbuck are similar in shape and size, but have black on the forelegs and bushier tails. Uganda Kob has black on the forelegs.

REPRODUCTION *Gestation*: 240 days. *Young per Birth*: 1. *Weaning*: 6 months. *Sexual Maturity:* 12-14 months. *Life Span:* 17 years. Mating and births occur throughout the year with a peak during the summer rainy season, between the months of May and September, to ensure that offspring are born during the wet season. Territorial ♂ are polygynous and herd ♀ into their territories. Offspring are hiders, meaning that females leave them on their own in a hidden place rather than travel with them. Older calves come out of hiding and join the herd. ♀ do not have a strong bond with their young, and rarely defend their young or address the high-pitched bleating a calf may produce when calling for help.

BEHAVIOR *Family Group:* Small maternal groups of from 6 to 23 animals, but during the rainy season, many herds will come together, typically reaching around 50 ♀. Adult ♂ solitary or in bachelor groups of up to 40 individuals. *Diet:* Obligate grazers, grasses. *Main Predators:* Lion, leopard, hyena, Cape hunting dog. Puku are both diurnal and crepuscular, with activity peaks around dawn and dusk. Territorial ♂ maintain their territories emitting 3 to 4 whistles to warn other ♂ to keep away; this whistle is also used as a way to advertise to ♀. Territorial ♂ rub their horns on the grass to saturate the grass with their neck secretions. ♂ fight with their horns. Territories average 4 km² and are temporary, lasting from a few days to several months. Puku are relatively easy to approach during the dry season, when densely aggregated on floodplains, and are consequently very vulnerable to illegal hunting.

DISTRIBUTION *Native*: DR Congo, Malawi, Tanzania, Zambia. Found in SW Tanzania, E DR Congo, N Zambia, and Malawi, but it has been eliminated from large parts of its former range and reduced to fragmented, isolated populations, though some of these are still numerous. Large numbers now occur in only two countries, Tanzania and Zambia.

HABITAT Grasslands near permanent water within the savanna woodlands and floodplains of S-central Africa. Although associated with wet areas and swamp vegetation, they avoid deep standing water.

STATUS Near Threatened. Estimated Puku population of 130,000 in 1999.

PHOTO CREDITS ♂: *Gary Macfadyen*. Head ♂: *Jaime Chang*. ♀: *Nigel Voaden*. Young: *Robert van Brug* and *Thomas Retterath*. Juvenile: *Matt Floreen*. All photos: South Luangwa (Zambia).

Red Lechwe

KOBUS LECHE

BL: 150-175 cm (♂), 134-162 cm (♀). SH: 94-112 cm (♂), 87-101 cm (♀). TL: 35-40 cm. W: 88-135 kg (♂), 52-89 kg (♀). HL: 45-66 cm (♂). Pelage coarse, bright reddish brown; dorsum particularly bright, flanks and thighs paler. Males darken with age. Underparts, neck, chin, mouth, lips, and eye ring white. Short muzzle. Black-tipped tail has a bushy white flag on the underside. Foreleg has a black stripe. Broad white band above the hooves. Body is long, with hindquarters higher than shoulders. Hooves long and narrow. Horns only in males, diverge and extend backward from the skull, growing increasingly parallel and curving upward toward the tip; thin and back slanted, with upturned tips, ringed along most of their length. Female similar to male, more lightly built, without horns.

♀

Juvenile

♂

♂

Young

Kobus leche

OTHER NAMES Southern Lechwe, Zambezi Lechwe, Common Lechwe. *French*: Cobe de Lechwe. *German*: Letschwe, Litschi. *Spanish*: Antílope Lechwe, kob rojo. *Russian*: Рыжий личи. *Afrikaans*: Rooi lechwe, basterwaterbok. *Zulu*: Iphiva. *Sepedi*: Kwele. *Setswana*: Letswee, letsweng. *Swati*: Liphiva.

SUBSPECIES Monotypic. The name *K. leche* formerly included *K. leche* (Red Lechwe), *K. kafuensis* (Kafue Flats Lechwe), *K. smithemani* (Black Lechwe), and *K. anselli* (Upemba Lechwe) as subspecies: these are all elevated to full species here. *K. l. robertsi* is extinct. Includes *ambolloensis* (SE Angola) and *notatus* (Caprivi).

REPRODUCTION *Gestation*: 210-240 days. *Young per Birth*: 1. *Weaning:* 4-7 months. *Sexual Maturity*: 1.5 years (♀), 2.5 years (♂). *Life Span:* 15 years. The majority of births occur in the dry season (July-October), although breeding has been noted throughout the year. Lambs lie hidden for up to 2 months; once they are mobile they spend more time with other lambs than with their mothers.

BEHAVIOR *Family Group:* Usually in small groups of 1-5, but may form loose mixed and single-sex herds of 400 or more animals. *Diet*: Grasses, water plants. *Main Predators*: Lion, leopard, cheetah, hyena, Cape hunting dog, crocodile, python. More active in the morning and late afternoon. They are regularly seen grazing in shoulder-deep water. They are good swimmers, but prefer to wade while walking on boggy ground. On solid land, their long, soft hooves are a disadvantage. Therefore, as seasonal floods and droughts occur, herds move in step with the water, grazing on the periphery of the floodplain. Generally, ♀ and their young are found in the wetter areas, with ♂, whether solitary or in bachelor herds, inhabiting the drier zones. As vegetation grows plentifully in the floodplain environment, population densities may be extremely high, up to 200 individuals per km^2 in some cases. No strict social system exists, and often the only lasting bonds are between a mother and her recent offspring. Due to the constant fluctuations in their habitat, ♂ do not hold extended territories. Instead, lekking is observed, with 20-200 ♂ defending small patches (15-200 m in diameter) within a common arena. Each of these clusters is associated with a large herd of ♀. The smaller, centrally located patches are prone to intense competition due to greater reproductive success, and an individual rarely holds this area for more than a few days. When disturbed they flee into the water via a series of ungainly bounds. Lechwe is the second most aquatic antelope after the Sitatunga.

DISTRIBUTION *Native*: Angola, Botswana, Namibia, Zambia. Distribution is discontinuous, with major populations restricted to extensive wetlands in Botswana, Namibia, Angola, and Zambia. It is found in the Okavango Delta, and the Kwando-Linyanti-Chobe system of N Botswana; the Okavango, Kwando-Linyanti-Chobe, Mashi, and Zambezi River systems of NE Namibia; and the upper Zambezi and middle Kafue of Zambia.

HABITAT Seasonal floodplains bordering swamps, rivers, and marshes in S-central Africa.

STATUS Least Concern. Population is estimated at 98,000 animals, 85% in the Okavango Delta.

PHOTO CREDITS ♂: *Benjamin Hollis*, Kwarea (Botswana). Head ♀: *Nico Smit*, Chobe (Botswana). Head ♂: *Andreas Rutz*, Moremi (Botswana). ♀: *Nicole Rodgers*. Juvenile: Cherokee Trace Safari (USA). Young: *Jerry Oldenettel* (Namibia).

Kafue Flats Lechwe
KOBUS KAFUENSIS

BL: 130-180 cm. SH: 99-112 cm (♂), 90-106 cm (♀). TL: 30-45 cm. W: 87-128 kg (♂), 62-97 kg (♀). HL: 62-83 (♂). General form of the body similar to that of Red Lechwe, slightly larger. Long, rough, greasy coat red brown. Males darken with age. Underparts, inside surface of legs, and stripe that extends along the throat from the chest to the underside of jaw are all white. Clear white rings around the eyes, lips, and chin. Front surfaces of the forelegs are rich black in color, as are the fronts of the lower hind legs; in males, the foreleg markings extend upward, forming a dark patch on the shoulders and extending along the lower margins of the white throat stripe. Tail slender, with a black terminal tuft. Horns, longer than in other Lechwe species, sweep backward from the forehead and curve upward, diverging from base to tips. Horns are ringed along most of their length. Females almost indistinguishable from Red Lechwe females.

♀

Young

♂

♂

Juvenile

Kobus kafuensis

OTHER NAMES Brown Lechwe. *French*: Cobe de Kafue. *German*: Kafue-Litschi. *Spanish*: Kob de Kafue. *Russian*: Кафуйский личи.

SUBSPECIES Monotypic. Formerly considered a subspecies of *K. leche* (Lechwe). Includes *grandicornis*.

SIMILAR SPECIES Somewhat larger in body than the Red Lechwe, with considerably longer horns and a lighter overall color, actually a fulvous or tawny chestnut; adult ♂ has distinctive dark patches on its shoulders.

REPRODUCTION *Gestation*: 240 days. *Young per Birth:* 1. *Weaning:* 4 months. *Sexual Maturity:* 1.5-2 years (♀), 15-30 months (♂). *Life Span:* 15 years. Reproduction shows strong seasonal trends, although some mating occurs year-round. Breeding coincides with rising water levels. The majority of births occur in the dry season (July-October). The young lie up for several weeks after birth before joining their mothers.

BEHAVIOR *Family Group:* Loose mixed and single-sex herds of 400 or more animals. *Diet*: Grasses, water plants. *Main Predators*: Lion, leopard, cheetah, hyena, Cape hunting dog, crocodile, python. Peak activity times in the morning and late afternoon. They live in marshy habitats and prefer swamps and wetlands. Excellent swimmers, but prefer wading in shallow water and walking on boggy ground. Kafue Flats Lechwe are comfortable standing and feeding in water up to 80 cm. When frightened, Lechwe completely submerge, leaving only their nostrils exposed. There is no strict social structure because of their natural nomadic behavior, following rains and floodplains in Africa. ♀ do, however, often exhibit "lekking" or defending small patches within a common area. Kafue Flats Lechwe give a snorting cough as an alert signal and during mating displays.

DISTRIBUTION *Native*: Zambia. Largely restricted to protected areas within the Kafue Flats, occurring in Lochinvar and Blue Lagoon NP and the Kafue Flats Game Management Area. The national parks are also listed jointly as a Ramsar Wetland of International Importance, and are managed exclusively for conservation, while the Kafue Flats Game Management Area is also managed for sport hunting.

HABITAT Open grasslands and floodplains associated with lakes, floodwaters, and streams; rarely seen more than 3 km away from surface water.

STATUS Vulnerable. Estimated population of 60,000 in 1999, stable since then. Maintenance of a seasonal flooding regime is critically important to survival; significant alteration to the current hydrological status could prove catastrophic.

PHOTO CREDITS ♂, ♀: *Ulrike Joerres*, Zoo Gdansk (Poland). Head ♂ and young: *Janet M. Horsman*, Yorkshire Wildlife Park (UK). Head ♀: *Marc Baldwin* (Wildlife Online), Exmoor Zoo, Barnstaple (UK). Young: *Debs Haynes*, Knowsley Safari Park (UK). Juvenile: *Ulrike Joerres*, Rostock Zoo (Germany) and *Marie Hale*, Knowsley Safari Park (UK).

Upemba Lechwe
KOBUS ANSELLI

BL: 160-180 cm. SH: 85-110 cm. TL: 30-45 cm. W: 45-75 kg (♂), 40-60 (♀). HL: 62-83 cm (♂). Smaller than other Lechwes. Lightly built, resembling the Black Lechwe. Pelage of both sexes is bright reddish brown. Flanks and neck are paler. Underparts are white, and a white stripe is present on the underside of the neck, which generally terminates before reaching the upper third of the neck. Forelegs have a thin blackish-brown stripe on the anterior surface; the lower hind legs are dark. Forehead and bridge of the nose are darker and more richly colored than the rest of the pale reddish-brown face. Circles of white hair surround the eyes, lips, ears, and chin. Long tail with a black bushy terminal tuft. Relatively slender horns, found only in males, diverging outward and curving backward before becoming approximately parallel and bending upward at the tips. Strong annulations are found along most of the horn length.

Kobus anselli

OTHER NAMES *French*: Cobe d'Ansell. *German*: Upemba-Litschi. *Spanish*: Kob de Upemba. *Russian*: Личи Анселла.

SUBSPECIES Monotypic. Formerly considered a subspecies of *K. leche* (Lechwe).

SIMILAR SPECIES Most similar to the Black Lechwe and quite distinct from the Red Lechwe.

REPRODUCTION *Gestation*: 260 days. *Young per Birth*: 1. *Weaning*: 3 months. *Sexual Maturity*: 1 year (♀). *Life Span:* 15 years. The breeding season begins in December, with reproductive peaking in mid-February and continuing until March-April. ♂ occupy territories with raised ground to attract ♀. Births occur between November and January, coinciding with the start of the rainy season. The neonate remains hidden for a few days, with the mother close by, especially at night. After the infant is stable on its feet, mother and offspring return to floodplain grazing areas.

BEHAVIOR *Family Group:* Large herds of up to 2,500 animals containing both sexes, during the wet season. Herds of fewer than 500 animals during the dry season. *Diet*: Grasses, water plants. *Main Predators*: Lion, leopard, cheetah, hyena, Cape hunting dog, crocodile, python. It is active both day and night. Feeding activity is highest in the morning. Midday is spent resting; individuals will lie down if dry underground is available, but in flooded pastures all remain standing. Unusual among ungulates, populations are more concentrated during the wet season (December-April). Herd structure appears to be relatively loose and lacking cohesion. Territoriality occurs only during the breeding season, often clustered around raised dry islands within flooded habitats. These territories are vigorously defended, resulting in severe injury or death.

DISTRIBUTION *Native*: DR Congo. Restricted to the Upemba wetlands, Kamalondo depression, in the Katanga Province of SE DR Congo.

HABITAT Edges of permanent swamps, seasonally inundated floodplains, and associated peripheral grasslands. Areas covered in shallow water 2-6 m deep, following the seasonal rise and fall of water levels.

STATUS Critically Endangered. Current data suggest than fewer than 1,000 individuals survive. Intense poaching for meat is believed to be responsible for the decline in population numbers.

PHOTO CREDITS ♂: *Benjamin Hollis.* Head: *Andreas Rutz.*

Black Lechwe

KOBUS SMITHEMANI

BL: 160-180 cm. SH: 85-110 cm. TL: 30-45 cm. W: 45-75 kg (♂), 40-60 (♀). HL: 62-83 cm (♂). Not actually black, but old males may turn blackish brown on the back and sides. Belly, inner surfaces of the legs, inside of ears, lips, and above the eyes, are white. Narrow pale strip running along the underside of the neck from the throat to the chest. Dark stripes on the front of forelegs. Tail has a bushy tip. As males mature, the reddish areas darken to brownish black, accentuating the white markings; there is considerable variation in the extent of the dark coloration between males as well as between seasons; rufous patches typically remain on the forehead and upper neck, the rump, and upper hind legs. Lyre-shaped horns, shorter and thinner than in the other Lechwes, but have a stronger curve. Females and young males are a dark chestnut color, somewhat darker than a Red Lechwe.

♀

Young

♂

60

Kobus smithemani

OTHER NAMES Bangweulu Lechwe. *French*: Cobe du Bangweulu, cobe noir. *German*: Bangweulu-Litschi. *Spanish*: Kob negro. *Russian*: Чёрный личи.

SUBSPECIES Monotypic. Formerly considered a subspecies of *K. leche* (Lechwe).

REPRODUCTION *Gestation*: 260 days. *Young per Birth*: 1. *Weaning*: 3 months. *Sexual Maturity*: 1 year (♀). *Life Span:* 15 years. The breeding season begins in December, with reproductive peaking in mid-February and continuing until March-April. ♂ occupy territories with raised ground to attract ♀. Births occur between November to January, coinciding with the start of the rainy season. The neonate remains hidden for a few days, with the mother close by, especially at night. After the infant is stable on its feet, mother and offspring return to floodplain grazing areas.

BEHAVIOR *Family Group*: Large herds of up to 2,500 animals containing both sexes, during the wet season. Herds of fewer than 500 animals during the dry season. *Diet*: Grasses, water plants. *Main Predators*: Leopard, lion, cheetah, hyena, python, crocodile, dog. Active both day and night. Feeding activity is highest in the morning. Midday is spent resting; individuals will lie down if dry ground is available, but in flooded pastures all remain standing. Unusual among ungulates, populations are more concentrated during the wet season (December-April). Herd structure appears to be relatively loose and lacking cohesion. Territoriality occurs only during the breeding season, often clustered around raised dry islands within flooded habitats. These territories are vigorously defended, resulting in severe injury or death. If disturbed it runs at great speed, with impressive leaps, and takes refuge in water since it is a good swimmer.

DISTRIBUTION *Native*: Zambia. The area surrounding Lake Bangweulu in NE Zambia. At one time they were also found along the upper Chambeshi River in Zambia, but they no longer occur there.

HABITAT Edges of permanent swamps, seasonally inundated floodplains, and associated peripheral grasslands. Areas covered in shallow water 2-6 m deep, following the seasonal rise and fall of water levels. In extreme flooding, Lechwes take refuge in woodlands.

STATUS Vulnerable. Population was estimated at 75,000 individuals in 2011, split among five subpopulations around Lake Bangweulu.

PHOTO CREDITS ♂: *Ulrike Joerres* and *Nigel Voaden,* Bangweulu (Zambia). ♀: *Alex Meyer*. Heads: *Jonas Livet,* Albinyana (Spain). Young: Aitana Safari (Spain).

Nile Lechwe
KOBUS MEGACEROS

BL: 160-180 cm (♂), 130-170 cm (♀). SH: 100-105 cm (♂), 80-85 cm (♀). TL: 45-50 cm. W: 90-120 kg (♂), 60-90 kg (♀). HL: 50-87 cm (♂). Medium-sized antelope. Pelage relatively shaggy and long in both sexes. Hair on the cheeks particularly long, and males have even longer hair on their necks. Males become rich mahogany or brownish black as they age, appearing black at a distance. Mature males have a white saddle on shoulders and white markings on their otherwise dark faces. Ears are white. Tail long and slender, with a terminal tuft. Hooves elongated and spread out. Lyre-shaped long horns, found only in males, rise from the head and bend backward before curving upward at the tips, strongly ringed at their bases. Female is smaller, without horns, golden brown in color, without the white saddle on shoulders. Juveniles are also golden brown in color.

♀

Juvenile

♂

Young

♂ Juvenile

Kobus megaceros

OTHER NAMES Mrs. Gray's Lechwe. *French*: Lechwe du Nil, cobe de Madame Gray. *German*: Weißnacken-Moorantilope, Frau Grays Wasserbock. *Spanish*: Cobo del Nilo, lechwe del Nilo. *Russian*: Нильский личи.

SUBSPECIES Monotypic.

SIMILAR SPECIES The White-eared Kob, also found in Sudan, has similar sexual dimorphism: ♂ are very dark with white markings and ♀ are golden brown, but Nile Lechwe is larger and has a much shaggier coat, with a distinctive white shoulder patch.

REPRODUCTION *Gestation*: 240 days. *Young per Birth*: 1. *Weaning*: 5-6 months. *Sexual Maturity*: 19-20 months. *Life Span*: 21 years. In the wild, most births occur from November to January. After birth, infants are hidden away from the herd for approximately 2 weeks, and are visited by their mothers for nursing. Mothers are protective of their young and may threaten other herd members that approach their calf. ♀ typically breed every year. Horn development occurs more rapidly than the development of mature coloration.

BEHAVIOR *Family Group:* Large mixed groups with 50 to several hundred individuals; bachelor herds are also seen. *Diet:* Grasses and other marsh vegetation. *Main Predators:* The flooded habitat used by the Nile Lechwe has relatively few predators; rarely, lion, leopard, or crocodile may hunt this species. Diurnal, but with most activity early and late in the day. Eyesight and hearing are good, sense of smell only fair. Swims well. Depending on the water level, they may be found deep within a swamp, close to the edge, or sometimes even outside on dry ground. They are unable to run fast on dry land. They undergo short seasonal movements (30-40 km) to follow the rise and fall of floodwaters. ♂ in mixed herds form a dominance hierarchy based on coloration. ♂ which lack the fully mature white markings are usually tolerated, but two closely matched mature ♂ will fight vigorously, often clashing their horns with heads underwater. Dominant ♂ will urinate through their front legs onto their neck mane, and then may rub this onto ♀.

DISTRIBUTION *Native:* Ethiopia, Sudan. Found only in Sudan and Ethiopia. In Sudan, the bulk of the population is found in the Sudd swamps, with smaller numbers in the Machar marshes near the Ethiopia border. In Ethiopia, the Nile Lechwe occurs marginally in the SW, in Gambella NP, where its survival is probably highly precarious because of expanding human activities.

HABITAT Swamps and flooded grasslands in S Sudan and W Ethiopia, often found in shallow water 10-40 cm deep. They follow the fluctuating margins between floodwaters and drier ground, moving up and down the flood tide lines with the seasons.

STATUS Endangered. The total population is unknown, but an aerial survey in 2007 yielded an estimate of about 4,000 animals, and identified the Zeraf Reserve as the most important protected area for this species. The survival of the Ethiopian populations seems highly precarious due to poaching and habitat degradation by domestic livestock.

PHOTO CREDITS ♂ and ♀: *Josef Lubomir Hlasek*, Zoo Prag, Praha-Troja (Czech Republic). Head ♂: *Sergey Chichagov*, San Diego Safari Park (USA). Head ♀: *Mahmoud Mahdy*. Young: *Jonas Livet*, Zoo di Napoli (Italy) and *Leonardo Ancillotto*, Bioparco Roma (Italy). Juvenile: *Sergey Chichagov,* San Diego Safari Park (USA).

Southern Common Reedbuck

REDUNCA ARUNDINUM

BL: 130-160 cm (♂), 120-140 cm (♀). SH: 80-150 cm (♂), 65-95 cm (♀). TL: 18-30 cm. W: 60-95 kg (♂), 50-85 kg (♀). HL: 25-45 cm (♂). Medium-sized antelope. Coat fawn or buff in color, with some grizzling of gray and brown. Undersides are white, including the bushy lower surface of the tail. All 4 legs have a dark stripe on their lower fronts. At the base of the pointed ears lies a gland that, when active, appears as a black circle of bare skin. No other distinctive facial markings, although the lips, bottom of the jaw, and area around the eyes are often pale or white. Horns found only in males, and have a distinctive forward-curving arc from the ringed bases to the smooth tips, forming a "V" when viewed from the front; transverse rings occur on the basal two-thirds, and the tips are smooth. Female similar to the male, slightly smaller, without horns.

♀

Juvenile

♂

♂

Redunca arundinum

OTHER NAMES Southern Reedbuck, Common Reedbuck. *French*: Redunca des roseaux, grand cobe des roseaux. *German*: Grossriedbock. *Spanish*: Redunca meridional, antílope de los cañaverales. *Russian*: Южный большой редунка. *Afrikaans*: Rietbok. *Swahili*: Tohe ya kusini. *Zulu*: Inxala. *Sepedi*: Lekwena.

SUBSPECIES Monotypic. The name *R. arundinum* (Common Reedbuck) formerly included *R. arundinum* (Southern Common Reedbuck) and *R. occidentalis* (Northern Common Reedbuck) as subspecies: these are elevated to full species here. Includes *algoensis, caffra, cinerea, coerulescens, eleotragus, isabellina,* and *multiannulata,* with *arundinum* having priority.

SIMILAR SPECIES Larger than Mountain and Bohor Reedbuck. Horns of ♂ much longer than those of the other Reedbucks, and lack the distinctive hooked tips of Bohor Reedbuck. Zambian Reedbuck has a paler and grayer head and neck, a darker brown blaze along the bridge of the nose, and shorter and less curved horns.

REPRODUCTION *Gestation*: 233 days. *Young per Birth*: 1. *Weaning*: 1 year. *Sexual Maturity*: 12 months (♀), 18 months (♂). *Life Span*: 16 years. Breeding occurs throughout the year, but in South Africa the majority of births occur in the summer and fall months (November to April). During courtship, a ♂ will follow a receptive ♀, who will pause occasionally to allow contact. However, laufschlag, seen in other Reedbucks, is not performed. Young will spend its first 6 weeks hidden in dense grasses, where it is visited by its mother for nursing a few times daily. By 3 months, the youngster regularly moves with its mother, and by 1 year it is independent.

BEHAVIOR *Family Group*: Solitary, in pairs, or in small loose groups. During the dry season, they congregate around water sources, in temporary aggregations of as many as 20 individuals. *Diet:* Grasses. *Main Predators:* Lion, leopard, spotted hyena, African wild dog, Nile crocodile. Active both day and night, but especially around dawn and dusk; periods of inactivity typically take place in dense cover. Because this species prefers tall-grass habitats with low visibility, whistling vocalizations and scent trails are a principal form of social communication. Population densities are generally low (0.2 per km^2), but they may exceed 35 per km^2 in pockets of high-quality habitat. They inhabit year-round home ranges (0.22-0.54 km^2). ♂ are territorial throughout the year, defending resources such as food, water, and cover from other ♂ in order to attract ♀. When concentrated around water sources in the dry season, ♂ may occupy smaller overlapping home ranges; access to ♀ is determined by a dominance hierarchy.

DISTRIBUTION *Native*: DR Congo, Namibia, Botswana, Zimbabwe, Mozambique, South Africa, Swaziland, Angola, Gabon. *Possibly Extinct*: Congo.

HABITAT Savannas with tall grasses, but during the dry season woodlands and reed beds with year-round water are frequently used. Prefers burned areas for feeding.

STATUS Least Concern. Estimated population of 73,000 animals. It remains widespread in protected areas and other areas with low to moderate levels of settlement, with significant populations on private land in Zimbabwe, South Africa, and Namibia.

PHOTO CREDITS ♂ and ♀: *Brian Ogniets,* Welgevonden (South Africa). Head ♂: *Joshua Stack*, Kongola, Caprivi (Namibia). Head ♀ and juvenile: *Nigel Voaden*, Sakania (DR Congo).

Northern Common Reedbuck
REDUNCA OCCIDENTALIS

BL: 120-160 cm (♂), 120-140 cm (♀). SH: 80-95 cm (♂), 65-95 cm (♀). TL: 20-30 cm. W: 43-68 kg (♂), 32-50 kg (♀). HL: 20-40 cm (♂). Medium-sized antelope. Coat rusty gray or tawny. Head and neck paler and grayer than in Southern Common Reedbuck. A blaze of darker brown runs along the bridge of the nose. Ears are large, and a black glandular patch is present beneath each ear base in both sexes. Limbs and tail tend to be suffused with gray. Undersides are white, extending to the buttocks. Very bushy tail, white underneath and the same color as the coat on the upper side. Legs with a black stripe on their front surfaces. Horns, found only in males, have a distinctive forward-curving arc from the ringed bases to the smooth tips; these are shorter and less curved than those of the Southern Common Reedbuck. Female similar to the male, a little smaller, without horns.

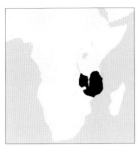

Redunca occidentalis

OTHER NAMES Zambian Reedbuck, Malawi Reedbuck. *French*: Redunca de Zambie. *German*: Sambia-Riedbock. *Spanish*: Redunca de Zambia. *Russian*: Северный большой редунка. *Swahili*: Tohe Ndope.

SUBSPECIES Monotypic. Formerly considered a subspecies of *R. arundinum* (Reedbuck). Includes *thomasinae*, with *occidentalis* having priority.

SIMILAR SPECIES Southern Common Reedbuck has a darker head and neck, larger and more curved horns, and lacks the dark brown blaze along the bridge of the nose, but otherwise, very similar. Bohor Reedbuck is smaller and has a yellowish or tan pelage.

REPRODUCTION *Gestation*: 233 days. *Young per Birth*: 1. *Weaning*: 1 year. *Sexual Maturity*: 12 months (♀), 18 months (♂). *Life Span*: 16 years. There is no specific information available for this subspecies, but presumably similar to the Common Reedbuck.

BEHAVIOR *Family Group*: Solitary, in pairs, or in small loose groups. During the dry season, Reedbucks will congregate around water sources, in temporary aggregations of as many as 20 individuals. *Diet:* Grasses. *Main Predators:* Lion, leopard, spotted hyena, African wild dog, Nile crocodile. Semi-gregarious and semi-social. There is no strict family bonding among members and little physical social contact ever occurs. Mating partners are seldom found in close proximity. Home ranges of non-territorial Common Reedbuck are relatively small and are seldom larger than 100 ha. They do not migrate seasonally but, on occasion, might move a distance of up to 80 km in search of a new home range when a habitat becomes unsuitable. Primarily crepuscular and nocturnal. They are reluctant to leave their resting places unless closely approached by a potential threat. During dry winters their activity extends into daylight. Although water dependent, they do not readily enter deeper water but limit themselves to grazing on vegetation growing in shallow water about 20 cm deep. They use fixed pathways to move between grazing grounds and water on a daily basis, so that the same animals are frequently seen at the same sites. During most of the daylight hours they lie in hollows between reeds or tall grass. When danger approaches from a distance, Common Reedbuck frequently give a sharp high-pitched whistle through their noses, similar to that of the Mountain Reedbuck and Gray Rhebok. This is a very distinctive sound often heard in the evening. If approached more closely, it remains lying motionless until the very last moment and then rapidly gallops off. The running speed is relatively slow in comparison to those of most other African antelope and they rely on their cryptic camouflage to remain unseen. It is extremely difficult to approach Common Reedbuck without being seen, as they feed mainly at head height, giving them a constant view of their surroundings.

DISTRIBUTION *Native*: Zambia, Malawi, Tanzania, Mozambique.

HABITAT Savannas, including floodplains and montane grasslands, with ready access to water.

STATUS Least Concern. Over 6,700 animals are believed to live in protected areas in Malawi.

PHOTO CREDITS *Lubomír Prause* and *Dave Appleton*, Nyika NP (Malawi), *Rudy Algera*, Gorongosa (Mozambique).

Nagor Reedbuck
REDUNCA REDUNCA

BL: 100-135 cm. SH: 68 cm. TL: 18-20 cm. W: 43-65 kg (♂), 35-45 kg (♀). HL: Up to 25 cm (♂). Smallest species of Bohor Reedbuck. Coat is relatively long, uniform golden yellow to brown color, with minimal grizzling. Undersides white. Legs are the same color as the body and characteristically lack any dark markings. Short tail, not particularly bushy, with a white underside. Pale ring of hair around the eyes and along lips, lower jaw, and upper throat. Subauricular glands are visible as dark circles beneath the ears. Horns, found only in males, short and very stout, sharply hooked forward and inward. Females without horns.

♀

♂
Juvenile

♂

Redunca redunca

OTHER NAMES Western Bohor Reedbuck, Senegal Reedbuck. *French*: Cobe des roseaux, nagor, rédunca commun. *German*: Senegal-Riedbock, Isabellantilope. *Spanish*: Redunca occidental. *Russian*: Нагорский обыкновенный редунка.

SUBSPECIES Monotypic. The name *R. redunca* (Bohor Reedbuck) formerly included *R. bohor* (Eastern Bohor Reedbuck), *R. cottoni* (Sudan Reedbuck), *R. nigeriensis* (Nigerian Reedbuck), and *R. redunca* (Western or Nagor Reedbuck) as subspecies: these are all elevated to full species here.

SIMILAR SPECIES Buffon's Kob is larger, with longer horns, golden brown to orange in color, has a vertical black stripe on the front of all four limbs, and conspicuous white-colored facial markings. Nigerian Bohor Reedbuck is larger, with slightly larger horns and dark markings on forelegs.

REPRODUCTION *Gestation*: 210-240 days. *Young per Birth*: 1. *Weaning*: Unknown. *Sexual Maturity*: 12 months (♀), 3-4 years (♂). *Life Span:* 10 years. There is no specific information available for this species, but likely similar to other Bohor Reedbuck.

BEHAVIOR *Family Group*: Typically solitary. Two to 7 adult ♀ and one mature ♂ occupy a shared home range but rarely associate together for long periods of time. Larger groups may form during the dry season; these may number over 100 animals in Sudan. Immature ♂ form bachelor groups. *Diet:* Grass. *Main Predators:* Lion, leopard, spotted hyena, African wild dog, Nile crocodile. There is no specific information available for this species, but likely similar to other Bohor Reedbuck. Active throughout the day and night, but often rest in long grass during midday. When threatened, they usually remain motionless or retreat slowly into cover, only fleeing once the threat is very close. Population densities in Benin as low as 0.14-0.7 Reedbuck per km^2.

DISTRIBUTION *Native*: Benin, Burkina Faso, Gambia, Ghana, Guinea, Guinea-Bissau, Mali, Mauritania, Nigeria, Senegal, Togo. *Possibly Extinct*: Côte d'Ivoire. Found in W Africa, from Senegal to SW Nigeria. The Niger River is used to separate its distribution from that of the Nigerian Bohor Reedbuck.

HABITAT Savanna woodlands near permanent water sources, with a preference for areas with tall grass. Riverine areas are used extensively during the dry season. They may colonize abandoned agricultural areas.

STATUS Least Concern. Numbers are very low and fragmented across much of its distribution. Viable populations are restricted to protected areas (Boucle du Baoule and Bafing Protected Areas in Mali, Niokolo-Koba NP in Senegal, Arly-Singou Protected Area and Nazinga Game Ranch in Burkina Faso, and Pendjari NP in Benin). Main threats include overhunting, habitat destruction, desertification, and competition with domestic livestock.

PHOTO CREDITS ♂ and ♀: *Robert Henno*, Pendjari NP (Benin). Head ♂ and juvenile: *Jonas Van de Voorde*, Pendjari NP (Benin).

Sudan Bohor Reedbuck
REDUNCA COTTONI

BL: 100-135 cm. SH: 65-89 cm. TL: 18-20 cm. W: 43-65 kg (♂), 35-45 kg (♀). HL: 33-40 cm (♂). Largest Bohor Reedbuck species. Pelage is golden brown, typically shaggy and oily, with white underparts. Grayish stripe extending down the front of the forelegs, more prominent in males. Round light grayish patch of bare skin below the ear. Tail short, very bushy, fawn above and white below. Horns, found only in males, are long, thin, widely divergent, with the outside spread often being greater than the horn length, but there is a good deal of individual variation and several different horn types may sometimes be seen in the same area. Females similar to males, with thinner necks, and without horns.

♀

♂

Redunca cottoni

OTHER NAMES Nile Reedbuck. *French*: Rédunca du Nil. *German*: Sudan-Riedbock. *Spanish*: Redunca del Nilo. *Russian*: Суданский обыкновенный редунка.

SUBSPECIES Monotypic. Formerly considered a subspecies of *R. redunca* (Bohor Reedbuck). Includes *dianae* (NE DR Congo).

SIMILAR SPECIES Loder's Kob, broadly sympatric, is much more robustly built, taller and redder, and is a social species. White-eared Kob may be readily distinguished by its black and white color.

REPRODUCTION *Gestation*: 210-240 days. *Young per Birth*: 1. *Weaning:* Unknown. *Sexual Maturity:* 12 months (♀), 3-4 years (♂). *Life Span:* 10 years. No specific information is available for this species, but likely similar to other Bohor Reedbuck. Breeding is probably seasonal. Courtship begins with the ♂ circling the ♀, and making a peculiar bleating noise, described as the sound of a toy trumpet. ♂ calves are driven away from the herd after 6 months, and form bachelor herds until they become fully mature. Young have been seen accompanying adults in February (dry season).

BEHAVIOR *Family Group*: Typically solitary. Two to 7 adult ♀ and one mature ♂ occupy a shared home range but rarely associate together for long periods of time. Larger groups may form during the dry season; these may number over 100 animals in Sudan. Immature ♂ form bachelor groups. *Diet:* Exclusively a grazer, feeding on fresh grass. *Main Predators:* Lion, leopard, spotted hyena, African wild dog, Nile crocodile. No specific information is available for this species, but likely similar to other Bohor Reedbuck. They are generally migratory, and seasonal movements are driven by changing water levels and vegetation abundance. During the rainy season, when forage is plentiful, they disperse across floodplains. During the dry season, half of the population may be found in extremely large herds. When a potential threat is detected, they use the typical predator avoidance strategy of Reedbucks: freezing in position, crouching low to the ground, or slowly retreating to cover. Choruses of variable whistles are frequently heard throughout the night, and leaps, which differ in height, length, and style, are a characteristic form of communication.

DISTRIBUTION *Native*: DR Congo, Ethiopia, Uganda. Found in S Sudan and the Gambella/Akobo River region of extreme W Ethiopia, and probably in NE DR Congo and N Uganda.

HABITAT Prefers grasslands within the moist savanna and forest/savanna zones, as it needs to drink daily or at least regularly.

STATUS Least Concern. Estimated total population of 14,000 individuals, with the majority occurring outside protected areas in the Jonglei area.

PHOTO CREDITS *Ludwig Siege*, Gambela (Ethiopia).

Eastern Bohor Reedbuck

REDUNCA BOHOR

BL: 100-135 cm. SH: 75-89 cm (♂), 69-76 cm (♀). TL: 18-20 cm. W: 43-55 kg (♂), 35-45 kg (♀). HL: 25-35 cm (♂). Medium-sized antelope, light and graceful. Golden-brown pelage, typically shaggy and oily. Undersides white. Dark stripe on the front of each foreleg. Pale ring of hair around the eyes and along lips, lower jaw, and upper throat. Subauricular glands present, and round bare black patches below the base of ears, inconspicuous when inactive. Tail short, very bushy, fawn above and white below. Males are readily distinguished from females by their thick necks and a pair of horns. Horns tend to be short and stout, extending backward from the forehead before hooking sharply inward and forward at the tips.

Redunca bohor

OTHER NAMES Abyssinian Bohor Reedbuck. *French*: Rédunca d'Abyssinie. *German*: Bohor-Riedbock. *Spanish*: Redunca bohor, ciervo cabra redunca. *Russian*: Абиссинский обыкновенный редунка. *Swahili*: Tohe. *Acholi*: Abut, dinka, keau. *Ful*: Konkoromaare, bawla-reedu. *Galla*: Baroufa. *Gbaya*: Kòk-te. *Hausa*: Kwanta rafi. *Sindebele*: Umziki. *Wolof*: Padala.

SUBSPECIES Monotypic. Formerly considered a subspecies of *R. redunca* (Bohor Reedbuck). Includes *tohi* (SE Kenya and E Tanzania), and *wardi* (E DR Congo, Uganda, SW Kenya, Rwanda, Burundi, and W Tanzania).

SIMILAR SPECIES Common Reedbuck is larger, darker with a duller color, grows much larger horns that are evenly curved and do not form hooks at the ends, and exhibits much more basal pulp, which is the incipient white horn material at the base of the horns. Chanler's Mountain Reedbuck is rather gray in color, and its body size and horn length are both much smaller.

REPRODUCTION *Gestation*: 210-240 days. *Young per Birth*: 1. *Weaning*: Unknown. *Sexual Maturity*: 12 months (♀), 3-4 years (♂). *Life Span:* 10 years. During courtship, a ♂ approaches a ♀ with his neck stretched out low and his head tilted so that his nose is elevated. For the first few months after birth, young remain hidden in dense vegetation. This habit makes determining birth seasonality a challenge; it appears that the species breeds year-round in E Africa, but with fewer births during the dry season.

BEHAVIOR *Family Group*: Typically solitary. Two to 7 adult ♀ and 1 mature ♂ occupy a shared home range but rarely associate together for long periods of time. Larger groups may form during the dry season; these may number over 100 animals in Sudan. Immature ♂ form bachelor groups. *Diet*: Grass. *Main Predators*: Lion, leopard, spotted hyena, African wild dog, Nile crocodile. Active throughout the day and night, but often rest in long grass during midday. When threatened, they usually remain motionless or retreat slowly into cover, only fleeing once the threat is very close. The alarm call is a shrill whistle. Adult ♂ maintain territories 0.2-0.3 km^2 in size, enforcing the boundaries through patrols and displays instead of marking them. Population densities in E Africa are typically 10–21 Reedbuck per km^2.

DISTRIBUTION *Native*: Burundi, DR Congo, Ethiopia, Kenya, Rwanda, Sudan, Tanzania, Uganda. Found in E DR Congo, SE Sudan, S and W Kenya, W Ethiopia, E Rwanda, E Burundi, and Tanzania.

HABITAT Floodplain and woodland habitats, with a preference for areas of tall grass near permanent water.

STATUS Least Concern. Estimated total population of 37,000 individuals in Tanzania.

PHOTO CREDITS ♂: *Dominique Mignard*, Bale NP (Ethiopia). Head ♂: *Karen Peacock*, Maasai Mara (Kenya). Head ♀: *Frédéric Slein*, Mikumi (Tanzania). ♀: *Achim Mittler*, Serengeti (Tanzania).

Nigerian Bohor Reedbuck
REDUNCA NIGERIENSIS

BL: 100-135 cm. SH: 65-89 cm. TL: 18-20 cm. W: 43-65 kg (♂), 35-45 kg (♀). HL: 23-27 cm (♂). Medium-sized antelope, larger than the Nagor Reedbuck, closely resembling the Eastern Bohor Reedbuck. Uniform golden-fawn thick pelage, with the midline of the back usually more richly colored. Undersides white. Dark stripe on the front of each foreleg. Pale ring of hair around the eyes and along lips, lower jaw, and upper throat. Round light grayish patch of bare skin below the ear. Tail short, very bushy, fawn or sometimes dark above, and white below. Horns, found only in males, larger than in Nagor Reedbuck, ringed, stout at the base, extending backward from the forehead before hooking sharply inward and forward at the tips. Tips often depressed below the level of the frontal plane. Females have a thinner neck, and no horns.

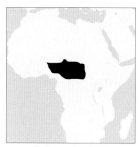

Redunca nigeriensis

OTHER NAMES *French*: Rédunca nigérian. *German*: Tschad-Riedbock. *Spanish*: Redunca de Nigeria. *Russian*: Нигерийский обыкновенный редунка.

SUBSPECIES Monotypic. Formerly considered a subspecies of *R. redunca* (Bohor Reedbuck). Considered by some authors to be the same species as *R. bohor*.

SIMILAR SPECIES Southern Reedbuck is larger, slenderer, and less intensely colored, with longer horns with a gentle curve, lacking a distinct hook at the tips. Mountain Reedbuck is rather gray in color; its body size and horn length are both much smaller.

REPRODUCTION *Gestation*: 210-240 days. *Young per Birth*: 1. *Weaning*: Unknown. *Sexual Maturity*: 12 months (♀), 3-4 years (♂). *Life Span*: 10 years. No specific information is available for this species, but likely similar to other Bohor Reedbuck. Courtship begins with the ♂ circling the ♀, and making a peculiar bleating noise, described as the sound of a toy trumpet. ♂ calves are driven away from the herd after 6 months, and form bachelor herds until they become fully mature at the age of 4 years.

BEHAVIOR *Family Group*: Typically solitary. Five to 6 adult ♀ and 1 mature ♂ occupy a shared home range but rarely associate together for long periods of time. Larger groups may form during the dry season. Immature ♂ form bachelor groups. *Diet:* Grass. *Main Predators:* Lion, leopard, spotted hyena, African wild dog, Nile crocodile. Active throughout the day and night, but often rest in long grass during midday. No specific information is available for this species, but likely similar to other Bohor Reedbuck. ♂ have a distinctive whistling, and ♀ a frog-like croaking. These animals become most verbose during ritual mating displays.

DISTRIBUTION *Native*: Cameroon, Central African Republic, Chad, DR Congo, Niger, Nigeria, Sudan. Found in Nigeria, N Cameroon, S Chad, the Central African Republic, and the adjacent N edge of DR Congo.

HABITAT Grasslands and wooded savannas close to permanent water, principally along watercourses.

STATUS Least Concern. Estimated total population of 7,500 individuals in Cameroon and Central African Republic. Populations are very low in Chad and Nigeria, where it has been extirpated from large parts of its former distribution. Main threats include expansion of human activities, uncontrolled hunting, and desertification.

Western Mountain Reedbuck

REDUNCA ADAMAUAE

BL: 97-110 cm. SH: 58-73 cm. TL: 12-20 cm. W: 35-60 kg. HL: 13 cm (♂). The smallest Mountain Reedbuck. Coat is thick and relatively long, bright reddish brown in color, with a yellowish cast to the flanks. Belly and inner aspects of the upper legs are white. In males, outer surface of legs marked with a brown stripe with a border of pale hairs. Tail is bushy with a white underside. Head is same color as the body, cheeks are reddish. Brown blaze from the muzzle to base of horns. Chin and throat are pale to white. Slender ears. Bare black subauricular glands. Horns, found only in males, more slender and parallel than on other Reedbucks, with a slight forward curve. Females are smaller than males, with a drab grayish-brown color.

Redunca adamauae

OTHER NAMES Adamaoua Mountain Reedbuck, Adamawa Reedbuck. *French*: Rédunca de l´Adamaoua. *German*: Adamaoua-Bergriedbock. *Spanish*: Redunca de Adamawa. *Russian*: Западный горный редунка.

SUBSPECIES Monotypic. Formerly considered a subspecies of *R. fulvorufula* (Mountain Reedbuck).

SIMILAR SPECIES Bohor Reedbuck is distinctively larger and has a light brown rather than gray coat, with longer horns with hooked tips.

REPRODUCTION *Gestation*: 240 days. *Young per Birth*: 1. *Weaning*: Before 1 year. *Sexual Maturity*: 9-18 months (♀), 15 months (♂). *Life Span*: 12 years. There is no specific information available for this species, but probably similar to other Mountain Reedbuck.

BEHAVIOR *Family Group*: Small groups of 2-5 ♀ and their young accompanied by a single adult ♂, although solitary individuals and pairs are sometimes seen. Immature ♂ may form small bachelor groups. *Diet:* Soft green grass, avoiding dry grass leaves and stems; drinks water regularly. *Main Predators:* Most sympatric large carnivores. There is no specific information available for this species, but probably similar to other Mountain Reedbuck. Not discovered by Europeans until 1961; very little is known about it. Active throughout day and night. The alarm call is a whistling snort. It is extremely agile on steep, rough slopes and generally flees uphill when threatened, disappearing over rocky summits.

DISTRIBUTION *Native*: Cameroon, Nigeria. Found only in mountain grassland on Chappal Waddi, Chappal Delam, and the Hendu-Shirigu-Yumti highlands in the Gashaka Forest Reserve of E Nigeria, and on the nearby Adamaoua Massif in Cameroon.

HABITAT High-elevation montane grasslands interspersed with rocky terrain and scattered woodland, at elevations of 1,300-1,900 m.

STATUS Endangered. Total numbers are estimated at 450 animals. It has been reduced to small, declining, remnant subpopulations within a relatively restricted range. Main threats include the expansion of human settlement, poaching, widespread disturbance by cattle herders and their livestock, and hunting by dogs.

Southern Mountain Reedbuck

REDUNCA FULVORUFULA

BL: 100-124 cm. SH: 60-83 cm. TL: 13-20 cm. W: 22-37 kg (♂), 22-35 kg (♀). HL: 18-22 cm (♂). Soft, woolly coat of grayish-fawn fur, brighter and largely tinged with rufous on the neck and head. Chin and upper throat are pale. Underparts are bright white, with a sharp demarcation with the gray upper parts. Inner parts of legs are white, while outer surfaces are gray, lacking conspicuous markings. Tail with a bushy white underside. Round bare patch of black skin (a scent gland) is located beneath the long, slender ears. Body condition may vary between seasons, with a decline in body weight in winter. Horns, found only in males, ringed at the base, are short and possess a slight forward curve. Female similar to the male, but much grayer, slightly smaller, with shorter tail, and without horns.

♀

♀
Young

♂

♂
Juvenile

Redunca fulvorufula

OTHER NAMES *French*: Rédunca de montagne. *German*: Bergriedbock. *Spanish*: Redunca de montaña. *Afrikaans*: Rooiribbok. *Russian*: Южный горный редунка. *Xhosa*: Inxala. *Zulu*: Inxala, ingxala, inhlangu. *Sepedi*: Letlabo. *Sesotho*: Letlabo, lebele.

SUBSPECIES Monotypic. The name *R. fulvorufula* (Mountain Reedbuck) formerly included *R. fulvorufula* (Southern Mountain Reedbuck), *R. chanleri* (Chanler's Mountain Reedbuck), and *R. adamauae* (Western Mountain Reedbuck) as subspecies: these are all elevated to full species here.

SIMILAR SPECIES Larger and somewhat redder in color than other Mountain Reedbuck, but otherwise similar. Common Reedbuck is larger and longer limbed, with much longer horns. Bohor Reedbuck is larger and has a light brown rather than gray coat, with longer horns with hooked tips. Rhebok is similarly sized, but thinner, with much longer ears, and horns lack the forward curve.

REPRODUCTION *Gestation*: 240 days. *Young per Birth*: 1. *Weaning*: Before 1 year. *Sexual Maturity*: 18-24 months (♀), 27 months (♂). *Life Span*: 14 years. In regions of South Africa with harsh winters most births occur in the austral summer (especially November). Infants are tucked away in dense vegetation by their mothers for at least 1 month, and remain hidden there unless visited for nursing.

BEHAVIOR *Family Group*: ♀ and young live in small groups of 3-12 animals. ♂ are solitary and territorial, but associate with ♀ as they pass through their territory. Immature ♂ live in small bachelor groups. *Diet:* Grass. *Main Predators*: Most sympatric large carnivores. Active throughout the day and night, showing the most activity around dawn and dusk. They frequently rest when temperatures are high. Groups are not stable: individuals may switch groups regularly. ♀ occupy home ranges of 0.36-0.76 km², which overlap several smaller ♂ territories. Body posturing and vocalizations are used to maintain boundaries between neighboring ♂. ♀ appear to prefer territories with steep slopes (used to escape from predators), regardless of the presence of food or water. Population densities are typically 5-7 animals per km² in South Africa.

DISTRIBUTION *Native*: Botswana, Lesotho, Mozambique, South Africa, Swaziland. Found discontinuously in E South Africa: the Transvaal except for the NE and W, Natal, S and E Orange Free State, and E Cape Province. There also are limited distributions in the Lobatsi area of SE Botswana, Swaziland, Lesotho, and in the Lobombo Mountains of SW Mozambique. Reports of its occurrence in N Botswana and Zimbabwe have been discredited.

HABITAT Steep rocky slopes with grass cover and scattered bushes and trees, at elevations between 1,400 and 2,400 m. In South Africa it is found as high as 2,400 m in the Drakensberg Mountains, on rocky hills in Zululand not far above sea level, and at all intermediate elevations.

STATUS Least Concern. Estimated total population of 33,000 animals. Populations are stable or increasing on private land and in protected areas.

PHOTO CREDITS ♂: *Alex Meyer*, Kronberg Zoo (Germany). Head: *Ruslou Koorts*, Zwartkloof Game Reserve (South Africa). ♀: *Benjamin Tupper*, Marakele NP, Limpopo (South Africa). Juvenile: *Derek Keats*, Borakalalo NP (South Africa). Young: *Jeff Blumberg*.

Chanler's Mountain Reedbuck

REDUNCA CHANLERI

BL: 100-136 cm. SH: 65-76 cm. TL: 18-20 cm. W: 22-38 kg (♂), 19-35 kg (♀). HL: 14-35 cm (♂). Smaller than the Southern Mountain Reedbuck, with a grayer and paler body, with very little reddish tint, contrasting noticeably with its reddish neck and head. A line of sharp contrast separates the gray upper parts from the white underparts. Bushy tail with a white underside. Some individuals with a dark stripe from between the eyes to the nose. Chin, lips, and upper throat are pale. Prominent glandular patch of bare black skin beneath each ear. Horns, found only in males, ringed at the base, shorter than in Southern Mountain Reedbuck. Females usually more drab in coloration than males, smaller, and without horns.

♀

♂

Redunca chanleri

OTHER NAMES *French*: Rédunca de Chanler, cobe de Chanler. *German*: Ostafrika-Bergriedbock. *Spanish*: Redunca de Chanler. *Russian*: Горный редунка Чанлера. *Swahili*: Tohe ya milima. *Maasai*: Enkakuluo.

SUBSPECIES Monotypic. Formerly considered a subspecies of *R. fulvorufula* (Mountain Reedbuck).

SIMILAR SPECIES Bohor Reedbuck is distinctively larger and has a light brown rather than gray coat, with longer horns with hooked tips.

REPRODUCTION *Gestation*: 240 days. *Young per Birth*: 1. *Weaning*: Before 1 year. *Sexual Maturity*: 9-18 months (♀), 15 months (♂). *Life Span*: 12 years. Breeding occurs year-round, although a peak in births occurs in the March-May rainy season. A territorial ♂ approaches a ♀ to ascertain her reproductive status, and she responds by stopping, lowering her head, and lifting her tail, allowing the ♂ to smell and lick the vulva. Courtship consists of stiff foreleg kicks directed between the hind legs of the ♀.

BEHAVIOR *Family Group:* ♀ and young live in small groups of 3-7 animals. ♂ are solitary and territorial, but associate with ♀ as they pass through their territory. Immature ♂ live in small bachelor groups. *Diet:* Soft green grass, avoiding dry grass leaves and stems; drinks water regularly. *Main Predators:* Most sympatric large carnivores. Active during the day and night, with patterns influenced by temperature, being more active during cooler periods, especially when raining. Diurnal activity mainly in the early morning and late afternoon, when ascending and descending hills. ♂ tend to be more active and less likely to lie down than ♀. Main vocalizations are a shrill whistle and a clicking noise, while scent trails through the tall grass are thought to be the main identifiers of the whereabouts of individuals.

DISTRIBUTION *Native:* Ethiopia, Kenya, Sudan, Tanzania, Uganda. Found discontinuously, from Awash NP in Ethiopia (its northernmost limit) southward along the Rift Valley in Ethiopia and W Kenya to NE Tanzania. It also occurs in extreme NE Uganda and extreme SE Sudan.

HABITAT Hillside savannas and thickets. In Ethiopia, it is found mainly from 1,200 to 3,000 m along the Rift Valley, occupying isolated hills on the valley floor and on the slopes of both the walls. In Kenya and Tanzania it is commonest from about 1,800 m up.

STATUS Vulnerable. Estimated total population of 3,000 animals or more, mostly in Kenya. Main threats include illegal hunting and habitat destruction.

PHOTO CREDITS Reconstruction by *Jose R. Castello*, based on photos from Nairobi NP (Kenya).

Rhebok

PELEA CAPREOLUS

BL: 105-125 cm. SH: 70-80 cm. TL: 10-20 cm. W: 18-30 kg. HL: 20-29 cm (♂). Small, graceful antelope with a long, slender neck. Dense, woolly, gray coat with whitish underparts, lacking any distinguishing markings. Legs and head tend to be more fawn in color than the body, and fronts of the lower legs are often darker. Bushy tail with a fluffy white underside. A very distictive bulbous black rhinarium; this bare nasal skin extends back a considerable distance from the nostrils, and contrasts with white hairs on the muzzle. No bare, glandular patches below the ears. Eyelids are black and the eyes are surrounded by whitish hairs. Ears extremely long and narrow and stand straight up. Horns, found only in males, are straight and slender, ringed only at the base, and rise vertically and parallel from the forehead. Female similar to the male, slightly smaller, without horns.

♀

♂
Juvenile

♂

Pelea capreolus

OTHER NAMES Vaal Rhebok, Ribbok, Gray Rhebok, Rhebuck. *French*: Péléa. *German*: Rehantilope. *Spanish*: Antílope cabrío, pelea. *Russian*: Косулья антилопа. *Afrikaans*: Vaalribbok. *Zulu*: Iza, ilinxala. *Sesotho*: Letsa, pshiatla. *Setswana*: Phele. *Swati*: Liza.

SUBSPECIES Monotypic.

SIMILAR SPECIES Mountain Reedbuck are similarly sized and are found in the same habitat, but their ears are much shorter, and the horns have a distinct forward hook.

REPRODUCTION *Gestation*: 210 days. *Young per Birth*: 1. *Weaning*: 6-8 months. *Sexual Maturity*: 16 months (♀), 18-24 months (♂). *Life Span*: 10 years. Rhebok breed seasonally; most mating activity occurs in the summer or autumn, but this varies by region. Births in W South Africa are usually in August, and in E South Africa occur between November and February. ♀ leave the herd to give birth. Infants lie hidden in grassy cover for their first 3 weeks, and by 6 weeks are fully mobile.

BEHAVIOR *Family Group*: Harem groups of up to 12-15 animals, with 1 ♂, 1-6 ♀, and their offspring. Other ♂ are solitary. *Diet*: Leaves from shrubs and ground-level forbs. Flowers, roots, and seeds may be eaten if present, and small amounts of grass are eaten year-round. *Main Predators:* Lion, leopard, hyena, Cape hunting dog, python, jackal. Active throughout the day and night, spending about half of their time foraging or moving. Rest usually occurs in open areas rather than in cover. When traveling, a ♀ will usually lead the herd, with the harem ♂ bringing up the rear. ♂ are very protective of their herds, and defend an exclusive territory of approximately 0.6 km^2 that is marked with dung. ♂ are extremely aggressive. Used fully during the winter, only a portion of this territory is used in the summer. Encounters between ♂ involve chasing and stabbing with their sharp horns. A swift runner and an accomplished leaper, clearing barriers easily. While running, it has a distinct rocking gait. Very wary and alert. Alarm call is a sharp cough or snort.

DISTRIBUTION *Native*: Lesotho, South Africa, Swaziland. Endemic to a small region in S Africa, inhabiting montane and plateau grasslands of South Africa, Swaziland, and Lesotho. In South Africa, their distribution is discontinuous and patchy, and they no longer occur N of the Orange River in the Northern Cape, or in parts of the North West Province. They remain fairly common in Malolotja Nature Reserve and still survive locally in unprotected areas. In Lesotho they have been reduced to a few scattered remnant populations. They responded well to protection in Sehlabathebe NP.

HABITAT Rocky hills with good grass cover, at elevations of 1,400-3,300 m in South Africa. Prefers north-facing slopes. It utilizes a more open and exposed habitat than the Mountain Reedbuck.

STATUS Least Concern. Approximately 10,000-18,000 individuals are thought to survive in the wild, and these numbers appear stable. Because they live in rugged habitats, they are less susceptible to habitat loss than other ungulates. This is the most common ungulate in Lesotho.

PHOTO CREDITS *Diane Smillie*, Komsberg Wilderness Nature Reserve (South Africa), *Mike Richardson* and *Sarah Winch*, Mpumalanga (South Africa), *Peter Boardman*, Gondwana Reserve (South Africa).

South African Springbok
ANTIDORCAS MARSUPIALIS

BL: 112-127 cm. SH: 68-82 cm. TL: 20-30 cm. W: 20-38 kg (♂), 20-28 kg (♀). HL: 28-44 cm (♂), 16 cm (♀). Medium-sized gazelle. The smallest Springbok. White and rich chestnut-brown color, with a deep brown stripe extending along each side from the shoulder to inside the thigh. Head white except for a very thin brown stripe from eye to muzzle. Skin fold normally closed, but when the animal is excited it opens to form a fan of stiff, white hairs. Brown or fawn on forehead not extending in front of the level of the eyes, and not sharply bordered anteriorly. Nose white or with a brown smudge. Lyre-shaped horns, found in both sexes, smaller than in other subspecies, parallel at the base, project upward and slightly backward, and turn sharply toward each other at the tips, forming two hooks. Horns in females are exceptionally short.

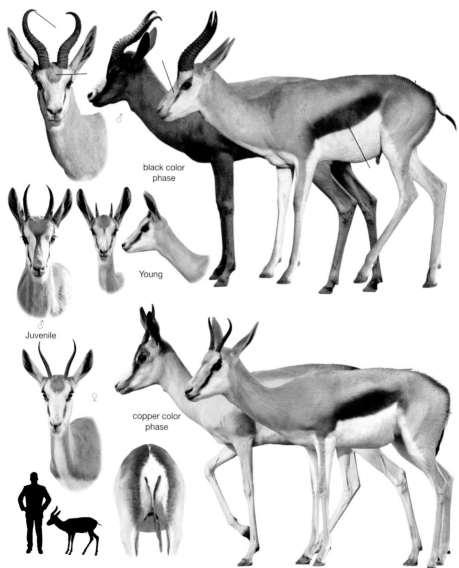

♂

black color
phase

Young

♂
Juvenile

♀

copper color
phase

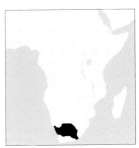

Antidorcas marsupialis

OTHER NAMES Karoo Springbok, Southern Springbok, Cape Springbok, Springbuck. *French*: Euchore, gazelle à poche dorsale. *German*: Springbock. *Spanish*: Gacela saltarina, springbok de Sudáfrica. *Russian*: Южноафриканский спрингбок. *Zulu*: Insephe. *Sepedi*: Tshêphê. *Swati*: Inswephe. *Herero*: Menyeh.

SUBSPECIES Monotypic. The name *A. marsupialis* (Springbok) formerly included *A. angolensis* (Angolan Springbok), *A. hofmeyri* (Kalahari Springbok), and *A. marsupialis* (Southern or Cape Springbok) as subspecies: these are all elevated to full species here. Interbreeding between Springbok species has taken place. Black, White, and Copper Springbok are not subspecies, but different color phases of the South African Springbok, developed by selective breeding.

SIMILAR SPECIES Kalahari Springbok is larger, with longer horns, lateral band usually nearly black, pygal band very dark brown, and face-stripes thick, rich dark brown, but is otherwise similar.

REPRODUCTION *Gestation*: 165-180 days. *Young per Birth*: 1. *Weaning*: 3 months. *Sexual Maturity*: 11-12 months. *Life Span*: 7-10 years. Usually mate during the dry season.

BEHAVIOR *Family Group:* 5-100 individuals during dry winter periods; aggregate into temporary mass herds in summer. *Diet*: Short sweet-grass, forbs, succulents, and browse. *Main Predators:* Cheetah, leopard, black-backed jackal, hyena, python. Diurnal and most active in the early morning, the late afternoon, and the early, dark evening hours. Hot midday hours are mostly spent lying down or standing and ruminating. When a ♂ shows off his strength to attract a mate, or to ward off predators, he starts off in a stiff-legged trot, jumping up into the air with an arched back every few paces and lifting a pocket-like skin flap along his back (pronking). Lifting the flap causes the long white hairs under the tail to stand up in a conspicuous fan shape, which in turn emits a strong scent of sweat. Social and gregarious. A family herd consists of adult ewes, subadult ♀, and juveniles of both sexes. Adult ♂ become territorial only during the rut; alternatively they join family herds or become solitary nomads. Family herds pass through several different ♂ territories during one mating season. Family herds tend to stay in a fixed home range. Individuals tend to keep a distance between each other and have little bodily contact. They groom themselves.

DISTRIBUTION *Native*: South Africa. Its natural distribution in recent times covered most of Cape Province, the Orange Free State, and the southern Transvaal. It was exterminated in many areas, but has been so widely reintroduced that its present range is not too dissimilar. It has also been introduced in parts of South Africa where it did not occur naturally.

HABITAT Dry grasslands, bushland, and shrubland of SW and S Africa, migrating sporadically in vast herds in some of the S parts of its range. These migrations or treks no longer occur.

STATUS Least Concern. Estimated population at 1,000,000 animals in the Karoo and about 100,000 in the Cape provinces outside of the Karoo.

PHOTO CREDITS ♂: *Warren Stevenson*, Karoo NP (South Africa). ♀ and young: *Kathy*, Western Cape (South Africa). Head ♂: *David Steele*, Mountain Zebra NP (South Africa). Head ♀: *Ali Bentley*, Western Cape (South Africa). Black ♂: *David Batzofin*, Heia Safari Ranch (South Africa). ♀: *Nico Smit* (South Africa).

Kalahari Springbok
ANTIDORCAS HOFMEYRI

BL: 120-140 cm. SH: 74-89 cm. TL: 20-30 cm. W: 25-45 kg (♂), 20-30 kg (♀). HL: 28-48 cm (♂), 16-28 cm (♀). Medium-sized gazelle. The largest Springbok species. White and light fawn color, with a dark brown to nearly black lateral band, extending along each side from the shoulder to inside the thigh. Pygal band medium brown, thin. Head white except for a narrow dark brown stripe from eye to muzzle. Brown on forehead extending anteriorly in front of the level of the eyes, with no anterior border, so the transition to the white not sharply demarcated. Dark smudge on the nose from dark to absent. Well-developed lyre-shaped horns, found in both sexes, larger than in other subspecies. Females similar to males, but smaller and have smaller, thinner, straighter horns, farther apart at the base.

♂

♂
Juvenile

♀

Young

Antidorcas hofmeyri

OTHER NAMES Western Springbok. *French*: Euchore, gazelle à poche dorsale. *German*: Kalahari-Springbock. *Spanish*: Gacela saltarina, springbok del Kalahari. *Russian*: Калахарский спрингбок. *Zulu*: Insephe. *Sepedi*: Tshêphê. *Swati*: Inswephe. *Herero*: Menyeh.

SUBSPECIES Monotypic. Formerly considered a subspecies of *A. marsupialis* (Springbok). Interbreeding between Springbok species has taken place.

SIMILAR SPECIES South African Springbok is smaller, with shorter horns, due to a harsher environment and poorer nutrition in most of its range, usually more rich chestnut brown in color, flank stripe deep brown, face white with stripes very thin, not dark, but is otherwise similar.

REPRODUCTION *Gestation*: 165-180 days. *Young per Birth*: 1. *Weaning*: 3 months. *Sexual Maturity*: 11-12 months. *Life Span*: 7-10 years. They normally mate during the early dry season, and give birth during the beginning of the rainy season, when food is usually abundant. For the first 2 days young lie tightly in the cover of bushes or grass clumps.

BEHAVIOR *Family Group:* 5-100 individuals during dry winter periods; aggregate into temporary mass herds in summer; smaller herds may contain ♂ and ♀ but bachelor herds are common, as are solitary ♂. *Diet*: Grazes in summer and browses more in winter and when veld is dry; eats grasses, broad-leaved plants, bushes, seeds, pods, fruits, and flowers, and digs for roots and bulbs. They can eat plants that are toxic to other animals. Wild melons and cucumbers are eaten for their water content, and soil for minerals. *Main Predators:* Cheetah, leopard, black-backed jackal, hyena, python. In some areas of Namibia and Botswana there are movements related to rainfall and new plant growth. ♂ are territorial during the rut and they attempt to hold ♀/young groups within their area. But territories are generally only held for short periods and ♂ then circulate freely. May be active day and night, but generally lie up during the hottest hours. Kalahari Springboks make regular use of natural licks. They have a considerable habitat tolerance, from savanna to the desert. They like firm footing and do not follow the Gemsbok onto the dunes of the SW Kalahari. Springboks are fast sprinters. They can reach a speed of 80 kmph and jump more than 10 m. The Latin name *marsupialis* comes from the presence of the pocket-like skin flap which opens the crest of white erected hair on its back.

DISTRIBUTION *Native*: Botswana, Namibia, South Africa. Found in NW South Africa, N of the Orange River, from the Upington district (N Cape) via the Sandfontein district through Botswana to S Namibia.

HABITAT Open, arid plains with grass or low scrub and can be independent of water, but will drink. It is absent from mountains and rocky hills and avoids woodlands with tall, dense vegetation.

STATUS Least Concern. Estimated population of 730,000 animals in Namibia, 100,000 in the Botswana, and 150,000 in South Africa.

PHOTO CREDITS ♂: *Alta Oosthuizen*, Kalahari Desert (South Africa). ♀: *Chris Kruger*, Kalahari Desert (South Africa). Head ♂: *Cam Lewis* (Namibia). Head ♀: *Michael Ian Gardner*, Kgalagadi Transfrontier Park (South Africa). Young: *Mogens Trolle* and *Leon Molenaar*, Kgalagadi (South Africa). Juvenile: *Cameron Ewart-Smith* and *Heindrich Albertyn*, Kgalagadi (South Africa).

Angolan Springbok
ANTIDORCAS ANGOLENSIS

BL: 112-127 cm. SH: 75 cm. TL: 25 cm. W: 26-41 kg (♂), 20-30 kg (♀). HL: 28-48 cm (♂), 16-28 cm (♀). Intermediate in body and horn size between the South African and Kalahari Springboks. White and brown-tawny color, with a dark brown to nearly black lateral stripe extending along each side from the shoulder to inside the thigh. Pygal band very dark brown. Head white except for a dark brown stripe from eye to muzzle. Ears are longer than in other species. Well-developed lyre-shaped horns, found in both sexes, parallel at the base, project upward and slightly backward, and turn sharply toward each other at the tips, forming 2 hooks, heavily grooved for 60-75% of the length. Horns in females are angled and relatively large. Females smaller than males.

♂

Juvenile

♂

♀

Young

86

Antidorcas angolensis

OTHER NAMES Springbuck. *French*: Euchore, gazelle à poche dorsale. *German*: Springbock. *Spanish*: Gacela saltarina, springbok. *Russian*: Ангольский спрингбок. *Zulu*: Insephe. *Sepedi*: Tshêphê. *Swati*: Inswephe. *Herero*: Menyeh.

SUBSPECIES Monotypic. Formerly considered a subspecies of *A. marsupialis* (Springbok). Interbreeding between Springbok species has taken place.

SIMILAR SPECIES Angolan Springbok is intermediate in body and horn size between the South African and Kalahari Springboks, and its ears are said to be longer in proportion to its body. It is otherwise similar. Females of Angolan Springbok have the largest horns.

REPRODUCTION *Gestation*: 168 days. *Young per Birth*: 1. *Weaning*: 3 months. *Sexual Maturity*: 6 months (♀), 12 months but mate at 18-24 months (♂). *Life Span*: 19 years. Usually mate during the dry season. For the first couple of days the youngster remains hidden in a bush or long grass before it joins a nursery herd with its mother. ♀ will remain with the herd whereas young ♂ will join a bachelor herd.

BEHAVIOR *Family Group*: 5-100 individuals during dry winter periods; aggregate into temporary mass herds in summer. *Diet*: Short sweet-grass, forbs, succulents, and browse. *Main Predators*: Cheetah, leopard, black-backed jackal, hyena, python. Diurnal and most active in the early morning, the late afternoon, and the early, dark evening hours. Hot, midday hours are mostly spent lying down or standing and ruminating. When a ♂ shows off his strength to attract a mate, or to ward off predators, he starts off in a stiff-legged trot, jumping up into the air with an arched back every few paces and lifting a pocket-like skin flap along his back (pronking). Lifting the flap causes the long white hairs under the tail to stand up in a conspicuous fan shape, which in turn emits a strong scent of sweat. Social and gregarious. A family herd consists of adult ewes, subadult ♀, and juveniles of both sexes. Adult ♂ become territorial only during the rut; alternatively they join family herds or become solitary nomads. Family herds pass through several different ♂ territories during one mating season. Family herds tend to stay in a fixed home range. Individuals tend to keep a distance between each other and have little bodily contact. They groom themselves.

DISTRIBUTION *Native*: Angola, Namibia. Found in N Namibia and S Angola, where it survives in greatly reduced numbers.

HABITAT Dry grasslands, bushland, and shrubland of SW and S Africa, migrating sporadically in vast herds in some of the S parts of its range. These migrations or treks no longer occur.

STATUS Least Concern. Estimated population at 10,000 animals in Angola.

PHOTO CREDITS Head ♂: *Dominique Van Geem*. Head ♀: *Tom Kelly* (www.tomkellyphoto.com). Young and juvenile: *Nadel* and *Ingrid Peters*.

Addra Gazelle
NANGER DAMA RUFICOLLIS

BL: 140-165 cm. SH: 88-108 cm. TL: 25-35 cm. W: 40-75 kg. HL: 20-43 cm. The largest of the true gazelles, slender, with a long neck and legs, and short, thick horns. Coat bright white, with reddish brown or chestnut on the neck. Neck reddish brown with a white spot just below the throat. The reddish brown coloration is often restricted to the neck, or may go some way along the back. The red and the white are not sharply demarcated from each other. Face completely white. Horns found in both sexes, generally larger and thicker in males, S-shaped, slanting backward, then curling upward. Males slightly larger than females, with stronger necks.

Young

Nanger dama ruficollis

OTHER NAMES Dama Gazelle, Nubian Gazelle, Red-necked Gazelle. *French*: Gazelle dama. *German*: Damagazelle. *Spanish*: Gacela dama, gacela Adra. *Russian*: Сахарская газель-дама. *Arabic*: Ariel, mhorr. *Dinka*: Riel. *Hausa*: Farin gindi. *Kirundi*: Intaramuyi. *Maasai*: Olwargas, oloibor riadi. *Peulh*: Jabare, diaoure.

SUBSPECIES Considered as a subspecies of *N. dama* (Dama Gazelle): *N. d. mhorr* (Mhorr Gazelle), *N. d. ruficollis* (Addra Gazelle). *N. d. dama is* extinct. Some authors treat the species as monotypic, with a cline of variation across its range.

SIMILAR SPECIES Mhorr Gazelle is darker, being at least rufous from the back to the flanks with extensions to the legs; rump always white, but across the thigh, a rufous band, sometimes contiguous to the dark back.

REPRODUCTION *Gestation*: 165-180 days. *Young per Birth*: 1. *Weaning*: 6 months. *Sexual Maturity*: 9-12 months (♀), 18-24 months (♂). *Life Span*: 12 years. In the wild, offspring are usually born from April through June. The newborns are hidden away from the herd, but a couple of days after birth, the offspring are usually strong enough to follow the dam.

BEHAVIOR *Family Group*: Mixed herds of about 15-20 animals. *Diet*: Desert shrubs and acacias. In times of drought they also eat rough desert grasses. Most of their water is obtained from plants. *Main Predators*: Cheetah, Cape hunting dog, lion, leopard, hyena, python. The social organization and behavior is greatly affected by the seasons. Herds typically spend the dry season in the Sahel where they occur in small groups (up to 15 individuals) or singly. With the rains, they migrate N into Chad where in the past, groups could swell to 200 or more individuals. It is also believed that ♂ are seasonally territorial. In captivity, the ♂ especially show marking behavior (defecation, urination, and marking with scent glands). Addra Gazelles communicate through vocalizations, body position, and scent gland marking. To maximize the amount of food available, these gazelles may stand on their hind legs in a manner reminiscent of the Gerenuk in order to reach leaves above the normal browsing height.

DISTRIBUTION *Native*: Chad, Mali, Niger. *Regionally Extinct*: Libya, Mauritania, Morocco, Nigeria, Tunisia. *Reintroduced*: Senegal. Formerly widespread in the Sahara and Sahel zones, but their range and numbers have been extremely reduced. In North Africa, Addra Gazelle are now probably extinct, although they may survive in the Drâa, and in the Tassili de Tin Rehror in S Algeria. S of the Sahara, Addra Gazelle are still present in E Mali, Air and Termit-Tin Toumma in Niger, and in the Chadian Manga and Ouadi Rimé Ouadi Achim Nature Reserve in Chad.

HABITAT Sahel, the sub-Saharan desert/semi-desert regions characterized by low and erratic rainfall with little vegetation, most of which is seasonal.

STATUS Critically Endangered. Still present in the wild but quickly declining. Estimated population is fewer than 2,500 individuals. The catastrophic decline is due to extensive habitat destruction by natives and nomadic cattle as well as uncontrolled hunting with vehicles and modern firearms.

PHOTO CREDITS ♂ and ♀: *Craig Salvas,* Smithsonian National Zoological Park (USA). Head ♀: *Gilles Malo*.

Mhorr Gazelle

NANGER DAMA MHORR

BL: 140-165 cm. SH: 90-120 cm. TL: 25-35 cm. W: 40-75 kg. HL: 20-43 cm. Similar to the Addra Gazelle. Coat bright white, with reddish brown or chestnut on the neck. Neck reddish brown with a white spot just below the throat. Reddish brown coloration on the forehead, back, fetlocks, and on the front of the forelegs. Face has relatively few markings, with thin black stripes running from the eyes to the corners of the mouth. Body supported by thin legs, neck long and slender. Horns found in both sexes, generally larger and thicker in males, S-shaped, slanting backward, then curling upward.

Juvenile

Young

♀

♂

Nanger dama mhorr

OTHER NAMES Dama Gazelle. *French*: Gazelle dama. *German*: Damagazelle. *Spanish*: Gacela mor. *Russian*: Марокканская газель-дама. *Arabic*: Ariel, mhorr. *Dinka*: Riel. *Hausa*: Farin gindi. *Kirundi*: Intaramuyi. *Maasai*: Olwargas, oloibor riadi. *Peulh*: Jabare, diaoure.

SUBSPECIES Considered as a subspecies of *N. dama* (Dama Gazelle): *N. d. mhorr* (Mhorr Gazelle), *N. d. ruficollis* (Addra Gazelle). *N. d. dama is* extinct. Some authors treat the species as monotypic, with a cline of variation across its range.

SIMILAR SPECIES Addra Gazelle is lighter in color, only the neck and a saddle on the shoulder being rufous, being almost entirely white.

REPRODUCTION *Gestation*: 165-180 days. *Young per Birth*: 1. *Weaning*: 6 months. *Sexual Maturity*: 9-12 months (♀), 18-24 months (♂). *Life Span*: 12 years. Breeding takes place from March to June, and the young are born around December.

BEHAVIOR *Family Group*: Mixed herds of about 15-20 animals. Often found with Dorcas Gazelles. *Diet*: Acacia and bush leaves, grasses. Drinks water, but can do without it for long periods. *Main Predators*: Cheetah, Cape hunting dog, lion, leopard, hyena, python. A diurnal species, this gazelle requires more water than others adapted to its dry habitat, although it can survive long periods of drought. Like most desert species, the Mhorr Gazelle is highly nomadic, ranging widely in order to obtain sufficient nutrition. In addition, these gazelles undertake large seasonal migrations, moving N into the Sahara Desert during the rainy season, and retreating S into the Sahel during the dry season. To maximize the amount of food available, these gazelles may stand on their hind legs in a manner reminiscent of the Gerenuk in order to reach leaves above the normal browsing height. Adult ♂ are believed to be territorial during the breeding season. Eyesight, hearing, and sense of smell are very good.

DISTRIBUTION Extinct in the wild, it was distributed in the past from Morocco, Western Sahara, Mauritania, and Senegal in the W of Africa to Egypt and Sudan in the E. There are several reintroduction projects occurring.

HABITAT Semidesert areas in pockets across N-central Africa.

STATUS Extinct in the Wild. Mhorr Gazelle is probably extinct in the wild but present in breeding programs in Europe and America. The catastrophic decline is due to extensive habitat destruction by natives and nomadic cattle as well as uncontrolled hunting with vehicles and modern firearms.

PHOTO CREDITS ♂ and head: *José R. Castelló*, Madrid Zoo (Spain). ♀: *Jim Capaldi*, Philadelphia Zoo (USA). Head ♀: *Ken Wewerka,* Phoenix Zoo (USA). Young: *Thomas Schwenker*, Diergaarde Blijdorp (Netherlands) and Frankfurt Zoo (Germany). Juvenile: *Jonathan Beilby* and *Nick Karpov*, Berlin Tierpark (Germany).

Nubian Soemmerring's Gazelle
NANGER SOEMMERRINGII SOEMMERRINGII

BL: 125-150 cm. SH: 85-92 cm. TL: 18-28 cm. W: 35-45 kg. HL: To 58 cm (♂), to 40 cm (♀). Upper body uniform tawny red, with head and neck lighter. Underside, inside of legs, and tail bright white. White rump patch normally extends onto the sides. The different back and belly colors meet along the flank with a sharp, crisp line. Head has dark markings of the traditional gazelle pattern, including a wide dark stripe down the nose and dark lines running from the eyes to the nose, separated by white stripes. Tail is short and tapered and terminates with a black tuft. Both sexes carry the lyre-shaped horns, which turn inward at the tips. Those in females are straighter, thinner, and smoother. Horns in males are considerably larger and heavier, and strongly ringed.

♂

Young

♀

Juvenile

*Nanger soemmerringii
soemmerringii*

OTHER NAMES Sudan Soemmerring's Gazelle. *French*: Gazelle de Soemmerring. *German*: Sömmerringgazelle. *Spanish*: Gacela de Soemmerring nubiana. *Russian*: Суданская (нубийская) сомалийская газель (Газель Зёммеринга).

SUBSPECIES Considered as a subspecies of *N. soemmerringii* (Soemmerring's Gazelle): *N. s. berberana* (Somali Soemmerring's Gazelle), *N. s. soemmerringii* (Sudan or Nubian Soemmerring's Gazelle), *N. s. butteri* (Borani Soemmerring's Gazelle).

SIMILAR SPECIES Somali Soemmerring's Gazelle (*berberana*) is slightly larger, with larger horns and a darker facial blaze. Borani Soemmerring's Gazelle (*butteri*) has an ill-defined band along the flanks and a dark band bordering the white patch on the rump. The gazelles of Dahlak Kebir Island (Eritrea) are smaller than their conspecifics living on the continent.

REPRODUCTION *Gestation*: 198 days. *Young per Birth*: 1. *Weaning*: 6 months. *Sexual Maturity*: 1.5 years. *Life Span*: 14 years. The mating season takes place during the light rains in about October. Births occurs at the peak of the main rains, in April, in Somalia. After birth, baby gazelles lie hidden in the grass away from their mothers.

BEHAVIOR *Family Group:* Mixed herds of between 5 and 20 individuals, rarely up to 150. *Diet*: Primarily grasses. *Main Predators:* Cheetah, Cape hunting dog, lion, leopard, hyena, python. Soemmerring's Gazelles migrate annually in the Sudan, relocating to areas with more food and water. ♂ are territorial, though this may be on a temporary basis. Defended ranges are staked out via dung middens, while the small-slitted preorbital glands do not seem to play a role in marking. When confronting rival ♂, they flick their heads, and when fights arise they yank their hooked horns sideways in an attempt to make the opponent lose his balance. When herding ♀, ♂ make a nasal croak. During the courting of a receptive ♀, the ♂ drives her at a walking pace with his head raised. Instead of the typical gazelle foreleg kick, the ♂ does a stiff-legged "trot in place." Copulation occurs while walking, with both partners keeping their heads up and the ♂ trailing after the ♀ on 2 legs.

DISTRIBUTION *Native*: Eritrea. *Possibly Extinct*: Sudan. Formerly widely distributed throughout NE and central Sudan, and lowland areas of Eritrea. The population on Dahlak Kebir Island was probably introduced over 100 years ago. Uncontrolled hunting and habitat destruction have most probably eliminated this species from its historic range in Sudan. It still occupies substantial parts of its historic range in Eritrea, but at lower densities and as isolated populations.

HABITAT Arid coastal plains and mudflats, arid and semi-arid acacia savannas, and semi-arid grassland plains. Tends to prefer rough hilly country, but also found in open bush savannas, and thinly wooded grasslands.

STATUS Vulnerable. Estimated population of fewer than 1,000 individuals in continental Eritrea, and 4,000-4,500 on Dahlak Kebir Island.

PHOTO CREDITS ♂: *Jim Frazee*, San Diego Zoo (USA). ♀: *Scott Hanko*, San Diego Zoo (USA). Young: *Dyrk Daniels*, San Diego Zoo (USA). Juvenile: *Queen-of-the-mountain* and *Sergey Chichagov*, San Diego Zoo (USA).

Somali Soemmerring's Gazelle

NANGER SOEMMERRINGII BERBERANA

BL: 125-150 cm. SH: 85-92 cm. TL: 18-28 cm. W: 35-45 kg. HL: To 58 cm (♂), to 40 cm (♀). Largest subspecies, with the longest horns. Darkest facial blaze, being black or dark brown rather than reddish brown. Upper body uniform tawny red, with head and neck lighter. Underside, inside of legs, and tail bright white. White rump patch normally extends onto the sides. The different back and belly colors meet along the flank with a sharp, crisp line. Tail is short and tapered and terminates with a black tuft. Both sexes carry the lyre-shaped horns, which turn inwardsat the tips. Those in females are straighter, thinner, and smoother. Horns in males are considerably larger and heavier, and strongly ringed.

Nanger soemmerringii berberana

Nanger soemmerringii butteri

OTHER NAMES *French*: Gazelle de Soemmerring. *German*: Sömmerringgazelle. *Spanish*: Gacela de Soemmerring Somali. *Russian*: Берберская сомалийская газель (Газель Зёммеринга) *(berberana),* Боранийская сомалийская газель (Газель Зёммеринга) *(butteri).*

SUBSPECIES Considered as a subspecies of *N. soemmerringii* (Soemmerring's Gazelle): *N. s. berberana* (Somali Soemmerring's Gazelle), *N. s. soemmerringii* (Sudan or Nubian Soemmerring's Gazelle), *N. s. butteri* (Borani Soemmerring's Gazelle). Includes *erlangeri* (Awash Valley in Ethiopia) and *berberana* (N Somalia and the Ogaden region of Ethiopia), with *berberana* having priority. Borani Soemmerring's Gazelle may be extinct.

SIMILAR SPECIES Sudan Soemmerring's Gazelle (*soemmerringii*) is slightly smaller, with smaller horns and a lighter facial blaze. Borani Soemmerring's Gazelle (*butteri*) is smaller, and has an ill-defined band along the flanks and a dark band bordering the white patch on the rump.

REPRODUCTION *Gestation*: 198 days. *Young per Birth:* 1. *Weaning*: 6 months. *Sexual Maturity*: 1.5 years. *Life Span:* 14 years. The mating season takes place during the light rains, between September and October. Births occur at the peak of the main rains, in April, in Somalia. After birth, baby gazelles lie hidden in the grass away from their mothers.

BEHAVIOR *Family Group:* Mixed herds of between 5 and 20 individuals, rarely up to 150. *Diet*: Primarily grasses, drinks regularly when water is available. *Main Predators:* Cheetah, Cape hunting dog, lion, leopard, hyena, python. There is no specific information available for this subspecies, but it may be like *N. s. soemmerringii.*

DISTRIBUTION *Native:* Djibouti, Ethiopia, Somalia. Distributed throughout most of Djibouti, in Awash Valley in Ethiopia and the Ogaden region, including the Webi Shebeli valley, and near Dolo on the Genale River, in far NW Somalia near Djibouti, S of the N coastal (Guban) mountains from about Burao eastward, along the E (Indian Ocean) coast from about Ras Hafun almost to Mogadishu, and in the Webi Shebeli and Juba valleys. *Butteri* is found in S Ethiopia, Dana Valley, Boran-Gallaland.

HABITAT Grassy plains or light bush, rough hilly country with scattered evergreen thickets and *Acacia/Commiphora* steppe, as well as open, short-grass plains.

STATUS Vulnerable. Estimated population of fewer than 1,000 individuals in Somalia, 1,000 to 1,500 in Djibouti, and fewer than 3,000 in Ethiopia. The population in Djibouti can probably be considered stable over recent years and may even be slightly increasing. However, in Ethiopia (Ogaden) and Somalia the decline must have been drastic over the past 50 years. The largest population occurs in Awash NP (Ethiopia). However, even within this protected area, seasonal cattle grazing occurs which may impact the gazelle's food supply. Of the 3 described subspecies, *soemmerringii* is kept in a few North American zoos, whereas *berberana* is only kept at Al Wabra Wildlife Preservation (Qatar).

PHOTO CREDITS ♂: *Jonas Livet*, Al Wabra Wildlife Preservation (Qatar). ♀: *Tim Melling*, Awash NP (Ethiopia).

Southern Grant's Gazelle
NANGER GRANTI GRANTI

BL: 155 -166 cm. SH: 75-95 cm. TL: 20-28 cm. W: 55-80 kg (♂), 35-45 kg (♀). HL: 50-80 cm
(♂), 30-43 cm (♀). The largest subspecies of Grant's Gazelle. The upper half of the body is
fawn or light cinnamon colored; the lower half and rump are white with a black stripe running
down the thigh. Males do not have a black flank band or it is very faint, but the nose spot and
pygal stripes are well defined. In females and young individuals, the flank band is usually,
but not always, better expressed. Males have thicker necks than females. Lyre-shaped, wide-
spreading horns found in both sexes, stout at the base, clearly ringed. Males have longer,
thicker, and more strongly ringed horns.

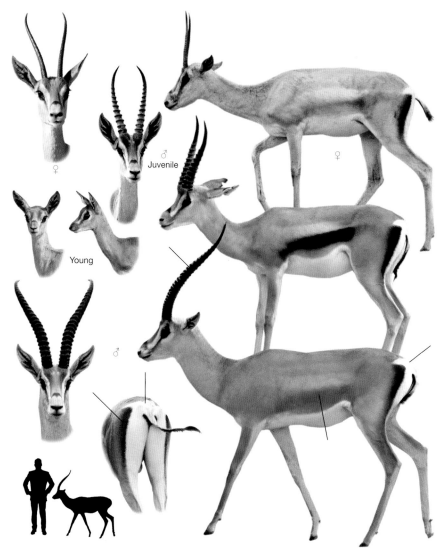

Nanger granti granti

OTHER NAMES Grant's Gazelle. *French*: Gazelle de Grant. *German*: Grant-Gazelle, Tansania-Grantgazelle. *Spanish*: Gazela de Grant. *Russian*: Южная газель Гранта. *Swahili*: Swala granti. *Acholi*: Lagweta. *Amharic*: Yegrant Medafeyel. *Galla*: Hidi. *Maasai*: Oloiborsiadi. *Kikuyu*: Thwara, irong'ha, karongha. *Kirundi*: Intaramvyi.

SUBSPECIES Considered as a subspecies of *G. granti* (Grant's Gazelle): *N. g. granti* (Southern Grant's Gazelle), *N. g. robertsi* (Robert's Gazelle). Includes *granti* (S Dodoma, Tanzania), *roosevelti* (Athi Plains, Kenya) and *serengetae* (S Kenya, near Taveta), with *granti* having priority. *N. granti* formerly also included: *N. notata* (Northern Grant's Gazelle) and *N. petersi* (Peters's Gazelle), which now have been elevated to full species.

SIMILAR SPECIES Larger than Thomson's Gazelle, with longer and heavier horns, with white above the tail, and usually with no conspicuous band on flank (when this band exists there is a "shadow band" below). Southern Grant's Gazelle is the largest subspecies, with the longest horns of any Grant's, or any other gazelle. *Roosevelti* race usually smaller, *serengetae* have narrower spreading horns and a narrow fawn-brown stripe that splits the white rump patch and reaches the root of the tail.

REPRODUCTION *Gestation*: 198 days. *Young per Birth*: 1. *Weaning*: 6 months. *Sexual Maturity*: 18 months. *Life Span*: 14 years. Births peak in January and February. A ♀ will leave her herd and find a well-hidden place to give birth. ♀ that have recently given birth will stay together for protection. Fawns are immobile for the first few days. When the fawn can walk, it leaves with its mother to find a herd.

BEHAVIOR *Family Group*: Herds can be ♀, ♀ and young, bachelor groups, or, outside the breeding season, mixed. ♀ with newborn calves and territorial ♂ do not join the herd. *Diet*: Dietary generalists, eating whatever is greenest (herbs, foliage from shrubs, short grasses, and shoots, depending on the season). *Main Predators*: Cheetah, wild dog, jackals (fawn). Outside the breeding season, Grant's Gazelles form mixed groups that contain both sexes; during the breeding season, ♂ become territorial, marking their territory with dung and urine. At this time, territories are defended from all other mature ♂. This usually begins with threat displays and can escalate to intense fighting between neighboring territorial ♂. Territorial ♂ will attempt to keep ♀ within their territories with displays but will not venture into the territory of another ♂ when the ♀ leave. Grant's Gazelles are extremely fast (97 kmph).

DISTRIBUTION *Native*: Kenya, Tanzania. Found in N Tanzania (down to Ruaha) to S Kenya. Those in the Athi Plains (Nairobi NP) have been described as *roosevelti*; those near Taveta (S tip of Tsavo West) have been described as *serengetae*.

HABITAT Semi-desert and open savannas.

CONSERVATION STATUS Least Concern.

PHOTO CREDITS ♂: *Moth Clark*, Lake Nakuru (Kenya). ♀: *Dianne Erskine-Hellrigel*. Juvenile: *Johannes Pfleiderer*, San Diego Zoo (USA) and *Esther Horwich*, Maasai Mara (Kenya). Young: *Steffen Foerster* and *Olivier Delaere*, Maasai Mara (Kenya).

Roberts's Gazelle
NANGER GRANTI ROBERTSI

BL: 155-166 cm. SH: 75-95 cm. TL: 20-28 cm. W: 55-80 kg (♂), 35-45 kg (♀). HL: 50-80 cm (♂), 30-43 cm (♀). Similar to *granti*, except that the male's horns may bend sharply outward at a point about one-third of their length from the base, so that the tips are very far apart, and the tips then bend either downward or backward, although there is a great deal of variation and horns may be lyrate as in *granti*. Coat is a beige orange on the back with a white belly. Males do not have a dark flank band. In females flank bands are either absent or very faint. The black pygal band is usually narrower than in Southern Grant's Gazelle. Females have normal horns.

♂
Juvenile

horn variation

♀

♂

Nanger granti robertsi

OTHER NAMES Wide-horned Grant's Gazelle. *French:* Gazelle de Robert. *German:* Robert Grant-Gazelle, Weithorn-Grantgazelle. *Spanish:* Gazela de Robert. *Russian:* Газель Робертса. *Swahili:* Swala Granti.

SUBSPECIES Considered as a subspecies of *G. granti* (Grant's Gazelle): *N. g. granti* (Southern Grant's Gazelle), *N. g. robertsi* (Roberts's Gazelle). Formerly included also: *N. notata* (Northern Grant's Gazelle), *N. petersi* (Peters's Gazelle), which now have been elevated to full species.

SIMILAR SPECIES Similar to the Southern Grant's Gazelle, except that the ♂'s horns are not lyrate. ♂ with *robertsi*-type horns are often found in the same area with others that have typical *granti*-type horns, and individual animals may exhibit considerable variation in horn configuration. It is likely that the two subspecies interbreed. Eastern Thomson's Gazelle has no white above the tail, is slightly smaller, and the horns curve backward rather than straight upward.

REPRODUCTION *Gestation*: 198 days. *Young per Birth*: 1. *Weaning*: 6 months. *Sexual Maturity*: 18 months. *Life Span*: 14 years. There is no specific information available for this subspecies, but it may be like *N. g. granti*.

BEHAVIOR *Family Group:* Herds can be ♀, ♀ and young, bachelor groups, or, outside the breeding season, mixed. ♀ with newborn calves and territorial ♂ do not join the herd. *Diet*: Dietary generalists, eating whatever is greenest (herbs, foliage from shrubs, short grasses, and shoots, depending on the season). *Main Predators*: Cheetah, wild dog, jackals (fawn). Outside the breeding season, Grant's Gazelles form mixed groups that contain both sexes; during the breeding season, ♂ become territorial, marking their territory with dung and urine. At this time, territories are defended from all other mature ♂. This usually begins with threat displays and can escalate to intense fighting between neighboring territorial ♂. Territorial ♂ will attempt to keep ♀ within their territories with displays but will not venture into the territory of another ♂ when the ♀ leave. Roberts's Gazelles are extremely fast (97 kmph).

DISTRIBUTION *Native*: Kenya, Tanzania. Found in N Tanzania generally W of the Rift Valley (Serengeti, Ngorongoro and a small part of Natron) to S Kenya in Maasai Mara and Loita Plains.

HABITAT It is more likely to be seen in Ngorongoro, and the Seronera area of Serengeti, but is rarely seen in the area in between (the short-grass plains).

CONSERVATION STATUS Least Concern.

PHOTO CREDITS ♂: *Richard Toller,* Ngorongoro Conservation Area (Tanzania). ♀: *Tom and Louisa,* Serengeti Conservation Area (Tanzania). Head ♀: *Greg Heffron* (Tanzania). Juvenile: *Cédric Charest* and *Chris Lira,* Ngorongoro Conservation Area (Tanzania).

Peters's Gazelle

NANGER PETERSI

BL: 155-166 cm. SH: 75-95 cm. TL: 20-28 cm. W: 55-80 kg (♂), 35-45 kg (♀). HL: 50-80 cm (♂), 30-43 cm (♀). A small and darker gazelle. The fawn-brown body color extends from neck to tail in a wide band that divides the white rump patch. Differs from Southern Grant's Gazelle, which has a much larger white rump patch divided by a narrow brown stripe. The rump patch is narrower and shorter than in other forms of Grant's Gazelle, reaching only to the anus. Pygal stripes are well developed. Facial stripes are faded, there is a whitish band above the eye, and a brown nose spot. The horns are short and almost straight, diverging only slightly.

Young

♀

Juvenile

♂

♂

petersi   granti

Nanger petersi

OTHER NAMES Tana Gazelle. *French*: Gazelle de Peters. *German*: Östliche Grant-Gazelle, Peters Grantgazelle. *Spanish*: Gazela de Peters. *Russian*: Газель Петерса.

SUBSPECIES Monotypic. Formerly considered a subspecies of *G. granti* (Grant's Gazelle).

SIMILAR SPECIES Larger than Thomson's Gazelle, with longer and heavier horns, and usually with no conspicuous band on flank. Southern Grant's Gazelle is usually larger, lighter in color, has a larger white rump patch, and more divergent horns.

REPRODUCTION *Gestation*: 198 days. *Young per Birth*: 1. *Weaning*: 6 months. *Sexual Maturity*: 18 months. *Life Span*: 14 years. Births peak in January and February. A ♀ will leave her herd and find a well-hidden place to give birth. ♀ that have recently given birth will stay together for protection. Fawns are immobile for the first few days. When the fawn can walk, it leaves with its mother to find a herd.

BEHAVIOR *Family Group:* Herds can be ♀, ♀ and young, bachelor groups, or, outside the breeding season, mixed. ♀ with newborn calves and territorial ♂ do not join the herd. *Diet*: Dietary generalists, eating whatever is greenest (herbs, foliage from shrubs, short grasses, and shoots, depending on the season). *Main Predators:* Cheetah, wild dog, jackals (fawn). Outside the breeding season, Grant's Gazelles form mixed groups that contain both sexes; during the breeding season, ♂ become territorial, marking their territory with dung and urine. At this time, territories are defended from all other mature ♂. This usually begins with threat displays and can escalate to intense fighting between neighboring territorial ♂. Territorial ♂ will attempt to keep ♀ within their territories with displays but will not venture into the territory of another ♂ when the ♀ leave. They are extremely fast (97 kmph).

DISTRIBUTION *Native*: Kenya, Somalia. Found in Tana River Valley to Tsavo East, NE Kenya (coastal Kenya), and SE Somalia.

HABITAT Semi-desert and open savannas.

CONSERVATION STATUS Least Concern.

PHOTO CREDITS ♂ and ♀: *Philippe Boissel,* Tsavo East (Kenya). Head ♀: *Alessia Zof,* Tsavo East (Kenya). Juvenile: *Francesca Solimini*, Tsavo East (Kenya). Young: *Jaap Bloot* (Kenya).

Northern Grant's Gazelle

NANGER NOTATA

BL: 155-166 cm. SH: 75-95 cm. TL: 20-28 cm. W: 55-80 kg (♂), 35-45 kg (♀). HL: 50-80 cm (♂), 30-43 cm (♀). Smaller than *granti*, with horns that are usually, but not always, smaller and more parallel. Coat is tan colored on the back, darker than in other forms of Grant's Gazelle, with a white belly, and usually a well-marked lateral flank band in males and females, so there is little difference in color between sexes. The flank band may be absent in both sexes in some areas (*brighti* and *lacuum* populations). Pygal band extends only halfway down, so it does not completely separate color of the haunch from the white of the buttock. Both sexes have horns; those of the male being longer, thicker, and more strongly ringed. Horns are usually straighter than in Southern Grant's Gazelle, diverging only slightly.

coat variation

Young

raineyi

Nanger notata

OTHER NAMES Bright's Gazelle. *French:* Gazelle de Bright. *German*: Nördliche Grant-Gazelle, Lorigi-Grantgazelle. *Spanish*: Gazela de Bright. *Russian*: Северная газель Гранта.

SUBSPECIES Monotypic. Formerly considered a subspecies of *G. granti* (Grant's Gazelle). Includes *brighti* (SE Sudan, SW Ethiopia W of the Omo River, NE Uganda, NW Kenya W of Lake Turkana), *lacuum* (S of Lake Zwai, Ethiopia), *notata* (W slope of Lorogi Mountains, Kenya), and *raineyi* (Isiolo Valley, Kenya), with *notata* having priority. Rainey's Gazelle (*raineyi*) is usually lighter in color, with horns almost straight. Bright's Gazelle (*brighti*) is smaller and paler, with small horns, with the pygal stripes either absent or very faint.

SIMILAR SPECIES Southern Grant's Gazelle is slightly lighter in color, larger, has no conspicuous flank band in adults, and has more diverging horns. Thomson's Gazelle is smaller, with shorter horns.

REPRODUCTION *Gestation*: 198 days. *Young per Birth*: 1. *Weaning*: 6 months. *Sexual Maturity*: 18 months. *Life Span*: 14 years. Breeding occurs in September-October. Births peak in April.

BEHAVIOR *Family Group:* Herds of 20-30 individuals, composed of ♀, ♀ and young, bachelor groups, or, outside the breeding season, mixed. ♀ with newborn calves and territorial ♂ do not join the herd. *Diet*: Dietary generalists, eating whatever is greenest (herbs, foliage from shrubs, short grasses, and shoots, depending on the season). *Main Predators:* Cheetah, wild dog, jackals (fawn). Outside the breeding season, Bright's Gazelles form mixed groups that contain both sexes; during the breeding season, ♂ become territorial, marking their territory with dung and urine. At this time, territories are defended from all other mature ♂. This usually begins with threat displays and can escalate to intense fighting between neighboring territorial ♂. Territorial ♂ will attempt to keep ♀ within their territories with displays but will not venture into the territory of another ♂ when the ♀ leave.

DISTRIBUTION *Native*: Ethiopia, Kenya, Sudan, Uganda. N of the equator and W of Lake Turkana in Kenya, Ethiopia E and W of the Omo River, NE Uganda. Those E of the Omo River in Ethiopia have been described as *lacuum*; those near Isiolo have been described as *raineyi*. Bright's Gazelle (*brighti*) is found in extreme SE Sudan and adjoining parts of extreme SW Ethiopia W of the Omo River, NE Uganda, and NW Kenya W of Lake Turkana.

HABITAT Sparse grasslands with acacia woodlands and bush.

CONSERVATION STATUS Least Concern.

PHOTO CREDITS ♂: *Elise Ney*, Kicheche Conservancy, Ol Pejeta (Kenya). ♀: *Ariadne Van Zandbergen,* Ol Pejeta (Kenya) and *Volker Sthamer,* South Omo Region (Ethiopia). Young: *Volker Sthamer,* South Omo Region (Ethiopia).

Eastern Thomson's Gazelle

EUDORCAS THOMSONI

BL: 92-107 cm (♂), 89-107 cm (♀). SH: 58-70 cm (♂), 58-69 cm (♀). W: 17-25 kg (♂), 13-20 kg (♀). TL: 20-28 cm. HL: 25-43 cm (♂), 7-15 cm (♀). A medium-sized gazelle. Upper parts are sandy rufous, with a lighter flank band below, and below that a distinctive wide black band, in immediate contact with the white underparts. White rump, bordered by narrow black pygal stripes. Tail all black. Chestnut blaze from the base of the horns to the muzzle, a white eye ring continuing as a stripe to the muzzle, and a reddish cheek stripe below the eye. Preorbital glands well developed in males, producing a thick, black secretion. Horns found in both sexes, significantly larger and strongly ringed in males, often nearly straight, curving slightly backward for most of their length, with the tips bending a little forward and upward. Female similar to male, slightly lighter, with horns short, straight, and relatively weak, often deformed or broken.

♀

♂
Juvenile

Young

♂

Eudorcas thomsoni

OTHER NAMES "Tommy." *French*: Gazelle de Thomson. *German*: Thomson-Gazelle. *Spanish*: Gacela de Thomson. *Russian*: Газель Томсона. *Swahili*: Swala tomi, lala. *Kinyaturu*: Sasunga. *Kikuyu*: Thwara. *Kirangi*: Mpefe. *Maasai*: Enkopera. *Kijita*: Nindala. *Turkana*: Nauren, Katebe.

SUBSPECIES Monotypic. The name *E. thomsoni* (Thomson's Gazelle) formerly included *E. thomsoni* (Eastern Thomson's Gazelle), and *E. nasalis* (Serengeti Thomson's Gazelle) as subspecies: these are elevated to full species here.

SIMILAR SPECIES Grant's Gazelle is much larger, with longer and heavier horns, a white rump patch that extends above the tail, and usually no conspicuous band on flank. Serengeti Thomson's Gazelle from W of the Rift Valley has more divergent horns, a well-defined black nose spot, a black eye stripe, and wider, more distinct pygal stripes, while Eastern Thomson's Gazelle, from E of the Rift Valley, has more parallel horns, no nose spot, a reddish eye stripe, and narrow, less distinct pygal stripes, and is less rufous.

REPRODUCTION *Gestation*: 180-230 days. *Young per Birth*: 1. *Weaning*: 2 months. *Sexual Maturity*: 7-12 months (♀), 16 months (♂). *Life Span*: 15 years. Mating takes place in winter, with births taking place in spring. ♀ can give birth twice a year, which is unusual for ungulates. The ♀ leaves the herd a few days before giving birth. She may stay alone with her baby for up to 3 weeks. Young ♂ are expelled from the herd to go and join a bachelor herd. This helps to avoid inbreeding.

BEHAVIOR *Family Group*: Over 200 animals. *Diet*: Grass, other low vegetation, shrubs. Most of their required water comes from vegetation. *Main Predators*: Lion, cheetah, jackal, leopard, wild dog, spotted hyena. More sedentary than the Serengeti Thomson's Gazelle. Social animals, living in herds, and may congregate with other hoofed animals (zebra, other antelopes). During migration, thousands of gazelles will travel together in search of water during the dry season. Their territories may overlap with those of other species of ungulates with no problems. However, some may be more territorial and defend their territories vigorously if challenged. The defending ♂ will clash horns with his opponent. They mark the boundaries of their territory with a small secretion from scent glands located beneath their eyes. They deposit the secretion onto blades of grass around 6 m apart daily. They are very fast and can outrun their predators (up to 80 kmph for 15-20 minutes). As the gazelles race along in their escape, they perform sudden bounding leaps in high arcs (pronking or stotting), making it more difficult for them to be brought down by their predator. When a gazelle spots a stalking predator, it will pronk or stot to alert other gazelles to the danger and can also startle the predator.

DISTRIBUTION E of Rift Valley in Kenya and Tanzania, SW via the Arusha district to Lake Eyasi, the Wembere Plains, and Shinyanga.

HABITAT Open plains with scattered trees and short grasses, on dry ground. It avoids long-grass areas but goes into these areas when they have been burned and new grass is sprouting.

STATUS Near Threatened.

PHOTO CREDITS ♂: *The Rohit*, Amboseli (Kenya). ♀: *Ken Wewerka*, Amboseli (Kenya). Head ♂: *Randall Knox,* Amboseli (Kenya). Head ♀: *Heather Paul*. Juvenile: *Jennifer Hall*, Amboseli (Kenya). Young: *Julianne Waddell*, Amboseli (Kenya).

Serengeti Thomson's Gazelle

EUDORCAS NASALIS

BL: 70-90 cm. SH: 66 cm. W: 15-17 kg (♀). TL: 22-24 cm. HL: 25-43 cm (♂), 7-15 cm (♀). Smaller than Eastern Thomson's Gazelle. Sandy, light brown color with a white rump and underside. Characteristic black flank stripe down the side of the body, along with the black tail. Facial markings darker than in Eastern Thomson's Gazelle, consisting of a chestnut blaze from the base of the horns to the muzzle, a blackish nose spot, a white eye ring continuing as a stripe to the muzzle, and a blackish cheek stripe below the eye. Preorbital glands well developed in males. White rump bordered by wider, more distinct black pygal stripes. Horns found in both sexes, significantly larger and strongly ringed in males, running relatively straight with a slight S-shaped curvature. Female similar to male, slightly lighter, with horns short, straight, and relatively weak, often deformed, broken, or absent.

♀

Juvenile

♂

♂

Young

Eudorcas nasalis

OTHER NAMES "Tommy." *French*: Gazelle de Lönnberg. *German*: Westliche Thomson-Gazelle. *Spanish*: Gacela del Serengeti. *Russian*: Черноносая газель Томсона.

SUBSPECIES Monotypic. Formerly considered a subspecies of *E. thomsoni* (Thomson's Gazelle).

SIMILAR SPECIES More rufous and much smaller in size than Eastern Thomson's Gazelle, but the horns not much less in ♂, face stripes darker, nose spot much more prominent, white crown extending as a V down the center of the forehead.

REPRODUCTION *Gestation*: 165-180 days. *Young per Birth*: 1. *Weaning*: 2 months. *Sexual Maturity*: 19-21 months. *Life Span*: 12 years. Both birth and mating peaks occur during the rains, with a secondary peak 6 months later. ♀ remain alone in relatively heavy cover after giving birth. The fawn lies with its head and neck stretched out along the ground. When the ♀ approaches to suckle, she stops 20 m away and calls for the fawn. The young remain with their mothers until 8 months of age.

BEHAVIOR *Family Group*: Over 200 animals. *Diet*: Almost entirely a grazer, although it browses to some extent; requires water daily when the grass is dry, but can go without it when feeding on new grass. *Main Predators*: Cheetah, jackal (fawn), African wild dog. Highly territorial and actively defend their territory, but they also migrate with the Wildebeest, Zebras, and Topi as well as trek long distances back and forth to water; in this state they are more sociably flexible. They form ♀ herds, with little interaction between them, which move through ♂ territories. A ♂ will try to prevent ♀ groups from leaving his territory, rounding them up and trying to move them toward the center of the territory. ♂ may be seen to cock their heads against a tall grass blade, marking territory using the preorbital glands, which are situated in front of the eye and deposit a black secretion. Territorial ♂ usually maintain a distance of 100-300 m from each other; territories are typically around 10-30 ha, but they may be as small as 2.5 ha or as large as 300 ha. Territorial encounters between ♂ are somewhat ritualized, with grazing duels and chasing. When a predator has been detected, all of them gather to look at it, and move with it, often walking back and forth in a small circle, keeping it in view, so that the predator loses the advantage of surprise. They are one of the fastest gazelles over shorter distances (up to 80 kmph for 15-20 minutes). As they race along in their escape, they perform sudden bounding leaps in high arcs (pronking or stotting), making it more difficult to be brought down by their predator. When a gazelle spots a stalking predator, it will pronk or stot to alert other gazelles to the danger and can also startle the predator.

DISTRIBUTION Serengeti and Kenya Rift Valley.

HABITAT Short-grass plains, although it will enter tall grasslands and woodlands during migration or to feed or drink.

STATUS Near Threatened. Estimated population at 175,000 for the Serengeti ecosystem and 40,000 in the Maasai Mara in 2003.

PHOTO CREDITS ♂: *Nick Leonard*, Maasai Mara (Kenya). ♀: *Dr. Caesar Sengupta*, Maasai Mara (Kenya). Head ♂: *Gavin Trimble* (Kenya). Head ♀: *Stuart Farmer*, Maasai Mara (Kenya). Juvenile: *Mark Dumont* and *Xinyi Xu*, Serengeti (Tanzania). Young: *Ian Loyd*, Maasai Mara (Kenya).

Mongalla Gazelle
EUDORCAS ALBONOTATA

BL: 80-120 cm. SH: 55-82 cm. W: 20-35 kg (♂), 15-25 kg (♀). TL: 15-27 cm. HL: 26 cm (♂), 7-13 cm (♀). Medium-sized gazelle. Color is ochery brown with a white belly and buttocks. Forehead white and eyes surrounded with a white ring, and usually a nose spot. Tips of ears pointed. Black lateral band is broad, with a rufous shadow stripe beneath it. Knee tuft large. Black tail. Pygal band is faint. Horns short and prominently ringed in males, curving backward and then slightly forward, and turning slightly inward at the tips. Female similar to male, with much shorter and thinner horns.

Eudorcas albonotata

OTHER NAMES *French*: Gazelle de Mongalla. *German*: Mongalla-Gazelle. *Spanish*: Gacela de Sudán. *Russian*: Монгальская газель.

SUBSPECIES Monotypic. Formerly considered a subspecies of *E. thomsoni* (Thomson's Gazelle) or *E. rufifrons* (Red-fronted Gazelle).

SIMILAR SPECIES Red-fronted Gazelle, occurring W of the Nile and absent in the Sudd ecosystem, is redder with face stripes buffy, and a very thin black flank band. Thomson's Gazelle is smaller in size, with longer horns in ♂, forehead with less white, and a more conspicuous pygal band. Grant's Gazelle is larger and paler, with longer horns, and in South Sudan is found at the very N of its range.

REPRODUCTION *Gestation*: 184-189 days. *Young per Birth*: 1. *Weaning*: 2 months. *Sexual Maturity*: 19-21 months. *Life Span*: 12 years. There is no specific information available for this species, but most young are born in the early wet season, from April to June.

BEHAVIOR *Family Group*: Groups of 10-50 animals, especially in prime feeding areas, where groups of more than 30 individuals often occur. *Diet*: Mainly a grazer, but also browses leaves and twigs of herbs and bushes during the dry season when the nutritive value of herbaceous vegetation is very low. *Main Predators*: Lion, cheetah, hyena; eagles and larger vultures may take young. Gregarious. Adult ♂ are territorial. ♀ form groups of more than 5 individuals; young ♂ live in bachelor herds. During the wet season, it aggregates in high population densities with other migratory species such as White-eared Kob and Tiang.

DISTRIBUTION *Native:* South Sudan. Found in SE Sudan, E of the Nile, but not reaching the Ugandan and Kenyan borders. It has been recorded from the Omo region in SW Ethiopia, but there is no recent information on its occurrence in this country. It is present in Boma NP and in Mongalla Game Reserve.

HABITAT Floodplain and savanna grasslands in South Sudan. It is adapted to following a nomadic annual cycle over the E Sudd floodplains, an ecologically peculiar region where extensive floods are followed by extreme aridity.

STATUS Least Concern. Estimated population of 100,000 to 278,000 in South Sudan. This species is rather safe from extinction due to its harsh habitat, which makes exploitation and poaching difficult, though it has a very narrow range.

PHOTO CREDITS *Michael French*, Mango Camp (South Sudan).

Red-fronted Gazelle
EUDORCAS RUFIFRONS

BL: 90-110 cm. SH: 65-70 cm. TL: 20-30 cm. W: 25-30 kg. HL: 22-40 cm (♂), 15-40 cm (♀). Medium-sized gazelle. Coat red fawn to chestnut in color, except for the undersides and rump, which are white. Narrow, 2-4 cm high black band from the elbow to the hind leg; a band of rufous hair separates the dark stripe from the white underparts. Pygal stripes are indistinct or absent. Tail with a black tuft. The rich red center of the face is bordered by a pair of white stripes that run from the eye to the corner of the mouth, echoed by a dark stripe beneath. Nose spot indistinct or absent. Horns found in both sexes, with a slight S-curve. In females, horns are smooth, thin, and fairly straight. In males, horns are much thicker and have deep rings. Male and female are similar in size.

♀

♂

♂
Juvenile

Eudorcas rufifrons

OTHER NAMES Korin Gazelle. *French*: Gazelle à front roux, gazelle corinne. *German*: Rotstirngazelle. *Spanish*: Gacela de frente roja. *Russian*: Краснолобая газель. *Dinka*: Nyer. *Hausa*: Jan Barewa; *Nuer*: Ngar. *Peulh:* Leoual. *Tigre*: Tel-Badu.

SUBSPECIES Monotypic. Formerly included the following subspecies: *E. r. rufifrons* (Senegal Red-fronted Gazelle, Senegal to Mali): reddish chestnut, midface bright rufous, light face stripes light buff, dark ones rufous, no dark spot on the nose, thin red stripe present below the black flank-band. *E. r. laevipes* (Nubian Red-fronted Gazelle, Niger and central Sudan W of the White Nile and E Sudan): large, less reddish, light face stripes, whitish in color. *E. r. kanuri* (S of Lake Chad, Waza NP in Cameroon): smaller; cinnamon colored. Includes *centralis* (E Chad), and *hasleri* (N Nigeria). *E. tilonura* (Heuglin's Gazelle), formerly considered as a subspecies of *E. rufifrons*, is now considered as a full species.

SIMILAR SPECIES Thomson's Gazelle has wider black side stripes. Dorcas Gazelle, which shares parts of the range, lacks the black side stripe (it is reddish instead), and has more curved horns. Mongalla Gazelle is browner in color, with horns curving backward and then slightly forward. Heuglin's Gazelle is smaller in size, with much reduced sexual dimorphism, horns more slender, much shorter in ♂ than ♀ and suddenly hooked in toward the tips, and knee tufts.

REPRODUCTION *Gestation*: 184-189 days. *Young per Birth*: 1. *Weaning*: 3 months. *Sexual Maturity*: 9 months (♀), 18 months (♂). *Life Span:* 14 years. Breeding in the wild occurs throughout most of the year. In typical behavior for "hider" species, infants are cached by their mothers and visited for nursing.

BEHAVIOR *Family Group*: Solitary, or in pairs or small groups. Herds usually have no more than 6 individuals. *Diet*: Primarily grasses, also leaves from trees and shrubs. *Main Predators*: Cheetah, wild dog, lion, leopard, hyena. They are not well adapted to arid conditions. They will feed along the S edge of the Sahara during the rains, but must migrate S during the dry season in order to find sufficient water. Even where they are relatively common, population densities are generally low (0.3-0.7 animals per km^2). When alarmed, this species produces a series of short "wheezy snorts" while pinching the nostrils forward.

DISTRIBUTION *Native*: Burkina Faso, Cameroon, Central African Republic, Chad, Eritrea, Ethiopia, Mali, Mauritania, Niger, Nigeria, Senegal, Sudan. *Regionally Extinct*: Ghana. This species formerly occurred throughout dry grasslands and Sahelian bushlands from Mauritania and N Senegal to the W side of the Nile River in Sudan. They have lost much of their habitat and now survive in small, fragmented populations.

HABITAT Open grassy habitats interspersed with thorny brush and trees for shade. They avoid heavily wooded areas. Found in the Sahelian zone, which stretches across the African continent along the S edge of the Sahara Desert.

STATUS Vulnerable. Estimated population of 20,000 individuals in 1999, with large numbers known to survive in Niger and Mali.

111

Heuglin's Gazelle

EUDORCAS TILONURA

BL: 80-120 cm. SH: 67 cm. TL: 15-27 cm. W: 20-35 kg (♂), 15-25 kg (♀). HL: 22-35 cm (♂), 15-25 cm (♀). Smaller and redder than the Red-fronted Gazelle. Upper coat is a dark reddish-fawn color. Below there is a broad, buff-colored flank band from shoulder to hip, and below that a strongly marked black flank band, and a reddish-fawn band separating this dark stripe from the white underparts. Pygal stripes are absent. Undersides and rump are white. Tail is black. Large knee brushes. Large white rings around the eyes. Forehead is reddish. Midline of the face is dark. No nose spot. Ears are long and light colored. Reduced sexual dimorphism. Horns found in both sexes; in males they are slender and short, with a marked inward hook toward the tips. In females, horns are almost as long as in males, much thinner, but similarly shaped. Male and female are similar in size.

♀

♂

Young

Eudorcas tilonura

OTHER NAMES Eritrean Gazelle. *French*: Gazelle de Heuglin. *German*: Heuglin-Gazelle. *Spanish*: Gacela de Eritrea. *Russian*: Газель Хойглина.

SUBSPECIES Monotypic. Formerly considered a subspecies of *E. rufifrons* (Red-fronted Gazelle). It has been assumed that this species has hybridized with *E. rufifrons*.

SIMILAR SPECIES Dorcas Gazelle, which shares parts of the range, lacks the black side stripe (it is reddish instead), and has more curved horns. Red-fronted Gazelle is larger, with larger horns, and without knee tufts. Heuglin's horns are said to be its distinguishing characteristic, with tips that turn sharply inward to form distinct hooks; however, this is not always the case, as many individuals have horns that are identical to those of the Red-fronted.

REPRODUCTION *Gestation*: 184-189 days. *Young per Birth*: 1. *Weaning*: 3 months. *Sexual Maturity*: 9 months (♀), 18 months (♂). *Life Span:* 14 years. There is no specific information for this species, but probably similar to the Red-fronted Gazelle.

BEHAVIOR *Family Group*: Probably solitary, or in pairs or small groups. *Diet*: Probably both a grazer and a browser. *Main Predators*: Cheetah, wild dog, lion, leopard, hyena. There is no specific information for this species, but probably similar to the Red-fronted Gazelle. Crepuscular, resting during the heat of the day in its arid habitats. These gazelles prefer open habitats, and hence may be found in close proximity with humans and their cultivated areas. Breeding ♂ defend territories from other ♂, marking the boundaries with dung piles and secretions from the preorbital glands. Although it can obtain most of its moisture requirements from the plants that it eats, it is more water dependent than most other species of gazelles which live in the same region.

DISTRIBUTION *Native*: Eritrea, Ethiopia, Sudan. Found in E-central Sudan, E of the Nile River, Rahad and Atbara river basins, in N Eritrea, N of the Setit River, as far as the Bogos River, and extreme NW Ethiopia.

HABITAT Highland plateaus, semi-arid and fairly open areas.

STATUS Vulnerable. Estimated population of 3,500-4,000 individuals. Main threats include ongoing hunting, competition with domestic livestock, and habitat degradation. Its habitat in Dinder NP is utilized intensively by camel herders who trespass into the park in the dry season and destroy the gazelle's favorite shade trees to feed their camels and goats.

PHOTO CREDITS ♂: *Peter Luptak*, Warsaw Zoo (Poland). Head ♂: *Dr. Jens-Ove Heckel*, Al Wabra Wildlife Preservation (Qatar). ♀, head ♀, and young: *Jonas Livet*, Al Wabra Wildlife Preservation (Qatar).

Southern Blackbuck
ANTILOPE CERVICAPRA CERVICAPRA

BL: 100-150 cm. SH: 56-64 cm. TL: 10-17 cm. W: 20-50 kg (♂), 19-33 kg (♀). HL: 35-73 cm (♂). Smaller than the Rajputan Blackbuck, with shorter and less divergent horns. Pronounced sexual dimorphism. Back, sides, neck, part of the face, and outside of legs are black in adult males. Dark color of the upper side runs down all the limbs to the hooves. White underparts, including insides of the legs and lower chest, white ring surrounding the eye, narrowed above the eye, and a white chin. Females and young are yellowish fawn on their back and head, and are generally hornless. Slender body, short tail. Long horns, found only in males and appearing before their pronounced color change, twisted in a tight spiral with up to 5 turns, ringed laterally.

♂

Young

♂
Juvenile

♀

Antilope cervicapra cervicapra

OTHER NAMES Indian Antelope. *French*: Antilope cervicapra. *German*: Hirschziegenantilope. *Spanish*: Sasin, Cervicabra meridional, antilope de cuello negro. *Russian*: Южная гарна. *Bengali*: Krishnosar mriga.

SUBSPECIES Considered as a subspecies of *A. cervicapra* (Blackbuck): *A. c. cervicapra* (Southern Blackbuck), *A. c. rajputanae* (Rajputan Blackbuck). Includes *centralis* (central India), and *rupricapra* (Uttar Pradesh).

SIMILAR SPECIES Rajputan Blackbuck is larger, with longer roughened pelage, shanks largely white, with little or no extension of the dark color from the upper limb segments, white eye ring broad all around the eye, horns longer, more divergent, and more closely spiraled.

REPRODUCTION *Gestation*: 150-180 days. *Young per Birth*: 1. *Weaning*: 5-6 months. *Sexual Maturity*: 1.5-2 years. *Life Span*: 12 years, rarely up to 18. Mating can take place throughout the year, but the peak periods are March-April and August-October. The young are able to run about soon after birth.

BEHAVIOR *Family Group*: Large herds composed of both sexes, smaller harems led by a mature ♂, and bachelor groups of immature ♂. *Diet*: Essentially a grazer, but does browse at times. *Main Predators*: Cheetah, wolf, rarely tiger and leopard. Active all day except during very hot weather when it will rest in shade at midday. Usually prefers open plains, but also found in open woodland. Very alert, with keen eyesight. Its senses of smell and hearing are not highly developed. Extremely fast, able to run 80 kmph. Breeding ♂ are territorial, marking and guarding their territories from other ♂. They establish a territory by regularly depositing feces in particular places, and are extremely aggressive during this time and drive all other ♂ from their territory by a throaty grunt and an occasional horn fight. Mainly sedentary, but in summer may move long distances in search of water and forage.

DISTRIBUTION *Native*: India. Confined to areas in Andhra Pradesh, Bihar, Chhattisgarh, Goa, Gujarat, Haryana, Jharkhand, Karnataka, Madhya Pradesh, Maharashtra, Orissa, Punjab, Rajasthan, Tamil Nadu, Uttar Pradesh, and West Bengal. In Nepal, the last surviving population is found in the Blackbuck Conservation Area south of Bardia NP.

HABITAT Grassland and lightly wooded country. They require water daily, which restricts distribution to areas where surface water is available for the greater part of the year.

STATUS Endangered. Its habitat is subject to heavy pressure from human population growth, increasing numbers of domestic livestock, and economic development.

PHOTO CREDITS ♂ and juvenile: *Viswanath S,* Jayamangali Blackbuck Sanctuary, Maidenahalli (India). ♀: *Casey's Korner,* Jayamangali Blackbuck Sanctuary, Maidenahalli (India). Head ♂: *Ashan Hafeez Awan*. Head juvenile: *Sumanth Suryanarayan,* Jayamangali Blackbuck Sanctuary, Maidenahalli (India).

Rajputan Blackbuck
ANTILOPE CERVICAPRA RAJPUTANAE

BL: 100-150 cm. SH: 60-85 cm. TL: 10-17 cm. W: 20-56 kg (♂), 19-33 kg (♀). HL: 35-73 cm (♂). Pronounced sexual dimorphism. Back, sides, neck, part of the face, and outside of legs are black in adult males. White underparts, including insides of the legs and lower chest, white ring surrounding the eye, and a white chin. Females and young are yellowish fawn on their back and head, and are generally hornless. Males gradually darken from tan to deep brown or black with age, beginning after 2 years. Slender body, short tail. Long horns, found only in males and appearing before their pronounced color change, twisted in a tight spiral with 3 to 5 turns, ringed laterally. Females smaller than males.

Young

Juvenile

♂

♀

Antilope cervicapra rajputanae

OTHER NAMES Indian Antelope. *French*: Antilope cervicapra. *German*: Hirschziegenantilope. *Spanish*: Sasín, cervicabra del Rajputan, antílope de cuello negro. *Russian*: Раджастханская гарна. *Bengali*: Krishnosar Mriga.

SUBSPECIES Considered as a subspecies of *A. cervicapra* (Blackbuck): *A. c. cervicapra* (Southern Blackbuck), *A. c. rajputanae* (Rajputan Blackbuck).

SIMILAR SPECIES Southern Blackbuck is smaller, with short hair, dark color of the upper side running down all the limbs to the hooves, white eye ring narrowed above the eye, horns relatively short, not very divergent, with a relatively open spiral.

REPRODUCTION *Gestation*: 150-180 days. *Young per Birth*: 1. Weaning: 5-6 months. *Sexual Maturity*: 1.5-2 years. *Life Span*: 12 years, rarely up to 18. Although breeding can occur throughout the year, there are peak periods in March-May and August-October.

BEHAVIOR *Family Group*: Mixed herds with 5-50 animals, generally with 3 or fewer ♂. Bachelor herds are known. *Diet*: Grasses, leaves, buds, field fruits. *Main Predators*: Cheetah, wolf, rarely tiger and leopard. During the cooler seasons, Blackbuck are diurnal, and active intermittently throughout the hours of daylight. As the temperature rises, they are more often seen grazing in the open in the early morning and late afternoon, sheltering from the sun for the rest of the day. When a potential threat is spotted, the alert ♀ are usually first to sound the alarm, with one individual leaping into the air. This motion is followed by the entire herd, although after a few large bounds the herd reduces its pace to a normal gallop. One of the fastest land mammals (80 kmph). Population densities are approximately 1 animal per 2 ha. During the breeding season ♂ become territorial, defending an area usually ranging in size from 1 to 17 ha from rival ♂, and attempting to keep the largest group of ♀ within it for the longest period of time. This territoriality can last anywhere from 2 weeks to 8 months. Dominance among ♂ within a herd is achieved primarily with posturing and threatening gestures; fights with the sharp horns are rare.

DISTRIBUTION *Native*: India, Pakistan. *Introduced*: Argentina, United States, Australia. Confined to parts of Gujarat, Hatyana, Punjab, and Rajasthan. It has been annihilated from Bangladesh, Nepal, and Pakistan. Attempted reintroductions have taken place in Pakistan and Nepal. Introduced populations are thriving in Texas, Argentina, and Australia.

HABITAT Range of habitats from tropical and subtropical woodland, dry deciduous forest, open plains (grassland), riverbanks, semi-desert habitats, cropland, and pastureland.

STATUS Endangered. Estimated total population at 50,000 in India and Pakistan. Introduced populations may number 43,000.

PHOTO CREDITS ♂: *Malay Nandy*, Blackbuck NP, Velavadar (India). ♀: *Heather Paul*, San Diego Zoo, CA (USA). Head ♂: *Hector Arencibia*. Head ♀: *Matthew Musgrove*, Fossil Rim Wildlife Center, TX (USA). Young: *Jonas Livet*, Zoo Alt Camp (Spain). Head juvenile: *Snehitdesign* and *Sahana Chattopadhyay*, Blackbuck NP, Velavadar (India).

Deccan Chinkara

GAZELLA BENNETTII

BL: 90-110 cm. SH: 58-61 cm. TL: 10-20 cm. W: 23 kg (♂), 15-18 kg (♀). HL: 18-34 cm (♂), 10-15 cm (♀). The smallest Indian gazelle. Smooth, dull reddish-brown coat, distinctly longer in winter than in summer and more brightly colored than in Gujarat Chinkara, with distinct contrasts. The upper parts are reddish brown or tawny, as are the lower flanks, with the area in between lighter and duller. Median dorsal region and lower flanks abruptly darker, tawny. Poorly expressed flank and rump stripes. Haunches and legs are paler than the body. Face with distinctive dark chestnut stripes running from the inner corner of the eyes to the mandible bordered by sharply defined white fur. Darker nose bridge. Ears are sandy gray. In males, horns are straight, with the tips turning slightly outward and the rings prominent. In females, horns are closer together, thinner, and straighter.

♀

Young

♂

♂
Juvenile

Gazella bennettii

OTHER NAMES Indian Gazelle, Idimi, Ravine Deer. *French*: Gazelle indienne. *German*: Dekkan-Chinkara, Bennetts Gazelle, Indische Gazelle. *Spanish*: Gacela de la India. *Russian*: Индийская (хинкара) газель (Газель Беннета). *Hindi*: Chinkara.

SUBSPECIES Monotypic. The name *G. bennettii* (Chinkara) formerly included *G. bennettii* (Deccan Chinkara), *G. christyi* (Gujarat Chinkara), *G. salinarum* (Salt Range Chinkara), *G. fuscifrons* (Eastern Jebeer), and *G. shikarii* (Western Jebeer) as subspecies: these are all elevated to full species here.

SIMILAR SPECIES Salt Range Chinkara is the largest Chinkara, with the longest horns, but the ♀ are relatively smaller, rich tobacco brown in color, with no contrasting zone on the back, but a contrasting flank band. Gujarat Chinkara is paler, almost silvery drab brown, with only the very restricted median dorsal and lower flank zones slightly darker, with little seasonal variation. The Tibetan Gazelle (*Procapra picticaudata*) is restricted to the Tibetan Plateau and is restricted in India to Ladakh and Sikkim, has distinctive horns, rising vertically and curving sharply backward, and has a white rump patch. Blackbuck is larger, adult ♂ have a dark brown to black coat with longer spiral horns, and ♀ are hornless and lack the dark face stripe.

REPRODUCTION *Gestation*: 165 days. *Young per Birth*: 1-2. *Weaning*: 2 months. *Sexual Maturity*: 2 years. *Life Span*: 15 years. There is no regular breeding time. Infants are left lying stretched out and flattened on the ground, in the middle of bare, stony areas, and if picked up and put down again, they resume the same position.

BEHAVIOR *Family Group*: Either as solitary animal or in small groups, averaging 2-5 animals per herd; during the monsoon months the size of herds increases greatly. *Diet*: Grass, leaves, and succulent fruits; they are better browsers than grazers. They can live without water for long periods of time. *Main Predators*: Jackal, wolf. They are almost nocturnal in foraging habits. They can also raid at night in the nearby crop fields for foraging. Generally shy and avoid open agricultural areas. They are less gregarious than Blackbuck. They prefer using open habitats, where visibility is high, and they may be observed resting around forest roads.

DISTRIBUTION *Native*: India. Found in central and W India, from the Ganges Valley S to the Deccan Plateau.

HABITAT Open scrub jungle, low foothills, and ravines, with open access to open, often cultivated, areas.

STATUS Least Concern. Numbers in India have been estimated at more than 100,000 individuals. Chinkaras may decline rapidly if the Eastern Deccan Plateau moist forest habitat is not secured away or reserved from humans.

PHOTO CREDITS ♂: *Shashwat Jaiswal*, Mayureshwar Wildlife Sanctuary (India). ♀: Mayureshwar Wildlife Sanctuary (India). Head ♀: *Dr. Caesar Sengupta,* Mayureshwar Wildlife Sanctuary (India). Juvenile: *Chaltanya Shukla*, Mayureshwar Wildlife Sanctuary (India). Young: *Kwokwai Chan*, Ranthambore NP (India).

Salt Range Chinkara
GAZELLA SALINARUM

BL: 75-125 cm. SH: 58-61 cm. TL: 15-20 cm. W: 23 kg (♂), 15-18 kg (♀). HL: 25-30 cm (♂), 12-17 cm (♀). Largest species of Chinkara, with a relatively long neck, legs, and ears. Rich tawny tobacco-brown color. Contrasting dark band along the flanks, separating this color from the white of the underside, but no contrasting zone on the back. Coat is short, with little seasonal variation. Face with distinctive hazelnut stripes running from the inner corner of the eyes to the mandible, bordered by sharply defined white fur. Tail is dark brown, bordered by a thinner patch of white fur. Horns found in both sexes, quite straight and slightly divergent, tips not inturned. Females slightly smaller than males, with horns closer together, thinner, and straighter.

♀

♂

Gazella salinarum

OTHER NAMES Indian Gazelle, Hossai. *French*: Gazelle du Punjab. *German*: Rajasthan-Gazelle, Punjab-Chinkara. *Spanish*: Gacela del Salt. *Russian*: Пенджабская (хинкара) газель. *Hindi*: Chinkara.

SUBSPECIES Monotypic. Formerly considered a subspecies of *G. bennettii* (Chinkara).

SIMILAR SPECIES Gujarat Chinkara is paler in color, with a contrasting zone on the back, but no contrasting flank band, and is smaller in size, with slightly shorter horns, with the tips inturned, but ♀ are similar in size. Deccan Chinkara in the E is the smallest Indian gazelle, with longer coat in winter.

REPRODUCTION *Gestation*: 150-165 days. *Young per Birth*: 1-2. *Weaning*: 3 months. *Sexual Maturity*: 12 months. *Life Span*: 15 years. There is no strict seasonality, and most births occur mainly in April, with a second peak in autumn. The young may remain with the mother for as long as 12 months, until she breeds again.

BEHAVIOR *Family Group*: Solitary ♂, ♀ groups of 2-3 individuals, occasionally up to 10 individuals, but unlike sympatric Persian Gazelles, they do not congregate in large herds. *Diet*: It browses on bushes, and grasses during the rainy season; during the monsoons and winter it eats more grass and other ground vegetation; it may drink from surface water, but a great deal of its water requirement comes from its diet, which may include fruits and succulent stems, being capable of going for long periods without drinking. *Main Predators*: Leopard, dhole. Mainly nocturnal in foraging activity, emerging to start feeding before sunset and retreating by day to its desert habitat. Adult ♂ are territorial, demarcating their territory by fecal mounds deposited in regular spots. Fighting methods among males include butting, pushing, locking horns and trying to lever the opponent, forward and sideways swinging with the horns, and attempting to deliver a forward-downward blow. Shy of human beings; if approached, it gives a series of snorts and prances away with a peculiar bounding gait.

DISTRIBUTION *Native*: India, Pakistan. Found in Pakistan, Punjab Province, and E as far as Delhi, and Indian Punjab, Haryana in NW India, Salt Range.

HABITAT Sand deserts, flat plains, and hills, dry scrub and light forest, from sea level to stony plateaus and low, hilly regions up to 1,200 m.

STATUS Least Concern. It is common in the Salt Range and in the Kalabagh Reserve; populations in S Haryana are small.

PHOTO CREDITS Reconstruction based on photos from Punjab (Pakistan).

Gujarat Chinkara

GAZELLA CHRISTYI

BL: 75-110 cm. SH: 58-61 cm. TL: 15-20 cm. W: 23 kg (♂), 15-18 kg (♀). HL: 22-35 cm (♂), 10-14 cm (♀). Graceful, elegant gazelle with a relatively long neck, legs, and ears. Smooth, dull light brown color, paler than in other Chinkaras, with only the very restricted median dorsal and lower flank zones slightly darker. Coat is very short, with little seasonal variation. Face with distinctive hazelnut stripes running from the inner corner of the eyes to the mandible, bordered by sharply defined white fur. Black stripe beginning a few inches above the coccyx widens as it reaches the tail, where it is bordered by a thinner patch of white fur. Horns found in both sexes, quite straight and slightly divergent, with the tips curving a little forward and inward, 10-25 pronounced rings. Females smaller than males, with horns closer together, thinner, and straighter.

Gazella christyi

OTHER NAMES Indian Gazelle, Hossai. *French*: Gazelle du Thar. *German*: Gujarat-Chinkara, Christies Gazelle. *Spanish*: Gacela de Gujarat. *Russian*: Гуджаратская (хинкара) газель. *Hindi*: Chinkara.

SUBSPECIES Monotypic. Formerly considered a subspecies of *G. bennettii* (Chinkara).

SIMILAR SPECIES Salt Range Chinkara is larger, with longer horns, with the tips not inturned, but ♀ are relatively smaller, rich tobacco brown in color, with no contrasting zone on the back, but a contrasting flank band. Deccan Chinkara is the smallest Indian gazelle, with horns comparable in size, and a coat that is longer in winter and more brightly colored, with distinct contrasts.

REPRODUCTION *Gestation*: 165 days. *Young per Birth*: 1-2. *Weaning*: 3 months. *Sexual Maturity*: 2 years. *Life Span*: 15 years. There is no strict seasonality. Rut in 2 seasons, one lasting from the end of the monsoon up to early October and the other in the late spring from March to the end of April. Births occur mainly in April. The young may remain with the mother for as long as 12 months, until she has another fawn.

BEHAVIOR *Family Group*: Solitary ♂, ♀ groups of 3-4 individuals, and mixed groups of up to 25 that seem to be temporary aggregations at a food source; unlike sympatric Persian Gazelles, they do not congregate in large herds. *Diet*: It browses on bushes; during the monsoons and winter it eats more grass and other ground vegetation; it does drink from surface water, but a great deal of its water requirement comes from its diet, and it is capable of going for long periods without drinking. *Main Predators:* Leopard, dhole. Mainly nocturnal in foraging activity, though it will emerge to start feeding before sunset. Adult ♂ are territorial and remain in a demarcated plot of ground; they chase other ♂ away but attempt to retain visiting ♀. Fighting methods among males include butting, pushing, locking horns and trying to lever the opponent, forward and sideways swinging with the horns, and attempting to deliver a forward-downward blow. The territory is demarcated by fecal mounds. Shy of human beings; if approached, it gives a series of snorts and prances away with a peculiar bounding gait. When alarmed, the herd takes off at a frantic pace, then stops 100-200 m away to discover the cause of the alarm.

DISTRIBUTION *Native*: India, Pakistan. Found in NW India (Gujarat, E as far as Ahmedabad, N into Rajasthan, and W into the Thar Desert) and SW Pakistan.

HABITAT Dry deciduous and thorn forest and scrub. Arid areas, including sand deserts, flat plains, and hills, dry scrub and light forest, from sea level to stony plateaus and low, hilly regions up to 1,500 m.

STATUS Least Concern. Estimated population of more than 100,000, found in 25 protected areas in 5 sanctuaries in Gujarat, and in Rajasthan. An increase in livestock has greatly reduced their numbers in the Thar Desert.

PHOTO CREDITS ♂: Based on photos from *Sarbjit32101*, Tal Chhapar Sanctuary (India). Head ♂: *Bernard Castelein*, Lohawat (India). ♀: *Dinodia Photos,* Kutch, Gujarat (India). Head ♀: *Sumeet Moghe,* Tal Chhapar Sanctuary (India).

Eastern Jebeer
GAZELLA FUSCIFRONS

BL: 100 cm. SH: 58-64 cm. TL: 15-22 cm. W: 18-30 kg. HL: 19-30 cm (♂), 0-23 cm (♀). Coat is rather long, especially in winter, sandy gray in color. In summer, coat is brownish bay fawn in color. Flank band is barely visible. Face markings well developed. Central facial band is strongly marked. Cheeks and front of the neck are gray. Conspicuous nose spot. Back of the neck, sides, haunches, and legs are sandy. Belly and rump are whitish. Ears are long. Long black knee brushes. In males, horns are long, more or less upright, with narrow spread, very close together at the base, and more strongly annulated than in other Chinkaras, bending forward and very slightly inward at the tips. Females are noticeably smaller than males, and have especially long horns.

♀

♂

Young

Gazella fuscifrons

OTHER NAMES Jebeer Gazelle, Baluchistan Gazelle, Kennion Gazelle. *French*: Gazelle du Baluchistan. *German*: Belutschistan-Chinkara. *Spanish*: Gacela jebeer oriental, gacela de Kennion. *Russian*: Белуджистанская (хинкара) газель (Газель Кенниона).

SUBSPECIES Monotypic. Formerly considered a subspecies of *G. bennettii* (Chinkara). It was also previously considered as a subspecies of *G. dorcas* (Dorcas Gazelle). Includes *hayi* and *kennioni*.

SIMILAR SPECIES Goitered Gazelle is larger, with a relatively stocky body and short legs, with longest horns with a more pronounced curve, similar in color, and female is hornless. There is very little overlap between the ranges of the Jebeer and the Goitered Gazelle. Salt Range and Gujarat Chinkaras are slightly larger, while Deccan Chinkara is smaller.

REPRODUCTION *Gestation*: 150-165 days. *Young per Birth*: 1-2. *Weaning*: 2 months. *Sexual Maturity*: 2 years. *Life Span*: 15 years. Rut takes place in November and the young are born in April, but there may be more than one breeding season, with some females dropping fawns in autumn. ♀ go off on their own to drop their young, seeking out broken, sheltered terrain.

BEHAVIOR *Family Group*: Small groups, usually fewer than 5 individuals; in winter the groups become larger, up to 20 individuals, but they never form the large aggregations of the Goitered Gazelle. *Diet*: Perennial shrubs. *Main Predators*: Leopard, dhole. ♂ are territorial during the rut and they set up their territories mainly around springs. During the summer, they are dependent on water and take advantage of natural springs. Out on the plains the vegetation is too low to offer shade, so in summer, during the middle of the day, Jebeer will commonly move into the foothills to rest. They do not visit springs where there is a lot of disturbance or where there is permanent human settlement. The Jebeer is thinly distributed over its range, and does not perform any seasonal movement.

DISTRIBUTION *Native*: Afghanistan, Iran, Pakistan. Found in the deserts of S and SE Iran (Hormogazan and Sistan and Baluchistan provinces) to S Afghanistan and SW Pakistan.

HABITAT Arid areas, including sand deserts, flat plains, and hills, dry scrub and light forest, from sea level to stony plateaus and low, hilly regions up to 1,000 m. Replaced by the Goitered Gazelle at higher elevations.

STATUS Least Concern. Populations have dwindled both in Iran and Pakistan. Main threats include human activity, cultivation, and competition with domestic sheep and goats.

PHOTO CREDITS *Jonas Livet,* Al Wabra Wildlife Preservation (Qatar) and Al Wabra Wildlife Preservation (Qatar).

Western Jebeer

GAZELLA SHIKARII

BL: 75-125 cm. SH: 65 cm. TL: 15-20 cm. W: 25 kg. HL: 25-30 cm (♂), 18-19 cm (♀). Pale reddish-sandy color, with white underparts. Little or no trace of a dark band along the flanks. Dark face stripes very poorly expressed. Forehead is no darker than the rest of the pelage. Nose spot is faint. Belly and rump are whitish. Ears are long. Knee tufts well developed. Horns found in both sexes. In males, horns slope backward, then spread somewhat outward, the tips pointing slightly inward. Females have long horns, thinner and less markedly ringed than in males.

Gazella shikarii

OTHER NAMES *French*: Gazelle de Shikari. *German*: Iran-Chinkara, Shikaris Gazelle. *Spanish*: Gacela jebeer occidental. *Russian*: Иранская (хинкара) газель. *Farsi*: Jabir.

SUBSPECIES Monotypic. Formerly considered a subspecies of *G. bennettii* (Chinkara). The taxonomy of this species in Iran has been poorly understood, and there are currently two different species of Chinkara recognized in Iran: the dark-colored Eastern Jebeer (*G. fuscifrons*) in the SE and along the Makran coast, and the pale Western Jebeer (*G. shikarii*) from the N and W central districts.

SIMILAR SPECIES Horns more depressed and more widely spread, with tips more slightly inturned than in Eastern Jebeer, lighter in color, with facial markings less expressed, and larger in size.

REPRODUCTION *Gestation*: 150-165 days. *Young per Birth*: 1-2. *Weaning*: 2 months. *Sexual Maturity*: 2 years. *Life Span*: 15 years. There may be 2 breeding seasons, with most births occurring in March-May, and in autumn.

BEHAVIOR *Family Group*: Small groups, usually fewer than 5 individuals; in winter the groups become larger, up to 20 individuals, but they never form the large aggregations of the Goitered Gazelle. *Diet*: Desert shrubs. *Main Predators:* Leopard, dhole. When disturbed, they jump away with high bounds, similar to the stotting of Mountain Gazelles, but the jumps are longer, not as high, and often zig-zagging. ♂ are territorial during the rut.

DISTRIBUTION *Native*: Iran. Found in W and N Iran, from Kavir NP, SE Tehran, as far E as Touran Protected Area and as far SE as Bahram-e Gour Protected Area, and S as far as Dehkuyeh. The range is bordered to the W by the Zagros Mountains, to the N probably by the Alborz mountain range and its easterly outliers, to the SE by the beginning of the Kavirs, and to the SW by the decrease in elevation where the Iranian Plateau approaches the sea.

HABITAT The margin of the cold deserts of the Iranian Plateau, with low-growing desert shrubs, and little or no surface water.

STATUS Least Concern. There are an estimated 1,400 individuals in Iran, most of them in 9 protected areas. Main threats include hunting for meat, and in some cases, for trophies.

PHOTO CREDITS *Frans Lanting,* Kavir NP (Iran).

Mountain Gazelle
GAZELLA GAZELLA

BL: 100-125 cm. SH: 60-65 cm. TL: 8-13 cm. W: 17-30 kg. HL: 22-30 cm (♂), 6-11 cm (♀). A small gazelle, with very slender body, and relatively long neck and legs. Coat is fawn to dark brown on the back, neck, and head. Belly and buttocks are pure white, being separated on the flanks by a dark narrow band. Coat is short, sleek, and glossy in summer. In winter the pelage is much longer, dense, and rainproof, and not glossy. Face with 2 conspicuous white stripes extending from the eyes toward the nostrils with dark brown to black lower margins, coupled usually with a black spot on the muzzle above the nose. Horns in males quite long, straight and thick basally, with a slight lyrate form and prominent rings. Horns in females shorter, unringed, irregular in shape, and often bent, crooked, or broken.

♀

Young

♂

Gazella gazella

OTHER NAMES Arabian Gazelle, Edmi Gazelle, Idmi, Palestine Mountain Gazelle, True Gazelle. *French*: Gazelle de montagne. *German*: Edmigazelle. *Spanish*: Gacela arábiga, gacela índica. *Russian*: Палестинская (горная) газель. *Arabic*: Edmi, admi, edem. *Hebrew*: Zwi mazui. *Kirundi*: Intaramvyi.

SUBSPECIES Monotypic. The name *G. gazella* (Mountain Gazelle) formerly included: *G. gazella* (Palestine Mountain Gazelle), *G. acaciae* (Acacia Gazelle), *G. arabica* (Arabian Mountain Gazelle), *G. erlangeri* (Arabian Coastal Gazelle), *G. farasani* (Farasan's Gazelle), *G. muscatensis* (Muscat Gazelle), and *G. dareshurii* (Farrur Gazelle) as subspecies: these are all elevated to full species here.

SIMILAR SPECIES It is the largest Mountain Gazelle species, with longer horns. Acacia Gazelle (*acaciae*), also found in Israel, has facial markings more strongly expressed. Arabian Mountain Gazelle (*arabica*) is lighter and redder in color. Arabian Coastal Gazelle (*erlangeri*) and Farasan's Gazelle (*farasani*) are darker in color, very dark brown, and have a large well-defined nose spot. Muscat Gazelle (*muscatensis*) is darker in color, very dark-brown, and smaller, but the horns are very slender.

REPRODUCTION *Gestation*: 180 days. *Young per Birth*: 1. *Weaning*: 3-6 weeks. *Sexual Maturity*: 1-2 years. *Life Span*: 8-13 years. Breeding throughout the year, but there are 2 birth peaks: in March-May and in October, though most young of the autumn peak will die. During hot summers and cold winters females give birth very rarely. They have births later (April-June) and mostly once a year. A ♀ leaves a herd several days before birth and stays alone, together with her young, after the birth for up to 2 months. While ♀ may remain with their mother for life, ♂ leave the maternal herd at around 6 months old to join a herd of young bachelor ♂.

BEHAVIOR *Family Group:* Small groups of 3-8 individuals, up to 40 animals. *Diet*: Mainly a grazer; diet comprises grasses, herbs, and shrubs. They may dig for succulent underground plants where there is no surface water. *Main Predators*: Golden jackal, wolf, red fox, feral dog. Their social structure consists of territorial solitary ♂, which stay and keep their territory all year-round; temporary or quite permanent groups of 1 to several ♀ with their young; and small bachelor ♂ herds. They are diurnal, though they may graze during moonlit nights where natural conditions are disrupted. Normally they feed at dawn and dusk and rest during the hottest part of the day.

DISTRIBUTION *Native*: Israel. Formerly occurred across the N part of the Arabian Peninsula, from the Sinai Peninsula to S Syria. Currently confined to central and N Israel, the Golan Heights, Ramot Naftali, the Galilee, in the coastal plain, S-central Turkey (Hatay region). It is not clear if any population survives in Lebanon, Jordan, or Syria.

HABITAT Low mountains, sometimes in very steep terrain. They prefer plateaus, hilly relief, foothills and valleys between mountains, the coastal plain of Israel, and the hot, dry areas of the Jordan Valley.

STATUS Vulnerable. Estimated population of 3,000-10,000 individuals in Israel. Main threats include habitat loss and hunting.

PHOTO CREDITS ♂: *Sergey Chichagov,* Tel-Aviv University Zoo (Israel). ♀: *Sergey Chichagov*, Jerusalem Zoo (Israel) and *Alex Kantorovich*, Meir Segals Garden University Zoo (Israel). 129

Acacia Gazelle
GAZELLA ACACIAE

BL: 111-116 cm. SH: 60-65 cm. TL: 11-14 cm. W: 18-21 kg (♂). HL: 22-30 cm (♂), 6-11 cm (♀).
A very slender and small gazelle, with long neck and legs. Coat is dark earth brown, paler in summer than in winter. Belly and buttocks are white, being separated on the flanks by a dark narrow band. Usually no pygal stripe. Facial marking strongly expressed, with pale stripes nearly white. Conspicuous black nose spot. Ears long and broad. Tail long and bushy. Horns in males are long, comparatively slender, bowing slightly outward in the middle and coming closer together at the tips. Horns in females shorter.

♀

Young

♂

Gazella acaciae

OTHER NAMES Arava Gazelle. *French*: Gazelle de l'Arava. *German*: Akaziengazelle. *Spanish*: Gacela del valle de Árava. *Russian*: Акациевая газель.

SUBSPECIES Monotypic. Formerly considered a subspecies of *G. gazella* (Mountain Gazelle). The taxonomy of Mountain Gazelles is controversial, and some gazelle populations in the Arabian Peninsula are not considered pure, but rather the result of crossbreeding between two or more species or subspecies.

REPRODUCTION *Gestation*: 180 days. *Young per Birth*: 1. *Weaning*: 14 weeks. *Sexual Maturity*: 1-2 years. *Life Span*: 8-13 years. Breeding during the whole year, with a peak of fawning in spring (March-May) and in autumn (October). The fawn is hidden for 6 weeks. Fawning is prolific but fawn survival rate is low, and most of the young born in autumn do not survive. ♀ rarely give birth during the hot summers and the cold winters.

SIMILAR SPECIES Larger and darker than Arabian Desert Gazelle (*G. arabica*). Sympatric Dorcas Gazelle (*G. dorcas*) has a lighter flank stripe.

BEHAVIOR *Family Group:* Small groups of 1-4 individuals; dominant ♂ solitary. *Diet*: They need no surface water as they get water from their food: leaves, young shoots, flowers, and pods of acacias and bushes. *Main Predators*: Red fox, wolf, and possibly hyena. Dominant ♂ hold territories of 0.3-0.6 km². The rest of the ♂ live in small bachelor herds. ♀ herds are small, made of related females, and they forage mainly inside territories. Gazelles shelter from the rain under acacia trees, standing close to the trunk. When moving through groves of acacias, they slip under branches in a sort of squat-walk. At night, they sleep on the slopes above the valley, digging out a shallow depression in the ground.

DISTRIBUTION *Native*: Israel, Jordan. This species represents a relict population that became isolated at the end of the last glacial period. Restricted to a very small area in the Arava Rift Valley, in S Negev Desert, in Israel and Jordan. It is not known whether the distribution extends E into Saudi Arabia.

HABITAT Dense acacia stands with abundant shrubs bordering on salt marshes.

STATUS Critically Endangered. Estimated population of 20-50 individuals. In the 1940s hundreds of animals inhabited the Hazeva area (N Arava), but during the 1960s massive gazelle hunting in the Negev destroyed the N Arava population. During the 1980s the Acacia Gazelles living between Eilat and Timna were eliminated, particularly in the Evrona playa. Virtually the entire population inhabits an area about 6 km² in the Yotvata Hai-Bar Nature Reserve.

PHOTO CREDITS *Klaus Rudloff*, Yotvata Hai-Bar Nature Reserve (Israel).

Arabian Desert Gazelle

GAZELLA ARABICA

BL: 100 cm. SH: 60 cm. TL: 9 cm. W: 15-20 kg. HL: 15-27 cm (♂), 5.8-11.5 cm (♀). A small gazelle, with very slender body, and relatively long neck and legs. Coat is reddish brown in color. Striking contrast between the darker-colored body and the white rump and legs. Distinctly dark flank stripe and facial markings. Dark nose spot also conspicuous. Black eyelids and eyelashes. Older animals develop a white spot on the forehead between the horn bases. Short tail, cylindrical, with a black terminal tuft. Horns straight with the tips curved forward and slightly inward, strongly ringed. Females are slightly smaller than males, with horns shorter, without rings, thin and fragile.

Young

♀

♂

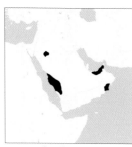

Gazella arabica

OTHER NAMES Arabian Mountain Gazelle. *French*: Gazelle cora. *German*: Arabische Wüstengazelle. *Spanish*: Gacela arábiga de desierto. *Russian*: Аравийская (пустынная) газель.

SUBSPECIES Monotypic. Formerly considered a subspecies of *G. gazella* (Mountain Gazelle). *G. cora* is considered as a synonym of *G. arabica*.

SIMILAR SPECIES Muscat Gazelle (*muscatensis*) is dark rufous fawn, with a dark flank band; the median face stripe is deep rufous with a blackish nose patch, and the pale lateral stripes are narrow and well defined; relatively short horns, with the tips turning markedly inward. This gazelle is confined to the Al Batinah coastal plain of NW Oman.

REPRODUCTION *Gestation*: 180 days. *Young per Birth*: 1. *Weaning*: 3-6 weeks. *Sexual Maturity*: 1-2 years. *Life Span*: 8 years. Mating takes place at any time of the year and fawns are born throughout the year, with peaks in spring and autumn. ♀ may remain with their mother for the whole of their life, but ♂ will leave at 6 months to join a bachelor herd.

BEHAVIOR *Family Group:* Solitary ♂, small groups of ♀ and their young, from 1-4 animals, and small bachelor herds. *Diet*: Primarily a grazer. Commonly reaches acacia branches by standing on its hind legs and leaning its front hooves on the trees. It will also dig for bulbs and corms when water is scarce. *Main Predators*: Jackal, wolf, fox (fawn). Sedentary, with strict territorial tendencies. ♂ form and defend territories for extended periods of time, and are intolerant of other ♂ and chase them when they infiltrate into the territory. ♂ are on the lookout for ♀ in estrus, will prevent them from leaving the territory, and will start courting them. ♂ will herd a ♀ for a prolonged period of time, sometimes more than an hour, before mating. They normally feed at dawn and dusk and rest during the hottest part of the day, but weather conditions and geographical locality may influence activity patterns. They use the shelter of trees and shrubs to take cover from solar radiation. They can reach speeds of 65 kmph if they need to escape danger.

DISTRIBUTION *Native*: Oman, Saudi Arabia, United Arab Emirates, Yemen. They range in fragmented populations in Saudi Arabia (Harrat al Harrah and Al Khunfah protected areas, Tihama coastal plain, and the Hejaz and Sarawat mountains), Yemen (Thiama coastal strip and Wadi Rima in the W Highlands), Oman (Jiddat al-Harasis, coastal areas to the E, Wahibah Sands, and the foothills of the Musadam Mountains), and United Arab Emirates (mountains in the N and deserts).

HABITAT Mountains, foothills, and coastal plains. Coral ravines and coral hills, where there is ample vegetation and the deep crevices in the rocks provide good cover. They favor areas with ample cover where they are protected from human disturbance and the sun.

STATUS Vulnerable. Estimated population of 9,500 in Oman, and 400-750 in Saudi Arabia. Populations are in decline due to poaching for meat, and hunting for sport and for private collections.

PHOTO CREDITS *Klaus Rudloff* (Biolib.cz), Arabia's Wildlife Center (United Arab Emirates). Young: *Carter S'*, Al-Maha (United Arab Emirates).

Arabian Coastal Gazelle

GAZELLA ERLANGERI

BL: 110-125 cm. SH: 52-61 cm. TL: 15-20 cm. W: 15-35 kg. HL: 17-23 cm (♂). A small and dark gazelle with a stout body and short legs. Coat is very dark brown on the back, neck, and head, becoming sharply paler, ochery brown on the haunches and legs. Face is dark, with clear white and black longitudinal stripes and a large nose spot. Tail with a thick black tuft. Ears long. Eyes large and oddly pale. Horns in male are quite long, slender, more or less parallel, and nearly straight, tending to turn slightly in at the tips, and narrow across the bases. The subspecies *farasani* is smaller. Horns in females shorter, unringed, irregular in shape, and often bent, crooked, or broken.

♀

Young

♂

ssp. erlangeri

ssp. farasani

Gazella erlangeri erlangeri

Gazella erlangeri farasani

Gazella erlangeri hanishi

OTHER NAMES Erlanger's Gazelle, Neumann's Gazelle, Farasan's Gazelle. *French*: Gazelle d'Erlanger. *German*: Arabische Küstengazelle. *Spanish*: Gacela arábiga de costa. *Russian*: Газель Неймана *(erlangeri)*, Газель Фаразанских островов *(farasani)*, Газель острова Ханиш *(hanishi)*.

SUBSPECIES Three subspecies are recognized: *G. e. erlangeri* (Neumann's Gazelle): found along the Red Sea coast of the Arabian Peninsula. *G. e. farasani* (Farasan's Gazelle): found only on Saudi Arabia's Great Farasan and Zifaf islands on the Red Sea. *G. e. hanishi* (Hanish Gazelle): less rufous and has a larger nose spot, found only on Great Hanish Island. This species was formerly considered as a subspecies of *G. gazella* (Mountain Gazelle). The Arabian Coastal Gazelle is treated as a distinct species here; since the entire taxonomy of Arabian Gazelles is currently under review, the present classification may change with further research. To complicate matters, some gazelle populations in the Arabian Peninsula are not considered pure, but rather the result of crossbreeding between two or more species or subspecies. A fairly similar gazelle, *G. bilkis* (Yemen or Queen of Sheba's Gazelle), formerly inhabited the Yemen highlands, but it is now considered extinct.

REPRODUCTION *Gestation*: 180 days. *Young per Birth*: 1. *Weaning*: 3-6 weeks. *Sexual Maturity*: 1-2 years. *Life Span*: 8-13 years. There in no information available for this subspecies, but likely similar to other Mountain Gazelles.

BEHAVIOR *Family Group:* Small groups of 5-8 individuals. On the Farasan Islands, single or in mother-young pairs. *Diet*: Grazers and browsers. They obtain water by feeding at dawn and dusk, when there is condensation on the leaves. *Main Predators*: Jackal, wolf, fox (fawn). They spend the day in cover and emerge to graze at night, or at dawn and dusk.

DISTRIBUTION *Native*: Saudi Arabia, Yemen. *Erlangeri* is found along the Red Sea coast of the Arabian Peninsula. *Farasani* is found only on Saudi Arabia's Great Farasan and Zifaf islands on the Red Sea.

HABITAT Barren areas around Ma'abar at 2,300 m and the lava plains N of Aden at sea level. On the Farasan Islands, the habitat is flat gravel plain, with little vegetation, and desert grasses in the wadis.

STATUS Mainland populations (*erlangeri*) must be considered Endangered, although there is no recent information on wild populations. On Farasan Islands (*farasani*) it still occurs at high densities, but only about 500 individuals. There are no natural predators on the Farasan Islands so overgrazing is a potential future problem if the population increases. Hunting and live trapping are the main threats but the effect of these has fallen since the islands were declared a reserve. At present, there are only two known facilities keeping Arabian Coastal Gazelles: King Khalis Wildlife Research Center (Saudi Arabia) and Al Wabra Wildlife Preservation (Qatar).

PHOTO CREDITS *G. e. erlangeri*: Based on photos from Al Wabra Wildlife Preservation (Qatar). Head *G. e. farasani*: Délirante Bestiole, Farasan Island (Saudi Arabia).

Muscat Gazelle
GAZELLA MUSCATENSIS

BL: 100 cm. SH: 53-56 cm. TL: 15-16 cm. W: 17-20 kg. HL: 15-27 cm (♂), 5.8-11.5 cm (♀). A small gazelle, with slender body and relatively long neck and legs. Coat is dark rufous fawn, darker than in other species, with a dark flank band. Median face stripe is deep rufous with a blackish nose patch. Well-defined narrow pale lateral strips. Brownish knee tufts. Limbs darker in color than usual, being white only on the inner surface of the upper legs. Relatively short horns, outbowed, turn markedly inward. Females are slightly smaller than males, with horns slightly shorter, scarcely ringed.

Gazella muscatensis

OTHER NAMES *French*: Gazelle de Muscat. *German*: Maskat-Gazelle. *Spanish*: Gacela de Muscat. *Russian*: Маскатская газель.

SUBSPECIES Monotypic. Formerly considered a subspecies of *G. gazella* (Mountain Gazelle). The taxonomy of Mountain Gazelles is controversial, and some gazelle populations in the Arabian Peninsula are not considered pure, but rather the result of crossbreeding between two or more species or subspecies.

SIMILAR SPECIES Dorcas Gazelles are smaller, with shorter hind legs, and horns with a wider basal gap and round cross section (elliptical in Mountain Gazelles). Goitered Gazelles are larger, with longer horns, usually widely divergent at the tips and lyrate, and have a goiter-like throat swelling in the breeding season. Mountain Gazelle (*G. gazella*) has straighter horns and is lighter in color.

REPRODUCTION *Gestation*: 180 days. *Young per Birth*: 1. *Weaning*: 3-6 weeks. *Sexual Maturity*: 1-2 years. *Life Span*: 8 years. There is no information available for this species but likely similar to the Mountain Gazelle (*G. gazella*).

BEHAVIOR *Family Group:* Solitary ♂, small groups of ♀ and their young, from 1 to 4 animals, and small bachelor herds. *Diet*: Primarily a grazer; it eats fruits and leaves, dicotyledons, and grasses during the growing season. *Main Predators*: Jackal, wolf, fox (fawn). Crepuscular, mainly active at dawn and dusk during the hot season.

DISTRIBUTION *Native*: Oman. Confined to the Al Batinah coastal plain of Oman, NW of Muscat.

HABITAT Mountains, foothills, and coastal plains.

STATUS Vulnerable. Estimated population of fewer than 250 individuals. The Batinah population has declined during the past few decades, probably because of development and severe fragmentation of its habitat, competition from domestic livestock, and illegal hunting.

Farrur Gazelle
GAZELLA DARESHURII

BL: 100 cm. SH: 53-56 cm. TL: 15-16 cm. W: 17-20 kg. HL: 15-27 cm (♂), 5.8-11.5 cm (♀). A small gazelle, with slender body and relatively long neck and legs. General color is apparently a pale sandy brown. Closely related to the Muscat Gazelle, but slightly larger, with similar outwardly bowed horns, the tips turned inward. Horns longer and broader across the base in both sexes. Brownish knee tufts. Females are slightly smaller than males.

Gazella dareshurii

OTHER NAMES Dareshuri Gazelle. *French*: Gazelle de Dareshuri. *German*: Farrur-Gazelle. *Spanish*: Gacela de Farur. *Russian*: Газель острова Фаррур.

SUBSPECIES Monotypic. Formerly considered a subspecies of *G. gazella* (Mountain Gazelle). The taxonomy of Mountain Gazelles is controversial, and some gazelle populations in the Arabian Peninsula are not considered pure, but rather the result of crossbreeding between two or more species or subspecies.

REPRODUCTION *Gestation*: 180 days. *Young per Birth*: 1. *Weaning*: 3-6 weeks. *Sexual Maturity*: 1-2 years. *Life Span*: 8 years. There is no information available for this species but likely similar to the Mountain Gazelle (*G. gazella*).

BEHAVIOR *Family Group:* Solitary ♂, small groups of ♀ and their young. *Diet*: Most likely primarily a grazer, with some seasonal browsing of locally abundant leaves and fruits. *Main Predators*: Jackal, wolf, fox (fawn). There is no information available for this species, but it is probably crepuscular, mainly active at dawn and dusk during the hot season.

DISTRIBUTION *Native*: Iran. Found only on Farrur Island, in the Persian Gulf (Iran).

HABITAT Desert scrub.

STATUS Vulnerable. Its population in Farrur is stable, having recovered well from a population crash due to drought in 1986.

Speke's Gazelle
GAZELLA SPEKEI

BL: 95-105 cm. SH: 50-60 cm. TL: 15-20 cm. W: 15-25 kg. HL: 25-31 cm (♂), 15-25 cm (♀). A small gazelle. Fawn or light tan upper coat, separated from white belly by black flank stripe, which generally has a lighter band above it. White undersides encompass the buttocks, as well as the insides of the legs. The nose is the most unique feature: 3-5 folds of skin, which lie just behind the nostrils across the bridge of the nose, can be inflated into a sac. Small horns in both sexes. In males horns curve backward in an S, heavily ringed, slightly divergent. Females are smaller than males, but have thinner horns, much straighter and steeper.

♀

♂
Juvenile

♂

Young

Gazella spekei

OTHER NAMES Flabby-nosed Gazelle. *French*: Gazelle de Speke. *German*: Spekegazelle. *Spanish*: Gacela de Speke. *Russian*: Газель Спика, или вислоносая газель. *Arabic*: Ariel. *Somali*: Aoul, dero.

SUBSPECIES Monotypic.

SIMILAR SPECIES It may be differentiated from other gazelles by the presence of a flabby, corrugated patch of pale gray skin on the muzzle that can be inflated when alarmed. Pelzeln's Gazelle (*G. dorcas pelzelni*) occurs sympatrically in coastal N Somalia, but has lyrate horns, and its flank band is dark reddish. Soemmerring's Gazelle (*Nanger soemmerringii*) is larger and lacks a dark flank.

REPRODUCTION *Gestation*: 169-190 days. *Young per Birth*: 1. *Weaning*: 2-3 months. *Sexual Maturity*: 9 months (♀), 18 months (♂). *Life Span*: 12 years. Breeding is aseasonal and copulations and newborns have been recorded in every month of the year. Sexual activity is bimodal with the peaks coinciding with the middle of the growing season.

BEHAVIOR *Family Group*: Small herds of 5-20 animals; occasionally larger groups will form in response to more abundant grazing. *Diet*: Grass, forbs, shrubs, and succulents. Water requirements unknown, but probably slight. *Main Predators*: Cheetah, lion, Cape hunting dog, leopard, hyena, python. Like most dwellers in a hot and dry environment, Speke's Gazelle is primarily active in the early morning and evening, resting during the heat of the day. This gazelle has a sac on its nose which is inflated when the gazelle is excited. The signature call of the Speke's Gazelle, a loud, gunshot-like sneeze, is thought to be amplified by this makeshift resonance chamber. Muscles surrounding the preorbital glands dispense secretions during periods of heightened excitement. Speke's gazelles are social animals, living in small herds. These smaller groups may merge into herds of up to 20 animals. There are two typical kinds of herds: one is composed of an adult ♂ with his harem of ♀, with which he breeds; the ♀ determine the direction in which the herd grazes; the dominant ♂ works to keep his harem within the boundaries of his home range, an area of 1.5-8 km². A second type of herd is the bachelor herd, made up of juvenile ♂ and young adult ♂ that don't have harems. Eyesight, hearing, and sense of smell are good. Shy and watchful.

DISTRIBUTION *Native*: Somalia. *Possibly Extinct*: Ethiopia. Inhabits the 20-40 km wide grassland plain that extends along the Indian Ocean coastline of Somalia. N limit delimited by steep hills of the Gulis Range.

HABITAT Stony brush, grass steppes, and semi-deserts, between 900 and 1,800 m elevation, in Ethiopia and Somalia.

STATUS Endangered. Only slightly more than 1,000 animals are currently thought to live in the wild. There are currently no protected areas within the range of Speke's Gazelles. The conservation status of this species is expected to decline further in the absence of protection and management of wild populations and their habitat.

PHOTO CREDITS ♂: *Adam Fagen*, National Zoological Park, Smithsonian Institution (USA). Head ♂: *David Valenzuela*, San Diego Zoo (USA). ♀ and head: *Sergey Chichagov*, Los Angeles Zoo (USA). Juvenile: *Hammer*, Al Wabra Wildlife Preservation (Qatar). Young: *Jonas Livet*, Al Ain Wildlife Park and Resort (United Arab Emirates), and *Tyler Blackwood*, Los Angeles Zoo (USA).

Saharan Dorcas Gazelle

GAZELLA DORCAS OSIRIS

BL: 90-110 cm. SH: 55-65 cm. TL: 15-20 cm. W: 15-20 kg. HL: 25-38 cm (♂), 15-25 cm (♀). A small gazelle. Upper pelage pale beige or sandy red, undersides and rump white. Wide rufous stripe along the lower flank between the front and rear legs, separating the white belly from the upper coat. A similarly colored stripe occurs on the upper hind legs, creating a border for the white rump. Head with same beige color as the body. White eye ring, and a pair of white and dark brown stripes running from each eye to the corners of the mouth. Forehead and bridge of the nose light reddish tan in color. Old males may develop a fold of skin across the bridge of their nose. Ridged, lyre-shaped horns found in both sexes. In males bent sharply backward, curved upward at the tips, ringed alrnost to the tips. Horns in females much thinner, straighter, and shorter, with fewer rings.

♀

ssp. *massaesyla*

♂

Young

ssp. *osiris*

Gazella dorcas osiris

Gazella dorcas massaesyla

Gazella dorcas dorcas

OTHER NAMES Ariel Gazelle. *French*: Gazelle Dorcade. *German*: Dorkasgazelle. *Spanish:* Gacela dorcas. *Russian*: Сахарская газель-доркас. *Arabic*: Ghazal, rajal, hemar. *Baluchi*: Ahu. *Bambara*: Sinè. *Baori*: Porsya. *Brahui*: Khazm. *Canarese*: Budari Tiska. *Hebrew*: Zwi ha Negev. *Somali*: Phero. *Tuareg*: Ahankod. *Wolof*: Kéwél.

SUBSPECIES Considered as a subspecies of *G. dorcas* (Dorcas Gazelle): *G. d. dorcas* (Egyptian Dorcas Gazelle), *G. d. isabella* (Isabelline Gazelle), *G. d. massaesyla* (Moroccan Dorcas Gazelle), *G. d. osiris* (Saharan Dorcas gazelle), *G. d. beccarii* (Eritrean Dorcas Gazelle). Includes two generally recognized subspecies: *neglecta* (plateau areas of W and central Sahara) and *osiris* (S and E Sahara). Dorcas Gazelle subspecies need further study.

SIMILAR SPECIES Rhim Gazelle has a paler coloration, no conspicuous head markings, and different shape of the horns. Cuvier's Gazelle is considerably larger and heavier, with a rough and thick coat, a darker fawn coloration, more pronounced markings on the head and flank, and thicker and relatively shorter horns. Red-fronted Gazelle is larger and has a conspicuous black lateral band. Moroccan or Egyptian Dorcas Gazelles are considerably smaller, with shorter horns.

REPRODUCTION *Gestation*: 180 days. *Young per Birth*: 1, rarely 2. *Weaning*: 2-3 months. *Sexual Maturity*: 9 months (♂), 18 months (♀). *Life Span*: Up to 12.5 years. After birth the young lie concealed away from their mother for 2-6 weeks.

BEHAVIOR *Family Group*: Single-sex herds with up to 40 animals, mixed herds of up to 100. *Diet*: Grasses, leaves, blossoms, succulents. *Main Predators:* Cheetah, lion, leopard, spotted hyena, python. Desert adapted, they may go their entire lives without drinking any water, obtaining all needed moisture from the plants they eat. They can withstand very high temperatures, although during hot weather they are primarily active at dawn, dusk, and throughout the night. Herds wander over large areas searching for food, and tend to congregate in areas where recent rainfall has stimulated plant growth. Adult ♂ are territorial, and establish dung middens throughout their range. A conspicuous display is used in the formation of these fecal piles, with the ♂ first pawing at the ground, then stretching over the scraped area to urinate, and then crouching with his anus just above the ground, at which point he deposits his dung.

DISTRIBUTION *Native*: Algeria, Burkina Faso, Chad, Egypt, Libya, Mali, Mauritania, Morocco, Niger, Sudan, Syria, Tunisia, Western Sahara, *Extinct*: Senegal, Nigeria. Found across the entire Sahara region S of the Atlas Mountains and west of the Nile, except for the ranges of the Moroccan and Egyptian Dorcas Gazelles. Egyptian Dorcas Gazelle (*dorcas*) is found in W (Libyan) desert of Egypt, which lies W of the Nile, and perhaps extending into E Libya. Moroccan Dorcas Gazelle (*massaesyla*) is found on the Moroccan high plateau and in the Atlantic Sahara.

HABITAT Savannas, semi-desert, and true desert.

STATUS Vulnerable.

Isabelline Dorcas Gazelle

GAZELLA DORCAS ISABELLA

BL: 90-110 cm. SH: 61-65 cm. TL: 15-20 cm. W: 20-23 kg. HL: 25-38 cm ($\male$), 15-25 cm ($\female$). A larger subspecies of Dorcas Gazelle. General color is brownish. Undersides and rump white. Flank band may be indistinct. Upper surface of the tail is reddish brown rather than black. Head with same beige color as the body. White eye ring, and a pair of white and dark brown stripes running from each eye to the corners of the mouth. Forehead and bridge of the nose light reddish tan in color. Older individuals may develop a dark nose spot. The shape of the horns is very variable, but tends to be other than perfectly lyrate, with the tips turned sharply inward. Horns in females much thinner, straighter, and shorter, with fewer rings.

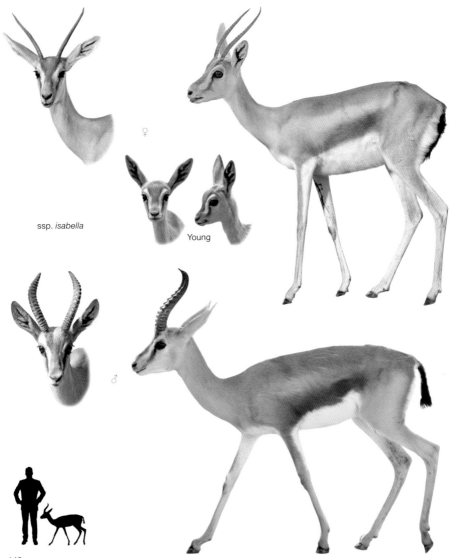

$\female$

ssp. *isabella*

Young

$\male$

Gazella dorcas isabella

Gazella dorcas beccarii

OTHER NAMES Eritrean Dorcas Gazelle, Isabelline Gazelle. *French*: Gazelle Dorcade. *German*: Dorkasgazelle. *Spanish*: Gacela dorcas. *Russian*: Изабелловая газель-доркас, Эритрейская газель-доркас. *Arabic*: Ghazal, rajal, hemar. *Baluchi*: Ahu, ask, ast. *Bambara*: Sinè. *Baori*: Porsya. *Brahui*: Khazm. *Canarese*: Mudari, budari tiska. *Hebrew*: Zwi ha Negev. *Somali*: Phero. *Tuareg:* Ahankod.

SUBSPECIES Considered as a subspecies of *G. dorcas* (Dorcas Gazelle): *G. d. dorcas* (Egyptian Dorcas Gazelle), *G. d. isabella* (Isabelline Gazelle), *G. d. massaesyla* (Moroccan Dorcas Gazelle), *G. d. osiris* (Saharan Dorcas gazelle), *G. d. beccarii* (Eritrean Dorcas Gazelle). Includes *isidis* and *littoralis*.

SIMILAR SPECIES Egyptian Dorcas Gazelle (*dorcas*) is smaller, rich fawn in color, with flank band well expressed, a clear pygal band, and lyrate long horns. Saharan Dorcas Gazelle (*osiris*) is paler in color, flank band poorly expressed but bordered above with a very pale band, paler facial markings with no nose spot, and long horns both in ♂ and ♀. Moroccan Dorcas Gazelle (*massaesyla*) is richer, more ochery in color, with a poorly expressed nose spot. Horns in Isabelline Gazelle are shorter, S-shaped rather than lyrate, and have tips that hook inward. Eritrean Dorcas Gazelle (*beccarii*) is richer, more chestnut colored than *isabella*, flank band is red brown, and nose spot is absent.

REPRODUCTION *Gestation*: 164-174 days. *Young per Birth*: 1, rarely 2. *Weaning*: 2-3 months. *Sexual Maturity*: 9 months (♂), 18 months (♀). *Life Span*: Up to 12.5 years. Breeding occurs from September to November. After birth the young lie concealed away from their mother for 2-6 weeks.

BEHAVIOR *Family Group*: In harsh conditions, found in pairs but will move in small herds with 1 dominant ♂ and several ♀ and young, when food is plentiful. *Diet*: Leaves, pods, bark, and flowers of acacia trees, as well as stems and tubers of lilies. *Main Predators:* Jackal, fox, sand cat, hyena, wolf, eagle. There is no specific information available for this subspecies, but probably similar to other Dorcas Gazelle subspecies. Well adapted to an arid environment. They can go their entire lives without drinking, as they obtain moisture from the plants they eat, but they will drink, if water is available. Graze mainly at dawn, dusk, and throughout the night. The preorbital glands, although functional, are not used for marking. The alarm call, which sounds like a duck's quack, is made through the nose, which inflates during the process in a fashion similar to that of Speke's Gazelle, although not as prominent.

DISTRIBUTION *Native*: Djibouti, Egypt, Eritrea, Ethiopia, Israel, Sudan. Found in N Eritrea, S in Ethiopia through the E Danakil Desert and lower Awash Valley to about the N border of Djibouti, E Desert and Red Sea Hills in Egypt, extending S through the Nubian Desert and Red Sea Hills in Sudan. Separated by the Nile from the Egyptian Dorcas Gazelle in Egypt and the Sahara Dorcas Gazelle in Sudan. Eritrean Dorcas Gazelle is found only in Eritrea, in the highlands of the upper Anseba River.

HABITAT Savannas, semi-desert, and true desert.

STATUS Vulnerable. Populations of all Dorcas subspecies are in decline due to illegal hunting, habitat loss through expanding agriculture, and hunting by domestic dogs.

PHOTO CREDITS ♂: *Jonas Livet,* Al Ain Zoo (United Arab Emirates). ♀: *Ilona Ignatova,* Al Ain Zoo (United Arab Emirates).

Pelzeln's Gazelle

GAZELLA PELZELNI

BL: 100-120 cm. SH: 61-64 cm. TL: 18-22 cm. W: 20-23 kg. HL: 25-38 cm (♂), 15-25 cm (♀). General color is reddish fawn, with the underparts white. Broad, dark reddish flank band usually present, though not always (its presence or absence does not depend or age or sex). Dark reddish blaze on the forehead and upper face, a whitish stripe from the horn base over the eye to the muzzle, a short and indistinct brown cheek stripe below the eye, and no nose spot. Evenly divergent horns, present in both sexes, ringed almost to the tips, rising nearly straight from the head, with only a slight backward curve and an upward or forward bend at the tips. Female has smaller and thinner horns.

Gazella pelzelni

OTHER NAMES Lowland Gazelle. *French*: Gazelle de Pelzeln. *German*: Pelzelns-Gazelle. *Spanish*: Gacela de Pelzeln. *Russian*: Газель-доркас Пельцельна. *Somali*: Dero.

SUBSPECIES Monotypic. Formerly considered a subspecies of *G. dorcas* (Dorcas Gazelle), elevated to full species here.

SIMILAR SPECIES It is distinctive in comparison with other species of Dorcas Gazelle; it is about the same size as the Isabelline Dorcas Gazelle. Speke's Gazelle is slightly smaller, with a dusky brown or black flank band, instead of dark reddish as in the Pelzeln Gazelle. Beira is smaller, with horns present only in ♂, and lacks the white stripes on the face.

REPRODUCTION *Gestation*: 169-181 days. *Young per Birth*: 1, rarely 2. *Weaning*: 2-3 months. *Sexual Maturity*: 9 months (♂), 18 months (♀). *Life Span*: Up to 12.5 years. There is no specific information available for this subspecies, but probably similar to other Dorcas Gazelle subspecies.

BEHAVIOR *Family Group*: Small herds of about 2 to 12 individuals. Older ♂ usually solitary. *Diet*: They browse on shoots of acacias and desert bushes. *Main Predators:* Jackal, fox, sand cat, hyena, wolf, eagle. There is no specific information available for this subspecies, but probably similar to other Dorcas Gazelle subspecies. Well adapted to an arid environment. They can presumably subsist with a minimum of water, getting the moisture they need from the plants they eat. Depending on food conditions, they travel in pairs or groups consisting of 1 ♂, several ♀, and their young.

DISTRIBUTION *Native*: Djibouti, Somalia. Found in Djibouti, and E along the maritime plains of N Somalia as far as Bosaso. Found only within about 32 km of the seacoast (farther inland it is replaced by the Speke's Gazelle).

HABITAT Rocky and sandy deserts with few or no bushes, at low elevations, below 750 m.

STATUS Vulnerable. A total estimation of about 4,000 is assumed for Djibouti. Its numbers appear to be stable. Main threats include habitat loss and hunting.

PHOTO CREDITS ♂: *Patrice Gachet* (Djibouti). ♀: *Jonas Livet,* Al Wabra Wildlife Preservation (Qatar).

Slender-horned Gazelle
GAZELLA LEPTOCEROS

BL: 100-110 cm. SH: 65-72 cm. TL: 15-20 cm. W: 20-30 kg. HL: 30-41 cm (♂), 20-38 cm (♀). A small pale gazelle. Cream or yellow-white body (the palest gazelle species). Undersides pure white, faint flank stripe. Facial markings relatively faint, composed of a reddish nose stripe and bands running from the eyes to the nose. Ears very large, elongated, and pale. Tail blackish brown, very distinct against pale rump. Hooves somewhat broadened to ease travel on long stretches of sand. Horns, found in both sexes, are long, slender, and slightly S-shaped. In females, horns significantly smaller and slimmer. Males, on average, larger and heavier than females.

Young

♀

♂

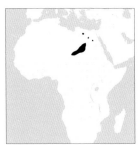

Gazella leptoceros leptoceros

Gazella leptoceros loderi

OTHER NAMES Rhim Gazelle, Sand Gazelle, Loder's Gazelle, White Gazelle. *French*: Gazelle de Rhim, gazelle des sables, gazelle à cornes fines. *German*: Dünengazelle. *Spanish*: Gacela blanca, gacela de Loder, gacela rim. *Russian*: Песчаная (тонкорогая) газель. *Arabic*: Rim, ghazal abyad, thim, riehm, abiad. *Kirundi*: Intaramvyi. *Tuareg*: Akukri.

SUBSPECIES *G. l. leptoceros* (Rhim Gazelle): W desert of Egypt; smaller, longed horned, darker coloration. *G. l. loderi* (Loder's Gazelle): Tunisia, E Algeria, and probably Mali, Libya, and Niger; larger, lighter coloration, shorter horned. The validity of these subspecies has been questioned by some authors.

SIMILAR SPECIES Dorcas Gazelle has a darker coloration and different horn shape. Mountain Gazelle has much shorter, stockier horns, is darker, and has distinct facial markings.

REPRODUCTION *Gestation*: 156-169 days. *Young per Birth*: 1. *Weaning*: 3 months. *Sexual Maturity*: 6-9 months (♀), 18 months (♂). *Life Span*: 14 years. Breeds May-June.

BEHAVIOR *Family Group*: ♂ and ♀ groups of 2-20 individuals. *Diet*: Grasses, leaves. *Main Predators:* Cheetah, Cape hunting dog, lion, leopard, spotted hyena, where still present in range. Due to the extreme heat of its desert environment, the Slender-horned Gazelle feeds mostly at night and in the early morning. At these times they are able to exploit the dew which has formed on the leaves and the higher water content in the plants. All needed water is obtained in this fashion; Slender-horned Gazelles rarely need to drink water. Nomadic species, wandering the dunes in search of vegetation. The main cooling mechanisms are the reflective white coat and a specially adapted nasal passage which allows for cooling of the blood. Deceptively mild mannered in appearance, Slender-horned Gazelles are known to become aggressive in captivity. ♂ often battle fiercely when defending the loose territories they establish. Eyesight, hearing, and sense of smell are very good. Their large, splayed hooves permit them to travel in deep sand where enemies cannot follow. The presence of Slender-horned Gazelles is often detected by the distinctive track lines they leave on the dunes, and by characteristic dung middens, which are used repeatedly by adult males, and possibly others too.

DISTRIBUTION *Native*: Algeria, Chad, Egypt, Libya, Mali, Niger, Sudan, Tunisia. Occurs across the Sahara, W of the Nile River. It has disappeared from most of its former range in Egypt's Western Desert. The center of its distribution is found in the Great Western Erg, the Great Eastern Erg, the sandy zone which stretches from the Hamada de Tinrhert in Algeria to the Fezzan in Libya, and the smaller ergs in the periphery of the central Saharan massifs of the Hoggar and the Tassili des Ajjers.

HABITAT Areas of dunes (ergs) and interdunal depressions. Ranges widely in search of ephemeral vegetation.

STATUS Endangered. Numbers are believed to have undergone a serious decline due to uncontrolled hunting. Estimated sub-Saharan Africa population could be as low as a few hundred and is unlikely to exceed a few thousand.

PHOTO CREDITS ♂: *David Ellis*, Cincinnati Zoo (USA). ♀: *Sergey Chichagov*, Bronx Zoo (USA). Young: Cleveland Metroparks Zoo (USA).

Cuvier's Gazelle

GAZELLA CUVIERI

BL: 95-105 cm. SH: 60-70 cm. TL: 15-20 cm. Weight: 20-35 kg (♂), 15-20 kg (♀). HL: 25-37 cm (♂), 25-30 (♀). A small, dark gazelle, one of the darkest. Grayish-brown upper parts. Wide blackish band from hind legs to front legs, dividing the upper parts from the white belly. White rump bordered on each side by a narrow pygal black stripe. Thin tail, entirely black. Face is striped: dark line from inside corner of eye to corner of mouth, bordered on top by wider whitish stripe. Conspicuous black spot sits across the bridge of the nose. Knee tufts are present. Horns found in both sexes, comparatively thick at the base and strongly ringed, rather upright and parallel, with a small upward and forward bend at the tips. Females are similar to males, but smaller, and have smaller, smoother, straighter horns.

♂

♂
Juvenile

♀

Young

Gazella cuvieri

OTHER NAMES Edmi Gazelle, Atlas Gazelle. *French*: Gazelle de Cuvier. *German*: Cuviergazelle, Echtgazelle. *Spanish*: Gacela de Cuvier, gacela del Atlas. *Russian*: Атласская газель (Газель Кювье). *Arabic*: Edmi, admi, edem.

SUBSPECIES Monotypic. Considered as a subspecies of *G. gazella* (Mountain Gazelle) by some authors. Others regard it as conspecific with *G. rufifrons* (Red-fronted Gazelle) or *G. thomsoni* (Thomson's Gazelle).

SIMILAR SPECIES Among the gazelles, only the Dorcas Gazelle and Slender-horned Gazelle have similar ranges. Both of these gazelles are much lighter in color compared to Cuvier's Gazelle; their side stripes are faint and reddish instead of dark and blackish. The horns of the Dorcas Gazelle are more lyre shaped, while those of the Slender-horned Gazelle are much longer.

REPRODUCTION *Gestation*: 165 days. *Young per Birth*: 1-2. *Sexual Maturity*: 7 months (♀). *Life Span*: 12 months. Most Cuvier's Gazelles are born between March and May, although there is a second birthing season in October; these 2 periods have the most rainfall. Mothers will separate themselves from the herd prior to giving birth. At around 1 month old, infants will start eating solid food, although they will still nurse from their mothers.

BEHAVIOR *Family Group*: Small mixed-sex groups with around 4 animals, sometimes up to 8. *Diet*: Both a grazer and a browser. Grasses, herbs, and leaves from shrubs. Drinks water where available, otherwise obtains moisture from dew and rain. *Main Predators*: Jackals prey on young (other large predators have been exterminated). Cuvier's Gazelles generally spend the days in brushy areas, emerging at night to graze in open valleys. They may also enter farmers' fields to eat crops, especially wheat. Some populations stay in the same area year-round, but others appear to be nomadic (wandering) or migratory between regions. Territories are held by ♂ in early winter; these are marked with dung piles. The preorbital glands may be used to mark objects as well. Eyesight, hearing, and sense of smell are good. Good climbers.

DISTRIBUTION *Native*: Algeria, Morocco, Tunisia, Western Sahara. Endemic to mountains and hills of the Atlas and neighboring ranges of NW Africa. Overhunting and habitat degradation have greatly reduced the former range and led to fragmented populations, most of which live in Morocco. In Algeria, the distribution is limited to the N part of the country. The most E populations are found in the Aurès, the Némentcha Mountains, and the hills near the Tunisian border. In Tunisia the population has increased in and around Chambi NP.

HABITAT Open semi-arid Mediterranean forests, maquis, and steppes, from sea level to 2,600 m.

STATUS Endangered. Estimated total population: 1,400-2,500 (Algeria: 560, Morocco: 600-1,500, Tunisia: 300-400). Major threats are fragmentation and loss of habitat, overgrazing by livestock, and poaching.

PHOTO CREDITS ♂: *Chris Hogan*, Living Desert Zoo and Gardens (USA). ♀: *Will Ferguson*, San Diego Zoo (USA). Head ♂: *Sergey Chichagov*, San Diego Zoo (USA). Head ♀: *Karl Drilling*, San Diego Zoo (USA). Young: *Jonas Livet*, Parque de Rescate de Fauna Sahariana (Spain).

Persian Goitered Gazelle

GAZELLA SUBGUTTUROSA

BL: 90-115 cm. SH: 60-80 cm. TL: 15-20 cm. W: 18-33 kg. HL: 25-43 cm (♂). A medium-sized gazelle with a heavily built body, thick neck, relatively short legs, and large hooves. Short summer coat sandy fawn, becoming much paler in the long, rough winter coat. Flank band and rump stripes are indistinct. Pygal stripes somewhat pronounced. Facial marking typical of gazelles only in juveniles; with age forehead and nose bridge turn white, with only the brown eye-nose stripe remaining. Underparts, inner legs, and buttocks up to the base of the tail are white. Black tail, conspicuous against the white buttocks, carried erect while running. Horns only in males, black in color and sharply diverging, S-shaped, bending up backward, and turning in at the tips. Females somewhat smaller than males and usually hornless. During the rut, the larynx of males bulges outward, resembling a goiter.

Young

♀

♂

Juvenile

♂

winter coat

summer coat

Gazella subgutturosa

OTHER NAMES Persian Gazelle. *French*: Gazelle à goitre, gazelle de Perse. *German*: Kropfgazelle. Spanish: Gacela persa, gacela de bocio. *Russian*: Персидский джейран. *Iranian*: Ahu, jeebir. *Local names*: Jairan, kik, saikik, jhar suult zeer.

SUBSPECIES Monotypic. The name *G. subgutturosa* (Goitered Gazelle) formerly included *G. subgutturosa* (Persian Gazelle), *G. s. gracilicornis* (Turkmen Gazelle), *G. yarkandensis* (Yarkand Gazelle), and *G. marica* (Sand Gazelle) as subspecies: these are all elevated to full species here. Includes *seistanica* (Seistan Gazelle of E Iran).

REPRODUCTION *Gestation*: 150-180 days. *Young per Birth*: 1-2, rarely up to 4. *Weaning*: 4-5 months. *Sexual Maturity*: 9 months (♀), 18 months (♂). *Life Span*: 10-12 years. A restricted breeding season, from November to January, with the resulting births taking place in April-May. The young lie camouflaged away from their mothers for the first 2 weeks, gaining strength and stability on their wobbly legs. The mother returns to nurse 3 times each day.

BEHAVIOR *Family Group*: In summer, small family groups of 2-5 animals; in winter, large herds with dozens or even hundreds of individuals. *Diet*: Grasses, leaves, and shoots. *Main Predators*: Leopard, wolf. During the summer, most activity takes place in the late afternoon and early morning, consisting of leisurely walking and simultaneous grazing. At midday, herds take shelter in the shade, where they excavate shallow oval-shaped pits to lie in. During the cooler winter months, this midday break is significantly reduced. If disturbed from its shelter, it rapidly flees for 200-300 m, pausing to assess the danger from this distance. A broad circular path is then taken back to the original resting spot. Extremely speedy (up to 60 kmph). They consume about 30% of their body weight in green matter per day, and can derive most of their needed moisture from it. In the spring and summer, groups may travel to water sources, but even still they rarely drink daily. Herds cover 10-30 km per day in the winter. Throughout much of their range, they undergo seasonal migrations. During the breeding season, adult ♂ become territorial, using dung middens placed at strategic locations to indicate ownership. At this time, ♂ emit hoarse bellows, and glandular activity increases significantly, with the result that the ♂ are often seen smearing secretions on objects.

DISTRIBUTION *Native*: Afghanistan, Azerbaijan, Iran, Iraq, Kazakhstan, Kyrgyzstan, Pakistan, Tajikistan, Turkey, Turkmenistan. Found in SE Turkey, Azerbaijan, Syria, N and E Iraq, Iran, S Afghanistan, and W Pakistan.

HABITAT Deserts, semi-deserts, hilly plains, and plateaus.

STATUS Vulnerable. Population estimated at 120,000 in 2001.

PHOTO CREDITS ♂ summer: *M. Reza Besmeli* (Iran). Head ♂: *Andrey Kotkin*, Moscow Zoo (Russia). ♂ winter: *Sergey Chichagov*, Helsinki Zoo (Finland). ♀: *Ferdi de Gier*, Zoo Parc Overloon (Netherlands). Head ♀: *Maxime Thué*, Plzen Zoo (Czech Republic). Young: *Nick Karpov*, Moscow Zoo (Russia).

Turkmen Goitered Gazelle
GAZELLA GRACILICORNIS

BL: 110-116 cm (♂), 98-110 cm (♀). SH: 64-75 cm (♂), 60-68 cm (♀). TL: 15-20 cm. W: 23-33 kg (♂), 18-28 kg (♀). HL: 25-43 cm (♂). A medium-sized gazelle, similar to the Persian Goitered Gazelle. Summer coat is short, sandy brown to sandy gray in color, becoming longer and paler in winter. Flank band and rump stripes somewhat pronounced. Underparts, inner legs, and buttocks up to the base of the tail are white. Facial markings indistinct in adults, with an incomplete dark lateral eye stripe and dark brown patch on the nose fading into white with age. Black tail, conspicuous against the white buttocks. Horns only in males, sharply diverging, S-shaped, bending up backward, and turning in at the tips. Very wide across the bases of the horns. Females smaller than males and usually hornless, but may develop small knobs.

Gazella gracilicornis

OTHER NAMES *French*: Gazelle tadjike. *German*: Turkmenistan-Kropfgazelle. *Spanish*: Gacela de Turkmenistán. *Russian*: Туркменский джейран.

SUBSPECIES Monotypic. Formerly considered a subspecies of *G. subgutturosa* (Goitered Gazelle). Considered by some authors to be a synonym of *G. subgutturosa*.

REPRODUCTION *Gestation*: 165-180 days. *Young per Birth*: 1-2, rarely up to 4. *Weaning*: 6 months. *Sexual Maturity*: 8-18 months (♀), 18 months (♂). *Life Span*: 10-12 years. Breeding season in October-November. Births take place in secluded places. The young stand in the first day after birth, being able to run after the first week.

BEHAVIOR *Family Group*: In summer, small family groups of 2-5 animals; in winter, large herds with dozens or even hundreds of individuals. *Diet*: Grasses; in summer they prefer succulents. *Main Predators*: Leopard, wolf. During the summer, most activity takes place in the late afternoon and early morning, consisting of leisurely walking and simultaneous grazing. At midday, herds take shelter in the shade, where they excavate shallow oval-shaped pits to lie in. During the cooler winter months, they graze throughout the day, sometimes with a break in the middle of the day. If disturbed from their shelter, they run without the high bounds or stotting seen in other species of gazelles. Throughout much of their range, they undergo seasonal migrations. During the breeding season, the larynx of ♂ bulges outward, and they become territorial, using dung middens placed at strategic locations to indicate ownership.

DISTRIBUTION *Native*: Kazakhstan, Tajikistan, Turkmenistan, Uzbekistan. Found in Kazakhstan in the E to about Lake Balkash, Turkmenistan, Tajikistan, and probably Uzbekistan. Boundaries with the Yarkand Gazelle are unclear. They still occur in small numbers at Badkhyz Nature Reserve (fewer then 1,000 individuals), in S Turkmenistan, and the Amudarya State Nature Reserve in NE Turkmenistan.

HABITAT Deserts, semi-deserts, hilly plains, and plateaus. It may ascend mountains to 3,000 m.

STATUS Vulnerable. Population was estimated as not more than 6,000 individuals in 2001. In Turkmenistan and Kazakhstan, the population has almost disappeared in recent years, mainly because of poaching and the development of roads, which interrupts migration routes and isolates smaller populations. There have been reintroductions in Uzbekistan, using animals from the Djeiran Ecocenter (Uzbekistan).

PHOTO CREDITS Reconstruction based on photos from *Alex Meyer* and Djeiran Ecocenter (Uzbekistan).

Yarkand Gazelle

GAZELLA YARKANDENSIS

BL: 90-110 cm. SH: 69 cm. TL: 10-15 cm. W: 20-30 kg. HL: 28-30 cm (♂). A medium-sized gazelle with a heavily built body, thick neck, relatively short legs, and large hooves. General color is dark fawn to pale sandy, with less of a reddish hue than in Persian Goitered Gazelle. Underparts, inner legs, and buttocks up to the base of the tail are white. Black tail, conspicuous against the white buttocks, carried erect while running. Facial markings well developed, dark muzzle blaze extending up the forehead and splitting to end at the horn bases. Horns are relatively shorter but stouter than in Persian Goitered Gazelle. About 14 horn rings, seldom exceeding 16. Ears longer than in the Persian Goitered Gazelle, and white area of the rump is larger, extending upward on each side of the root of the tail. Females always hornless. During the rut, the larynx of males bulges outward, resembling a goiter.

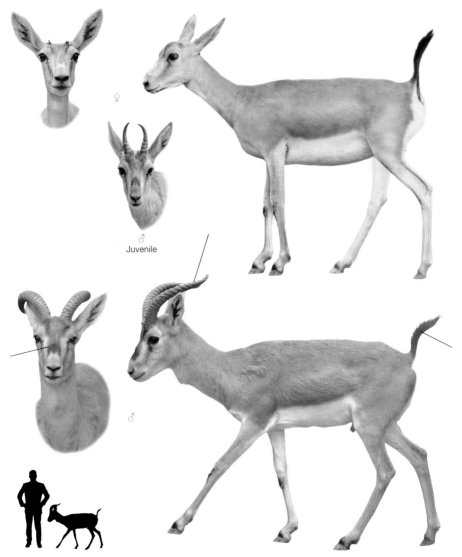

♀

♂
Juvenile

♂

Gazella yarkandensis

OTHER NAMES Saikik Gazelle, Mongolian Goitered Gazelle, Black-tailed Gazelle, Hilier Goitered Gazelle. *French*: Gazelle à goitre de Yarkand. *German*: Yarkand Kropf-Gazelle. *Spanish*: Gacela de bocio de Yarkand. *Russian*: Яркендский (монгольский) джейран. *Chinese*: Oe-hou-lin. *Mongol*: Khar, süült.

SUBSPECIES Monotypic. Formerly considered a subspecies of *G. subgutturosa* (Goitered Gazelle). Includes *hillieriana* (Hillier Goitered Gazelle, from Gobi Desert), *mongolica* (Mongolia), *reginae* (Qaidam), *sairensis* (Sair Mountains, Junggar), and *yarkandensis* (Xinjiang).

SIMILAR SPECIES Similar in size and appearance to the Persian Goitered Gazelle, but the horns are much shorter and stouter. Its range overlaps that of the Mongolian Gazelle (*Procapra gutturosa*) in the E Gobi region, but it can be distinguished by its smaller size, its smaller goiter, different coloration, and much longer black tail, which it carries erect when running. Normally the two species occupy different terrain and keep to themselves; however, they are sometimes found together.

REPRODUCTION *Gestation*: 150-180 days. *Young per Birth*: 1-2, rarely up to 4. *Weaning*: 4-5 months. *Sexual Maturity*: 9 months (♀), 18 months (♂). *Life Span*: 10-12 years. There is no specific information for this subspecies. Fawns are born in late June and the young may be left to sleep on the ground, where they are perfectly camouflaged by their coats, while their mothers feed on desert shrubs and search for water.

BEHAVIOR *Family Group*: In summer, small family groups of 1 to 12 animals; in winter, groups of 20-30 animals, sometimes larger, for protection against wolves. They may form mixed herds with Mongolian Gazelles (*Procapra gutturosa*), but never with other livestock. *Diet*: Desert plants. *Main Predators*: Leopard, wolf. There is no specific information for this subspecies.

DISTRIBUTION *Native*: China, Mongolia. Found in plains and deserts of NW and N China (Xinjiang, Qinghai, Gansu, N Shaanxi, and Nei Mongo), and Mongolia.

HABITAT Steppes, alpine grasslands, and semi-deserts.

STATUS Vulnerable. It is one of the largest numbered population of Goitered Gazelle species, with estimated numbers higher than 60,000. Illegal hunting for meat and sport is the primary threat.

PHOTO CREDITS ♂ and ♀: *Jonas Livet*, Beijing Zoological Gardens (China). Head ♀ and juvenile: *Sergey Chichagov* and *Alex Kantorovich,* Beijing Zoological Gardens (China).

Sand Gazelle

GAZELLA MARICA

BL: 97 cm. SH: 55-60 cm. TL: 15 cm. W: 22 kg (♂), 18 kg (♀). HL: 27 cm (♂), 15 cm (♀). Smaller than the Persian Goitered Gazelle, but comparatively robustly built, with a whitish or pale yellow-brown color. Only rudimentary face and body markings. There is no darker stripe between the white underside and beige flanks and back. Face and forehead tend to be white, especially in old animals. Black tail. White underparts. Legs long and slender, with black, narrow hooves. Horns in males curve upward and backward, with the sharp tips closing inward or slightly forward. Females are slightly smaller and have well-developed horns that are straight, shorter, and do not widen in a lyrate curve like horns of males. Both sexes have a goiter-like swelling at the throat, more prominent in males, which enables the animals to emit loud calls during courtship.

Young

♀

♂
Juvenile

♂

Gazella marica

OTHER NAMES Arabian Goitered Gazelle, Arabian Sand Gazelle, Reem Gazelle. *French*: Gazelle marica, gazelle à goître d'Arabie. *German*: Sandgazelle. *Spanish*: Gacela árabe de dunas, gacela de bocio. *Russian*: Аравийский джейран.

SUBSPECIES Monotypic. Formerly considered a subspecies of *G. subgutturosa* (Goitered Gazelle).

REPRODUCTION *Gestation*: 150-180 days. *Young per Birth*: 1-2, rarely up to 4. *Weaning*: 5 months. *Sexual Maturity*: 9 months (♀), 18 months (♂). *Life Span*: 6-12 years. Breeding occurs from September to January. The young are hidden in vegetation from predators. Twins are separated from one another and are led to new hiding places after each nursing. At 2.5 months young are able to follow their mother.

BEHAVIOR *Family Group*: In summer, small family groups of 2-10 animals; in winter, large herds with dozens or even hundreds of individuals. Diet: Grasses, leaves, and young shoots. *Main Predators*: Leopard, wolf. During summer they graze largely between dusk and dawn, digging shallow pits, where the earth is cooler, in which to rest. Small groups of up to 10 animals are formed in summer and grow to large herds in winter. A dominant ♂ guards up to 30 ♀ and their young, marking his territory with urine and dung, while subadult ♂ form bachelor herds. After the breeding season the gazelles gather in mixed groups of up to 50 animals. By spring, both ♂ and ♀ form separate groups and pregnant ♀ become solitary, as the time to give birth draws close. Most of their water needs are gained through the plants they eat. To keep cool and reduce water loss via the body, desert gazelles can store body heat during the day, without panting or sweating, and release it at night. Sand Gazelles are very quick and excellent jumpers and use their speed and agility to evade the attention of predators.

DISTRIBUTION *Native*: Bahrain, Iraq, Jordan, Oman, Saudi Arabia, Syria, United Arab Emirates, Yemen. *Regionally Extinct*: Kuwait. Formerly occurred in the Arabian Peninsula N to Iraq and Kuwait. Currently found in Bahrain (Hawar Island and S part of Bahrain Island), Oman (Dhofar, edge of Rub al Khali to Arabian Oryx Sanctuary), United Arab Emirates (Umm al Zummur area), N Saudi Arabia, NE Jordan, S Syria, SW Iraq, and Yemen.

HABITAT Sandy deserts, bordering gravel plains, limestone plateaus, basaltic lava fields, sedimentary escarpments, and coastal flats.

STATUS Vulnerable. In decline due to illegal hunting, expanding agriculture, competition for food with livestock, and fragmentation of habitat through development. The population is estimated to be fewer than 10,000 mature individuals, mostly in Saudi Arabia, in four populations, all in protected areas.

PHOTO CREDITS ♂: *Klaus Rudloff*, Arabia's Wildlife Centre, Sharjah (United Arab Emirates). ♀: *Mike Barth* (www.flickr.com/photos/ mikebarth), Dubai (United Arab Emirates). Head ♂: *Mohsen Jafar*. Young: *Stephen James*, Empty Quarter (United Arab Emirates). Juvenile: *Danny McLaughlin London (UK)*, Dubai (United Arab Emirates).

Southern Gerenuk
LITOCRANIUS WALLERI

BL: 140-160 cm. SH: 85-105 cm. TL: 25-35 cm. W: 30-50 kg. HL: 25-44 cm (♂). A long-necked antelope, with skinny body supported by long, slender legs. Reddish-fawn smooth coat, underparts and front of neck white. Along the back is a darker band or saddle, which reaches partly down the sides. Very long and slender neck. Band of reversed hairs directed toward the neck, on the dorsal midline of the neck. Head wedge shaped and somewhat flattened. Ring of white around the eye, ears long and skinny. Short tail terminating in a black tuft. Horns found only in males, curve backward and upward, terminating with hooked tips, ringed around their circumference. Females similar to males, but without horns and with a dark patch on the crown.

♀

♂
Juvenile

♂

Young

Litocranius walleri

OTHER NAMES Waller's Gazelle, Giraffe Gazelle. *French*: Gazelle de Waller, antilope girafe. *German*: Südliche Giraffengazelle. *Spanish*: Gerenuc, gacela jirafa meridional, gacela de Waller. *Russian*: Южный геренук. *Swahili*: Swala twiga. *Galla*: Gugufto. *Kikamba*: Katwilagamia. *Maasai*: Nanjaart. *Ndorobo*: Ligu, enanjaart. *Samburu*: Riko. *Somali*: Gerenuk.

SUBSPECIES Monotypic. The name *L. walleri* (Gerenuk) formerly included *L. walleri* (Southern Gerenuk), and *L. sclateri* (Northern Gerenuk) as subspecies: these are elevated to full species here.

SIMILAR SPECIES Dibatag has a more slender neck and longer tail, held differently, and the facial markings and the shape of the horns are different. Northern Gerenuk is slightly larger, with a somewhat larger neck, general color lighter and less red, with less contrast between the darker back and lighter flanks, and the white area on the back of the rump is smaller. Impala has a similar color pattern, but easily identified by its shorter neck and legs.

REPRODUCTION *Gestation*: 203-210 days. *Young per Birth*: 1. *Sexual Maturity*: 1 year (♀), 1.5 years (♂). *Life Span*: 10-12 years. During courtship, the ♂ simply walks behind the ♀ with nose lifted; he then stands behind the ♀ and makes a very ritualized "laufschlag" or mating kick: the foreleg is slowly raised and the hooves are spread apart; he then rubs the ♀ with his preorbital glands. He then stands on his hind legs, walks forward bipedally behind the walking ♀, and performs intromission in this position. The newborn takes an hour to be able to stand securely; it is kept hidden in thick bushes. It can stand bipedally after a month.

BEHAVIOR *Family Group*: Solitary or in single-sex groups of up to 10 animals. *Diet*: Leaves of bushes and trees, shoots, buds, fruits, and blossoms; largely independent of water. *Main Predators*: Cheetah, leopard, lion, Cape hunting dog, hyena. The diurnal Gerenuk requires very little water, and may not drink at all during its life. It is exclusively a browser. To reach leaves on taller trees, it stands on its hind legs, resting its forelegs on the branches of the tree to steady itself. From this position, it plucks the tender leaves from the branches with its long upper lip and tongue. When a Gerenuk sees a strange object, it freezes and hides behind a bush, looking over the cover with the help of its long neck. When startled, the Gerenuk runs off in a crouched trot with its head held level with its body. Population densities average about 0.6 animals per km^2. Home range sizes vary from 1.5 to 3.5 km^2, with the edges overlapping. Mature ♂ become territorial, marking their areas with urine, feces, and glandular secretions.

DISTRIBUTION *Native*: Ethiopia, Kenya, Somalia, Tanzania. The S edge of Ethiopia, E of the Omo River and S and W of the Webi Shebeli River, E of the Rift Valley in Kenya and N Tanzania, and S Somalia W of the Webi Shebeli River.

HABITAT Bushland, thickets, semi-arid and arid thornbush, avoiding dense woodlands and very open grass-dominated habitats.

STATUS Near Threatened. Estimated population of 95,000 in 1999 for both species of Gerenuk.

PHOTO CREDITS ♂: *Andrew Cosand*, Samburu National Reserve (Kenya). Head ♂: *Sergey Chichagov*, San Diego Zoo (USA). ♀: *Van Swearingen*, Los Angeles Zoo (USA). Juvenile: *Lisa P.*, Disney's Animal Kingdom (USA).

Northern Gerenuk
LITOCRANIUS SCLATERI

BL: 140-160 cm. SH: 80-120 cm. TL: 22-35 cm. W: 31-52 kg (♂), 28-45 kg (♀). HL: 25-44 cm (♂). A long-necked antelope. Slightly larger than the Southern Gerenuk, with a somewhat longer neck. Reddish-fawn smooth coat, underparts and front of neck white. Slightly paler and less rufous than the Southern Gerenuk, with less contrast between the dark back and lighter flanks, and the white area on the back of the rump is smaller. There is no hair reversal on the neck. The knee tufts are usually brown rather than black. Females similar to males, but without horns and with a dark patch on the crown.

Litocranius sclateri

OTHER NAMES Sclater's Gazelle. *French*: Gazelle de Sclater. *German*: Nördliche Giraffengazelle. *Spanish*: Gerenuc septentrional, gacela jirafa septentrional. *Russian*: Северный геренук.

SUBSPECIES Monotypic. Formerly considered a subspecies of *L. walleri* (Gerenuk).

SIMILAR SPECIES The Dibatag has a more slender neck and longer tail, held differently, and the facial markings and the shape of the horns are different. Southern Gerenuk is rather similar in color, but slightly smaller, with a somewhat shorter neck, and a band of reversed of hairs directed toward the neck, on the dorsal midline of the neck.

REPRODUCTION *Gestation*: 203 days. *Young per Birth*: 1. *Sexual Maturity*: 1 year (♀), 1.5 years (♂). *Life Span*: 13 years. Mating probably any time of the year. The ♀ will give birth in a secluded place away from the others in her group. The young spends the first 2 weeks lying in the bush while its mother is away feeding.

BEHAVIOR *Family Group*: Small groups of 2-6 ♀, along with a single ♂. Sometimes a group may consist only of related ♀ and their young, or all ♂, and occasionally a ♂ will live by himself. *Diet*: Exclusive browser: leaves of bushes and trees, shoots, buds, fruits, and blossoms; largely independent of water. *Main Predators*: Cheetah, leopard, lion, Cape hunting dog, hyena. There is no specific information available for this subspecies, but probably much like the Southern Gerenuk, which is more active during the day, especially so around dawn or dusk. During the heat of the day, they often stand or lie in shaded areas. Much of the rest of their time is spent feeding or searching for food.

DISTRIBUTION *Native*: Djibouti, Ethiopia, Somalia. The S Danakil region of Ethiopia SE of the Awash River and N of the Chercher Mountains, S Djibouti, the Ogaden region of Ethiopia NE of the Webi Shebeli River, and central and N Somalia E of the Webi Shebeli River.

HABITAT Bushland, thickets, semi-arid and arid thornbush, below 1,600 m, avoiding dense woodlands and very open grass-dominated habitats.

STATUS Near Threatened. No population estimates are available, and there are fewer protected areas within its range than in that of the Southern Gerenuk.

PHOTO CREDITS *Jonas Livet* and Al Wabra Wildlife Preservation (Qatar).

Dibatag
AMMODORCAS CLARKEI

BL: 152-168 cm. SH: 80-88 cm. TL: 30-36 cm. W: 22-35 kg. HL: 15-25 cm (♂). A small, slender antelope with a long, slim neck and long legs. General coloration of the upper parts grayish fawn, rump and undersides white. Facial markings similar to those of true gazelles, consisting of a white stripe running from above the eye to the muzzle. Streak along the bridge of the nose deep chestnut, mouth opening very small. The most conspicuous feature is its long, heavily furred black tail, which raises like a baton when fleeing. Horns, found only in males, are like those of the Reedbuck, angling back from the forehead, and curving around vertically so that the tips face forward, brownish black, lower half with 6-10 well-developed rings, upper half smooth and pointed. Females carry only a patch of dark hair at the crown, and are generally smaller than males.

Ammodorcas clarkei

OTHER NAMES Clarke's Gazelle. *French*: Antilope de Clarke, dibatag. *German*: Stelzengazelle, Lamagazelle, Dibatag. *Spanish*: Dibatag, gacela de Clark. *Russian*: Дибатаг. *Somali*: Dibatag.

SUBSPECIES Monotypic.

SIMILAR SPECIES The Gerenuk has a longer and heavier neck and shorter tail, held differently, and the facial markings and the shape of the horns are different.

REPRODUCTION *Gestation*: 180-210 days. *Young per Birth*: 1. *Sexual Maturity*: 12-18 months. *Life Span:* 10-12 years. Breeding takes place year-round, but seems to peak during the rainy season. Births occur in October and November, after which the fawn lies concealed for 2 weeks.

BEHAVIOR *Family Group*: Solitary, in pairs, or in family parties with 3-6 animals. May be in loose association with other species such as Soemmerring's Gazelle and Gerenuk. *Diet*: Leaves of bushes and trees, shoots; can survive without free water. *Main Predators:* Cheetah, lion, hyena, Cape hunting dog. Active early and late, resting during the midday heat. Hearing and sense of smell are very good, eyesight less so. Very shy and alert. Remains motionless until discovered. When it first senses danger, the Dibatag conceals itself behind vegetation, standing motionless while peering over the top to keep track of the threat. Its coloration, long, skinny legs and neck, and sharply pointed head match the natural cover so well as to render the animal virtually invisible. Once detected and advanced upon, the Dibatag flees with its head arched back and its tail carried erect like a baton. It has a pronounced ambling gait in the form of a cross-trot (opposite legs moving together), and rarely does it gallop. ♂ are territorial, marking their ranges with dung piles, which are visited daily. ♀ are sometimes marked using preorbital gland secretions. Due to the fragility and shape of their horns, Dibatag ♂ take special precautions when sparring. Tucking their nose between their forelegs, they push and shove against their opponent's horns and neck, attempting to throw the other off balance. Its long neck is used to reach higher vegetation. However, if the leaves are still out of reach, the Dibatag will, like the Gerenuk, stand up on its hind legs, supporting itself with its forefeet on the tree.

DISTRIBUTION *Native*: Ethiopia, Somalia. Endemic to the Ogaden region of SE Ethiopia and adjoining areas of central Somalia. Formerly widespread in the Haud of N Somalia, but no longer found there.

HABITAT Sandy areas with scattered thorn scrub and grass.

STATUS Vulnerable. Estimated population of about 1,500 in the Ogaden in 2006. The total surviving population is unknown, but is clearly not large. Threatened by war in its Somalia range, hunting, drought, and habitat loss. There are currently no protected areas within its range, and no captive breeding populations.

PHOTO CREDITS ♂: Based on photos by *Charles Carpenter*, Field Museum Library and *F. Wilhelmi*. Heads: *Anne Petersen*, Chicago Field Museum of Natural History (USA).

Tibetan Gazelle

PROCAPRA PICTICAUDATA

BL: 91-105 cm. SH: 54-65 cm. TL: 8-9 cm. W: 13-16 kg. HL: 26-33 cm (♂). A small gazelle, with a slender and compact body, and long and fine limbs. Grayish-brown color over most of the body, with the summer coat being noticeably grayer than the winter one. White abdomen. Short, black-tipped tail in the center of a heart-shaped white rump patch. The fur lacks an undercoat, consisting of long guard hairs only, and is noticeably thicker in winter. Large eyes. Long, narrow, pointed ears. Hooves anteriorly compressed and posteriorly wide and rounded. Males have long, tapering, ringed horns, positioned close together on the forehead, which rise more or less vertically until they suddenly diverge toward the tips. Females have no horns, and neither sex has distinct facial markings.

Procapra picticaudata

OTHER NAMES Goa, Ragao. *French*: Gazelle du Tibet. *German*: Tibetgazelle. *Spanish*: Gacela del Tibet. *Russian*: Тибетский дзерен, или гоа. *Chinese*: Zang yuan ling.

SUBSPECIES Monotypic.

SIMILAR SPECIES: Przewalski's Gazelle is larger and has shorter, more curvaceous horns, with a different shape. Mongolian Gazelle is larger and longer, and has smaller horns. Goitered Gazelle is larger with a more pronounced color pattern (face with black stripes).

REPRODUCTION *Gestation*: 180 days. *Young per Birth:* 1. *Sexual Maturity*: 18 months. *Life Span*: 5 years. For much of the year, the sexes remain separate, with the ♀ grazing in higher-altitude terrain than the ♂. The ♀ descend from their high pastures around September, prior to the mating season in December. During the rut, the ♂ are largely solitary, scent marking their territories and sometimes butting or wrestling rival ♂ with their horns. Horn-to-horn combat between rutting ♂ is aggressive and involves face-offs, horn clashes, and pushing and twisting with locked horns. Specific courtship and copulatory behaviors have not been described, but they may be similar to those of Przewalski's Gazelles, which are unique among ungulates and include a courtship performance during which ♂ dance on their hind legs, followed by a brief intromission with no locking of the front legs by the ♂. ♀ separate themselves from other ♀ and seek a secluded place to give birth, often moving up in elevation. The infants remain hidden with their mother for the first 2 weeks of life, before rejoining the herd.

BEHAVIOR *Family Group*: Single or in small groups of 3-20 animals, gathering in larger herds during migrations to higher summer pastures. *Diet*: Primarily forbs and legumes, supplemented by relatively small amounts of grasses and sedges. *Main Predators*: Wolf. Unlike some other ungulates, Tibetan Gazelle do not form large herds. Although they occasionally gather into larger aggregations, most groups contain no more than 10 individuals, and many are solitary. They have been noted to give short cries and calls to alert the herd to the approach of a predator or other perceived threat. They are generally crepuscular, with 2 feeding and moving periods early and late in the day and resting during midday, although feeding throughout the day is not uncommon. Tibetan Gazelles do not move great distances between seasonal ranges. Some ♀ groups move seasonally from low-elevation breeding and winter ranges to high-alpine mesic summer ranges to give birth. ♂ stay in lowland, grass-dominated habitats.

DISTRIBUTION *Native*: China, India. Most animals occur in China, but some very small populations exist in India. Occurs across virtually the whole Qinghai-Tibetan Plateau (China), extending a small distance into two adjoining areas of India (Ladakh, Sikkim).

HABITAT Alpine meadow and alpine steppe, between 4,000 and 5,500 m, but uses other lower-elevation plains and valleys.

STATUS Near Threatened. Estimated population in 2003 in China on the Qinghai-Tibet Plateau may be around 100,000. Habitat loss and illegal hunting are reducing the population, but at what rate is not clear.

PHOTO CREDITS ♂: *Coke and Som Smith*, Qinghai (China). ♀: *Stephen Davis*, Qinghai (China). Back: *Jan Reurink*, Qinghai (China).

Przewalski's Gazelle

PROCAPRA PRZEWALSKII

BL: 109-160 cm. SH: 50-70 cm. TL: 7-12 cm. W: 17-32 kg. HL: 18-26 cm (♂). A relatively small gazelle, Yellowish brown, more noticeably grayish in winter, with a white underside and a white heart-shaped patch on its rump. A narrow light brown line runs down the back to the upper surface of the tail. There are no pronounced lateral and facial markings. Males darker than females. Large eyes and short, pointed ears. Short tail, often entirely hidden by fur. Fronts of limbs are brownish with no knee tufts. Males have ringed horns, which rise between the eyes and curve inward at the tips. Females are hornless and generally smaller and lighter than males.

Procapra przewalskii

OTHER NAMES Chinese Gazelle, Qinghai Gazelle. *French*: Gazelle Przewalski. *German*: Przewalski-Gazelle. *Spanish*: Gacela de Przewalski. *Russian*: Дзерен Пржевальского.

SUBSPECIES *P. p. przewalskii*: Restricted to a few small isolated populations around the Qinghai Lake (China). *P. p. diversicornis*: Formerly found in Gansu and the Ordos region, now spread to the Qinghai Lake region; larger size and darker, more reddish color, with more-spreading horns with less incurved tips. *P. przewalskii* is considered by some authors as a subspecies of *P. picticaudata*.

SIMILAR SPECIES: Tibetan Gazelle is smaller and has longer, less curvaceous horns. Mongolian Gazelle is larger and longer, and has smaller horns. Goitered Gazelle is larger with a more pronounced color pattern (face with black stripes). Przewalski's Gazelle may be distinguished by the shape of its horns.

REPRODUCTION *Gestation*: 6 months. *Young per Birth:* 1. *Sexual Maturity*: 18 months. *Life Span*: 8 years. Rut from late December to early January. ♂ scent mark small territories and clash with rivals, fighting with their horns. ♀ have also been observed fighting for access to ♂. Courtship consists of the ♂ moving toward the ♀ while standing on his hind legs, followed by a brief copulation. The young are born around May or June, usually in thickets or areas of tall grass where they can be concealed from potential predators. The newborn young are able to follow their mother within a few minutes of birth, although they may remain concealed for a few days before rejoining the herd.

BEHAVIOR *Family Group:* Small groups of from 2-8 individuals, rarely more than a dozen individuals. *Diet*: Sedges and grasses, supplemented by herbs and shrubs. They are often found foraging together with Tibetan Gazelles, but do not compete for resources, because the latter animal prefers legumes. *Main Predators*: Wolf. They usually travel in small groups, although much larger herds were reported in the 19th century, when the overall population was higher. ♂ are often solitary, or travel in small groups of 2-3 individuals for much of the year, but gather together in small herds with the ♀ during the winter rut. Przewalski's Gazelles are generally quiet, but have been reported to make short bleating sounds. Combats among ♂ involve face-offs, horn clashes, and fighting with locked horns similar to the behavior described for Tibetan Gazelles. ♂ establish breeding "leks" in late autumn to display to ♀ and regularly scent mark them by urinating in a deep crouch of their hindquarters. ♀ may fight and chase, with an apparently dominant ♀ driving a subordinate ♀ from a group.

DISTRIBUTION *Native*: China. Formerly occurred in W China from Qinghai Lake through Gansu to Ningxia and Ordos. Now confined to six isolated subpopulations around Qinghai Lake: Bird Island on the W side; Shadao-Gahai and Hudong-Ketu on the E; Yuanzhe on the SE; near Gonghe across the mountains on the S side of the lake, and W of Tianjun, about 120 km NW of the lake.

HABITAT Semi-arid grassland steppe, stable sand dunes, and the desert-shrub ecotone between them.

STATUS Endangered. Estimated population of 250-500 in 2003. This species is under major threat of extinction.

PHOTO CREDITS *Yilun Qiao* (China).

Mongolian Gazelle
PROCAPRA GUTTUROSA

BL: 100-150 cm. SH: 54-84 cm. TL: 8-12 cm. W: 20-39 kg. HL: 25-40 cm (♂). The largest Asian gazelle, intermediate in characteristics between the Goitered Gazelle and the Tibetan and Przewalski's Gazelles. Light brown or buff coat with pinkish tones in the summer, longer and paler in winter. Darker upper coat gradually fading into the white underparts; sharply demarcated heart-shaped patch of white hair on the rump. Muzzle, chin, and jowls white. Bridge of the nose slightly darker than the body color. During the breeding season, males develop a swollen throat, which resembles the condition of goiter, and are also said to have a bulbous muzzle. Eyes small, protruding from the head. Only males have dark gray, lyre-shaped horns, which curl backward from the forehead and then run virtually parallel to the back, slightly ringed along most of their length. Horns diverge along their length, such that the tips are 6-10 times farther apart than the bases.

Procapra gutturosa gutturosa

Procapra gutturosa altai

OTHER NAMES Dzeren, White-tailed Gazelle. *French*: Gazelle à queue blanche, gazelle de Daourie. *German*: Mongolische Gazelle, Mongoleigazelle. *Spanish*: Gacela de Mongolia, zeren. *Russian*: Монгольский дзерен *(gutturosa),* Алтайский дзерен *(altai). Chinese*: Mongu-hiang-yang. *Mongolian*: Zeer, zagan zeer.

SUBSPECIES *P. g. altaica* (Altai Gazelle): from the Altai Mountains; slightly darker coat, broader skull, larger molars, and more widely spreading horns; otherwise, very similar. *P. g. gutturosa*: from the rest of the species range.

SIMILAR SPECIES It differs from typical gazelles by the absence of flank bands, pygal stripes, and the usual gazelle facial markings. Its range overlaps that of the Goitered Gazelle in the Gobi Desert and Inner Mongolia. It can be distinguished from the Goitered Gazelle by its larger size, different coloration, much shorter tail, and differently shaped horns. Normally the two species occupy different terrain; however, they are sometimes found together.

REPRODUCTION *Gestation*: 185 days. *Young per Birth*: 1-2, rarely 3. *Weaning*: 5 months. *Sexual Maturity*: 1.5-2 years. *Life Span*: 7 years. Mating season from November to January, with the resulting births occurring from May to July. Mating occurs within the herds, with harem behavior not evidenced. The young lie hidden for their first few days of life, joining their mothers after 4-8 days.

BEHAVIOR *Family Group*: Single-sex herds of 20-30 animals; during the winter they may be as large as 120. *Diet*: Grasses and herbs. *Main Predators*: Wolf. In autumn and winter, these gazelles are active during the daylight hours, grazing in the morning and late afternoon. Beds are excavated in the lee of bushes where the animals are sheltered from the wind. Very speedy, they can gallop up to 65 kmph, and sustain this speed for 12-15 km, leaping up to 2 m into the air at intervals. They are good swimmers and can negotiate large rivers. Large-scale migrations are undertaken by this species. Herds of 6,000-8,000 animals of both sexes gather in the spring, when the northerly movements begin, covering 200-300 km in a single day. The summer pastures are reached in June, at which point the sexes segregate themselves, and the ♀ prepare to give birth. Herds generally use several hundred km² as a summer home range, regularly shifting their position in the search for food. Even outside of the migration, they will cover in excess of 20 km per day. Normally silent, males may make a loud bellow during the rut.

DISTRIBUTION *Native*: China, Mongolia, Russian Federation. *Regionally Extinct*: Kazakhstan. Occurs in E Mongolia and adjacent areas of Russia and NE China. Smaller populations are still found in central and W Mongolia. There is a translocated population on Homin Tal steppe in Zavkhan Province of W-central Mongolia.

HABITAT Grassy steppe and subdeserts of Mongolia, N China, and S Russia.

STATUS Least Concern. Population estimates over the last 10 years have ranged from 400,000 to 2,700,000. Even though the species seems to be doing all right now, heavy hunting in combination with some unexpected event could put it in a vulnerable position.

PHOTO CREDITS *Yashnov V. I.* and *Vadim Kiriliuk,* Trans-Baikal (Russian Federation). *Lkhagvasuren Badamjav* (Mongolia). Head ♂: *Marcel Huijser*, Khentii (Mongolia).

Russian Saiga
SAIGA TATARICA

BL: 108-146 cm. SH: 60-80 cm. TL: 6-13 cm. W: 21-51 kg. HL: 20-38 cm. A rather odd-looking antelope, build rather robust, with legs relatively short and thin. Large head, with a remarkable nose. Coat composed of a woolly underlayer and a coarse set of bristly hairs. Summer coat is sparse, yellowish red in color. Winter coat is thicker and longer, pale, dull in color. Underparts, including the underside of the tail, always light. Dark brownish patch around the sacrum. Small mane on the underside of the neck. The most notable feature is the inflatable, humped nose, which has a wide range of mobility and a unique internal structure, with convoluted bones, and numerous hairs and mucos-secreting glands. Eyes appear to stand out on small, bony protrusions. Males have semi-translucent, wax-colored horns, almost vertical, slightly lyrate, ringed on their lower two-thirds.

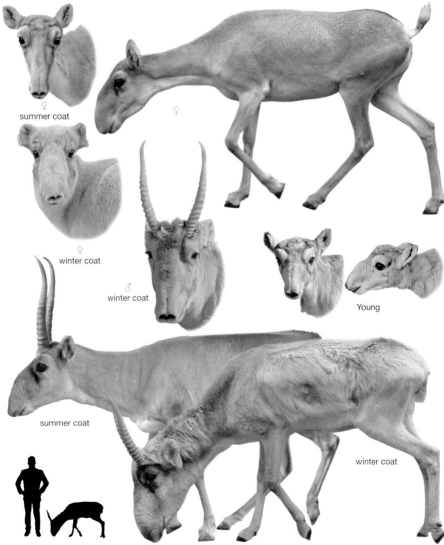

♀
summer coat

♀

♀
winter coat

♂
winter coat

Young

summer coat

winter coat

Saiga tatarica

OTHER NAMES Western Saiga. *French*: Saïga de Russie. *German*: Saiga. *Spanish*: Saiga de las estepas, saiga de Rusia. *Chinese*: Gao-bi-lin-yang. *Russian*: Западный сайгак, или русская сайга.

SUBSPECIES Monotypic. The name *S. tatarica* (Saiga) formerly included *S. tatarica* (Russian Saiga), and *S. mongolica* (Mongolian Saiga) as subspecies: these are all elevated to full species here.

SIMILAR SPECIES Mongolian Saiga is smaller, with shorter and thinner horns with weakly expressed rings, a less raised nasal opening, a sandy-gray summer coat, and a larger, more sharply bordered brown spot in the lumbar region.

REPRODUCTION *Gestation*: 140 days. *Young per Birth*: In the first year 1, subsequently 2 is normal. *Weaning:* 3-4 months. *Sexual Maturity:* 8 months (♀), 20 months (♂). *Life Span:* 6-10 years. Mating season is December-January. Births March-April, with all the ♀ in a herd dropping their calves within a few days. The young lie concealed and immobile for the first 3 days, moving around, bleating, and eating a bit of green food from the fourth day of life.

BEHAVIOR *Family Group*: Streams of over 200,000 animals in spring migrations, 30-40 in summer. *Diet*: Herbs, lichens, plants containing salt. *Main Predators*: Wolf, fox, birds of prey. Active mostly during the day, although it may rest at midday. A nomadic species, extremely good runner, up to 80 kmph. Populations undertake seasonal migrations, moving N in the spring to the summer grazing grounds, and returning S in the fall. Covering 80-120 km per day, marching with their heads low to the ground, with their specialized noses filtering out the stirred-up dust from the air. The rut begins in the wintering grounds, with ♂ becoming territorial and attempting to gather a harem of ♀. Fierce fights break out among rival ♂, which often result in death (up to 97% may not survive). At the end of April, surviving ♂ start off the seasonal spring migration, forming herds of 10-2,000 animals and setting out N. In the meantime, ♀ wander in huge herds to a suitable birthing ground, where they all drop their calves within about a week of each other. Just 8-10 days after the peak in births, the ♀ and new babies set off after the ♂, in congregations exceeding 100,000 animals. Once the migration is finished, the streams of animals break up and disperse in smaller herds. The large groups return in the autumn, and the Saiga move en masse back. A timid species, it can be easily startled, causing immediate flight, even in the huge migrating herds. Sense of hearing is poorly developed; senses of sight and smell are exceptional.

DISTRIBUTION *Native*: Kazakhstan, Russian Federation, Turkmenistan, Uzbekistan. *Regionally Extinct:* China, Moldova, Poland, Ukraine. Currently, there is one population in Russia (Kalmykia) and three in Kazakhstan, although in winter some animals reach Uzbekistan and even N Turkmenistan. A small captive breeding herd is kept at the Wuwei Endangered Animal Breeding Center, Gansu Province (China).

HABITAT Steppes and semi-desert regions.

STATUS Critically Endangered. Estimated population at 50,000 animals. In 2015 more than 120,000 Saiga died from a mysterious epizootic illness in Kazakhstan, representing more than a third of the total population.

PHOTO CREDITS ♂: *Jonas Livet*, Köln (Germany) and *Dmytro Pylypenko*. ♀: *Andrey Kotkin*, Moscow Zoo (Russia). Head: *Veranis*, *Igor Sphilenok* and *Andrey Kotkin*. Young: *terr-bo*. 171

Mongolian Saiga
SAIGA MONGOLICA

BL: 104-136 cm. SH: 57-79 cm. TL: 6-12 cm. W: 21-51 kg. HL: To 22 cm. Smaller in size than Russian Saiga. Summer coat sandy gray, dorsal region not darkened, large brown spot in the lumbar region, sharply bordered. Winter coat is thicker and longer and lighter in color. Underparts, including the underside of the tail, light. The most notable feature is the inflatable, humped nose, with the nasal opening less raised than in Russian Saiga. Eyes appear to stand out on small, bony protrusions. Less curved horns, relatively short, thin, with weakly expressed rings, only in males. Females are similar to males, without horns.

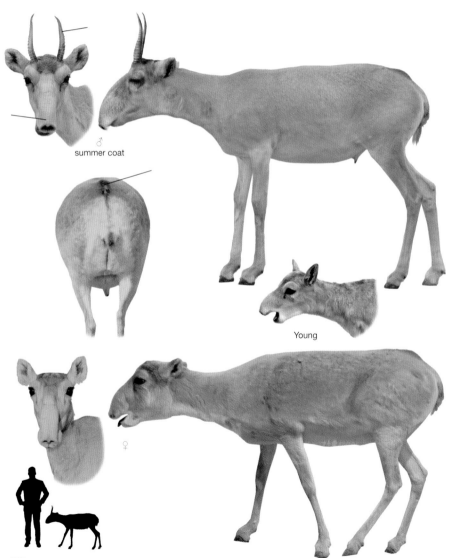

summer coat

♂

Young

♀

Saiga mongolica

OTHER NAMES *French:* Saïga de Mongolie. *German*: Mongolei-Saiga. *Spanish*: Saiga de Mongolia. *Chinese:* Gao-bi-lin-yang. *Mongolian*: Bökhön. *Russian*: Восточный сайгак, или монгольская сайга.

SUBSPECIES Monotypic. Formerly considered a subspecies of *S. tatarica* (Saiga).

SIMILAR SPECIES Russian Saiga is larger, with strongly ringed, thicker, and more curved horns, nasal opening more raised, and darker zones on the shoulders and loins.

REPRODUCTION *Gestation*: 130-140 days. *Young per Birth*: 2 in years of good environmental condition, 1 otherwise. *Weaning*: 3-4 months. *Sexual Maturity*: 7-8 months (♀), 19 months (♂). *Life Span:* 6-10 years. Rut takes place in December-January, and during this period the Saiga are mainly organized into small harem herds. Pregnant ♀ leave their groups and remain solitary during this period. ♀ usually give birth from mid-June to early July. Saiga is a typical hider species and the young remain secluded from the mother up to about 10 days of age.

BEHAVIOR *Family Group*: Groups of from 2 to 50 individuals, with much larger groups in winter. Small groups are more common in arid environments, where food is likely to be sparsely distributed. *Diet*: Herbs, lichens, plants containing salt. *Main Predators*: Fox, raptors, lynx. While the Russian Saiga undertakes large-scale migration tracking greenness of vegetation, the Mongolian Saiga does not show nomadic behavior with pronounced seasonal movements. There are no dominant animals except for during the rut period, where ♂ become leaders of a harem of 5-15 ♀. Ferocious fights between ♂ occur in the rut period, which occasionally result in the death of one of them. After the rut, adult ♂ occur in small groups of 5 to 10, whereas the rest of the animals may form larger groups. During the winter they are active throughout the day, while in summer they are mostly inactive, feeding at dawn and the evening. They scratch the earth with their hooves, sniff at the earth, and wait a short period before lying down to rest. It has been suggested that their locomotion is somewhat different from that of the Russian Saiga.

DISTRIBUTION *Native*: Mongolia. They now occupy only 20% of their former range and are restricted to four small regions in W Mongolia: the majority of the population occurs in and around Sharga Nature Reserve in the Mongol Altai Mountain Range; the remaining subpopulations are found in Mankhan Nature Reserve, Huisiin Gobi, and Hüren Tal in the Great Lakes Depression.

HABITAT Semi-desert and dry steppe depressions in W Mongolia.

STATUS Endangered. Estimated population of 5,000-7,000 individuals in 2010. One-quarter occurs within protected areas. Main threats include illegal hunting for the horns, used in traditional medicines, and competition with livestock due to overgrazing, disease transmission, and probable competition for pasture and water resources. Population appears stable, probably owing to enhanced protection and favorable climate.

PHOTO CREDITS Based on photographs from *Bayarbaatar Buuveibaatar, Chimeddorj Buyanaa*, WWF Mongolia, and *Buyanbat Thegmed* (Mongolia).

Beira
DORCATRAGUS MEGALOTIS

BL: 76-86 cm. SH: 50-76 cm. TL: 6-7.5 cm. W: 9-11.5 kg (♂), 9-13 kg (♀). HL: 7.5-10 cm (♂). A small long-legged and long-necked antelope, with enormous ears. Coarse coat reddish gray on top, underparts white. Dark band extends along each side from elbow to rear leg. Fawn-colored legs, long and slender. Yellowish-red head, accentuated with black eyelids and white rings around the eyes. Ears large and prominent, growing 15 cm long and 7.5 cm wide; white inside of ears covered with a layer of white hair, interrupted by dark bare radial stripes. Bushy and short tail. Horns, only in males, are straight spikes which rise vertically from near the sides of the ear. No crest between the horns. Hooves very short, with a broad and thick internal pad. Female similar to male, but larger, without horns.

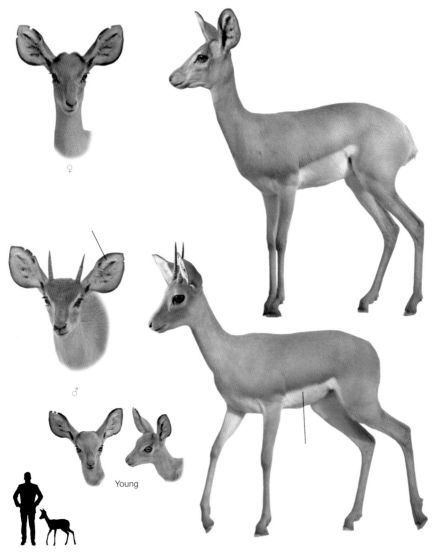

♀

♂

Young

Dorcatragus megalotis

OTHER NAMES Beira Antelope. *French*: Beira. *German*: Beira. *Spanish*: Beira. *Russian*: Бейра. *Amharic*: Beira. *Somali*: Baira.

SUBSPECIES Monotypic.

REPRODUCTION *Gestation*: 180 days. *Young per Birth*: 1. Births have only been recorded in April, at the height of the rains, but may be capable of breeding in other periods of the year. Beira may breed twice a year. Neonates are hidden.

BEHAVIOR *Family Group*: Pairs or small parties with a single ♂. Larger groups are probably meetings between families. *Diet:* Mainly leaves of bushes, also grasses. *Main Predators:* Lion and leopard where existent, caracal, hyena, jackal. Like most antelope, Beira are active mostly in the morning and evening, while at midday they rest. Beira are exceptionally wary, and are alerted to the slightest disturbance by their large ears. When startled they move off with great speed across the loose stones, bounding from rock to rock in a goat-like fashion on steeper, more secure territory. Beira are adapted to a dry habitat, obtaining all needed water from their food supply. Beira have no face glands, so they mark territories by urination-defecation sites; the ♀ arrives at the site and squats to urinate and defecate, then the ♂ sniffs the ground, scrapes vigorously with his forelegs, squats to urinate, then squats again to defecate. ♂ of different groups are intolerant and chase each other, whereas ♀ are not antagonistic toward each other. Beira live in non-overlapping territories, with a surface area averaging 0.7 km², composed of a single adult ♂, and from 1 to 3 adult ♀. Collective sequences of linked urination and defecation are frequent. Members of neighboring units rarely meet and interact, chasing behavior occurring mainly between adult ♂.

DISTRIBUTION *Native*: Ethiopia, Somalia, Djibouti. Endemic to NE Africa. Most of the distribution area lies in N Somalia, from the Nogaal Valley N (Asse hills-Lahan Sheik, Garoowe area, Wagar, Buuraha, and Golis mountains, Araweina, Ali Haidh, and Guban region). The area of distribution in Djibouti is about 250 km² and located in the mountainous Ali Sabieh - Arrey - Assamo region. In Ethiopia, the species is known from the Marmar Mountains along the border with NW Somalia.

HABITAT Rocky or stony hillsides, rarely steep slopes, where the dominant vegetation is a woody steppe of mixed acacia scrub, at altitudes up to 2,000 m.

STATUS Vulnerable. Estimated population in 1999 was 7,000.

PHOTO CREDITS *Jonas Livet*, Al Wabra Wildlife Preservation, Al Shahaniah (Qatar).

Southern Oribi
OUREBIA OUREBI

BL: 97-115 cm (♂), 89-105 (♀). SH: 51-64 cm. TL: 7.5 cm. W: 10-17 kg (♂), 8-17 kg (♀). HL: 8-18 cm (♂). Small antelope with a long, slender neck and legs. Coat color is bright sandy rufous, more rufous than in other subspecies, without conspicuous speckling, with white underparts. Crown mark small but conspicuous. Tail is black. Horns fairly long. Hindquarters are slightly higher than forequarters. Ears are long and oval. Males have large preorbital glands, situated close to the inner corners of the eyes, that produce a copious black secretion. Both sexes have glands on the carpus and tarsus, covered by a brush of long hair, and on forefeet and hind feet. There is a bare patch below the ear, as in Reedbucks. Only males have short, straight horns, which are ringed at the base. Only subspecies in which males are larger than females.

Ourebia ourebi

OTHER NAMES South African Oribi. *French*: Ourébi du Cap. *German*: Südliches Oribi. *Spanish*: Oribi meridional. *Russian*: Южный ориби. *Afrikaans*: Oorbietjie. *Swahili*: Taya. *Ndebele*: Insinza. *Setswana*: Phuduhudu-kgamane. *Zulu*: Iliwula. *Wolof*: Biabare.

SUBSPECIES Monotypic. The name *O. ourebi* (Oribi) formerly included *O. quadriscopa* (Western Oribi), *O. montana* (Sudan Oribi), *O. hastata* (Central Oribi), and *O. ourebi* (Southern Oribi) as subspecies: these are all elevated to full species here.

SIMILAR SPECIES Gray Duiker may be distinguished by color, long head, short neck, and presence of a crest between the horns. Steenbok and Grysbok are more lightly built, have broader ears, a shorter tail, and no bare patch below the ear. Reedbuck is larger and heavier, and has quite different horns.

REPRODUCTION *Gestation Period*: 192-210 days. *Young per Birth*: 1. *Weaning*: 4-5 months. *Sexual Maturity*: 10-14 months. *Life Span*: 8-14 years. It exhibits an extended breeding season. However it usually has distinct peaks that coincide with the rainy season: in Zimbabwe this occurs between August and November, and in South Africa, in November and December.

BEHAVIOR *Family Group*: ♂ and ♀ pairs, often with 1 young present; multiple ♀, or multiple ♂ with multiple ♀, have also been observed. *Diet*: A selective grazer, relies on fresh green grasses but feeds also on forbs, legumes, and tree foliage when fresh grass is unavailable; water independent. *Main Predators*: Lion, leopard, caracal, hyena, African wild dog, jackal, crocodile, python. ♂ are extremely territorial and will defend their territories against other ♂; yearling ♂ are excluded from groups. Territories appear to be seasonal in South Africa. They may abandon territoriality entirely in the driest, coolest, or least productive parts of the range. ♂ defend their territories by means of object horning, and chasing opponents; dominant ♂ may also maintain an erect posture with their head raised and neck nearly vertical. ♂ are more alert than ♀. While this territory is maintained and advertised by both sexes through olfactory markings, the ♂ is the more active marker. Dung middens are also utilized for territorial marking. Home range varies between 28 and 60 ha. When a predator is sighted, they sink to the ground and hide, lying undetected prone with their head folded; they then flush from cover at the last moment and run.

DISTRIBUTION *Native*: Namibia, South Africa, Swaziland, Zimbabwe. Patchy distribution S of the Zambezi River; E South Africa from the Eastern Cape, parts of KwaZulu-Natal and the Free State to the Limpopo River, and W via W Zimbabwe to E Namibia.

HABITAT Open grasslands and wooded grasslands. They favor moist grassland on flat to gently undulating terrain with actively growing short grass (for food) adjacent to long grass, which is required to provide cover from the elements and predators. Oribi seldom use agricultural lands or pastures, as do common Reedbuck.

STATUS Least Concern. Vulnerable in the South African Red Data Book. Eliminated from some parts of the range by agriculture and excessive hunting.

PHOTO CREDITS ♂: *Dries and Marilize de Wet* (www.dewetswild. com), Chelmsford Nature Reserve, KwaZulu-Natal Province (South Africa). ♀: *Ann and Steve Toon,* Mlilwane Nature Reserve (Swaziland).

Sudan Oribi
OUREBIA MONTANA

BL: 96-97 cm. SH: 50-67 cm. TL: 8-10 cm. W: 11-17 kg (♂), 8-20 kg (♀). HL: 8-18 cm (♂). Small antelope with a long, slender neck and legs. Coat color from dark clay to orange buff, speckled, with white underparts. Dark crown mark may be absent. Tail darker but not usually black, unlike in other subspecies. Hindquarters are slightly higher than forequarters. Ears are long and oval. Males have large preorbital glands, situated close to the inner corners of the eyes, that produce a copious black secretion. There is a bare patch below the ear, as in Reedbucks. Only males have short, straight horns, which are ringed at the base. Females are slightly larger than males.

♀

Young

♂

Ourebia montana

OTHER NAMES Uganda Oribi. *French*: Ourébi du Nil. *German*: Sudan-Oribi. *Spanish*: Oribi oriental. *Russian*: Восточноафриканский ориби. *Afrikaans*: Oorbietjie. *Swahili*: Taya. *Ndebele*: Insinza. *Setswana*: Phuduhudu-kgamane. *Arabic*: Um Digdig. *Zulu*: Iliwula.

SUBSPECIES Monotypic. Formerly considered a subspecies of *O. ourebi* (Oribi). Includes *aquatoria* (N Uganda, S Sudan), *dorcas* (Chad and Central African Republic), *gallarum* (central Ethiopia), *goslingi* (N Congo), *masakensis* (S Uganda, N Rwanda, NW Tanzania), *montana* (SE Sudan, W Ethiopia, extreme NW Kenya), *pitmani* (Ankole), and *ugandae* (Uganda Oribi, from Uganda, Gondokoro South Sudan), with *montana* having preference.

SIMILAR SPECIES Gray Duiker may be distinguished by color, long head, short neck, and presence of a crest between the horns. Steenbok and Grysbok are more lightly built, have broader ears, a shorter tail, and no bare patch below the ear. Reedbuck is larger and heavier, and has quite different horns. Sudan Oribi is considerably larger than the Western Oribi, but horns are not longer, and the tail is usually not black.

REPRODUCTION *Gestation Period*: 180-210 days. *Young per Birth*: 1. *Weaning*: 4-5 months. *Sexual Maturity*: 10-14 months. *Life Span*: 8-14 years. Birth peak in May-July. During the breeding season, the ♂ will mate with all the ♀ who share his territory. Usually only 1-2 ♀ are present in each territory. For the first 8-10 weeks the ♀ hides her young in thick grass, where it will lie motionless if approached. The mother returns periodically to suckle her offspring.

BEHAVIOR *Family Group:* Small monogamous groups of a ♂ with 1-4 ♀, but commonly these family groups join into small loose aggregations. *Diet:* Primarily a grazer, occasionally browses on forbs; largely independent of water. *Main Predators:* Lion, leopard, caracal, hyena, African wild dog, jackal, crocodile, python. Groups are territorial, and actively defend their territories of 25-100 ha in size. Territorial ♂ spend most of the time scent marking by depositing preorbital secretion along the border, as well as inside the territory. ♂ who approach each other assume an erect posture with neck arched forward, and may horn the ground, and the other male usually flees. ♀, but not ♂, fight by head butting. Territorial ♂ evict young ♂ from their family group, whereas young ♀ remain longer until they can form their own pair bonds. Oribi display a distinctive "stotting" action when alarmed, which entails vertical leaps with straight legs. Family members communicate with a soft whistling sound, and express alarm with a loud whistle.

DISTRIBUTION *Native:* Central African Republic, Chad, Ethiopia, Kenya, Nigeria, Rwanda, Sudan, Tanzania, Uganda. Found from N Nigeria, E into Ethiopia, and S into Uganda and Rwanda.

HABITAT Savanna woodlands, floodplains, and other open grasslands. They reach their highest density on floodplains and moist tropical grasslands, especially in association with large grazers.

STATUS Least Concern.

PHOTO CREDITS ♂: *David Beadle*, Murchison Falls NP (Uganda). ♀: *Ludwig Siege,* Senkele (Ethiopia). Head ♂: *Lee Boddie*, Murchison Falls NP (Uganda). Head ♀ and young: *J. A. Kok,* Murchison Falls NP (Uganda).

Central Oribi
OUREBIA HASTATA

BL: 92-140 cm. SH: 50-67 cm. TL: 6.5-10.5 cm. W: 11-17 kg (♂), 8-20 kg (♀). HL: 8-18 cm (♂).
Small antelope with a long, slender neck and legs. Coat is rich yellow ocher in color, speckled, with white underparts. Tail is usually black, even on the underside. Face with darker patches on forehead and crown, a dark bare patch below the ear, white markings on either side of the nostrils, and white crescent-shaped bands above eyes. Preorbital glands open into a small depression in front of each eye, slightly larger in males. Ears are long and oval. Hindquarters slightly higher than forequarters. Only males have short, straight horns, which are ringed at the base. Females are larger than males.

Young

♀

♂

Ourebia hastata

OTHER NAMES Peters's Oribi. *French:* Ourébi du Mozambique. *German:* Serengeti-Oribi. *Spanish:* Oribí central. *Russian:* Центральноафриканский ориби. *Afrikaans:* Oorbietjie. *Swahili:* Taya. *Ndebele:* Insinza. *Setswana:* Phuduhudu-kgamane. *Arabic:* Um Digdig. *Zulu:* Iliwula. *Wolof:* Biabare.

SUBSPECIES Monotypic. Formerly considered a subspecies of *O. ourebi* (Oribi). Includes *haggardi* (Haggard's Oribi), *hastata,* and *rutila* (Angolan Oribi), with *hastata* having priority.

SIMILAR SPECIES Haggard's Oribi is much lighter in color, lacking the darker patches on forehead and crown, with thicker horns deeply ringed at the base. Sudan Oribi is similar, with smaller horns, tail usually not black, and dark crown may be absent. Southern Oribi is the only subspecies in which ♂ are larger than ♀, color more rufous, without conspicuous speckling, crown small but conspicuous, tail black, horns fairly long. Western Oribi is speckled gray fawn to deep orange; only ♀ have a small dark crown mark, tail black. Steenbok is smaller and does not have a black patch behind the ear. Reedbuck is larger and all species have curved horns.

REPRODUCTION *Gestation Period:* 180-210 days. *Young per Birth:* 1. *Weaning:* 4-5 months. *Sexual Maturity:* 10 months (♀), 14 months (♂). *Life Span:* 8-14 years. Birth peaks are in August-November in Zambia. For the first 8-10 weeks the ♀ Oribi hides her young in thick grass, where it will lie motionless if approached. The mother returns periodically to suckle her offspring.

BEHAVIOR *Family Group:* Monogamous pairs, or groups of 1 or 2 ♂ with 2 or more ♀. Occasionally, family groups up to a dozen, but these aggregations break up when disturbed. *Diet:* Grass, mainly fresh young grass; also leaves, buds, twigs, bark, fruits, seeds, and seedpods. *Main Predators:* Lion, leopard, caracal, hyena, African wild dog, jackal, crocodile, python. There are activity peaks early and late in the day, with rest during the heat of the day. Territorial, with territory sizes of 30 ha, marked intensely by ♂ along borders they share with other territorial ♂, and little marking along the unshared borders. Marking is done with preorbital glands, dung, and urine.

DISTRIBUTION *Native:* Angola, Botswana, Kenya, Mozambique, Namibia, Somalia, Tanzania, Zambia, Zimbabwe. Found in SW Somalia and coastal Kenya (Haggard's Oribi), SW Kenya via the Serengeti ecosystem S to N Mozambique and W to Angola, although there are gaps in the distribution in most of Tanzania and in N Zambia.

HABITAT Woodlands, with rocky outcrops. They move close to rocks in the dry season and into long grass areas in the wet season. They avoid open grasslands.

STATUS Least Concern. Estimated population of fewer than 10,000 individuals, and the population is declining.

PHOTO CREDITS ♂: *Rudy Algera*, Gorongosa (Mozambique). ♀: *Jason Duplessis, Fish Eagle Safaris Inc.* Head ♀: *Bill Higham*, Gorongosa (Mozambique). Head ♂: *Joaquim Muchaxo*, Gorongosa (Mozambique). Young: *Leon Marais*, Gorongosa (Mozambique).

Western Oribi
OUREBIA QUADRISCOPA

BL: 92-140 cm. SH: 50-67 cm. TL: 6-10.5 cm. W: 11-17 kg (♂), 8-20 kg (♀). HL: 10 cm (♂). Small antelope with a long, slender neck and legs, short tail, a narrow-base rhinarium, and large ears. Hindquarters slightly higher than forequarters. Coat color quite distinct from that of other subspecies, from a speckled gray fawn to deep orange. White underparts. Only females have a small dark crown mark. Tail is black. Males have large preorbital glands, situated close to the inner corners of the eyes, that produce a copious black secretion. Both sexes have glands on the carpus and tarsus, covered by a brush of long hair, and on forefeet and hind feet. Bare patch below the ear. Only males have short, straight horns, which are ringed at the base. Females are slightly larger than males.

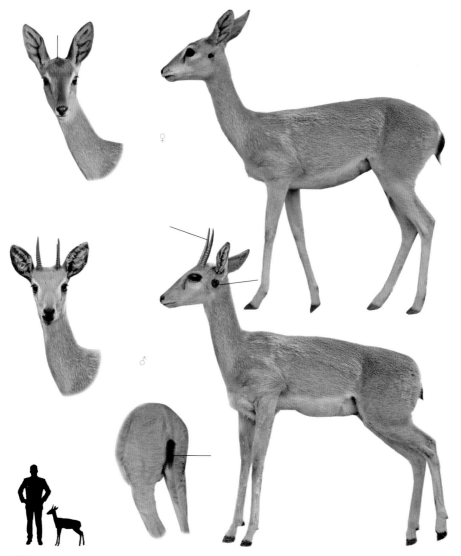

♀

♂

Ourebia quadriscopa

OTHER NAMES *French*: Ourébi occidental. *German*: Senegal-Oribi. *Spanish*: Oribi occidental. *Russian*: Западноафриканский ориби.

SUBSPECIES Monotypic. Formerly considered a subspecies of *O. ourebi* (Oribi). As many as 13 subspecies of Oribi have been proposed, to account for the considerable variation in body size and coloration across the species' range. Animals in E Africa appear larger and darker than W, N, and S conspecifics, but this trend, and the validity of many proposed subspecies distinctions, have not been tested.

SIMILAR SPECIES Sudan Oribi is larger, and the tail is not black.

REPRODUCTION *Gestation Period*: 180-210 days. *Young per Birth*: 1. *Weaning*: 4-5 months. *Sexual Maturity*: 10-14 months. *Life Span*: 8-14 years. During the breeding season, August-December, the ♂ will mate with all the ♀ who share his territory. Usually only 1-2 ♀ are present in each territory. For the first 8-10 weeks the ♀ Oribi hides her young in thick grass, where it will lie motionless if approached. The mother returns periodically to suckle her offspring.

BEHAVIOR *Family Group:* Small monogamous groups of a ♂ with 2 ♀. *Diet*: Primarily a grazer, occasionally browses on forbs. *Main Predators:* Lion, leopard, caracal, hyena, African wild dog, jackal, crocodile, python. Groups are territorial, and actively defend their territories of 25-100 ha in size. Territorial ♂ evict young ♂ from their family group, whereas young ♀ remain longer until they can form their own pair bonds. Since it is important to maintain social bonds, a family regularly performs a dunging ceremony, although dung middens are not maintained. Oribi display a distinctive "stotting" action when alarmed, which entails vertical leaps with straight legs.

DISTRIBUTION *Native*: Benin, Burkina Faso, Ghana, Guinea, Ivory Coast, Mali, Niger, Nigeria, Senegal, Togo. The exact E boundary is not known.

HABITAT Savanna woodlands, floodplains, and other open grasslands. They reach their highest density on floodplains and moist tropical grasslands, especially in association with large grazers.

STATUS Least Concern.

PHOTO CREDITS Based on photos from Konkombouri Reserve (Burkina Faso) and Pendjari (Benin).

Cape Grysbok
RAPHICERUS MELANOTIS

BL: 70-75 cm. SH: 54-56 cm. TL: 4-8 cm. W: 8-13 kg. HL: 6-8 cm (♂). A small, rather stout antelope with its rump a little higher than its shoulders. Coat is reddish brown, flecked with white hairs that give it a grizzled appearance. Down the neck and flanks, the white hairs are less numerous and the underparts are a much lighter shade of brown. There is a white patch on the throat. Small lateral hooves are present. Large, pointed ears are positioned prominently on the black-tufted crown. There are large preorbital glands that secrete a black fluid. The tail is almost invisible. Males have short, sharp, straight, needle-like horns, which are smooth. Males and females are the same size.

Raphicerus melanotis

OTHER NAMES Southern Grysbok, Grys Steenbok. *French*: Raphicère du Cap. *German*: Kap-Greisbock. *Spanish*: Grysbok de El Cabo, raficero de El Cabo. *Russian*: Капский грисбок. *Afrikaans*: Kaapse grysbok. *Chibisa*: Katili. *Swahili*: Inhlengana. *Sotho*: Gsamempa. *Zulu*: Inxamazane eci sh'uku-fama negadu.

SUBSPECIES Monotypic.

SIMILAR SPECIES Sharpe's Grysbok, formerly considered as a subspecies of Cape Grysbok, is smaller, has white underparts, and lacks false hooves. Steenbok is somewhat larger. Oribi is larger and has a different color, a longer tail with a black tuft, smaller oval-shaped ears, and a bare patch below the ear.

REPRODUCTION *Gestation*: 180-192 days. *Young per Birth:* 1-2. *Weaning:* 3 months. *Sexual Maturity*: 6-7 months (♀), 9 months (♂). *Life Span*: probably 10-12 years. Although breeding can take place at any time during the year, most births take place between September and December. Under good conditions a sexually mature ♀ will give birth to 2 lambs a year. Along with mating, this is the only other time that Cape Grysbok are not solitary.

BEHAVIOR *Family Group*: Solitary; in pairs during the mating season. *Diet:* Predominantly browser, although it will also graze on succulent grass and enter into plantations to feed on young shoots and fruit; it has limited water requirements. *Main Predators*: Leopard, caracal, crowned eagle, python. Mainly nocturnal and relies its acute senses of smell, hearing, and touch to navigate the dense bush safely and efficiently at night. During the day it rests, but is sometimes active in the early morning or late afternoon, if there is little disturbance. Normally solitary, this species is entirely dependent on its own cunning and is an expert in avoiding detection and evading danger. When under perceived threat, rather than running, it hides motionless in the vegetation and will not flee until the last moment. If chased, it will bolt in an erratic zigzag run that is extremely tricky for a pursuer to follow. ♂ hold territories of 1.5-4.8 ha, ♀ have home ranges of 1 ha. ♂ will mark out well-defined territories in several ways including urinating and defecating in dung piles, scraping the dung with their hooves, and marking stalks and grass stems with a scent produced by preorbital glands. Furthermore, rival ♂ will fiercely defend a territory by actively fighting each other with their horns.

DISTRIBUTION *Native*: South Africa. Endemic to South Africa, where largely confined to the Cape Floristic Region. It remains widespread and locally common within its historical range in the Western Cape and Eastern Cape provinces.

HABITAT Thickets, shrublands, and the fynbos biome. Dense cover is an important habitat requirement. Their presence in the high-altitude grasslands of the NE Cape is conditional on the proximity of forest fragments and bush clumps, although they may also use long grass for cover. They also enter developed areas such as vineyards and agricultural areas.

STATUS Least Concern. Estimated population of 250,000 in the Cape Floristic Region (2003).

PHOTO CREDITS *Neal Cooper*, near Cape Town (South Africa) and *Johannes Pfleiderer*, Tygerberg Zoo (South Africa).

Sharpe's Grysbok
RAPHICERUS SHARPEI

BL: 65-75 cm. SH: 45-60 cm. TL: 4-8 cm. W: 6.5-11 kg. HL: 3-4.5 cm (♂). A small antelope, with its rump somewhat higher than its shoulders. Body color rufous brown, flecked with distinctive speckles of white giving the animal a grizzled appearance, especially along the flanks. Sides of the face, forehead, upper parts of the muzzle, and outer parts of the limbs are yellowish brown. Belly, underside of the neck, and inside of the legs and ears are white. Whitish ring around the eyes extends as a line down the sides of the muzzle to the rhinarium. Ears large. Tail very short, rufous brown on the upper side, white on the underside. Lateral hooves absent. Horns very short, conical, rising vertically from forehead. Females are similar to or slightly larger than males, with no horns.

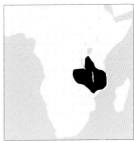

Raphicerus sharpei

OTHER NAMES Northern Grysbok. *French:* Raphicère de Sharpe. *German*: Sharpe-Greisbock, Nördliches Greisbökchen. *Spanish*: Raficero de Sharpe. *Russian*: Грисбок Шарпе. *Shona*: Himba. *Swahili*: Dondoro.

SUBSPECIES Monotypic. The name *R. sharpei* formerly included *R. sharpei* (Sharpe's Grysbok), and *R. colonicus* (Limpopo Grysbok) as subspecies: these are all elevated to full species here.

SIMILAR SPECIES Cape Grysbok has false hooves and longer horns and is slightly larger, with underparts less white. Limpopo Grysbok is somewhat larger, overall color is richer and darker, with legs lighter, more reddish underparts, including the throat, more buff. Steenbok is less stocky, with proportionally longer legs and larger ears, and its fur has no whitish flecks and is slightly shorter. Bush Duiker is larger, has a black stripe down the face, and a longer tail. Natal Duiker has red, rather than white, underparts, and has a longer tail. Oribi is considerably larger, with a distinctive black patch beneath the ears.

REPRODUCTION *Gestation*: 168-210 days. *Young per Birth*: 1-2. *Weaning*: 3 months. *Sexual Maturity*: 6-19 months. *Life Span*: 10-12 years. Breeding throughout the year, but most births take place at the beginning of the rains.

BEHAVIOR *Family Group*: Solitary, except during the mating season. *Diet*: Leaves and buds, but also fruits, seeds, and grass. Seems to require water regularly. *Main Predators*: Lion, cheetah, brown hyena, spotted hyena, side-striped jackal, black-backed jackal, caracal, birds of prey. They are mostly nocturnal, but are sometimes active during the early morning and late afternoon, particularly in overcast conditions. ♂ and ♀ form monogamous pairs that defend a territory, but they are generally seen alone, except during the mating season. Shy and secretive, they are seldom seen even where common. When disturbed, they run off low to the ground and dart into a bush, disappearing into the thick vegetation.

DISTRIBUTION *Native*: DR Congo, Malawi, Mozambique, Tanzania, Zambia. Found in Zambia (except W of the Zambezi), E of the Luangwa River, Malawi, NW Mozambique, and SW Tanzania. The precise limits of distribution with the Limpopo Grysbok are not very clear.

HABITAT Thick scrub and grass up to 0.5 m high, and areas of miombo woodland with good ground cover. Occasionally on cultivated land.

STATUS Least Concern. It is common and widespread, and there are no major threats that might result in a significant population decline. Hunting with dogs and snares outside protected areas poses a threat.

PHOTO CREDITS ♂: Based on photos from Gonarezhou NP and South Luangwa NP (Zambia). ♀: *Tim Randall* and *Thomas Retterath*, South Luangwa NP (Zambia). Heads: *Edward Selfe*, South Luangwa NP (Zambia).

Limpopo Grysbok
RAPHICERUS COLONICUS

BL: 71-80 cm. SH: 45-60 cm. TL: 4.5-7 cm. W: 6.4-9 kg. HL: 5 cm (♂). Similar to Sharpe's Grysbok, but larger, with a rufous to reddish-brown color, richer and darker. Numerous white hairs interspersed among the browner ones. Legs are paler, more reddish in tone. Underparts and throat are more buff, with the boundary line less distinct on the sides of the belly. Short dark band on top of the muzzle extends from the rhinarium to the front of the eyes. Sides of the face, outer parts of limbs, forehead, and upper parts of muzzle are yellowish brown, lacking the white grizzling. Ears large, with buffy-white hair inside, dark on the outside. Tail very short. Lateral hooves absent. Horns very short, conical, rising vertically from forehead, similar in size to those of Sharpe's Grysbok. Females are similar to or slightly larger than males, with no horns.

♀

♂

♂

Juvenile

Raphicerus colonicus

OTHER NAMES South African Grysbok. *French*: Raphicère du Limpopo. *German*: Natal-Greisböckchen. *Spanish*: Raficero de Sharpe meridional. *Russian*: Грисбок Лимпопо. *Afrikaans*: Sharpe se grysbok, tropiese grysbok. *Ndebel*: Isanempa. *Setswana*: Phuduhudu. *Shona*: Himba. *Swati*: Mawumbane. *Xitsonga*: Pitsipitsi.

SUBSPECIES Monotypic. Formerly considered a subspecies of *R. sharpei* (Sharpe's Grysbok).

SIMILAR SPECIES Cape Grysbok has false hooves and longer horns and is slightly larger, with underparts less white. Steenbok has slightly shorter fur with no white flecks.

REPRODUCTION *Gestation*: 168-210 days. *Young per Birth*: 1-2. *Weaning*: 3 months. *Sexual Maturity*: 6-19 months. *Life Span*: 10-12 years. Breeding throughout the year, but most births take place between November and December, coinciding with the start of the spring rains in S Africa.

BEHAVIOR *Family Group*: Solitary, except during the mating season. *Diet:* Leaves, roots, tubers, wood, bark, stems, fruit. Seems to require water regularly. *Main Predators:* Lion, cheetah, brown hyena, spotted hyena, side-striped jackal, black-backed jackal, caracal, birds of prey. They are secretive animals, usually spending most of the day lying in thick cover. Generally nocturnal and solitary, although adult pairs or a ♀ with offspring may be seen throughout the year. Territorial, usually defending territories alone, although pairs may defend a single territory together. The ♂ territorial fighting is less ritualistic than in most antelopes, simply involving a straight, forward stride into battle, a lowering to the knees, and stabbing or meeting of the short horns. When frightened by a predator, they rarely run, instead lying flat with an outstretched head and neck in thick undercover until a predator may be nearly on top of them. In the chance that they may have to run, such fleeing takes place with a deliberate crouch and the animal stays low to the ground. They are known to use old burrows, especially those of aardvarks, when in search of protection from predators. They possess preputial, eye, and facial glands that are used in scent-based communication. They also use tactile communication in fighting and mating, as well as between mothers and their offspring.

DISTRIBUTION *Native*: Botswana, Mozambique, Namibia, South Africa, Swaziland, Zimbabwe. Found in N and E Transvaal in South Africa, Zimbabwe, S Mozambique (S of the Zambezi River), NE Namibia (Caprivi Strip), extreme N Botswana (Chobe and Okavango regions), and E Swaziland.

HABITAT A variety of habitats, most often in rocky, hilly country. They seem to avoid large areas of grass more than 50 cm tall, and appear to require some shrub thickets and areas with undercover, as are often found in secondary-growth forest.

STATUS Least Concern. Estimated total population of 95,000 for both Limpopo and Sharpe's Grysbok.

PHOTO CREDITS ♂: *Frank Oldham*, Singita Reserve (South Africa). ♀: *Nick Dean*, Kruger NP (South Africa). Head ♂: *Johann du Preez*, Kruger NP (South Africa). Head ♀: *Bernard Dupont*, Kruger NP (South Africa). Juvenile: *Thomas Kalcher*, Kruger NP (South Africa).

South African Steenbok

RAPHICERUS CAMPESTRIS CAMPESTRIS

BL: 70-95 cm. SH: 49 cm (♂), 51 cm (♀). TL: 5-10 cm. W: 9-13 kg (♂), 11-13 kg (♀). HL: 7-19 cm (♂). A small antelope, slim and slender, with a short, conical head, and long legs. Smaller than other subspecies. Coat is orange rufous. Broad white area on the underparts, not extending down the inside of the limbs. White patch on the throat less extensive than in other subspecies. Cheek and legs are ochraceous tawny. Light-colored eye ring. Slender black triangle starts at the nose and tapers upward. Dark brown horseshoe-like patch on the crown. Ears large. Tail short, colored above like the back, white below. Lateral hooves present. Horns, found only in males, are straight, sharp, and very upright. Female similar to male, sometimes heavier, without horns.

♀

♂

♂ Juvenile

*Raphicerus campestris
campestris*

OTHER NAMES Cape Steinbok, Steenbuck, Steinbuck. *French*: Steenbok de l'Ouest. *German*: Südafrikanisches Steinböckchen. *Spanish*: Raficero de Sudáfrica. *Russian*: Восточный южноафриканский стенбок. *Afrikaans*: Vlakbok. *Swahili*: Isha, dondor. *Zulu*: Iqhina. *Xhosa*: Itshabanqa. *Sepedi*: Pudubudu. *Sesotho*: Thiane. *Swati*: Lingcina.

SUBSPECIES Considered as a subspecies of *R. campestris* (Steenbok): *R. c. campestris* (South African Steenbok), *R. c. fulvorubescens* (Albany Steenbok), *R. c. natalensis* (Natal Steenbok), *R. c. capricornis* (Short-horned Steenbok), *R. c. neumanni* (East African Steenbok), *R. c. steinhardti* (Kalahari Steenbok). Includes *pediotragus* (Western Cape Province, South Africa). The described subspecies are not strongly distinct and appear to overlap in all features.

SIMILAR SPECIES *R. c. fulvorubescens* is rather lighter in color, amber brown, and white on the throat extends almost to the chin. *R. c. natalensis* has longer horns. *R. c. capricornis* is amber brown in color, with face much lighter. Common Duiker is similar in size and color, but more grizzled, grayer in appearance; face usually marked by a black blaze which runs from the top of the head right down to the nose; smaller, more slender ears. Oribi are similar in color and form, but are larger and more slender; there is a distinctive black patch at the base of the ear, and no black on the front of the face.

REPRODUCTION *Gestation*: 170 days. *Young per Birth*: 1. *Weaning*: 3 months. *Sexual Maturity*: 6-7 months (♀), 9 months (♂). *Life Span*: 12 years. Breeding mainly in summer, but may take place year-round. Lambs are dropped in the shelter of tall grass, shrubs or among rocks, and concealed there while the mother feeds nearby.

BEHAVIOR *Family Group*: Solitary, although a stable pair (which meets up solely for breeding) shares one territory. *Diet*: Selective grazers and browsers; leaves and fine stems of forbs and woody plants, but also berries, fruit, and pods; dig for tubers and bulbs; fairly independent of water and obtain most of their moisture requirements from the food they eat. *Main Predators*: Larger eagles, jackal, caracal, serval, and other predators. They are most active during the day, especially in the cool of early mornings and late afternoons. They are fast runners and zigzag when taking flight. They enjoy resting up in stands of dense grass and under low bush. They are also known to take refuge underground in old aardvark holes. Steenbok have the unusual habit of scratching sand over their scat. When alarmed, they dash away for a short distance. If not pursued, they will stop and look back to try to identify the cause of the disturbance. They settle in territories which they will defend against other Steenbok.

DISTRIBUTION *Native*: South Africa. Found in S and W Cape Province (South Africa).

HABITAT Bushveld savanna and grassveld with adjacent bush and shrub; they do not generally occur in thick forests or in rocky mountains.

STATUS Least Concern.

PHOTO CREDITS ♂: *Sergey Chichagov*, Los Angeles Zoo (USA). ♀: *Sailer Schnizler*, Western Cape (South Africa). Head ♀: *Nathan Rupert*, San Diego Zoo (USA). Juvenile: *Greg Goebel*, San Diego Zoo (USA).

Short-horned Steenbok

RAPHICERUS CAMPESTRIS CAPRICORNIS

BL: 70-95 cm. SH: 45-60 cm. TL: 5-10 cm. W: 9-16 kg. HL: 13 cm (♂). A small antelope, slim and slender, with a short, conical head, and long legs. General color is amber brown, with face much lighter. White extends continuously from the throat to the chin, and more extensively elsewhere below. Light-colored eye ring. Conspicuous bare rhinarium. Small preorbital glands, larger in males. Ears are notably large. Tail very short, a mere stump. Lateral hooves present. Horns, found only in males, are straight, sharp, and very upright, usually shorter than in other subspecies. Female similar to male, sometimes heavier, without horns.

Juvenile

*Raphicerus campestris
capricornis*

OTHER NAMES *French*: Steenbok du Mozambique. *German*: Südafrikanisches Steinböckchen. *Spanish*: Raficero de cuernos cortos, raficero de Mozambique. *Russian*: Мозамбикский (короткорогий) стенбок. *Afrikaans*: Vlakbok.

SUBSPECIES Considered as a subspecies of *R. campestris* (Steenbok): *R. c. campestris* (South African Steenbok), *R. c. fulvorubescens* (Albany Steenbok), *R. c. natalensis* (Natal Steenbok), *R. c. capricornis* (Short-horned Steenbok), *R. c. neumanni* (East African Steenbok), *R. c. steinhardti* (Kalahari Steenbok).

SIMILAR SPECIES *R. c. campestris* is more orange rufous in color, and white patches on the throat less extensive. *R. c. fulvorubescens* is rather lighter in color, amber brown, less rufous, and white on the throat extends almost to the chin. *R. c. natalensis* has longer horns.

REPRODUCTION *Gestation*: 170 days. *Young per Birth*: 1. *Weaning*: 3 months. *Sexual Maturity*: 6-7 months (♀), 9 months (♂). *Life Span*: 12 years. Breeding season has not been clearly defined. Births have been recorded year-round. Lambs are concealed for the first 3-4 months, during which time the mother only makes contact in the early morning and evening to feed and groom the infant. To conceal the infant's presence, the mother eats her lamb's feces and drinks its urine during her visits; this keeps the hiding place relatively odor free and protected from predators.

BEHAVIOR *Family Group*: Solitary, although a stable pair (which meets up solely for breeding) shares one territory. *Diet*: Purely browsers by preference, and not mixed feeders as previously suggested. *Main Predators*: All major predators, including wild cats and pythons. Most active during the day, although when temperatures peak at midday they may seek refuge in shade. ♂ and ♀ defend and share a territory, although they are mainly solitary. ♂ mark off their territories with urine and secretions from gland under the chin as well as with dung. Mean home range area is 0.6 km². They are the only Bovid that scrape the ground before and after urination and defecation. ♂ are known to use roads and telephone lines as boundaries. They have excellent hearing. They may scavenge meat from carcasses as well as kill the young of ground birds but this is due to severe shortages of food. At times they take refuge in ant-bear holes, and use these to bear their young.

DISTRIBUTION *Native*: Mozambique, South Africa, Swaziland, Zambia, Zimbabwe. Found in Transvaal, South Africa, Zimbabwe, and Mozambique. The isolating barrier with the East African Steenbok is the tall miombo woodlands of central Zambia, Malawi, and N Mozambique.

HABITAT Open savanna country where they are reliant on adequate cover in the form of taller grass and clumps of bushes. Absent or rarely seen in forests, mountains, dense woodlands, and rocky areas.

STATUS Least Concern. Estimated population of 20,000 animals in Kruger NP.

PHOTO CREDITS ♂: *Paul Barnard*, Mpumalanga (South Africa). ♀: *Josh M. London*, Kruger NP (South Africa). Head ♂: *Rob Keulemans*, Kruger NP (South Africa). Head ♀: *Kristofor and Rebekah*, Kruger NP (South Africa). Juvenile: *Mahesh Rao* and *Colin Michaelis*, Kruger NP (South Africa). 193

Albany Steenbok
RAPHICERUS CAMPESTRIS FULVORUBESCENS

BL: 70-95 cm. SH: 45-60 cm. TL: 5-10 cm. W: 7-16 kg. HL: 7-19 cm (♂). A small antelope, slim and slender, with a short, conical head, and long legs. Coat is amber brown, lighter than that of South African and Natal Steenbok. White on the throat extends almost to the chin. Lower lip is whitish. Underparts are white, extending down inside of the upper part of the legs. Light-colored eye ring. Slender black triangle starts at the nose and tapers upward. Ears extremely large. Tail very short, a mere stump. Lateral hooves present. Horns, found only in males, are straight, sharp, and very upright. Natal Steenbok usually has larger horns. Female similar to male, sometimes heavier, without horns.

*Raphicerus campestris
fulvorubescens*

Raphicerus campestris natalensis

OTHER NAMES Kafue Steenbok, Zulu Steenbok. *French*: Steenbok du Nord, steenbok du Natal. *German*: Südafrikanisches Steinböckchen. *Spanish*: Raficero común. *Russian*: Западный южноафриканский стенбок *(fulvorubescens)*, Натальский стенбок *(natalensis)*. *Afrikaans*: Vlakbok. *Swahili*: Isha, dondor. *Zulu*: Iqhina. *Xhosa*: Itshabanqa. *Sepedi*: Pudubudu. *Sesotho*: Thiane. *Swati*: Lingcina.

SUBSPECIES Considered as a subspecies of *R. campestris* (Steenbok): *R. c. campestris* (South African Steenbok), *R. c. fulvorubescens* (Albany Steenbok), *R. c. natalensis* (Natal Steenbok), *R. c. capricornis* (Short-horned Steenbok), *R. c. neumanni* (East African Steenbok), *R. c. steinhardti* (Kalahari Steenbok).

SIMILAR SPECIES *R. c. campestris* is orange rufous in color, and white patches on the throat less extensive. *R. c. capricornis* is amber brown in color, with face much lighter. Common Duiker is similar in size and color, but more grizzled, grayer in appearance; face usually marked by a black blaze which runs from the top of the head right down to the nose; smaller, more slender ears. Oribi are similar in color and form, but are larger and more slender; there is a distinctive black patch at the base of the ear, and no black on the front of the face.

REPRODUCTION *Gestation*: 170 days. *Young per Birth*: 1. *Weaning*: 3 months. *Sexual Maturity*: 6-7 months (♀), 9 months (♂). *Life Span*: 12 years. Breeding appears to take place year-round.

BEHAVIOR *Family Group*: Solitary, although a stable pair (which meets up solely for breeding) shares one territory. *Diet*: Mostly leaves from shrubs and trees, also fruits and grasses, seemingly independent of water. *Main Predators*: All major predators, including wild cats and pythons. Most active during the day, although when temperatures peak at midday they may seek refuge in shade.

DISTRIBUTION *Native*: South Africa. *R. c. natalensis:* S KwaZulu-Natal, Drakensberg District (South Africa). *R. c. fulvorubescens:* Eastern Cape Province, Albany District (South Africa).

HABITAT Open grassland with light tree cover across most of S Africa. Another population lives in the stonier acacia grasslands of E Africa.

STATUS Least Concern. Estimated total population of 600,000 (1999), but this may be an underestimate (census methods are too unreliable for this cryptic species).

PHOTO CREDITS Head ♂: *Chris Fourie*, Mountain Zebra NP (South Africa). Head ♀: *Ariadne Van Zandbergen,* Kwandwe Game Reserve (South Africa).

Kalahari Steenbok

RAPHICERUS CAMPESTRIS STEINHARDTI

BL: 70-95 cm. SH: 45-60 cm. TL: 5-10 cm. W: 7-16 kg. HL: 7-19 cm (♂). A small antelope, slim and slender, with a short, conical head, and long legs. Coat is light golden brown color, paler than in other subspecies, with white parts more extensive. Undersides are white. Few distinctive markings: light-colored eye ring, dark crescent-shaped coronal mark, and a slender black triangle which starts at the nose and tapers upward. Ears extremely large. Tail very short, a mere stump. Lateral hooves present. Horns, found only in males, are straight, sharp, and very upright. Female similar to male, sometimes heavier, without horns.

♀

Juvenile ♂

♂

Raphicerus campestris steinhardti

OTHER NAMES Steinhardt Steenbok. *French*: Steenbok du Botswana. *German*: Kalahari-Steinböckchen. *Spanish*: Raficero común del Kalahari. *Russian*: Калахарский стенбок. *Afrikaans*: Vlakbok. *Swahili*: Isha, dondor. *Zulu*: Iqhina. *Xhosa*: Itshabanqa. *Sepedi*: Pudubudu. *Sesotho*: Thiane. *Swati*: Lingcina.

SUBSPECIES Considered as a subspecies of *R. campestris* (Steenbok): *R. c. campestris* (South African Steenbok), *R. c. fulvorubescens* (Albany Steenbok), *R. c. natalensis* (Natal Steenbok), *R. c. capricornis* (Short-horned Steenbok), *R. c. neumanni* (East African Steenbok), *R. c. steinhardti* (Kalahari Steenbok). Includes *bourquii* (Calundungu, Angola), *cunenensis* (S Omuhonga Mountains), *hoamihensis* (S Ombombo, Namibia), *kelleni* (S Angola), *ugabensis* (Omaruru, Namibia), *zukowskyi* (Bubos, Namibia).

SIMILAR SPECIES Gray Duiker similar in size and color, but more grizzled (grayer) in appearance; face usually marked by a black blaze which runs from the top of the head right down to the nose; smaller, more slender ears. Oribi are similar in color and form, but are larger and more slender; there is a distinctive black patch at the base of the ear, and no black on the front of the face.

REPRODUCTION *Gestation*: 170 days. *Young per Birth*: 1. *Weaning*: 3 months. *Sexual Maturity*: 6-7 months (♀), 9 months (♂). *Life Span*: 12 years. Breeding appears to take place year-round. Young may be born throughout the year, and can stand and walk just a few minutes after birth. The infant is usually hidden away by its mother for a few weeks before beginning to follow her around.

BEHAVIOR *Family Group*: Solitary, although a stable pair (which meets up solely for breeding) shares one territory. *Diet*: Mostly leaves from shrubs and trees, also fruits and grasses, seemingly independent of water. *Main Predators*: All major predators, including wild cats and pythons. Most active during the day, although when temperatures peak at midday they may seek refuge in shade. Live in monogamous pairs which share a territory some 4-100 ha in size; however, the two animals are usually found apart and only come together to breed. They bury their dung fully under loose soil. They may be seen scratching the ground where urine and dung are dropped. When threatened, Steenbok will hide by lying on the ground and freezing in order to avoid the danger. If the threat continues to approach, they will rocket away for a short distance and then try to hide again. Aardvark burrows may be used as refuges.

DISTRIBUTION *Native:* Angola, Botswana, Namibia. Found in Botswana, Angola, N Namibia, Orange River N to Ovamboland.

HABITAT Generally an arid-habitat species, but in Botswana they are found in the Okavango Delta.

STATUS Least Concern.

PHOTO CREDITS ♂: *Mark Piazzi*, Namib Rand Nature Reserve (Namibia). Heads: *Yathin S. Krishnappa*, Etosha NP (Namibia). ♀: *Mark Piazzi*, Etosha NP (Namibia). Juvenile: *Kayla Stevenson*, Central Kalahari Game Reserve (Botswana), Etosha (Namibia).

East African Steenbok
RAPHICERUS CAMPESTRIS NEUMANNI

BL: 72-87 cm. SH: 45-60 cm. TL: 5 cm. W: 7-16 kg. HL: 7-11 cm (♂). A small antelope, slim and slender, with a short, conical head, and long legs. Smooth coat, rufous brown in color, paler than in other subspecies. Undersides are white, more clearly defined than in other subspecies. Legs have rufous outer sides, and inner sides that are white above the knee. Face with a distinctive triangle of black above the nose. No dark, crescent-shaped coronal mark. White eye ring large, complete. More white on the margin of the ears and lips. Tail very short, a mere stump. Horns, found only in males, are straight, sharp, very upright, ringed only at the base. Female similar to male, sometimes heavier, without horns.

♂

Young

♀

Raphicerus campestris neumanni

OTHER NAMES Neumann Steenbok, Maasailand Steenbok, Tanganyika Steenbok. *French*: Raphicère champètre, steenbok du Sud du Kenya. *German*: Ostafrikanisches Steinböckchen. *Spanish*: Raficero común de África oriental. *Russian*: Восточноафриканский стенбок. *Swahili*: Isha, dondor.

SUBSPECIES Considered as a subspecies of *R. campestris* (Steenbok): *R. c. campestris* (South African Steenbok), *R. c. fulvorubescens* (Albany Steenbok), *R. c. natalensis* (Natal Steenbok), *R. c. capricornis* (Short-horned Steenbok), *R. c. neumanni* (East African Steenbok), *R. c. steinhardti* (Kalahari Steenbok). Includes *stigmatus* (Kilimanjaro, Kenya).

SIMILAR SPECIES This subspecies lacks a dark crescent between its ears and has large, complete white eye rings. Otherwise is very similar. Kirk's Dik-dik is much smaller and has a longer, flexible nose. Oribi is slightly larger, with a longer neck and a distinctive black spot below the ear. Sharpe's Grysbok has shorter legs, more rounded hindquarters, smaller ears, and white hairs in the coat. Common Duiker can also have a reddish coat, but has a much longer tail and a prominent black stripe down the face.

REPRODUCTION *Gestation*: 170 days. *Young per Birth*: 1. *Weaning*: 3 months. *Sexual Maturity*: 6-7 months (♀), 9 months (♂). *Life Span*: 12 years. Breeding appears to take place year-round. Young may be born throughout the year, and can stand and walk just a few minutes after birth. The infant is usually hidden away by its mother for a few weeks before beginning to follow her around.

BEHAVIOR *Family Group*: Solitary, although a stable pair (which meets up solely for breeding) shares one territory. *Diet*: Mostly leaves from shrubs and trees, also fruits and grasses, seemingly independent of water. *Main Predators*: All major predators, including wild cats and pythons. Active both during the day and night. They live in monogamous pairs that share a territory of 5-60 ha. Pairs commonly move and rest separately, although usually stay within 200-300 m of each other.

DISTRIBUTION *Native*: Kenya, Tanzania. *Regionally Extinct*: Uganda. Found in central Kenya, S Tanzania northward throughout the highlands of the Rift Valley and coast drainage area to the N slopes of Mount Kenya and Mount Elgon, E as far as the coast lowlands and W to the shores of the Victoria-Nyanza in Kenya. They no longer occur in Uganda, where most suitable habitat is now cultivated.

HABITAT A variety of habitats, from semi-desert to alpine moorland zones up to altitudes of 3,500 m on Mount Kenya. They occur widely in drier savannas, grasslands, and scrublands. They also frequently inhabit farmland and occasionally occur in semi-urban environments. They avoid thick woodland and forest.

STATUS Least Concern. The main threats are habitat loss and illegal hunting, although populations are stable inside most protected areas.

PHOTO CREDITS ♀: Maasai Mara (Kenya). ♂: *Phil Gould* (Tanzania). Head ♀: *Mike Lane* (Tanzania). Young: *Graeme Guy*, Serengeti (Tanzania).

Günther's Dik-dik
MADOQUA GUENTHERI

BL: 55-71 cm. SH: 35-40 cm. TL: 3-5 cm. W: 3-5 kg. HL: To 9.8 cm (♂). A very small, slender antelope with long neck and small head. Hindquarters usually higher than the shoulder. Pelage is soft, with coloration ranging from yellowish gray to reddish brown on the dorsal side, finely speckled gray, underparts pinkish buff. Short tail, hairy on the dorsal, naked on the ventral side. Eyes large and black. Eyelids and preorbital glands also black. Ears large, white on the inside. Both sexes have a crest of hair, in males more brightly colored and longer. Another distinguishing feature is the elongated snout, which can be turned in all directions. Legs are slender and long, with black hooves pointed anteriorly; accessory hooves are diminutive. Males have black horns, short, straight or curved backward, sometimes hidden by a tuft of hair on the forehead; more circular toward the tips, ringed. Females are larger and do not possess horns.

Madoqua guentheri

OTHER NAMES Long-snouted Dik-dik. *French*: Dik-dik de Günther. *German*: Günther Dik-dik, Rüsselantilope. *Spanish*: Dik-dik de Günther. *Russian*: Дикдик Гюнтера.

SUBSPECIES Monotypic. The name *M. guentheri* (Günther's Dik-dik) formerly included *M. guentheri* (Günther's Dik-dik), and *M. smithii* (Smith's Dik-dik) as subspecies: these are elevated to full species here. Includes *hodsoni* (Hodson's Dik-dik, S Ethiopia, Mount Mega) and *wroughtoni* (Central Ethiopia, Webi Valley, Gallaland).

SIMILAR SPECIES Distinguished from Kirk's Dik-dik by their longer nose. Smith's Dik-dik is more reddish, with underparts buffy white, otherwise very similar.

REPRODUCTION *Gestation:* 168-180 days. *Young per Birth:* 1. *Weaning:* 4-5.3 months. *Sexual Maturity*: 6-12 months. *Life Span*: 17.5 years. During parturition, the head appears first and the forelegs are laid back alongside the body (this differs from births among other ruminants, except the mouse deer). Young are nursed for 3-4 months. Fawns, however, can start to eat solid food after about a week. The ♀ stays with her young for the first few days after birth. For a few months, young fawns accompany both parents. The ♂ takes no part in providing food. Fawns are contacted using calls made by the mother. The young are silent during the day but may whistle at night. The coloration of Dik-diks at birth is identical to that of adults. Between 7 and 9 weeks, horns appear, although at first the crest hides them. The horns reach their full size at 2 years of age. At 34 weeks, horn annulations appear.

BEHAVIOR *Family Group*: 3 animals (an adult pair and 1 immature fawn). *Diet:* Young leaves and buds, fruit, roots and tubers, fallen leaves, and green grass. They are able to survive on the moisture from the vegetation they eat, and may go for long periods without drinking. *Main Predators*: Hyena, leopard, cheetah, caracal, other cats, jackal, baboon, eagle, and python. Territories are determined by heaps of dung about 30 cm in diameter deposited by Dik-diks relative to the boundaries of the territory. Postorbital gland secretions are also used to mark territories. An intrusion in their territory causes the Dik-diks to bounce and then whistle upon landing (sounds like "zik-zik" or "dik-dik," hence their name). The ♂ also grates tree trunks with the corrugations on his horns to mark a territory. Fights between ♂ for territory are usually symbolic and infrequent. These are shy animals that will look for cover at the least bit of an alarm; they will seek out vegetation and then crouch flat on the ground. They are chiefly diurnal, and are mostly active at night and in the evening. The elongated snout is a thermoregulatory device; arterial blood is diverted to membranes in the snout and, through an evaporative process, is cooled.

DISTRIBUTION *Native:* Ethiopia, Somalia. Found in S and E Ethiopia, NE from Lake Stephanie, and Somalia, except the coast. It is not known to occur within 30 km of the coast, being replaced there by Kirk's Dik-dik.

HABITAT Low thicket vegetation, including arid and semi-arid thornbush, savanna grassland-woodland, and riverine grassland-woodland, from near sea level to 2,100 m.

STATUS Least Concern. Total population estimate of 511,000 animals (1999).

PHOTO CREDITS *Hans Bauer*, Nechisar NP (Ethiopia).

Smith's Dik-dik

MADOQUA SMITHII

BL: 55-71 cm. SH: 35-40 cm. TL: 3-5 cm. W: 3-5 kg. HL: To 9.8 cm (♂). General color grizzled yellowish gray, slightly fading to grayish brown, light rust red or sandy on the flanks, more reddish than Gunther's Dik-dik. White to sandy white on the chin, throat, underparts, and inside of legs. Short tail. Eyes large and black. Eyelids and preorbital glands also black. Ears large, white on the inside. Both sexes have a crest of hair, in males more brightly colored and longer. Another distinguishing feature is their elongated snout, which can be turned in all directions. Legs are slender and long, with black hooves pointed anteriorly; accessory hooves are diminutive. Males have black horns, short, straight or curved backward, sometimes hidden by a tuft of hair on the forehead; more circular toward the tips, ringed. Females are larger and do not possess horns.

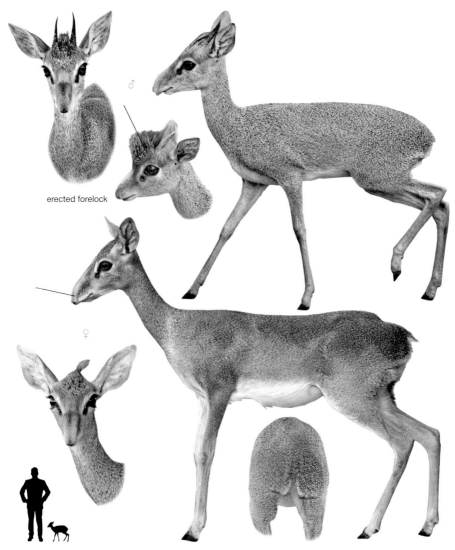

erected forelock

Madoqua smithii

OTHER NAMES Long-snouted Dik-dik, Kenyan Gunther's Dik-dik, Large-snouted Dik-dik. *French*: Dik-dik de Smith. *German*: Smith Dik-dik, Rüsselantilope. *Spanish*: Dik-dik de Smith. *Russian*: Дикдик Смита.

SUBSPECIES Monotypic. Formerly considered a subspecies of *M. guentheri* (Günther's Dik-dik). Includes *nasoguttatus* (Kenya, W of Lake Baringo).

SIMILAR SPECIES Distinguished from Kirk's Dik-dik by their longer nose. Günther's Dik-dik is smaller, less reddish, with underparts pinkish buff, otherwise very similar.

REPRODUCTION *Gestation:* 168-180 days. *Young per Birth:* 1. *Weaning:* 4-5.3 months. *Sexual Maturity:* 6-12 months. *Life Span:* 17.5 years. During parturition, the head appears first and the forelegs are laid back alongside the body (this differs from births among other ruminants, except the mouse deer). Young are nursed for 3-4 months. Fawns, however, can start to eat solid food after about a week. The ♀ stays with her young for the first few days after birth. For a few months, young fawns accompany both parents. The ♂ takes no part in providing food. Fawns are contacted using calls made by the mother. The young are silent during the day but may whistle at night. The coloration of Dik-diks at birth is identical to that of adults. Between 7 and 9 weeks, horns appear, although at first the crest hides them. The horns reach their full size at 2 years of age. At 34 weeks, horn annulations appear.

BEHAVIOR *Family Group:* 3 animals (an adult pair and 1 immature fawn). *Diet:* Young leaves and buds, fruit roots, and tubers, fallen leaves, and green grass. They are able to survive on the moisture from the vegetation they eat, and may go for long periods without drinking. *Main Predators*: Hyena, leopard, cheetah, caracal, other cats, jackal, baboon, eagle, and pythons. Territories are determined by heaps of dung about 30 cm in diameter deposited by Dik-diks relative to the boundaries of the territory. Postorbital gland secretions are also used to mark territories. An intrusion in their territory causes the Dik-diks to bounce and then whistle upon landing (sounds like "zik-zik" or "dik-dik," hence their name). The ♂ also grates tree trunks with the corrugations on his horns to mark a territory. Fights between ♂ for territory are usually symbolic and infrequent. These are shy animals that will look for cover at the least bit of an alarm; they will seek out vegetation and then crouch flat on the ground. They are chiefly diurnal, and are mostly active at night and in the evening.

DISTRIBUTION *Native:* Ethiopia, Kenya, Sudan, Uganda. Driest, hottest arid, and semi-arid scrublands in NE Africa: SE Sudan (E of the Nile), NE Uganda, N Kenya, E in SW Ethiopia to about as far as Lake Stephanie.

HABITAT Low thicket vegetation, including arid and semiarid thornbush, savanna grassland-woodland, and riverine grassland-woodland. Driest, hottest arid and semi-arid scrublands in NE Africa.

STATUS Least Concern. Total population estimate of 511,000 animals (1999).

PHOTO CREDITS ♂: *C. Lundqvist*, Mago NP (Ethiopia). ♀: *Sérgio Nogueira*, Omo Valley (Ethiopia). Heads: *Volker Sthamer*, South Omo Region (Ethiopia).

Kirk's Dik-dik
MADOQUA KIRKII

BL: 55-77 cm. SH: 35-45 cm. TL: 4-6 cm. W: 2.7-6.5 kg. HL: To 11.4 cm (♂). A very small and slender antelope, with the nose moderately elongated. The coat is yellow olive to reddish olive, while the head, legs, and flanks are paler chestnut. The forehead and tuft are marbled with black. Undersides, including the insides of the legs and bottom of the chin, are white. The white on the underside does not reach as far down the legs as in other subspecies. Bright ring of white hair around the large eye, reaching well in front of the eye. Only males bear sharp, corrugated horns. These may be slightly hidden by the erectile forelock. Female similar to male, slightly larger, without horns.

♀

erected forelock

♂

Madoqua kirkii

OTHER NAMES Taita Dik-dik. *French*: Dik-dik de Kerk. *German*: Kirk-Dikdik, Zwerg-Rüsselantilope. *Spanish:* Dicdic de Kirk. *Russian*: Дикдик Керка. *Afrikaans*: Damaralandse Bloubokkie. *Swahili*: Suguya, Digidigi. *Damara*: Ihauib. *Herero*: Thini, okatini. *Kikuyu*: Thuni. *Maasai*: Eronko. *Ovambo*: Okabundja. *Turkana*: Ethuro.

SUBSPECIES Monotypic. The name *M. kirkii* (Kirk's Dik-dik) formerly included *M. k. kirkii* (Kirk's Dik-dik), *M. cavendishi* (Cavendish's Dik-dik), *M. thomasi* (Thomas's Dik-dik), and *M. damarensis* (Damara Dik-dik) as subspecies: these are all elevated to full species here. Includes *nyikae*.

SIMILAR SPECIES: Slightly smaller than other subspecies, and paler in color, yellow olive. Günther's Dik-dik is sympatric in Kenya and Somalia, but has a larger nose. Silver and Salt's Dik-diks are sympatric in Somalia, but both are smaller and have shorter noses. Klipspringer, broadly sympatric, is larger, with a more upright stance; close to rocky terrain.

REPRODUCTION *Gestation*: 5-6 months. *Young per Birth*: 1. *Weaning*: 3-4 months. *Sexual Maturity*: 6-8 months (♀), 8-9 months (♂). *Life Span*: 10 years. Birthing peaks occur from November to December and April to May. After birth, kids lie concealed away from their mother for 2-3 weeks. Although they grow up with their parents, the young are ejected from the home territory at 7-8 months. ♀ may bear up to 2 young per year.

BEHAVIOR *Family Group:* Permanent breeding pairs. *Diet:* Leaves of bushes and shrubs, buds, shoots, fruits, grasses. Needs much salt and little water. *Main Predators*: Lion, leopard, cheetah, caracal, hyena, Cape hunting dog, jackals, ratel, crocodile, python. Young are also taken by eagles, baboons, and genets. Primarily active in the morning and late afternoon, although some activity may continue throughout the night. Mated pairs defend a territory 5-30 ha in size, and if no unexpected unfavorable conditions arise, this pair may occupy the same territory for life. Definite trails run through the thick cover, which are used with some regularity. Along the boundaries of the territory, and in other places important to the animals, they deposit dung heaps approximately 30 cm in diameter. Both sexes mark the range of their territory with secretions from their preorbital glands, although this is done much more frequently by ♂. Despite joint marking, only the ♂ defends the family range, chasing away any intruders of the same species, including other ♀. When startled, Dik-diks make quick zigzag leaps, dashing for cover while making a call that resembles "zik-zik" or "dik-dik." Population density in the Serengeti is about 24 animals per km².

DISTRIBUTION *Native*: Kenya, Somalia, Tanzania. Found in NE and SE Kenya from N Esawo Ngiro to the coast at Lamu, into Somalia as far as Mogadishu, and N and NE Tanzania, as far as the Mount Kilimanjaro and the Pare-Usambara Mountain system in the S.

HABITAT Dry terrain with dense, high brush and kopjes in E Africa, with a small, isolated population along the coast of SW Africa.

STATUS Least Concern. Total population estimate of 971,000 animals (1999), but this may be an underestimate.

PHOTO CREDITS ♂: *Leon Bell*. ♀: *Roger Smith* (rogersmithpix flickr). Head ♀: *Arturo Pardavila III*. Head ♂: *Robbin Merritt* and *Tim Randall*. All photos from Samburu (Kenya).

Thomas's Dik-dik

MADOQUA THOMASI

BL: 55-77 cm. SH: 35-45 cm. TL: 4-6 cm. W: 2.7-6.5 kg. HL: To 11.4 cm (♂). Similar to Kirk's Dik-dik, more rufous on the flanks, contrasting to white underparts. Coat is speckled rabbit gray in color, with rufous sides. Rump and thighs are grayer. Legs and lower flanks are chestnut, extending to the shoulder, with a narrow transition zone to the main body color on the flanks. Underside and inner side of the upper limbs are white, with the white extending down to the knee on the forelimbs, and usually beyond the hock on the hind limbs. Head, forehead, and the tuft between the ears are chestnut, often mixed with black and off-white. Prominent eye rings, usually going completely around the eyes. Only males bear sharp, corrugated horns. These may be slightly hidden by the erectile forelock. Females slightly larger than males, without horns.

Madoqua thomasi

OTHER NAMES Ugogo Dik-dik. *French*: Dik-dik de Thomas. *German*: Thomas-Dikdik. *Spanish:* Dicdic de Thomas. *Russian*: Дикдик Томаса. *Swahili*: Digidigi, suguya ugogo.

SUBSPECIES Monotypic. Formerly considered a subspecies of *M. kirkii* (Kirk's Dik-dik).

SIMILAR SPECIES Kirk's Dik-dik is slightly smaller, paler in color, yellow olive, rufous only on rump and back. Cavendish's Dik-dik has a darker gray color, with a wide transition zone on the flanks to the pale zone, with less sexual dimorphism in size. Damara's Dik-dik has the anterior part of the body paler, and the crest more blackish. Günther's Dik-dik has a larger nose. Steenbok is significantly larger and has a reddish coat, a smaller, shorter nose, and larger ears. Suni is uniformly colored.

REPRODUCTION *Gestation*: 166-174 days. *Young per Birth:* 1. *Weaning:* 3-4 months. *Sexual Maturity*: 6-8 months (♀), 8-9 months (♂). *Life Span*: 10 years. There is no specific information for this subspecies, but probably like Kirk's Dik-dik.

BEHAVIOR *Family Group:* Permanent breeding pairs, with 1 or 2 young. *Diet:* Leaves of bushes and shrubs, buds, shoots, fruits, grasses. Needs much salt and little water. *Main Predators*: Lion, leopard, cheetah, caracal, hyena, Cape hunting dog, jackals, ratel, crocodile, python. Young are also taken by eagles, baboons, and genets. Primarily active in the morning and late afternoon, although some activity may continue throughout the night. There is no specific information for this subspecies, but probably like Kirk's Dik-dik.

DISTRIBUTION *Native*: Tanzania. Found in NW Tanzania (the Serengeti ecosystem excluded), from Mwanza, Olduvai, and Lake Manyara to the Kondoa, Dodoma, Bugogo, Irangi, and Tabora districts.

HABITAT Thicket and acacia bushlands.

STATUS Least Concern.

PHOTO CREDITS ♀: *Nigel Voaden* and *Sha Sha Shu*, Lake Manyara (Tanzania). ♂: Lake Manyara (Tanzania). Head ♀: *Ganesh Raghunathan*, Lake Manyara (Tanzania). Head ♂: *Keith Liscinsky*, Lake Manyara (Tanzania).

Cavendish's Dik-dik

MADOQUA CAVENDISHI

BL: 55-77 cm. SH: 35-45 cm. TL: 4-6 cm. W: 2.7-6.5 kg. HL: To 11.4 cm (♂). Similar to Kirk's Dik-dik, somewhat larger, darker gray coloration, with a wide transition zone on the flanks to the pale chestnut zone of the lower flanks and the legs. Rufous sides. The white zone on the underside reaches farther down the inner sides of the limbs than in other species. On the head, only the nose is chestnut. The eye ring reaches well in front of the eye. The forehead and tuft are marbled with black. Only males bear sharp, corrugated horns. Female similar to male, without horns, with no sexual dimorphism in size.

Madoqua cavendishi

OTHER NAMES Naivasaha Dik-dik. *French*: Dik-dik de Cavendish. *German:* Cavendish-Dikdik. *Spanish:* Dicdic de Cavendish. *Russian:* Наивашский дикдик. *Swahili*: Digidigi.

SUBSPECIES Monotypic. Formerly considered a subspecies of *M. kirkii* (Kirk's Dik-dik). Includes *langi* (Lang's Dik-dik), and *minor* (Northern Dik-dik).

SIMILAR SPECIES Kirk's Dik-dik is paler in color, yellow olive, rufous only on back and rump. Thomas's Dik-dik is rabbit gray in color, with red tones, and has a larger nose. Damara's Dik-dik has the anterior part of the body paler, and the crest more blackish. Günther's Dik-dik has a larger nose. Steenbok is significantly larger and has a reddish coat, a smaller, shorter nose, and larger ears. Suni is uniformly colored.

REPRODUCTION *Gestation*: 150-180 days. *Young per Birth:* 1. *Weaning:* 3-4 months. *Sexual Maturity*: 6-8 months (♀), 8-9 months (♂). *Life Span*: 10 years. Birthing peaks occur from November to December and April to June. After birth, the young stand within 15 minutes, and start nursing within the first couple of hours. They remain hidden in thickets during the first 2-3 weeks, and then join their parents.

BEHAVIOR *Family Group:* Permanent breeding pairs. *Diet:* High in browse, especially trees and shrubs. Independent of surface water, getting their moisture from plants, dew, and rain. *Main Predators*: Lion, leopard, cheetah, caracal, hyena, Cape hunting dog, jackals, ratel, crocodile, python. Young are also taken by eagles, baboons, and genets. When cover is scarce, they tend to be more nocturnal, whereas in areas with more extensive cover they are active both day and night. The members of the pair, when resting, often face in opposite directions, intermittently putting their heads down and closing their eyes. Cavendish's Dik-diks conserves water by producing very dry feces and concentrated urine, and obtains its water needs mostly from its food plants.

DISTRIBUTION *Native*: Kenya, Tanzania, Uganda. Found in the Kenya-Rift Valley, extending into the Serengeti-Mara ecosystem in SW Kenya and NW Tanzania: Lake Elmenteita, Enterit River, S end of Lake Nakuru, Lake Naivasha, Kijabe, Kedong River, Olorgesailie, Amala River, Loita Plains, NW of Narok, Sotik, S Guaso Nyiro, Grumeti River, and Banagi.

HABITAT On the Serengeti, they occur frequently on kopjes. In Lake Nakuru NP they prefer shrub habitats, but they live also in forest and open grassland. Where sympatric with Günther's Dik-dik, this species favors less arid areas.

STATUS Least Concern. Estimated population of 32,000 individuals in the Serengeti.

PHOTO CREDITS ♂: *tomandlousia*, Serengeti NP (Tanzania). Head ♂: *Enrico Penolazzi*, Serengeti NP (Tanzania). ♀: *Robert Cave* and *Olivier Delaere*, Maasai Mara (Kenya). Head ♀: *Robert Cave*, Maasai Mara (Kenya).

Hinde's Dik-dik
MADOQUA HINDEI

BL: 55-77 cm. SH: 35-45 cm. TL: 4-6 cm. W: 2.7-6.5 kg. HL: To 11.4 cm (♂). Similar to Cavendish's Dik-dik. Body color is reddish olive, with the dorsum redder and more finely speckled than the rest of the body. Legs and flanks are paler chestnut, not extending to the shoulder, with a narrow transition zone with the general body color. The white zone on the underside does not reach farther down the inner sides of the limbs. Muzzle is paler. Forehead and tuft are marbled with black. The eye ring reaches well in front of the eye, more than in Thomas's Dik-dik. Only males bear sharp, corrugated horns. Unlike other Dik-diks, females are smaller than males, without horns.

Madoqua hindei

OTHER NAMES Ukamba Kirk Dik-dik. *French*: Hinde-Dik-dik. *German:* Hinde-Dikdik. *Spanish*: Dicdic de Hinde. *Russian*: Укамбский (красно-оливковый) дикдик.

SUBSPECIES Monotypic. Formerly considered a subspecies of *M. kirkii* (Kirk's Dik-dik).

SIMILAR SPECIES Cavendish's Dik-dik is larger and grayer, with the white on the limbs reaching farther down, but otherwise very similar. Thomas's Dik-dik is more rufous. Maasai Klipspringer (*Oreotragus schillingsi*) is larger, yellow grey in color, with a more upright stance; although sympatric, it is found close to rocky terrain. Smith's Dik-dik (*M. smithii*) has a much longer nose.

REPRODUCTION *Gestation*: 150-180 days. *Young per Birth:* 1. *Weaning:* 3-4 months. *Sexual Maturity*: 6-8 months (♀), 8-9 months (♂). *Life Span:* 10 years. There is no specific information available for this species, but probably similar to Cavendish's Dik-dik.

BEHAVIOR *Family Group:* Permanent breeding pairs. *Diet:* High in browse, especially trees and shrubs. Independent of surface water, getting their moisture from plants, dew, and rain. *Main Predators*: Lion, leopard, cheetah, caracal, hyena, Cape hunting dog, jackals, ratel, crocodile, python. Young are also taken by eagles, baboons, and genets. There is no specific information available for this species, but probably similar to Cavendish's Dik-dik. It is likely crepuscular, as well as nocturnal at some times of the year, tending to alternate feeding and resting bouts throughout the day. It lives in mated pairs in a territory, from 0.05 to 30 ha in size, although more than one adult ♀ may occupy a territory in places where densities are especially high. Territories increase in size or can be abandoned during the dry season when food is scarce.

DISTRIBUTION *Native*: Kenya, Tanzania. Found in highland regions in SE Kenya and N and NE Tanzania, probably bounded by the Tana River, Mount Kilimanjaro, the Para-Usambara Mountains system, and the Rift Highlands. Found in Tarangire, Tsavo East, Tsavo West, and Arusha National Parks.

HABITAT Heavy arid bush.

STATUS Least Concern. Estimated population in Tarangire about 5,000 individuals.

PHOTO CREDITS ♂ and heads: *John H. Gavin*, Tsavo NP (Kenya). ♀: *Pigl3t,* Tsavo NP (Kenya).

Damara Dik-dik

MADOQUA DAMARENSIS

BL: 55-77 cm. SH: 40 cm. TL: 4-6 cm. W: 5.1 kg (♂), 5.6 kg (♀). HL: To 8.0 cm (♂). A very small and slender antelope, with the nose moderately elongated, somewhat larger than the Kirk's Dik-dik. Upper parts of the body are yellowish gray in color, the hairs with subterminal whitish or pale yellow annulations and dark tips. The hair on the face, the crown of the head, and around the ears is a pale rusty color. Chest and belly and inside of the thighs are white to off-white. White rings around the eyes. A tuft of long hair on the forehead becomes erect when the Dik-dik is alarmed or displaying. Large prominent preorbital glands in front of the eyes. Only the males carry the spike-like horns, which are stout at the base, ringed, and longitudinally grooved. Female similar to male, slightly larger, without horns.

Madoqua damarensis

OTHER NAMES *French*: Dik-dik du Damaraland. *German*: Damara-Dikdik. *Spanish*: Dicdic de Damara. *Russian*: Дамарский дикдик. *Afrikaans*: Damara Dik-dik.

SUBSPECIES Monotypic. Formerly considered a subspecies of *M. kirkii* (Kirk's Dik-dik). Includes *hemprichianus* and *variani*.

SIMILAR SPECIES Somewhat larger than the Kirk Dik-dik, it is darker on the back and a brighter reddish-fawn color on the flanks. Steenbok is much larger, rufous brown above rather than gray brown, and lacks the distinctive crest of long hair on the forehead.

REPRODUCTION *Gestation*: 166-174 days. *Young per Birth*: 1. *Weaning*: 4 months. *Sexual Maturity*: 6-8 months (♀), 8-9 months (♂). *Life Span*: 16 years. In contrast to Kirk's Dik-dik, they only reproduce once a year. During courtship, ♂ approach ♀ in a stiff-legged walk, the head held low, the nose pointed forward, and the crest on the forehead fully erected. ♀ react to this in a crouching, supplicatory pose with tail raised. Birthing peaks occur during the rainy seasons, between January and March. ♂ do not help with the rearing of young and cover the ♀'s scent markings with their own in order to maintain the pair bond. Infants stay hidden in patches of thick cover for the first 3 weeks of life, before beginning to accompany their parents. Mothers visit to suckle and clean them at about 6-hour intervals.

BEHAVIOR *Family Group:* They occur singly, in pairs, or in family parties of 3, except during the dry season when groups of up to six may be seen together. *Diet:* Shoots, leaves, fruits, and flowers; they eat small quantities of the tips of grass leaves during the rainy season and also eat freshly fallen leaves and fruit. *Main Predators:* Leopard, caracal, hyena, Cape hunting dog, jackals, ratel, crocodile, python; eagle, baboon, genet (young). Shy species; when suddenly disturbed, give vent to a single explosive whistle as they run for cover to the deepest part of the thicket. In reaction to sudden fright they may also bound away stiff legged, stotting, with their legs tucked up under their bodies. They spend as much as half of their time inactive during the day, standing or lying down in thick shady cover ruminating, often in situations overlooking open glades. Active at sunrise, in the late afternoon, and at dusk, with some activity after dark. Independent of drinking water, but will drink from puddles when they are available. Territorial, marking their territories using a secretion produced by glands which are found in front of their eyes, as well as with dung and urine. Vocalizations include a sharp alarm whistle, bleats, and grunts.

DISTRIBUTION *Native*: Angola, Namibia. Distributed through SW Angola, central and NW Namibia (from Kaokoland S to Brukkaros Mountain in the central hilly parts of the country; in the N they occur as far E as the Grootfontein District; in the NW they penetrate into the coastal Namib Desert down watercourses with associated thickets.

HABITAT Dense shrubs and thickets with closed canopy cover, which provide shade and protection. Rocky areas with little grass are also frequented. Penetrates into desert along river flows.

STATUS Least Concern.

PHOTO CREDITS ♂: *Scott Lamont,* Etosha NP (Namibia). ♀: *Thomas Jenny,* Etosha NP (Namibia). Head ♂: *Christine Lamberth* (Namibia). Head ♀: *Glenda Rees*, Etosha NP (Namibia).

Silver Dik-dik

MADOQUA PIACENTINII

BL: 45–50 cm. SH: 30-33 cm. TL: 3-4 cm. W: 2-3 kg. A small antelope with a short, squared-off, furry nose, large eyes, and very thin legs, the hind legs being longer than the forelegs. It is the smallest species of Dik-dik, with very soft, thin fur. Its back and flanks are grizzled silvery, while the limbs, ears, and muzzle are ochraceous in color. The forehead is gray, and the bridge of the nose is often a vivid russet. There is no conspicuous white ring around the eye. The hairs are more agouti banded than in other species. There is a distinctive black rim around the back surface of the ears. Males have ringed spike-like horns, which are stout at the base. Female similar to the male, slightly larger, without horns.

Madoqua piacentinii

OTHER NAMES Somali Dik-dik. *French*: Dik-dik argenté. *German*: Silber-Dikdik. *Spanish*: Dicdic de Piacentini. *Russian*: Серебристый дикдик (Дикдик Пъячентини).

SUBSPECIES Monotypic. It was formerly considered a subspecies of the Salt's Dik-dik (*M. swainei piacentinii* or *M. saltiana piacentinii*).

SIMILAR SPECIES The smallest Dik-dik. Salt's Dik-dik is larger and its coat varies from reddish brown to yellowish gray, and it has a conspicuous white ring around the eye. Silver Dik-dik has a reddish tuft on the top of the head and a reddish spot on the nose, usually separated by gray fur on the forehead. In Salt's Dik-dik, the red color on the head forms a single patch and the forehead is largely reddish. In Silver Dik-dik the white circle around the eyes is less apparent than in Salt's Dik-dik.

REPRODUCTION There is no information available for this species.

BEHAVIOR *Family Group*: Probably they live in small family groups which consist of a pair of monogamous partners and their youngest offspring. *Diet*: Shoots and foliage of shrubs and herbs in undergrowth of the Obbia littoral thicket. *Main Predators*: Hyena, leopard, cheetah, caracal, several other cats, jackal, baboon, eagle, and python. This is probably the most primitive and least arid-adapted Dik-diks.

DISTRIBUTION *Native:* Ethiopia, Somalia. The range of the Silver Dik-dik is usually given as being confined to the central coastal plain of Somalia, where its range does not appear to extend for more than 10 km inland from the coast. Recently, this species has been reliably reported farther up the Shebelle River valley and in the valley bottoms of its seasonal tributaries in the Ogaden of Ethiopia.

HABITAT The Silver Dik-dik occurs in very low, dense thickets growing along the central Somali coastal littoral on fertile, sandy soils under a powerful offshore wind which has a cooling and moisturizing effect. In the SE part of the Ethiopian Ogaden, Silver Dik-dik have been observed in dense to semi-dense *Acacia-Commiphora* bushland.

STATUS Data Deficient. In 1999, the estimated total population was 30,000, perhaps an overestimate, since hunting pressures and other disturbances are relatively high within the Silver Dik-dik's restricted range.

PHOTO CREDITS ♂: *Ekaterina Morozova,* Park of Birds Vorobji (transferred to the Moscow Zoo in 2009) (Russia). ♀: *Andrey Kotkin* and *Alex Kantorovich,* Moscow Zoo (Russia).

Salt's Dik-dik
MADOQUA SALTIANA

BL: 52-67 cm. SH: 30-40.5 cm. TL: 3.5-5.5 cm. W: 2.5-4 kg. HL: To 9 cm (♂). A small antelope with a short, squared-off, furry nose, large eyes, and very thin legs, the hind legs being longer than the forelegs. Largest species of Salt's Dik-dik group. Coat on the neck and back is thick and harsh, often grizzled gray. Flanks are bright cinnamon rufous, less thick, soft, and more sleek. Blaze, forehead, and back of ears bright rufous. Underparts white, sometimes washed with fulvous. Limbs rufous to fulvous. Brush-like crest of erectile hairs on the forehead. Conspicuous white ring around the eye, and black bare patch in front of the eye. Small accessory hooves. Inconspicuous tail, of the same color as the back. Males with ringed spike-like horns, stout at the base, with slight longitudinal grooves, somewhat concealed by the small tuft of hair on the forehead. Female similar to the male, slightly larger, without horns.

erected forelock

♂

♀

216

Madoqua saltiana

OTHER NAMES Eritrea Dik-dik. *French*: Dik-dik de Salt. *German*: Eritrea-Dikdik, Windspielantilope, Rotbauchdikdik. *Spanish*: Dicdic de Salt. *Russian*: Горный дикдик. *Amharic*: Yesolt enshoo, inshu. *Arabic*: Um Digdig. *Somali*: Sakaro.

SUBSPECIES Monotypic. The name *M. saltiana* (Salt's Dik-dik) formerly included *M. saltiana* (Salt's Dik-dik), *M. hararensis* (Harar Dik-dik), *M. lawrancei* (Lawrance's Dik-dik), *M. phillipsi* (Phillips's Dik-dik), and *M. swaynei* (Swayne's Dik-dik) as subspecies: these are all elevated to full species here. Includes *madoqua* (Ethiopia).

SIMILAR SPECIES Günther's Dik-dik (*M. guentheri*), sympatric in Somalia and Ethiopia, has a much larger and elongated proboscis.

REPRODUCTION *Gestation*: Probably 150-180 days. *Young per Birth*: 1. *Weaning*: 1.5-4 months. *Sexual Maturity*: 6-9 months. *Life Span*: 14 years. ♀ Dik-diks give birth to 1 young twice a year. The newborn is hidden for at least 2-3 weeks. After 1 week, the infant is able to eat solid food. However, it continues to nurse for 3-4 months. At the age of 1 month, the ♂ begins to grow his horns. The young are adult size after 8 months and stop growing completely after 12 months. Once sexual maturity is reached, they establish a territory with a mate.

BEHAVIOR *Family Group*: Small family groups which consist of a pair of monogamous partners and their 2 youngest offspring. *Diet*: Herbivorous browsers: leaves of scrub, bushes, buds, flowers, fruit, and herbs. However, they browse mainly on acacia bushes. *Main Predators*: Hyena, leopard, cheetah, caracal, several other cats, jackal, baboon, eagle, and pythons. Salt's Dik-dik are most active in the morning and late afternoon. On occasion, they will remain active through the afternoon into the night. For the most part, Dik-diks are shy and elusive. The family group works together to maintain a territory. Within these territories they use well-defined paths, or runs. These runs are used to navigate through thick vegetation. Runs can also be used to mark territory boundaries with droppings. When they are alarmed, they erect the tuft of hair on their forehead and run away in a zigzag pattern. They also make an alarm call which sounds like the words "dik-dik."

DISTRIBUTION *Native*: Djibouti, Eritrea, Ethiopia, Sudan. Found in Sudan, from the Atbara River to the S Red Sea Hills, and along the Red Sea coast through Eritrea and Ethiopia N of the Highlands, as far as the Chester Mountains.

HABITAT Found in various types of semi-desert scrub. Occurs from sea level to 1,500 m.

STATUS Least Concern. Current population status is unknown.

PHOTO CREDITS ♂: *Frederick B. Cook* (Djibouti) and *Ignacio Yúfera*, Awash NP (Ethiopia). ♀ : *Volker Sthamer,* Ali Dege Plains (Ethiopia) and *Ignacio Yúfera*, Awash NP (Ethiopia). Heads: *Volker Sthamer,* Ali Dege Plains (Ethiopia).

Swayne's Dik-dik

MADOQUA SWAYNEI

BL: 52-67 cm. SH: 30-40.5 cm. TL: 3.5-5.5 cm. W: 2.1 kg (♂), 2.3-2.5 kg (♀). HL: To 9 cm (♂). Smallest species of Salt's Dik-dik group. Coat is thick with a dull speckled gray-brown color on the back, similar to Salt's Dik-dik. Bright rufous nose patch may not be continuous with the crest, which may be either rufous or dull earthy brown. Underparts white, sometimes washed with fulvous. Limbs rufous to fulvous. Brush-like crest of erectile hairs on the forehead. White ring around the eyes. In front of the eye, a black bare patch. Small accessory hooves. Inconspicuous tail, of the same color as the back. Males have ringed spike-like horns, which are stout at the base. The horns have slight longitudinal grooves, but these are somewhat concealed by the small tuft of hair on the forehead. Female similar to the male, slightly larger and heavier, without horns.

218

Madoqua swaynei

OTHER NAMES *French*: Dik-dik de Swayne. *German*: Kleindikdik. *Spanish*: Dicdic de Swayne. *Russian*: Дикдик Суэйна. *Amharic*: Yesolt enshoo, inshu. *Arabic*: Um Digdig. *Somali*: Sakaro.

SUBSPECIES Monotypic. Formerly considered a subspecies of *M. saltiana* (Salt's Dik-dik). Includes *erlangeri* (Erlanger Dik-dik, Ethiopia, left bank of the Webi River) and *citernii*.

SIMILAR SPECIES Somewhat larger than the other short-snouted races, but has slightly smaller horns. Silver dik-dik is grizzled silvery, while the limbs, ears and muzzle are ochraceous in color.

REPRODUCTION *Gestation*: Probably 150-180 days. *Young per Birth*: 1. *Weaning*: 1.5-4 months. *Sexual Maturity*: 6-9 months. *Life Span*: 14 years. No specific information is available for this species, but probably similar to other Salt's Dik-diks.

BEHAVIOR *Family Group*: Monogamous pairs on territories defended by ♂. *Diet*: Herbivorous browsers: leaves of scrub, bushes, buds, plants, flowers, fruit, and herbs; however, they browse mainly on acacia bushes; apparently they do not drink, getting all the moisture from their food. *Main Predators*: Hyena, leopard, cheetah, caracal, several other cats, jackal, baboon, eagle, and python. No specific information is available for this species, but probably similar to other Salt's Dik-diks. More active at night, but depending on the season, they also may be crepuscular. They are monogamous, and the pairs occur together most of the time. Offspring may lick their father's face as a submissive gesture. For the most part, Dik-diks are shy and elusive. The family group works together to maintain a territory. Within these territories they use well-defined paths, or runs. These runs are used to navigate through thick vegetation. Runs can also be used to mark territory boundaries with droppings.

DISTRIBUTION *Native*: Ethiopia, Kenya, Somalia. Found in the Jubba Valley region of S Ethiopia, S Somalia, and far N Kenya.

HABITAT Dry land with barren scrub and areas with acacia tree and dense underbush, and also in mountainous slopes covered with scrub.

STATUS Least Concern. Current population status is unknown. Subsistence hunting is a factor across the range. Hunting pressure is heavier in areas of civil and military conflict. In Somalia, hunting of all Dik-dik species is more intensive, with meat, skins, and live animals exported to the Gulf states.

PHOTO CREDITS *Franck Boyer* (Ethiopia).

Phillips's Dik-dik

MADOQUA PHILLIPSI

BL: 53 cm. SH: 36 cm. TL: 8 cm. W: 2.5 kg (♂), 3 kg (♀). HL: To 9 cm (♂). Smaller than Salt's Dik-dik, and somewhat paler and more contrastingly colored. It has the reddest coloration of all Dik-diks. Upper parts are pale gray agouti. Legs, underparts, and lower flanks are pale orange, the orange extending onto side of shoulders. Rufous brush-like crest of erectile hairs on the forehead. White ring around the eye. Black bare patch in front of the eye. Small accessory hooves. Inconspicuous tail. Spike-like horns, found only in males. Female similar to the male, slightly larger and heavier, without horns.

Madoqua phillipsi

OTHER NAMES *French*: Dik-dik de Lawrance. *German*: Lawrance-Dikdik. *Spanish*: Dicdic de Lawrance. *Russian*: Дикдик Филлипса. *Amharic*: Yesolt enshoo, inshu. *Arabic*: Um Digdig. *Somali*: Sakaro.

SUBSPECIES Monotypic. Formerly considered a subspecies of *M. saltiana* (Salt's Dik-dik).

SIMILAR SPECIES Somewhat larger than the other short-snouted races, but has slightly smaller horns. Silver Dik-dik is grizzled silvery, while the limbs, ears, and muzzle are ochraceous in color.

REPRODUCTION *Gestation*: Probably 150-180 days. *Young per Birth*: 1. *Weaning*: 1.5-4 months. *Sexual Maturity*: 6-9 months. *Life Span*: 14 years. No specific information is available for this species, but probably similar to other Salt's Dik-diks.

BEHAVIOR *Family Group*: Monogamous pairs or small groups including parents and young, on territories defended by ♂. *Diet*: Herbivorous browsers: leaves of scrub, bushes, buds, flowers, fruit, and herbs; however, they browse mainly on acacia bushes; apparently they do not drink, getting all the moisture from their food. *Main Predators*: Hyena, leopard, cheetah, caracal, several other cats, jackal, baboon, eagle, and pythons. No specific information is available for this species, but probably similar to other Salt's Dik-diks. More active at night, but depending on the season, they also may be crepuscular. They are monogamous, and the pairs occur together most of the time. For the most part, dik-diks are shy and elusive. The family group works together to maintain a territory. Within these territories they use well-defined paths, or runs. These runs are used to navigate through thick vegetation. Runs can also be used to mark territory boundaries with droppings. When they are alarmed, they erect the tuft of hair on their forehead and run away in a zigzag pattern. They also make an alarm call which sounds like the words "dik-dik." They have a variety of visual communication mechanisms. These include an alert posture where the animal stands rigid with the neck arched, and a dominance posture in which the animal stands with back hunched and the neck drawn back.

DISTRIBUTION *Native*: Somalia. Found in N Somalia, from the border with Ethiopia and Djibouti, S at least to the Golis Mountains.

HABITAT Semi-desert vegetation, including bushland and thickets.

STATUS Least Concern. Current population status is unknown.

PHOTO CREDITS *Brian McMorrow*, Sheikh (Somaliland), *CS-Hammer* and *Jonas Livet*, Al Wabra Wildlife Preservation (Qatar).

Harar Dik-dik
MADOQUA HARARENSIS

BL: 52-67 cm. SH: 33-40.5 cm. TL: 3-4 cm. W: 2.1 kg (♂), 2.3-2.5 kg (♀). HL: To 9 cm (♂). Same size as the Swayne's and Phillips's Dik-diks. Flanks and shoulder patches are bright reddish brown, much darker than the pale orange flares of the Phillips's Dik-dik, contrasting sharply with the grizzled gray of the cheeks, neck, and rump. The reddish color spreads across the back to give it a grizzled ginger coloration. In the western part of its range it loses the contrast, becoming browner overall. Top of the face, head tuft, and legs are reddish. Underparts are white. Males have ringed spike-like horns. Female similar to the male, slightly larger and heavier, without horns.

Madoqua hararensis

OTHER NAMES *French*: Dik-dik de Harar. *German*: Harar-Dikdik, Rotbauchdikdik. *Spanish*: Dicdic de Harar. *Russian*: Харарский диқдик. *Amharic*: Yesolt enshoo, inshu. *Arabic*: Um Digdig. *Somali*: Sakaro.

SUBSPECIES Monotypic. Formerly considered a subspecies of *M. saltiana* (Salt's Dik-dik).

SIMILAR SPECIES Somewhat larger than the other short-snouted races, but has slightly smaller horns. Silver Dik-dik is grizzled silvery, while the limbs, ears, and muzzle are ochraceous in color.

REPRODUCTION *Gestation*: Probably 150-180 days. *Young per Birth*: 1. *Weaning*: 1.5-4 months. *Sexual Maturity*: 6-9 months. *Life Span*: 14 years. No specific information is available for this species, but probably similar to other Salt's Dik-diks.

BEHAVIOR *Family Group*: Monogamous pairs on territories defended by ♂. *Diet*: Herbivorous browsers: leaves of scrub, bushes, buds, flowers, fruit, and herbs; however, they browse mainly on acacia bushes; apparently they do not drink, getting all their moisture from their food. *Main Predators*: Hyena, leopard, cheetah, caracal, several other cats, jackal, baboon, eagle, and pythons. No specific information is available for this species, but probably similar to other Salt's Dik-diks. More active at night, but depending on the season, they also may be crepuscular. They are monogamous, and the pairs occur together most of the time. For the most part, Dik-diks are shy and elusive.

DISTRIBUTION *Native*: Ethiopia, Somalia. South of the Chercher Mountains in Ethiopia, extending from the Webi Shebeli River eastward to the Somali border, and into NW Somalia perhaps as far as the Golis Mountains. The extent of its range in the Ogaden region S and SE of the Chercher Mountains is not known. It appears to overlap with Phillips's Dik-dik at the N end of the Golis Mountains, and with Swayne's Dik-dik to the E of Harar.

HABITAT Dry land with barren scrub and areas with acacia trees and dense underbush, and also on mountainous slopes covered with scrub.

STATUS Least Concern. Estimated total population for all Salt's Dik-dik group at 485,600 individuals (1999), but there is no current data available for many regions. It occurs in a few protected areas like Awash and Yangudi Rassa NP in Ethiopia. Rather common in the Ogaden. Its status is secure in Djibouti; however, its density appears to be much lower in comparison to that in other countries like Ethiopia, and in areas with human impact its numbers are locally decreasing. However, the taxonomic status of different species remains unclear.

Lawrance's Dik-dik
MADOQUA LAWRANCEI

BL: 52-67 cm. SH: 33-40.5 cm. TL: 3-4 cm. W: 2.1 kg (♂), 2.5-3 kg (♀). HL: To 9 cm (♂). Similar to the Phillips's Dik-dik. Short, squared-off, furry nose, large eyes, and very thin legs, the hind legs being longer than the forelegs. Coat is thick with a pale silvery agouti color on the back. Legs and shoulder flares are a deep reddish orange, sharply distinct from the back color. Bright rufous nose patch. Underparts white. Brush-like crest of erectile hairs on the forehead, rufous or dull earthy brown in color. White ring around the eye. Black bare patch in front of the eye. Small accessory hooves. Inconspicuous tail. Spike-like horns, found only in males. Female similar to the male, slightly larger and heavier, without horns.

Madoqua lawrenci

OTHER NAMES *French*: Dik-dik de Lawrance. *German*: Lawrance-Dikdik. *Spanish*: Dicdic de Lawrance. *Russian*: Дикдик Лоуренса. *Amharic*: Yesolt enshoo, inshu. *Arabic*: Um Digdig. *Somali*: Sakaro.

SUBSPECIES Monotypic. Formerly considered a subspecies of *M. saltiana* (Salt's Dik-dik).

SIMILAR SPECIES Somewhat larger than the other short-snouted races, but has slightly smaller horns. Silver Dik-dik is grizzled silvery, while the limbs, ears, and muzzle are ochraceous in color.

REPRODUCTION *Gestation*: Probably 150-180 days. *Young per Birth*: 1. *Weaning*: 1.5-4 months. *Sexual Maturity*: 6-9 months. *Life Span*: 14 years. No specific information is available for this species, but probably similar to other Salt's Dik-diks.

BEHAVIOR *Family Group*: Monogamous pairs on territories defended by ♂. *Diet*: Herbivorous browsers: leaves of scrub, bushes, buds, flowers, fruit, and herbs; however, they browse mainly on acacia bushes; apparently they do not drink, getting all the moisture from their food. *Main Predators*: Hyena, leopard, cheetah, caracal, several other cats, jackal, baboon, eagle, and pythons. No specific information is available for this species, but probably similar to other Salt's Dik-diks. Predominantly a nocturnal and crepuscular species, lying up in dense shade during the day. Predation must be the main factor suppressing bright colors in the western part of their range. Colors appear to correspond with color-coding for aggressive and submissive gestures. Subordinates of both sexes lower their forequarters and expose their grayer backs. Dominant animals flare their red or yellow crests and strut in high-stepping, side-on displays of the red or yellow limbs and flanks. Very commonly occur in pairs or small family groups. The family group works together to maintain a territory. Within these territories they use well-defined paths, or runs. These runs are used to navigate through thick vegetation. Runs can also be used to mark territory boundaries with droppings. When they are alarmed, they erect the tuft of hair on their forehead and run away in a zigzag pattern. They also make an alarm call which sounds like the words "dik-dik.".

DISTRIBUTION *Native*: Somalia. Found in E and SE Somalia. Its distribution to the W is limited by arid country.

HABITAT Evergreen and semi-deciduous bushlands and thickets in the Horn of Africa.

STATUS Least Concern. Current population status is unknown.

Cape Klipspringer
OREOTRAGUS OREOTRAGUS

BL: 83 cm. SH: 42 cm. TL: 7-13 cm. W: 9-12 kg (♂), 11-18 kg (♀). HL: 7.5-9 cm (♂). Largest subspecies of Klipspringer, with particularly short horns. Short coat, speckled overall color. Middle of the underside is pale, and the chin and throat are pale yellowish. Dark brown patch above each hoof. Ears relatively short, whitish, with a thick black line along the rim. Forehead reddish brown. Very large, slit-like preorbital glands, especially in males, with bare dark skin surrounding them. Tail very short, reduced to a mere stump. Horns, found in males, are wide-set on the forehead and rise vertically as spikes, shorter than in other subspecies; ringed at the base. Little sexual dimorphism, females being the same size as males, without horns.

Oreotragus oreotragus

OTHER NAMES *French*: Oréotrague du Cap. *German:* Kap-Klippspringer. *Spanish:* Saltarrocas de El Cabo. *Russian:* Капский клипшпрингер. *Afrikaans:* Klipbokkie.

SUBSPECIES Monotypic. The name *O. oreotragus* (Klipspringer) formerly included *O. oreotragus* (Cape Klipspringer), *O. transvaalensis* (Transvaal Klipspringer), *O. stevensoni* (Zimbabwean Klipspringer), *O. tyleri* (Angolan Klipspringer), *O. centralis* (Zambian Klipspringer), *O. aceratos* (Southern Tanzanian Klipspringer), *O. schillingsi* (Maasai Klipspringer), *O. aureus* (Golden Klipspringer), *O. saltatrixoides* (Ethiopian Klipspringer), *O. somalicus* (Somali Klipspringer), and *O. porteousi* (Nigerian Klipspringer) as subspecies: these are all elevated to full species here.

SIMILAR SPECIES Bush Duiker is also similar in outline, though taller and heavier, and has much smaller, backward-pointing horns. Steenbok has larger ears, and more slender build.

REPRODUCTION *Gestation*: 150-210 days. *Young per Birth*: 1. *Weaning:* 4-5 months. *Sexual Maturity:* 1 year. *Life Span*: 15 years. Breeding seasonality varies according to local conditions.

BEHAVIOR *Family Group*: Most commonly in pairs, also solitary individuals or in small family groups, although slightly larger groups may congregate temporarily at feeding sites. *Diet:* Browsers and concentrate selectors with a very wide dietary range. They eat flowers, fruits, young shoots, leaves, and also bones and the soil from termite mounds. They stand on their hind legs to reach higher. Not dependent on drinking water. *Main Predators:* Leopard, caracal, serval, hyena, jackal, large snakes. Active in the early morning and more especially in the late afternoon. Like other Klipspringers, they run with a jerky, bounding gait, and jump from rock to rock. They stand motionless for long periods of time on top of rocks, scanning the surroundings, their four feet together. They leave the rocks to feed on the surrounding lowlands. They are territorial. Territories are 15-49 ha in area, and are occupied permanently by a ♂ and a ♀ and their young, but it is the ♂ that chases off trespassers. The owners may wander outside their territory to specific feeding sites, including salt licks. Territories are marked by dung piles, especially around borders, and both sexes mark with preorbital glands; the ♀ marks first, pushing the end of a twig into her gland, followed by the ♂, who overmarks the twig.

DISTRIBUTION *Native*: South Africa. Found S of Northern, Western, and Eastern Cape Provinces, South Africa.

HABITAT Mountainous regions, rocky hills, kopjes, gorges, moving between quite widely spaced rocky areas.

STATUS Least Concern.

PHOTO CREDITS ♂: *Jean-Marc Strydom* and *Craig Adams*, Augrabies NP (South Africa). Head ♂: *NJR ZA*, Augrabies NP (South Africa). ♀: *Tudor Owen*, Augrabies NP (South Africa). Head ♂: *Jean-Marc Strydom*, Augrabies NP (South Africa).

Ethiopian Klipspringer
OREOTRAGUS SALTATRIXOIDES

BL: 75-115 cm. SH: 43-60 cm. TL: 6.5-10.5 cm. W: 8-18 kg. HL: To 15 cm (♂). A small subspecies of Klipspringer. General color is golden, more deeply colored on the neck. Well speckled, less extensive on the rump. Belly and insides of the ears are white. Ears have a conspicuous black border. Nose is black, as are the large preorbital glands. Body is sturdy and the hindquarters are overdeveloped. Tail very short, reduced to a mere stump. The hooves look like vertical cylinders; the animal walks on the blunt hoof tips. Horns, found in males, are wide-set on the forehead and rise vertically as short spikes; ridged at the base. Females somewhat larger and heavier than males, generally without horns, except those from Bale Mountains.

Oreotragus saltatrixoides

OTHER NAMES Abyssinian Klipspringer. *French*: Oréotrague d'Éthiopie. *German*: Äthiopien-Klippspringer. *Spanish*: Saltarrocas etíope. *Russian*: Эфиопский клипшпрингер.

SUBSPECIES Monotypic. Formerly considered a subspecies of *O. oreotragus* (Klipspringer).

SIMILAR SPECIES Nigerian Klipspringer is very similar in pelage color, varying from dull yellowish to darker, more golden. Dorsal stripe is broad and gray, sometimes reduced to speckling down the midline of the back. Crown and upper muzzle are golden. Thighs and legs are grayish, with the upper part of forelegs paler. Horns found only in ♂.

REPRODUCTION *Gestation*: 210 days. *Young per Birth*: 1. *Weaning*: 4-5 months. *Sexual Maturity*: 1 year. *Life Span*: 15 years. Seasonal breeder, with the degree of seasonality varying according to local conditions, probably in August-September.

BEHAVIOR *Family Group*: Monogamous pairs with young offspring; occasionally live singly. *Diet*: Mainly browsers, because shrubs are much more common than grasses in their habitat. *Main Predators*: Leopard, caracal, serval, hyena, jackal, large snakes. ♂ are much more vigilant than ♀, standing like statues for up to half an hour. A pair are usually only 2 m apart. The ♀ is usually the first to begin moving; the ♂ stays close, but actual contact is rare, usually just an approach and a sniff of the face and rump, or rubbing the muzzles together. They make alarm calls in duet. Those living in the gorge begin moving and feeding early in the morning, when the sun reaches them, while those living on the escarpment remain in shelter, out of the wind, until the sun reaches them. At midday, those in the gorge go behind the rocks and bushes out of the sun, spending more time resting, less time feeding, whereas those on the escarpment remain active until late afternoon. Pairs have exclusive territories of 8 ha in size, which they defend fiercely. These territories contain dung piles up to 3 m in diameter, 10 cm high, usually on flat ground 10 to 100 m apart, with smaller piles between. Urination and defecation are not ritualized. Twigs are often marked with the preorbital secretion, including after defecation; the secretion is thick and tarry.

DISTRIBUTION *Native*: Ethiopia. Found in Ethiopia, S to Lake Turkana and E to Harar.

HABITAT Steep rocky terrain in savannas in Ethiopia, as high as 3,300 m, where temperatures fall to freezing at night.

STATUS Least Concern.

PHOTO CREDITS ♂: *Tim Strater*, Rotterdam Zoo (Netherlands). Head ♂: *Jonas Livet,* Bioparc Valencia (Spain). ♀: *Quartl*, Frankfurt Zoo (Germany). Head ♀: *Joachim S. Müller,* Frankfurt Zoo (Germany) and Bale Mountains (Ethiopia).

Nyasa Klipspringer
OREOTRAGUS ACERATOS

BL: 75-115 cm. SH: 43-60 cm. TL: 6.5-10.5 cm. W: 8-18 kg. HL: 9.5 cm (♂). The forequarters are more yellowish or ocher, and only the hindquarters olive, much less yellow, with the 2 zones quite well separated. Legs are gray. Belly and insides of the ears are white. Ears have a conspicuous black border. Nose is black, as are the large preorbital glands. Body is sturdy and the hindquarters are overdeveloped. Tail very short, reduced to a mere stump. The hooves look like vertical cylinders; the animal walks on the blunt hoof tips. Horns, found in males, are wide-set on the forehead and rise vertically as short spikes; ridged at the base. Little sexual dimorphism, females being the same size as males, without horns.

Oreotragus aceratos

OTHER NAMES Noack's Klipspringer, Southern Tanzanian Klipspringer. *French*: Oréotrague de Noack. *German*: Tansania-Klippspringer. *Spanish*: Saltarrocas de Noack. *Russian*: Клипшпрингер Ноака. *Swahili*: Mbuzimawe kati.

SUBSPECIES Monotypic. Formerly considered a subspecies of *O. oreotragus* (Klipspringer).

SIMILAR SPECIES Zambian Klipspringer (*O. centralis*) is very similar, and differs only in the larger size of the ♀. Oribi is similar in outline, though taller and heavier, with a more slender build and a distinctive black patch below the ears. Bush Duiker is also similar in outline, though taller and heavier, and has much smaller, backward-pointing horns. Steenbok has larger ears, and more slender build.

REPRODUCTION *Gestation*: 210 days. *Young per Birth*: 1. *Weaning*: 4-5 months. *Sexual Maturity*: 1 year. *Life Span*: 15 years. There is no specific information available for this species, but probably similar to other Klipspringers. Seasonal breeder, with the degree of seasonality varying according to local conditions. Young are kept hidden for the first 2-3 months.

BEHAVIOR *Family Group*: Typical groups consists of an adult pair; in some cases a pair of ♀ or single individuals; group sizes of up to 5 can occur in exceptional cases. *Diet:* Like other Klipspringers, mainly browsers, because shrubs are much more common than grasses in their habitat. *Main Predators:* Leopard, caracal, serval, hyena, jackal, large snakes. There is no specific information available for this species, but probably like other Klipspringers. Mainly active during the early morning and late afternoon, resting during the hottest part of the day among rocks or beneath overhangs. Remarkable agility among the steep rocks of native kopjes, attributed to a set of unique feet; they stand on the very tips of their almost circular hooves, each about 15-20 mm in diameter. The strong back legs can project them up a smooth wall, and they can jump with all four feet. Pairs have exclusive territories of 8-49 ha in size, which they defend fiercely. Both sexes are involved in marking with their preorbital glands. When alarmed, a sentinel within the group emits a shrill whistle to alert the other animals, at which they head for cover. Intruding ♂ are chased by the territorial ♂, and there may be a fight, with slow approaches followed by head butting and occasional wounding.

DISTRIBUTION *Native*: Tanzania. Found in S Tanzania.

HABITAT Rocky areas, like other Klipspringers.

STATUS Least Concern.

PHOTO CREDITS *Jos van de Leijgraaf*, Ruaha NP (Tanzania).

Transvaal Klipspringer
OREOTRAGUS TRANSVAALENSIS

BL: 80-88 cm. SH: 45-60 cm. TL: 7-13 cm. W: 9-12 kg (♂), 11-18 kg (♀). HL: 8.7-12.7 cm (♂). A large subspecies of Klipspringer. Body is sturdy and the hindquarters are overdeveloped. Color is bright golden yellow, with strongly contrasting white underparts. Feet above the hooves are brown. Ears short. Nose is black, as are the large preorbital glands. Tail very short, reduced to a mere stump. Horns, found in males, very long, among the largest of all Klipspringers, contrasting strongly with those of Cape Klipspringer (*O. oreotragus*). Females somewhat larger and heavier than males, without horns.

♀

Young

♂

230

Oreotragus transvaalensis

OTHER NAMES *French*: Oréotrague du Transvaal. *German*: Transvaal-Klippspringer. *Spanish*: Saltarrocas de Transvaal. *Russian*: Трансваальский клипшпрингер. *Afrikaans*: Klipbokkie. *Swahili*: Ngurunguru, mbuzi mawe.

SUBSPECIES Monotypic. Formerly considered a subspecies of *O. oreotragus* (Klipspringer).

SIMILAR SPECIES Oribi is similar in outline, though taller and heavier, with a more slender build and a distinctive black patch below the ears. Bush Duiker is also similar in outline, though taller and heavier, and has much smaller, backward-pointing horns. Steenbok has larger ears, and more slender build.

REPRODUCTION *Gestation*: 210 days. *Young per Birth*: 1. *Weaning*: 4-5 months. *Sexual Maturity*: 1 year. *Life Span*: 15 years. Courtship and mating in July, suggesting a stronger seasonality than in other Klipspringers. Births during the rains in November-December.

BEHAVIOR *Family Group*: Most commonly in pairs, also solitary individuals or in small family groups, although slightly larger groups may congregate temporarily at feeding sites. *Diet*: Selective browsing of flowers, tender green shoots, and fruits of a wide variety of shrubs and herbs; hardly ever feeds on grass. Not dependent on drinking water. *Main Predators*: Leopard, caracal, serval, hyena, jackal, large snakes. Both the ♂ and the ♀ scent mark their ranges. A pair of preorbital glands below the eyes produces the scent. The secretion produced is a sticky milky substance that is deposited on a suitable twig. Most activity is early and late in the day, also on moonlit nights. Stands on its hind legs to reach foliage. Drinks when water is available, but can do without it by obtaining moisture from vegetation. Its eyesight and hearing are good, more important than its sense of smell. Often seen keeping watch from the top of a rock. Its characteristic pose is to stand with its back hunched and all four hooves almost touching. Warning call is a sharp whistle. Able to run up and down steep cliffs and leap from rock to rock in a phenomenal manner. Its gait is a series of abrupt, jerky hops.

DISTRIBUTION *Native*: Botswana, Mozambique, South Africa, Swaziland, Zimbabwe. Found in KwaZulu-Natal and Transvaal, South Africa, Swaziland, SE Zimbabwe, and probably in neighboring areas of Botswana and Mozambique.

HABITAT Well adapted to live in rocky conditions, confined to rocky outcrops, kopjes, and mountains.

STATUS Least Concern.

PHOTO CREDITS ♂: *Dt Stephen Williams*, Kruger NP (South Africa). Head ♂: *Ian White*, Limpopo (South Africa). ♀: *Frik Erasmus*, Kruger NP (South Africa). Young: *Jonathan Keytel*, Marakele (South Africa).

Maasai Klipspringer
OREOTRAGUS SCHILLINGSI

BL: 77-84 cm. SH: 45-60 cm. TL: 7-13 cm. W: 10 kg (♂), 13 kg (♀). HL: 8-8.7 cm (♂), 6.7-9.5 cm (♀). A large subspecies of Klipspringer with horned females. General color very rich, bright orange, with contrasting gray legs and dark pasterns. Midback region is darker. There may be some variation in color. Big rounded ears, with a conspicuous black border, white inside with radiating dlark lines. Nose is black, as are the large preorbital glands. Body is sturdy and hindquarters are overdeveloped. Tail very short, reduced to a mere stump. The hooves look like vertical cylinders; the animal walks on the blunt hoof tips. Horns, found in both sexes, widely spaced. Females larger and heavier than males, with slender necks and slightly smaller preorbital glands.

Oreotragus schillingsi

OTHER NAMES Tanzanian Klipspringer, Northern Klipspringer, Schillings's Klipspringer, Maasailand Klipspringer. *French*: Oréotrague de Schillings. *German*: Massai-Klippspringer. *Spanish*: Saltarrocas de Schillings. *Russian*: Масайский клипшпрингер. *Maasai*: Enkine, o soito. *Swahili*: Mbuzimawe kaskazi.

SUBSPECIES Monotypic. Formerly considered a subspecies of *O. oreotragus* (Klipspringer). Considered as a synonym of *O. saltatrixoides* by some authors.

SIMILAR SPECIES Oribi is similar in outline, though taller and heavier, with a more slender build and a distinctive black patch below the ears. Bush Duiker is also similar in outline, though taller and heavier, and has much smaller, backward-pointing horns. Steenbok has larger ears, and more slender build.

REPRODUCTION *Gestation*: 210 days. *Young per Birth*: 1. *Weaning*: 4-5 months. *Sexual Maturity*: 1 year. *Life Span*: 15 years. After hiding for up to 3 months, calves stay close to mother, nursing twice a day for 7 to 8 minutes, during which father remains on highest alert.

BEHAVIOR *Family Group*: Monogamous pairs with young offspring. *Diet:* Grasses, leaves, blossoms, fruit, lichens. *Main Predators:* Leopard, caracal, serval, hyena, jackal, large snakes. The territories of this subspecies average less than 2 ha, whereas in all other subspecies territories are much larger, suggesting than ♀, being large and having horns, are as competitive as the ♂ or more so. These territories may be seasonal; during the dry season, a group of kopjes may be unoccupied, but after the rains Klipspringers reestablish themselves there. Klipspringers may typically spend their adult lifetimes within the territory. Families venture outside their territories only when drawn to new growth or a salt lick. If fires burn off their cover and food, Klipspringers will evacuate their territories and take up temporary residence in places they normally avoid. When alarmed they retreat into the rocks for safety. Amazingly agile, they can often be observed bounding up impossibly rough rock faces. They are most active just before and after midday. Both sexes are involved in marking with their preorbital glands. When alarmed, a sentinel within the group emits a shrill whistle to alert the other animals, at which they head for cover.

DISTRIBUTION *Native*: Kenya, Tanzania, Uganda. *Possibly Extinct:* Burundi. Kenya, S of Mount Kenya, Uganda as far W as Dodoth Hills, Tanzania S to Rukwa, and presumably Rwanda and formerly Burundi.

HABITAT Rocky outcrops in Tsavo, Amboseli, Maasai Mara, Marsabit, and Meru reserves.

STATUS Least Concern.

PHOTO CREDITS ♂: *John H. Gavin*, Tsavo NP (Kenya). Head ♂: *Stan Darling*, Lemala North Camp, Serengeti (Tanzania). ♀: Serengeti (Tanzania). Head ♀: *Jan Sevcik*, Tsavo NP (Kenya).

Golden Klipspringer
OREOTRAGUS AUREUS

BL: 75-84 cm. SH: 45-60 cm. TL: 6-9.5 cm. W: 10-18 kg. HL: To 8.3-10.4 cm (♂). A small species of Klipspringer, distinguished from the Maasai Klipspringer only by hornless females. General color is golden yellow, with a very slight difference between the body and the legs. The belly and insides of the ears are white. The crown of the head is reddish, in marked contrast to the body color. Ears have a conspicuous black border. Nose is black, as are the large preorbital glands. Tail very short. The hooves look like vertical cylinders. Horns, found in males, are wide-set on the forehead and rise vertically as short spikes; ringed at the base. Females are slightly smaller than males, without horns.

Oreotragus aureus

OTHER NAMES Marsabit Klipspringer. *French*: Oréotrague de Heller. *German*: Kenia-Klippspringer. *Spanish*: Saltarrocas dorado. *Russian*: Золотистый клипшпрингер.

SUBSPECIES Monotypic. Formerly considered a subspecies of *O. oreotragus* (Klipspringer). Golden Klipspringer is considered as a synonym of Maasai Klipspringer (*schillingsi*) by some authors.

SIMILAR SPECIES Oribi is similar in outline, though taller and heavier, with a more slender build and a distinctive black patch below the ears. Bush Duiker is also similar in outline, though taller and heavier, and has much smaller, backward-pointing horns. Steenbok has larger ears, and more slender build.

REPRODUCTION *Gestation*: 150-210 days. *Young per Birth*: 1. *Weaning*: 4-5 months. *Sexual Maturity*: 1 year. *Life Span*: 15 years. After birth, the young remain concealed in crevices for 2-3 months.

BEHAVIOR *Family Group*: Monogamous pairs with young offspring. *Diet*: Grasses, leaves, blossoms, fruit, lichens. *Main Predators*: Leopard, caracal, serval, hyena, jackal, large snakes. Mainly active during the early morning and late afternoon, resting during the hottest part of the day among rocks or beneath overhangs. Remarkable agility among the steep rocks of native kopjes, attributed to a set of unique feet, standing on the very tips of its almost circular hooves, each about 15-20 mm in diameter. The strong back legs can project them up a smooth wall, and they can jump with all four feet. Pairs have exclusive territories of 8-49 ha in size, which they defend fiercely. Both sexes are involved in marking with their preorbital glands. When alarmed, a sentinel within the group emits a shrill whistle to alert the other animals, at which they head for cover.

DISTRIBUTION *Native*: Kenya, Uganda. Found from the drainage area of the N Ewaso Ng´iro River and the N slopes of Mount Kenya northward to Lake Rudolf, W as far as Mount Elgon, and E in the lower desert region to S of the Tana River, and also from the Ankole region in SW Uganda.

HABITAT Rocky areas including mountainous regions, rocky hills, kopjes, and gorges, like other Klipspringers.

STATUS Least Concern.

PHOTO CREDITS *Dino J. Martins/Dudu Diaries*, Laikipia, Ol Malo and Lentille Conservancy (Kenya).

Angolan Klipspringer
OREOTRAGUS TYLERI

BL: 77-91 cm (♂). SH: 50-57 cm (♂). TL: 6.5-10 cm. W: 5-16 kg. HL: 8.5-10 cm (♂). A medium-sized subspecies of Klipspringer. General color is weakly speckled pale sandy ocher. Legs are gray, with no noticeable speckling. Underparts are extensively white, as in Transvaal and Zimbabwean Klipspringer. Region above the hooves is conspicuously dark brown. Ears are yellow inside and out, longer than in southern and eastern subspecies. Nose is black, as are the large preorbital glands. Tail very short, reduced to a mere stump. Hooves look like vertical cylinders. Horns, found only in males, rise vertically as short spikes; ringed at the base. Females larger than males, without horns.

Oreotragus tyleri

OTHER NAMES Tyler's Klipspringer. *French*: Oréotrague de Tyler. *German*: Angola-Klippspringer. *Spanish*: Saltarrocas de Angola. *Russian*: Ангольский клипшпрингер.

SUBSPECIES Monotypic. Formerly considered a subspecies of *O. oreotragus* (Klipspringer). Includes *cunenensis* (Angola, Kambele Falls, N bank of Cunene River, and Namibia, Kaokoveld) and *steinhardti* (Namibia, Otjongombe, W of Kaoko Otavi).

SIMILAR SPECIES Oribi is similar in outline, though taller and heavier, with a more slender build and a distinctive black patch below the ears. Bush Duiker is also similar in outline, though taller and heavier, and has much smaller, backward-pointing horns.

REPRODUCTION *Gestation*: 150-214 days. *Young per Birth*: 1. *Weaning*: 4-5 months. *Sexual Maturity*: 1 year. *Life Span*: 15 years. Young are born in a protected rocky recess and remain hidden for 2-3 months. Horns begin to develop at 6 months and are fully grown at 17-18 months. Young reach adult size after 1 year, and are evicted from the group.

BEHAVIOR *Family Group*: Monogamous pairs with young offspring. *Diet:* Selective browsing of flowers, tender green shoots, and fruits of a wide variety of shrubs and herbs; hardly ever feeds on grass. Not dependent on drinking water. *Main Predators:* Leopard, jackal, spotted hyena; calves are vulnerable to eagles and baboons. Mainly active during the early morning and late afternoon, resting during the hottest part of the day among rocks or beneath overhangs. Because Klipspringers must often leave their refuges to forage, they are very alert to predators and to alarm signals of other species. They react by fleeing to higher ground with or without first calling, the ♀ leading. Once safe, they give whistling alarm calls in duet. ♂ and ♀ form lasting bonds and both sexes defend their permanent territories. At most, groups of up to 8 can be seen together, which are probably family groups from neighboring territories. Pairs have exclusive territories, which they defend fiercely. Territories are larger than in other subspecies, averaging 100 ha. The hollow bristly hair of Klipspringers has the function of regulating their temperature; it insulates them against extreme cold and heat, and reflects the heat from their surroundings during the hotter times of the day.

DISTRIBUTION *Native*: Angola, Namibia. Found in the Kaokoveld in S Angola, and the Naukluft and Kuiseb Canyon in Namibia, in the central highlands and W escarpment, but not in the far N of the Caprivi Strip. Exact limits and degree of intergradation with the Cape Klipspringer (*O. oreotragus*) are unclear.

HABITAT Rocky areas including mountainous regions.

STATUS Least Concern.

PHOTO CREDITS ♂: *Kate Boydell* (Namibia). Head ♂: *Thomas Eisenhut (www.xeta.at)*, Ai-Ais Richtersveld Transfrontier Park (Namibia). ♀: *Erongo Mountains (Namibia)*. Head ♀: *Paul Moquin* (Namibia).

Zimbabwean Klipspringer

OREOTRAGUS STEVENSONI

BL: 82-92 cm (♂), 88-100 cm (♀). SH: 49-52 cm (♂), 50-54 cm (♀). TL: 6.5-10 cm. W: 9-11.6 kg (♂), 5-16 kg (♀). HL: 9-11.5 cm (♂). One of the smallest species of Klipspringer. Short coat made of hollow, brittle hairs. Color much duller than that of Transvaal Klipspringer, being strongly grizzled, with black on the dorsum but not on the flanks, and the head is much darker. Undersides extensively white, as in Transvaal Klipspringer. Ears have a conspicuous black border. Nose is black, as are the large preorbital glands. Tail very short, reduced to a mere stump. The hooves look like vertical cylinders. Horns, found only in males, are particularly long, rising vertically as short spikes; ringed at the base. Females slightly larger than males, without horns.

♀

Young

♂

238

Oreotragus stevensoni

OTHER NAMES Stevenson's Klipspringer. *French*: Oréotrague de Stevenson. *German*: Simbabwe-Klippspringer. *Spanish*: Saltarrocas de Stevenson. *Russian*: Антилопа-прыгун (клипшпрингер) Стивенсона. *Afrikaans*: Klipbokkie. *Swahili*: Ngurunguru, mbuzi mawe.

SUBSPECIES Monotypic. Formerly considered a subspecies of *O. oreotragus* (Klipspringer).

SIMILAR SPECIES Oribi is similar in outline, though taller and heavier, with a more slender build and a distinctive black patch below the ears. Bush Duiker is also similar in outline, though taller and heavier, and has much smaller, backward-pointing horns.

REPRODUCTION *Gestation*: 150-214 days. *Young per Birth*: 1. *Weaning*: 4-5 months. *Sexual Maturity*: 1 year. *Life Span*: 15 years. Mating has been observed in July, and lambing coinciding with the wet season. The ♂ follows the ♀ closely, with laufschlag, and blocks her movement, standing with arched neck; ♀ may bite ♂, and they circle tightly before mating. Birth occurs in dense vegetation or among rocks; the young lie quietly for 2-3 months, and walk unsteadily.

BEHAVIOR *Family Group*: Monogamous pairs with young offspring. *Diet:* Leaves, new shoots, berries, fruits, seedpods, flowers of woody plants, forbs, and some new grass. Generally all moisture is obtained from their food. *Main Predators:* Leopard, caracal, serval, hyena, jackal, large snakes. Very vigilant, reacting to the alarm call of other species. They give alarm whistles or flee silently, usually to a higher vantage point, where they begin continuous trumpeting alarm calls, made through the nose. Mainly active during the early morning and late afternoon, resting during the hottest part of the day among rocks or beneath overhangs. Remarkable agility among the steep rocks of native kopjes, attributed to a set of unique feet; they stand on the very tips of their almost circular hooves, each about 15-20 mm in diameter. The strong back legs can project them up a smooth wall, and they can jump with all four feet. Pairs have exclusive territories of 8-49 ha in size, which they defend fiercely. Both sexes are involved in marking with their preorbital glands.

DISTRIBUTION *Native*: Botswana, Zimbabwe. Found in W Zimbabwe and N and E Botswana.

HABITAT Rocky areas including mountainous regions, rocky hills, kopjes, and gorges.

STATUS Least Concern.

PHOTO CREDITS ♂: *Isaac Hsieh*, San Diego Zoo (USA). Head ♂: *Christian Dionne*, Dallas Zoo (USA). ♀: San Diego Zoo (USA). Head ♀: *Lorraine Paulhus*, San Diego Zoo (USA). Young: *Lazzete Gifford*, Omaha Zoo (USA) and Lincoln Park Zoo (USA).

Zambian Klipspringer
OREOTRAGUS CENTRALIS

BL: 75-115 cm. SH: 45-60 cm. TL: 7-13 cm. W: 10-18 kg. HL: 7.5-12.5 cm (♂). General color is deep reddish to orange to yellow gray, with some individuals exhibiting a dazzling black and yellow effect. The belly and insides of the ears are white. Legs are gray, contrasting with the body color. In some individuals, there is no black above the hooves. Ears have a conspicuous black border. Nose is black, as are the large preorbital glands. Body is sturdy and the hindquarters are overdeveloped. Tail very short, reduced to a mere stump. The hooves look like vertical cylinders. Horns, found in males, rise vertically as short spikes; ringed at the base. Females somewhat larger and heavier than males.

Oreotragus centralis

OTHER NAMES Southern Klipspringer. *French*: Oréotrague de Zambie. *German*: Sambia-Klippspringer. *Spanish*: Saltarrocas de Zambia. *Russian*: Замбийский (центральноафриканский) клипшпрингер. *Swahili*: Mbuzimawe kusi.

SUBSPECIES Monotypic. Formerly considered a subspecies of *O. oreotragus* (Klipspringer). Includes *saltator* (Sassa Antelope, E DR Congo from Katanga and NW of Lake Tanganyika).

SIMILAR SPECIES Oribi is similar in outline, though taller and heavier, with a more slender build and a distinctive black patch below the ears. Bush Duiker is also similar in outline, though taller and heavier, and has much smaller, backward-pointing horns. Steenbok has larger ears, and more slender build.

REPRODUCTION *Gestation*: 150-210 days. *Young per Birth*: 1. *Weaning*: 4-5 months. *Sexual Maturity*: 1 year. *Life Span*: 15 years. Non-seasonal breeder; pregnant females have been recorded in all months, except in December-January. After birth, the young remain concealed in crevices for 2-3 months.

BEHAVIOR *Family Group*: Monogamous pairs with young offspring. *Diet*: Leaves, berries, fruits, seedpods, flowers. *Main Predators*: Leopard, caracal, serval, hyena, jackal, large snakes. Mainly active during the early morning and late afternoon, resting during the hottest part of the day among rocks or beneath overhangs. Remarkable agility among the steep rocks of native kopjes, attributed to a set of unique feet; they stand on the very tips of its almost circular hooves, each about 15-20 mm in diameter. The strong back legs can project them up a smooth wall, and they can jump with all four feet. Pairs have exclusive territories, which they defend fiercely. Both sexes are involved in marking with their preorbital glands. When alarmed, a sentinel within the group emits a shrill whistle to alert the other animals, at which they head for cover.

DISTRIBUTION *Native*: DR Congo, Malawi, Tanzania, Zambia, Zimbabwe. Found in Zambia, including the Luangwa Valley; probably also SE DR Congo (Katanga), N Malawi, SW Tanzania, and Zimbabwe.

HABITAT Rocky areas including mountainous regions, like other Klipspringers.

STATUS Least Concern.

PHOTO CREDITS ♂ and ♀: *Dave Appleton*, Nyika NP (Malawi). Heads: *BeechcraftMUC*, Lower Zambezi NP (Zambia).

Somali Klipspringer
OREOTRAGUS SOMALICUS

BL: 75-77 cm. SH: 51-53 cm. TL: 7-8 cm. W: 10-18 kg. HL: To 15 cm (♂). The smallest species of Klipspringer. Short coat made of hollow, brittle hairs that range in color from gray to yellow olive, giving the coat a grizzled appearance. There is little or no differentiation of color between foreparts and hind parts. The crown of the head is brown. Ears have a conspicuous black border. Nose is black, as are the large preorbital glands. Legs are contrastingly gray in front. The belly and insides of the ears are white. Tail very short, reduced to a mere stump. The hooves look like vertical cylinders. Horns, found only in males, are particularly large. Females much larger and heavier than males, without horns.

Oreotragus somalicus

OTHER NAMES *French*: Oréotrague de Somalie. *German*: Somalie-Klippspringer. *Spanish*: Saltarrocas de Somalia. *Russian*: Сомалийский клипшпрингер.

SUBSPECIES Monotypic. Formerly considered a subspecies of *O. oreotragus* (Klipspringer). Considered as a synonym of *O. saltatrixoides* by some authors.

SIMILAR SPECIES Oribi is similar in outline, though taller and heavier, with a more slender build and a distinctive black patch below the ears. Bush Duiker is also similar in outline, though taller and heavier, and has much smaller, backward-pointing horns.

REPRODUCTION *Gestation*: 150-210 days. *Young per Birth*: 1. *Weaning*: 4-5 months. *Sexual Maturity*: 1 year. *Life Span*: 15 years. There is no specific information available for this species, but probably like other Klipspringers. Given the habitat and climate of its range, breeding is likely to be seasonal. After birth, the young remain concealed in crevices for 2-3 months.

BEHAVIOR *Family Group*: Monogamous pairs with young offspring. *Diet*: Grasses, leaves, blossoms, fruit, lichens. *Main Predators*: Leopard, caracal, serval, hyena, jackal, large snakes. Mainly active during the early morning and late afternoon, resting during the hottest part of the day among rocks or beneath overhangs. Remarkable agility among the steep rocks of native kopjes, attributed to a set of unique feet; they stand on the very tips of its almost circular hooves, each about 15-20 mm in diameter. The strong back legs can project them up a smooth wall, and they can jump with all four feet. Pairs have exclusive territories of 8-49 ha in size, which they defend fiercely. Both sexes are involved in marking with their preorbital glands. When alarmed, a sentinel within the group emits a shrill whistle to alert the other animals, at which they head for cover.

DISTRIBUTION *Native*: Djibouti, Eritrea, Ethiopia, Somalia, Sudan. Found in N Sudan through Eritrea and N Somalia to N Ethiopia.

HABITAT Rocky areas including mountainous regions, like other Klipspringers.

STATUS Least Concern.

Nigerian Klipspringer
OREOTRAGUS PORTEOUSI

BL: 75-115 cm. SH: 43-60 cm. TL: 6.5-10.5 cm. W: 8-18 kg. HL: 9-11 cm (♂). A small subspecies of Klipspringer. General color varies from dull yellowish to darker, more golden, very similar to the Maasai Klipspringer. Dorsal stripe is dark and gray, reduced to speckling down the midline of the back. Crown and upper muzzle are golden. Belly is white. Ears are gray. Upper parts of the forelegs are paler, and the lower parts are gray. Thighs and legs are grayish. Tail very short. The hooves look like vertical cylinders; the animal walks on the blunt hoof tips. Horns are wide-set on the forehead and rise vertically as short spikes; ringed at the base. Degree of sexual dimorphism is unknown.

Oreotragus porteousi

OTHER NAMES Western Klipspringer. *French*: Oréotrague de Porteous. *German*: Nigeria-Klippspringer. *Spanish*: Saltarrocas de Nigeria. *Russian*: Западный (нигерийский) клипшпрингер.

SUBSPECIES Monotypic. Formerly considered a subspecies of *O. oreotragus* (Klipspringer). Includes *hyatti* (Hyatt's Klipspringer, from N Nigeria). Considered as a synonym of Ethiopian Klipspringer (*O. saltatrixoides*) by some authors.

REPRODUCTION *Gestation*: 210 days. *Young per Birth*: 1. *Weaning*: 4-5 months. *Sexual Maturity*: 1 year. *Life Span*: 15 years. There is no specific information available for this species.

BEHAVIOR *Family Group*: Monogamous pairs with young offspring; occasionally live singly. *Diet:* Grasses, leaves, blossoms, fruit, lichens. *Main Predators:* Leopard, caracal, serval, hyena, jackal, large snakes. There is no specific information available for this species, but probably crepuscular, with most activity in the early morning and late afternoon. Probably territorial, like other Klipspringers.

DISTRIBUTION *Native*: Nigeria. Found only on the Jos Plateau, in central Nigeria; it is known to occur in Lame-Burra Game Reserve and in Gashaka-Gumti NP; there is a population of Klipspringers in the Central African Republic which may belong to this species.

HABITAT Steep rocky areas.

STATUS Endangered. Estimated population is fewer than 250 mature individuals, and it may eventually decline to extinction.

Southern Bush Duiker

SYLVICAPRA GRIMMIA CAFFRA

BL: 70-105 cm (♂), 90-115 cm (♀). SH: 40-65 cm. TL: 10-20 cm. W: 10-22 kg (♂), 10-26 kg (♀). HL: 7-18 cm (♂). Largest subspecies. Coat color is a pale grayish brown, grizzled with black. Lower parts colored like the back. Chin, belly, and insides of the upper legs are whitish. Short tail is black on the top, contrasting sharply with the fluffy white underside. Forelegs are black. Face is reddish with a dark brown nose stripe, not reaching the top of the head. Ears are long, with narrow pointed tips, separated by a tuft of hair on the forehead. Head is long and narrow. Sharply pointed horns are usually found only in males, more vertically oriented than in other Duiker species, the longest horns of any Bush Duiker. Females are usually larger than males.

♀

♂

Juvenile

Young

Sylvicapra grimmia grimmia

Sylvicapra grimmia caffra

OTHER NAMES Gray Duiker, Common Duiker, Grimm's Duiker. *French*: Céphalophe couronné. *German*: Kronenducker. *Spanish*: Duiqueo o cefalofo común sudafricano, duiquero gris, duiquero de sabana. *Russian*: Капский кустарниковый дукер *(grimmia)*, Натальский кустарниковый дукер *(caffra)*. *Afrikaans*: Gewone Duiker. *Swahili*: Nsya.

SUBSPECIES Southern Bush Duiker includes a number of local subspecies from considerably different habitats and climates: *S. g. grimmia*, *S. g. caffra* (Limpopo Bush Duiker), *S. g. steinhardti* (Kalahari Bush Duiker). East African Bush Duiker: *S. g. nyansae*, *S. g. madoqua*, *S. g. orbicularis*, *S. g. hindei*, *S. g. altivallis*, and *S. g. lobeliarum*. West African Bush Duiker: *S. g. pallidior* (Sahel Duiker), *S. g. coronata* (Crowned Duiker), *S. g. campbelliae* (Northern Bush Duiker). Angolan Common Duiker: *S. g. splendidula*. Invalid southern subspecies include: *burchelli, shirensis,* and *transvaalensis.*

SIMILAR SPECIES Different from the other Duikers in color, general features, and shape of horns. Klipspringer has a shorter and more conic head and broader ears. Oribi is sandy rufous to brownish fawn, with a short head, long neck, no crest between the horns, a naked patch below the eye, and tufts of long hairs on the knees.

REPRODUCTION *Gestation*: 180-210 days. *Young per Birth*: 1. *Weaning*: 2 months. *Sexual Maturity*: 8-10 months (♀), 12 months (♂). *Life Span*: 14 years. After birth, the young lie up in dense cover for a number of weeks.

BEHAVIOR *Family Group*: Usually solitary, although pairs are occasionally sighted. *Diet*: Tree and bush foliage, fruits, seeds, occasionally carrion. *Main Predators*: Large predators, small cats, baboon, crocodile, python, eagle. Feeding predominantly from dusk until dawn, it rests in favorite hiding places in scrub or grass during the day. It has exceptional speed and stamina, and is usually able to outrun dogs that chase after it. The home ranges of individuals of the same sex rarely overlap. However, there is substantial common land in the ranges of individuals of opposite sex. ♂ are territorial, marking their defended areas with preorbital secretions and attacking other ♂ that intrude. The favorite resting place of these ♂ is a high spot overlooking their territory. Juveniles make a loud bleat if caught, which brings the parents running.

DISTRIBUTION *S. g. grimmia:* S South Africa. *S. g. caffra:* S Mozambique, E Zimbabwe, Swaziland, Lesotho, NE South Africa.

HABITAT Sparse forests, brushy steppe, savanna, and mountainous regions throughout sub-Saharan Africa.

STATUS Least Concern.

PHOTO CREDITS ♂ and head: *Alex Meyer,* Lowry Park Zoo (USA). ♀: *Arno Meintjes* (South Africa). Head ♀: *Bernard Dupont,* Kruger (South Africa). Young: *Johannes Pfleiderer* (South Africa).

Kalahari Bush Duiker

SYLVICAPRA GRIMMIA STEINHARDTI

BL: 70-100 cm (♂), 90-115 cm (♀). SH: 50-60 cm. TL: 10-20 cm. W: 15-18 kg (♂), 16-22 kg (♀). HL: 7-18 cm (♂). Coat color is very pale, sandy colored or fawn, with speckling very reduced, with the contrast between the light and the dark bands obliterated, and very few black tips, even in the middorsal region. Facial blaze reaching the level of the eyes, but not reaching the top of the head. Forehead pale ocher. Very large ears. Chest and throat buffy. Underside off-white. Only the upper parts of the inner limb surfaces white, the rest pale buff. Leg stripes broad and black, reaching the knees and the hocks. Pasterns black. Tail black for the terminal two-thirds. Sharply pointed horns, heavily grooved at the base, found only in males. Females are usually larger than males, without horns. Immature animals are darker and grayer.

Sylvicapra grimmia steinhardti

OTHER NAMES Steinhardt's Bush Duiker, Kalahari Common Duiker. *French*: Céphalophe couronné. *German*: Kronenducker. *Spanish*: Duiqueo o cefalofo común del Kalahari. *Russian*: Калахарский кустарниковый дукер. *Afrikaans*: Gewone Duiker.

SUBSPECIES Considered as a subspecies of *S. grimmia* (Bush Duiker): *S. g. grimmia* (Southern Bush Duiker), *S. g. caffra* (Limpopo Bush Duiker), *S. g. steinhardti* (Kalahari Bush Duiker), *S. g. nyansae*, *S. g. madoqua*, *S. g. orbicularis*, *S. g. hindei*, *S. g. altivallis*, *S. g. lobeliarum*, *S. g. pallidior* (Sahel Duiker), *S. g. coronata* (Crowned Duiker), *S. g. campbelliae* (Northern Bush Duiker), *S. g. splendidula* (Angolan Common Duiker). Includes *cunenensis* (N Kaokoveld, Namibia), *omurabae* (Grootfontein District, Namibia), *ugabensis* (N Damaraland, Namibia), *bradfieldi* (Damaraland, Namibia), and *vernayi* (Kalahari, Botswana).

REPRODUCTION *Gestation*: 180-210 days. *Young per Birth*: 1. *Weaning*: 2 months. *Sexual Maturity*: 8-10 months (♀), 12 months (♂). *Life Span*: 14 years.

BEHAVIOR *Family Group*: Usually solitary, although pairs are occasionally sighted. *Diet*: Opportunistic feeders, taking fruits, seeds, and leaves, as well as crops, small reptiles, and amphibians. *Main Predators*: Large predators, small cats, baboon, crocodile, python, eagle. There is no information available for this subspecies, but probably like other Bush Duikers. Mainly nocturnal, although often seen in daylight. Feeding predominantly from dusk until dawn, they rest in favorite hiding places in scrub or grass during the day. They get their water needs from their fodder, as they are the only savanna-dwelling Duikers. Unlike other Duikers, they can run fast for some distance, and it is probably improved gaits and longer leg proportions that explain why they carry their spinal column straight. It is as dependant as the other Duikers on freezing or crouching to escape detection unless they are discovered, in which case they will dash for the nearest thicket. They are solitary, with both the ♂ and ♀ having their own permanent individual territories and home ranges that are heavily defended. ♂ and ♀ do not form permanent or lifetime breeding bonds. A single ♂'s home range borders the home ranges of 2-3 adjacent ♀; these are only entered sporadically in order to determine the estrus status of the ♀. If ♀ is in estrus, the union lasts for 2-4 days, after which the ♂ returns to its own territory. If not in estrus, she will fight aggressively and force him to leave. The ♀ and her lamb form a family unit that lasts until shortly before the next birth, when the subadult leaves its mother to establish its own territory and home range. Many of these temporarily nomadic subadults fall prey to large predators, and others are run over while crossing roads.

DISTRIBUTION *Native:* Angola, Botswana, Namibia, South Africa. Found everywhere in Namibia, except the Namib Desert, S as far as Por Nolloth, W Cape (NW South Africa), N to Namburi and Cahama (S Angola), E to Kazungula, the Chobe District, and Kuka Pan (W Botswana).

HABITAT Tolerates most habitats except for the true forest and very open country, and tolerantes nearby human settlements.

STATUS Least Concern.

PHOTO CREDITS ♂: *Terry Thormin*, N'Kwazi Camp (Namibia). Head ♂: *Peter Boardman,* Rietfontein, Northern Cape (South Africa). ♀: *Stacey Ann Alberts* (Namibia). Head ♀: *Gordon Balfour* (Namibia).

East African Bush Duiker

SYLVICAPRA GRIMMIA NYANSAE

BL: 70-105 cm (♂), 90-115 cm (♀). SH: 40-65 cm. TL: 10-20 cm. W: 10-22 kg (♂), 10-26 kg (♀). HL: 7-18 cm (♂). Medium-sized to fairly large Duiker. Coat color is yellowish gray through bright tawny, with a little black speckling. Undersides are whitish, while the muzzle and forelegs are black. Coat longer and shaggier at higher elevations (*altivallis, lobeliarum*). Black nose stripe from the rhinarium to the top of the head, more pronounced than in Southern Bush Duiker. Whitish ring around the eyes (*orbicularis*). Short tail is black on the top, contrasting sharply with the fluffy white underside. Long, pointed ears are separated by a tuft of hair on the forehead. Sharply pointed horns are usually found only in males, somewhat shorter than in the Southern Common Duiker. Females usually larger than males.

♀

Young

♂

Sylvicapra grimmia orbicularis
and *hindei*

Sylvicapra grimmia nyansae

Sylvicapra grimmia madoqua

Sylvicapra grimmia altivallis and
lobeliarum

OTHER NAMES Gray Duiker, Bush Duiker, Grimm's Duiker. *French*: Céphalophe couronné. *German*: Kronenducker. *Spanish*: Duiquero o cefalofo común de África Oriental, duiquero gris, duiquero de sabana. *Russian*: Восточноафриканский кустарниковый дукер. *Afrikaans*: Gewone Duiker. *Swahili*: Nsya.

SUBSPECIES East African Bush Duiker includes a number of local subspecies from considerably different habitats and climates: *S. g. nyansae*, *S. g. madoqua*, *S. g. orbicularis*, *S. g. hindei*, *S. g. altivallis*, and *S. g. lobeliarum*. Southern Bush Duiker: *S. g. grimmia*, *S. g. caffra* (Limpopo Bush Duiker), *S. g. steinhardti* (Kalahari Bush Duiker). West African Bush Duiker: *S. g. pallidior* (Sahel Duiker), *S. g. coronata* (Crowned Duiker), *S. g. campbelliae* (Northern Bush Duiker). Angolan Common Duiker: *S. g. splendidula*. Invalid East African subspecies include: *abyssinicus, deserti, lutea, roosevelti,* and *uvirensis*.

REPRODUCTION *Gestation*: 180-210 days. *Young per Birth*: 1. *Weaning*: 2 months. *Sexual Maturity*: 8-10 months (♀), 12 months (♂). *Life Span:* 14 years.

BEHAVIOR *Family Group:* Usually solitary, although pairs are occasionally sighted. *Diet:* Tree and bush foliage, fruits, seeds, occasionally carrion. *Main Predators:* Large predators, small cats, baboon, crocodile, python, eagle.

DISTRIBUTION *S. g. nyansae:* SE Sudan, W Ethiopia, E Uganda, W Kenya. *S. g. hindei:* SE Kenya, N Tanzania. *S. g. madoqua:* W Ethiopia, W Eritrea. *S. g. orbicularis:* S Somalia, E Kenya, Tanzania, E Zambia, Malawi, N Mozambique. *S. g. altivallis:* central Kenya (higher parts of the Aberdares and Mount Kenya). *S. g. lobeliarum:* E Uganda, W Kenya (higher parts of Mount Elgon).

HABITAT Sparse forests, brushy steppe, savanna, and mountainous regions throughout sub-Saharan Africa.

STATUS Least Concern.

PHOTO CREDITS ♂: *Lo Fion,* Mount Kenya Safari Club (Kenya). ♀: *Ariadne Van Zandbergen,* Lake Baringo (Kenya). Head ♂: *Cliff Buckton*, Dinsho (Ethiopia). Head ♀: *Jeff Vize*, Aberdare NP (Kenya). Young: *Jeffrey Kerby*, Guassa Plateau (Ethiopia) and *Courtney Quirin*, Didibe (Ethiopia).

West African Bush Duiker

SYLVICAPRA GRIMMIA CORONATA

BL: 70-105 cm (♂), 90-115 cm (♀). SH: 40-65 cm. TL: 10-20 cm. W: 10-22 kg (♂), 10-26 kg (♀). HL: 7-18 cm (♂). Medium-sized to fairly large Duiker, with western individuals tending to be larger than those from eastern parts. Coat is generally pale sandy brown or buff, paler than that of other subspecies, with a weakly speckled appearance. The undersides and inner surfaces of the legs are whitish, extending down to the hooves. Forelegs have a diffuse dark stripe on their front surface. Distal half of tail is black, the underside is white. Dark facial blaze extending from the muzzle to the top of the head. Crest of long hair at the top of the head. Horns present only in males. Females usually larger than males.

Sylvicapra grimmia pallidior

Sylvicapra grimmia campbelliae

Sylvicapra grimmia coronata

OTHER NAMES Sahel Duiker, Crowned Duiker, Chad Crowned Duiker. *French*: Céphalophe du Sahel. *German*: Sahel-Kronenducker. *Spanish*: Duiquero o cefalofo del Sahel. *Russian*: Западный кустарниковый дукер. *Afrikaans*: Gewone Duiker. *Swahili*: Nsya.

SUBSPECIES West African Bush Duiker includes a number of local subspecies from considerably different habitats and climates: *S. g. pallidior* (Sahel Duiker), *S. g. coronata* (Crowned Duiker), and *S. g. campbelliae* (Northern Bush Duiker). East African Bush Duiker: *S. g. nyansae*, *S. g. madoqua*, *S. g. orbicularis*, *S. g. hindei*, *S. g. altivallis*, *S. g. lobeliarum*. Southern Bush Duiker: *S. g. grimmia*, *S. g. caffra* (Limpopo Bush Duiker), *S. g. steinhardti* (Kalahari Bush Duiker). Angolan Common Duiker: *S. g. splendidula*.

SIMILAR SPECIES *S. g. coronata* is the smallest subspecies, bright orange yellow in coloration, with the middorsal region darker, and the deep red facial blaze runs from the muzzle to the eyes, but it does not extend to the top of the forehead.

REPRODUCTION *Gestation*: 180-210 days. *Young per Birth*: 1. *Weaning*: 2 months. *Sexual Maturity*: 8-10 months (♀), 12 months (♂). *Life Span*: 14 years. There is no specific information for these subspecies, but likely similar to other Bush Duikers.

BEHAVIOR *Family Group*: Usually solitary, although pairs are occasionally sighted. *Diet*: Tree and bush foliage, fruits, seeds, occasionally carrion. *Main Predators*: Large predators, small cats, baboon, crocodile, python, eagle. There is no specific information for these subspecies, but likely similar to other Bush Duikers, presumably diurnal or crepuscular.

DISTRIBUTION *S. g. pallidior*: S Chad, N Central African Republic, central Sudan, W Ethiopia. *S. g. campbelliae*: E Guinea, S Mali, N Côte d'Ivoire, S Burkina Faso, N Ghana, Togo, Benin, S Niger, Nigeria, N Cameroon, S Chad, Central African Republic, SW Sudan, W Uganda, Rwanda, Burundi. *S. g. coronata* (Crowned Duiker): Senegal, Gambia, Guinea-Bissau, Guinea.

HABITAT Sahelo-Sudanian savannas with interspersed woodland. Areas with secondary grass growth are preferred, and the color of the coat provides excellent camouflage in dry grass. Sufficient cover is a necessary habitat component.

STATUS Least Concern.

Angolan Bush Duiker
SYLVICAPRA GRIMMIA SPLENDIDULA

BL: 70-105 cm (♂), 90-115 cm (♀). SH: 40-65 cm. TL: 10-20 cm. W: 10-22 kg (♂), 10-26 kg (♀). HL: 7-18 cm (♂). Medium-sized to fairly large Duiker. Back not conspicuously hunched, often nearly straight. Legs longer than in any other species of Duiker. Coat is generally pale reddish brown to grizzled gray, depending on the geographical location. The undersides are whitish, while the muzzle, nose bridge, and forelegs are black. Short tail is black on the top, contrasting sharply with the fluffy white underside. Long, pointed ears are separated by a tuft of hair on the forehead. Sharply pointed horns are usually found only in males, and are more vertically oriented than in other Duiker species (due to the more open habitat). Females are usually larger than males.

Sylvicapra grimmia splendidula

OTHER NAMES *French*: Céphalophe couronné. *German*: Kronenducker. *Spanish*: Duiquero o cefalofo común de Angola. *Russian*: Ангольский кустарниковый дукер. *Afrikaans*: Gewone Duiker. *Swahili:* Nsya.

SUBSPECIES Angolan Common Duiker: *S. g. splendidula*. West African Bush Duiker: *S. g. pallidior* (Sahel Duiker), *S. g. coronata* (Crowned Duiker), *S. g. campbelliae* (Northern Bush Duiker). East African Bush Duiker: *S. g. nyansae*, *S. g. madoqua*, *S. g. orbicularis*, *S. g. hindei*, *S. g. altivallis*, *S. g. lobeliarum*. Southern Bush Duiker: *S. g. grimmia*, *S. g. caffra* (Limpopo Bush Duiker), *S. g. steinhardti* (Kalahari Bush Duiker).

SIMILAR SPECIES Different from the other Duikers in color, general features, and shape of horns. Klipspringer has a shorter and more conic head and broader ears. Oribi is sandy rufous to brownish fawn, with a short head, long neck, no crest between the horns, a naked patch below the eye, and tufts of long hairs on the knees.

REPRODUCTION *Gestation*: 180-210 days. *Young per Birth*: 1. *Weaning*: 2 months. *Sexual Maturity*: 8-10 months (♀), 12 months (♂). *Life Span*: 14 years. There is no specific information for these subspecies, but likely similar to other Bush Duikers.

BEHAVIOR *Family Group:* Usually solitary, although pairs are occasionally sighted. *Diet:* Leaves, small branches, fruit, flowers, seeds, and vegetables. Seldom drinks water. *Main Predators:* Large predators, small cats, baboon, crocodile, python, eagle. There is no specific information for these subspecies, but likely similar to other Bush Duikers. A solitary animal except in the mating season. Forages in the early morning and late afternoon until dark. Active for longer periods on cool cloudy days. Lies down in dense shelter, underneath shrubs or in tall grass during the hottest part of the day. Waits until the very last moment before it runs away, head down and with characteristic jumping and swerving movements. Acute sense of smell and sight. Defensive and aggressive attacks on humans have been documented. A nasal snort as an alarm call, a loud scream when in danger.

DISTRIBUTION SE Gabon, S Congo, S DR Congo, N Angola, E Botswana, W Zambia, W Zimbabwe.

HABITAT Prefers woodland with sufficient undergrowth and thickets. Important requirements are thickets of shrubs or tall grass on which it feeds, and where it rests and shelters when in danger. Avoids open woodland, short-grass veld, and dense mountain or coastal forests. Independent of water.

STATUS Least Concern.

Black Duiker
CEPHALOPHUS NIGER

BL: 80-100 cm. SH: 44-50 cm. TL: 9-14 cm. W: 19-23 kg (♂), 17-26 kg (♀). HL: 7-9 cm (♂), 2-3 cm (♀). Medium-sized and heavily built Duiker. Rather thick and soft coat, black in color. Long body, with short, stocky legs. Underparts are slightly paler than the back, except for the underside of the tail which is bright white. Neck becomes increasingly gray near the head, such that the throat and chin are pale gray. Face is often reddish in color, with a bright red tuft of hair on the forehead. The insides of the ears are whitish and the backs are black. Both sexes have straight, pointed horns which angle back from the forehead; in females they are much shorter. Females tend to be slightly larger than males, but otherwise the sexes are similar.

♂

♂
Juvenile

Young

♀

Cephalophus niger

OTHER NAMES Black Deer. *French*: Céphalophe noir. *German*: Schwarzducker. *Spanish*: Duiquero o cefalofo negro. *Russian*: Чёрный дукер. *Akan*: Ewi. *Akpafu*: Duiyaya. *Brisa*: Gyami. *Bron*: Wio. *Dyula:* Tuba. *Fanti*: Twi. *Ful*: Paseneyel-'baleyel. *Lehemi*: Kedu. *Nkonya*: Kuma, mo. *Wolof*: Baroom, badoom.

SUBSPECIES Monotypic. *C. pluto* is an invalid synonym for *C. niger*.

SIMILAR SPECIES The related Abbott's Duiker is similarly dark in color with a bright rufous forehead crest, but it is much larger and is restricted to the mountains of Tanzania. The coloration of the Black Duiker readily distinguishes this species from all other antelope from the same region.

REPRODUCTION *Gestation*: 210 days. *Young per Birth*: 1. *Weaning*: 3-5 months. *Sexual Maturity*: 9-12 months (♀), 12-18 months (♂). *Life Span*: 14 years. Breeding year-round, although in Ghana there is a peak in births in November, December, and January. Birth weights average 1.94 kg. ♂ tend to grow more quickly than ♀, but both sexes double in weight in their first month. Duikers are considered precocial but are concealed in vegetation by their mother for several weeks after birth.

BEHAVIOR *Family Group*: Typically solitary; sometimes observed in pairs. *Diet*: Mostly fruit; also leaves and shoots, roots, fungi, and animal matter. *Main Predators*: Leopard, rock python, Libyan wild cat, civet cat, crocodile, eagle, golden cat, large owls, monitor, serval. Most active around dawn and dusk (crepuscular); in undisturbed areas it may be more diurnal, while increased human activity may cause a shift toward a more nocturnal existence. Resting spots are typically found in dense thickets or in between buttress roots of large trees. It has been suggested that this species is territorial. Its territory is generally about 0.1 ha. They are frequently observed in farmland, where they are often considered pests: they will raid crops on a regular basis. Cultivated crops make up a large proportion of the diet in some regions (as determined from the stomachs of individuals killed for bushmeat). Less secretive than most forest Duikers.

DISTRIBUTION *Native*: Côte d'Ivoire, Ghana, Guinea, Liberia, Nigeria, Sierra Leone, Togo. It ranges in forested and formerly forested areas from SW Guinea eastward through Sierra Leone to the Niger River.

HABITAT Lowland rainforest habitats, although individuals have been observed in riverine galleries, isolated forest patches, and semi-deciduous forests at the margins of the species' range. Primary forest is rarely used. Mixed farmland and thicket, and regenerating areas of cultivation are frequently inhabited; its ability to colonize such areas allows the Black Duiker to persist in areas where typical forest habitats have been destroyed.

STATUS Least Concern. The wild population is estimated at 100,000 individuals. Unlike many other Duikers, the Black Duiker does well in disturbed forests around agricultural areas. It is one of the most common Duikers in Ghana.

PHOTO CREDITS ♂: *Ronald McRae*, Los Angeles Zoo and Botanical Gardens (USA). Head ♂: *José R. Castelló*, Miami Zoo (USA). ♀: *David Ellis*, Colombus Zoo and Aquarium (USA). Head ♀: *Ronald McRae*, Los Angeles Zoo & Botanical Gardens (USA). Young: *Grahm S. Jones*, Columbus Zoo and Aquarium (USA). Juvenile: *Sergey Chichagov*, San Diego Zoo (USA).

Red-flanked Duiker

CEPHALOPHUS RUFILATUS

BL: 70 cm. SH: 35-48 cm. TL: 7-10 cm. W: 11-14 kg. HL: 6-9.5 cm (♂), 3-4 cm (♀). Medium-sized Duiker. Coat orange rufous, with no marked difference in coloration on the ventral surface. Broad bluish-gray stripe located along the middorsal line, gradually merging with the rufous pelage on the upper flanks. Lower legs dark blue gray in color. Narrow tail ending with a black tuft. Profile of the nose is straight, with the largest and deepest preorbital gland pits for its head size of any red-colored Duiker. Blue-black stripe running down front of face, ending at the black muzzle. Dark nose and black lower lip, white upper lip and underside of the jaw. Prominent vertical tuft of dark hair on the forehead. Horns are simple spikes, smooth and pointed, in the same plane as the forehead; may be found in both sexes, but regularly lacking in females, may be hidden by forehead tuft. Males larger than females (unusual for Duikers).

♂

Young

♀

Cephalophus rufilatus rufilatus

Cephalophus rufilatus rubidior

OTHER NAMES *French*: Céphalophe à flancs roux. *German*: Rotflankenducker, Blaurückenducker. *Spanish*: Duiquero o cefalofo de flancos rojos. *Russian*: Западноафриканский рыжебокий дукер *(rufilatus),* Ценральноафриканский рыжебокий дукер *(rubidior).* *Madi*: Tili. *Hausa*: Gadan-Kurmi, makurna. *Yoruba*: Esuru. *Fulani:* Jabare. *Twi*: Akogyei, asebee. *Dyula*: Konani. *Banda-Linda*: Wuge. *Basari*: Awúma. *Ewondo-Beti*: Zom. *Foulada*: Kubeyel-bodeyel. *Ful*: Bollere, boleere. *Gbaya*: Bàn. *Sango*: Wuga. *Wolof*: Hamfurde.

SUBSPECIES *C. r. rufilatus* (Western Red-flanked Duiker): Gambia, Senegal to the Chari and Benue valleys. *C. r. rubidior* (Congo Red-flanked Duiker): DR Congo (Uele Valley-Uele River in Eastern Province), Central African Republic (Chari to Nile valleys), S Chad, SW South Sudan; dorsal band darker.

REPRODUCTION *Gestation*: 223-245 days. *Young per Birth*: 1. *Weaning*: 5 months. *Sexual Maturity*: 9 months. *Life Span:* 15 years. Young animals have been reported in the dry season or early wet season. After birth, the single young is concealed by its mother in dense vegetation, where it stays still, even if approached closely. Fecundity is likely high due to the observed maintenance of population numbers despite heavy hunting.

BEHAVIOR *Family Group*: Solitary or in mating pairs. *Diet*: Browser, feeding mostly on leaves but also on twigs, flowers, and fruits. *Main Predators*: Leopard, eagle, python. Inhabits riverine/riparian forests and savanna areas near vegetative cover. Usable habitat requires only dense vegetation growth, and as a result it may be found far from true forest along drainage lines. It rarely leaves areas with cover. Very sedentary; animals occupy small home ranges, which may be maintained for many months provided there is no disturbance. These home ranges are marked with secretions from the preorbital gland, which is relatively large compared to that of other red Duikers. Reports regarding the primary time of activity vary from primarily diurnal through crepuscular to nocturnal, with some activity occurring in the early mornings and late afternoon. It is shy and wary, when disturbed rushing with a bouncing gait to nearest cover, keeping the head low. The alarm call is a shrill bark.

DISTRIBUTION *Native*: Benin, Burkina Faso, Cameroon, Central African Republic, Chad, DR Congo, Côte d'Ivoire, Gambia, Ghana, Guinea, Guinea-Bissau, Mali, Niger, Nigeria, Senegal, Sierra Leone, Sudan, Togo, Uganda. This Duiker formerly occurred throughout the band of savanna woodlands that stretches across W and central Africa from Senegal and Gambia to the Nile Valley. Formerly widespread in NW Uganda, as far E as the Albert Nile; a small relict population was discovered in the Bugungu Game Reserve, immediately south of Murchison Falls NP.

HABITAT Forest edges, gallery forest, and savanna thickets. Not in primary rainforest.

STATUS Least Concern. More resilient to habitat loss than other Duiker species. Nevertheless, this species is threatened outside of well-managed areas due to encroachment of agricultural lands and increased hunting pressure. The total population is estimated at 170,000 individuals.

PHOTO CREDITS ♂: Oregon Zoo (USA). Head ♂: *Glenn Nagel*. ♀: *F. Douglas Martin* (Guinea). Head ♀: *Johannes Pfleiderer*, Los Angeles Zoo (USA). Young: *Tony Rao*, Bouaké (Côte d'Ivoire).

Natal Red Duiker
CEPHALOPHUS NATALENSIS

BL: 75-87 cm. SH: 40-46 cm. TL: 9-14 cm. W: 12-15 kg. HL: 4.5-8 cm (♂), 2-4.4 cm (♀).
Medium-sized Duiker. General color almost uniform bright rufous chestnut all over, somewhat
paler on the underparts. Neck may be red or pale gray. Margin of the ears, chin, throat, and
underside of the tail are white. Upper side of the tail, ears, and muzzle are black. In front of
each eye sits a conspicuous long, thin scent gland. Both male and female have short, straight,
backward-sloping horns, hidden among a tuft of long and bushy chestnut-black hair. The horns
of the male are around twice the length of those of the female. Females are slightly larger than
the males.

♂

Young

♀

Cephalophus natalensis

OTHER NAMES Red Forest Duiker, Natal Duiker. *French*: Céphalophe du Natal. *German*: Rotducker, Natalducker. *Spanish*: Duiquero o cefalofo de Natal. *Russian*: Красный дукер. *Afrikaans*: Rooiduiker. *Swahili*: Funo, ngarombwi. *Ndebele*: Ipunzi ebovu. *Xhosa*: Impunzi. *Zulu*: Umsumpe. *Sepedi*: Mungulwi, kutsoa. *Sesotho*: Phuthi e kgubedu. *Swati*: Umsumbi. *Xitsonga*: Mhunti. *Tshivenda*: Tshipiti.

SUBSPECIES Monotypic. Includes *amoenus* (Transvaal), *lebombo* (NE Natal), *natalensis* (S Natal), *robertsi* (Mozambique and N to SE Tanzania), and *walkeri* (Malawi). Aders's and Harvey's Duiker are considered by some authors as subspecies of *C. natalensis*.

SIMILAR SPECIES Lacks the white flecking of either Sharpe's Grysbok or Suni. A tapered tuft of long hair grows on the top of the head whereas no tuft exists in Sharpe's Grysbok or Suni.

REPRODUCTION *Gestation*: 210 days. *Young per Birth*: 1. *Sexual Maturity*: 18-24 months. *Life Span:* 8-15 years. Breeding throughout the year, with most births possibly during spring and summer. Calving interval is about 9 months. ♂ take no part in rearing young but both sexes will respond to a distress call from the calf.

BEHAVIOR *Family Group*: Solitary or in pairs. *Diet*: Fallen fruit, plus foliage and insects. *Main Predators*: Lion, leopard, hyena, large raptors. Most active in the midmorning, late afternoon, and early evening, but in highly disturbed areas it may become nocturnal. A shy animal, like other Duikers, diving into cover at the slightest disturbance. Avoids predators by freezing and dashing away when closely approached. Generally, it is seen on its own, but occasionally a pair or a ♀ with her offspring may be observed. It is territorial, with mated pairs defending territory of 3 to 9.5 ha. When Duikers do meet, they greet each other by rubbing their facial scent glands together; these scent glands are also used to mark branches, twigs, and tree trunks within their range. Only occasionally a meeting between Duikers may escalate into a fight, when the small, sharp horns can be used to inflict considerable wounds. They have been seen under trees where troops of monkeys are feeding, taking advantage of the plentiful, carelessly dropped fruit.

DISTRIBUTION *Native*: Malawi, Mozambique, South Africa, Swaziland, Tanzania, Zambia. The Natal Red Duiker formerly occurred widely in coastal and riverine forests and thickets, escarpments, and montane forests from SE Tanzania to NE KwaZulu-Natal in South Africa. Presently, it is found in S Tanzania, including the Selous Reserve, the Nyika area of extreme NE Zambia, Mozambique, SE Malawi, possibly in SE Zimbabwe, Swaziland, and the E Transvaal and Natal in South Africa.

HABITAT Evergreen forest, tropical/subtropical forest patches, thickets, thickly wooded ravines, and dense coastal bush.

STATUS Least Concern. Total population estimate of about 42,000, although actual numbers could be considerably greater. It has disappeared from large parts of its former range, largely as a result of the loss of suitable habitat, as well as hunting. Nonetheless, it remains locally common within its former range.

PHOTO CREDITS ♂: *4028mdk09*, Zoo Landau, Rheinland-Pfalz (Germany). Head ♂: *Cameron Ewart-Smith*, Lubombo (Swaziland). ♀: *Alex Meyer,* Berlin Zoo (Germany). Head ♀: *Joachim S. Müller,* Valencia Bioparc (Spain). Young: *Lucas Leite/L8 Photos*, Hoedspruit (South Africa).

257

Harvey's Duiker
CEPHALOPHUS HARVEYI

BL: 85-95 cm. SH: 38-47 cm. TL: 8-11 cm. W: 9-14 kg. HL: 6-9 cm (♂). Medium-sized Duiker, slightly larger than the Natal Red Duiker, with much brighter coloration and slightly longer horns. General color is a rich red becoming lighter below. Black stripe from nose to forehead, including the head tuft, and continuing down the back of the neck, where it gives way to a dark speckling. Legs vary in color from brownish to brownish black. Specimens from the highlands of Kenya tend to be larger, brighter, and redder, with more extensive black leg markings and face blaze than those from lowlands. Horns, found in both sexes, similar to those of the Natal Red Duiker, being short, thick, conical, strongly ringed at the base, and inclined backward in the plane of the face. Females similar to males, but slightly larger in body and with smaller horns.

Cephalophus harveyi harveyi

Cephalophus harveyi bottegoi

OTHER NAMES *French*: Céphalophe de Harvey. *German*: Harveyducker, Harvey-Rotducker. *Spanish*: Duiquero o cefalofo de Harvey. *Russian*: Дукер Харви *(harveyi),* Сомалийский красный дукер *(bottegoi)*. Swahili: Funo.

SUBSPECIES *C. h. bottegoi*: Somalia. *C. h. harveyi*: Kenya, Tanzania, N Malawi, N Zambia. There is some debate as to whether the Natal Red Duiker and Harvey's Duiker are subspecies or full species. Harvey's Duiker has more black on the legs and face and its body color is a darker red. However, the two are known to hybridize in the forests around Dar es Salaam.

SIMILAR SPECIES Natal Red Duiker is smaller, legs slightly gray or not at all, facial midline darker. Weyns's Duiker is larger, with longer, more arched muzzle and duller orange-red coloring. Aders's Duiker is smaller, with white underparts, white freckling on the lower limbs, and a broad white band on the rump. Black-fronted Duiker has longer legs and darker, finely freckled pelage.

REPRODUCTION *Life Span*: 17 years. It breeds year-round in N Malawi. There is no more information available for this species, but it may be similar to the Natal Red Duiker.

BEHAVIOR *Family Group*: Solitary, but occasionally seen in pairs. *Diet*: Leaves, fruits, and blossoms. Literature available on this Duiker is very scarce, and almost nothing is known of the ecology of the species. Diurnal, with two distinct periods of activity: early morning and late afternoon, foraging in open areas adjacent to forest. They may use soft barks as contact calls.

DISTRIBUTION *Native*: Kenya, Somalia, Tanzania, Zambia, Malawi, probably Ethiopia. It is the most widespread red Duiker in E Africa, occurring in central and NE Tanzania, locally in central and SE Kenya, and in SW Somalia, especially along the lower Juba River, to N Tanzania and Malawi. There have been reports in the Harenna forest in the S Bale Mountains in Ethiopia, but this needs further study.

HABITAT Lowland and montane forests, isolated forest patches, riverine forest, coastal scrub, thickets and other habitats with thick cover, to 3,400 m.

STATUS Least Concern. Total population estimate of about 20,000 individuals, but this is likely to be a substantial underestimate. Main threats are habitat loss due to timber extraction and encroachment of settlement, especially in the many coastal and montane forests. It continues to be heavily hunted throughout most of its range, using both dogs and wire snares.

PHOTO CREDITS ♂: *Andy Poole,* Arusha NP (Tanzania). ♀: Based on photos from *Adam Scott Kenney*, Mikumi NP (Tanzania).

Aders's Duiker
CEPHALOPHUS ADERSI

BL: 66-72 cm. SH: 30-40 cm. TL: 9-12 cm. W: 7-12 kg. HL: 3-5 cm (♂), 1-3 cm (♀). Medium-sized to small Duiker. Body covered with soft, silky hair. Back and rump are brownish red in color, becoming increasingly gray on the neck. Undersides are bright white, and the line where the red and white meet on the sides is continued by a distinctive wide band of white that crosses the thighs and buttocks. Legs are reddish, turning black near the hooves; they are marked with irregular white spots, especially the front legs. Face with no distinct markings, but with a tuft of bright red hair on the forehead. Muzzle is pointed, and the nose has a flat front. Both sexes have short, pointed horns. Females are similar to males in size and appearance, with slightly shorter horns.

Cephalophus adersi

OTHER NAMES Zanzibar Duiker, Dwarf Red Duiker. *French*: Céphalophe de Aders. *German*: Adersducker. *Spanish*: Duiquero o cefalofo de Aders. *Russian*: Занзибарский дукер. *Arabuko-Sokoke*: Nunga. *Swahili*: Paa Nunga, Funo mwekundu Unguja. *Kipokomo*: Kungu marara. *Giriama:* Harake.

SUBSPECIES Monotypic. Considered by some authors as a subspecies of Natal Red Duiker, Harvey's Duiker, Peters's Duiker, or a hybrid of a combination of these.

SIMILAR SPECIES May be confused with the Suni or Harvey's Duiker which are similar in size and color. However, neither possesses the distinctive white band on the rump. Aders's Duiker is sympatric with Harvey's Duiker on the mainland and with Blue Duiker (*Philantomba monticola sundevalli*) on Zanzibar, although nothing is known regarding their ecological separation. Natal Red Duiker has a red, rather than white, belly and lacks both the white stripe across the rump and speckling on the legs.

REPRODUCTION *Gestation*: Unknown. *Young per Birth*: 1. *Sexual Maturity*: Unknown. *Life Span*: Unknown. Very little is known about the reproductive habits of this species. Pregnancies are known to occur between June and November, but it is not known whether Aders's Duiker breeds year-round. Young remains hidden in vegetation for the first few weeks of life.

BEHAVIOR *Family Group*: Typically solitary, or found in small groups of 2 or 3. *Diet:* Leaves and fallen fruit. *Main Predators:* Leopard and python (where still present). Primarily diurnal. Individuals begin feeding around dawn and continue until midday, when they stop to rest and ruminate. Foraging resumes in midafternoon and continues until nightfall. Like many Duikers, this species will follow birds or monkeys in order to feed on food items dropped from the trees. Aders's Duiker can obtain sufficient moisture from its food and does not need to drink regularly. This species is very shy, alert, and has a keen sense of hearing.

DISTRIBUTION *Native*: Kenya, Tanzania. They are found in only three small areas: Boni-Dodori and Arabuko-Sukoke in Kenya, and in Zanzibar, Tanzania (on the large island of Unguja, as well as two introduced populations on Chumbe and Mnemba islands).

HABITAT Woodlands and thickets, where dense vegetation provides shelter.

STATUS Critically Endangered. It is one of the most endangered antelopes, having experienced a decline in numbers of over 75% in the past 20 years. Only 1,000 individuals are thought to survive in Zanzibar and Arabuko-Sukoke, although the newly discovered population in Boni-Dodori (Kenya) appears to be larger. It is threatened by hunting and habitat destruction.

PHOTO CREDITS ♂: based on photos from *Thomas Struhsaker* and *Brent Huffman*. ♀ and heads: *Brent Huffman*, Mnemba Island, Zanzibar (Tanzania).

Black-fronted Duiker

CEPHALOPHUS NIGRIFRONS AND RELATED SPECIES

BL: 85-107 cm. SH: 48-58 cm. TL: 10-16 cm. W: 13-18 kg. HL: 6.5-9.5 cm (♂), 1.3-5.2 cm (♀). Medium-sized Duiker with relatively long legs and a coarse coat. General color rich chestnut. Back of neck darkening to blackish. No dorsal band. Underparts of the same color as the back. Distinguished from other Duikers by the wide black nose stripe connecting to the black forehead, and by the blackish lower legs and feet. The black facial blaze contrasts strongly with the lighter eyebrow streak and the reddish sides of the face. Crest mostly black, sparingly mixed with rufous hairs. Tail moderately long, with a conspicuous tuft, black with a white tip. Hooves are elongated and the false hooves are large, which are adaptations for walking on soft marshy ground. Horns, found in both sexes, thick at the base, strongly ringed, oval in cross section, with very thin straight tips, growing backward in the plane of the face. Females are similar to males, slightly larger, with smaller horns.

Cephalophus nigrifrons

Cephalophus rubidus

Cephalophus hypoxanthus

Cephalophus fosteri and hooki

OTHER NAMES *French*: Céphalophe à front noir, céphalophe rouge. *German*: Schwarzstirnducker. *Spanish*: Duiquero de frente negra. *Russian*: Чернолобый дукер. *Bila*: Nge. *Ewondo-Beti*: Nzumbi. *Ful*: Kubeyel meelde. *Kikongo*: Mbambi. *Kiladi*: Ncoombe. *Kirundu*: Igisaho. *Lomongo*: Mpambi. *Maasai*: Erong'o. *Punu*: Tsambi. *Teke*: Ntsuumi. *Yoruba*: Ekulu.

SUBSPECIES *C. n. nigrifons*: SE Nigeria and from S Cameroon to N Angola, E to E DR Congo. *C. n. kivuensis*: Virunga Volcanoes in Uganda, Rwanda, Burundi, and E DR Congo; the entire leg is grayish black, thick pelage. The following were formerly considered as subspecies of *C. nigrifons*, but now has been elevated to full species: *C. rubidus* (Ruwenzori Red Duiker): Ruwenzori Mountains in W Uganda; thick rich rufous fur, grayish-brown dorsal stripe, underparts much paler than the body, black hind legs, considered as a full species by some authors. *C. hypoxanthus* (Itombwe Duiker): Itombwe Mountains in DR Congo, W of Lake Tanganyika; pale yellowish-chestnut color, distinctly paler, hair long and soft, limbs only slightly darker than the body. *C. fosteri* (Mount Elgon Duiker): Mount Elgon in E Uganda and W Kenya; smaller subspecies, face and neck paler. *C. hooki* (Mount Kenya Duiker): Mountains of central Kenya; duller in color, with longer, softer, and thicker pelage. At one time Black-fronted Duiker was regarded as a subspecies of Natal Red Duiker.

REPRODUCTION *Life Span*: 17 years. There is no more information available for this species.

BEHAVIOR *Family Group*: Solitary, but occasionally seen in pairs. *Diet*: Primarily frugivorous, but consumes more vegetation (leaves and stems) than other Duikers. Territorial and at least partly diurnal. This Duiker frequently uses pathways in dense vegetation alongside marshy areas. It may disperse far into the swamps during the day to forage, especially in the dry season. It has been observed swimming across rivers.

DISTRIBUTION *Native*: Angola, Burundi, Cameroon, Central African Republic, Congo, DR Congo, Equatorial Guinea, Gabon, Kenya, Nigeria, Rwanda, Uganda. It occurs widely in swamp forests and alongside watercourses within the equatorial forest zone, from SE Nigeria to the Albertine Rift, and in isolated montane forests in E Africa. The Nigerian population occurs in the Niger Delta and is probably disjunct from the nearest known population in Cameroon. *C. rubidus* is confined to the Ruwenzori Mountains at altitudes of 1,300-4,200 m.

HABITAT Tropical forests of central Africa ranging from lowland swamp forest and seasonally flooded forest with poorly drained or permanently saturated soils, where it is frequently encountered along streams and in marshy areas, to montane forests, subalpine vegetation zones, bamboo, and moorland on Mounts Elgon and Kenya and the Aberdares (Kenya).

STATUS Least Concern. Total population estimate of about 300,000. *C. rubidus* is Endangered, with an estimated population of few thousands.

PHOTO CREDITS Based on photos from *Greg* and *Yvonne Dean*, Bwindi Impenetrable Forest (Uganda), Mgahinga Gorilla NP (Uganda), and *John Warburton-Lee*, Mount Kenya NP (Kenya).

Zebra Duiker
CEPHALOPHUS ZEBRA

BL: 85-90 cm. SH: 40-50 cm. TL: 15 cm. W: 15-23 kg. HL: 4-5 cm (♂), 2-3 cm (♀). Medium-sized Duiker, rather stockily built, with a highly distinctive coat. Pale orange to reddish-brown body, marked with 12-16 black or dark brown transverse stripes from the shoulders to the rump. This striping pattern is unique to each individual. Shoulders and lower legs are darker than the rest of the body, and blackish bands encircle the upper legs. Undersides are pale. Tail is rufous and lacks stripes. Face is an overall deep chestnut-brown color; there are no distinctive markings, but the muzzle is black and the lower jaw whitish. Head tuft is very short or absent. Horns are short, smooth, sharp cones in both males and females; they may be concealed by the coronal tuft. Females are similar to males, but have shorter, slimmer horns.

Cephalophus zebra

OTHER NAMES Banded Duiker, Striped Duiker, Zebra Antelope, Marked Deer, Mountain Deer. *French*: Céphalophe zèbre, céphalophe rayé. *German*: Zebraducker, Streifenducker. *Spanish*: Duiquero o cefalofo cebrado, duiquero de Doria. *Russian*: Зебровый дукер. *Local names:* Were, nemmeh.

SUBSPECIES No subspecies are recognized. *C. doria* and *C. zebrata* are invalid synonyms.

SIMILAR SPECIES The extinct Tasmanian Tiger (*Thylacinus cynocephalus*) is the only recent species with a similar striped coat. In Zebra Duikers, the stripes from the shoulders to the hips all extend well down the sides, and past the hips they become very narrow and disappear before the tail. In the Tasmanian Tiger, the stripes are often very short and narrow from the shoulders to the midback, and past the hips they remain wide and continue onto the tail.

REPRODUCTION *Gestation*: 221-229 days. *Young per Birth*: 1. *Weaning*: 95 days. *Sexual Maturity*: Approximately 2 years. *Life Span*: 14 years. Zebra Duikers breed year-round, conceiving shortly after giving birth. Mothers hide their baby for the first 2-3 weeks after birth, leaving the infant tucked away in dense vegetation and visiting it, on average, 4 times daily for nursing. Young Zebra Duikers have a bluish cast to their coat and very closely spaced stripes. Beginning at 2 months of age, the coat gradually turns golden; adult coloration is reached by 7-9 months.

BEHAVIOR *Family Group*: Mainly solitary, though sometimes in small family groups or breeding pairs. *Diet*: Mostly fruits and seeds, also leaves and sometimes animal matter. *Main Predators*: Leopard. A diurnal species, but is shy and rarely seen in the wild. The normal social unit appears to be a breeding pair; the pair bond is reinforced with mutual rubbing, licking, and scent marking. This species is thought to be territorial, and, based on heavy scars in many individuals, appears to fight quite vigorously. Seems to move about in a fairly large area, appearing infrequently but repeatedly over a period of time in the same places. Although generally quiet, both sexes may make throaty grunting sounds during courtship.

DISTRIBUTION *Native*: Côte d'Ivoire, Guinea, Liberia, Sierra Leone. It occurs from E Sierra Leone to SW Côte d'Ivoire; its presence in SE Guinea was confirmed by a report from the Ziama-Diecke Forest Reserves.

HABITAT Closed-canopy rainforests in W Africa. They are very sensitive to forest disturbance, and their range, centered around Liberia, continues to decline.

STATUS Vulnerable. Highly dependent on mature rainforest, and is thus one of the first species to disappear with logging. Recent population estimates suggest that only 15,000 individuals may survive in the wild.

PHOTO CREDITS ♂: *Brent Huffman*, Cincinnati Zoo (USA). ♀: Based on photos from Cincinnati Zoo (USA).

Peters's Duiker
CEPHALOPHUS CALLIPYGUS

BL: 80-115 cm. SH: 45-60 cm. TL: 10-16 cm. W: 15-24 kg. HL: 8-10 cm (♂), 4.0-5.8 cm (♀). A medium-sized Duiker. Yellowish brown in front, becoming reddish behind. Underparts are paler than the body. Black dorsal line beginning between shoulders and running along the spine, expanding to cover the rear flanks. Legs, shoulders, neck also dark. Underside of the tip of the tail is white. Two pale spots are found below and behind the eyes. Muzzle blackish; forehead and crest rufous brown. Sides of face grayish brown. Lips, chin, and throat white. A rich russet tuft of hair surrounds the horns. Both sexes have spike-like horns that extend backward from the forehead, thick and heavily ringed at the base. Females similar to males, but somewhat larger and with smaller horns.

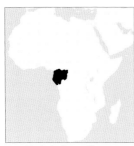

Cephalophus callipygus

OTHER NAMES Gabon Duiker. *French*: Céphalophe de Peters. *German*: Schönsteiss-Rotducker, Petersducker. *Spanish*: Duiquero de Peters, cefalofo de Peters. *Russian*: Конголезский дукер (дукер Петерса). *Local names*: Mbindi, zumbi, momjombi.

SUBSPECIES Monotypic. Some authorities consider the Weyns's Duiker to be a subspecies of Peters's Duiker.

SIMILAR SPECIES Red Duikers are often difficult to tell apart, especially as they flee. A dorsal stripe that expands over the rump and haunches is characteristic of Peters's Duiker. Bay Duiker is nocturnal and has a dorsal stripe which narrows to the width of the tail. Similarly, Ogilby's Duiker can be recognized by its narrow dorsal stripe. White-bellied Duiker has a dorsal stripe that widens in the center of the back and the belly is noticeably pale and whitish. Black-fronted Duiker and Weyns's Duiker do not possess a dorsal stripe.

REPRODUCTION *Gestation* period: 240 days. *Young per Birth*: 1. *Weaning*: Likely around 4 months. *Sexual Maturity:* Probably around 18 months. *Life Span:* Unknown. Reproduction occurs year-round, although more births occur early in the dry seasons (May-June and December) when fruit is most abundant. Infants are dark brown in color and possess the black dorsal stripe of adults.

BEHAVIOR *Family Group:* Often solitary, but 1 ♂ and several ♀ usually live in the same area and have a social system. *Diet:* Principally fruit; also leaves, flowers, fungi, and animal matter. *Main Predators:* Large and medium carnivores (leopard). Active during the day and spend the night resting or sleeping. These diurnal habits allow them to coexist with the nocturnal, but otherwise very similar, Bay Duiker. This species usually feeds in open areas, but flees into dense cover if threatened. Daytime resting areas are typically in thickets, but sleeping spots at night are often in areas with minimal undergrowth. An adult ♀ occupies a home range of approximately 40 ha; this overlaps with those of several other ♀ and a ♂. ♂ are thought to keep other ♂ away from their territories. Population densities range from 0.6 to 15.5 animals per km².

DISTRIBUTION *Native*: Cameroon, Central African Republic, Congo, Equatorial Guinea, Gabon. Found in S Cameroon, extreme SW Central African Republic, Equatorial Guinea, Gabon, and Congo. It is found W of the Congo and Ubangi rivers, being replaced to the E by the Weyns's Duiker.

HABITAT Lowland rainforests in W-central Africa. Dense undergrowth is an important habitat characteristic, providing shelter.

STATUS Least Concern. The estimated total population is 382,000 animals.

PHOTO CREDITS Head ♂: *Philipp Henschel/Panthera* (Gabon). ♀: *Jean-Louis Albert* (Gabon).

Ogilby's Duiker
CEPHALOPHUS OGILBYI

BL: 85-115 cm. SH: 55 cm. TL: 12-16 cm. W: 14-20 kg. HL: 8-12 cm (♂), 4-6 cm (♀). Medium-sized Duiker, long legged, with powerful hindquarters. Overall color is golden brown, although the belly is paler. Thin black stripe, 1-6 cm wide, running along the midline of the back, beginning at the shoulders and narrowing as it approaches the base of the tail. Tail is otherwise golden brown on top and white underneath, with a tuft of mixed white, black, and brown hairs at the tip. Legs are usually darker than the body. Ocher face with a dark muzzle, white lower jaw, and distinct chestnut eyebrows. Forehead is bright rufous in color, topped with a sparse crest of longer hairs. Both sexes bear short, upward-curving horns, strongly ringed and thick at the base. Females similar to males, though a little larger and with smaller horns.

Cephalophus ogilbyi

OTHER NAMES *French*: Céphalophe d'Ogilby. *German*: Ogilbyducker. *Spanish*: Duiquero de Ogilby, cefalofo de Ogilby. *Russian*: Дукер Оджильби. *Local names:* Odabohene, n'chumjbi.

SUBSPECIES Monotypic. The name *C. ogilbyi* (Ogilby's Duiker) formerly included *C. brookei* (Brooke's Duiker), *C. ogilbyi* (Ogilby's Duiker), and *C. crusalbum* (White-legged Duiker) as subspecies: these are all elevated to full species here.

SIMILAR SPECIES Much larger than the Blue Duiker, which is also found on Bioko Island.

REPRODUCTION Nothing is known about the breeding or development of this Duiker.

BEHAVIOR *Family Group*: Solitary or in pairs. *Diet*: Fruits and seeds, flowers, and leaves. *Main Predators*: Leopard and small cats; on Bioko, drills and pythons are the principal predators. One of the least-known Duikers. They are diurnal in nature, showing very little activity in the hours of darkness, but are very secretive. Foraging typically occurs in the morning and late afternoon. They may follow monkeys moving through the forest canopy in order to feed on fruits, seeds, and flowers that fall to the ground. The midday is often spent resting. Individuals maintain small home ranges, approximately 0.1 km^2 in size. The same areas are returned to nightly for sleeping, and latrine spots are used. The principal vocalization is a "wheet" call.

DISTRIBUTION *Native*: Cameroon, Equatorial Guinea, Nigeria. Found in central Africa, including extreme SE Nigeria E of the Cross River, far W Cameroon near the Nigerian border, and Bioko Island (formerly Fernando Po) in Equatorial Guinea.

HABITAT Primary rainforest, usually with a closed forest canopy. On Bioko Island, they may be found in montane as well as in lowland forests, and even at higher altitudes, up to at least 2,260 m.

STATUS Least Concern. Estimated total population is 12,000 animals. It is one of the principal sources of bushmeat on Bioko Island.

Brooke's Duiker
CEPHALOPHUS BROOKEI

BL: 100 cm. SH: 42-51 cm. TL: 12 cm. W: 14-20 kg. HL: 5.1-9.3 cm (♂), 2.3 cm (♀). Medium-sized Duiker, similar to but paler than the Ogilby's Duiker. General color is a dull golden brown, with dorsal surface brighter. Undersides very pale. Dorsal midline black stripe wider than in Ogilby's Duiker, from the shoulders, terminating on the rump as a very thin line, not extending to the tail. Legs are the same color as the body, with narrow black lines or smears down the front. Small lateral hooves are present. May have a reversal of hair on the neck. Coronal tuft is reddish ocher. Tail with a distinctive terminal tuft of black and white hairs. Both sexes bear short, upward-curving horns, strongly ringed and thick at the base. Females similar to males, though a little larger and with smaller horns. Infant coat is speckled.

Cephalophus brookei

OTHER NAMES *French:* Céphalophe de Brooke. *German*: Brooke-Ducker. *Spanish*: Duiquero de Brooke, cefalofo de Brooke. *Russian*: Дукер Брука. *Asanti*: Odabohene.

SUBSPECIES Monotypic. Formerly considered a subspecies of *C. ogilbyi* (Ogilby's Duiker).

REPRODUCTION Nothing is known about the breeding or development of this Duiker.

BEHAVIOR *Family Group:* Solitary or in pairs. *Diet*: Fruits and seeds, flowers, and leaves. *Main Predators:* Leopard and small cats; on Bioko, drills and pythons are the principal predators. One of the least-known Duikers. They are diurnal in nature, showing very little activity in the hours of darkness, but are very secretive. Foraging typically occurs in the morning and late afternoon. They may follow monkeys moving through the forest canopy in order to feed on fruits, seeds, and flowers that fall to the ground. The midday is often spent resting. Individuals maintain small home ranges, approximately 0.1 km^2 in size. The same areas are returned to nightly for sleeping, and latrine spots are used. The principal vocalization is a "wheet" call.

DISTRIBUTION *Native*: Côte d'Ivoire, Ghana, Liberia, Sierra Leone. Found from Sierra Leone to Ghana W of the Volta River.

HABITAT Primary forest in moist lowlands; rarely observed in secondary forest. They may enter farmland adjacent to forest to feed on crops.

STATUS Vulnerable. Estimated total population is 5,000 animals, and declining. It appears to be highly susceptible to the effects of habitat loss and hunting.

White-legged Duiker
CEPHALOPHUS CRUSALBUM

BL: 96.5-104.1 cm. SH: 55 cm. TL: 13-16 cm. W: 20 kg. HL: 8.7-11 cm (♂), 5 cm (♀). Medium-sized Duiker. Overall color is golden brown. Hindquarters and rump are darker than the sides, and neck and forequarters have a grayish tint. Belly is gray. Black dorsal stripe, wider than in Ogilby's Duiker, from the shoulders to the rump, extending as a narrow line to the tail tip. Scattered black hairs may form a secondary band near the tail. Hair on the nape of the neck may be reversed. Tail with a long, narrow terminal tuft of gray-brown hairs. All legs are distinctly white below the carpus and tarsus, with a narrow brown stripe down the front. Throat and lower jaw are white. Head is gray, with a darker brown forehead with a dark chestnut coronal tuft. Muzzle is blackish. Bright chestnut arch above each eye. Horns found in both sexes. Females similar to males, though a little larger and with smaller horns. Juveniles are speckled.

Cephalophus crusalbum

OTHER NAMES *French*: Céphalophe à pattes blanches. *German*: Weißbeinducker. *Spanish*: Duiquero de patas blancas, cefalofo patiblanco. *Russian*: Белоногий дукер.

SUBSPECIES Monotypic. Formerly considered a subspecies of *C. ogilbyi* (Ogilby's Duiker).

SIMILAR SPECIES Peters's Duiker is marginally sympatric, but differs from the White-legged Duiker by its black dorsal stripe, which broadens on the rump and extends down the back of the hams and legs, and its darker color. The striking white lower legs distinguish the White-legged Duiker from all other species of Duikers.

REPRODUCTION Nothing is known about the breeding or development of this Duiker.

BEHAVIOR *Family Group:* Solitary or in pairs. *Diet*: Fruits and seeds, flowers, and leaves; frequently observed under trees in which primates are feeding, consuming fallen or dropped matter. *Main Predators:* Leopard and small cats; on Bioko, drills and pythons are the principal predators. One of the least-known Duikers. Diurnal, with an abrupt reduction in activity at sundown and an equally abrupt resumption of activity at sunrise. The times of greater activity are just after dawn and in the afternoon.

DISTRIBUTION *Native*: Congo, Gabon. Found from coastal Gabon, mostly S of the Ogooué River, to W Congo.

HABITAT Rainforest blocks and forest patches within savanna-forest mosaic.

STATUS Least Concern. Estimated total population is 18,000 animals, with stable population numbers throughout most of its range. However, increasing human occupation may eventually reduce it to protected areas, such as Lope and Gamba.

PHOTO CREDITS *Philipp Henschel/Panthera* (Gabon).

White-bellied Duiker
CEPHALOPHUS LEUCOGASTER AND CEPHALOPHUS ARRHENII

BL: 92-105 cm. SH: 42-51 cm. TL: 10-15 cm. W: 14-21 kg. HL: 2.1-6.9 cm (♂), 1.8-2.9 cm (♀). Medium-sized Duiker. General color is sandy brown, lighter than that of other species. Underparts are white, blending gradually with the color of the flanks. Head with a dark blackish-brown forehead and blaze, contrasting with the lighter sides. Crest mainly rufous mixed with black. Blackish median band from the nape of the shoulder, broadening on the middle of the back, then narrowing progressively on the rump, where it is sharply defined. Neck, shoulder, and flanks warm brownish to grayish, blending gradually with the dorsal band on the back and with the whitish underparts. Rump and thighs tinged with rufous. Buttocks white. Limbs brownish, darkening on lower half. Tail rather longish, with a conspicuous black and white tuft. Horns short, tapering, heavily ringed at the base. Females slightly heavier than males.

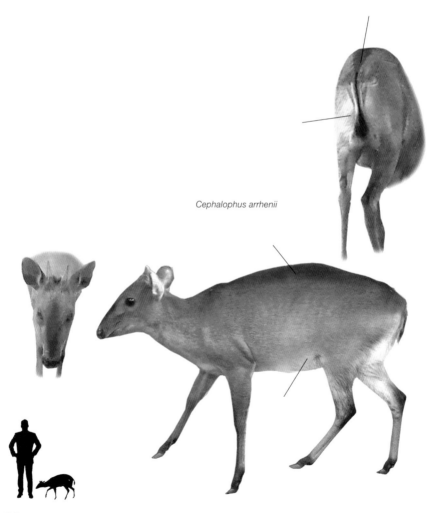

Cephalophus arrhenii

Cephalophus arrhenii

Cephalophus leucogaster

OTHER NAMES Gabon Duiker, Uele White-bellied Duiker. *French*: Céphalophe à ventre blanc, céphalophe du Gabon, céphalophe d'Arrhenius. *German*: Gabun-Ducker, Weissbauchducker, Uëlle-Weissbauchducker. *Spanish*: Duiquero de vientre blanco occidental, duiquero de Gabón, cefalofo de Gabón, duiquero de vientre blanco del Uele, cefalofo de vientre blanco oriental. *Russian*: Восточный белобрюхий дукер, Западный белобрюхий дукер. *Bila*: Seke. *Ewondo-Beti:* Mie. *Kibali*: Sesi, seke. *Kingwane*: Sonde. *Lise*: Tau. *Maasai*: Erong'o. *Teke*: Opese.

SUBSPECIES Monotypic. The name *C. leucogaster* (White-bellied Duiker) formerly included *C. leucogaster* (Western White-bellied Duiker), and *C. arrhenii* (Eastern White-bellied Duiker) as subspecies: these are elevated to full species here. Previously considered as a subspecies of the Eastern Bay Duiker (*C. castaneus*).

SIMILAR SPECIES Eastern White-bellied Duiker is slightly larger, paler and browner than the Western White-bellied Duiker, and the black dorsal stripe is broader. Hocks of hind limbs are marked with black. White-bellied Duikers are distinguished from the Bay Duiker by the shape of the black median band, and the white belly and buttocks.

REPRODUCTION *Gestation*: Unknown. *Young per Birth*: 1. *Life Span*: Unknown. There is very little information available on the reproductive habits of these Duikers. Breeding likely occurs throughout the year, although a peak in births has been noted in August-November (the rainy season). Pelage in infants is pale gray; the dorsal stripe is less prominent than in mature animals.

BEHAVIOUR *Family Group*: 1 or 2 individuals (a juvenile traveling with its mother). Diurnal. These Duikers occupy large home ranges. When disturbed, it will freeze in position and attempt to locate the source of noise or movement, and then seek safety by bounding away in a zigzag pattern.

HABITAT Undisturbed primary forest. Moist lowland equatorial forests and mature closed-canopy forest; also present in older secondary forests, but absent from swamp forest, gallery forest, forest-savanna mosaics, and cleared areas. It appears to prefer mono-dominant stands of *Gilbertiodendron* forest in areas such as Nouabale-Ndoki in Congo-Brazzaville and the Ituri Forest in DR Congo.

DISTRIBUTION Western White-bellied Duiker ranges in the W from S Cameroon, S of the Sanaga River, through Gabon, Equatorial Guinea, N and SW Congo, and extreme SW Central African Republic, and restricted to the E by the Congo and Ubangi rivers. Eastern White-bellied Duiker is found in S Central African Republic, and DR Congo NE of the Congo River.

STATUS Least Concern. Total population estimate of 287,000 animals for both species. Like most other Duikers of the central African lowland equatorial forests, its numbers are generally stable in areas remote from settlement, but decreasing elsewhere because of forest degradation and bushmeat hunting. Main threats include snare and net hunting by locals.

PHOTO CREDITS *Aebischer Thierry,* Chinko Protection Area (Central African Republic).

Weyns's and Lestrade's Duiker
CEPHALOPHUS WEYNSI AND CEPHALOPHUS LESTRADEI

BL: 94-100 cm. SH: 56 cm. TL: 13-20 cm. W: 14-20 kg. HL: 9-11 cm (♂), 3-5.5 cm (♀). A medium-sized Duiker, with a long, narrow muzzle, and a soft, fine coat. General color is a dull brown or reddish brown, with no belly stripe or facial blaze. No dorsal stripe (some specimens may have a dorsal stripe). Hair on the nape of the neck directed forward. Short head tuft is reddish with no black in it, forehead is reddish black, cheeks are pale brown above and whitish below, and muzzle is chocolate brown. Short, round ears are brown with whitish edges. Legs are darker than the body, becoming almost black at the hooves. Horns, found in both sexes, cone shaped and heavily ringed and thick at the base. Females similar to males, but have smaller horns. Infant coloration is browner than in adults, with a speckled appearance.

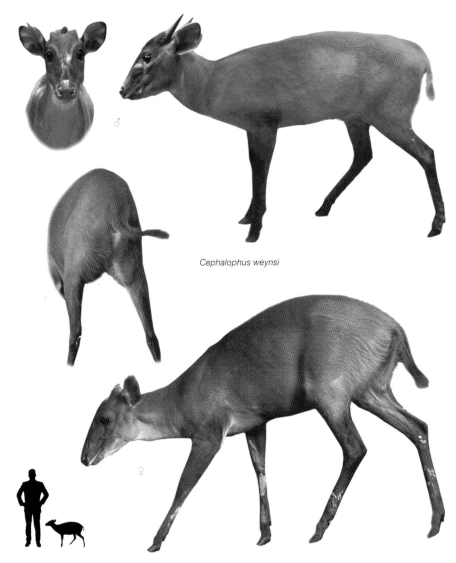

Cephalophus weynsi

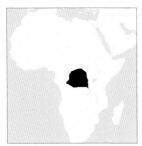

Cephalophus weynsi

Cephalophus lestradei

OTHER NAMES *French*: Céphalophe de Weyns, Céphalophe de Lestrade. *German*: Weynsducker, Lestrade-Ducker. *Spanish*: Duiquero de Weyns, cefalofo de Weyns, Duiquero de Lestrade, cefalofo de Lestrade. *Russian*: Заирский дукер, Руандский дукер.

SUBSPECIES Monotypic. The name *C. weynsi* (Weyns's Duiker) formerly included *C. w. johnstoni* (Johnston's Duiker), *C. w. lestradei* (Lestrade's Duiker), and *C. w. weynsi* (Weyns's Duiker) as subspecies: these are all elevated to full species here. Weyns's Duiker is considered by some authors as a subspecies of Peters's Duiker, Harvey's Red Duiker, or Natal Red Duiker.

SIMILAR SPECIES Lestrade's Duiker is intermediate in size between the closely related Weyns's Duiker and Johnston's Duiker. General color is dark gray brown with reddish tones, darker than Weyns's Duiker, with underparts pale gray, and yellowish tints in the inguinal and axillary regions, and a prominent black dorsal stripe, starting diffusely on the neck and becoming more intense and wider toward the rump, and a dark wash on the hindquarters. Dark tail with a terminal black and white tuft. Forehead is dark brown, with a well-developed rufous-chestnut frontal crest. Neck with very short hair, reversed along the dorsal midline.

REPRODUCTION *Gestation*: Unknown. *Young per Birth*: 1. *Weaning*: Unknown. *Sexual Maturity*: Unknown. *Life Span:* 15 years. There is no specific breeding season, although there is a peak in births from September to December, when fruits are most abundant.

BEHAVIOR *Family Group*: Solitary, or occasionally in pairs. *Diet*: Primarily fruits and seeds, but also leaves, fungi, flowers, and even animal matter (invertebrates, eggs, and birds). *Main Predators*: Leopard, african golden cat, crowned eagle. Diurnal. May develop group living, which is unusual in forest Duikers and separates this species from the closely related Peters's Duiker. The small individual home ranges, in combination with a generalized diet, may permit this Duiker to control areas of relatively higher food availability and may contribute to anti-predator defense. Both ♂ and ♀ frequently utter whistled contact calls, in addition to loud bleating calls that they, as well as other Duikers, utter when distressed.

DISTRIBUTION Weyns's Duiker is widespread in DR Congo, including large areas of contiguous range N of the Congo River, from the Ubangui in the W, to W Uganda, W Rwanda and Burundi, and W Tanzania (Mahali Mountains and Gombe). Lestrade´s Duiker is found in found in W Rwanda, W Burundi, and S to W Tanzania.

HABITAT Mixed primary and secondary forest, principally in large continuous blocks of closed forest. It does not use gallery forest or forest savanna mosaics.

STATUS Least Concern. They are likely gradually declining due to the effects of hunting.

PHOTO CREDITS *Aebischer Thierry*, Chinko Protection Area (Central African Republic).

Johnston's Duiker

CEPHALOPHUS JOHNSTONI

BL: 90 cm. SH: 56 cm. TL: 10 cm. W: 14-20 kg. HL: 8.8-10.7 cm (♂), 3.5-3.7 cm (♀). A medium-sized Duiker, smaller and lighter than the Weyns's Duiker. General color is deep reddish brown, becoming darker and less reddish on the shoulders and neck. Coat is thick and both darker and woollier than in Weyns's Duiker. Legs are brown and darken to almost black at the hooves. Underparts are brown. Tail is white on the underside, with a terminal white and brown tuft. Deep chestnut coronal tuft. Muzzle is dark, while chin and lips are contrastingly white. Ears are white inside, and brown outside with a white border. Horns, found in both sexes, are short and straight. Infants are darker and browner, with a speckled appearance due to dark bands on the hairs.

Cephalophus johnstoni

OTHER NAMES Uganda Red Duiker. *French*: Céphalophe de Johnston. *German*: Johnston-Ducker. *Spanish*: Duiquero de Johnston, cefalofo de de Johnston. *Russian*: Угандский дукер (Дукер Джонстона).

SUBSPECIES Monotypic. Formerly considered a subspecies of *C. weynsi* (Weyns's Duiker). It may hybridize with Harvey's Duiker in Kenya. Includes *barbertoni* (Elgon Harvey's Duiker, from Mount Elgon to Kakamega Forest in Kenya), *ignifer* (Isaac's Duiker, westward in Kenya from Mount Kenya), and *rutshuricus* (Rutshuru Harvey's Duiker, DR Congo-Uganda border).

REPRODUCTION *Gestation*: Unknown. *Young per Birth*: 1. *Weaning*: Unknown. *Sexual Maturity*: Unknown. *Life Span*: 15 years. There is no specific breeding season, although there is a peak in births from September to December, when fruits are most abundant.

BEHAVIOR *Family Group:* Solitary, or occasionally in pairs. *Diet*: Primarily fruits and seeds, but also leaves, fungi, flowers, and even animal matter (invertebrates, eggs, and birds). *Main Predators*: Leopard, african golden cat, crowned eagle. There is no specific information available on this species, but probably similar to Weyns's Duiker. Diurnal. Densities in the Ituri Forest (DR Congo) average 11 animals per km^2, and are highest in unhunted areas.

DISTRIBUTION *Native*: DR Congo, Kenya, Sudan, Uganda. Found in forests from the E edge of DR Congo (Rutshuru region, Kivu region) through Uganda, W of the Rift Valley Province in Kenya, and W base of Mount Elgon eastward to Ruwenzori.

HABITAT Forest, bush thickets, and grassy jungles, up to 3,000 m.

STATUS Least Concern. It is common in Uganda, where it is one of the dominant herbivores in forest patches, but its status is unknown elsewhere.

Abbott's Duiker
CEPHALOPHUS SPADIX

BL: 100-140 cm. SH: 65-75 cm. TL: 8-13 cm. W: 50-60 kg. HL: 8-12 cm. A large Duiker with short legs and a thick neck. Short and glossy coat is an overall very dark brown or black in color. Undersides are pale brown, usually with a reddish tone, and the throat and face are pale grayish brown. No conspicuous facial markings, but the upper lip is whitish and the forehead deep brown in color. A distinctive bushy crest of long hair grows at the top of the head between the ears; this may vary in color from pale brown to deep chestnut, but it usually has a bright reddish hue. Tail tipped with white. Sharp spike-like horns, present in both sexes, directed backward from the top of the head in line with the forehead. Although the horns are long compared to those of most other Duikers, they are sometimes entirely hidden by the thick forehead tuft.

Cephalophus spadix

OTHER NAMES *French*: Céphalophe d'Abbott. *German*: Abbottducker. *Spanish:* Duiquero de Abbott, cefalofo de Abbott. *Russian*: Танзанийский дукер (дукер Аббота). *Kiswahili*: Minde. *Maasai*: Erong'o.

SUBSPECIES Monotypic. Closely related to the Yellow-backed Duiker (*C. silvicultor*).

SIMILAR SPECIES The Yellow-backed Duiker is similar in size and coloration, but has a distinctive yellow wedge from midback to rump and has a much shorter and sparser forehead crest. Ignoring the substantial difference in size, Abbott's Duiker and Black Duiker are remarkably similar in appearance, both being dark with reddish crests. They are easily distinguished on the basis of their native ranges (W Africa versus Tanzania).

REPRODUCTION Presumably similar to the closely related Yellow-backed Duiker. Infants have been observed in September and October, but this species is probably able to breed year-round.

BEHAVIOR *Family Group:* Solitary. *Diet:* Principally fruit, but also leaves, flowers, and animal matter. *Main Predators*: Leopard, lion, spotted hyena; African crowned eagle and pythons may hunt youngsters. Activity patterns drawn from reports and camera-trapping results suggest the species is nocturnal, likely spending the day resting in dense undergrowth. Hunters are well aware of this Duiker's use of regular pathways (which usually run diagonally along hillsides) and often hunt the species with snares. If pursued, individuals may swim to evade the threat, and if cornered they may aggressively defend themselves. Abbott's Duiker is rare across its range. Even in optimal habitat, the maximum population density is 1.3 individuals per km^2; in less suitable areas, population densities may be only 0.1 per km^2.

DISTRIBUTION *Native*: Tanzania. Endemic to Tanzania, found in a few montane and submontane forests and one lowland forest in the E Arc Mountains (W Usambara Mountains and Udzungwa Mountains), Mount Kilimanjaro, and S Highlands. A small population is still present on Mount Rungwe and the Livingstone Forest within the new Kitulo NP. The Udzungwa Mountains and Mount Kilimanjaro might hold the only two viable populations.

HABITAT Dense montane forests, usually at altitudes of 1,300-2,700 meters.

STATUS Endangered. It is a difficult species to survey on account of its shyness and nocturnal nature. There are an estimated 1,500 individuals remaining in the wild. However, populations are extremely fragmented, and only two viable populations may remain. They are seriously threatened by habitat destruction, human encroachment, and poaching with nets, traps, and dogs.

Western Yellow-backed Duiker
CEPHALOPHUS SILVICULTOR

BL: 115-145 cm. SH: 65-80 cm. TL: 11-20 cm. W: 45-80 kg. HL: 8.5-21 cm. Large and heavyset Duiker, with slender legs. Short, glossy coat dark brown to black. Distinctive white to orange wedge of erectile hair on the back, contrasting with the dark background. Muzzle and sides of face are light gray in color, and lips are white. Eyes and ears are small. Crest well developed, orange or rufous, sometimes blackish. Tail short, thin, with a small black tuft. Both sexes have faintly ringed, wedge-shaped horns, which curve down slightly at the tips. Females are similar to males, somewhat larger and with smaller horns. Young are born dark brown, with spots on their sides and a reddish tinge on the underparts; the center of the back remains jet black until 5-9 months of age, at which point the yellow hairs start to grow.

Young

Cephalophus silvicultor silvicultor

Cephalophus silvicultor longiceps

Cephalophus silvicultor ruficrista

OTHER NAMES *French*: Céphalophe à dos jaune, céphalophe géant. *German*: Gelbrückenducker, Riesenducker. *Spanish*: Duiquero de lomo amarillo o silvicultor. *Russian*: Западный желтоспинный дукер. *Azande*: Gangono, m'bio. *Bila*: Moimbo. *Duala*: Njibo. *Ewondo-Beti*: Zib. *Foulado*: Kubeyel. *Ful*: Ku'beyel. *Gbaya*: Mbò. *Kirundu*: Igisaho. *Lomongo*: Lisoko. *Manza*: Mboko. *Peui*: Monteval. *Punu*: Nzibu. *Shaba*: Ntundu. *Teke*: Bimba. *Wolof*: Mbill. *Yoruba*: Gidigidi, agugugbu.

SUBSPECIES *C. s. silvicultor*: S Senegal to W Nigeria (W of Niger River). *C. s. longiceps:* E Nigeria (E of Niger River) to S Chad and SW Sudan, S to Congo River. *C. s. ruficrista:* DR Congo S to Congo River, Angola, Zambia. Includes *coxi* (Rhodesian Yellow-backed Duiker, NW Zimbabwe, Zambia), *ituriensis* (Ituri Yellow-backed Duiker, DR Congo, Ituri Forest), *melanoprymnus* (Gabon), *punctulatus* (Sierra Leone), *sclateri* (Liberia), *silvicultrix* (White-backed Bush Goat, Sierra Leone) and *thomasi*.

SIMILAR SPECIES One of the three large Duikers, the others being Jentink's and Abbott's Duikers. It is actually somewhat smaller than the Jentink's, to which it is similar in its stocky build. Juvenile Yellow-backed and Jetink's Duikers may be confused where they are sympatric (Liberia, W Côte d'Ivoire). Adult Yellow-backed Duiker has a characteristic yellow rump patch.

REPRODUCTION *Gestation*: 210 days. *Young per Birth*: 1, rarely 2. *Weaning*: 5 months. *Sexual Maturity*: 9-12 months (♀), 12-18 months (♂). *Life Span*: 12 years. After birth, the newborn lies hidden for over a week, after which it begins to venture out and nibble vegetation.

BEHAVIOR *Family Group*: Solitary or in pairs. *Diet*: Foliage, fruit, seeds, fungi, grasses. *Main Predators:* Leopard, python, crocodile, civet. Generally nocturnal, these Duikers lie up singly during the day in "forms," which are regularly used beds found under fallen tree trunks, in root forms at the bases of trees, and in dense tangles. They have also been observed resting on top of termite mounds, suggesting a regular surveillance of the surroundings. Broken horns in ♀ suggest that they actively defend their territories, which they are thought to share with a single ♂ in a semi-detached pair relationship. The Yellow-backed Duiker marks its territory with its maxillary glands. Adults communicate by means of shrill bleats and resonant grunts. When alarmed, it erects its bright dorsal crest and whistles a shrill alert, then flees into the underbrush.

DISTRIBUTION *Native*: Angola, Benin, Burkina Faso, Cameroon, Central African Republic, Congo, DR Congo, Côte d'Ivoire, Equatorial Guinea, Gabon, Ghana, Guinea, Guinea-Bissau, Liberia, Nigeria, Senegal, Sierra Leone, Togo, Zambia. *Regionally Extinct*: Gambia. The Yellow-backed Duiker has the widest distribution of the forest Duikers, ranging from SW Senegal through all W African countries to SW Sudan, S to N Angola (including Cabinda) and Zambia. They are now considered extinct in Gambia.

HABITAT Forests with heavy undergrowth in W-central Africa.

STATUS Least Concern. Total population estimate of about 160,000.

PHOTO CREDITS ♂: *Alex Meyer*, San Diego Zoo (USA). Head ♂: *Sergey Chichagov*, Los Angeles Zoo (USA). ♀: *Debra Turner*, Sacramento Zoo (USA) and *Arthur Ramos*, Los Angeles Zoo (USA). Head ♀: Columbus Zoo (USA). Young: *Stephanie Adams,* Houston Zoo (USA) and Dallas Zoo (USA).

Eastern Yellow-backed Duiker
CEPHALOPHUS CURTICEPS

BL: 115 cm. SH: 65 cm. TL: 11 cm. W: 45 kg. Similar to the Western Yellow-backed Duiker although much smaller. Short, glossy coat dark brown to black, generally darker than that of the Western Yellow-backed Duiker. Distinctive bright gold to very dark golden-brown wedge of erectile hair on the dorsum, narrowest toward the head, ending in an abrupt line at the hip, narrower and darker than in the Western Yellow-backed Duiker. Smaller gold-colored spots are found behind this triangle. Sides of neck and cheeks paler than the body. Prominent coronal tuft, often reddish. Tail short, thin, with a small black tuft. Both sexes have faintly ringed, wedge-shaped horns, which curve down slightly at the tips. Females are similar to males, somewhat larger and with smaller horns.

Cephalophus curticeps

OTHER NAMES *French*: Céphalophe du Sabinio. *German*: Östlicher Gelbrückenducker. *Spanish*: Duiquero o cefalofo de lomo amarillo oriental. *Russian*: Восточный желтоспинный дукер.

SUBSPECIES Monotypic. Formerly recognized as a subspecies of *C. silvicultor* (Yellow-backed Duiker).

SIMILAR SPECIES One of the three large Duikers, the others being Jentink's and Abbott's Duikers. It is actually somewhat smaller than the Jentink's, to which it is similar in its stocky build. Juvenile Yellow-backed and Jetink's Duikers may be confused where they are sympatric (Liberia, W Côte d'Ivoire). Adult Yellow-backed Duiker has a characteristic yellow rump patch.

REPRODUCTION *Gestation*: 210 days. *Young per Birth*: 1, rarely 2. *Weaning*: 5 months. *Sexual Maturity*: 9-12 months (♀), 12-18 months (♂). *Life Span*: 12 years. There is no specific information available for this species, but probably similar to the Western Yellow-backed Duiker.

BEHAVIOR *Family Group*: Solitary or in pairs. *Diet:* Foliage, fruit, seeds, fungi, grasses. *Main Predators:* Leopard, python, crocodile, civet. There is no specific information available for this species, but probably similar to the Western Yellow-backed Duiker. Probably active both night and day. Generally nocturnal, these Duikers lie up singly during the day in "forms," which are regularly used beds found under fallen tree trunks, in root forms at the bases of trees, and in dense tangles. They have also been observed resting on top of termite mounds, suggesting a regular surveillance of the surroundings. Broken horns in ♀ suggest that they actively defend their territories, which they are thought to share with a single ♂ in a semi-detached pair relationship. The Yellow-backed Duiker marks its territory with its maxillary glands. Adults communicate by means of shrill bleats and resonant grunts. When alarmed, the Yellow-backed Duiker erects its bright dorsal crest and whistles a shrill alert, then flees into the underbrush.

DISTRIBUTION *Native*: Burundi, Kenya, Rwanda, Uganda. Found between W and E Rift Valleys, in S Uganda, Rwanda, Burundi, and W Kenya (Mau Forest, Kericho, Molo, Masi).

HABITAT Montane forests and bamboo stands, as well as some protected forest at lower elevations.

STATUS Least Concern. It is considered endangered in Uganda, rare in Kenya, and may be extinct in Rwanda.

PHOTO CREDITS *Marcell Claassen*, Bwindi Impenetrable NP, Buhoma (Uganda).

Jentink's Duiker
CEPHALOPHUS JENTINKI

BL: 130-150 cm. SH: 80-89 cm. TL: 15 cm. W: 57-91 kg. HL: 14-21 cm. The largest Duiker. Stockily built and strikingly marked: head and neck are glossy brownish black, with the muzzle gray, and back, flanks, and rump grizzled gray, with the legs paler; the inside of the legs and the tip of the tail are whitish. White collar runs around the shoulders and lower chest, separating the black and gray around the shoulders. Slit in front of each eye holds a glandular patch. There is no tuft of hair on the forehead. Both males and females have sturdy spike-like horns that slope backward from the forehead, lightly ringed at the base but otherwise smooth. Horns are long when compared with those of other Duiker species. Females are similar to males, probably somewhat larger in body, and with smaller horns.

Cephalophus jentinki

OTHER NAMES White-shouldered Duiker, Black-headed Duiker. *French*: Céphalophe de Jentink. *German*: Jentinks Ducker. *Spanish:* Duiquero o cefalofo de Jentink. *Russian*: Чепрачный дукер. *Krio*: Gidi-gidi. *Mende*: Kaikulowulei. *Creole*: Dikidiki. *Côte d'Ivoire*: Nienagbé.

SUBSPECIES Monotypic. In the past, Jentink's Duiker was thought to be only a variation in color of Yellow-backed Duiker.

SIMILAR SPECIES Yellow-backed Duiker is the only Duiker of similar size that lives in W Africa. Although adult Jentink's Duikers are easily distinguished by their black and gray coats, juveniles of the two species are very similar. Coloration of the Asian tapir (*Tapirus indicus*) is superficially similar, but the elongated proboscis, black legs, and much larger size of the tapir readily distinguish it from Jentink's Duiker.

REPRODUCTION *Gestation*: Probably 240 days. *Young per Birth*: 1. *Weaning*: Probably 3-4 months. *Sexual Maturity*: Unknown. *Life Span*: 21 years. Very little is known of the breeding patterns of Jentink's Duiker. In captivity, ♂ may occasionally puncture the perineal or tail-head region of the ♀ during courtship, although these wounds heal readily. Infants are born dark brown, and do not obtain the black and gray coloration of adults until 1 year of age.

BEHAVIOR *Family Group:* Solitary, although pairs are occasionally seen. *Diet*: Primarily leaves and stems; also fruit when available. *Main Predators*: Leopard. It appears to be sedentary and is supposedly territorial. Primarily nocturnal, although captive individuals may be active during the daytime as well. Very wary and secretive. Sheltered spots like hollow or fallen tree trunks and the buttresses of large trees are typically used when resting or sleeping. Although it can run quickly if threatened, this species has poor stamina and typically does not run far. Like most Duikers, Jentink's Duiker is thought to live in a stable home range; it is unknown whether or not these areas are defended from other individuals as territories. This species is typically hunted at night, when hunters can use torches to pick up the eye shine of the animals.

DISTRIBUTION *Native*: Côte d'Ivoire, Liberia, Sierra Leone. Confined to the W part of the Upper Guinean forest block, from Sierra Leone through Liberia to W Côte d'Ivoire.

HABITAT Closed-canopy rainforests in W Africa, although secondary forests are sometimes used and nighttime foraging may occur in farmland. Basic habitat requirements appear to be a diversity of fruiting trees and very dense shelter. Due to human encroachment on forested land, much of the habitat remaining is fragmented and restricted to areas inaccessible to most human activity.

STATUS Endangered. The estimated total population is no more than 3,500 individuals; some experts believe that fewer than 2,000 remain. Main threats include loss of its habitat and bushmeat trade. Duikers are highly sought after by hunters as they are easily shot or captured, easily transported by foot, and have sufficient meat to be highly profitable. Without action, it could be extinct within the next few years.

PHOTO CREDITS *Jim C. Smith* and *Jonathan Beilby*, Gladys Porter Zoo (USA).

Western Bay Duiker

CEPHALOPHUS DORSALIS

BL: 76-103 cm. SH: 45-52 cm. TL: 8-12 cm. W: 18-24 kg. HL: 5-8 cm. Medium-sized Duiker. Bright reddish-brown coat, with a very bold black stripe that runs along the spine from the back of the head to the tail. Legs are dark brown, and the tail is black above and white below. Underparts are the same color as the sides, but a dark stripe runs along the center line of the belly. Head with a much-reduced crest, dark brown. Reddish face has a dark blaze that extends from the nose to the top of the forehead. White spots are present above the eyes and on the lips and chin. Cheek muscles very large and powerful. Both sexes have a pair of short, spike-like horns that extend backward from the forehead. Females are typically larger than males, with shorter horns, a narrower dorsal stripe, and less extensive black markings. Entirely dark at birth; the chestnut color and black markings develop after several months.

Cephalopus dorsalis

OTHER NAMES Western Black-backed Duiker, Black-striped Duiker. *French*: Céphalophe bai, céphalophe à bande dorsale noir. *German*: Schwarzrückenducker. *Spanish*: Duiquero bayo, cefalofo de dorso oscuro. *Russian*: Западный черноспинный дукер. *Fanti*: Dabo. *Twi*: Odabo. *Ashanti*: Odabo, abedee. *Nkonya*: Abere. *Kibali*: Sinzambi, Kuwa. *Kibudu*: Endo, kupa. *Kibira*: Kufa.

SUBSPECIES Monotypic. The name *C. dorsalis* (Bay Duiker) formerly included *C. dorsalis* (Western Bay Duiker), and *C. castaneus* (Eastern Bay Duiker) as subspecies: these are elevated to full species here. Includes *breviceps*.

SIMILAR SPECIES Red Duikers are often difficult to tell apart based on fleeting glimpses. Bay Duiker's bright white spots above each eye are distinctive. Ogilby's Duiker has paler underparts and dorsal stripe that ends at the shoulders and is not distinct on the neck. White-bellied Duiker has a less well-defined dorsal stripe that widens in the center of the back, and a pale belly. The dorsal stripe of Peters's Duiker begins at the shoulders and becomes very wide, covering the entire rump. Bay Duiker's dorsal stripe readily distinguishes it from the stripeless Black-fronted Duiker and Weyns's Duiker.

REPRODUCTION *Gestation*: 240 days. *Young per Birth*: 1. Weaning: 3.5 months. *Sexual Maturity*: 18 months (♀). *Life Span*: 17 years. There is no specific breeding season, although in central Africa there is a peak in births in January and February. Infants are born a uniform dark brown color, and begin to acquire the bright chestnut adult coloration at 5-6 months. For the first few weeks of life, an infant will remain hidden in dense vegetation while its mother forages.

BEHAVIOR *Family Group:* Solitary. *Diet*: Primarily fruits and seeds, but also leaves, fungi, flowers, and even animal matter (invertebrates, eggs, and birds). *Main Predators*: Leopard. A nocturnal species, which provides some ecological separation from similarly sized Duikers that live in the same habitat. During the day, individuals rest in dense thickets or in the buttresses of trees. ♀ have home ranges 0.2-0.4 km² in size; ♂ may range over twice that area. Population densities are typically 1.5–8.7 individuals per km². Bay Duikers are very scent oriented, using their noses to find food, detect danger, and communicate with others of their own species through the use of preorbital gland secretions, urine, and feces. If a threat is detected, Bay Duikers usually freeze in position and observe; if startled, they flee with a bounding gait into dense cover.

DISTRIBUTION *Native*: Cameroon, Côte d'Ivoire, Ghana, Guinea, Guinea-Bissau, Liberia, Nigeria, Sierra Leone, Togo. Found from Guinea-Bissau to Togo, with an isolated population in E Nigeria (E of the Cross River) and W Cameroon.

HABITAT Tracts of moist primary forest interspersed with dense thickets in W and central (equatorial) Africa.

STATUS Least Concern. This species is no longer common as a result of habitat loss and overhunting. It is only common in protected areas in Liberia and Ghana.

PHOTO CREDITS ♂: *Jonas Livet*, Kumasi Zoo (Ghana). ♀: *Brent Huffman*, Ellen Trout Zoo (USA). Head ♀: *Alex Meyer*, Lowry Park Zoo (USA).

285

Eastern Bay Duiker

CEPHALOPHUS CASTANEUS

BL: 88-103 cm. SH: 45-52 cm. TL: 8-12 cm. W: 18-24 kg. HL: 5-9.2 cm. Medium-sized Duiker. Larger, heavier, and darker than the Western Bay Duiker. General color is a uniformly deep chestnut brown, with the undersides slightly brighter than the back. Wide black dorsal stripe extending from the neck to the rump, wider than in Western Bay Duiker, narrowing to a thin line that extends to the end of the tail. Legs are dark brown. Tail is black with a white terminal tuft. Throat and upper neck are whitish. Chestnut-red face, white lips and chin, and pronounced cheek muscles. White spot usually present above the eye. Dark reddish frontal blaze and crest, less black than in Western Bay Duiker. Ears are dark brown on the back, paler inside, larger than in Western Bay Duiker. Horns, present in both sexes, are parallel and smooth from base to tip. Females are slightly larger than males, with shorter horns. Infants are blackish brown, with less apparent white facial spots.

♀

♂

286

Cephalophus castaneus

OTHER NAMES Eastern Black-backed Duiker. *French*: Céphalophe bai, céphalophe à bande dorsale noir. *German*: Kongo-Schwarzrückenducker. *Spanish*: Duiquero o cefalofo de dorso oscuro oriental. *Russian*: Восточный черноспинный дукер. *Local names*: Senge, mbon, ngendi, dengbe, gbaide.

SUBSPECIES Monotypic. Formerly considered a subspecies of *C. dorsalis* (Bay Duiker). Includes *kuha* (Ituri District, DR Congo), *leucochilus* (southward from Cameroon to the mouth of the Congo River and perhaps into Angola), and *orientalis* (Uele Valley, DR Congo).

REPRODUCTION *Gestation*: 240 days. *Young per Birth*: 1. Weaning: 3.5 months. *Sexual Maturity*: 2.5 years (♀). *Life Span*: 17 years. Polygynous. Breeding throughout the year, with a peak in births in the rainy seasons (May and October) as well as in the short dry season (January-February). During courtship, a male pursues a female with his head outstretched, licking the anogenital region. Receptive females remain quiet during courtship, while unreceptive females puff at approaching males, and may retire to a sheltered spot. Estrus last for less than 24 hours, and copulation duration is 1-2 seconds. Ritualized foreleg kicking has not been observed.

BEHAVIOR *Family Group:* Solitary. *Diet*: Primarily fruits and seeds, but also leaves, fungi, flowers, and even animal matter (invertebrates, eggs, and birds). *Main Predators*: Leopard. Nocturnal, with activity starting slightly before sunset, and ceasing before dawn. During the day they hide in areas with restricted visibility, such as in buttress roots of large trees, hollow logs, and recent deadfall, which may be reused day to day. They often remain hidden in resting sites even when approached. They are never found resting with others. ♂ may travel 4 km per night, significantly more than ♀. Home ranges may vary from 0.07 to 0.8 km^2, being generally larger during the dry seasons, and may overlap with others. Density estimates are 1.5-8.7 individuals per km^2. ♂ mark tree trunks with secretion from their preorbital glands, which crystallizes, but also with urine or feces. These Duikers tend to move slowly with the head stretched out at shoulder height, dropping the head so that the nose is at ground level. Detection of danger is by hearing and smell; when threatened, they will freeze in position, and will flee into dense cover with the head stretched forward, and will then observe while standing stock-still. Vocalizations are rare, and there is no alarm vocalization.

DISTRIBUTION *Native*: Angola, Cameroon, Central African Republic, Congo, DR Congo, Equatorial Guinea, Gabon. *Possibly Extinct*: Uganda. S Cameroon, S Central African Republic to E DR Congo, S to N Angola. Formerly occurred throughout the equatorial lowland forests of W and central Africa, extending to a limited extent into forest patches in the adjoining forest-savanna mosaic.

HABITAT Closed-canopy forest, most frequently in moist lowland areas.

STATUS Least Concern. It is common in most of its range; however, its status in Angola is unknown, and it may be extinct in Uganda. Main threats include habitat loss and degradation, and poaching.

PHOTO CREDITS ♀: *Brent Huffman*, Limbe Wildlife Centre (Cameroon).

Maxwell's Duiker
PHILANTOMBA MAXWELLI AND PHILANTOMBA WALTERI

BL: 55-76 cm. SH: 35-42 cm. TL: 8-15 cm. W: 5-10 kg. HL: 5 cm. Smooth coat, slate-gray or gray-brown color, paling on the underside of the neck and belly. Facial markings much darker and the head more angular than in the Blue Duiker. Forehead and nose bridge are dark brown or charcoal in color, bordered by whitish-gray stripes which run from above the eyes down to the nose. Maxillary gland, found on the cheek in front of the eye, is extremely large and conspicuous. Tail is thin and fringed with white hairs. Short, spike-like horns, found in both sexes, rising almost vertically from between the ears, corrugated at the base, may be hidden by the dark brown forehead tuft. Female larger than the male, with smaller horns or hornless.

Philantomba maxwelli maxwelli

Philantomba maxwelli danei

Philantomba walteri

OTHER NAMES *French*: Céphalophe de Maxwell. *German*: Maxwell-Ducker. *Spanish*: Duiquero o cefalofo de Maxwell. *Russian*: Дукер Максвелла (*maxwelli*), Дукер Уолтера (*walteri*). *Hausa*: Gadan Kurmi. *Twi*: Otwe. *Yoruba*: Etu. *Dyula*: Diafi, forni. *Achande*: Muvru. *Bambara*: Nkokunan, manunkalan. *Banda-Linda*: Mbelé. *Fid*: Kubeyel.

SUBSPECIES *P. m. maxwelli*: Senegal and Gambia to E Ghana (W of the Volta River). *P. m. danei*: Yatward and Sherbo islands (Sierra Leone). *P. walteri* (Verheyen's Duiker): Togo, Benin, Nigeria, E Ghana (E of the Volta River); smaller, longer tail, dark dorsum gradually fading into the paler haunches. Maxwell's Duiker is sometimes considered as a subspecies of the Blue Duiker.

SIMILAR SPECIES Similar to the Blue Duiker, but twice as heavy, with a more uniform mouse-gray color; the rump is the same color as the body, whereas in the Blue Duiker it is whitish, with somewhat larger horns.

REPRODUCTION *Gestation*: 120 days. *Young per Birth*: 1. *Weaning*: 5 months. *Sexual Maturity*: 9-12 months (♀), 12-18 months (♂). *Life Span*: 12 years. Most births occur from January to March, with a second period occurring in August-September. Young are able to stand very soon after birth, and can walk within a few hours. They generally remain with their parents for their first year.

BEHAVIOR *Family Group*: Bonded pairs, possibly forming a lifetime bond. *Diet*: Fruit, herbs, shrubs, and new growth, probably some animal matter. *Main Predators:* Leopard, golden cat, serval, Libyan wild cat, civet, large raptors, crocodile, monitor, python. Nocturnal. The general mode of locomotion is a jerky walk, generally accompanied by flicks of the tail. When startled, these antelope bound for cover. Pairs inhabit home ranges whose boundaries are actively marked by both sexes with secretions from the preorbital glands. These are believed to be defended territories, as neighboring pairs do not usually overlap their ranges. The ♂ is territorial and highly aggressive, fiercely attacking and driving away other ♂ and larger animals. Mutual marking between two individuals (generally a bonded pair) is common, and is accomplished by rubbing their heads together. Special sites are used as latrines, and several well-defined trails lead to these from frequently used sleeping areas.

DISTRIBUTION *Native*: Benin, Burkina Faso, Côte d'Ivoire, Gambia, Ghana, Guinea, Guinea-Bissau, Liberia, Nigeria, Senegal, Sierra Leone, Togo. Presently, it is found in SW Senegal, W Gambia, Guinea-Bissau, Guinea, Sierra Leone, Liberia, Côte d'Ivoire, extreme SW Burkina Faso, S Ghana, central and S Togo, central and S Benin, and SW Nigeria W of the Niger River. E of the Niger River it is replaced by the Blue Duiker.

HABITAT Rainforest areas, relict forests in savannas, secondary-growth forests and clearings in rainforests. They prefer dense foliage where they can remain concealed, and rarely stray more than 30 m from cover.

STATUS Least Concern. Total population estimate of 2,137,000, likely a conservative estimate. Within its distribution range the Maxwell's Duiker is the commonest of the forest Duikers.

PHOTO CREDITS ♂: *Johan Bordonné*, Antwerp Zoo (Belgium). Head ♂: *Dan Doucette,* Atebubu (Ghana). Head ♀: *Jonas Livet*, Kumasi Zoo (Ghana).

Cape Blue Duiker

PHILANTOMBA MONTICOLA

BL: 50-75 cm. SH: 30-35 cm. TL: 7-10 cm. W: 4 kg (♂), 4.6 kg (♀). HL: 4.7 cm (♂), 3 cm (♀). Color varies from dark reddish brown to dark grayish brown, paler than Zimbabwe Blue Duiker. Rump is not particularly dark. Legs reddish tan, with very little transition between the haunches and the croup. Belly, throat, chest, and inner legs slightly lighter in color. Tail is not very dark, white underneath. Rounded ears, front is white, back is dark gray. Preorbital glands on the sides of the face, below the eyes. Face colored similarly to the body, with the cheeks and underside of jaw paler. Light eyebrow ridge curves up to the base of the horns. Horns are present in both sexes, larger than in Zimbabwe Blue Duiker. Females are generally larger than males, sometimes without horns.

♀

♂

Young

Philantomba monticola

OTHER NAMES *French*: Céphalophe bleu. *German*: Blauducker, Rotfussducker. *Spanish:* Duiquero o cefalofo azul del Cabo. *Russian*: Капский голубой дукер. *Afrikaans*: Bloubokkie. *Swahili:* Paa, ndimba, chesi. *Ndebele*: Ipunzi ehlaza. *Xhosa*: Iphuthi. *Zulu*: Iphithi. *Setswana*: Photi. *Swati*: Imphunzi. *Xitonga*: Mhunti. *Tshivenda*: Ntas ya muvhala wa lutombo. *Damara*: Dôas.

SUBSPECIES Monotypic. The name *P. monticola* (Blue Duiker) formerly included *P. aequatorialis* (Eastern Blue Duiker), *P. anchietae* (Angolan Blue Duiker), *P. bicolor* (Zimbabwe Blue Duiker), *P. congica* (Western Blue Duiker), *P. defriesi* (Zambian Blue Duiker), *P. hecki* (Malawi Blue Duiker), *P. lugens* (Mountain Blue Duiker), *P. melanorhea* (Bioko Blue Duiker), *P. monticola* (Cape Blue Duiker), *P. simpsoni* (Simpson's Blue Duiker) as subspecies: these are all elevated to full species here.

REPRODUCTION *Gestation*: 225 days. *Young per Birth*: 1, rarely 2. *Weaning:* 5 months. *Sexual Maturity*: 16-17 months (♀), 9 months (♂). *Life Span*: 12 years. They breed throughout the year, and may take temporary mates or mate for life. During courtship ♂ prances before the ♀, nibbling at her back and shoulders, rubbing his preorbital glands against her cheeks and presenting his horns. Young lie concealed away from the mother for 2-3 months. At this point their coat changes from reddish brown to the gray-blue color of adults.

BEHAVIOR *Family Group*: In pairs, sometimes with subadult offspring. *Diet*: Fruit, leaves, and soft stems of the rooikans branches; also eat a variety of leaves of the underbush, ferns, shoots, forest herbs, and fallen fruits found in the forest; they drink plenty of water. *Main Predators*: Caracal, mountain leopard, crowned eagle, python. Very shy, secretive, silent, timid creatures that are seldom seen. Most active in the early morning and late afternoon. At night they come into less sheltered areas at the forest's edge. During daytime they are very alert and approach these areas with great caution. Duikers leave well-marked trails or paths, as they need to drink water every day, so they are easily trapped in snares. A snared or otherwise caught Duiker gives utterance to pitiful, loud, and strangely cat-like meowing. Highly territorial, each breeding pair usually remains within a limited area of between 4 and 6 ha. Both ♂ and ♀ scent markings are present in their chosen territory. They usually forage, sleep, and rest close to or next to one another. Established pairs groom each other frequently and often go through extensive greetings (rubbing noses, preorbital glands, head tufts and shoulders). Like other Duikers, the Blue Duiker has a jerky, zigzag action as it darts through the bush. Being so small, it can move freely below the undergrowth, and it is well camouflaged, making it almost invisible; it may be spotted only, due to the constant flicking of its tail, which exposes the white in tiny flashes.

DISTRIBUTION S South Africa, in East and West Cape.

HABITAT Dense bush, thickets, or forests where water is readily available.

STATUS Least Concern. The destruction of the Southern Cape's indigenous forest has severely limited its range in this area.

PHOTO CREDITS ♂, ♀: *Claire J. Hamilton*, Plettenberg Bay (South Africa). Head ♀: *Tony Makepeace*, Featherbed Nature Reserve (South Africa). Young: *Amy* and *Mikhail Perfilov*, Featherbed Nature Reserve (South Africa). 291

Eastern Blue Duiker

PHILANTOMBA AEQUATORIALIS

BL: 60-67 cm. SH: 31-38 cm. TL: 7-12 cm. W: 3.9-5 kg (♂), 4.2-6.5 kg (♀). HL: 2-4.6 cm (♂), to 3.3 cm (♀). The smallest of all Duikers. Overall color is drab brown, with a bluish sheen on the back. Underparts, inner legs, rump, and underside of the tail are pale gray to whitish. Dark patch on the upper haunches on either side of the tail base. Head sparsely covered with hairs, of the same color as the body; there is a light eyebrow ridge which curves up to the base of the horns. Opening of facial glands underneath the eye is curved, and not straight as in other Duikers. Crest very short. Legs of the same color as the body or more or less tinged with rufous fawn, contrasting with the body. Tail rather long, bushy, black, bordered with white. Horns are strongly ringed and short, sometimes absent in females, or hidden by the short head crest. Females are slightly larger than males.

♀

Young

♂

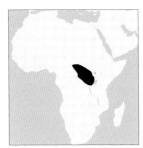

*Philantomba aequatorialis
aequatorialis*

*Philantomba aequatorialis
musculoides*

*Philantomba aequatorialis
sundevalli*

OTHER NAMES Equatorial Blue Duiker, Zanzibar Blue Duiker. *French*: Céphalophe équatorial. *German*: Ostafrika-Blauducker, Rotfussducker. *Spanish*: Duiquero azul oriental, cefalofo azul de Zanzibar. *Russian*: Восточный голубой дукер. *Afrikaans*: Bloubokkie. *Swahili*: Paa, ndimba, chesi. *Ndebele*: Ipunzi ehlaza. *Xhosa*: Iphuthi. *Zulu*: Iphithi. *Setswana*: Photi. *Swati*: Imphunzi. *Xitonga*: Mhunti. *Tshivenda*: Ntas ya muvhala wa lutombo. *Damara*: Dôas.

SUBSPECIES *P. a. aequatorialis*: ♀ usually hornless; found from C Central African Republic and E DR Congo (E from Lisala, S to Upemba) to SW Sudan and W Uganda, with an isolated population in Imatong Mountains in S Sudan; range bordered to the S and W by the Congo River. *P. a. musculoides*: darker on dorsum than *aequatorialis*, but flanks lighter, haunch stripe less well marked; ♀ always hornless; found in E Uganda, W Kenya (E to the Rift Valley), and NW Tanzania. *P. a. sundevalli*: paler subspecies, light brownish in color, white below, with longest horns; found on Zanzibar, Pemba, and Mafia islands (Tanzania), coastal mainland Kenya and Tanzania; individuals from Pemba Island are sometimes listed as the separate subspecies *pembae*. Formerly considered a subspecies of *P. monticola* (Blue Duiker). This species intergrades with Angolan Blue Duiker (*P. defriesi*). Includes *pembae* (Pemba Blue Duiker, from Pemba Island).

REPRODUCTION *Gestation*: 225 days. *Young per Birth*: 1, rarely 2. *Weaning*: 5 months. *Sexual Maturity*: 9-12 months (♀), 12-18 months (♂). *Life Span*: 12 years. It likely breeds year-round. Kids lie concealed away from the mother for 2-3 months. At this point their coat changes from reddish brown to the gray-blue color of adults.

BEHAVIOR *Family Group*: Solitary or in mating pairs. *Diet*: Leaves, buds, shoots, grasses, fruit, insects, eggs. *Main Predators*: Leopard, small cats, civet, eagle, crocodile, python, monitor. Diurnal; mostly active around dawn and dusk. Bonded pairs patrol their territory, which are 2.5-4 ha in size, regularly marking them with scent clues from their pedal glands (situated between the hooves) and facial glands, and from defecating. Both sexes chase off any intruders, but will remain tolerant of their own young until they reach 18 months of age. The mother and young make contact through soft groaning calls, both freezing at the slightest alarm. ♂ may emit a whistle or a sneezing sound to raise the alarm.

DISTRIBUTION *Native*: Central African Republic, DR Congo, Kenya, Sudan, Tanzania, Uganda. Widely distributed in central Africa, from Central African Republic to W Kenya and NW Tanzania. Also present on the islands of Pemba, Zanzibar, and Mafia.

HABITAT Forested habitats, including lowland rainforest, montane forest, and dry thickets, from sea level to 3,000 m.

STATUS Least Concern. Intense hunting pressure has led to localized declines in the coastal forests of Tanzania and in the forests of W Kenya, but it is probably common in the undisturbed forests in central DR Congo.

PHOTO CREDITS ♂: *Hartmut Inerless*. Head ♂: *Terry Costales*. ♀: *Sergey Chichagov*. Young: *Nicki Miller*.

Western Blue Duiker

PHILANTOMBA CONGICA

BL: 56-66 cm. SH: 32-38 cm. TL: 7-8 cm. W: 3.9-5 kg (♂), 4.2-6.1 kg (♀). HL: 2.8-4.5 cm (♂), 0-3 cm (♀). Color pale grayish, with a bright, strong gray-brown to black dorsum. Underparts, inner legs, rump, and underside of the tail are whitish. Horizontal black stripe on the haunches marking the sharp transition from the blackish brown of the croup to the paler haunch. Cheeks red tinged. Opening of facial glands underneath the eye is curved, and not straight as in other Duikers. Crest very short. Median nuchal hair reversal is frequent. Tail rather long, bushy, black, bordered with white. Legs are gray or brownish gray, with dark marks above the hooves. Face is dark, with reddish cheeks. Horns are short, sometimes absent in females, or hidden by the short head crest. Females are generally larger than males.

♂

Young

♀

Philantomba congica

Philantomba melanorhea

OTHER NAMES Congo Blue Duiker, Cameroon Blue Duiker. *French*: Céphalophe bleu du Cameroun. *German*: Kamerun-Blauducker. *Spanish*: Duiquero azul de Camerún, cefalofo azul de Camerún. *Russian*: Конголезский голубой дукер *(congica),* Западный голубой дукер *(melanorhea).*

SUBSPECIES Monotypic. Formerly considered a subspecies of *P. monticola* (Blue Duiker). Includes *schultzei* (Cameroon Blue Duiker, from Bumba Valley, SW Cameroon).

SIMILAR SPECIES It is about half as large as the Maxwell Duiker, and the rump area is whitish (same color as the body in Maxwell Duiker). Bioko Blue Duiker is similar, but even more contrasty, with a black dorsum and pinkish-gray flanks, long, thick fur, smaller size, and very long horns.

REPRODUCTION *Gestation*: 204 days. *Young per Birth*: 1. *Weaning*: 5 months. *Sexual Maturity*: 9-12 months (♀), 12-18 months (♂). *Life Span*: 12 years. Breeds year-round, with peaks during the 2 dry seasons, around January and July. A male courts a female by pursuing her and licking at her tail region during the chase, with ritualized foreleg kicks (laufschlag) prior to copulation. Males may be quite aggressive to other animals in the vicinity during this time.

BEHAVIOR *Family Group*: A mating pair, sometimes with 1 or 2 offspring. *Diet:* Frugivorous; foliage may be consumed in the form of fallen leaves. *Main Predators*: Leopard, small cats, civet, eagle, crocodile, python, monitor. Strictly diurnal, with a peak during the early morning and late afternoon. At night, they retire to regularly used resting places, which are often smelled and scraped briefly with the hooves before lying down. Activity increases during the dry seasons, as reduced food resources require increased foraging time. While active, they constantly flick their tails up and down, flashing the white underside. Soft, brief calls help maintain contact between family members. They occupy stable territories, averaging 0.04 km² in size. Both sexes are territorial, each defending the area against others of the same sex. Territory edges are marked with horn scrapings on tree trunks and with scent marks. When confronted with a potential threat, they freeze in position just before flight. A loud whistle is used as an alarm call.

DISTRIBUTION *P. congica* (Western Blue Duiker): Nigeria to W Central African Republic and DR Congo, S to coastal S Congo. *P. melanorhea* (Bioko Blue Duiker): Bioko Island (Equatorial Guinea).

HABITAT Wide range of forested habitats: high forest, secondary forest, and forest edges. Large open areas are avoided, but pockets of gallery forest within savannas may be used. They enter dense forest only if alarmed.

STATUS Least Concern.

PHOTO CREDITS ♂: *Antoine Rabussier*, Krefeld Zoo (Germany). Head ♂: *Maxime Thué*, Zoo d'Asson (France). ♀: *Lee Buck*, Colchester Zoo (UK). Head ♀: *Philip Harris*, Colchester Zoo (UK). Young: *Thomas Schwenker,* Burgers Zoo (Netherlands) and Zoo d'Asson (France).

Zimbabwe Blue Duiker

PHILANTOMBA BICOLOR

BL: 57-64 cm. SH: 32-37 cm. TL: 7-9 cm. W: 3.9-5.4 kg (♂), 3.8-6.5 kg (♀). HL: 3.4-4.2 cm (♂), 2.3-2.9 cm (♀). Coat color dark gray brown to bluish gray, with variable amounts of gray. Sides paler and brighter than the dorsal surface, with a distinct rufous tone. Rump and base of the tail darker. Legs are rusty brown, fetlocks are dark with pale reddish patches above the hooves. Undersides are white. Tail is dark brown on the upper surface, white on the underside. Forehead and bridge of the nose are dark brown, cheeks are pale gray with a rufous tinge, extending around the eyes, forming a supraciliary streak. Throat is warm gray with an orange tinge. Ears are dark brown outside and white inside, with a white spot at the base. Short coronal tuft on the forehead. Horns found in both sexes, strongly ringed in males. Females slightly larger than males, with shorter horns.

Philantomba bicolor

OTHER NAMES Zulu Blue Duiker, Natal Blue Duiker. *French*: Céphalophe bicolore. *German*: Simbabwe-Blauducker. *Spanish*: Duiquero azul de Zimbabue, cefalofo azul de Zimbabue. *Russian*: Южный голубой дукер. *Afrikaans*: Blouduiker. *Zulu*: Iphithi.

SUBSPECIES Monotypic. Formerly considered a subspecies of *P. monticola* (Blue Duiker). Includes *fuscicolor* (Southeastern Rhodesia Blue Duiker) and *ruddi* (from Sibedeni, NW Eshowe, Zululand, KwaZulu-Natal).

SIMILAR SPECIES Darker than Malawi Blue Duiker, but not as dark as Mountain Blue Duiker.

REPRODUCTION *Gestation*: 197-215 days. *Young per Birth*: 1, rarely 2. *Weaning*: 5 months. *Sexual Maturity*: 8-12 months (♀), 11-14 months (♂). *Life Span*: 6-7 years. Breeds year-round. ♂ court ♀ by closely following or chasing them, and may become very aggressive toward other conspecifics. ♂ perform ritualized leg kicks (laufschlag) between ♀ hind legs. Copulation is brief, but occurs up to 5 times. ♀ choose a secluded, sheltered area in which to give birth.

BEHAVIOR *Family Group*: Solitary or in mating pairs. *Diet*: Principally folivorous, but also frugivorous; it feeds principally on freshly fallen leaves instead of browsing; not dependent on drinking water. *Main Predators*: Leopard, small cats, civet, eagle, crocodile, python, monitor. Diurnal, with the highest activity levels after dawn and prior to dusk. Between bouts of activity, it frequently retires to resting spots. It tends to be more active in higher-quality habitats: although foraging time is reduced, the time spent patrolling territorial boundaries and defending territories is higher. Small home ranges, averaging 7,000 m², are occupied year-round, with the central area with bed sites used for refuge, rest, and rumination. Home ranges are shared by a family group of an adult ♂ and ♀, plus their offspring. Each territory is transected by a number of regularly used pathways, which makes the animals especially vulnerable to snares. Population densities are about 150 individuals per km². They avoid predators by staying motionless and then suddenly dashing away when approached too closely.

DISTRIBUTION *Native*: Mozambique, South Africa, Zimbabwe. Found in Mozambique, and E Zimbabwe S of Zambezi River to E South Africa (Limpopo and KwaZulu-Natal).

HABITAT Lowland evergreen forests, coastal forest, dune forest, and montane forest up to 1,370 m. Areas with dense underbrush are used for cover.

STATUS Least Concern. Uncommon or rare in Zimbabwe and Mozambique, with populations continuing to decline due to poaching. Most of the population is found in KwaZulu-Natal.

PHOTO CREDITS ♂: Mlilwane Wildlife Sanctuary (Swaziland). ♀: *Johannes Pfleiderer*, Montecasino Bird Gardens (South Africa). Head ♀: *Scott N. Ramsay*, Mlilwane Wildlife Sanctuary (Swaziland).

Mountain Blue Duiker
PHILANTOMBA LUGENS

BL: 65 cm. SH: 30-40 cm. TL: 10 cm. W: 5 kg. HL: 4.3 cm (♂), 3.2 cm (♀). Larger than the neighboring Eastern Blue Duiker and Malawi Blue Duiker. Pelage is a uniform dark gray brown across the back, sides, and legs, except for a pale streak down the front of the limbs. Rump darkens to black above the tail, but this marking is not conspicuous because the haunches are also quite dark. Underparts are pale brownish gray, with groins paler, and there may be a narrow streak of white along the midline. Face is brown, forehead and the top of muzzle are nearly black, chin and underside of the jaw are white. Whitish supraciliary streak. Ears are nearly black. Crown of the head with a very long crest of black hairs. Horns are present in both sexes, longer than in other species of Blue Duiker.

Philantomba lugens

OTHER NAMES Usangu Blue Duiker, Urori Duiker. *French*: Céphalophe de montagne. *German*: Tansania-Blauducker. *Spanish*: Duiquero azul de montaña, cefalofo azul de montaña. *Russian*: Узамбарский голубой дукер.

SUBSPECIES Monotypic. Formerly considered a subspecies of *P. monticola* (Blue Duiker). This species intergrades with Malawi Blue Duiker (*P. hecki*). Includes *schusteri* (Uluguru Blue Duiker, from Uluguru Mountains in E Tanzania).

SIMILAR SPECIES Suni is similar in size and appearance, but has a paler coat, larger ears, and the tail is bushy, uniformly brown above, and with no white stripe down the center.

REPRODUCTION *Gestation*: 225 days. *Young per Birth*: 1, rarely 2. *Weaning*: 5 months. *Sexual Maturity*: 9-12 months (♀), 12-18 months (♂). *Life Span*: 12 years. There is no specific information available for this species, but probably similar to other Blue Duikers.

BEHAVIOR *Family Group*: Solitary or in mating pairs. *Diet:* Leaves, buds, shoots, grasses, fruit, insects, eggs. *Main Predators:* Leopard, small cats, civet, eagle, crocodile, python, monitor. Presumably diurnal. There is no specific information available for this species, but probably similar to other Blue Duikers.

DISTRIBUTION *Native*: Tanzania. Found in the highlands of Tanzania, from Usambara Mountains S to Irangi, and to borders of Malawi at Tukuyu; also known from Uhehe, Kigoma District. The Nyika Plateau population is difficult to assign with certainty to either *P. lugens* or *P. hecki*.

HABITAT Montane forest in the highlands of Tanzania.

STATUS Least Concern. Populations of this species appear to be severely affected by hunting. Habitat loss through human encroachment is another significant threat.

Simpson's Blue Duiker

PHILANTOMBA SIMPSONI

BL: 60 cm. SH: 30-40 cm. TL: 10 cm. W: 5 kg. HL: 4.4 cm (♂), 2.7 cm (♀). A small Blue Duiker. General color is reddish brown, darkening to blackish brown in a stripe along the midline of back. Underparts are white, extending up the sides and blending gradually with the color of the flanks. Legs are rufous brown, with the inner surfaces pale, but not white. Haunches are redder than the body. Face has a dark brown blaze running from the muzzle to the top of the forehead. Opening of facial glands underneath the eye is curved. Well-defined, bright rufous supraciliary streaks. Underside of jaw is white. Tail rather long, bushy, black, bordered with white. Spike-like horns, usually present in both sexes, but occasionally lacking in females.

Philantomba simpsoni

OTHER NAMES Middle Congo Blue Duiker. *French*: Céphalophe de Simpson. *German*: Simpson-Blauducker. *Spanish*: Duiquero azul de Simpson, cefalofo azul de Simpson. *Russian*: Голубой дукер Симпсона.

SUBSPECIES Monotypic. Formerly considered a subspecies of *P. monticola* (Blue Duiker).

REPRODUCTION *Gestation*: 225 days. *Young per Birth*: 1, rarely 2. *Weaning*: 5 months. *Sexual Maturity*: 9-12 months (♀), 12-18 months (♂). *Life Span*: 12 years. There is no specific information available for this species, but probably similar to other Blue Duikers. It likely breeds year-round. Kids lie concealed away from the mother for 2-3 months. At this point their coat changes from reddish brown to the gray-blue color of adults.

BEHAVIOR *Family Group*: Solitary or in mating pairs. *Diet*: Leaves, buds, shoots, grasses, fruit, insects, eggs. *Main Predators*: Leopard, small cats, civet, eagle, crocodile, python, monitor. There is no specific information available for this species, but probably similar to other Blue Duikers. Probably diurnal; mostly active around dawn and dusk.

DISTRIBUTION *Native*: DR Congo. Found in central DR Congo: Salonga NP, Equateur Province, Eastern Province, W Kasai and E Kasai, with a range confined by the Congo and Kasai rivers.

HABITAT Rainforest and riverine forest, dense thickets, and montane forests up to 3,000 m.

STATUS Least Concern. There is no estimate of population size of this species.

Malawi and Zambian Blue Duiker

PHILANTOMBA HECKI AND PHILANTOMBA DEFRIESI

BL: 50-65 cm. SH: 30-37 cm. TL: 8 cm. W: 4-5.2 kg (♂), 4.3-6.2 kg (♀). HL: 4.3 cm (♂), 2.8 cm (♀). Malawi Blue Duiker has a reddish pelage. Dorsum is rufous gray to brown, blending into pale rufous flanks. Rump is dark brown, and is especially dark at the sides of the tail. Sharp demarcation between the dark rump and the pale red haunches. Legs with a reddish tone. Underparts from white to pale reddish gray with white patches in the axillary and inguinal regions and along the midline. Forehead is dark brown. Rufous supraciliary streaks. Rufous patch at the base of ears. Opening of facial glands underneath the eye is curved. Tail rather long, bushy, black, bordered with white. Short, straight horns, present in both sexes. Females larger than males, with shorter horns.

Philantomba hecki

Philantomba defriesi

OTHER NAMES Coast Blue Duiker, Mozambique Blue Duiker, Heck's Blue Duiker, Northeastern Rhodesia Blue Duiker. *French*: Céphalophe de Heck, céphalophe de De Fries. *German*: Malawi-Blauducker, Sambia-Blauducker. *Spanish*: Duiquero azul de Malawi, duiquero azul de Zambia. *Russian*: Малавийский голубой дукер *(hecki),* Катангский голубой дукер *(defriesi).*

SUBSPECIES Monotypic. Formerly considered as subspecies of *P. monticola* (Blue Duiker). Malawi Blue Duiker intergrades with Mountain Blue Duiker *(lugens);* includes *nyasae* (Nyasa Blue Duiker). Zambian Blue Duiker intergrades with Eastern Blue Duiker *(aequatorialis);* includes *ludlami* (NW Rhodesia Blue Duiker).

SIMILAR SPECIES Zambian Blue Duiker is one of the largest Blue Duikers. Pelage is gray brown, paler that of the neighboring Malawi Blue Duiker. Dorsum is darker gray over the midline. Flanks have a reddish tint. Forequarters are bluish gray. Tail and rump are dark, and this coloration extends laterally onto the upper hind legs, where there is a clearly defined line between this dark patch and the reddish haunches. Legs are distinctly rufous. Horns are present in both sexes.

REPRODUCTION *Gestation*: 225 days. *Young per Birth*: 1, rarely 2. *Weaning*: 5 months. *Sexual Maturity*: 9-12 months (♀), 12-18 months (♂). *Life Span*: 12 years. Births have been recorded in June, August, and October.

BEHAVIOR *Family Group*: Solitary or in mating pairs. *Diet:* Selective forager that feeds on fallen fruit and leaves; it generally feeds from the forest floor, but it may occasionally browse directly from plants. *Main Predators:* Crowned hawk-eagle, leopard, small cats, civet, eagle, crocodile, python, monitor. Presumably diurnal.

DISTRIBUTION Malawi Blue Duiker: *Native*: Malawi, Mozambique, Zambia. Found in NE Malawi, NE Zambia E of the Luangwa Valley, N Mozambique, Rovuma and from the Witu District and the mouth of the Tana River S through the forest area of the coast to Mozambique. Zambian Blue Duiker: *Native*: Angola, DR Congo, Zambia. Found in Central Africa, between Lake Mweru and Lake Tanganyika, N Zambia, Katanga, N to Lukonzolwa and Kinda, including S DR Congo (S of Upemba NP), and E Angola.

HABITAT Rainforest and riverine forest, dense thickets, and montane forests. Preferred habitats are correlated with a balance between high canopy and dense undergrowth.

STATUS Least Concern. There is no estimate of population size of this species, but its distribution is considerably fragmented as a result of habitat destruction, and numbers have been reduced by overhunting.

Angolan Blue Duiker
PHILANTOMBA ANCHIETAE

BL: 60-67 cm. SH: 30-40 cm. TL: 7-11 cm. W: 5 kg. HL: 4-4.6 cm (♂), 2.6 cm (♀). The largest species of Blue Duiker. General color is pale gray brown, with the darkening of the dorsal surfaces, typical of this genus, restricted to the base of the tail. Sides are pale gray, blending to red on the posterior haunches. Transition between the red haunches and the dark at the tail base is well marked but not extensive. Tail rather long, bushy, black on the upper surface and white underneath. Legs are pale brownish. Underparts and proximal half of inner legs are grayish white. Opening of facial glands underneath the eye is curved. Horns are found in both sexes, but may be absent in females.

Philantomba anchietae

OTHER NAMES Anchieta's Antelope. *French*: Céphalophe d'Angola. *German*: Angola-Blauducker. *Spanish*: Duiquero azul de Angola. *Russian*: Ангольский голубой дукер.

SUBSPECIES Monotypic. Formerly considered a subspecies of *P. monticola* (Blue Duiker).

REPRODUCTION *Gestation*: 225 days. *Young per Birth*: 1, rarely 2. *Weaning*: 5 months. *Sexual Maturity*: 9-12 months (♀), 12-18 months (♂). *Life Span*: 12 years. There is no specific information available for this species, but probably similar to other Blue Duikers. It likely breeds year-round. Kids lie concealed away from the mother for 2-3 months. At this point their coat changes from reddish brown to the gray-blue color of adults.

BEHAVIOR *Family Group*: Solitary or in mating pairs. *Diet*: Leaves, buds, shoots, grasses, fruit, insects, eggs. *Main Predators*: Leopard, small cats, civet, eagle, crocodile, python, monitor. There is no specific information available for this species, but probably similar to other Blue Duikers. Probably diurnal; mostly active around dawn and dusk.

DISTRIBUTION *Native*: Angola, DR Congo. Found in NW Angola throughout the mountainous area, and SW DR Congo.

HABITAT Forests, thickets, and dense coastal brush.

STATUS Least Concern. There is no estimate of population size of this species, but it is believed to be widespread in N Angola.

Barbary Sheep
AMMOTRAGUS LERVIA

BL: 130-165 cm. SH: 75-110 cm. TL: 15-20 cm. W: 30-145 kg. HL: Up to 88 cm (♂). Medium-sized sheep. Short, bristly outer coat reddish to sandy brown in color. Underparts are moderately lighter. Both sexes have a heavy fringe of hair on the throat, although in males this extends down the neck to encompass the chest and front legs. Tail is also fringed. Body quite thick and sturdy. Thick, triangular-based horns, found in both sexes, although slightly larger in males. Horns have numerous fine rings, although in older individuals these may be worn down, causing the horn surface to look smooth. They curve in a semi-circle over the back. Female much smaller and lighter with a reduced fringe of hairs, and horns less developed.

♀

Young

♂

302

Ammotragus lervia

Ammotragus lervia angusi

Ammotragus lervia lervia

Ammotragus lervia ornatus

OTHER NAMES Aoudad. *French:* Mouflon à manchettes, mouflon de Barbarie, aoudad, arui. *German:* Mähnenspringer, Mähnenschaf, Berberschaf, Aoudad. *Spanish:* Arrui, carnero de berbería. *Russian:* Гривистый баран. *Arabic:* Arwi, kabsh gabali, audan, aroui el Maghreb. *Peulh:* Edda.

SUBSPECIES *A. l. angusi* (Aïr Aoudad): NW Niger. *A. l. blainei* (Kordofan Aoudad): Sudan, NE Chad, SE Libya. *A. l. lervia* (Atlas Aoudad): Morocco, N Algeria, N Tunisia. *A. l. fassini* (Libyan Aoudad): S Tunisia, NW Libya. *A. l. ornatus* (Egyptian Aoudad): Egypt; probably extinct. *A. l. sahariensis* (Saharan Aoudad): S Morocco, W Sahara, S Algeria, SW Libya, NE Mali, SE Niger, NW Mauritania, NW Chad.

REPRODUCTION *Gestation*: 160 days. *Young per Birth*: 1, rarely up to 3. *Weaning*: 3-4 months. *Sexual Maturity*: 18 months. *Life Span*: 20 years. Although breeding can occur throughout the year, there is a peak from September to November, with the young being born from March to May. ♀ may give birth twice per year. Newborns are able to negotiate rocky hills almost immediately after birth.

BEHAVIOR *Family Group*: Generally solitary or in small groups. *Diet*: Sparse grasses, bushes, acacia, lichens. *Main Predators*: Leopard, caracal. Like most desert dwellers, the Barbary Sheep is most active in the cooler hours of dawn and dusk, seeking shade and shelter during the day. Barbary sheep are exceptionally sure footed and have such jumping power that they can clear a 2 m obstacle with ease from a standing start. The lack of vegetation for cover in their habitat has caused the Barbary Sheep to conceal itself by freezing in the presence of danger. Although they can generally obtain all needed moisture from their food, if water is available Barbary Sheep drink and wallow liberally.

DISTRIBUTION *Native*: Algeria, Chad, Egypt, Libya, Mali, Mauritania, Morocco, Niger, Sudan, Tunisia. *Introduced:* Mexico, Spain, United States. Formerly widespread in rugged and mountainous terrain from deserts and semi-deserts to open forests in N Africa, but has suffered a strong decline. It has been introduced into the United States, N Mexico, Spain (mainland and the Canary Islands). *A. l. lervia* occurs in the mountains of Morocco, except the W half of the Rif, and in N Algeria and N Tunisia. *A. l. ornata* was formerly quite widespread throughout the E and W Desert of Egypt; there is evidence of its presence in both the Elba Protected Area and the Western Desert. *A. l. blainei* is currently restricted to the Red Sea hills of E Sudan, and in the Ennedi and Uweinat Mountains in NE Chad; it may also be present in SE Libya. *A. l. fassini* is found only in extreme S Tunisia and in Libya. *A. l. angusi* inhabits the Aïr Massif and Termit Massif (Niger). *A. l. sahariensis* has the largest range of the subspecies, including S Morocco and Western Sahara, S Algeria, SW Libya, Sudan, the mountains of the Adrar de Iforas in Mali, Niger, Mauritania, and the Tibesti Massif.

HABITAT Rocky arid mountains in isolated pockets throughout N Africa.

STATUS Vulnerable. Although this sheep is becoming more and more difficult to find in its native North Africa, introduced populations in Spain and the southern United States are flourishing.

PHOTO CREDITS ♂: *Marco Zhiehl*, Madrid Zoo (Spain). Head ♂: *Bill Hill*, Fossil Rim and Dinosaur Valley (USA). ♀: *Darshan Karia*, Six Flags Wild Safari (USA). Head ♀: *Cathy Rattu*, Toronto Zoo (Canada). Young: *Tony*, Toronto Zoo (Canada).   303

Libyan Barbary Sheep

AMMOTRAGUS LERVIA FASSINI

BL: 175-190 cm (♂), 145-160 cm (♀). SH: 90-100 cm (♂), 75-90 cm (♀). TL: 20-25 cm (♂), 15-20 cm (♀). W: 100-140 kg (♂), 40-55 kg (♀). HL: Up to 88 cm (♂), up to 40 cm (♀). Medium-sized sheep, strongly built, with a prominent mane along underside of neck. General color is tawny to brown, darker in males, with underparts paler. Beard with a blackish tinge, as in *blainei*. Lower legs and feet pale, hooves dark. Profuse mane of long hair running from throat down underside of neck to forelegs, more apparent in male than female, paler than underparts, sometimes with blackish areas. Short mane on neck and shoulders. Face darker than body. Horns, less depressed than in other subspecies, smooth, thick, triangular in cross section, and curved to form a semi-circle over the neck. Females are much smaller than males and lighter in color, with less hair and much smaller horns.

Young

Ammotragus lervia fassini

OTHER NAMES Libyan Aoudad. *French:* Mouflon à manchettes du Libye, mouflon de Barbarie, aoudad, arui. *German:* Mähnenspringer, Mähnenschaf, Berberschaf, Aoudad. *Spanish:* Arrui, carnero de berbería. *Russian:* Ливийский гривистый баран. *Arabic:* Arwi, kabsh gabali, audan, aroui el Maghreb. *Peulh:* Edda.

SUBSPECIES Considered as a subspecies of *A. lervia* (Barbary Sheep): *A. l. angusi* (Aïr Aoudad), *A. l. blainei* (Kordofan Aoudad), *A. l. lervia* (Atlas Aoudad), *A. l. fassini* (Libyan Aoudad), *A. l. ornatus* (Egyptian Aoudad), *A. l. sahariensis* (Saharan Aoudad).

SIMILAR SPECIES Morphological differences between subspecies are not well defined, and there are several apparent zones of hybridization. Libyan Barbary Sheep has a darker beard, horns less flattened than in *ornata* and *sahariensis*, and lacks a dark band in the face, although this area may be darker.

REPRODUCTION *Gestation*: 150-165 days. *Young per Birth*: 1, rarely up to 3. *Weaning*: 3-4 months. *Sexual Maturity*: 18 months. *Life Span*: 20 years. Breeds mainly from September to November, but there is some activity throughout the year, with the young being born from March to May. ♀ may give birth twice per year. Newborns are able to get about in moderately rugged terrain almost at once.

BEHAVIOR *Family Group*: Usually lives in small family groups of 5-6 animals with an adult ♂. Old ♂ and pregnant ♀ may be solitary. *Diet*: Sparse grasses, bushes, acacia, lichens. *Main Predators*: Largely exterminated; leopard, caracal. Feeds early morning and late afternoon, resting in shade at midday. Eats grasses and foliage, sometimes standing on its hind legs to browse. Drinks water where available, otherwise obtains moisture from its food. Will descend from rocky terrain in evening to feed on plains. Eyesight and hearing are very good, sense of smell is good. Alert and wary. An agile climber and jumper. They probably make small migratory movements in relation to food availability.

DISTRIBUTION *Native*: Libya, Tunisia. Found only in extreme S Tunisia and in Libya.

HABITAT Rocky and often precipitous arid mountains. They also require rocks or sparse tree cover for shade, and might wander far from water sources for long periods of time.

STATUS Vulnerable. There are no population estimates available for Libya and Tunisia, but it is generally regarded as very rare and almost certainly declining. Major threats include poaching and habitat destruction, mainly from livestock grazing, fuelwood collection, and drought and desertification.

PHOTO CREDITS ♂: *Klaus Rudloff*, Barcelona Zoo (Spain). ♀: *Francisco Javier Guerra Hernando*, Barcelona Zoo (Spain). Head ♀: *Tomasz Doron*, Barcelona Zoo (Spain). Young: *Jonas Livet*, Terra Natura Murcia (Spain).

Saharan Barbary Sheep

AMMOTRAGUS LERVIA SAHARIENSIS

BL: 175-190 cm (♂), 145-160 cm (♀). SH: 90-100 cm (♂), 75-90 cm (♀). TL: 20-25 cm (♂), 15-20 cm (♀). W: 100-140 kg (♂), 40-55 kg (♀). HL: Up to 88 cm (♂), up to 40 cm (♀). Coat is tawny to sandy colored, darker in males, with underparts paler. Lighter in color than the other subspecies. No flank stripe. Lower legs and feet pale, hooves dark. Profuse mane of long hair running from throat down underside of neck to forelegs, more apparent in male than female, paler than underparts, uniformly sandy colored. Short mane on neck and shoulders. Horns are strongly depressed, turning sharply downward before bending backward. Females are much smaller than males and lighter in color, with less hair and much smaller horns.

♀

Young

♂
Juvenile

♂

Ammotragus lervia sahariensis

OTHER NAMES Saharan Aoudad, Saharan Arrui. *French*: Mouflon à manchettes du Sahara. *German:* Mähnenspringer, Mähnenschaf, Berberschaf, Aoudad. *Spanish*: Arrui del Sahara. *Russian*: Сахарский гривистый баран. *Arabic*: Arwi, kabsh gabali, audan, aroui el Maghreb. *Peulh*: Edda.

SUBSPECIES Considered as a subspecies of *A. lervia* (Barbary Sheep): *A. l. angusi* (Aïr Aoudad), *A. l. blainei* (Kordofan Aoudad), *A. l. lervia* (Atlas Aoudad), *A. l. fassini* (Libyan Aoudad), *A. l. ornatus* (Egyptian Aoudad), *A. l. sahariensis* (Saharan Aoudad).

SIMILAR SPECIES Morphological differences between subspecies are not well defined, and there are several apparent zones of hybridization. Coat and mane are a uniform sandy color, somewhat lighter than in *ornata*. Horns similar to those of *ornata*.

REPRODUCTION *Gestation*: 150-165 days. *Young per Birth*: 1, rarely up to 3. *Weaning*: 3-4 months. *Sexual Maturity*: 18 months. *Life Span*: 20 years. Breeds mainly from September to November, but there is some activity throughout the year, with the young being born from March to May. ♀ may give birth twice per year. Newborns are able to get about in moderately rugged terrain almost at once.

BEHAVIOR *Family Group*: Usually lives in small family groups of 6-7 animals with an adult ♂. Old ♂ and pregnant ♀ may be solitary. *Diet*: Sparse grasses, bushes, acacia, lichens. *Main Predators*: Largely exterminated; leopard, caracal, feral dog. Although able to exploit high-mountain water sources out of reach to other large mammals, they also live in areas where there is no permanent water, obtaining moisture from the plants they eat. With their heavy horns, they have been observed ramming trees to dislodge nutritious acacia seedpods. They will shelter from the midday heat and wind behind boulders, in caves or on sheltered plateaus. They may dust themselves in specially excavated scrapes. If disturbed, they quickly flee for rocky slopes and safety. When undisturbed, they may leave the safety of the mountains to feed and seek shade in neighboring wadis.

DISTRIBUTION *Native*: Algeria, Libya, Mali, Mauritania, Morocco, Niger, Sudan, Western Sahara. It has the largest range of the subspecies, including S Morocco and Western Sahara, S Algeria, SW Libya, Sudan, the mountains of the Adrar de Iforas in Mali, Niger, Mauritania, and the Tibesti Massif. Outside Africa, it has been introduced in Almeria (Spain).

HABITAT Very dry deserts, deep canyons, and plateaus as high as 3,000 m in the Moroccan High Atlas. Mountains and low hills throughout most of the Sahara.

STATUS Vulnerable. Estimated population of 800-2,000 animals in Morocco, 4,200 in Niger, and several thousand in Algeria. Low numbers survive in Chad, Mauritania, Mali, Libya, Western Sahara, Sudan, and Tunisia.

PHOTO CREDITS *José R. Castelló*, Jerez Zoo (Spain).

Kordofan Barbary Sheep

AMMOTRAGUS LERVIA BLAINEI

BL: 175-190 cm (♂), 145-160 cm (♀). SH: 90-100 cm (♂), 75-90 cm (♀). TL: 20-25 cm (♂), 15-20 cm (♀). W: 100-140 kg (♂), 40-55 kg (♀). HL: Up to 88 cm (♂), up to 40 cm (♀). Pelage color differs from that of the other subspecies. Coat is brownish, less red, darker in males, with underparts paler. Beard with a blackish tinge, as in *fassini*. No flank stripe. Lower legs and feet pale, hooves dark. Profuse light brown mane of long hair running from throat down underside of neck to forelegs, more apparent in male than female, paler than underparts. Short mane on neck and shoulders. Face darker than the body. Horns, found in both sexes, strongly depressed, but not bent backward, smooth, thick, triangular in cross section. Females are much smaller than males and lighter in color, with less hair and much smaller horns.

♀

Juvenile

♂

Ammotragus lervia blainei

OTHER NAMES Kordofan Aoudad, Sudan Barbary Sheep. *French*: Mouflon à manchettes du Sahara. *German*: Mähnenspringer, Mähnenschaf, Berberschaf, Aoudad. *Spanish*: Arrui del Sahara. *Russian*: Кордофанский гривистый баран. *Arabic*: Arwi, kabsh gabali, audan, aroui el Maghreb. *Peulh*: Edda.

SUBSPECIES Considered as a subspecies of *A. lervia* (Barbary Sheep): *A. l. angusi* (Aïr Aoudad), *A. l. blainei* (Kordofan Aoudad), *A. l. lervia* (Atlas Aoudad), *A. l. fassini* (Libyan Aoudad), *A. l. ornatus* (Egyptian Aoudad), *A. l. sahariensis* (Saharan Aoudad).

SIMILAR SPECIES Morphological differences between subspecies are not well defined, and there are several apparent zones of hybridization. Coat and mane are less reddish than in other subspecies.

REPRODUCTION *Gestation*: 150-165 days. *Young per Birth*: 1, rarely up to 3. *Weaning*: 3-4 months. *Sexual Maturity*: 18 months. *Life Span*: 20 years. No specific information is available for this subspecies, but probably similar to other Barbary Sheep. During breeding season, males compete for females. Backing away from each other, the males charge one another and meet head on. The impact of the collision seldom results in injuries.

BEHAVIOR *Family Group*: Usually lives in small family groups of fewer than 10 animals with an adult ♂. Old ♂ and pregnant ♀ may be solitary. *Diet*: Grasses, forbs, and shrubs. Apparently, they can survive for long periods without access to fresh water; however, when water is available they utilize it for both drinking and bathing. *Main Predators*: Largely exterminated; leopard, caracal, feral dog. No specific information is available for this subspecies, but probably similar to other Barbary Sheep. Gregarious, gathering in small groups as their barren surroundings cannot support large aggregates of animals. Especially active at dawn and dusk, they seek shade during the hottest hours. They freeze in the presence of danger, probably in order to remain unnoticed by predators. Excellent, sure-footed jumpers and climbers; their heavy horns help them with balance.

DISTRIBUTION *Native*: Sudan. It was once relatively widespread from W Sudan to the Red Sea coast, but currently is probably restricted to the Red Sea hills of E Sudan. It may also occur in the Ennedi and Uweinat mountains in NE Chad, and in SE Libya.

HABITAT Rocky and precipitous areas, from sea level up to the extent of snow-free areas at about 3,000 m. They prefer woodlands during summer, grasslands during autumn and winter, and protective rocky slopes during spring. They tend to prefer open lands during breeding season.

STATUS Vulnerable. There are no population estimates available for this subspecies in Sudan, but it is generally regarded as very rare and almost certainly declining. Main threats include poaching, habitat destruction, and desertification.

PHOTO CREDITS ♂ and ♀: *Brett Cortesi*, Roger Williams Park Zoo (USA). Juvenile: *Sergey Chichagov*, San Diego Zoo Safari Park (USA).

Arabian Tahr

ARABITRAGUS JAYAKARI

BL: 93-95 cm. SH: 60-64 cm. TL: 8.4-10 cm. W: 38-45 kg (♂), 17-20 kg (♀). HL: To 32 cm. The smallest species of Tahr. Stocky build. Coat consists of long, reddish-brown hair, with a dark stripe running down the back. Males possess impressive manes which extend right down the back and grow longer with age. Older males also grow such a grand mane with a black muzzle and darker eye stripes. No beard. Two white stripes run from their forehead to nose and a black stripe down their back. Rubbery hooves. Backward-arching horns, found in both sexes. Females much less robust than males, with shorter hair, usually a reddish sandy depending on season and local habitat, and shorter horns with less curvature.

Young

Arabitragus jayakari

OTHER NAMES *French*: Tahr d'Arabie. *German*: Arabische Tahr. *Spanish*: Tahr árabe. *Russian*: Аравийский тар.

SUBSPECIES Monotypic. This species has been removed from *Hemitragus* and has been allocated to the monotypic genus *Arabitragus*. It is more closely related to Barbary Sheep (*Ammotragus lervia*) than to the other two Tahr species (*Hemitragus jemlahicus* and *Nilgiritragus hylocrius*).

REPRODUCTION *Gestation*: 140–145 days. *Young per Birth*: 1-2. *Sexual Maturity*: 2-3 years. *Life Span*: 22 years. In captivity births have occurred in all months of the year, but in the wild the season is from September to November. A second rut is reported to occur in February in years when there is good forage after early rainfall. Instead of forming herds during seasonal ruts, they reproduce in small, dispersed family units.

BEHAVIOR *Family Group*: Unlike other species of Tahrs, the Arabian Tahr is solitary or lives in small groups consisting of a ♀ and a kid, or a ♂. *Diet*: Browsers, feeding on grass, shrubs, leaves, and fruits of most trees. *Main Predators*: Once preyed on by Arabian leopards, and human. Diurnal, grazing in the early morning and late afternoon. Although it can survive long periods without drinking if good vegetation is available, in summer it will come down to drink every 2 or 3 days. There is widespread anecdotal evidence of Tahrs drinking at night from the sources of the "falaj" channel irrigation systems. Arabian Tahr ♂ mark their territory by scratching their hooves on the ground and urinating. The average area covered by an Arabian Tahr is 0.3 km², which usually contains water and vegetation. When this water supply is not enough, they temporarily travel outside of their territory. Shy and retiring, difficult to see in the wild because their coat keeps them camouflaged.

DISTRIBUTION *Native*: Oman. *Possibly Extinct*: United Arab Emirates. The entire world population of Arabian Tahr occurs in the mountains of N Oman and the United Arab Emirates. There are small scattered populations throughout a 600 km crescent in N Oman, from the limestone massifs of the Musandam, through the Hajar Mountains as far as Jebel Qahwan due S of Sur. The most important populations occur near Nakhl, the Wadi As Sareen Nature Reserve, and Jebel Qahwan in the Ja'alan.

HABITAT North-facing slopes between 1,000 and 1,800 m that are characterized by relatively high rainfall, cool temperatures, and diverse vegetation. They have been seen at altitudes down to sea level, especially during the rut when ♂ are known to move long distances between known populations to find ♀.

STATUS Endangered. Estimated population of 2,500 mature individuals. No subpopulation contains more than 250 mature individuals, and there is probably a continuing decline in the number of individuals. The greatest threat to the survival of the species is loss of habitat, poaching, and competition with livestock, primarily domestic goats.

PHOTO CREDITS ♂: *Malik Ghulam Sarwar*, Al Ain Zoo (United Arab Emirates). ♀: *Dr. An Pas*, Sharjah (United Arab Emirates). Heads: *Jonas Livet*, Oman Mammal Breeding Centre (Oman). Young: *Jonas Livet*, Sharjah (United Arab Emirates).

Himalayan Bharal

PSEUDOIS NAYAUR NAYAUR

BL: 115-165 cm. SH: 75-91 cm. TL: 13-20 cm. W: 60-75 kg (♂), 35-55 kg (♀). HL: 38-80 cm (♂), 10-20 cm (♀). Medium-sized sheep. In winter, coat is thick and woolly, bluish gray in color, while in summer, coat is short and finer, brownish gray in color. Underparts and backs of the legs are white, while the chest and fronts of the legs are black. Separating the gray back and white belly is a charcoal-colored stripe. Small ears. Bridge of the nose dark. No beard. No fringe of hair on neck, throat, or forelegs. Broad, flat tail with a bare central surface. Large dewclaws. Smooth horns, found in both sexes, ringed on the upper surface. In males, they grow upward, then turn sideways and curve backward, looking somewhat like an upside-down moustache. Females are smaller, with much shorter and straighter horns.

Pseudois nayaur nayaur

OTHER NAMES Tibetan Bharal, Himalayan Blue Sheep, Nepal Blue Sheep, Tibetan Blue Sheep, Naur, Greater Blue Sheep. *French*: Bharal du Tibet, mouton bleu. *German*: Tibet Blauschaf, Bharal. *Spanish*: Baral del Tibet, cabra azul del Himalaya. *Russian*: Гималайский голубой баран (бхарал). *Tibetan*: Napu, na, nawa. *Hindi*: Burrhe. *Kulu*: Myatu. *Nepali*: Naur, nahoor, nahur. *Chinese*: Yanyang, banyang.

SUBSPECIES Considered as a subspecies of Bharal (*P. nayaur*): *P. n. szechuanensis* (Chinese Blue Sheep), *P. n. nayaur* (Himalayan Blue Sheep). The validity and geographic characteristics of these subspecies remain unclear. Dwarf Bharal (*P. schaeferi*) is considered to be a full species.

SIMILAR SPECIES Chinese Bharal is smaller, with a lighter color and less black on front of neck and chest, a narrower black lateral band, and smaller horns, growing outward horizontally, with little downward curve, then turning backward with the tips inclined upward. Dwarf Bharal is much smaller, with a drab coloration and very small horns.

REPRODUCTION *Gestation*: 160 days. *Young per Birth*: 1, rarely 2. *Weaning*: 6 months. *Sexual Maturity*: 1.5 years, although ♂ do not reach their full potential before age 7. *Life Span*: 15 years. Mating occurs between October and January, with the young being born from May to July. Crèches, in which a larger number of nursing young temporaryly associate with a few ♀, have been documented. ♂ join ♀ to form mixed groups and actively court ♀ with a variety of courtship displays. Dominant ♂, older than 5 years old, do most of the mating.

BEHAVIOR *Family Group*: Solitary or in small groups of fewer than 20 animals which consist of almost entirely 1 sex. *Diet*: Grasses, lichens, hardy herbaceous plants, mosses. *Main Predators*: Snow leopard, leopard, mountain fox, tawny eagle. Active throughout the day, alternating between feeding and resting on grassy mountain slopes. Due to their excellent camouflage and the absence of cover in their environment, Bharal remain motionless when approached. Once they have been noticed, however, they scamper up to the precipitous cliffs, where they once again freeze, melting into the rock face. ♂ have the usual ungulate behaviors such as lip curling, low-stretch twisting, kicking, penis mouthing, mounting, horn pulling, and neck fighting. Other aggressive caprine behaviors such as broadside display, horning vegetation, jerking and lunging, head shaking, jumping, butting, and clashing are also seen, with slight variation from those of other caprines. ♀ also behave aggressively toward other ♀.

DISTRIBUTION *Native*: Bhutan, China, India, Myanmar, Nepal, Pakistan. Found in the Himalayan region of NE Pakistan, NW India, Nepal, and Bhutan, in scattered populations throughout Tibet, and in China (S Xinjiang, W Qinghai, extreme NW Yunnan W of the Yangtze River). Boundaries with the Chinese Bharal to the E are unclear.

HABITAT Montane regions in the Himalayas at 3,000-5,550 m.

STATUS Least Concern.

PHOTO CREDITS Based on photographs from Hemis Wildlife Sanctuary, Ladakh (India).

Chinese Bharal

PSEUDOIS NAYAUR SZECHUANENSIS

BL: 104-154 cm. SH: 68-85 cm. TL: 13-20 cm. W: 52-72 kg (♂), 32-51 kg (♀). HL: 38-80 cm (♂), 10-20 cm (♀). Medium-sized sheep, lighter in color and slightly smaller than Himalayan Bharal. Coat is buffy brown in color, darker and thicker in winter. Facial mask is light brown, sides of face whitish, sides of neck light buff. Less black on front of neck and chest, black lateral band narrower, stopping several inches behind the shoulder instead of almost joining the dark chest patch, as in Himalayan Bharal. Horn length and circumference smaller, but tip-to-tip length greater. Horns grow outward horizontally, with little downward curve, then turn backward with the tips inclined upward, rounded throughout their length, with only the frontal-nuchal edge sharply defined. Females are smaller, with much shorter and straighter horns.

Young

♀

♂

♂

Juvenile

314

Pseudois nayaur szechuanensis

OTHER NAMES Northern Blue Sheep, Sichuan Blue Sheep, Naur. *French*: Bharal de Chine, mouton bleu. *German*: Chinesischer Blauschaf. *Spanish*: Baral de China, cabra azul de China. *Russian*: Китайский голубой баран (бхарал). *Tibetan*: Napu, na, nawa. *Hindi*: Burrhe. *Kulu*: Myatu. *Nepali*: Naur, nahoor, nahur. *Chinese*: Yanyang, banyang.

SUBSPECIES Considered as a subspecies of Bharal (*P. nayaur*): *P. n. szechuanensis* (Chinese Blue Sheep), *P. n. nayaur* (Himalayan Blue Sheep). The validity and geographic characteristics of these subspecies remain unclear. Dwarf Bharal (*P. schaeferi*) is considered to be a full species.

SIMILAR SPECIES Bharal are distinguished from true sheep by the absence of preorbital glands and interdigital glands. Himalayan Bharal is slightly larger, darker in color, with more black on front of neck and chest, and a wider black lateral band, with larger horns with a downward curve. Dwarf Bharal is much smaller, with a drab coloration and very small horns.

REPRODUCTION *Gestation*: 160 days. *Young per Birth*: 1, rarely 2. *Weaning*: 6 months. *Sexual Maturity*: 1.5 years, although ♂ do not reach their full potential before age 7. *Life Span*: 15 years. Mating occurs between October and January, with the young being born from May to July.

BEHAVIOR *Family Group*: Solitary or in small groups of fewer than 30 animals, consisting of all ♂, all ♀, ♀ with young and yearling, or ♀ and ♂ both adult and young; sometimes up to 400 animals. *Diet*: Grasses, herbs, lichens, mosses. *Main Predators*: Snow leopard, wolf, common leopard. Most active in the early morning, in the late afternoon, and briefly around midday. Bharal freeze when a potential predator is in their vicinity; their excellent camouflage often results in them being overlooked as part of the landscape. Bharal flee if a predator does manage to spot them.

DISTRIBUTION *Native*: China. Found in central China (central and E Qinghai, W Sichuan, Gansu, and SW Ningxia). Boundaries with the Himalayan Bharal to the W are unclear.

HABITAT Treeless slopes and alpine meadows and shrub zones above timberline in the Himalayas and in the Sichuan region of China at 3,000-5,550 m. It prefers relatively gentle hillsides covered with grasses and sedges, but usually remains within 200 m of cliffs up which it can climb to escape from predators. Dwarf Bharal inhabits the steep, arid, lower slopes of the Yangtze River valley, at elevations of 2,600-3,200 m, and is cut off from the Bharal populations of the upper grassy altitudes of the same region by a thick, scrubby forest 5-6 km across and covering 450 m of elevation.

STATUS Least Concern.

PHOTO CREDITS *Sergey Chichagov*, Tallinn Zoo (Estonia) and Suzhou Zoo (China). Juvenile: *Pierre de Chabannes*, Tierpark Berlin (Germany) and *Sergey Chichagov*, Tallinn Zoo (Estonia).

Dwarf Bharal

PSEUDOIS SCHAEFERI

BL: 106-140 cm. SH: 50-80 cm. TL: 7-17 cm. W: 28-35 kg (♂), 25 kg (♀). HL: 28-55 cm (♂), 10-20 cm (♀). Much smaller than other Bharal species, with a drab coloration and smaller horns. Winter coat is bright silver gray, with the colors more pronounced, and there is a thin black stripe separating flanks from belly. Summer coat is a dull brownish gray, with the head, dorsal area, tail tip, and front of legs darker. Underparts, inside of legs, and inside of ears are whitish, and there is a light ring around the eyes. Horns, found in both sexes, are much smaller than in other blue sheep. In males the thick horns curve out to the sides, with the tips pointing upward and outward. Females have very small, straight horns.

Pseudois schaeferi

OTHER NAMES Dwarf Blue Sheep, Sichuan Blue Sheep, Pygmy Blue Sheep. *French:* Bharal nain. *German:* Zwergblauschaf. *Spanish*: Baral enano, cabra azul enana. *Russian*: Карликовый голубой баран.

SUBSPECIES Monotypic. Formerly considered a subspecies of Bharal (*P. nayaur*).

SIMILAR SPECIES Himalayan and Chinese Bharal are larger, with more distinct black markings on front of neck and chest and a wider black lateral band, and larger horns with a downward curve. Females of the two species are very similar.

REPRODUCTION *Gestation*: 160 days. *Young per Birth*: 1, rarely 2. *Weaning*: 6 months. *Sexual Maturity*: 1.5 years. *Life Span*: Unknown. The breeding season is thought to occur between mid-November and mid-December. Births occur between late May and late June.

BEHAVIOR *Family Group*: Formerly 10-36 animals, but now usually fewer than 15, as a result of overhunting and competition with livestock; ♂ sometimes form all ♂ groups or sometimes mix with ♀ and young. *Diet*: Grasses, low shrubs, club moss, lichens. *Main Predators*: Wolf, dhole, leopard, large raptors. Wary animals, very difficult to observe. They tend to be active in the morning and late afternoon, resting during midday in shallow beds scraped out with their front legs. During the summer, nearly a third of their time is spent feeding and foraging. Population densities range between 0.5 and 1.0 individuals per km².

DISTRIBUTION *Native*: China. Found in China, in Upper Yangtze Gorge in W Sichuan and adjacent parts of Tibet and N Yunnan. It has been also reported from Deqin County (NW Yunnan), Derong (SW Sichuan), Baiyu, to the N of Batang, and Markam (E Xizang), but the status of Dwarf Bharal in these areas is in some dispute, and requires more investigation. Its primary range is in a narrow area along the Jinshajiang Valley, which forms part of the upper reaches of the Yangtze River.

HABITAT Steep rocky slopes between 2,700 and 3,200 m above sea level; occasionally range into conifer forest and forest clearings. This species is isolated from the alpine habitat of *P. nayaur* by a belt of oak forest, into which it has not been documented to enter.

STATUS Endangered. Estimated population in 1998 was 7,000 individuals, bur recent estimations report only a few hundred. Its population has fallen drastically, due to overhunting and habitat destruction and degradation. Much of its range falls within a protected reserve, although the principal threats to its survival continue to occur within its borders.

PHOTO CREDITS Reconstruction by *José R. Castelló*.

Himalayan Tahr

HEMITRAGUS JEMLAHICUS

BL: 90-155 cm. SH: 65-100 cm. TL: 9-12 cm. W: 70-140 kg (♂), 30-50 kg (♀). HL: To 45 cm. Medium-sized, powerfully built Tahr. Dense, woolly winter coat reddish to dark brown, with a thick undercoat. With their winter coat, males also grow a long, shaggy mane around the neck and shoulders which extends down the front legs. After the spring molt, the coat is much shorter and lighter in color. Face always dark brown. Legs relatively short, and head proportionally small. Eyes large, ears small and pointed. Short horns, triangular in cross section, found in both sexes, curving upward, backward, and then inward, usually larger in males. Females smaller than males, lack a mane, have different coloration, and shorter horns. Young uniformly brown except for the fronts of their legs, which are black.

♀

♂

Juvenile

summer coat

winter coat

♂

Young

Hemitragus jemlahicus

OTHER NAMES *French*: Jharal, tahr de l'Himalaya. *German*: Himalaya-Tahr. *Spanish*: Tar del Himalaya. *Russian*: Гималайский тар. *Kashmiri*: Jagla, kras. *Kulu and Chamba*: Kart. *Kunuwar*: Jhula. *Nepali*: Jharal. *Sutley Valley*: Esbu. *Tibetan*: Radong Nak. *Urdu*: Tehr, jehr. *West Himalaya*: Tehr, jehr.

SUBSPECIES Monotypic. Includes *schaeferi*. It is closely related to wild goats.

REPRODUCTION *Gestation*: 7 months. *Young per Birth*: 1, rarely 2. *Weaning*: 6 months. *Sexual Maturity*: 2-3 years. *Life Span*: 21 years. Breeding season occurs from October to January.

BEHAVIOR *Family Group*: Mixed herds of about 15 animals, with up to 80 in one group. Old ♂ usually solitary. *Diet*: Grasses, leaves. *Main Predators*: Leopard, snow leopard. Most active during the early morning and late afternoon, spending the middle of the day resting among rocks and vegetation. Prefers to live on steep slopes that are more or less timbered. ♀ prefer open summit areas, ♂ the wooded cliffs below. It has remarkable climbing ability on the steepest cliffs. Does not like snow, keeping below it to as low as 2,200 m, then following it up as it melts. Very shy and wary, they are difficult to approach, especially from downhill. When startled, they flee with confidence, speeding sure footedly across the uneven terrain of their habitat. They may migrate down the mountain during the winter, resting in denser cover at lower altitudes as protection from the elements. When competing for breeding privileges, ♂ lock horns and attempt to throw each other off balance, although compared to other ungulates this is done in a somewhat half-hearted manner. With the introduced groups in New Zealand, the population density varies from 4.5-6.8 animals per km^2.

DISTRIBUTION *Native*: China, India, Nepal. *Introduced*: New Zealand, South Africa. In China, Tahr appear to be found in only a few spots along the S Tibetan border near the Qubuo River, extending S into the Himalayas, and can be expected in extreme W Tibet adjacent to known populations in India. In India, it occurs in timberline regions across the S forested slopes of the Himalaya from Jammu and Kashmir to Sikkim. It is patchily distributed from S-central Kashmir, eastward through the S part of Kulu District (Himachal Pradesh) between 2,000 and 3,270 m, and more widely present at similar elevations through N Uttarakhand to the Nepalese border. Small numbers are also found in E and W Sikkim near the borders with Nepal and Bhutan. Outside Asia, it has been introduced in the wild on the South Island of New Zealand and in parts of South Africa, and on private properties in the United States, Argentina, and Austria. Other introductions in Scotland and Canada have failed.

HABITAT Rugged mountain country and montane woodlands in the Himalayan mountains.

STATUS Near Threatened. There is no global population estimate. For China, estimated population is 400-500 individuals. For India, about 130 individuals in the Kanawar Wildlife Sanctuary and more than 100 in Great Himalayan NP. For Nepal, 1,000 individuals in Sagamatha, Makalu-Barun, and Langtang NP.

PHOTO CREDITS ♂: *Klaus Rudloff* and *Alex Meyer*, Berlin Zoo (Germany). Head ♂: *Asanbonsam* (Germany). ♀: *Jonathan Beilby*. Head ♀: *David Ellis*, Akron Zoo (USA). Young: *Tomoko Ichishima*, Tama Zoo (Japan). Juvenile: *Bruce Zidar,* Table Mountain (South Africa).

Flare-horned Markhor

CAPRA FALCONERI FALCONERI

BL: 132-186 cm. SH: 65-107 cm. TL: 8-20 cm. W: 91-102 kg (♂). HL: 80-160 cm (♂), to 36 cm (♀). A medium-sized sturdy goat. Largest subspecies. Coat is long and coarse in winter, with very little underwool, much shorter in summer, grizzled reddish gray to brown in color. Older males tend to be whitish. Males have long hair on the chin, throat, chest, and shanks. Thick legs and broad hooves. Lower legs have a black and white pattern. Dark tail short. Horns in Astor Markhor are massive, flaring very widely just above the base, with 1 to 1-1/2 twists, with the first turn being very large. Horns in Kashmir Markhor are larger, with less flare and 2-3 spiral twists. Intermediate forms are seen. Females are smaller and redder and have small black beards, no manes, and small, slender horns with usually 1 to 1-1/4 twists and tips that diverge outward.

Astor
(*falconeri*)

♀

Kashmir
(*cashmirensis*)

♂

Capra falconeri falconeri

OTHER NAMES Screw-horned Goat, Astor Markhor, Pir Panjal Markhor, Kashmir Markhor. *French*: Markhor d'Astor, markhor de Cachemire. *German*: Astor Schraubenziege, Kaschmir Schraubenzeige. *Spanish*: Markor de Astor, markor de Cachemira. *Baluchi*: Pachin, sarah. *Brahui:* Matt, rezkuh. *Ladakhi*: Raphoche. *Pashto*: Maar Khur. *Russian*: Раскинуторогий мархур (включая подвиды: Асторский мархур, Кашмирский мархур). *Tamil*: Kàttu àtu. *Tibetan*: Rira.

SUBSPECIES Considered as a subspecies of *C. falconeri: C. f. falconeri* (Astor Markhor), *C. f. heptneri* (Bukhara, Tadjik, or Russian Markhor), *C. f. megaceros* (Straight-horned or Kabul Markhor). It includes *cashmiriensis* (Kashmir or Pir Panja Markhor), which is not considered as a valid subspecies here.

REPRODUCTION *Gestation*: 135-170 days. *Young per Birth*: 1 or 2, rarely 3. *Weaning:* 5-6 months. *Sexual Maturity:* 18-30 months. *Life Span:* 12 years. Mating occurs during winter, with the subsequent births occurring from late April to early June.

BEHAVIOR *Family Group*: ♀ and young live in herds of around 9 animals; adult ♂ are usually solitary. *Diet:* Primarily grasses and forbs during spring and summer months, while in the winter it feeds primarily on browse for nourishment; it may stand on its hind legs to reach the top leaves of trees. *Main Predators*: Wolf, snow leopard, leopard, lynx, human. Mainly crepuscular. It forages 8-12 hours daily, and it is usually active all day except for several hours in the middle of the day, when it rests and chews its cud. Years ago herds with 100 or more animals, usually consisting of ♀ and young, were common, but the average herd size today is 9, with some as large as 35. Although some adult ♂ remain with the ♀ throughout the year, most ♂ only join the ♀ during the rut. Population densities in Pakistan range from 1 to 9 animals per km^2.

DISTRIBUTION *Native*: Afghanistan, India, Pakistan. Astor Markhor (*falconeri*): The Gilgit region of N Pakistan on the slopes of Nanga Parbat and along the Indus River and its tributaries, among them the Gilgit, Astor, and Hunza rivers. Along both banks of the Indus from Jalkot upstream to about Tungas near Skardu. Along the Gilgit as far upstream as Gakuch. Along the Astor as far as the Parashing Valley. Along the Hunza as far as Chalt. Kashmir Markhor (*cashmiriensis*): Laghman Province and the Bashgul River area in Afghanistan. In Pakistan in Chitral District, along the Kunar River from Shogore to Arandu on the W bank and to Drosh on the E bank, and up its tributary the Mastuj River as far as Barenis; Dir District, along the upper Panjkora River; and Swat District on the cliffs E of Mankial. In India, in the Shamsberi, Kaj-i-Nag, and Pir Panjal ranges.

HABITAT Steep slopes at lower to medium elevation, in temperate coniferous forests and adjacent alpine meadows.

STATUS Endangered. Estimated population of 3,000 individuals in 2011, with the largest concentration in the Chitral District in Pakistan, with 800-1,000 animals. Domestic livestock create competition for forage.

PHOTO CREDITS Based on photos by *Kees Otte, Michael Lane, Mario Pineda,* and Chitral Gol NP (Pakistan).

Bukhara Markhor

CAPRA FALCONERI HEPTNERI

BL: 132-186 cm. SH: 86-90 cm. TL: 8-20 cm. W: 80-90 kg (♂), 45-50 kg (♀). HL: 75-82 cm (♂), to 38 cm (♀). Intermediate in horn and body size between the Flare-horned and Straight-horned Markhors. Coat is short, grizzled reddish gray in summer, growing longer and thicker in winter, grayer in color with black hair tips. Older males tend to be whitish. Males have a black beard and shaggy mane of long dark hairs, hanging from the neck. Lower legs have a black and white pattern. Dark tail short and not as bushy as that of Ibexes. Tightly curled, corkscrew-like horns, found in both sexes, starting close together at the head, but spreading toward the tips. Females about half of the size of mature males, redder in color, with shorter hair, a short black beard, no mane, with very small horns, with 1 to 1-1/2 twists near the tip.

Young

♀

♂

♂ Juvenile

winter coat

summer coat

Capra falconeri heptneri

OTHER NAMES Tajik Markhor, Tadzhid Markhor, Turkmenian Markhor, Uzbek Markhor, Russian Markhor, Heptner's Markhor, Turkomen Markhor. *French*: Markhor de Bukhara. *German*: Bukhara Schraubenziege. *Spanish*: Markor de Bukhara. *Baluchi*: Pachin, sarah. *Brahui:* Matt, rezkuh. *Ladakhi*: Raphoche. *Pashto*: Maar Khur. *Russian*: Таджикский (бухарский) мархур (включая подвиды: Таджикский мархур, Туркменский мархур). *Tamil*: Kàttu àtu. *Tibetan*: Rira.

SUBSPECIES Considered as a subspecies of *C. falconeri: C. f. falconeri* (Astor Markhor), *C. f. heptneri* (Bukhara, Tadjik, or Russian Markhor), *C. f. megaceros* (Straight-horned or Kabul Markhor). It includes *ognevi* (Turkomen Markhor).

REPRODUCTION *Gestation*: 135-170 days. *Young per Birth*: 1 or 2, rarely 3. *Weaning*: 5-6 months. *Sexual Maturity*: 18-30 months. *Life Span*: 12 years. Mating occurs during winter, with the subsequent births occurring from late April to early June.

BEHAVIOR *Family Group*: ♀ and young live in herds of around 9 animals; adult ♂ are usually solitary. *Diet:* Grasses, leaves. *Main Predators*: Wolf, snow leopard, leopard, lynx, human. Mainly active in the early morning and late afternoon. During the spring and summer months it is a grazer, while in the winter it turns to browse for nourishment. It often stands on its hind legs in order to reach high vegetation. Population densities in Pakistan range from 1 to 9 animals per km^2. During the rut ♂ fight for breeding rights. These competitions involve lunging and locking the horns, followed by the combatants twisting and pushing in an attempt to make the other lose his balance. The alarm call resembles the nasal "a" popularized by the common domestic goat.

DISTRIBUTION *Native*: Afghanistan, Tajikistan, Uzbekistan. Found only in two or three scattered populations in the Kugitang Range of extreme E Turkmenistan and SE Uzbekistan, in the area between the Pyandzh and Vakhsh rivers in SW Tajikistan, and in the NW part of the Darwaz Peninsula of NE Afghanistan near the Tajik border.

HABITAT Steppe mountain conditions and regions of meager erratic rainfall, from 600 m elevation in the completely treeless hot and arid hills up to 3,600 m in the Himalayas in association with juniper and birch scrub forest. They avoid the higher altitudes frequented by the Ibex and stick to the more precipitous mountainsides, never feeding on the more open alpine slopes frequented by the latter species. The main habitat requirements are the presence of cliffs, absence of deep snow, and accessibility of areas below 2,200 m where temperatures are not extrerne in the winter. Its habitat overlaps with that of the Siberian Ibex (*C. sibirica*) and Bukhara Urial (*Ovis bochariensis*).

STATUS Critically Endangered. Total population estimated to be fewer than 700 animals in the 1990s. Main threats include poaching for meat and for horns, which are used for medicinal purposes in the large Asian market, habitat loss, disturbance, and forage competition from domestic livestock. This is the subspecies commonly seen in zoos worldwide.

PHOTO CREDITS ♂ and head ♂: *Sergey Chichagov,* Riga Zoo (Latvia). ♀ and head ♀: *Sergey Chichagov,* Tallinn Zoo (Estonia). Young: *David Munro,* Highland Wildlife Park (UK) and *Alisha Van Scyoc*, Columbus Zoo (USA). Juvenile: *Sarah Bell*, Highland Wildlife Park (UK).

Straight-horned Markhor

CAPRA FALCONERI MEGACEROS

BL: 132 cm. SH: 89-91 cm. TL: 8-20 cm. W: 68 kg (♂), 32-50 kg (♀). HL: 80-160 cm (♂), 15-18 cm (♀). Smallest subspecies, with a comparatively short body and shorter horns. Coat is grizzled reddish gray to brown in color, short, coarse and thick in winter, short and smooth in summer. Older males may be whitish. Ruff is shorter and less conspicuous than in other subspecies. Lower legs have a black and white pattern. Dark tail short. Horns in Suleiman Markhor are straight, forming 2-3 complete spiral turns, resembling a corkscrew. Horns in Kabul Markhor are straight, with up to 3 complete spiral turns in an open twist. Females are smaller, redder in color, with a short black beard and much smaller horns, showing 1 twist.

♀

Kabul
(*megaceros*)

♂

Suleiman
(*jerdoni*)

Capra falconeri megaceros

OTHER NAMES Kabul Markhor, Suleiman Markhor. *French*: Markhor du Kabul, markhor du Suleiman. *German*: Kabul Schraubenziege, Suleiman Schraubenziege. *Spanish*: Markor de Kabul, markor de Suleiman. *Baluchi*: Pachin, sarah. *Brahui*: Matt, rezkuh. *Ladakhi*: Raphoche. *Pashto*: Maar Khur. *Russian*: Прямарогий мархур (включая подвиды: Кабульский мархур, Сулейманский мархур). *Tamil*: Kàttu àtu. *Tibetan*: Rira.

SUBSPECIES Considered as a subspecies of *C. falconeri*: *C. f. falconeri* (Astor Markhor), *C. f. heptneri* (Bukhara, Tadjik, or Russian Markhor), *C. f. megaceros* (Straight-horned or Kabul Markhor). It includes *jerdoni* (Suleiman Markhor), which is not considered as a valid subspecies here. The Suleiman Markhor was first given subspecific status on the basis of its tightly spiraling horns; paradoxically, such horns appear to be in the minority in most of its range.

SIMILAR SPECIES Chiltan Wild Goat is believed to be a hybrid between Suleiman Markhor and Wild Goat (*C. aegagrus blythi*) or Domestic Goat (*C. hircus*) or a subspecies of Wild Goat (*C. aegagrus chialtanensis*); ♂ do not have a ruff, and may have dark brown or almost black chests, and sometimes a dark shoulder stripe, like *C. aegagrus*; horns are intermediate in shape between those of a Markhor and a Wild Goat: they are flattened in cross section, sharply keeled in front (in Markhors keeled in back), forming a long, open spiral. It is found only in Hazarganji-Chiltan NP, with an estimated population of fewer than 500 individuals.

REPRODUCTION *Gestation*: 135-170 days. *Young per Birth*: 1 or 2, rarely 3. *Weaning*: 5-6 months. *Sexual Maturity*: 18-30 months. *Life Span*: 12 years. Mating occurs during winter, with the subsequent births occurring from late April to early June.

BEHAVIOR *Family Group*: ♀ and young live in herds of around 9 animals; adult ♂ are usually solitary. *Diet*: Grasses, leaves. *Main Predators*: Wolf, snow leopard, leopard, lynx, human. Mainly active in the early morning and late afternoon.

DISTRIBUTION *Native*: Afghanistan, Pakistan. Kabul Markhor (*megaceros*): Found in Afghanistan only in the Kabul Gorge and the Kohi Safi area of Kapissa Province, and in isolated pockets in between. As of 1987 in Pakistan, it was still found in the Safed Koh Range, the areas near Mardan and Sheikh Buddin, and possibly between Pezu and the Gumal River. Suleiman Markhor (*jerdoni*): Found in Pakistan, S of the Gumal River, mainly in the Suleiman Range and the Torghar hills of the Toba-Kakar Range (Zhob District), and in the Takatu Hills (Quetta District).

HABITAT Desert mountains not usually higher than 3,000 m.

STATUS Endangered. Estimated population in Pakistan of fewer than 2,000 individuals, restricted mainly to the Province of Balochistan, surviving in discontinuous and isolated pockets, with the main concentration in the Toba Kakar and Torghar hills. Population in Afghanistan is much lower, perhaps 50-80 in the Kohi Safi region, with a few in other isolated pockets. Main threats include excessive hunting by local people and forage competition with livestock, as well as significant habitat loss caused by logging.

PHOTO CREDITS Based on photos by *Kees Otte, Peter Hopper,* and *Andreev Oleg,* Torghar, Balochistan (Pakistan).

West Caucasian Tur

CAPRA CAUCASICA

BL: 150-165 cm (♂), 120-140 cm (♀). SH: 95-109 cm (♂), 78-90 cm (♀). TL: 10-14 cm. W: 65-80 kg (♂), 50-60 kg (♀). HL: 66-74 cm (♂), to 30 cm (♀). A large goat, with a massive body with short and strong legs. Summer coat rusty gray to rufous brown, winter coat grayish brown, lighter in older animals, yellowish gray or dirty white underparts. Front surfaces of legs deep brown color, becoming darker toward the hooves. Short tail covered with dark hairs. Face of males darker and browner than the body. Dense, long, curly hair grows on the foreheads of males, especially in winter. Beard of moderate length, short and dark brown in summer, longer and fuller in winter. Horns of males relatively short, but very thick; bent like a scimitar in a single plane, diverge in a wide V laterally from their base. Front surfaces strongly ringed. Females smaller and lighter than males, with thin and relatively weak horns.

♀

♂

Juvenile

Young

winter coat

summer coat

Capra caucasica dinniki

Capra caucasica caucasica

OTHER NAMES Kuban Tur. *French*: Bouquetin de Caucase, tour du Caucase occidental, chèvre du Caucase. *German*: Westkaukasischer Steinbock, Kuban-Tur. *Spanish*: Tur del Cáucaso occidental. *Abkhazian*: Abg-adzhma. *Russian*: Кубанский (западно-кавказский) тур.

SUBSPECIES *C. c. dinniki* (West Caucasian Tur): W Caucasus, W of Mount Elbrus; slightly taller, shorter beard. *C. c. caucasica* (Mid-Caucasian Tur): Central Caucasus, from Mount Elbrus east to Mount Dykhtau; darker, with a dark dorsal streak; considered by some authors as a hybrid between West and East Caucasian Tur.

REPRODUCTION *Gestation*: 150-160 days. *Young per Birth*: 1, rarely 2. *Weaning*: 3-4 months. *Sexual Maturity*: 2 years. *Life Span*: 12 years. Seasonal breeders, rut extending from November to early January. Births occur from mid to late May through June. Captive ♀ are capable of breeding every year. ♀ do not retreat to a sheltered locale prior to parturition, but instead give birth in accessible areas; infant gains its footing within a few hours and is fleet footed after only a day. ♀ will generally hang back from the herd for the first 10 days after birth, with the kid following her closely.

BEHAVIOR *Family Group*: Several dozen individuals, although large herds of up to several hundred may form. *Diet*: Grasses, including sweet vernal grass, foxtail, mountain fescue, and meadow grass; shoots and leaves of willow and birch during summer; salt licks are visited regularly. *Main Predators*: Wolf, lynx. For most of the year, adult ♂ and ♀ live separately, with mixed herds forming during the rut and remaining together for 1-2 months afterward. Most active between the late afternoon and early morning. Grazing continues throughout the night, alternating with periods of rest. In cloudy weather or on rainy days, Tur may be seen foraging in the open throughout the day. Home range varies in size from dozens of hectares to several km^2; size is somewhat dependent on season. Seasonal migrations between summer and winter ranges are documented, and may cover vertical distances of 1,500-2,000 m. Tur vocalize using sharp, intermittent whistling, which sounds almost like a high-pitched sneeze.

DISTRIBUTION *Native*: Georgia, Russian Federation. Endemic to the W part of the Great Caucasus Mountains in Georgia and Russia. Its range stretches in a narrow stripe from the Tchugush Mountain massif to the Balkar Cherek River headwaters on the N slope and Inguri River headwaters on the S slope, just E of the Mount Elbrus massif. Its range is the smallest of any in the genus Capra.

HABITAT Subalpine and alpine regions between 800 and 4,000 m above sea level. The permanent snowline restricts them to heights of 1,500-3,000 m. Forest-covered slopes, often near steep rocky crags, are the primary habitat of this species. Adult ♂ typically inhabit higher, less accessible altitudes than ♀ and young. During harsh winters, Tur concentrate on sunny slopes, with most animals staying below timberline; during summer, Tur expand their distribution to slopes of different exposures.

STATUS Endangered. Total population in 2004 was 5,000-6,000 animals, and might now be lower.

PHOTO CREDITS ♂ *Bodlina*, Prague Zoo (Czech Republic) and *Dean Leverett*, Edmonton Valley Zoo (Canada). Head ♂: *Pavanravela*, Toronto Zoo (Canada). ♀ and young: *Ulrike Joerres*, Tallinn Zoo, Tallinn (Estonia). Head ♀: *L.C. Willis*, Toronto Zoo (Canada). Juvenile: *Sergey Chichagov*, Tallinn Zoo (Estonia). 327

East Caucasian Tur

CAPRA CYLINDRICORNIS

BL: 178-192 cm (♂), 135-141 cm (♀). SH: 79-104 cm (♂), 65-80 cm (♀). TL: 11-15 cm. W: 100-143 kg (♂), 48-64 kg (♀). HL: 70-90 cm (♂), 20-22 cm (♀). A large goat, with a thick and stout body, supported by short legs. Marked sexual dimorphism in size, pelage, and horn development. In males, coat from chestnut brown with lighter underparts in the winter, to an overall lighter rusty-brown color in summer. In females and juveniles, coat is the same year-round, sandy yellow with whitish ventral body and dark brown stripes on front of legs. Short beard, directed slightly forward, found on males, most noticeable in winter. Skull does not have a bulge on the forehead below the horns. Smooth and rounded horns, curving above and behind the neck, with the tips turning inward and upward, similar to those of Bharal, but more massive. Horn base is cylindrical. Females smaller and lighter than males, with short, thin horns that grow outward, upward, and back.

Juvenile

♀

♂

Young

♂

summer coat

winter coat

Capra cylindricornis

OTHER NAMES Dagestan Tur, Pallas Tur, Caucasian Bharal. *French*: Chèvre du Caucase oriental. *German*: Ostkaukasische Steinbock, Daghestan-Tur. *Spanish*: Tur del Cáucaso oriental. *Russian*: Дагестанский (восточно-кавказский) тур. *Caucasus*: Abg-ab, abg-adshma.

SUBSPECIES Monotypic. It is still unclear whether or not *C. caucasica* and *C. cylindricornis* are two separate species, or are a single species with geographically dependent variability.

SIMILAR SPECIES West Caucasian Turs are larger and more massive; the winter color of ♂ East Caucasian Tur is brown, being grayish yellow in West Caucasian Tur. East Caucasian Turs differ from other species of Caprids by having much shorter beards. ♂ also lack the stripes on their forelegs that are typical of Siberian Ibex, Nubian Ibex, and Wild Goat. Alpine Ibex can be distinguished by differences in their horns.

REPRODUCTION *Gestation*: 150-160 days. *Young per Birth*: 1, rarely 2. *Weaning*: 2-4 months. *Sexual Maturity*: 2-4 years. *Life Span*: 15 years. East Caucasian Turs breed seasonally in December or January. ♂ and ♀ live separately except during the breeding season when ♂ come down from the higher elevations to breed. Adult ♂ fight furiously against each other for access to ♀. ♀ can also be violent during this time, chasing younger ♂ away if they try to breed. Young ♂ do not attempt to breed until after adult ♂ have done so. ♀ isolate themselves before birth and keep their young hidden for 3-4 days after birth. Home ranges of ♂ overlap those of ♀, but ♂ are highly territorial with other ♂ during the breeding season. Animals form mixed, adult ♂-♀ groups in November, just prior to rut. These disband by mid-January or the beginning of February at the latest, and adult ♂ and ♀ live separately until the next rutting season.

BEHAVIOR *Family Group*: ♀ form incoherent groups of approximately a dozen individuals. *Diet*: Grass and shrubs; grasses are eaten in autumn and beginning of winter. *Main Predators*: Wolf, lynx. There is a seasonal migration covering a vertical distance of 1,500-2,000 m with an upward thrust in May and a retreat downward in October. The solitary adult ♂ generally inhabit higher altitudes than groups of ♀ and their young, descending to join them in the breeding season. Young Turs are extremely agile, being able to scamper about steep slopes after only a day of life.

DISTRIBUTION *Native*: Azerbaijan, Georgia, Russian Federation. Endemic to the E part of the Great Caucasus along the borders of Russia, Georgia, and Azerbaijan. Its range begins around the headwaters of the Baksan River E of Mount Elbrus and stretches for some 600 km eastward along both slopes of the Greater Caucasus to Babadagh Mountain.

HABITAT Elevations between 1,000 and 4,000 m. Forests up to 2,600 m, and in subalpine and alpine meadows and rocky talus slopes at higher elevations. They avoid thick forests on gentle slopes, but stay readily in open forests growing on steep precipitous slopes.

STATUS Near Threatened. Estimated population at 14,000-20,000.

PHOTO CREDITS ♂ winter: *Ulrike Joerres*, Tallinn Zoo (Estonia) and *Iakov Filimonov*. ♀, ♂ summer, young, and juvenile: *Sergey Chichagov*, Tallinn Zoo (Estonia). Head ♂: *Iakov Filimonov*.

Walia Ibex
CAPRA WALIE

BL: 140-170 cm. SH: 75-110 cm (♂), 65-100 cm (♀). TL: 20-25 cm. W: 100-125 kg (♂), 80 kg (♀). HL: 89-114 cm (♂), to 13 cm (♀). A small Ibex. Chestnut-brown color, strongest on the back, and fades to gray on the flanks before merging with the pale underparts, including the throat and chin. Fronts of legs black, with striking white bands above the hooves and, on the forelegs, above the knees. Only males have a black beard on the chin. Older males also have very dark chests and a dark band along the flanks. Both sexes grow horns, which are flattened laterally, diverge slightly, and grow upward in a scimitar-shaped curve. Males have semi-circular horns, very massive, with pronounced knobs on the front surfaces (mature males may have over 10 knobs). Females significantly smaller than males, with slender and slightly arched horns.

♀

♂
Juvenile

♂

Young

Capra walie

OTHER NAMES Walia, Ethiopian Ibex, Abyssinian Ibex. *French*: Bouquetin d'Abyssinie, bouquetin d'Ethiopie. *German*: Äthiopischer Steinbock, Waliasteinbock. *Spanish*: Cabra montesa de Etiopía, íbice de Walia. *Russian*: Эфиопский (абиссинский) козёл.

SUBSPECIES Monotypic. Considered by some authors as a subspecies of the Nubian Ibex (*C. nubiana*).

SIMILAR SPECIES Easily distinguished based on range and coloration. Nubian Ibex to the N tends to be smaller, sandier in color, and has longer and more slender horns.

REPRODUCTION *Gestation*: 150-165 days. *Young per Birth*: 1, rarely 2. *Weaning*: Not known. *Sexual Maturity*: Likely at 2 years. *Life Span*: 12 years. Breeding season is between March and May, although some breeding occurs year-round, particularly in younger animals. The typical mating system is polygyny, with dominant ♂ siring a disproportionate number of offspring during the breeding season. These ♂, because of their large size and fighting experience, are able to monopolize ♀ by obtaining exclusive access to overlapping ♀ home ranges. The majority of offspring are born in September and October. When a ♀ gives birth, a group of adults will combine to protect her offspring from eagles.

BEHAVIOR *Family Group*: Variable throughout the year. Typically small mixed groups, averaging 3 individuals. Larger groups with at least 11 individuals have been seen. Atypical of most mountain sheep, ♂ tend to be more sociable than ♀ outside of the breeding season. This pattern of association is reversed during the rut season, with ♀ forming nursery groups and ♂ isolating themselves from one another in competition. Older ♂ more solitary, though they will remain within a short distance of the main herd most of the time and during the mating season and rejoin with the herd for breeding purposes. *Diet*: Leaves (especially young leaves) of trees and shrubs, grasses, and lichens. *Main Predators*: None; leopards and hyenas inhabit the forests at the bases of the cliffs, but the inaccessible habitat affords significant protection; birds of prey may take young kids. Typically most active in the early morning and late afternoon, with a distinct resting period in the middle of the day. While foraging on plateaus, they frequently associate with gelada baboons and will respond to alarm calls made by the primates. Home ranges for ♂ may be greater than 3 km^2, while ♀ tend to inhabit smaller areas (one observed ♀ used 0.5 km^2). Herds may travel 0.5-2 km per day.

DISTRIBUTION *Native*: Ethiopia. Found only in the Simien Mountains of N Ethiopia, mostly within Simien Mountains NP. Within the park, they are most often seen along a 25 km stretch of the N escarpment.

HABITAT Precipitous mountain slopes where there is considerable moisture and vegetation, usually at altitudes of 2,300-2,900 m, but can be as high as 4,100 m.

STATUS Endangered. Estimated population is 500 individuals, with fewer than 250 mature animals. The population may be slowly increasing, but restricted habitat and encroachment by people are limiting factors.

PHOTO CREDITS ♂: *Christof Asbach*. ♀: *Dominique Mignard*. Juvenile: *Ignacio Yufera*. Young: *Ludwig Siege*. All photos from Simien Mountains (Ethiopia).

Nubian Ibex

CAPRA NUBIANA NUBIANA

BL: 119-160 cm (♂), 90-120 cm (♀). SH: 75-110 (♂), 65-100 cm (♀). TL: 6-17 cm. W: 50-85 kg (♂), 25-50 kg (♀). HL: 88-127 cm (♂), to 35 cm (♀). Smaller and more lightly built than other true Ibexes, with slender, scimitar-shaped horns. Coat light sandy brown with the hindquarters lighter. Underparts almost white. Rump patch small, narrow, and white. Tail black and tufted. Males have a dark stripe on their front legs and one down their back, as well as a dark beard. During the October rut, the neck, chest, shoulders, upper legs, and sides of males become dark brown to almost black in color. Ears are large. Semi-circular and rather narrow horns curve upward, backward, and finally down, forming three-fourths of a circle. Horns on males have 24-36 knobs on the outer curve. Females smaller and lighter than males, beardless, lacking dorsal and flank stripes, with smaller horns.

♀

♂

Juvenile

Young

winter coat

summer coat

Capra nubiana nubiana

OTHER NAMES Sudanese Nubian Ibex, African Nubian Ibex. *French*: Bouquetin de Nubie. *German*: Syrische Steinbock, Nubische Steinbock. *Spanish*: Íbice de Nubia. *Russian*: Нубийский (горный) козёл. *Arabic*: Taytal nubi.

SUBSPECIES Considered as a subspecies of *C. nubiana* (Nubian Ibex): *C. n. nubiana* (Nubian Ibex), and *C. n. sinaitica* (Sinai Ibex). Includes *arabica* (Sinai), *beden* (SW Arabia), *mengesi* (SE Arabia), *nubiana* (Upper Egypt, Red Sea, Sudan), and *sinaitica* (Sinai).

SIMILAR SPECIES Distinguished from other Ibexes by its narrower horns with their rounded outer edges, its white belly, and its contrasting black and white leg markings. It shares the characteristic of black and white leg markings with the Walia Ibex, but lacks the bony boss on the forehead. Barbary Sheep lacks the black and white markings on the legs, has a pronounced throat fringe, different coat color, and smooth, very differently shaped horns. Domestic Goat is much smaller, longer haired, and very differently and variably patterned.

REPRODUCTION *Gestation*: 150 days. *Young per Birth*: 1-2. *Weaning*: 3 months. *Sexual Maturity*: 2-3 years. *Life Span*: 17 years. Mating occurs during the late summer months, especially October. The majority of kids are born in March. The neonate remains secluded for several days and is fed periodically by the mother until it is mature enough to follow her and join a ♀ herd. ♂ tend individual ♀ and do not form harems. Older ♂ do most of the mating and by aggressive behaviors prevent younger subdominant ♂ from participating in the rut.

BEHAVIOR *Family Group*: Single-sex herds, with kids staying with their maternal herd until the age of 3 years. *Diet*: Grasses, leaves. *Main Predators*: Leopard, bearded vulture, eagle. In contrast to most desert animals, it drinks almost daily. The light, smooth, shiny coat is thought to reflect a large amount of incoming solar radiation, which allows the animals to remain active throughout the day, even during hot summer afternoons. During summer nights, it rests in high, open areas of slopes, allowing a variety of escape routes should danger present itself. During the cooler winter nights, herds rest in more sheltered places, like caves or under overhangs. Although equipped with a semi-waterproof coat, they do not like to get wet, seeking shelter if possible during rainstorms. Seasonal movements from lower areas in winter to higher areas in spring can occur during the rainy season. Daily movements are about 4-6 km, depending on forage availability and proximity to cover. Home ranges can be 0.5 km² or smaller, but some ♀ groups can range over an area of 15 km².

DISTRIBUTION *Native*: Egypt, Ethiopia, Eritrea, Sudan. *Introduced*: Syria. This species occurs in Egypt E of the Nile, NE Sudan, N Ethiopia and W Eritrea.

HABITAT Rocky, desert mountains with steep slopes in NE Africa and parts of Arabia.

STATUS Vulnerable. Major threats are habitat loss and degradation due to livestock in Egypt, Saudi Arabia, and Oman, limited water resources in Egypt, and hunting.

PHOTO CREDITS *Sergey Chichagov,* Tallinn Zoo (Estonia).

Sinai Ibex

CAPRA NUBIANA SINAITICA

BL: 102-136 cm (♂), 90-120 cm (♀). SH: 75-110 (♂), 65-100 cm (♀). TL: 5.6-8.3 cm. W: 50-85 kg (♂), 25-50 kg (♀). HL: 88-127 cm (♂), to 35 cm (♀). Similar to the Nubian Ibex, with less black on its legs. Summer coat is yellowish fawn. Underparts almost white. Winter coat is darker grayish brown in the male, with more black on the legs. Blackish stripe on the back, dark across the shoulders and chest. Black beard and tail. Ears rather large. Males with scimitar-shaped horns, with bold transverse knobs on the front surface. Females much smaller than males, beardless, lacking dorsal and flank stripes, with much smaller horns, more erect and smoother. Juveniles resemble females in color.

♀

♂

Juvenile

♂

summer coat

winter coat

334

Capra nubiana sinaitica

OTHER NAMES *French*: Bouquetin de Sinai. *German*: Sinai Steinbock. *Spanish*: Íbice del Sinaí, cabra del Sinaí. *Russian*: Синайский (горный) козёл. *Arabic*: Beden. *Hebrew*: Ya′el.

SUBSPECIES Considered as a subspecies of *C. nubiana* (Nubian Ibex): *C. n. nubiana* (Nubian Ibex), and *C. n. sinaitica* (Sinai Ibex).

SIMILAR SPECIES Sinai Ibex seems to differ from Nubian Ibex in having less black on its legs, regardless of age or winter pelage, with a wider and rounder build and longer horns that have less of a curve.

REPRODUCTION *Gestation*: 147-180 days. *Young per Birth*: 1-2. *Weaning*: 3 months. *Sexual Maturity*: 2-3 years. *Life Span*: 17 years. Mating occurs during the late summer months, especially October. A grouping pattern unique among all other Caprids has been observed: ♀ leave their kids unattended in nursery groups in a steep-walled canyon with many other kids. The nursery is most likely an accidental trap that the kids have fallen into and they cannot surmount the cliff walls to climb out. Mothers visit the nursery often to feed the kids, which stay in the nursery until they are mature enough to follow along on the steep cliffs.

BEHAVIOR *Family Group*: Single-sex herds, with young staying with their maternal herd until the age of 3 years. *Diet*: Grazers and browsers, sometimes standing on their hind legs only; they drink almost daily. *Main Predators*: Leopard, bearded vulture, eagle. Gregarious, they usually associate in small groups, with a single, old ♂ leading his harem and young during the rutting season. Most groups have ranges of only a few km², dominated by either ♀ or ♂ which will fight other encroaching members of the same sex. Rival ♂ fight by rising on their hind legs and with heads tilted, crashing their horns together. Outside the rutting season, ♂ and ♀ remain apart. Since the forelegs are somewhat shorter than the hind legs, they seek safety by running uphill. Most active in the twilight period; resting and ruminating occurs in the afternoon or at night. During the winter months, they will seek shelter such as rock outcroppings or caves to avoid the cold, wind, or rain. They often hollow out shallow depressions in the ground in which to rest. During warm periods, they will often lie down or occasionally turn on their sides to stay cool. They often spend the hot periods of the day in shaded areas.

DISTRIBUTION *Native*: Egypt, Israel, Jordan, Oman, Saudi Arabia, Yemen. *Regionally Extinct:* Lebanon. Found in Sinai Peninsula, Egypt, Dead Sea region, and Negev Desert, S to Eliat (Israel), Albian Mountains E of Aden Region in Yemen and Saudi Arabia. Isolated from the African Nubian Ibex by the Isthmus of Suez.

HABITAT Dry desert mountains, deep wadis, and steep cliffs, not far from water on which they depend.

STATUS Vulnerable. The Israeli population comprises approximately 1,000 individuals.

PHOTO CREDITS ♂: *Sergey Chichagov,* Tel-Aviv University Zoo and Yotvata Hai-Bar Nature Reserve (Israel). Head ♂: *Oren and Shimrit Nadir,* Negev Desert (Israel). ♀: *Eyal Gindi,* Negev Desert (Israel). Immature ♂: *hairy_bass,* Negev Desert (Israel).

Alpine Ibex

CAPRA IBEX

BL: 115-135 cm (♂), 55-100 cm (♀). SH: 65-94 cm. TL: 15-29 cm. W: 70-120 kg (♂), 40-50 kg (♀). HL: 75-100 cm (♂), to 35 cm (♀). A stocky Ibex, with a heavy body supported by short, sturdy legs, darker than those of other Ibexes. Color of adult males changes seasonally: in summer, coat is yellowish brown with darker legs, with lighter parts on the neck and flanks, and underparts white; in late summer, there is a gradual change in old males to a dark chestnut brown. Coat length varies seasonally, being short and fuzzy during the summer, and growing thicker wool and long guard hairs during the winter. Males have a short beard, 6-7 cm long. Saber-shaped horns, curving upward and bending toward the rear, are shorter, thicker, and straighter than those of other Ibexes. Females smaller and lighter than males, without beard, and much shorter horns. Female and young animals light ocher brown to pale brown.

♂

♀

♂
Juvenile

winter coat

summer coat

Capra ibex

OTHER NAMES European Ibex. *French*: Bouquetin, bouquetin des Alpes. *German*: Alpensteinbock, Gemeiner Steinbock. *Spanish*: Íbice, cabra salvaje de los Alpes, cabra alpina. *Russian*: Альпийский (горный) козёл.

SUBSPECIES Monotypic.

REPRODUCTION *Gestation*: 165-170 days. *Young per Birth*: 1, rarely 2. *Weaning*: Gradual (no cutoff). *Sexual Maturity*: 1-1.5 years (♀), 2 years (♂). *Life Span*: 14 years. Mating occurs in December-January. They have a serial polygynous mating system; ♂ can mate with more than one ♀ during a mating season but only guard and court one ♀ at a time. Dominant ♂ do most of the courting and mating and attempt to prevent other ♂ from mating with the guarded ♀. Prior to parturition, pregnant ♀ leave ewe herds and give birth in isolation in steep, rugged terrain where neonates are safer from predators and human interference. Infants can jump after their first day, after which they join kid groups.

BEHAVIOR *Family Group*: Maternal herds of 10-20 animals, ♂ in bachelor groups or solitary. *Diet*: Grasses, some woody plants, shrubs, and lichens. *Main Predators*: For kids, golden eagle, fox. Most active during the early morning and late afternoon, lying in the shade of rocks during midday. Strong jumpers and sure-footed climbers, which allows them to move with ease in their mountainous abode. During the winter, they are found at medium elevations on steep faces usually facing south. As the warm weather approaches, they follow the receding snowline up the mountains to the highest part of their habitat. Here they spend late spring, summer, and autumn. ♂ join the ♀ herds during late autumn, remaining through the winter and departing during early spring. The ♂ bachelor herds which form during the summer have a distinct hierarchy, based on age, size, and strength. Playful fights occur to clarify this ranking, with ♂ rearing up on their hind legs before crashing their horns together. During the rut, however, most high-ranking ♂ avoid each other, minimizing the number of serious conflicts. Population densities vary widely, from 1 to 9 per km².

DISTRIBUTION *Native:* Italy. *Reintroduced:* Austria, France, Germany, Switzerland. *Introduced:* Bulgaria; Slovenia. Endemic to Europe, where its native range is the Alps of France, Switzerland, Austria, Germany, and N Italy. It has been introduced to Slovenia and Bulgaria. It was driven very close to extinction in the early 19th century, and with the exception of the population in Gran Paradiso NP (Italy), all current populations originate from re-introductions or introductions. Although its range has increased over the last century as a result of translocations and natural colonization, its distribution is still rather patchy in the Alps.

HABITAT High montane pastures in the Alps, normally above the treeline and at or below the snowline, at an altitude of 1,600-3,200 m. Ibexes evolved in arid mountains with little snow, and were never widely distributed in the Alps. Good Ibex range is limited to mountains with little precipitation and with sunny, snow-free areas where the animals can survive the winter.

STATUS Least Concern. Estimated population of 34,000 in 2007.

PHOTO CREDITS ♂: *Alex Meyer*, Munich Zoo (Germany) and *Michelle Bender*, Helsinki Zoo (Finland). Head ♂: *Jan Stefka*, Munich Zoo (Germany). ♀: *Ulrike Joerres*, Dierenrijk Zoo (Netherlands). Head ♀: *Steve Boyton*, Omega Park, Quebec (Canada). Juvenile: *Sergey Chichagov*, Helsinki Zoo (Finland).

Siberian Ibex

CAPRA SIBIRICA SIBIRICA

BL: 103-135 cm (♂), 85-101 cm (♀). SH: 67-107 cm. TL: 13-22 cm. W: 80-100 kg (♂), 30-56 kg (♀). HL: 91-117 cm (♂), 19-39 cm (♀). A large Ibex, thick legged and stoutly built. Summer coat short, yellowish brown or grayish brown in color, with a darker dorsal stripe, dark underparts and legs, without a lighter saddle patch. Winter coat longer, coarse and brittle, with a dorsal crest and thick undercoat, relatively light, yellowish white, and usually a light saddle patch, but may be absent. Dorsal stripe, tail, and beard are blackish brown. Long, pointed chin beard. Large horns, curving around to form three-fourths of a circle and tapering to relatively slender points, flat on the front surface, with well-defined cross ridges, thinner than in Mid-Asian Ibex. Females grow short, thin horns and lack beards.

summer coat

winter coat

Capra sibirica sibirica

OTHER NAMES Altai Ibex, Asiatic Ibex. *French:* Yanghir, ibex de Sibérie. *German:* Sibirischer Steinbock. *Spanish:* Íbice siberiano. *Russian:* Сибирский (горный козёл) козерог. *Local names:* Skin, sakin (♂), danmo (♀).

SUBSPECIES Considered as a subspecies of *C. sibirica* (Asian Ibex): *C. s. hagenbecki* (Gobi or Mongolian Ibex), *C. s. sibirica* (Siberian or Altai Ibex), *C. s. alaiana* (Tian Shan Ibex), *C. s. sakeen* (Himalayan Ibex). Includes *altaica* (Irtish Altai), *fasciata* (NE Altai near Lake Telezko), *lydekkeri* (Katutay Range of Irtish Altai), *sibirica* (Sayan Mountains W of Lake Baikal), and *typica* (Tunkinskie Belki E of Irkutsk), with *sibirica* having priority.

SIMILAR SPECIES Gobi Ibex is quite close to Siberian Ibex in size and build, but it has relatively longer horns, ridges in middle portion of horns are larger, and lacks a light saddle. Mid-Asian Ibex is larger, with larger horns, and is darker in winter. Himalayan Ibex is also larger.

REPRODUCTION *Gestation:* 155-180 days. *Young per Birth:* 1 or 2, rarely 3. *Weaning:* Gradual, without a sharp cutoff. *Sexual Maturity:* 1.5-2 years. *Life Span:* 15 years. Mating season can start in October and extend into January, due to differences between ranges and weather conditions. A breeding hierarchy between ♂ is established through fighting, which includes clashes of horns, with both ♂ either facing each other or standing next to one another; mortality is rare during fights. ♂ begin courting females by approaching with a low-stretch pose, then sniffing and licking the ♀. This courtship behavior lasts over 30 minutes. Mature ♂ will establish and guard harems of 5-15 females. ♀ leave their groups and yearling for around a week before and after parturition and give birth in solitude. A few days following birth, the newborn is often left alone to hide from predators. Young generally stay close to their mothers for protection, and bleat at signs of danger. Young can graze like adults within 1.5 months of birth, but depending on when they are weaned, they can suckle for the first 5-8 months of life.

BEHAVIOR *Family Group:* Maternal and bachelor herds. *Diet:* Grasses, leaves and shoots of bushes and trees. *Main Predators:* Wolf, snow leopard, lynx, wolverine, brown bear, fox, golden eagle, human. Diurnal, with alternating periods of resting and activity throughout the day. Migration is associated with snow accumulation in autumn. This is due to limited access to food during times of high snow levels. They can migrate over 100 km between seasons, while also changing up to 2,000 m in elevation. They reach food covered by 30 to 40 cm of snow by digging with their hooves.

DISTRIBUTION *Native:* China, Kazakhstan, Mongolia, Russian Federation. Found in S Asian Russia, Altai Mountains, Sayan Mountains W of Lake Baikal, S Siberia, Mongolian Altai, China (Xinjiang), and Kazakhstan. Outside Asia, it has been introduced in New Mexico.

HABITAT Open, precipitous terrain at any altitude.

STATUS Least Concern.

PHOTO CREDITS ♂ winter: *Andrey Kotkin*, Krasnoyarsk Zoo (Russia). ♂ summer: *Alex Meyer*, Wroclaw Zoo (Poland). Head ♂: *Andrey Kotkin*, Novosibirsk Zoo (Russia). ♀: *Andrey Kotkin*, Krasnoyarsk Zoo (Russia).

339

Mid-Asian Ibex

CAPRA SIBIRICA ALAIANA

BL: 103-135 cm (♂), 85-101 cm (♀). SH: 67-110 cm. TL: 13-22 cm. W: 60-130 kg (♂), 30-56 kg (♀). HL: 100-148 cm (♂), 19-39 cm (♀). Largest subspecies with largest horns. There is a good deal of variation in color and markings. In winter, color is cinnamon brown of varying intensity, browner and duller on the flanks, shoulders, and thighs. Dark, well-developed dorsal stripe, but may be absent. Light-colored saddle patch, variable in size, shape, and location. Dark flank band separating the brown flanks from the whitish belly. Head grayish and lighter than flanks, beard is brown. Some animals darker or lighter, and some are a uniform light gray color. Summer coat is light grayish or reddish brown, and usually saddle patch is absent. Horns very long and relatively slender with comparatively small cross ridges. Females smaller than males, with no beards, smaller horns, and usually no saddle patch.

Young

♀

♂

Juvenile

♂

summer coat

winter coat

Capra sibirica alaiana

Capra sibirica sakeen

OTHER NAMES Tian Shan Ibex, Himalayan Ibex, Central Asian Ibex. *French:* Yanghir, ibex de Sibérie. *German:* Sibirischer Steinbock. *Spanish:* Íbice de Asia central, íbice de Cachemira, íbice del Himalaya. *Russian:* Среднеазиатский (горный козёл) козерог.

SUBSPECIES Considered as a subspecies of *C. sibirica* (Asian Ibex): *C. s. hagenbecki* (Gobi or Mongolian Ibex), *C. s. sibirica* (Siberian or Altai Ibex), *C. s. alaiana* (Tian Shan Ibex), *C. s. sakeen* (Himalayan Ibex). *C. s. alaiana* also includes *almasyi, merzbacheri,* and *transalaiana,* with *alaiana* having priority. *C. s. sakeen* includes *dementievi* and *hemalayanus.*

SIMILAR SPECIES The largest subspecies in size and has the largest horns. Its coloration is very different from that of the Siberian and Gobi Ibexes. Himalayan Ibex (*C. s. sakeen*) is similar to Mid-Asian Ibex, but smaller in size, lighter in color, with shorter horns, more massive at base. In contrast to horns of Nubian and Alpine Ibexes, horns of Asian Ibex have two marked edges with a broad flat surface between them frontally, and index of their bend is nearly twice as large. Cross section of horn is tetrahedral at base and more triangular toward top.

REPRODUCTION *Gestation:* 155-180 days. *Young per Birth:* 1 or 2, rarely 3. *Weaning:* Gradual, without a sharp cutoff. *Sexual Maturity:* 1.5-2 years. *Life Span:* 16 years. Mating occurs in October-January, with regional differences during rut. ♂ 5 years old and older do most of the courting and mating.

BEHAVIOR *Family Group:* Gregarious, living in herds of 40-50, sometimes more. Older ♂ are often solitary or in small groups of 3-4, frequently in more inaccessible terrain. *Diet:* Grazer: grasses, leaves and shoots of bushes and trees. *Main Predators:* Wolf, snow leopard, lynx, wolverine, brown bear, fox, golden eagle, human. Diurnal, with alternating periods of resting and activity throughout the day. Although they live at high elevations, and often climb up to the vegetation line at 5,000 m, as a rule they seek out lower slopes during the winter. These slopes are generally steep and southward facing, and snow has difficulty covering a large area over large stretches of time. However, when the snow cover is heavy, they must find food by pawing away the snow with their forelegs in order to reach the vegetation concealed below. If threatened, they flee to steep, rocky cliffs.

DISTRIBUTION *Native:* Afghanistan, China, India, Kazakhstan, Kyrgyzstan, Pakistan, Tajikistan. *C. s. alaiana:* Found in the Pamir, Alai, Transalai, and Tian Shan mountains in Afghanistan, Tajikistan, Kyrgyzstan, Kazakhstan, and China. *C. s. sakeen:* Found in the Himalaya, Pamirs, Hindu Kush, and Karakoram in N Pakistan and N India, and in China (Xinjiang, Xizang).

HABITAT Alpine meadows and crags in Central Asia. It occupies precipitous habitats in a range of environments from deserts, low mountains, and foothills, to high mountain ridges. It can also be found in areas with canyons, rocky outcrops, and steep "escape" terrain far from high mountains.

STATUS Least Concern. It is the most numerous subspecies of Asian Ibex. Population in the Tian Shan has been guessed at 40,000-50,000 individuals.

PHOTO CREDITS ♂: *Sergey Chichagov,* Tallinn Zoo (Estonia). Head ♂: *Nick Karpov,* Moscow Zoo (Russia). ♀ and head, young, and juvenile: *Sergey Chichagov,* Tallinn Zoo (Estonia).

Gobi Ibex

CAPRA SIBIRICA HAGENBECKI

BL: 103-125 cm (♂), 85-101 cm (♀). SH: 67-105 cm. TL: 12-15 cm. W: 80-100 kg (♂), 30-56 kg (♀). HL: 74-124 cm (♂), 16-38 cm (♀). A large Ibex, thick legged and stoutly built, slightly smaller than Siberian Ibex. General coat coloration is more gray and pale brown without a lighter saddle. In winter, adult males become much darker. Old males may become nearly white. Both sexes have a dark beard beneath the chin, less pronounced in females. No contrasting black and white markings on the legs. Horns slightly shorter and slimmer than in Siberian Ibex, but the cross ridges are often larger and closer together. Females have small horns, slightly arched toward the rear.

Young

Juvenile
♂

♀

old ♂

342

Capra sibirica hagenbecki

OTHER NAMES Mongolian Ibex. *French*: Ibex du Gobi, bouquetin du Gobi. *German*: Gobi Steinbock. *Spanish*: Íbice del Gobi, íbice mongol. *Russian*: Гобийский (монгольский) горный козёл. *Mongolian*: Yangir yamaa.

SUBSPECIES Considered as a subspecies of *C. sibirica* (Asian Ibex): *C. s. hagenbecki* (Gobi or Mongolian Ibex), *C. s. sibirica* (Siberian or Altai Ibex), *C. s. alaiana* (Tian Shan Ibex), *C. s. sakeen* (Himalayan Ibex). Some authorities believe these subspecies are synonymous, and taxonomy is not yet resolved.

SIMILAR SPECIES Siberian Ibex is very similar, slightly larger in size, with a light saddle patch in winter, and heavier horns, with less pronounced cross ridges. Tian Shan Ibex is the largest subspecies, with larger horns, and has a light-colored saddle patch.

REPRODUCTION *Gestation*: 155-180 days. *Young per Birth*: 1 or 2, rarely 3. *Weaning*: Gradual, without a sharp cutoff. *Sexual Maturity*: 1.5-2 years. *Life Span*: 16 years. Mating occurs in September-early October. ♀ give birth in June.

BEHAVIOR *Family Group*: Maternal and bachelor herds; up to 70 animals in winter. *Diet*: Grasses, leaves and shoots of bushes and trees. *Main Predators*: Wolf, snow leopard, lynx, wolverine, brown bear, fox, golden eagle, human. They share their pasture with domesticated goats and other species, which they follow onto lower slopes in winter. As the number of domesticated goats has grown, this species has moved to higher altitudes for summer grazing. Diurnal, with alternating periods of resting and activity throughout the day.

DISTRIBUTION *Native*: China, Mongolia. Found in Gobi and trans-Altai Gobi in central and S Mongolia, and Xinjiang (Tian Shan Mountains), W Nei Mongol and Gansu, in N China. At the NW boundary of Gansu Province with Xinjiang Uyghur Autonomous Region, the ranges of *hagenbecki, sibirica,* and *alaiana* almost meet just E of the town of Hami.

HABITAT Rocky, steep slopes at 3,500-6,000 m above sea level. It occupies precipitous habitats in a range of environments from deserts, low mountains, and foothills, to high mountain ridges. It can also be found in areas with canyons, rocky outcrops, and steep "escape" terrain far from high mountains.

STATUS Least Concern. Listed as Near Threatened in the Mongolian Red List of Mammals. Estimated total population is 19,000 animals in Gobi Gurvansikhan NP (Mongolia). Main threats include illegal and unsustainable hunting for meat, skins, and trophies, which are traded and exported.

PHOTO CREDITS ♂: *Zhou Fangyi*, Beijing Zoo (China). Old ♂, head ♀ juvenile, and young: *Otgonbayar Baatargal*, Gobi (Mongolia). ♀: *Sergey Chichagov,* Beijing Zoo (China).

Western Spanish Ibex

CAPRA PYRENAICA VICTORIAE

BL: 108-155 cm (♂). 97-130 cm (♀). SH: 65-89 cm (♂), 65-76 cm (♀). TL: 10-15 cm. W: 85-120 kg (♂), 31-41 kg (♀). HL: 42-101 cm (♂), 13-29 cm (♀). A medium-sized Ibex. Adult males are grayish to pale brown to whitish on the side of head, throat, and upper front sides of the neck, and upper sides of the body, extending to the hindquarters. Forehead, beard, chest, and front of the shoulders and legs are black. Middorsal stripe extending to the dark tail. The lower sides of the body, the front of the upper hind legs, and the lower front legs are black. Winter coat is darker and longer. Male horns are lyre shaped, growing upward, then curving out and back, with the tips pointing up, and a spiral turn of more than 180 degrees. Females smaller than males, with a uniform brown body, except for white underparts, and much shorter horns, growing up and back.

♂

♀

Young

♂

Juvenile

344

Capra pyrenaica victoriae

OTHER NAMES Gredos Ibex, Iberian Wild Goat, Central Plateau Ibex. *French*: Bouquetin des Pyrénées, bouquetin d'Espagne, bouquetin ibérique. *German*: Iberiensteinbock. *Spanish*: Cabra montés. *Russian*: Гредосский (пиренейский горный) козёл.

SUBSPECIES *C. p. victoriae* (Gredos or Western Spanish Ibex), *C. p. hispanica* (Southeastern Spanish or Beceite Ibex). *C. p. pyrenaica* (Pyrenean Ibex) and *lustanica* (Portuguese Ibex) are extinct.

SIMILAR SPECIES Southeastern Spanish Ibex is small, coat is less black, with smaller and more down-curved horns. Horn configuration and coat color are not uniform, with variations among a given herd.

REPRODUCTION *Gestation*: 161-168 days. *Young per Birth*: 1-2. *Sexual Maturity*: 1.5 years (♀), 3 years (♂). *Life Span*: 16 years. Breeding occurs from November through December, peaking in the first half of December. During the rut, ♂ battle with each other for the right to mate by butting heads. The peak birthing period is in mid-May. ♀ breed every year. ♀ often find a remote, inaccessible location with thick brush for birthing. After giving birth, ♀ and young congregate in groups.

BEHAVIOR *Family Group*: ♂ and ♀ with young are segregated into separate groups during most of the year. *Diet*: Browsers; their main forage is holm oak (*Quercus ilex*); they also feed on forbs and grasses. *Main Predators*: No natural predators except humans; eagles and foxes (young). They exhibit herding behavior. ♂ and ♀ with young are segregated into separate groups. The young of the year generally travel in the center of the group for protection from predators. ♀ tend to be solitary during the birthing season, but join the herd later. In the fall, mixed-sex herds of adults separate from mixed-sex herds of juveniles. In the adult herds, one dominant ♂ and up to several subordinate ♂ associate with multiple ♀. There is a strict dominance hierarchy among the ♂, and only the dominant ♂ breeds. The dominant ♂ defends his territory and herd of ♀ from other ♂. ♂ form the hierarchy and defend their territory by aggressive posturing and fighting by butting heads. After the breeding season, the adults again segregate into herds of ♂ and ♀. When danger is detected, usually by sight or smell, an alarm whistle is given and the herd flees in columns led by an adult ♂ or ♀.

DISTRIBUTION *Native*: Spain. *Reintroduced*: Portugal. Found in N and W Spain (Sierra de Gredos, Baturcas); reintroduced in N Portugal (Peneda-Gerês NP). It no longer occurs in the Pyrenees.

HABITAT Rocky habitats. Even small rocky patches in arable farmland and on the coast may be used, although cliffs and screes interspersed with scrub or pine trees are the most typical habitats. It often lives in very close proximity to humans. It disperses readily and can rapidly colonize new areas if appropriate habitat is available.

STATUS Vulnerable. About 15,000 animals live in Sierra de Gredos national game reserve. The biggest threat is tourism.

PHOTO CREDITS ♂: *Juan Luis Jiménez Cordero*, Sierra de Gredos (Spain). Head ♂: *Ruben Alvarez*, Sierra de Gredos (Spain). ♀: *Eva Gallud,* Sierra de Gredos (Spain). Head ♀: *Antonio Fernandez*, Sierra de Gredos (Spain). Young: *Juan M. Casillas*, La Pedriza, Madrid (Spain).

Southeastern Spanish Ibex
CAPRA PYRENAICA HISPANICA

BL: 90-140 cm (♂). 97-130 cm (♀). SH: 65-89 cm (♂), 65-76 cm (♀). TL: 15 cm. W: 35-80 kg (♂), 31-41 kg (♀). HL: 42-101 cm (♂), 13-29 cm (♀). A medium-sized Ibex, smaller and lighter in color than Western Spanish Ibex. Grayish to pale brown to whitish on the sides of head, throat, and upper front sides of the neck, and upper sides of the body, extending to the hindquarters. Forehead, beard, chest, and front of the shoulders and legs are black. Middorsal stripe extending to the dark tail. The lower sides of the body, the front of the upper hind legs, and the lower front legs are black. Horns in males grow backward from the skull, smaller and thinner than in Western Spanish Ibex. Females are smaller than males, have a uniform brown body, except for white underparts, and much shorter horns, growing up and back.

♀

Juvenile

♂

♂

♀

Juvenile

♂

Capra pyrenaica hispanica

OTHER NAMES Beicete Ibex, Ronda Ibex, Sierra Nevada Ibex, Iberian Wild Goat. *French*: Bouquetin des Pyrénées, bouquetin d'Espagne, bouquetin ibérique. *German*: Iberiensteinbock. *Spanish*: Cabra montés, íbice ibérico. *Russian*: Бесейтский (пиренейский горный) козёл.

SUBSPECIES *C. p. victoriae* (Gredos or Western Spanish Ibex), *C. p. hispanica* (Southeastern Spanish or Beceite Ibex). Includes *maritimus* (Beicete Ibex, Mountains of Beceite and Tortosa), *penibeticus* (Southeastern Ibex, Mountains of Almijara, Sierra Nevada, Lujar and Almería), and *meridionalis* (Ronda Ibex, Mountains of Ronda and Malaga). *C. p. pyrenaica* (Pyrenean Ibex) and *lustanica* (Portuguese Ibex) are extinct.

SIMILAR SPECIES Western Spanish Ibex is larger and darker, with more lyre-shaped horns. Horn size and shape vary considerably from place to place.

REPRODUCTION *Gestation*: 161-168 days. *Young per Birth*: 1-2. *Sexual Maturity*: 1.5 years (♀), 3 years (♂). *Life Span*: 16 years. Breeding occurs from November through December, peaking in the first half of December. During the rut, ♂ battle with each other for the right to mate by butting heads. The peak birthing period is in mid-May. ♀ often find a remote, inaccessible location with thick brush for birthing. After giving birth, ♀ and young congregate in groups.

BEHAVIOR *Family Group*: ♂ and ♀ with young are segregated into separate groups during most of the year. *Diet*: ♀ and youngsters usually eat grasses, herbs, and lichens; ♂ eat leaves of vines, shrubs, and olive trees (not the fruit); in late summer, they also feed on figs and the fruit of carob trees; in late autumn, they consume acorns before beginning their rutting season in early winter. *Main Predators*: No natural predators. During summer, the herds' movements are determined by the availability of water sources in the high elevations. It often lives in very close proximity to humans, and is a familiar and popular species. It disperses readily and can rapidly colonize new areas if appropriate habitat is available. It is an important trophy-hunting species. It can sometimes be an agricultural pest, causing damage to almond trees. There is a strict dominance hierarchy among the ♂, and only the dominant ♂ breeds. The dominant ♂ defends his territory and herd of ♀ from other ♂. ♂ form the hierarchy and defend their territory by aggressive posturing and fighting by butting heads.

DISTRIBUTION *Native*: Spain. *Regionally Extinct*: Andorra; France. Endemic to the Iberian Peninsula. Found in Mediterranean and S mountains of Spain (S and E Spain).

HABITAT Rocky mountainous regions at altitudes of 500-3,000 m.

STATUS Least Concern. Estimated population of 30,000 individuals. The main threat is human disturbance.

PHOTO CREDITS Head ♂ and ♂: *Gabriel Pérez Zenni*, Sierra de Cazorla, Jaen (Spain). ♀: *Francisco Javier Guerra Hernando*, Barcelona Zoo (Spain). Head ♀: *Nicolás Pérez Palma*, Almuñecar (Spain). Juvenile: *José L. Muñoz Ferrera de Castro* and *Ingeborg van Leeuwen*, Monachil (Spain).

Wild Goat

CAPRA AEGAGRUS

BL: 120-160 cm. SH: 73-100 cm (♂), 55-60 cm (♀). TL: 11-15 cm. W: 45-90 kg (♂), 25-55 kg (♀). HL: To 127 cm (♂), to 33 cm (♀). A large handsome goat. Coloration brownish, with typical black stripes through the shoulders and on the sides of the abdomen. Front sides of legs and tail also black, and the rear parts of legs and abdomen white. Around the eyes, on the neck, and on the sides of the body there are typical light areas. Dorsal stripe extending from the nape to the tail. Summer coat short and coarse and even in adult males is more reddish buff in color. Males have long black beards. Long, sweeping, scimitar-shaped horns in males, strongly keeled in front, sweep upward and outward, with the tips generally diverging. Females are smaller than males, tawny brown at all seasons, have a dark stripe from eye to muzzle, no beard, and shorter horns, lacking frontal knobs.

♂

♀

ssp. *blythi*

ssp. *aegagrus*

Capra aegagrus aegagrus

Capra aegagrus blythi

Capra aegagrus turcmenica (blythi)

Capra aegagrus chialtanensis

OTHER NAMES Persian Wild Goat, Bezoar Wild Goat. *French*: Chèvre à bézoard. *German*: Wildziege. *Spanish*: Cabra salvaje. *Baluchi*: Sair, phashin, pachin. *Brahui*: Chank. *Czech*: Koza bezoárová. *Greek*: Egagros, agrimi. *Iranian*: Kal, takeh, pasang. *Pashto*: Ghavza, borz. *Russian*: Синдский бородатый козёл (*blythi*), Туркменский безоаровый козёл (*turcmenica*). *Sindi*: Ter, sarah. *Slovakian*: Koza bezoárová. *Turkish*: Dag keçisi, yaban keçisi, kirmizi, kizil keçcisi. *Urdu*: Kail.

SUBSPECIES *C. a. aegagrus* (European Wild Goat or Bezoar Ibex): Caucasus Mountains (from Turkey to Afghanistan); reddish brown, turning brownish gray in winter, old ♂ ashy gray. *C. a. blythi* (Sindh Ibex): SW Pakistan; paler in color, somewhat smaller, horns closer together at the tips, without knobs on the front keel or with only a few small ones; may include *turcmenica* (Turkmen Wild Goat), found in Turkmenistan. *C. a. chialtanensis* (Chiltan Goat, Chiltan Markhor): NW Pakistan (only at Hazarganji-Chiltan NP); may be a hybrid between Wild Goat and Markhor (*C. falconeri x C. a. blythi*); horns flattened in cross section, sharply keeled in front, forming a long, open spiral. The validity of these subspecies is uncertain. The Wild Goat is considered the wild ancestor of Domestic Goats.

REPRODUCTION *Gestation*: 170 days. *Young per Birth*: 1-2. *Weaning*: 6 months. *Sexual Maturity*: 1.5-2.5 years (♀), 3.5-4 years (♂). *Life Span*: 14 years. Rut lasts from mid-December until the end of January. Birth season takes place from mid-June to mid-July. *C. a. chialtanensis*: Rut starts mid-October and is almost over by the third week of November.

BEHAVIOR *Family Group*: ♂ usually live alone and the ♀ gather with the young ones into flocks (up to 15 animals). *Diet*: Herbaceous plants and shrubs. *Main Predators*: Wolf, eagle. Diurnal or nocturnal, depending on predator and human activity, but older ♂ tend to sleep in hiding places, often caves, by day and feed at night. Sedentary, living in a small area. Both grazes and browses, often climbing trees to feed. Drinks water regularly when available, usually very early or late, or even after dark.

DISTRIBUTION *Native*: Armenia, Azerbaijan, Georgia, Iran, Pakistan, Russian Federation, Turkey, Turkmenistan. *Regionally Extinct*: Jordan, Lebanon, Syria. There is an introduced population in the Moravian region of the Czech Republic, in New Mexico (USA), and it is found on game ranches in many places.

HABITAT Mountainous areas, where there is a mixture of rocky outcrops (including scree slopes) and vegetation (shrubby maquis thickets or conifer forests). It tends to be found in relatively arid habitats, though it is a forest species in the Caucasus.

STATUS Vulnerable. *C. a. chialtanensis*: Critically Endangered (one population of about 480 animals in Hazarganji-Chiltan NP in 1990). The total population of Wild Goat is believed to be about 30,000 individuals. Its major threat is illegal hunting, competition for food with domestic livestock, and disturbance and habitat loss from logging and land clearing.

PHOTO CREDITS ♂: Turkey. ♀ and heads: *fofo*, Tehran Zoo (Iran). ♂ *blythi*: *Jim Shockey* (Pakistan).

Domestic Goat

CAPRA HIRCUS

BL: 115-170 cm. SH: 26-107 cm. W: 20-113 kg. There are many different breeds, with different attributes. Sexually dimorphic: males have a beard, horns, and are larger than females. The horns grow in either a scimitar or corkscrew shape. The hair is generally straight, but some breeds have a wool undercoat. Coat color varies, and can be black, white, red, and brown. Color patterns include solid color, spotted, striped, blended shades, and facial stripes. The nose can be either straight or convex. European breeds have erect ears and Indian breeds do not. The LaMancha breed has no external ears. The tail is short and curved upward. Almost all goats are born with horns, but most goats, except for Pygmies, are dehorned at a young age to protect both the goats and humans.

Feral
♂

Boer
♂

Rove
♂

Peacock
♀

♀

African Pygmy
♂

Jermasia
♂

Capra hircus

OTHER NAMES *French*: Chèvre domestique. *German*: Hausziege. *Spanish*: Cabra, chivo. *Russian*: Домашняя коза.

SUBSPECIES Domestic Goats are descendants of *C. aegagrus* (Wild Goat) and *C. falconeri* (Markhor). There are many different breeds of Domestic Goats. The six traditional breeds of goats are Nubian, Alpine, Saanen, Toggenburg, LaMancha, and Oberhasli. Other breeds which are growing in popularity include Pygmy, Boer, Cashmere, and Angora.

REPRODUCTION *Gestation*: 145-152 days. *Young per Birth*: 1-3. *Weaning*: 10 months. *Sexual Maturity*: 1 year (♀), 5 months (♂). *Life Span*: 15 years. It follows a polygynous reproductive system. ♂ goats compete for rank, and the highest-ranking ♂ have access to mate with the ♀. ♂ fight by butting heads. The breeding season is from late summer to early winter. In the tropics certain breeds reproduce all year long. The ♀ will separate from the rest of the flock when kidding time approaches. The young are born precocious and able to walk and follow the mother just hours after birth. ♀ may give a parturient call, consisting of a short, low-pitched bleating. If a strange kid should approach her, however, she will rebuke it.

BEHAVIOR *Family Group*: 5-10 members. *Diet*: Grasses and shrubs. Well adapted to limited water intake and short-term shortages, and can go without water for long periods of time. *Main Predators*: Coyote, dog, mountain lion, fox, eagle, bobcat. Domestic Goats are social animals. Herd sizes in the wild tend to be 5 to 20 members, but can be as high as 100. The herds can contain only ♂, only ♀ and young, or a mix of both. Goats are diurnal, and spend most of the day grazing in the herds. There is a rank structure in the herds. The ♂ butt heads for hierarchy status. Goats dislike water and would rather leap over streams and puddles. They are remarkable in their ability to climb and can move safely along narrow mountain paths to graze herbs. This ability can be a problem in farming, as goats will climb fence stays and jump over. They may also dig holes below fences to escape. They also like to dig areas to lie in and enjoy the sun. They do this especially on north-facing slopes which then start eroding.

DISTRIBUTION Since the domestication of this species, goats have been spread all over the world by humans.

HABITAT Domesticated animal, raised in almost all habitats. They require grass for grazing, but can thrive in areas of thin growth that would not support other grazers such as sheep or cows. They can be kept in dry lots as long as they are constantly fed by humans. Some sort of clean and ventilated shelter is necessary, but it does not have to be extravagant. For sleeping, they prefer a bedded area of at least 4.5 m. Goats require exercise; optimally a goat should have at least 2.5 m² per animal for this. As a domesticated species, *C. hircus* is very susceptible to predation. Therefore, it is best situated in a fenced-in area. Feral groups are found usually in rugged mountain country, rocky crags, and alpine meadows.

STATUS Domesticated.

PHOTO CREDITS Rove goat: *Eric Isselée*. Jermasia goat: *Prof. Dr. Ramli Bin Abdullah*, University of Malaya (Malaysia). Peacock goat: *Michelle Bender*, Zoo Basel, Basel (Switzerland). Boer goat: *Klaus Rudloff*, Cottbus Tierpark (Germany). Feral goat: *Joe King*, Glenealo Valley, Glendalough (Ireland). African Pygmy goat: *Ryan Somma*, Virginia Zoo, Norfolk (USA).

Cretan Wild Goat

CAPRA HIRCUS VAR. CRETICA

BL: 90 cm. SH: 60 cm (♂), 45 cm (♀). TL: 11 cm. W: 26-42 kg (♂). HL: To 90 cm (♂), to 33 cm (♀). A medium-sized goat. Blackish-brown markings contrast with the lighter overall color. Dark blackish areas include a dorsal stripe, shoulder stripes, flank stripes, front of legs, chest, tail, throat, face, and beard. Summer coat reddish brown, turning ashy gray in winter in adult males. Underparts and back of legs are white. Calluses on knees. Males have large, scimitar-shaped, laterally compressed horns. The front edge is a sharp keel with a number of bold, sharp-edged, widely separated knobs. Females are smaller than males, have short, slender horns and no beard; they are brownish tan at all seasons, with a dark stripe from eye to muzzle.

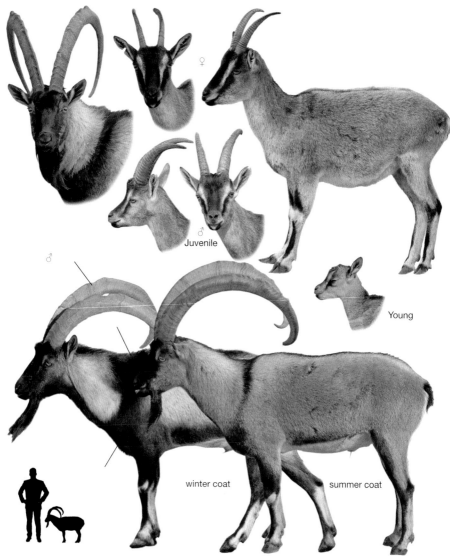

♀

♂

Juvenile

♂

Young

winter coat

summer coat

352

Capra hircus var. *cretica*

OTHER NAMES Kri-kri, Cretan Goat, Cretan Feral Goat, Cretan Ibex, Agrimi (♂), Sanada (♀). *French*: Chèvre sauvage crétoise. *German*: Kretische Wildziege. *Spanish*: Kri-kri. *Russian*: Критский безоаровый козёл, или агрими.

SUBSPECIES Formerly considered a subspecies of *C. aegagrus*, but molecular analysis suggests that it may be a feral variety of the Domestic Goat (*C. hircus*), which externally resembles its wild ancestor (*C. aegagrus*). Three races have been described: *cretica* (Cretan Wild Goat): White Mountains in W Crete; *pictus* (Aegean Wild Goat): Islet of Antimilos in NW Milos; and *dorcas* (Youra Wild Goat): Islet of Youra in N Sporades. Most populations appear to have undergone some degree of hybridization with Domestic Goats.

SIMILAR SPECIES The Cretan Wild Goat is smaller and more distinctly colored than the typical Wild Goat of Asia.

REPRODUCTION *Gestation*: 148-160 days. *Young per Birth*: 1, generally 2. *Weaning*: 6 months. *Sexual Maturity*: 2-2.5 years (♀), 1.5-3 years (♂). *Life Span:* 12 years. Breeding season in October-November, after the first substantial rainfalls, with single ♂ often chasing single ♀ even for several hours. Breeding behavior includes stomping, kicking, gobbling, tongue wagging, and mounting. Births occur in early spring, when chances for survival are maximized.

BEHAVIOR *Family Group:* Family Groups of 2-5 animals, composed of ♀ and offspring up to 2 years of age, sometimes up to 34 animals. Adult ♂ usually live alone. *Diet:* Browse on stems, buds, and leaves of shrubs and low trees, and grasses as well. They go out for pasture in early morning and toward evening, and during the day they rest in rocky recesses or caves with good visibility of the surroundings. There is a dominance hierarchy with older and larger ♂ being most dominant, which translates into more access to foraging and mates.

DISTRIBUTION *Native*: Greece. Found only on the islands of Crete (White Mountains of W Crete at Samaria NP) and the islets of Dia, Thodorou, and Agii Pandes. Recently some were introduced onto two more islands. It is not thought to be indigenous to Crete, but was imported during the time of the Minoan civilization.

HABITAT Mountainous areas, where there is a mixture of rocky outcrops or scree slopes and vegetation (shrubby maquis thickets or conifer forests). They tend to be found in relatively arid habitats, and are herbivorous, feeding on grasses, herbaceous plants, and shrubs.

STATUS Vulnerable. By 1960, population was below 200. Recent estimates vary widely, but some are as large as 2,000 individuals. The greatest threat is hybridization with recently feral Domestic Goats that are common even within Samaria NP.

PHOTO CREDITS ♂: *Sergey Chichagov*, Tallinn Zoo (Estonia) and *Will Papageorgiou,* Attica Zoological Park (Greece). Head ♂: *Alex Kantorovich*, Carmel Hai-Bar Nature Reserve (Israel). ♀, juvenile, and young: *Sergey Chichagov*, Tallinn Zoo (Estonia).

Majorcan Goat

CAPRA HIRCUS VAR. MAJORCAN

BL: 95-110 cm. SH: 63-79 cm (♂), 48-62 cm (♀). W: 39-57 kg (♂), 23-41 kg (♀). HL: To 100 cm (♂). Slightly smaller than Domestic Goats. Coat short and bright. Black markings, contrasting with the reddish-brown coat. Blackish areas in males include a distinct dorsal stripe, shoulder stripes, flank stripes, legs, chest, tail, face, and beard. Underparts usually black. Older males are darker. Large head, face convex, ears large in horizontal position, amber small eyes, long neck. Calluses on knees. Hooves are heavy and black. Males have thick, horizontal, curled horns, with subtriangular cross section. Females are smaller, with smaller and slightly diverging horns, no beard, a black dorsal stripe, black lower legs and abdomen, and a black line between the eye and the nose.

Capra hircus var. *majorcan*

OTHER NAMES Balearean Goat, Majorcan Agrimi. *French*: Chèvre balear. *German*: Mallorca Ziege. *Spanish*: Cabra mallorquina, boc balear, cabra cimarrón balear. *Russian*: Майоркская домашняя (одичавшая) коза.

SUBSPECIES Considered to be feral descendants of early Domestic Goats (*Capra hircus*). They were introduced to Mediterranean islands in prehistoric times and are clearly distinct from modern domestic and feral goats. Morphologically, the Majorcan Wild Goat is homogeneous and, against all the other Domestic Goats, displays only one phenotypic manifestation visible genetic characters, which is the expected one for a wild Caprid.

SIMILAR SPECIES Only goats depicting the clear "black cross over reddish brown coat" are considered Majorcan Wild Goat. Feral goats usually show three or more colors in a spotted pattern.

REPRODUCTION *Gestation*: 5 months. *Young per Birth*: 1, rarely 2. *Weaning*: 10 months. Sexual Maturity: 2 years (♀). *Life Span*: 15 years. Rut lasts from July until the end of October, with a peak in August and September.

BEHAVIOR *Family Group*: Small groups of 2-5 animals, composed of ♀ and offspring up to 2 years of age. Adult ♂ usually live alone. During the rut, mixed groups may include feral goats. *Diet*: Herbivorous, they browse on leaves, twigs, and weeds and are therefore highly destructive feeders. Able to climb trees and feed in the branches. *Predators*: Dog. They are diurnal and all senses are good.

DISTRIBUTION *Native*: Spain. Island of Mallorca (Spain), one of the Balearic Islands in the Mediterranean Sea, on the entire W coast and NW in the Sierra de Tramuntana and the Formentor, Alcudia, and Artá peninsulas.

HABITAT Mountainous areas, at elevations of 0-1,450 meters.

STATUS Estimated population in 2007 was 1,500-2,000 individuals, out of a total of 10,000, including hybrids and feral descendants of modern Domestic Goats. These animals are completely wild, the biggest threat to their existence being the crossbreeding with domestic livestock. The impressive horns have gained an economic value in recent years.

PHOTO CREDITS ♂: *Pau Coca*, Sierra de Tramuntana, Mallorca (Spain). ♀: *Matthias Buehler*, Torrent de Pareis, Mallorca (Spain). Head ♂: *Carlos Pache*, Sierra de Tramuntana, Mallorca (Spain). Head ♀: *Dani Alvarez Cañellas*, Alcudia, Mallorca (Spain).

Nilgiri Tahr
NILGIRITRAGUS HYLOCRIUS

BL: 150 cm (♂), 110 cm (♀). SH: 100-110 cm (♂), 80 cm (♀). TL: 9-15 cm. W: 80-100 kg (♂), 50 kg (♀). HL: To 44.5 cm (♂), to 30 cm (♀). Largest Tahr, stockily built, with coarse fur. Significant sexual dimorphism. Females and immature males yellowish brown to gray, with underparts paler, face with no distinctive markings, dark stripe running down the dorsal midline. As males age, their pelage darkens to a deep chocolate or blackish brown, with white knee spots marking the anterior surface of the front legs. Silvery saddle patch marks the back, becoming lighter and more defined with age. Face nearly black, fawn-colored ring encircling the eye, silvery stripe on side of face. No beard. Short curving horns in both sexes, rising nearly parallel before diverging and curling downward. Front surface highly convex with deeply transverse wrinkles. Females significantly lighter than males, with smaller horns.

Young

♀

♂

Juvenile

356

Nilgiritragus hylocrius

OTHER NAMES Nilgiri Ibex, South Indian Tahr. *French*: Tahr des monts Nilgiri. *German*: Nilgiritahr. *Spanish*: Tahr del Nilgiri. *Russian*: Нильгирийский тар. *Tamil*: Varai ádoo, varayadu, warri-adu. *Malayalam*: Mulla átu. *Canarese*: Kard-ardu.

SUBSPECIES Monotypic. Some authors have placed it as a subspecies of the Himalayan Tahr (*H. jemlahicus*).

SIMILAR SPECIES The largest of the three Tahr species, being just slightly larger than the Himalayan Tahr. Unlike the coat of the Himalayan Tahr, the coat of the Nilgiri Tahr is short, probably as an adaptation to the wet climate this species inhabits, and the horns also lack the ridged keel seen in Himalayan Tahr. ♀ have two nipples, unlike the two other species of Tahr, which have four.

REPRODUCTION *Gestation*: 178-190 days. *Young per Birth*: 1, rarely 2. *Weaning*: 4-6 months. *Sexual Maturity*: 3 years. *Life Span*: 9 years. The main breeding season is from June to August during the monsoons. There is a corresponding peak in births in the cool, clear weather of January and February. ♀ are highly protective of their offspring and will adopt threatening postures if other herd members approach too closely. For the first few weeks of life, the infant lies hidden while the mother forages, but by 2 months of age the kid follows its mother.

BEHAVIOR *Family Group*: Groups as small as 6 animals or as large as 150, but typically a herd contains 11-71 individuals. Mixed herds are common, as are all-♂ groups and maternal herds composed of adult ♀ and their young. *Diet*: Grazers, feeding on herbs and grasses. *Main Predators*: Leopard, dhole, tiger. Nilgiri Tahr inhabit montane grasslands at elevations of 1,200-2,600 m above sea level. The climate of the region is very wet, with approximately 4 m of precipitation falling every year. Active from dawn to late evening, grazing most frequently in the early morning and late afternoon. When the sun is at its peak, they retreat to higher, rockier terrain in order to rest in the relatively secure shade of cliffs. While the herd rests, at least one member (usually a ♀) remains alert, serving as a sentinel and watching for predators. These animals are sharp-sighted and able to spot danger approaching from below at a distance, but are less aware of danger descending from above. Alarm is sounded as a whistle or snort. If two ♂ are evenly matched, a fight will develop, but not before a ritualized pre-fight display, in which ♂ will lower their heads, arch their backs, and walk with a stiff-legged gait.

DISTRIBUTION *Native*: India. Limited to approximately 5% of the Western Ghats in S India, in Kerala and Tamil Nadu in S India. The animals are more or less confined to altitudes of 1200-2600 m.

HABITAT High elevations on cliffs, grass-covered hills, and open terrain.

STATUS Endangered. Estimated population is 2,000-2,500 individuals; current trends indicate that these numbers are in decline.

PHOTO CREDITS ♂: *Michael Smith*, Eravikulam NP (India). Head ♂: *Meera Rajesh*, Munnar (India). ♀: *Sivanagk*, Kerala (India). Head ♀: *Mugdha Srineet,* Anaimudi, Kerala (India). Young: *Paul Williams*, Kerala (India). Juvenile: *Paul Williams*, Western Ghats (India).

Dall's Sheep

OVIS DALLI DALLI

BL: 130-180 cm (♂), 130-160 cm (♀). SH: 91-109 cm (♂), 78-89 cm (♀). TL: 7-11.5 cm (♂), 7-9 cm (♀). W: 73-114 kg (♂), 45-50 kg (♀). HL: 80-100 cm (♂). Coat pure white or creamy white, although variation is present. A few black hairs on the tail may be present. Belly white, as are the backs of the legs. White rump patch. Pelage of a fine wool undercoat and stiff, long, and hollow guard hairs, thicker in winter. Characteristic yellowish-brown iris. Horns amber or almost transparent; in males massive and curled, flaring outward at the tips after making a full curl. As rams mature their horns form a circle. Horns slimmer than in other North American sheep, more triangular in cross section and relatively longer. Females lighter than males, with short, slender horns. Newborn lambs may have considerable amounts of brown in their coat.

Juvenile

♂   ♀

summer coat

Young

winter coat

Ovis dalli dalli

OTHER NAMES Dall Sheep, Thinhorn Sheep, White Sheep. *French*: Mouflon de Dall. German: Dall-Schaf, Alaska-Schneeschaf. *Spanish*: Carnero de Dall, muflón de Dall. *Russian*: Баран Далла.

SUBSPECIES Considered as a subspecies of *O. dalli*: *O. d. dalli* (Dall's Sheep), *O. d. stonei* (Stone Sheep). Includes *kenaiensis* (Kenai Sheep) of Alaska's Kenai Peninsula, not considered a valid subspecies by most authors.

REPRODUCTION *Gestation*: 173 days. *Young per Birth*: 1, rarely 2. *Weaning*: 4-5 months. *Sexual Maturity*: 30 months. *Life Span*: 19 years. Polygynous mating system in which dominant ♂ breed most often. Lambs are born in late May or early June. Ewes seek solitude and protection in the most rugged cliffs to bear their lamb. Ewes give birth and the mother-lamb pair remains in the cliffs until the lambs are strong enough to travel. Lambs are able to travel with their mother within 24 hours. Lambs are precocious and actively play among themselves.

BEHAVIOR *Family Group:* Ewes in flocks with other ewes, lambs, yearling and immature rams. Adult rams in bachelor bands that do not associate with ewes until the mating season. *Diet*: Herbivorous, grazing primarily on grasses and sedges, also lichens and mosses in smaller quantities; mineral licks. *Main Predators*: Wolf, coyote, golden eagle, grizzly bear, wolverine. Well-developed social system. Adult rams live in bachelor bands that do not associate with ewes until the mating season in late November and early December. Rams establish a dominance hierarchy in the summer, in which rank is determined by horn size. This ranking is not just for access to ♀, but also for social order. Larger rams typically win fights and the dominance hierarchy affects breeding opportunities. These fights include aggressive broadside displays, vigorous kicking, jump threats, and horn clashes. Some ♂ even throw competitors off cliffs. Most populations occupy distinct summer and winter ranges, although some are sedentary. Migrations are correlated with snow depth, temperature, and plant phenology. Most of the year is spent in the winter range in windswept areas that expose forage.

DISTRIBUTION *Native*: Canada, United States. Most of Alaska's mountain ranges; the extreme NW corner of British Columbia; the N and W Yukon Territory; and the Mackenzie Mountains in the NortWest Territories.

HABITAT Arctic and subarctic regions but occur mostly in high mountain ranges. They typically inhabit dry mountainous regions and select subalpine grasslands and shrublands. They are dependent upon steep, rugged cliffs and outcrops that provide escape terrain from predators. They use nearby open grass and meadows for feeding. In winter they prefer areas with light snowfall and strong winds that remove snow and expose forage.

STATUS Least Concern. Dal's Sheep numbers are high and are stable throughout their range. Estimated population was 60,000-90,000 animals in 2012.

PHOTO CREDITS ♂ summer: *Shumon Huque*, Denali NP and Preserve, Cantwell, AK (USA). ♂ winter: *Alex Meyer*, Denver Zoo (USA). Head ♂: Denver Zoo (USA). ♀: *Alaska National Parks*, Denali NP (USA). Head ♀: *Drew Avery*, Denver Zoo (USA). Young and juvenile: *Sergey Chichagov*, Tallinn Zoo (Estonia).

Stone Sheep

OVIS DALLI STONEI

BL: 130-180 cm (♂), 130-160 cm (♀). SH: 91-109 cm (♂), 78-89 cm (♀). TL: 7-11.5 cm (♂), 7-9 cm (♀). W: 73-122 kg (♂), 45-50 kg (♀). HL: To 127 cm (♂), 15-20 cm (♀). Slightly larger and stockier than Dall's Sheep, with a larger and wider head, and heavier, darker-colored horns. Coat varies greatly in color and pattern, ranging from almost white to gray and brown or nearly black; various colors may be found in the same group. Head and neck lighter in color than the body. Muzzle, belly, backs of legs, and rump white. Tail black, usually connected by a dark band to the dark hairs of the back. Older rams sometimes have a dark band partially across the white belly. Horns brown or dark amber, with considerable variation in size and shape. Females considerably smaller than males, with short, slim horns.

Young

♀

♂

Ovis dalli stonei

OTHER NAMES *French*: Mouflon du Stone. *German*: Steinschaf, Schwarzes Schneeschaf. *Spanish*: Carnero de Stone. *Russian*: Баран Стоуна.

SUBSPECIES Considered as a subspecies of *O. dalli: O. d. dalli* (Dall's Sheep), *O. d. stonei* (Stone Sheep). Includes *fannini* (Fannin Sheep) of N Yukon, *niger* (Black Sheep), *liardensis* (Liard Sheep), and *cowani* (Mount Logan Sheep), now considered color variations of Stone Sheep, not valid subspecies.

SIMILAR SPECIES Stone Sheep is somewhat larger and chunkier than Dall's Sheep, with a larger and relatively wider skull and heavier, darker-colored horns, and it is not black. Dall's and Stone Sheep intergrade, with a great many color variations resulting. In general, any sheep that is not pure white, other than the tail, is treated as Stone Sheep.

REPRODUCTION *Gestation*: 173 days. *Young per Birth*: 1, rarely 2. *Weaning*: 4-5 months. *Sexual Maturity*: 30 months. *Life Span*: 19 years. Most lambs are born in May, but lambing extends into June. Lambing habitat differs from non-breeding habitat in that there is always escape terrain, steep rugged cliffs or rock outcrops to which ewes and lambs can flee. Older ♂ often forage on the periphery of lambing areas and usually leave them for summer range before the nursery groups depart. ♀ seek seclusion in the cliffs to give birth.

BEHAVIOR *Family Group:* ♀ in flocks with other ♀, lambs, yearling and immature ♂. Adult ♂ in bachelor bands that do not associate with ♀ until the mating season. *Diet:* Herbivorous, grazing primarily on grasses and sedges, also lichens and mosses in smaller quantities; mineral licks of calcium phosphate or calcium magnesium concentrate, especially in the spring and summer. *Main Predators:* Wolf, coyote, golden eagle, grizzly bear, wolverine. Gregarious, uncommonly seen alone, although they may become widely scattered during summer. ♂ and nursery groups usually are apart during the summer months. There are relatively few aggressive interactions among ♀ over feeding or bedding sites. Dominance among ♂ helps determine access to ewes. Contests may last over 90 minutes, after which the ♂ will peacefully graze together. Struggles for dominance occur during summer.

DISTRIBUTION *Native*: Canada. N British Columbia N of the Peace River, extending N into the S Yukon Territory.

HABITAT Alpine areas and cliffs. Also inhabit lower-elevation subalpine brushlands and lower forested areas. The highest concentrations are found on lower mountain areas to the NE of high-elevation mountains, where the high precipitation and winds result in good graminoid production, winter snow removal, and summer drying.

STATUS Least Concern. Estimated population was 13,500 individuals in 2003.

PHOTO CREDITS ♂: *Travis Shinabarger*, Northern Rockies, British Columbia (Canada). ♀ and head ♀: *Arthur Chapman*, Muncho Lake, British Columbia (Canada) and *Travis Shinabarger*, Northern Rockies, British Columbia (Canada). Young: *Kathleen and Theo Mosman*, Muncho Lake, British Columbia (Canada) and *Kathleen I. Kent*, British Columbia (Canada).

Rocky Mountain Bighorn Sheep

OVIS CANADENSIS CANADENSIS

BL: 109-195 cm (♂), 96-126 cm (♀). SH: 102-112 cm (♂), 76-91 cm (♀). TL: 10-15 cm. W: 90-135 (♂), 45-79 kg (♀). HL: To 126 cm (♂), to 26 cm (♀). Largest sheep in North America. Heavy body. Smooth coat consisting of guard hairs and dense fleece, varying from dark brown to grayish. Back of legs, muzzle, and eye patch all white. Rump patch large and white, surrounding the dark tail. Dorsal stripe usually interrupted or absent. Belly white in the groin area, sometimes extending forward onto the chest. No neck ruff. Brown horns found in both sexes, much larger in males. In males, horns are massive and curl up, back over the ears, then down, forward, and up past the cheeks; very thick at the base, tending to carry the thickness throughout their length. In old males horns may begin a second curl. Females smaller and lighter than males, with slender and saber-like horns, never forming more than half a curl.

♀

♂

Juvenile

♂

Young

Ovis canadensis canadensis

OTHER NAMES Mountain Sheep, California Bighorn. *French*: Mouflon d'Amérique, mouflon du Canada, mouflon Pachycère. *German*: Dickhornschaf. *Spanish*: Borrego cimarrón, carnero del Canadá, carnero salvaje, musmón, carnero de las Rocosas, muflón de las montañas, muflón canadiense. *Russian*: Баран (толсторог) Скалистых гор. *Algonquin*: Manteenesh. *Apache*: Dibetii, bideém biyeshd nechaahi. *Chipewyan*: Bálayttëné. *Locheux*: Divii. *Navajo*: Tábaastiin. *South-Slavey*: Doo.

SUBSPECIES Considered as a subspecies of *O. canadensis* (Bighorn Sheep): *O. c. canadensis* (Rocky Mountain Bighorn Sheep), *O. c. nelsoni* (Desert Bighorn Sheep), *O. c. sierrae* (Sierra Nevada Bighorn Sheep).

REPRODUCTION *Gestation*: 175 days. *Young per Birth*: 1. *Weaning*: 4-6 months. *Sexual Maturity*: 2.5 years (♀), 3 years (♂), although they do not generally breed until age 7. *Life Span:* 14 years. In N populations, mating occurs in late November and early December, and parturition coincides with warmer temperatures and the growth of spring vegetation, in late May and early June. Newborn lambs have a woolly, light-colored coat and small horn buds. They stay hidden for about a week, then follow their mother. Within a few weeks, the lambs of the herd form bands of their own and seek out their mother for nursing only occasionally.

BEHAVIOR *Family Group*: Usually in single-sex herds of around 10 animals. In winter, mixed herds of 100 animals may form. *Diet*: More browse and less grass than other subspecies. *Main Predators*: Wolf, cougar, golden eagle, coyote, bear, bobcat, lynx. Extremely agile and nimble, able to move quickly over uneven, steep surfaces. Remarkable swimmers. These sheep are renowned for the spectacular competition among ♂ during the breeding season. Dominance hierarchies among ♂ are based on horn size, and ♂ with significantly smaller horns generally act subordinate to large-horned ♂. ♂ with similarly sized horns, however, battle among each other for breeding privileges in the style of a face-off. Facing each other from a distance, they run toward each other with heads lowered, rearing up and crashing their horns together. Population densities average 2 animals per km². N populations usually migrate seasonally between winter and summer home ranges, which can involve movements of 10-20 km. They are primarily diurnal and spend the better part of the day eating, then lying down to chew their cud (partially digested food). They retire for the night to their bedding areas, which may be used for many years. When temperatures rise, they will graze at night and rest during the heat of the day.

DISTRIBUTION *Native*: Canada, United States. W Alberta, British Columbia, SE Arizona, Colorado, W and central Idaho, W Montana, E, NE, and central Nevada, SW, N, and central New Mexico, NE Oregon, SW North Dakota, SW South Dakota (non-indigenous), NE Utah, SE Washington, NW and central Wyoming, NW Nebraska.

HABITAT Mountain ridges and basins, usually above timberline, but often in timbered areas as well.

STATUS Least Concern. Estimated population probably exceeds 55,000 individuals.

PHOTO CREDITS ♂: *Jean-Edouard Rozey*, Yellowstone NP (USA). Head ♂: *Shanesabin*. ♀, head ♀: *Lorrie Herric,* Radium (Canada). Young: *Rob Dodson*, Badlands NP (USA), *Tina Leatham*, Yellowstone NP (USA), and *Brandon Smith*, Alberta (Canada).

Desert Bighorn Sheep

OVIS CANADENSIS NELSONI

BL: 109-195 cm (♂), 96-126 cm (♀). SH: 83-97 cm (♂), 54 cm (♀). TL: 10-15 cm. W: 72-90 kg (♂), 34-58 kg (♀). HL: 91-107 cm (♂), 25-33 cm (♀). Smaller and slenderer than the Rocky Mountain Bighorn, with a smaller head, bigger ears, paler color, and shorter coat. General color from light buff to chocolate brown, with a deeper reddish tinge on the neck and shoulders, and more grayish tinge on the underparts. White rump patch smaller and usually divided by a dark tail stripe. Muzzle is lighter, almost white. Brown horns, almost as large as those of a Rocky Mountain Bighorn, tending to have more flare. Females smaller than males, with short, thin horns, larger than in Rocky Mountain Bighorn females.

♀

Young

♂ 2-3 years

♂

Ovis canadensis nelsoni

OTHER NAMES Desert Sheep. *French*: Mouflon du desert. *German*: Nuslen Dickhornschaf, Wüsten-Dickhornschaf. *Spanish*: Borrego cimarrón. *Russian*: Пустынный баран (толсторог).

SUBSPECIES Considered as a subspecies of *O. canadensis* (Bighorn Sheep): *O. c. canadensis* (Rocky Mountain Bighorn Sheep), *O. c. nelsoni* (Desert Bighorn Sheep), *O. c. sierrae* (Sierra Nevada Bighorn Sheep). Includes *nelsoni* (Nelson Bighorn), *mexicana* (Mexican Bighorn), *cremnobates* (Lower California or Peninsular Bighorn), and *weemsi* (Weems Bighorn), not considered valid subspecies by most authors.

SIMILAR SPECIES Smaller than Stone Sheep, Dall´s Sheep, and Siberian Snow Sheep.

REPRODUCTION *Gestation*: 150-180 days. *Young per Birth*: 1. *Weaning*: 4-6 months. *Sexual Maturity*: 18 months (♀), 3 years (♂), although they do not generally breed until age 7. *Life Span:* 14 years. Breeding may occur anytime in the desert due to suitable climatic conditions. Births occur from January through June, due to unpredictable precipitation patterns.

BEHAVIOR *Family Group*: Single-sex herds of 8-10 individuals, sometimes herds of 100 are observed. *Diet*: Grasses; when grasses are unavailable, they turn to other food sources, such as sedges, forbs, or cacti; while they may forage for considerable distances, they must return to drink every few days during hot weather. *Main Predators*: Mountain lion. Well adapted to living in the desert heat and cold, and their body temperature can safely fluctuate several degrees. Most active during daylight, moving to traditional bedding areas at night. During the summer they rest during the hot midday, on cliffs above their water source. Water is critical to survival. In early spring of years with good winter rains they get enough water from the grass they eat to go without drinking. At other times they must trek to a spring or water-holding depression at least every third day. Lactating ♀ need to drink almost every day. ♂ battle to determine the dominant animal, which then gains possession of the ♀. Facing each other, ♂ charge head-on from distances of 6 m or more, crashing their massive horns together with tremendous impact, until one or the other ceases. During the rut, ♂ snort loudly. The lambs bleat, and ♀ respond with a guttural "ba-aa." They also utter throaty rumbles when frightened. They have extremely acute eyesight, which aids in jumping in steep terrain.

DISTRIBUTION *Native*: Mexico, United States. Nelson Bighorn: SE California, S Nevada, SW Utah, and NW Arizona. Mexican Bighorn: most of Arizona, SW New Mexico, N Sonora, and locally in Chihuahua and Coahuila. Peninsular Bighorn: N Baja California Norte, extending northward into S California. Weems Bighorn: from S Baja California Norte, extending S through Baja California Sur.

HABITAT Desert mountains with sufficient permanent water.

STATUS Least Concern. In 1993, population was estimated at 19,000. Peninsular Bighorn Sheep, a distinct population segment, is Endangered, with an estimated population in 2008 of 800.

PHOTO CREDITS ♂ and head ♀: *Andrew Cattoir,* Lake Mead NRA (USA). Head ♂: *Sergey Chichagov*, San Diego Safari Park (USA). ♀: *David Scott Allen*, Arizona-Sonora Desert Museum (USA). Young: *waltarrrrr*, Los Angeles Zoo (USA). Juvenile ♂: *Michael T. Vaugh*, San Diego Safari Park (USA).

Sierra Nevada Bighorn Sheep

OVIS CANADENSIS SIERRAE

BL: 152 cm (♂), 96-126 cm (♀). SH: 91 cm (♂), 76 cm (♀). TL: 10-15 cm. W: 54-99 kg (♂), 45-67 kg (♀). HL: To 126 cm (♂), to 26 cm (♀). Stocky build, with relatively short legs. Considerably smaller than the Rocky Mountain Bighorn. Coat not as heavy, lighter in color, being more gray than brown. There is some seasonal change in coloration due to the shedding of a thicker winter layer. Normally a dark stripe extends from the dorsal area through the white rump patch to connect with the dark tail. Ears longer. Horns shorter and less massive, and tend to have more flare. Horns found in both sexes, much larger in males. In females, horns slender and saber-like, never forming more than half a curl. Males larger than females.

♀

♂
Juvenile

♂

ssp. *canadensis*   ssp. *sierrae*

Ovis canadensis sierrae

OTHER NAMES California Bighorn Sheep. *French*: Mouflon du California. *German*: California Dickhornschaf. *Spanish*: Borrego de California. *Russian*: Баран (толсторог) заснеженных гор.

SUBSPECIES Considered as a subspecies of *O. canadensis* (Bighorn Sheep): *O. c. canadensis* (Rocky Mountain Bighorn Sheep), *O. c. nelsoni* (Desert Bighorn Sheep), *O. c. sierrae* (Sierra Nevada Bighorn Sheep). Includes the California Bighorn (*O. c. californiana*), which is not considered a valid subspecies by most authors.

SIMILAR SPECIES Desert Bighorn has a tight narrow curl, while Sierra Nevada Bighorn has a more splayed horn conformation with a less pronounced curl. Rocky Mountain Bighorn has larger and less flared horns.

REPRODUCTION *Gestation*: 174 days. *Young per Birth*: 1, rarely 2. *Weaning*: 4-6 months. *Sexual Maturity*: 2.5 years (♀), 3 years (♂), although they do not generally breed until age 7. *Life Span*: 12 years. Breeding occurs during late fall and early winter, mostly November and December, when Bighorn Sheep are usually still at high elevations. Lambing occurs between late April and early July on precipitous rocky slopes where Bighorn are relatively safe from predators.

BEHAVIOR *Family Group*: Usually in single-sex herds of around 10 animals. In winter, mixed herds of 100 animals may form. *Diet:* Grasses, forbs, woody vegetation. *Main Predators:* Wolf, cougar, golden eagle, coyote, bear, bobcat, lynx. Primarily diurnal; nights generally are spent on rocky slopes, but may venture a short distance away from rocky escape terrain to feed during daylight. They may obtain needed moisture from forage or occasional consumption of snow. Gregarious, usually spatially segregated by sex, except during mating season. ♀ generally remain with the herd in which they were born. ♂ older than two years of age remain apart from ♀ and younger ♀ for most of the year. The groups come together in late fall and winter and concentrate in suitable winter habitat. During this time, ♂ compete for dominance with behaviors like horn clashes. Elevational migration allows Sierra Nevada Bighorn Sheep to increase their annual nutritional intake by following the new growth of forage from low-elevation winter ranges (early growth) to alpine summer ranges (later growth). Bighorn Sheep typically use the same winter and summer ranges each year, although variation exists in whether an individual winters high or low every year. Annual home ranges of Sierra Bighorn average about 50 km² for ♀ and 100 km² for ♂.

DISTRIBUTION Native: Canada, United States. S British Columbia, SW Idaho, NW Nevada, SE Oregon, N, central, and SE Washington, NW Utah. Present United States populations are largely the result of transplants from British Columbia. California Bighorn consists of only a small population located in the S and central Sierra Nevada (California, USA).

HABITAT Less steep and rough than that of the Rocky Mountain Bighorn, with more grass and less browse.

STATUS Endangered. In 2012 the population estimate was over 500 animals.

PHOTO CREDITS ♂: *Alan Broccolo,* British Columbia (Canada). Head ♂ and ♀: *Baker County Tourism,* OR (USA). Young: *June Gempler,* Malheur County, OR (USA).

Snow Sheep

OVIS NIVICOLA

BL: 136-188 cm (♂), 126-156 cm (♀). SH: 93-112 cm (♂), 90-94 cm (♀). TL: 7.5-13 cm. W: 56-120 kg (♂), 33-68 kg (♀). HL: 69-93 cm (♂), 23-28 cm (♀). Large sheep. Grayish-brown coat, accented by a small patch of light hair on the buttocks. Woolly winter coat light, milky coffee color. Fronts of the legs dark chocolate brown, while the rear edges may have whitish markings. Dark band, running across the nose between the eyes and muzzle, contrasting greatly with the bright white rostrum. Ears are small and dark gray in color. Horns, found in both sexes, lighter than those of the related Bighorn Sheep, with up to 35% less horn substance. The horns curl backward, downward, and upward around the ears, corkscrewing outward in old males as the horns begin their second revolution. Horns in females are thinner and shorter, curving backward in a saber-like fashion.

ssp. *borealis*

ssp. *koriakorum*

♂

ssp. *nivicola*

♀

ssp. *alleni*

368

Ovis nivicola nivicola, borealis

Ovis nivicola alleni

Ovis nivicola lydekkeri

Ovis nivicola koriakorum

OTHER NAMES Siberian Bighorn Sheep, Northeast Asiatic Thinhorned Sheep. *French*: Mouflon des neiges. *German*: Schneeschaf. *Spanish*: Oveja de las nieves, carnero nival. *Jakut*: Tschubuku, tschubukun. *Russian*: Снежный баран.

SUBSPECIES *O. n. nivicola* (Kamchatka Snow Sheep): Kamchatka Peninsula (Russia); grayish brown or grizzled, small white rump, muzzle white, but brown facial band almost lost, large horns. *O. n. borealis* (Putorana, Norilsk, or Syverma Snow Sheep): N-central Siberia, Putoran Mountains S of Taymyr Peninsula (Russia); dark grayish-brown winter coat, white belly, large white rump patch. *O. n. alleni* (Okhotsk and Kolyma Snow Sheep): E Siberia, Yablonovy and Stanovoy mountains, to Verkhoyansky District in the N (Russia); larger subspecies, light yellowish-gray summer coat, grizzled grayish brown in winter, largest white area on the forehead. *O. n. lydekkeri* (Yakutia Snow Sheep): NE Siberia, from Lena River in the W to Stanovoy Mountains in the E, and Verkhoyansky District in the S (Russia); similar to *O. n. alleni*, slightly smaller, less white on the forehead, the most widely distributed. *O. n. koriakorum* (Koryak and Chukotka Snow Sheep): Chukchi Peninsula and Koryak District (Russia); dwarf form of Kamchatka Snow Sheep, white muzzle and rump patch not as pronounced.

REPRODUCTION *Gestation*: 8.5 months. *Young per Birth*: 1. *Weaning*: 4-6 months. *Sexual Maturity*: 2 years (♀), 5 years (♂). *Life Span*: 18 years. The mating season occurs in November-December. ♀ isolate themselves from the herd before lambing, which occurs in rugged, rocky sites. Young ♂ are prevented from mating by older ♂. During rut, ♂ may travel up to 15 km a day in search of estrous ♀.

BEHAVIOR *Family Group*: Large groups generally segregated by sex. *Diet*: Grasses, lichens. *Main Predators*: Large carnivores. Diurnal. A well-adapted mountain dweller, extremely agile and nimble, able to move quickly over steep, uneven terrain. Within bachelor herds, a dominance hierarchy is formed based primarily on horn size. These hierarchies remain relatively stable, even in the breeding season, with larger ♂ getting the majority of the mating rights. However, if two ♂ have approximately equal-sized horns, the dominant/subordinate relationship is decided in combat. Facing each other from a distance, they run toward each other with heads lowered, rearing up and crashing their horns together in an attempt to throw their rival off balance.

DISTRIBUTION *Native*: Russian Federation. Distributed throughout most of the mountain regions of E Siberia (Russia). The main distribution area begins just E of the Lena River and stretches as far as the Tenkany Mountains on the Chukotsk Peninsula on the W edge of the Bering Strait. Also occurs in the volcanic mountains running down the Kamchatka Peninsula, and the S limit of the species appears to be in the Yablonovy Mountains, S of the Lena River. In addition, a totally isolated population (*O. n. borealis*) is restricted to the Putoran Mountains S of the Tamyr Peninsula, E of the Yenisey River, and separated from the nearest Yakutian population by about 1,000 km.

HABITAT Alpine meadows with rocky terrain in NE Russia.

STATUS Least Concern. Estimated population is 57,700 animals, 40,000 located in Yakutia.

PHOTO CREDITS *Andrey Kotkin*, Zoo Novosibirsk (Russia) and *Yuriy Yarovenko*, Kamchatcka (Russia).

Altai Argali

OVIS AMMON

BL: 172-200 cm (♂), 167-174 cm (♀). SH: 115-120 cm (♂), 100-114 cm (♀). TL: 9.5-12 cm. W: 101-175 kg (♂), 80-100 kg (♀). HL: To 180 cm (♂), 40-56 cm (♀). Largest wild sheep in the world, with the most massive horns. General color in winter is pale to dark brown tinged with white hairs. Large saddle-like white spots on the back. Rump patch, belly, lower legs, and face are white. Summer coat is much shorter and lighter, with the upper parts a uniformly speckled brown and white, and the rump patch only slightly lighter than the back. This subspecies does not grow a neck ruff. Massive horns, with rounded frontal edges, heavily corrugated, forming more than a complete circle when fully developed. Females are brown or grayish brown in summer, and gray or dark gray in winter, and have the longest horns among all Argali.

♀

♂

winter coat   summer coat

Ovis ammon

OTHER NAMES Siberian Argali. *French*: Mouflon Altai. *German*: Altai-Wildschaf. *Spanish*: Argalí del Altai. *Russian*: Алтайский аргали.

SUBSPECIES Monotypic. The name *O. ammon* (Argali) formerly included *O. ammon* (Altai Argali), *O. collium* (Kazakhstan, Karaganda, or Sair Argali), *O. jubata* (Shanxi, Northern China Argali), *O. darwini* (Gobi, Mongolian Argali), *O. hodgsoni* (Tibetan Argali), *O. karelini* (Tianshan, Ala Tau Argali), *O. nigrimontana* (Karatau Argali), *O. polii* (Marco Polo Argali, Pamir Argali), and *O. severtzovi* (Severtzov's Argali) as subspecies: these are all elevated to full species here. Includes *adametzi* (NW China), *altaica* (S Altai), *ammon* (Altai), *asiaticus* (upper Irtysh River), *daurica, mongolica, przewalskii,* and *typica,* with *ammon* having priority.

SIMILAR SPECIES The horns are shorter than in Marco Polo Argali, but are more massive. Altai Argali and Gobi Argali (*darwini*) lack throat ruff. Argali horns have two full circles of spiral, with tops always directed sideways, which is distinct from those of other *Ovis* species.

REPRODUCTION *Gestation*: 155-165 days. *Young per Birth*: 1. *Weaning*: 4 months. *Sexual Maturity*: 2.5 years (♀), 5 years (♂). *Life Span*: 13 years. Mating mainly occurs in November through mid-December. Lambs are born at the end of April and beginning of May.

BEHAVIOR *Family Group*: Herds of ♀ with lambs and yearlings of both sexes, up to 27 individuals. Mixed herds in the mating season. *Diet*: Grasses, herbs, sedges. *Main Predators*: Gray wolf. Active in broad daylight, even in summer, due to the cold habitats in which they live, alternating feeding and resting periods, with two peaks of activity, mornings and evenings. In winter, active throughout the day, with a period of rest at midnight.

DISTRIBUTION *Native*: China, Kazakhstan, Mongolia, Russia. Found mainly in the Altai Mountains of W Mongolia. Extends marginally N into the Gorno-Altai and Tuva republics of Siberian Russia, W into extreme NE Kazakhstan, and SW into N Xinjiang in China; however, these are mostly summer visitors that retreat back into Mongolia from September onward. Recent genetic studies may suggest that all Argali in Mongolia represent a single species, instead of the two species commonly recognized: Altai Argali (*O. ammon*) and Gobi Argali (*O. darwini*).

HABITAT Undulating terrain with adjoining rough, steep, rocky outcrops and scree that they can use as escape terrain. Arid steppe habitats, with minimal winter precipitation and low yearly temperatures. They avoid more humid habitats and tall vegetation.

STATUS Near Threatened. Estimated population of 9,000 animals in Mongolia, 600 in Russia, and probably fewer than several hundred in China and Kazakhstan. Major threats include competition with livestock and illegal hunting.

PHOTO CREDITS Head ♀: *Andrey Kotkin,* Novosibirsk Zoo (Russia). ♂ summer: Reconstruction by *José R. Castelló.* ♂ winter: *Baatargal Otgonbayar,* Ikh Nart National Reserve (Mongolia).

Tibetan Argali

OVIS HODGSONI

BL: 167 cm (♂), 148 cm (♀). SH: 115-132 cm (♂), 99-112 cm (♀). TL: 5.5 cm. W: 98-105 kg (♂), 68 kg (♀). HL: 86-140 cm (♂), 36-46 cm (♀). In winter, upper parts grayish brown, with the throat, chest, rump, underparts, and inside of legs white. Head is brown with a white muzzle. Males have a ruff of long white hairs on neck and throat, encompassing most of the neck's surface, and a dorsal crest, both of which are more prominent in the winter coat. Dark lateral strip dividing the upper parts from the white belly. Whitish rump patch surrounding the tail. Summer coat shorter and lighter. Horns less massive than in Altai or Gobi Argali, forming a tighter spiral with little or no flare, usually less than a full curl. Tips usually broken or broomed, surface wrinkles close together and only moderately prominent, frontal edges rounded. Females have a short, dark throat ruff, with horns much smaller.

♀

Young

♂

♂
Juvenile

summer coat

372

Ovis hodgsoni

OTHER NAMES Gansu Argali. *French*: Argali du Tibet, mouflon du Tibet. *German*: Tibet-Argali, Tibet-Wildschaf. *Spanish*: Argalí del Tibet. *Russian*: Тибетский аргали.

SUBSPECIES Monotypic. Formerly considered a subspecies of *O. ammon* (Argali). Includes *ammonoides* (Himalayas), *bambhera* (Nepal), *blythi* (Tibet), *brookei* (Ladakh), *henrii* (Tibet), *dalailamae* (Gansu Argali, N Tibetan Plateau), and *hodgsoni* (S Tibetan Plateau), with *hodgsoni* having priority. More research is required to clarify the taxonomy of Argali species.

SIMILAR SPECIES Altai and Gobi Argali are larger, with massive horns and no neck ruff.

REPRODUCTION *Gestation*: 155-160 days. *Young per Birth*: 1, rarely 2. *Weaning*: 4 months. *Sexual Maturity*: 2 years (♀), 5 years (♂). *Life Span*: 9 years. Mating is polygynandrous, and occurs in December-January. Just prior to parturition, ♀ separate from the herd and retreat to an inaccessible spot to give birth. Births take place in late May and early June. The mother and her newborn lamb remain separated from the herd for several days, during which the mother takes brief forays to graze, while the newborn mostly lies motionless.

BEHAVIOR *Family Group*: Small herds of 2 to 15 animals, but groups as large as 50 have been spotted; ♂ and ♀ congregate during the rut. *Diet*: Herbs, sedges, and grasses. *Main Predators*: Wolf, snow leopard, leopard, eagle (lambs). Gregarious. It prefers open and rolling terrain as it runs, unlike Wild Goats, which climb into steep cliffs to escape from predators. They are most active at dawn and dusk. However, they forage and rest alternately throughout the day, but rest for a longer period during midday. The Argali's primary vocalizations are an alarm whistle and a warning hiss, which the sheep produces by blowing air through its nostrils. It is a relatively fast runner.

DISTRIBUTION *Native:* Bhutan, China, India, Nepal. A very extensive range, covering Ladakh (N India), N Nepal, N Sikkah (India), possibly N Bhutan, most of Tibet, NW Sichuan (China), extreme SW Gansu (China), and S Qinghai (China) to the Kun Lun and Burhan Budai mountains.

HABITAT Open, rolling plateau country at altitudes of 3,600-5,100 m. It uses higher areas during summer and descends to lower slopes during winter, when upper reaches get covered with snow.

STATUS Near Threatened. Estimated population of fewer than 7,000 animals in 1998. Its preference for open areas, often close to human settlements, makes it especially vulnerable. Another serious threat is the increasingly large livestock populations encroaching upon large sections of the Argali's habitat range.

PHOTO CREDITS ♂ and head ♂: *YongXin Zhan*, Beijing Zoo (China). ♀: *Jonas Livet,* Beijing Zoo (China). Head ♀, young, and juvenile: *Sergey Chichagov*, Beijing Zoo (China).

Marco Polo Argali

OVIS POLII

BL: 160-180 cm (♂), 143 cm (♀). SH: 101-120 cm (♂), 87 cm (♀). TL: 8.5-11 cm. W: 100-135 kg (♂), 48-61 kg (♀). HL: To 190 cm (♂), 33-49.5 cm (♀). Large, long-legged, light-boned Argali, with the longest horns. Summer coat is light, speckled reddish brown to grayish brown, with face, chest, underparts, rump patch, and legs white. Winter coat is longer, upper parts are a somewhat darker brown, with full white neck ruff extending to the brisket. Long, slender, homonymous horns, forming up to 1-1/2 open spiral, triangular in cross section, with a sharp orbital-nuchal edge. Females are considerably smaller, lack the white neck ruff, and have smaller horns.

Juvenile

♀

♂

Young

summer coat

winter coat

Ovis polii

OTHER NAMES Pamir Argali, Marco Polo Sheep. *French*: Mouflon de Marco Polo. *German*: Marco Polo Argali, Pamir-Wildschaf. *Spanish*: Argalí de Marco Polo, argali del Pamir. *Russian*: Аргали Марко Поло. *Chinese*: Pan yan.

SUBSPECIES Monotypic. Formerly considered a subspecies of *O. ammon* (Argali). Includes *polii, sculptorium, typica,* and *humei* (Humei Argali), with *polii* having priority.

SIMILAR SPECIES Humei Argali is similar in body size and coloration, but its horns are shorter, heavier, and have less flare. Altai Argali (*O. ammon*) has more massive horns. The neighboring Tianshan (*O. karelini*) and Kazakhstan Argali (*O. collium*) are smaller.

REPRODUCTION *Gestation*: 155-165 days. *Young per Birth*: 1-2. *Weaning*: 4 months. *Sexual Maturity*: 1.5-2.5 years (♀), 4-5 years (♂). *Life Span*: 13 years. Mating occurs in December-January, and births in May-June. Although ♂ are known to herd ♀, during the rut ♂ pair off with ♀ to reproduce. ♂ will approach a flock of ♀ and smell the urine of possible mates. The ♂ then splits from the flock to copulate with his ♀ and afterward, will often stay with the flock for a month or two.

BEHAVIOR *Family Group:* Herds segregated by sex, except for breeding season, up to 100 animals. *Diet:* Grasses, herbs, sedges. *Main Predators*: Wolf, snow leopard, leopard, dog. Active throughout the day, with feeding periods alternating with resting periods. On sunny, warm days they are active in the morning and evening. When the rut begins, ♂ begin to fight for dominance among their flocks. Only mature ♂ (over 6 years old) fight for dominance; the young will sometimes threaten older ♂, but never charge them. Mature ♂ fight by standing next to each other and spinning around, then one steps back and charges; they rise up on their hind legs when they clash with opponents, which is not common in lowland sheep and similar to the fighting habits of goats. ♂ commonly emit grunts while fighting and often chip their horns or break their noses.

DISTRIBUTION *Native:* Afghanistan, China, Kyrgyzstan, Pakistan, Tajikistan. Found in the E part of the Wakhan Corridor in Afghanistan, the Pamir Plateau in E Tajikistan, extending N into SE Kyrgyzstan S of the Naryn River, and the adjacent Pamir region of far W China. The N limit is the Naryn River. Humei Argali is found to the N of *polii* in SE Kyrgyzstan and far W China.

HABITAT More arid and barren than that of most other sheep grounds. At altitudes of 4,600-5,800 m, rarely below 3,000 m.

STATUS Near Threatened. Major threats include illegal hunting, overgrazing by domestic livestock, and habitat destruction by fuelwood collection. Estimated population of 25,000 in Tajikistan, 5,000 in Kyrgyzstan, 2,500 in China, fewer than 150 in Pakistan, and fewer than 100 in Afghanistan.

PHOTO CREDITS ♂: *Klaus Rudloff*, Tierpark Berlin (Germany). ♀ and young: *Nick Karpov,* Moscow Zoo (Russia). Juvenile: *Andrey Kotkin*, Moscow Zoo (Russia).

Gobi Argali

OVIS DARWINI

BL: 133-159 cm. SH: 104-117 cm (♂). TL: 11-18 cm. W: 116-152 kg (♂), 48-66 kg (♀). HL: 113-132 cm (♂), 26-34 cm (♀). One of the largest Argali, similar to the Altai Argali. Upper parts are yellowish brown in summer, and chocolate brown in winter, with whitish patches on the shoulders, withers, and back, and smaller white areas on the neck. Flanks and fronts of thighs are a more uniform darker brown. Muzzle, sides of face, and upper throat are grizzled grayish brown. Rump patch light buff and diffuse. Tail with a brown center line. Belly is whitish. No neck ruff. Horns similar to those of Altai Argali, being nearly as massive but a little shorter. Females are smaller than males, with smaller horns.

♀

♂
Juvenile
Ovis jubata

♂

Ovis darwini

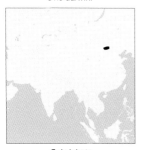

Ovis jubata

OTHER NAMES Mongolian Argali, Khangai Argali, Darwin Argali. *French*: Mouflon du Mongolie, argali du Gobi, argali du Khangai. *German*: Gobi-Wildschaf, Gobi Argali. *Spanish*: Argalí del Gobi, argalí de Kangai. *Russian*: Гобийский аргали (*darwini*), Северокитайский аргали (*jubata*).

SUBSPECIES Monotypic. Formerly considered a subspecies of *O. ammon* (Argali). Includes *darwini* (S Gobi), *dauricus, intermedia* (central Gobi), *kozlovi* (Ala Shan Mountains), *mongolica* (Mongolia), and *przevalskii* (Saylyugem Range), with *darwini* having priority. Sometimes considered a synonym of *O. a. ammon* (Altai Argali).

SIMILAR SPECIES Shanxi Argali or Northern Chinese Argali (*O. a. jubata*) is similar to the Gobi Argali, coat is dark fawn gray, flecked with white, but there is no white spotting on shoulders; yellow-brown to pale gray neck ruff, restricted to the front of the neck, and hair is also elongated on the dorsal line of the neck, extending to the shoulders.

REPRODUCTION *Gestation*: 155-165 days. *Young per Birth*: 1, rarely 2. *Weaning*: 4 months. *Sexual Maturity*: 2 years (♀), 5 years (♂). *Life Span*: 13 years. Rut occurs in late October-December. Births occur in late March-May, with a peak in April.

BEHAVIOR *Family Group*: Small herds segregated by sex, except for breeding season, from 2 to 11 animals. *Diet*: Shrubs, forbs, grasses. *Main Predators*: Gray wolf, domestic dog, Pallas's cat, red fox, raptors. There is no specific information for this subspecies, but probably similar to other Argalis, with two peaks of activity, mornings and evenings.

DISTRIBUTION *Native:* China, Mongolia. Found in N China, in Neimenggu and S Mongolia, S slopes of the Hurku Mountains and S and N borders of the Galbyn Gobi, Trans-Altai Gobi in S Gobi Desert. *O. a. jubata* is restricted to NE China; boundaries with the Gobi Argali, with which it has been confused, are unclear.

HABITAT Desert, semi-desert and steppe habitats, usually in gentle sloping to undulating landscapes, hilly regions, and canyon lands adjacent to montane areas, at elevations of 2,000-2,800 m. They also live in desert lowlands at 1,000-1,300 m, in mountains, and in areas interspersed with rocky, dry gullies and rock outcrops.

STATUS Near Threatened. Estimated population of 14,000 in Mongolia; status of population in China is unknown. Major threats include illegal hunting and competition for forage with domestic livestock. *O. a. jubata* may be extinct, and there is no known extant population that can definitely be anatomically relegated to this species.

PHOTO CREDITS *O. darwini*: based on several photos. Juvenile (*jubata*): *Sergey Chichagov,* Shanghai Zoo (China).

Karaganda Argali

OVIS COLLIUM

BL: 165-199 cm (♂), 136-160 cm (♀). SH: 108-135 cm (♂), 85-100 cm (♀). TL: 10-17 cm. W: 108-157 kg (♂), 43-62 kg (♀). HL: 94-154 cm (♂). Similar to the Tianshan Argali in body size and shape, with smaller horns. Coat is dark brown above, separated from the white belly by a dark flank band. Creamy white neck ruff, blending into the darker body hair. Distinct white rump patch, not extending above the root of the tail. Long tail, with a dark tip. Dark stripes down the front of hind legs, but not always down the front legs. Head darker than neck, with a dark facial mask. Horns are angular in cross section at the base, with a well-developed frontal-orbital edge in old males. Females smaller than males, with smaller horns.

♀

Young

♂

Ovis collium

OTHER NAMES Kazakh Argali, Kazakhstan Argali, Semipalatinsk Argali. *French*: Mouflon du Kazakhstane. *German*: Kasachstan-Wildschaf. *Spanish*: Argalí de Kazajistán. *Russian*: Карагандинский аргали.

SUBSPECIES Monotypic. Formerly considered a subspecies of *O. ammon* (Argali). Most authors have lumped it with the Tianshan Argali for years, but recently recognized as a distinct species.

REPRODUCTION *Gestation*: 150-160 days. *Young per Birth*: 1-2. *Weaning:* 4 months. *Sexual Maturity*: 2 years (♀), 5 years (♂). *Life Span:* 13 years. Rut occurs in the second half of October and lasts through November. Births occur from late March to early May.

BEHAVIOR *Family Group*: Small herds segregated by sex, except for breeding season, from 3 to 11 animals. *Diet*: Forbs; they may feed in cultivated grain fields. *Main Predators*: Gray wolf. Diurnal or crepuscular, as other subspecies. They migrate seasonally between mountain ranges. There are also irregular movements caused by droughts and steppe fires.

DISTRIBUTION *Native*: China, Kazakhstan. Found throughout the Karaganda Region in E and central Kazakhstan, extending W and N into Akmola, N into Pavlodar, and E into Semey (Semipalatinsk) regions. Stops short of the Tarbagatay Mountains and, therefore, does not mix with the Tianshan Argali. Found also in NW China. This Argali is geographically isolated from all other Argali subspecies.

HABITAT Occupies lower, more arid country than most Argalis, at 1,000-1,500 m above sea level.

STATUS Near Threatened. Population estimate was 8,000-12,000 animals in Kazakhstan in 2005, and is increasing. Most common threats include poaching, competition with livestock, and steppe fires.

PHOTO CREDITS *Klaus Rudloff,* Almaty Zoo (Kazakhstan).

Karatau Argali

OVIS NIGRIMONTANA

BL: 160-180 cm. SH: 86-97 cm (♂). TL: 10-12 cm. W: 101-160 kg (♂), 48-61 kg (♀). HL: 75-83 cm (♂). The second-smallest species of Argali. General body color is dark brown, with a paler neck. Short neck ruff, creamy white in color, blending gradually with the body hair. White belly, set off by a dark flank stripe. Fronts of forelegs are white. Fronts of the hind legs have dark stripes. White rump patch not extending beyond the base of the tail. No saddle patch or bib. Homonymous horns, strongly corrugated. Females are smaller than males, with smaller horns.

Ovis nigrimontana

OTHER NAMES Kyzyl Kum Sheep, Kara-Tau Sheep, Bokharan Argali. *French*: Mouflon du Severtzov. *German*: Kysylkum-Wildschaf. *Spanish*: Argalí de Kysylkum. *Russian*: Каратаусский аргали.

SUBSPECIES Monotypic. Formerly considered a subspecies of *O. ammon* (Argali).

REPRODUCTION *Gestation*: 150-160 days. *Young per Birth*: 1-2. *Weaning*: 4 months. *Sexual Maturity*: 2 years (♀), 5 years (♂). *Life Span*: 13 years. Rut occurs in October. Births occur on April.

BEHAVIOR *Family Group*: Small herds segregated by sex, except for breeding season, from 2 to 11 animals. *Diet*: Grasses, herbs, sedges, and some herbs and lichens. *Main Predators*: Gray wolf. Diurnal or crepuscular, as other subspecies. Sedentary. Seasonal migrations are uncommon, but in particularly snowy winters they move to areas with less snow, or even descend to plains.

DISTRIBUTION *Native*: Kazakhstan. Distributed only in the Syr Darya Karatau Mountains of Kazakhstan. In the SW Karatau, this subspecies has hybridized with Tianshan Argali that migrated from Talas Alatau; consequently, pure sheep remain only in the NW part of the mountains.

HABITAT Deep ravines, among cliffs and scree; they seldom use plateau areas because these are occupied by livestock. They rest in areas with high grass and brush, which is atypical of other subspecies.

STATUS Critically Endangered. Total population has gradually declined from approximately 150 individuals in 1976 to about 100 at present. The limiting factors are poaching, predation by wolves, and cattle grazing in the core habitat areas.

PHOTO CREDITS *Klaus Rudloff,* Almaty Zoo (Kazakhstan).

Severtzov's Argali

OVIS SEVERTZOVI

BL: 160-180 cm. SH: 86-97 cm (♂). TL: 10-12 cm. W: 101-160 kg (♂), 48-61 kg (♀). HL: 75-83 cm (♂). The smallest species of Argali. Morphologically intermediate between Urials and Argalis, as it exhibits characteristics of both. Winter coat is chestnut brown to dark brown above, slightly paler on the neck, and grayish brown on flanks and tail. Head darker than the neck. Rump patch, belly, and muzzle are white. Rump patch does not extend above the base of the tail. Lower legs are dirty white except for dark, reddish-brown stripes on the fronts. Short white neck ruff, tinged with gray. No saddle patch or bib. Homonymous horns, strongly corrugated. Females are smaller than males, with smaller horns.

Ovis severtzovi

OTHER NAMES Kyzyl Kum Sheep. *French*: Mouflon de Severtzov. *German*: Kysylkum-Wildschaf. *Spanish*: Argalí de Kysylkum. *Russian*: Аргали Северцова.

SUBSPECIES Monotypic. Formerly considered a subspecies of *O. ammon* (Argali). Formerly recognized as Severtzov's Urial (*O. vignei severtzovi*).

REPRODUCTION *Gestation*: 150-160 days. *Young per Birth*: 1-2. *Weaning*: 4 months. *Sexual Maturity*: 2 years (♀), 5 years (♂). *Life Span*: 13 years. Rut occurs from the end of October throughout mid-November. Births occur in April.

BEHAVIOR *Family Group*: Herds segregated by sex, except for breeding season, with a maximum of 54 animals. *Diet*: Grasses, herbs, sedges; they also dig up roots of plants. *Main Predators*: Gray wolf. Active in the early morning and evening during the warm time of the year. In winter they are active throughout the day. In summer, they prefer montane steppe mainly above 400 m on north-facing slopes, moving to south-facing slopes during winter.

DISTRIBUTION *Native:* Kyrgyzstan, Tajikistan, Uzbekistan. *Regionally Extinct:* Kazakhstan. Formerly had a wide distribution in Uzbekistan from the NW Pamiro-Alay Mountains through to the low mountains and hills of the Kyzylkum Desert. Today, almost all remaining animals are restricted to the higher mountains of Nuratau. In Kyrgyzstan it occurs in a small part of the Turkestan Range between the Tonuk Suu and Kara Suu rivers. It is also reported from the Turkestan Range in Tajikistan. This species is already extinct in Kazakhstan.

HABITAT Foothills and mountains with shrub and rocky outcrops at medium height in the Nuratau Range, up to 2,190 m.

STATUS Endangered. Competition with domestic livestock and illegal hunting are the major threats. Estimated population was 2,000 animals by the end of the 1990s. The species depends entirely on the Nuratau nature reserve.

Tianshan Argali

OVIS KARELINI

BL: 158-190 cm. SH: 103-112 cm (♂). TL: 12 cm. W: 97-152 kg (♂), 47-66 kg (♀). HL: 114-180 cm (♂), 26-34 cm (♀). Similar to the Marco Polo Argali, but darker, and its horns have a tighter curl and are generally thicker. Winter coat is light brown above, lightening gradually to the diffuse, grayish-brown rump patch. Muzzle and lower lip are white. Top of the head, sides, and front of the face are dark gray. Yellowish-white belly separated from the flanks by a wide dark line, more conspicuous in females. Dark dorsal line running from shoulders to loins. Neck mane is white, shaded with grayish brown. Females are smaller than males, with smaller horns.

Ovis karelini

OTHER NAMES Ala Tau Argali, Karelin Argali, Heins Argali, Hume Argali, Littledale Argali, Sair Argali, Kazakhstan Argali. *French*: Argali du Tian Shan. *German*: Tian Shan Argali, Tianshan-Wildschaf. *Spanish*: Argalí del Tian Shan, argalí de Karelini. *Russian*: Тянь-шанский аргали.

SUBSPECIES Monotypic. Formerly considered a subspecies of *O. ammon* (Argali). Includes *heinsii*, *karelini*, *littledalei* (E Xinjiang), *melanopyga*, and *nassanovi*, with *karelini* having preference.

REPRODUCTION *Gestation*: 155-165 days. *Young per Birth*: 1, rarely 2. *Weaning*: 4 months. *Sexual Maturity*: 2 years (♀), 5 years (♂). *Life Span*: 13 years. Rut from mid-October to mid-November. Births occur in late March and early April.

BEHAVIOR *Family Group*: Herds segregated by sex, except for breeding season, with a maximum of 54 animals. *Diet*: Grasses, herbs, sedges; in summer diets have higher forb content. *Main Predators*: Gray wolf, snow leopard. Formerly, animals migrated seasonally from higher mountain habitats in summer to wintering sites in lowlands and foothills with lower snowfall accumulation, but because these areas have been affected by livestock and human settlements, they remain at higher elevations year-round.

DISTRIBUTION *Native:* China, Kazakhstan, Kyrgyzstan. Found in Tian Shan Mountains in SE Kazakhstan and E Kyrgyzstan, E to about Urumqi in Xinjiang. Boundaries with the Marco Polo Argali to the S and W are unclear.

HABITAT Diverse habitats, ranging from lowland semi-deserts to typical highland montane steppes, subalpine meadows, and other subalpine areas, at altitudes of 200 to 4,000 meters above sea level.

STATUS Near Threatened. Estimated total population is 8,000 animals. A major challenge is the large number of domestic livestock throughout their range, which have displaced Argali populations.

Transcaspian Urial

OVIS ARKAL

BL: 127-160 cm (♂), 120-134 cm (♀). SH: 94-99 cm (♂), 72-88 cm (♀). TL: 11-13 cm. W: 62-91 kg (♂), 36-45 kg (♀). HL: To 105 cm (♂), 13 cm (♀). Medium-sized sheep. A large, bright-colored Urial. Overall color uniformly tawny brown. Rump patch, muzzle, belly, and lower legs are white, and there is a darker stripe separating belly and upper body. White bib and long, white neck ruff in adult males. Immature males have a smaller, dark neck ruff. No saddle patch, but some males have a dark shoulder spot in winter coat. Horns are rather long and homonymous, growing in a tight circle or forming an open spiral. Frontal horn surface is flat, with sharp angles and distinct ridges, triangular in cross section. Females are smaller, with short, straight horns.

♂

♀

Juvenile

♂

Young

summer coat

winter coat

Ovis arkal

OTHER NAMES Ustyurt Sheep, Arkal. *French*: Transcaspien urial. *German:* Transkaspischer Urialschaf. *Spanish*: Urial del Transcaspio, urial de Arkal. *Iran*: Kopet Dag urial. *Russian*: Закаспиский (транскаспиский) уриал.

SUBSPECIES Monotypic. Formerly considered a subspecies of *O. vignei* (Urial). Includes *arkal* (Ustyurt Plateau), *dolgopolovi* (near Astrabad in NE Iran), and *varentsowi* (Kopet Dag Range), with *arkal* having priority. Sometimes included under *cycloceros*.

REPRODUCTION *Gestation*: 150-160 days. *Young per Birth*: 1, 2 in areas with high forage production. *Weaning*: 5-6 months. *Sexual Maturity*: 1.5 years. *Life Span*: 11 years. The mating season occurs in November-December in colder climates, but can vary. Most births occur in mid-April to early May.

BEHAVIOR *Family Group*: ♀ and their offspring usually remain in groups separate from the male groups, except during mating season. *Diet*: Opportunistic herbivore, feeding on grasses and shrubs. *Main Predators*: Leopard, gray wolf, golden jackal, red fox, and feral and domestic dog. Feeding activity is confined to the early morning and evening in the summer months, often commencing well before dawn. During the day they rest, usually under an overhanging bush or rock where they are well concealed. Their sight, hearing, and sense of smell are all acutely developed. They are excessively wary, depending upon early detection of approaching danger and flight for their survival.

DISTRIBUTION *Native:* Kazakhstan, Uzbekistan, Turkmenistan, Afghanistan. Found in SW Kazakhstan, on the Ustyurt Plateau between the Caspian and Aral seas, and S in the Kopet Dag Range, W Uzbekistan, NW Turkmenistan, NE Iran, from the Kopet Dag Range through Khorasan Province in the NE, and in Afghanistan, in the extreme NW, bordering Iran and Turkmenistan. Boundaries to the E with the Afghan Urial are undetermined.

HABITAT Hilly terrain and rugged canyons in low-elevation, open areas that are often close to human settlements and thus heavily used by livestock, and readily accessible to hunters. From near sea level to above 3,000 m, rarely exceeding 4,000 m. Many occur in degraded habitats grazed by domestic livestock.

STATUS Vulnerable. Estimated total population of 1,500-2,000 in Tandureh NP (NE Iran), 1,500-2,300 in Heyadary protected area near Neyshabour, 800-1,500 in Salouk and Sarigul NP in Khorasan Shomali Province (Iran); there is also a population in Golestan NP (N Iran). Total population in Kazakhstan is about 6,000 individuals. Threats all derive from an increasing human population with concomitant demands for food and other natural resources.

PHOTO CREDITS ♂: *Sergey Chichagov*, Tallinn Zoo (Estonia). Head ♂: Saint Louis Zoo (USA). ♀: *Jeff Whitlock*, Saint Louis Zoo (USA). Head ♀: *Sergey Chichagov*, Tallinn Zoo (Estonia). Young and juvenile: *Sergey Chichagov*, Tallinn Zoo (Estonia).

Bukhara Urial

OVIS BOCHARIENSIS

BL: 135-160 cm (♂), 120-134 cm (♀). SH: 94-100 cm (♂), 82-88 cm (♀). TL: 11-13 cm. W: 62-90 kg (♂), 36-42 kg (♀). HL: To 73 cm (♂), 13 cm (♀). Medium-sized sheep. General color is sandy yellow or cinnamon yellow, paler in summertime. White throat and black neck ruff and a dark saddle patch in males, as in Ladakh Urial. Rump patch, muzzle, belly, back of hindquarters, and lower legs from the knee to the hooves usually white. Horns grow upward and sideways from the skull, and are crescent shaped in a single plane; outer rib is quite faint and transverse folds are small. Females with smaller horns.

♀

♂

♂
Juvenile

summer coat

winter coat

Young

386

Ovis bochariensis

OTHER NAMES Tadjik Urial, Turkestan Urial, Bokharan Urial, Panja Urial, Bukhara Sheep. *French*: Mouflon de Boukhara. *German*: Tadschikistan-Wildschaf. *Spanish*: Urial de Bujará. *Russian*: Таджикский (бухарский) уриал.

SUBSPECIES Monotypic. Formerly considered a subspecies of *O. vignei* (Urial). Sometimes included under *cycloceros*.

SIMILAR SPECIES Smaller than the Ladakh and Afghan Urials, with shorter horns, and seems to be lighter in pelage color.

REPRODUCTION *Gestation*: 150-160 days. *Young per Birth*: 1 (2-3 in older ewes). *Weaning*: 5-6 months. *Sexual Maturity*: 1.5 years. *Life Span*: 12 years. Breeding season in November-December, with most births occurring in May-June.

BEHAVIOR *Family Group*: Herds of related individuals, comprising ♀, lambs, and juveniles. *Diet*: Herbivorous: grasses and shrubs; also grains. *Main Predators*: Large eagles, canids, large felids (young sheep). There is no specific information available for this species, but probably similar to other Urials. Most active in the early morning and twilight hours, especially in summer.

DISTRIBUTION *Native*: Turkmenistan, Uzbekistan, Tajikistan, Afghanistan. Found in S Tajikistan, from Baldzhuan on upper courses of Kyzylsu, right tributary of the Pyandzha River, NE Turkmenistan, S Uzbekistan along the border with Turkmenistan, and probably N Afghanistan.

HABITAT Mountainous terrain with associated rough, precipitous habitats at elevations of 1,000-4,500 m.

STATUS Vulnerable. This is the scarcest Urial: Estimated total population is fewer than 200 animals. It has been extirpated over most of its historical distribution and now occurs in isolated populations. Major threats include illegal hunting, and habitat degradation.

PHOTO CREDITS ♂ summer and winter coat: *Sergey Chichagov*, Tallinn Zoo (Estonia). ♀, young, and juvenile: *Sergey Chichagov*, Riga Zoo (Latvia).

Afghan Urial

OVIS CYCLOCEROS

BL: 127 cm (♂), 94 cm (♀). SH: 75-81 cm (♂), 72 cm (♀). TL: 10.5-11 cm. W: 36 kg (♂), 26 kg (♀). HL: To 105 cm (♂), 13 cm (♀). Medium-sized sheep, smaller than Transcaspian Urial. Overall color varies from reddish buff to yellowish brown, lighter in summer than in winter. Underparts white. Clearly delineated white rump, restricted to below the base of the tail. Back of hindquarters and lower legs from the knee to the hooves usually white. Face bluish gray. Saddle mark generally very indistinct or lacking. Throat neck and ruff variable in color, usually white throat ruff and black neck ruff, longer and more developed than in other subspecies. Homonymous horns, triangular in cross section, strongly wrinkled, often develop more than a complete arc when viewed from the side, with tips bending slightly outward. Females are smaller, and have small, straight horns.

♀

Juvenile

♂

♂

Ovis cycloceros

OTHER NAMES Turkmen Urial, Turkmenian Sheep, Baluchi Urial. *French*: Urial du Afghanistan. *German*: Afghanischer Urialschaf. *Spanish*: Urial del Afganistan. *Russian*: Афганский (туркменский) уриал. *Astor*: Urin. *Baluchi*: Kar. *Ladakhi*: Arkars, shapo. *Iranian*: Ghuch-e-Uyreal. *Pashto*: Zahra hii Gada. *Turkish*: Yaban koyunu, Dag koyunu. *Urdu*: Jangli Dumba, Gud, Gad.

SUBSPECIES Monotypic. Formerly considered a subspecies of *O. vignei* (Urial). Includes *blandfordi* (Blandford's or Southern Afghan Urial, from Sind and Baluchistan in Pakistan).

REPRODUCTION *Gestation*: 150-160 days. *Young per Birth*: 1, 2 in areas with high forage production. *Weaning*: 5-6 months. *Sexual Maturity*: 1.5 years. *Life Span*: 10 years. The mating season may vary in desert populations. Most births occur in February and the rut occurs in August. Reproduction is dependent on summer precipitation in desert populations. During mating, ♂, which live in their own herds when not mating, will select 4-5 ♀. ♀ segregate themselves from the herd prior to giving birth. After giving birth, ♀ and their young remain apart from the herd for 3-7 days.

BEHAVIOR *Family Group:* Except for the mating season, adult ♂ and ♀ segregate into separate groups. Ram groups usually number fewer than 30, and are composed of 2-year-olds and older ♂; ♀ groups may exceed 100 animals, and consist of ewes, lambs, yearlings, and occasionally younger rams. *Diet:* Opportunistic herbivore, feeding on grasses and shrubs. *Main Predators:* Leopard, gray wolf, golden jackal, red fox, and feral and domestic dog. Mostly active during morning and afternoon. During the warmest period of the day, they seek thermal cover in tall vegetation. Adult rams form dominance hierarchies, with older, larger rams dominant over younger rams. Dominance hierarchies probably also occur among ewes.

DISTRIBUTION *Native:* Afghanistan, Pakistan, Turkmenistan. It has a greater distribution and occurs in a greater variety of habitats than any other subspecies of Urial. Found in central and NE Afghanistan, and in Pakistan, W of the Indus River and N of Quetta, but S of Chitral. Populations in S Turkmenistan, along the border with Iran and Afghanistan, are assigned by Russian authorities to this species. However, Iranian authorities consider populations on the Iranian side of the border to be *arkal*. It is likely that the two species intergrade to some degree in this region. Outside Asia, Afghan Urials have been introduced on private ranches in the United States.

HABITAT Hilly terrain and rugged canyons in low-elevation, open areas that are often close to human settlements and thus heavily used by livestock, and readily accessible to hunters. From near sea level to above 3,000 m, rarely exceeding 4,000 m.

STATUS Vulnerable. Estimated total population of 12,000, including *blandfordi*.

PHOTO CREDITS ♂: *Milos Andera* and *Jonas Livet*, Tierpark Berlin (Germany). Head ♂: *Jonas Livet*, Tierpark Berlin (Germany). ♀: *Lukas Blazek* and *Nick Hadad*, Tierpark Berlin (Germany). Head ♀: *Lukas Blazek*, Tierpark Berlin (Germany). Juvenile: *Maxime Thué*, Ménagerie du Jardin des Plantes (France).

Ladakh Urial

OVIS VIGNEI

BL: 135-160 cm (♂), 120-134 cm (♀). SH: 80-92 cm (♂), 68 cm (♂). TL: 11-13 cm. W: 62-90 kg (♂), 36-42 kg (♀). HL: 50-99 cm (♂), to 13 cm (♀). Medium-sized sheep. Coat color is rufous gray, less red than in other subspecies. Underparts and legs are whitish. Lighter coat in summer than in winter. Males have a white bib and a comparatively short black neck ruff. In older males neck ruff is gray or white in front passing into black behind. Males usually have a 2-colored saddle patch, dark in front followed by white. Horns are curved upward, backward and turned outward, but horn shape may vary. Wrinkles or corrugations are rather shallow and indistinct. Females are smaller and paler sandy brown, with small horns.

Ovis vignei

OTHER NAMES Shapu. *French*: Mouflon urial. *German*: Ladakh-Wildschaf. *Spanish*: Urial del Ladakh. *Russian*: Ладахский уриал. *Astor*: Urin. *Baluchi*: Kar. *Ladakhi*: Arkars, shapo, shap, shalugu, shalmar.

SUBSPECIES Monotypic. The name *O. vignei* (Urial) formerly included *O. arkal* (Transcaspian Urial), *O. bochariensis* (Bukhara Urial), *O. cycloceros* (Afghan Urial), *O. punjabiensis* (Punjab, Salt Range, or Kalabagh Urial), and *O. vignei* (Ladakh Urial) as subspecies: these are all elevated to full species here.

REPRODUCTION *Gestation*: 150-160 days. *Young per Birth*: 1 (2-3 in older ewes). *Weaning*: 5-6 months. *Sexual Maturity*: 1.5 years. *Life Span*: 10 years. Mating occurs in November-December, with most births in May and early June.

BEHAVIOR *Family Group*: Herds of related individuals, comprising ♀, lambs, and juveniles. *Diet*: Herbivorous: grasses and shrubs; also grains. *Main Predators*: Gray wolf, snow leopard. Gregarious, forming groups ranging from 1 to 30 individuals. ♂ and ♀ segregate during the non-rutting season. The animals are most active during morning and evening, and rest during midday on boulder-strewn slopes, merging completely with their surroundings. Well-developed eyesight, sense of smell, and hearing ability. Well-adapted to extreme cold and aridity. They are shy and highly alert, and when disturbed they run up slopes, stopping intermittently to assess the graveness of the threat. ♂ engage in fierce contests for ♀ during the rut.

DISTRIBUTION *Native*: India, Pakistan. Restricted to the Ladakh region along the Shyok, Nubra, and Indus river valleys and their tributaries in India, and W bank of the Kunar River from Chitral S to Drosh and areas near the cities of Skardo and Gilgit, in Pakistan.

HABITAT Along major river valleys, where they sometimes occupy a narrow band of low hills at elevations of 3,000-4,250 m. Gentle slopes with smooth to sometimes broken terrain; they generally use steep slopes or rocky terrain very little. Restricted to the higher-elevation zones even during winter, due to habitat destruction. It may descend to agricultural fields and damage crops, specially in spring. Snow cover is usually light. The higher elevations are occupied by Siberian Ibexes and Blue Sheep.

STATUS Vulnerable. Estimated population in India about 700 in 2002; its status in Pakistan is even more precarious. Habitat loss and degradation, and competition with domestic livestock are major threats.

PHOTO CREDITS Based on photos from *Kenny Ross*, Ladakh (India).

Punjab Urial
OVIS PUNJABIENSIS

BL: 109-116 cm (♂). SH: 78-92 cm (♂). TL: 11-12 cm. W: 40-45 kg (♂), 25 kg (♀). HL: 60-100 cm (♂), to 12 cm (♀). Medium-sized sheep, smaller and stockier in build compared with the Afghan Urial. General color is reddish gray, redder than that of other subspecies. Underparts and legs are whitish. Dark, narrow stripe between belly and upper body. Lighter coat in summer than in winter. Males lose their ruffs during the spring molt. Males have white bib and a black neck ruff in the winter coat, and usually a white saddle patch, but the patch can be bicolored or absent. Horns in males are sickle shaped, cervical, more massive at their base than in the Afghan Urial, but these never curve around in more than a complete arc. Females are smaller and paler sandy brown, with small horns.

Ovis punjabiensis

OTHER NAMES Salt Range Urial, Kalabagh Urial. *French*: Mouflon du Punjab. *German*: Punjab-Wildschaf, Punjab Urialschaf. *Spanish*: Urial del Punyab. *Russian*: Пенджабский уриал. *Punjabi*: Hureal, oorial.

SUBSPECIES Monotypic. Formerly considered a subspecies of *O. vignei* (Urial).

REPRODUCTION *Gestation*: 150-160 days. *Young per Birth*: 1 (2-3 in older ewes). *Weaning*: 5-6 months. *Sexual Maturity*: 1.5 years (♀), 2-4 years (♂). *Life Span*: 10 years. Mating occurs in October-November, and parturition occurs in early April. Urials are serially polygynous. Larger, dominant ♂ actively seek ewes in estrus. A ♂ mates with one estrous ♀ at a time; the ♂ do not form harems. Within a week after birth, lambs are able to follow their mothers even in rough terrain.

BEHAVIOR *Family Group*: Herds of 4-6 members, comprising ♀, lambs, and juveniles, sometimes up to 30-40 individuals. Most ♂ segregate into ram herds during the birthing period. *Diet*: Primarily grazers, feeding on grasses and sedges, but they can switch to browse during the autumn and winter when grasses have lost their nutritional value. Diet overlap with domestic livestock may be significant. *Main Predators*: Feral dog, red fox, golden jackal; gray wolf, caracal, and leopard have been extirpated from its range. They form larger groups in winter than in other seasons; in the winter when forage quality is low sheep use more open habitat and may decrease vigilance and increase bite rate by increasing group size. Diurnal. Animals begin feeding at sunlight and then retreat into shade. During the warm season, they may forage at night. During the winter they can remain in the open throughout the day, grazing and resting intermittently. They avoid domestic sheep and goats.

DISTRIBUTION *Native*: Pakistan. This Urial occurs only in Punjab Province of Pakistan, restricted to the Kala Chita and Salt ranges between the Jhelum and Indus rivers.

HABITAT Stony, rounded hills, interspersed with gullies and ravines, in dry, subtropical semi-evergreen scrub forest at 250-1,000 m above sea level. They usually prefer low vegetation cover, but may enter tall vegetation habitats for thermal and security cover and for foraging.

STATUS Vulnerable. Total estimated population is 800-1,000 animals. In recent decades it has undergone a severe decline in both range and numbers, disappearing from much of its historic range. One of the greatest threats is the overutilization of rangelands by domestic livestock.

Esfahan Mouflon

OVIS ISPHAHANICA

BL: 124 cm (♂), 119 cm (♀). SH: 65-82 cm. TL: 12-13 cm. W: 40-70 kg (♂), 35-50 kg (♀). HL: To 79 cm (♂), to 25 cm (♀). A small Mouflon. Short-haired coat. General color pale yellowish brown to tan, almost whitish, with a white saddle patch. In winter, males have a full-length black neck ruff extending to the brisket. There is no bib. Muzzle, chin, throat, and lower part of legs are white. Supracervical or cervical horns, similar to those of the Armenian Mouflon, but angled more vertically, with the tips growing inward toward the neck. Frontal-orbital horn edge is rounded, frontal-nuchal edge is sharp. Females smaller than males, usually hornless, but may have very small horns, similar in appearance to Armenian Mouflon females.

Ovis isphahanica

OTHER NAMES Isfahan Mouflon, Estafan Red Sheep, Isfahan Sheep. *French*: Mouflon d'Esfahan Laristan. *German*: Esfahan Mufflon, Isfahan-Wildschaf. *Spanish*: Muflón de Esfahan, mouflón de Isfahán. *Russian*: Исфаханский муфлон *(isphahanica)*. *Iranian*: Chuche-Armani.

SUBSPECIES Monotypic. Formerly considered a subspecies of *O. gmelini* (Mouflon).

SIMILAR SPECIES Laristan Mouflon is very similar, but frontal-orbital horn edge is sharp, and females usually have horns. Armenian Mouflon has less tightly curled horns, and the coloration is slightly different.

REPRODUCTION *Gestation*: 150-160 days. *Young per Birth*: 1, rarely 2. *Sexual Maturity*: 2.5-3.5 years. *Life Span*: 20 years. Mating occurs in November, birth season is March-April.

BEHAVIOR *Family Group*: Except for the breeding season, ♂ live in flocks separate from the mothers and their young. *Diet*: Grazes on short grasses, but in arid S Iran, browse probably predominates. *Main Predators*: Gray wolf, cheetah, feral dogs. There is no specific information available for this subspecies, but probably crepuscular, resting during the hot part of the day. In summer and autumn they migrate to higher elevations, where habitats are more suitable, whereas in winter and spring they descend to lower elevations; slopes over 30% and distance to water sources in summer are limiting factors for the distribution of this species.

DISTRIBUTION *Native*: Iran. Restricted to a very small area in W-central Iran, in the mountains SW and NW of the city of Esfahan. It occurs in the Gamishloo, Tange-Sayad, Kola-Ghazi Wildlife Refuge, Tandooreh NP, and Mooteh Wildlife Refuge.

HABITAT Lower, less precipitous portions of mountain regions, at elevations not exceeding 2000 m above sea level.

STATUS Vulnerable. Estimated population does not exceed 500 animals.

Laristan Mouflon

OVIS LARISTANICA

BL: 124 cm (♂), 119 cm (♀). SH: 50-82 cm. TL: 12-13 cm. W: 25-64 kg (♂), 35-50 kg (♀). HL: To 79 cm (♂), to 25 cm (♀). The smallest species, with both Urial characteristics (horns curl along the side of the head) and Mouflon characteristics (saddle patch present). Summer coat straw brown, turning darker brown with a narrow white saddle patch in winter, sometimes with a dark shoulder band. Thin-haired coat with a short black ruff on the lower neck and breast. Whitish saddle patch. Underparts white. Narrow brown flank band and brown markings on front of the upper legs. Dark line separating the white undersides from the body coloration. There is no bib. White muzzle and white circles around the eyes. Horns with a flat frontal surface with sharp edges, curving down by the side of the head, with the tips pointing forward. Females smaller than males, with very small horns.

ssp. *isphahanica*
♂

♀

ssp. *laristanica*

♀

♂

Ovis laristanica

OTHER NAMES Laristan Red Sheep, Shiraz Sheep, Kerman Sheep. *French*: Mouflon du Laristan. *German*: Laristan Mufflon, Laristan-Wildschaf. *Spanish*: Muflón de Laristan. *Russian:* Ларистанский муфлон. *Iranian*: Chuche-Armani.

SUBSPECIES Monotypic. Formerly considered a subspecies of *O. gmelini* (Mouflon).

SIMILAR SPECIES Esphahan Mouflon is very similar to Laristan Mouflon, but frontal-orbital horn edge is rounded, and frontal-nuchal edge is sharp, and ♀ are usually hornless. Kerman Sheep, considered as a hybrid between Laristan Mouflon and Blanford or Afghan Urial (*O. vignei cycloceros*), occurs naturally in the Kerman region of SE Iran; its winter coat is darker than that of the Laristan Mouflon; there is a white saddle patch but no bib; a black neck ruff is present, extending the full length of the neck in some animals but limited to just the lower half in others; the horns also show a flat frontal surface with sharp corners.

REPRODUCTION *Gestation*: 150-160 days. *Young per Birth*: 1, rarely 2. *Sexual Maturity*: 2.5-3.5 years. *Life Span*: 20 years. Mating occurs in November, birth season is March-April.

BEHAVIOR *Family Group*: Except for the breeding season, ♂ live in flocks separate from the mothers and their young. *Diet*: Grazes on short grasses, but in arid S Iran, browse probably predominates. *Main Predators*: Gray wolf, leopard, feral dogs. Gregarious, gathering in herds of sometimes up to 100 individuals. They avoid cities and villages. Most populations undergo seasonal movements. During the dry season, from April to autumn, they congregate around water holes. With the rainy season and abundance of food and water sources, they spread out more evenly across the landscape.

DISTRIBUTION *Native*: Iran. Found in S Iran, in Fars and Laristan provinces. Kerman Sheep is found in Kerman Province of Iran, in the Kabr-va-Rouchon Wildlife Refuge and E and S. Boundaries with the Laristan Mouflon to the W are unclear.

HABITAT Desert mountains and hills of Laristan and Fars provinces of S Iran, from valley bottoms to undulating and mountainous terrain, at an average altitude of 800 m; they usually are not sighted in steep, rocky terrain.

STATUS Vulnerable. Estimated population for Larestan Mouflon was fewer than 1,500 animals in 2011. It has been extirpated over widespread areas, and it is highly vulnerable to illegal hunting and transmission of diseases from domestic sheep and goats.

PHOTO CREDITS ♂: *Jonas Livet*, Kuwait Zoo (Kuwait) and Al Wabra Wildlife Preservation (Qatar). ♀: *Irvin Calicut*, Kuwait Zoo (Kuwait).

Armenian Mouflon

OVIS GMELINI GMELINI

BL: 128-140 cm (♂), 124-128 cm (♀). SH: 83-91 cm. TL: 11-13 cm. W: 55-67 kg (♂), 35-45 kg (♀). HL: To 85 cm (♂). A small and graceful sheep with relatively long, slender legs. Short-haired coat. General color reddish tan with a narrow, grayish-white saddle patch. Underparts, lower legs, and muzzle white. Chest dark brown. Narrow brown flank band and brown markings on front of the upper legs. In winter, there is a short black ruff on the lower neck and brisket. No bib. Supracervical horns, curving above and behind the neck, not flaring out at the end as in most wild sheep. Females considerably smaller than males, lacking a saddle patch; may be hornless or have small horns.

♀

♀ hornless

Young

♂

♂ Juvenile

Ovis gmelini gmelini

OTHER NAMES Transcaucasian Mouflon, Asiatic Mouflon, Arak Sheep, Gmelin Sheep, Iranian Red Sheep. *French*: Mouflon d'Armenie. *German*: Armenischer Mufflon. *Spanish*: Muflón de Armenia. *Russian*: Армянийский муфлон. *Azeri*: Erm ni muflon. *Iranian*: Quch-e-armani. *Turkish*: Ermeni Yaban.

SUBSPECIES The name *O. gmelini* (Mouflon) formerly included *O. g. gmelini* (Iranian Red Sheep, Armenian Mouflon), *O. isphahanica* (Esfahan Sheep), *O. laristanica* (Laristan Sheep), *O. aries* var. *musimon* (European Mouflon), *O. aries* var. *ophion* (Cypriot Mouflon, Agrino, Cyprian Wild Sheep), and *O. g. anatolica* (Turkish or Konya Mouflon) as subspecies. Includes *armeniana* (E Turkey), *gmelini* (E Turkey), and *urmiana* (Urmi Sheep, Kabudan Island in Lake Orumiyeh, NW Iran), with *gmelini* having priority. Armenian Mouflon is regarded by many authorities as the probable ancestor of the European Mouflon and the Domestic Sheep. Formerly classified as *O. orientalis*. Mouflons may cross with any other species of sheep, including Domestic Sheep.

SIMILAR SPECIES The Alborz Red Sheep is cosidered as a hybrid between Armenian Mouflon and Transcaspian Urial (*O. arkal*); its characteristics vary: saddle patch and bib may be present or not, neck ruff and horn configuration are variable, and color is light brown or tan, with individuals varying from very light grayish brown to light reddish brown.

REPRODUCTION *Gestation*: 150-210 days. *Young per Birth*: 1 or 2. *Sexual Maturity*: 2-3 years. *Life Span*: 18 years. Rutting season from late November to early December. Births in May.

BEHAVIOR *Family Group*: Except for the breeding season, ♂ live in flocks separate from the mothers and their young. *Diet*: Grazes on short grasses, heather, and shrubs. *Main Predators*: Bear, wolf, jackal. They tend to feed early in the morning and in the evening, resting during the day under an overhanging bush or rock, where they are well hidden. Mouflon are gregarious and form non-territorial herds grazing on grasses, unless food is scarce, when they will turn to browsing leaves and fruits. They live in small or larger herds, and in the summer the older ♂ live singly or in separate groups. Like all Eurasian sheep, they generally avoid cliffs but sometimes they do rest or even forage there. In Armenia, they reside year-round, don't move away in winter, and in the hot season are replenished by ♂ immigrating from Nakhichevan.

DISTRIBUTION Found in Armenia, extreme SW Azerbaijan, E Turkey, NE Iraq, NW Iran E to Tabriz and S to the central Zagros Mountains, and N Israel. The sheep on Kabudan Island (Iran) are said to have been introduced from the mainland. It has also been introduced on private ranches in USA. Alborz Red Sheep is found in N Iran, in the Alborz Mountains, plus an isolated population in the Kavir Desert of N-central Iran. Boundaries with the Armenian Mouflon to the W and the Transcaspian Urial to the E are unclear.

HABITAT Arid mountain grasslands with juniper and almond scrublands, subalpine and alpine meadows. Prefer open spaces alternating with rocky outcrops and canyons at 1,000-3,000 m above sea level.

STATUS Vulnerable. Estimated population is 2,250 animals.

PHOTO CREDITS ♂, ♀, young and juvenile: *Sergey Chichagov*, Tallinn Zoo (Estonia). Head ♂: *Alex Meyer*, San Diego Zoo (USA).

Turkish Mouflon

OVIS GMELINI ANATOLICA

BL: 105-140 cm (♂), 124-128 cm (♀). SH: 83-91 cm. TL: 11-13 cm. W: 45-74 kg (♂), 35-40 kg (♀). HL: To 77 cm (♂). A small and graceful sheep with relatively long, slender legs. Short-haired coat. General color varies from pale brown in summer to reddish brown in winter. Summer coat is short, thick, and sparse. Winter coat is long, thin, and dense. Dark flank stripe, separating the upper parts from the paler, cream-colored, underparts. Whitish saddle in older males. Dark gray to black marks on the chest, forelegs above the knees, and front side of upper hind legs, more pronounced during the rutting season. Horns in males similar to those of the Armenian Mouflon, with a wider distance between the horn apexes. Females more uniformly colored, lacking the distinct black markings of males, usually hornless, and considerably smaller.

♀

♂

♂
Juvenile

♂
Young

Ovis gmelini anatolica

OTHER NAMES Anatolian Sheep, Central Anatolian Mouflon, Konya Sheep. *French*: Mouflon d'Anatolia. *German*: Anatolischer Mufflon. *Spanish*: Muflón de Anatolia. *Russian*: Конийский муфлон. *Turkish*: Anadolu Yaban koyunu, dag koyanu.

SUBSPECIES Considered by some authors as conspecific with the Armenian Mouflon (*O. g. gmelini*), or with the European or Cyprian Mouflon. Considered here as a subspecies of *O. gmelini*. The Turkish Mouflon is geographically separated from the Armenian Mouflon (*O. g. gmelini*) of NW Iran and easternmost Turkey, and there is no evidence of connection at least in the last several hundred years. The Steppic corridor between central Turkey and W Iran was replaced by deciduous dry forest or woodland by about 6,000 years ago, possibly acting as a barrier to Mouflon dispersal.

SIMILAR SPECIES Armenian Mouflon is somewhat larger and darker, and ♀ are hornless, but otherwise, they are very similar. A minority of ♀ may have horns.

REPRODUCTION *Gestation*: 148 days. *Young per Birth*: 1 or 2. *Sexual Maturity*: 2-3 years. *Life Span*: 18 years. Breeding season from late November to early December. Births in May. Anatolian Mouflon shows a polygynous mating system. There is a strong inter-male competition for ♀ during the rutting season. The ♀ generally prefer the older and bigger-horned ♂.

BEHAVIOR *Family Group*: Except for the breeding season, ♂ rarely form groups with ♀ or their offspring. *Diet*: Grasses and herbs; may dig tubers in winter. *Main Predators*: None. They tend to feed early in the morning and in the evening, resting during the day under an overhanging bush or rock, where they are well hidden. The centers of activity of ♂ and ♀ are mostly separate throughout the year: sexual segregation, while there is continuous overlap in general area use. ♀ use mostly the areas to the W of Bagderesi, and ♂ use mostly the areas to the E of Bagderesi where the two areas seem to differ in ruggedness and altitude. ♀ show a shift in area use toward ♂ dominated areas during the rut, and ♂ extend their area use substantially towards the ♀-dominated areas during spring. Average home ranges are 2,000 ha.

DISTRIBUTION *Native*: Turkey. It is endemic to Turkey, restricted to Konya Bozda (Alagaglar Mountains) in central Turkey, not far from the town of Nidge. Former range included central Anatolia, in the W and central parts of the plateau.

HABITAT Rolling hills in the steppe-forest ecotone, sometimes of a drier or more rugged nature, and usually at an altitudinal range between 1,000-1,500 m.

STATUS Vulnerable. Estimated population was 700 individuals in 2008. Until 2005 there was only one known remaining population inside a fenced area. Since then, there have been successful reintroductions into the Karaman-Karada and Sariyar wildlife protection areas.

PHOTO CREDITS *Blickwinkel/Hartl* and *Images&Stories*, Konya Bozda (Turkey).

Domestic Sheep

OVIS ARIES

BL: 120-180 cm. SH: 65-127 cm. TL: 70-150 cm. W: 45-160 kg (♂), 45-100 kg (♀). Physical details vary greatly among breeds. Coloration from milky white to dark brown and black. Tail may be large and used as a fat reserve. Coat is a crimped, woolly fleece with occasional hair fibers. It may be short and neat or long and untidy, depending on the population and the stage of the molt cycle. Nose narrow and completely covered with short hair except on the margins of the nostrils and lips; ears pointed. Either sex may carry horns. In females they are slender, more or less erect, and curved backward; in males they are more massive, with broad anterior surfaces, and after curving back they spiral outward for up to 2 turns. Females smaller than males.

Jacob

♀

Merino

♂

400

Ovis aries

OTHER NAMES *French*: Mouton. *German*: Hausschaf. *Spanish*: Oveja. *Russian*: Домашняя овца.

SUBSPECIES DNA studies of European, African, and Asian Domestic Sheep suggest that there are three major and distinct lineages. These lineages are called Type A or Asian, Type B or European, and Type C, which has been identified in modern sheep from Turkey and China. All three types are believed to have been descended from different wild ancestor species of Mouflon, someplace in the Fertile Crescent. A Bronze Age sheep in China was found to belong to Type B, and is thought to have been introduced into China perhaps as early as 5000 BC. Several hundred breeds of sheep have been identified. Almost all Domestic Sheep are classified as being best suited to furnishing a certain product: wool, meat, milk, hides, or a combination in a dual-purpose breed. Other features used when classifying sheep include face color (generally white or black), tail length, presence or lack of horns, and the topography for which the breed has been developed.

REPRODUCTION *Gestation*: 148 days. *Young per Birth*: 1-2. *Sexual Maturity*: 1 year. *Life Span*: 12 years. *Ovis aries* breeds on a seasonal basis, determined by day length, with ♀ first becoming fertile in the early fall and remaining fertile through midwinter. ♂ are fertile year-round and most Domestic Sheep breeders use 1 ♂ to 25 to 35 ♀. Most lambs are born in midspring and are able to stand and suckle within a few minutes of birth.

BEHAVIOR *Family Group*: Large groups. *Diet*: Grasses, while in pastures, and can be fed a wide variety of hays and oats. *Main Predators*: Wolf, coyote, dog, felines, bear, birds of prey, raven, feral hog. *Ovis aries* has a highly developed flocking or herding instinct. Large groups of sheep (up to 1,000 or more) move over an area in groups, rather than as individuals. No "leaders" in the flock initiate grazing or other forms of behavior, including flight. This flocking instinct contributes to their economic significance, as a single shepherd can control a large flock of animals. Sheep become considerably stressed when separated from others, often calling and pawing at the ground. Mating occurs mainly in the early morning or in the evening. ♂ search for ♀ and if a ♂ suspects a ♀ is in estrus, he will nudge the ♀ in the perineum. The ♀ then assumes a mating stance if interested in the ♂ or walks away if not. If the ♀ is interested, the ♂ will conduct a short "foreplay" session, mount, and copulate. If not then he will move on to another ♀.

DISTRIBUTION Domestic Sheep live worldwide in association with humans. The first domesticated sheep resided mainly in the Middle East and Central Asia but since then have been introduced everywhere.

HABITAT Wide variety of habitats worldwide ranging from temperate mountain forests to desert conditions.

STATUS Domesticated.

PHOTO CREDITS Merino sheep: *Eric Isselée*, Life on White (Belgium). Merino sheep (head ♀): *Nikol Lohr* (USA). Jacob: *Eric Isselée*, Life on White (Belgium).

European Mouflon

OVIS ARIES VAR. MUSIMON

BL: 128-152 cm (♂), 120-130 cm (♀). SH: 66-76 cm. TL: 11-13 cm. W: 40-60 kg (♂), 30-40 kg (♀). HL: To 85 cm (♂). One of the smallest wild sheep, resembling a slim Domestic Sheep. Red-brown, short-haired coat with dark back stripes and light-colored, almost white, saddle patches. Underparts white as well as the bottom half of the legs. There can be a dark line separating the white undersides from the body coloration. White muzzle and white circles around the eyes. Males lack a bib and have a dark ruff extending from the front of the lower neck to the chest. Males are horned; most females are hornless. Horns usually grow in a tight circle, with the tips turned inward toward the face and broomed back to about a three-quarter curl. Horns do not flare out at the end as in most wild sheep. Females smaller than males.

♂

Juvenile

♀

♂

Young

summer coat

winter coat

Ovis aries var. *musimon*

OTHER NAMES Corsican Mouflon. *French*: Mouflon corse. *German*: Mufflon. *Spanish*: Muflón. *Russian*: Европейский муфлон. *Czech*: Mufloni zver. *Greek*: Agrioprovato.

SUBSPECIES Authors do not agree on the origin of the European Mouflon. Some regard it as the ancestor of the Domestic Sheep, others as a feral descendant from Domestic Sheep. Traditionally it has been regarded as indigenous to Corsica and Sardinia, and from there introduced on the European mainland and elsewhere. However, some authorities now believe it is descended from Domestic Sheep transplanted to Corsica and Sardinia by humans thousands of years ago. Some authorities consider it a full species, *O. musimon*, others as a subspecies of Asian Mouflon (*O. gmelini* or *O. orientalis*), and still others as a race of Domestic Sheep (*O. aries*) or even as a race of Argali (*O. ammon*). Mouflons may cross with any other species of sheep, including Domestic Sheep.

REPRODUCTION *Gestation*: 150-210 days. *Young per Birth*: 1 or 2. *Weaning*: 3 months. *Sexual Maturity*: 1 year (♀), 2.5-3.5 years (♂). *Life Span*: 14 years. Breeding season in October-November. They give birth in protected nooks and crannies such as dead tree stumps, brush country, or rock nests. The lambs follow their mothers within a few hours of birth.

BEHAVIOR *Family Group*: Except for the breeding season, ♂ live in flocks separate from the mothers and their young. *Diet*: Mainly a grazer, but browses to an extent. Drinks rarely. *Main Predators*: Feral dogs; eagles for young lambs. Gregarious. ♀ with young form year-round flocks; mature ♂ have separate flocks. During the mating season, individual ♂ join the ♀ after battling for dominance. It is the only sheep that is mainly nocturnal, resting by day in thick cover. A good runner.

DISTRIBUTION *Introduced*: Spain, France, Germany, Italy, Switzerland, Austria, the Netherlands, Belgium, Czech Republic, Poland, Slovakia, Slovenia, Hungary, Bulgaria, Romania, Sweden, Finland, Chile, Argentina, USA. Mouflon were introduced to the islands of Corsica and Sardinia during the Neolithic period, perhaps as feral domesticated animals, where they have naturalized in the mountainous interiors of these islands over the past few thousand years, giving rise to the subspecies known as European Mouflon. They were later successfully introduced into continental Europe.

HABITAT Steep mountainous woods near tree lines. In winter, they migrate to lower altitudes.

STATUS Vulnerable. A total of 800 animals has been estimated for Corsica. The total estimate of introduced populations on the mainland was 5,600 in 1989.

PHOTO CREDITS ♂ winter coat: *Michelle Bender*, Wildpark Frankenhof (Germany). ♂ summer coat, ♀, and young: *José R. Castelló*, Safari Aldea del Fresno (Spain). Head ♂: *José R. Castelló*.

Cyprus Mouflon

OVIS ARIES VAR. OPHION

BL: 128-152 cm (♂), 124-128 cm (♀). SH: 68 cm. TL: 11-13 cm. W: 35-42 kg (♂), 25-30 kg (♀). HL: 50-65 cm (♂). Small-sized sheep. In winter, thick coat, light reddish-brown color with light gray on the back, black patch on the neck. White saddle on the back, extending down to the flanks during the mating season, absent or indistinct in the summer coat. In summer, coat becomes short and smooth, with a uniform brown to light orange color and white underparts. There can be a dark line separating the white undersides from the body coloration. White muzzle. Males lack a bib. Very short tail, black on the upper side and white on the lower side. Horns of mature males are supracervical, heavy, and sickle shaped. Females are smaller than males, without horns.

404

Ovis aries var. *ophion*

OTHER NAMES Cypriot Mouflon, Agrino. *French*: Mouflon du Chypre. *German*: Zyprischen Mufflon. *Spanish*: Muflón de Chipre. *Russian*: Кипрский муфлон. *Greek*: Agrioprovato. *Turkish*: Kıbrıs muflon.

SUBSPECIES It is thought that the Cyprus Mouflon might actually be a feral version of an ancient domesticated sheep which was imported to the island of Cyprus during the Neolithic period, and the relationship between wild and domesticated sheep is unclear. Cyprus and European Mouflon are considered by some authors as a subspecies group of the wild sheep *O. aries*. Considered by other authors as a subspecies of *O. gmelini* (Mouflon).

REPRODUCTION *Gestation*: 150-160 days. *Young per Birth*: 1-2. *Sexual Maturity*: 2.5-3.5 years. *Life Span:* 20 years. Mating occurs from October to November. Births occur in April-May.

BEHAVIOR *Family Group*: During the mating period, mixed herds of 10-20 animals. In spring, these herds are divided into small groups of 2-3 animals. Old ♂ solitary. *Diet*: Grazes on short grasses, heather, and shrubs. *Main Predators*: Feral dogs. Active in early morning and late afternoon in summer, whereas in winter they are active over the entire day. During the summer, they live on the high mountains of the Paphos forest (Tripilos region). In winter, when the high peaks of the mountains are covered with snow, they come down to lower pastures in search of food. They may venture to the edge of the forest to search for food, when sources in the forest are scarce, and may cause considerable damage to various agricultural crops. Shy and agile, they move very fast on steep slopes and are very difficult to approach,especially when they are frightened.

DISTRIBUTION *Native*: Cyprus. Found only in the Paphos Forest Game Reserve, a mountainous area of 620,000 ha in the NW part of the Troodos Mountains, in Cyprus.

HABITAT Along with the Mouflon of Sardinia and Corsica (*O. g. musimon*), it is the only forest dweller among the Caprinae.

STATUS Endangered. Estimated population was 3,000 animals in 2012. Uncontrolled hunting and habitat destruction have almost driven this subspecies to extinction.

PHOTO CREDITS ♂: *Sandy Beach Cat*, Karamoullidhes (Cyprus). Head ♂: *Martin D. Parr*, Spilia (Cyprus). ♀: *Nigel Watson,* Paphos Zoo (Cyprus). Head ♀: *Catherine Dijon*, Stavros tis Psokas, Paphos (Cyprus).

Tibetan Antelope
PANTHOLOPS HODGSONII

BL: 120-130 cm. SH: 80-100 cm. TL: 18-30 cm. W: 35-40 kg (♂), 25-30 kg (♀). HL: 50-70 cm (♂). A very distinctive, medium-sized antelope. Overall coat color pink-tinted pale tan, with the underparts, including the chin, being creamy white. Fronts of the slender legs are dark brown to black. Face, including the forehead, bridge of the nose, and upper cheeks, is also dark brown to black. Nostrils are bulbous, with sacs on the sides which can be inflated to the size of small eggs. Hooves long and narrow, dewclaws small, but broad. Horns, found only in males, are long and slender, lyre shaped, black, ringed on the front surface, and rise nearly vertically from the head. Females smaller than males, without horns (unlike other Caprini).

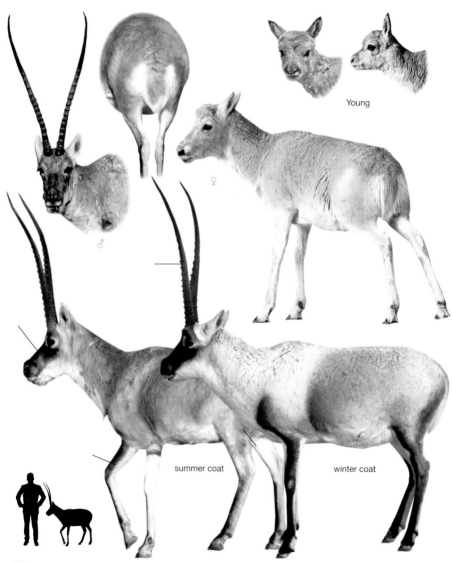

Young

♀

♂

summer coat

winter coat

Pantholops hodgsonii

OTHER NAMES Chiru. *French*: Chiru, Antilope du Tibet. *German*: Tschiru, Orongo, Tibetantilope. *Spanish*: Antílope tibetano. *Russian*: Тибетская антилопа, или чиру. *Chinese*: Zang-lin. *Nepali*: Chiru. *Tibetan*: Nawa, tsus, chuhu, chiru, tsö.

SUBSPECIES Monotypic. It has previously been classified together with Saiga (*Saiga tatarica*) in a separate tribe Saigini.

SIMILAR SPECIES It can be distinguished from the sympatric Tibetan Gazelle (*Procapra picticaudata*) and other Asiatic gazelles, such as Goitered Gazelle (*Gazella subgutturosa*) and Mongolian Gazelle (*Procapra gutturosa*), by the enlarged snout, fine undercoat of the pelage of both sexes, and long upright lyre-shaped horns of ♂. Saiga is of comparable mass, but horns of Tibetan Antelope are straighter and much longer.

REPRODUCTION *Gestation*: 180 days. *Young per Birth*: 1-2. *Weaning:* 10-11 months. *Sexual Maturity*: Presumably at 1.5-2.5 years. *Life Span*: Probably 10-15 years. The rut takes place in early winter (November-December). Courtship and mating are abrupt and brief, with cursory displays and contacts. Young are born in May and June. ♀ congregate at traditional birthing grounds. Neonates are precocial; they can arise and nurse 15 minutes postpartum and follow their mother 1 hour postpartum. Offspring grow rapidly: 15-month-old ♀ are almost indistinguishable from adult ♀, and ♂ are identified by their developing horns.

BEHAVIOR *Family Group*: Herds with 10-15 animals, adult ♂ solitary. *Diet*: Grasses and herbs. *Main Predators*: Wolf, Himalayan black bear. Extremely wary by nature, constantly on the alert, and hence difficult to approach. Feeding occurs primarily in the morning and evening. When resting, they excavate a shallow depression about 30 cm deep: this partially conceals the animal from predators, and helps to protect it from the harsh wind. Unlike in other Caprini, ♂ lack a graded system of rank based on horn length, and avoid serious horn-to-horn combat. Mature ♂ are not territorial but form harems. During the rut, ♂ rarely eat and are almost constantly in motion. Each attempts to control a harem of 10-20 ♀, and zealously guards them from rival ♂. Fights between ♂ break out frequently, and are extremely fierce. One or both of the contestants may perish as the result of wounds inflicted by the sharp horns. Local densities are around 0.2-1.5 animals per km². They are either migratory, moving up to 300–400 km, or sedentary; deep snows modify traditional migratory movements in search of forage and as a means of avoidance, as they are not suited for efficient travel through snow.

DISTRIBUTION *Native*: China (Qinghai, Xinjiang), India (Jammu-Kashmir). *Regionally Extinct*: Nepal. Formerly ranged across the whole Qinghai-Tibetan Plateau, China. Range decreased and now absent from all or most of the E plateau; the main stronghold of the species is in the remote Chang Tang area of NW Tibet. A small number occur seasonally in NE Ladakh, in the extreme N of India. Formerly occurred in a small area of NW Nepal.

HABITAT High-elevation alpine and desert steppe with flat to rolling terrain on the Tibetan Plateau at elevations of 3,700-5,500 meters.

STATUS Endangered. Estimated population is 100,000 animals.

PHOTO CREDITS *Coke Smith* and *G. B. Schaller*, Qinghai (China). Young: *Galen Rowell* and *Kate Harris*, Changtang National Reserve (China).

Pyrenean Chamois
RUPICAPRA PYRENAICA

BL: 100-130 cm. SH: 70-81 cm. TL: 3-4 cm. W: 23-50 kg (♂), 20-32 kg (♀). HL: 17-28 cm (♂). Small graceful goat-antelope. Summer coat reddish in color. Winter coat blackish brown with white markings on the throat, neck, shoulders, and flanks, much thicker. Dark middorsal stripe. Dark stripe extending from the base of the horns to the eyes and muzzle. Tail is black. Hoof padded with a slight depression and is somewhat elastic, helping to provide solid footing in rough terrain. Black horns, found in both sexes, set very close together, rise in a vertical fashion, and then bend backward sharply to form hooks. Horns of males have a greater basal girth, usually more hooked. Females smaller than males, otherwise little sexual dimorphism.

♀

Young

summer
coat

winter
coat

Juvenile

♂

winter coat

Rupicapra pyrenaica

OTHER NAMES Southern Chamois, Western Chamois, Isard. *French*: Izard, chamois des Pyrénées. *German*: Pyrenäen-Gämse. *Spanish*: Sarrio, isart. *Russian*: Пиренейская серна.

SUBSPECIES Monotypic. The name *R. pyrenaica* (Southern Chamois) formerly included *R. pyrenaica* (Pyrenean Chamois), *R. parva* (Cantabrian Chamois), and *R. ornata* (Apennine Chamois) as subspecies: these are all elevated to full species here.

SIMILAR SPECIES Larger and darker than the Cantabrian Chamois, with longer, thicker horns. Darker, with less white, and smaller than the Apennine Chamois.

REPRODUCTION *Gestation*: 170 days. *Young per Birth*: 1-2. *Weaning*: 6 months. *Sexual Maturity*: 8-9 years. *Life Span:* 20 years. The Pyrenean Chamois breeds seasonally, mating in the fall and giving birth in the spring. The young are born in a shelter of lichens and mosses. The young usually follow their mothers almost immediately after birth, and they rapidly improve their leaping ability during the first few days of their life.

BEHAVIOR *Family Group*: Herds of 15-30 individuals (♀ and young). *Diet*: Herbs and flowers. In the winter months they also eat lichens, mosses, and young pine shoots. *Main Predators*: Brown bear, golden eagle. The Pyrenean Chamois usually live with their mother's group until they are 2-3 years old. They live a nomadic lifestyle until they reach full maturity at 8-9 years, at which point they become attached to an area. ♀ and young form herds of 15-30 individuals, with the number in the herd varying with the seasons. In the winter months, ♀ isolate themselves to give birth in the spring. Adult ♂ live alone most of the year. During the late summer they join the herds, and during the autumn rut the older ♂ drive the younger ♂ from the herd, occasionally killing them. The Pyrenean Chamois are very graceful and nimble. They can jump nearly 2 m in height and a distance of 6 m. They can also run at speeds of 50 kmph on uneven ground.

DISTRIBUTION *Native*: Andorra, France, Spain. Found in the Pyrenees Mountains, along France' s border with Spain, including Andorra.

HABITAT Alpine meadows, rocky areas, and the forested valleys and lower slopes in mountainous regions. This species generally stays above 1,800 m in alpine meadows during the warmer months of the year. These animals make altitudinal migrations from the forests in the valleys to the more open alpine meadows. In late fall and winter they have been known to enter lands below 1,100 m, while usually staying on steep slopes, and rarely in forested areas.

STATUS Least Concern. The population and range of this subspecies increased markedly from 1989 to 2003, although there have subsequently been some declines. The 2003 estimate for the total number was 25,000-53,000 animals, but many Chamois populations have recently declined due to severe mortality caused by pestivirus, a viral disease.

PHOTO CREDITS ♂: Pyrenees (Spain). ♀: *Dave Watts*, Pyrenees (France) and *Jonas Livet*, Zoodysee (France). Head ♂: *Benoit Dandonneau*, Pyrenees (France). Young: *Gerard Mussot*, Pyrenees (Andorra) and *Manu Leopold*, Pyrenees (France). Juvenile: *Juliensa*, Pyrenees (France).

Cantabrian Chamois

RUPICAPRA PARVA

BL: 100-104 cm. SH: 72-74 cm. TL: 3-4 cm. W: 20-34 kg (♂), 24 kg (♀). HL: 17-28 cm (♂). Slim goat-antelope, the smallest subspecies, with the lightest coloration. Light cinnamon head, throat, and cheeks, with a dark mask design that crosses the big eyes. Dark brown back, chest, legs, and flanks, pale brown shoulders and hindquarters. In winter, the back and belly become paler in color and the flanks darker, giving a more contrasting color pattern. Tail is dark reddish brown, not black. Juveniles exhibit a less contrasting color pattern. Black horns, found in both sexes, shorter and slimmer than in other subspecies, set very close together, rise in a vertical fashion, and then bend backward sharply to form hooks. Horns in males more hooked and thicker than in females. Little sexual dimorphism.

Young

♀

summer coat

♂

♀

♂

summer coat

winter coat

Rupicapra parva

OTHER NAMES Southern Chamois. *French*: Chamois Cantabre. *German*: Cantabrischegemse. *Spanish*: Rebeco cantábrico, gamuza, robezu, rebezo. *Russian*: Кантабрийская серна.

SUBSPECIES Monotypic. Formerly considered as a subspecies of *R. pyrenaica* (Southern Chamois).

SIMILAR SUBSPECIES Smaller, summer pelage more reddish in color, tail dark reddish brown, not black, with shorter and slimmer horns than Pyrenean Chamois.

REPRODUCTION *Gestation*: 160-185 days. *Young per Birth*: 1, rarely 2. *Weaning*: 6 months. *Sexual Maturity*: 3-5 years (♀). *Life Span*: 21 years. Rut takes place from the end of October to the beginning of December. Birth season from mid-May to mid-June. The young are born in a shelter of lichens and mosses. The young usually follow their mothers almost immediately after birth, and they rapidly improve their leaping ability during the first few days of their life.

BEHAVIOR *Family Group*: Herds of 2-55 individuals (♀ and young); adult ♂ solitary except during the rut. *Diet*: Herbaceous and woody vegetation, and forest fruits. *Main Predators*: Wolf; young can be preyed on by fox and golden eagle. The Cantabrian Chamois usually live with their mother's group until they are 2-3 years old. They live a nomadic lifestyle until they reach full maturity at 8-9 years, at which point they become attached to an area. ♀ and young form herds of 15-30 individuals, with the number in the herd varying with the seasons. In the winter months, ♀ isolate themselves to give birth in the spring. Adult ♂ live alone most of the year. During the late summer they join the herds, and during the autumn rut the older ♂ drive the younger ♂ from the herd, occasionally killing them. The Cantabrian Chamois are very graceful and nimble. They can jump nearly 2 m in height and a distance of 6 m. They can also run at speeds of 50 kmph on uneven ground. Home ranges from 20-100 ha in ♂, and from 50-500 ha in ♀.

DISTRIBUTION *Native*: Spain. Endemic to Spain, found in NW Spain, in Cantabrian Mountains: from E Saja Reserve and Alto Asón to W Ancares Reserve.

HABITAT Subalpine, preference for the ecotone between forest and alpine meadow, with nearby cliffs as refuge-escape areas. It moves from alpine pastures in summer, to obtain higher quality feeding, to lower altitudes in winter. ♀ use higher altitudes and areas closer to escapes than ♂.

STATUS Least Concern. Estimated population was 17,000 animals in 2008. Diseases, such as sarcoptic mange, are currently the most important threat. Chamois is a major game species in Spain and is important socially and economically as a source of rural livelihoods.

PHOTO CREDITS ♂: *Julio Robles*, Picos de Europa (Spain). ♀: Picos de Europa (Spain). Head ♂: *Agel Ruiz Elizalde* (bicherioxtremo. blogspot.com), Fuente Dé, Cantabria (Spain). Head ♀: *Juan Lacruz*, Picos de Europa (Spain). Young: *Manuel Estebanez*, Picos de Europa (Spain).

Apennine Chamois

RUPICAPRA ORNATA

BL: 105-120 cm. SH: 76-80 cm. TL: 3-4 cm. W: 23-45 kg (♂), 14-32 kg (♀). HL: Up to 32 cm (♂). Small graceful goat-antelope. Winter coat thicker, blackish brown with a white throat patch, larger than other subspecies, and extensive white areas on the side and back of neck that extend to the shoulder. Summer coat smooth, short, reddish brown or tawny in color. Dark middorsal stripe. Dark stripe extending from the base of the horns to the eyes and muzzle. Hoof padded with a slight depression and is somewhat elastic, helping to provide solid footing in rough terrain. Black horns, found in both sexes, set very close together, rise in a vertical fashion, and then bend backward sharply to form hooks, larger than in other subspecies. Horns of males have a greater basal girth, usually more hooked. Little sexual dimorphism.

Young

winter coat

summer coat

Rupicapra ornata

OTHER NAMES Abruzzo Chamois, Southern Chamois. *French*: Izard, chamois des Abruzzes. *German*: Abruzzo-Gämse. *Spanish*: Gamuza de los Abruzzos, rebeco de los Apeninos, rebeco meridional. *Russian*: Апеннинская серна. *Italian:* Camoscio d'Abruzzo, camoscio appenninico.

SUBSPECIES Monotypic. Formerly considered a subspecies of *R. pyrenaica* (Southern Chamois).

SIMILAR SPECIES Horns are slightly longer and straighter than in Alpine Chamois, with different coloration. White throat patch and white areas on the sides and back are larger than in other subspecies.

REPRODUCTION *Gestation*: 170 days. *Young per Birth*: 1, rarely 2. *Weaning*: 6 months. *Sexual Maturity*: 2.5 years (♀), 3.5-4 years, fully mature at 8-9 years (♂). *Life Span*: 22 years. Births occur from May to the end of June, and in this period we see nurseries formed, where 1 or 2 ♀ guard a group of young, while the other mothers have the opportunity to graze peacefully nearby. If a mother is killed, her young are taken care of by other ♀.

BEHAVIOR *Family Group*: Herds of 15-30 individuals (♀ and young); adult ♂ are solitary, only approaching females during the mating season. Subadult ♂ tend to disperse from herds at the age of 2-3 years. There is seasonal variation in herd size, with herds being largest in summer but dispersing when moving to their winter ranges. *Diet*: Grasses, leaves, buds, shoots and fungi. *Main Predators*: Wolf, brown bear, golden eagle, red fox. It usually inhabits inaccessible areas, especially very steep rocky walls, where they can take refuge from predatory attacks. When frightened, they emit a type of alarm whistle. ♂ have little time to feed during the mating season, arriving at mid-December with limited fat reserves. For this reason, older ♂ may not survive the harsh winters. Home ranges may range from 113 ha for ♀ to 168 ha for ♂. ♀ rank is correlated with age, weight, and horn size, with body weight thought to be the most important factor in determining dominance.

DISTRIBUTION *Native*: Italy. Endemic to Italy, it survives only in three small populations in Abruzzo, Majella, and Gran Sasso-Monti della Laga NP in Italy.

HABITAT High-altitude pastureland, more than 1,700 m in summer, while in winter, they descend to steeply sloped forested areas, 1,000-1,300 m, with a southern exposure and, thus, less snow and a higher possibility for finding food.

STATUS Vulnerable. As a result of conservation action, including reintroductions and the establishment of two new populations, numbers have increased and the population is currently estimated at about 1,100 individuals. The main threats come from the low number and size of its populations and their low genetic variability, and food competition with livestock, especially domestic caprines.

PHOTO CREDITS ♂: *Abruzzo-Gemse*, Tierpark München-Hellabrunn (Germany) and *Fabio Pierboni,* Parco Nazionale d'Abruzzo (Italy). ♀: *Andrea R.*, Parco Nazionale d'Abruzzo (Italy). Head: *Gabriele Profita* (gabry.tnx.it), Parco Nazionale d'Abruzzo (Italy). Young: *Marco Cirillo*, Parco Nazionale d'Abruzzo (Italy).

Alpine Chamois

RUPICAPRA RUPICAPRA RUPICAPRA

BL: 100-130 cm. SH: 70-85 cm. TL: 8-15 cm. W: 14-62 kg. HL: 17-28 cm (♂). Small graceful goat-antelope. Short, smooth summer coat, overall tawny or reddish brown, while in winter it becomes a chocolate brown, with guard hairs measuring 10-20 cm long covering a woolly underlayer. Underparts pale. Legs usually darker. Slight mane on the throat. Jaw, cheeks, and nose bridge strikingly white. Black stripe running from the eye to the muzzle. Hooves with hard, sharp edges, and rubbery soles. Slender, black horns, found in both sexes, round in cross section, rising vertically from the forehead, curve sharply backward on their top third like hooks. Female's horns can be longer than the male's, but are slimmer and sometimes lack the hooks. Females about 30% smaller than males, but otherwise, little sexual dimorphism.

summer coat

♀

winter coat

Young

♂

winter coat

summer coat

Rupicapra rupicapra rupicapra

OTHER NAMES Northern Chamois. *French*: Chamois des Alpes. *German*: Alpen-Gämse, Gamswild. *Spanish*: Rebeco alpino, gamuza septentrional, gauza. *Italian*: Camoscio alpino. *Russian*: Обыкновенная серна.

SUBSPECIES Considered as a subspecies of *R. rupicapra* (Alpine Chamois): *R. r. rupicapra* (Alpine Chamois), *R. r. tatrica* (Tatra Chamois), *R. r. balcanica* (Balkan Chamois), *R. r. cartusiana* (Chartreuse Chamois). Includes *sylvatica* and *alpina*. *R. carpatica* (Carpathian Chamois) has been elevated to full species. *R. a. asiatica* (Anatolian or Turkish Chamois) and *R. a. caucasica* (Caucasian Chamois) are now considered subspecies of *R. asiatica* (Asia Minor Chamois).

REPRODUCTION *Gestation*: 170 days. *Young per Birth*: 1, rarely 2. *Weaning*: 6 months. *Sexual Maturity*: 2.5 years (♀), 3.5-4 years (♂). *Life Span*: 14-22 years. The young are born in late spring (May-June), and can follow their mothers almost immediately after birth.

BEHAVIOR *Family Group*: ♀ and young in small flocks of 5-30 animals, adult ♂ solitary. *Diet*: Both a browser and a grazer: grasses, leaves, buds, shoots, fungi. *Main Predators*: Lynx, wolf, bear, fox. Diurnal, feeding early and late, with the middle part of the day spent resting. A sentinel, usually a ♀, is posted to watch for danger, and will warn the others with shrill whistles. All senses are excellent, but eyesight is exceptional. Very agile and elusive, handling precipitous terrain with ease. During the summer months, herds of Chamois wander alpine meadows above 1,800 m in home ranges averaging 74 ha. As winter approaches there is a general downward shift to lower altitudes (below 1,100 m), where the Chamois may enter forested regions, although they remain near steep cliffs. When alarmed, they speed to the most inaccessible places, making leaps as high as 2 m and spanning as much as 6 m. Extremely nimble and sure-footed, they can travel up to 50 kmph over steep or uneven ground. Alarm signals include whistling through the nose, sneezing, and stamping their feet. During the autumn rut, old ♂ make an open-mouthed grunt. These breeding ♂ drive younger ♂ from the maternal herds, occasionally killing them.

DISTRIBUTION *Native*: Austria, France, Germany, Italy, Switzerland, Slovenia, Croatia, Liechtenstein. *Introduced:* Argentina, Czech Republic, New Zealand. Native to mountainous parts of central and S Europe.

HABITAT Rocky areas and alpine meadows.

STATUS Least Concern. This subspecies comprises the bulk of the global northern Chamois population, and is widespread and abundant in the Alps. Estimated total population was 500,000 individuals in 2009. Major threats include overharvesting of older ♂, poaching, and tourist development. In Austria, sarcoptic mange is a problem, and in Italy, competition with introduced Mouflon.

PHOTO CREDITS Winter coat: *Patrice Correia,* Vosges Mountain (France). Summer coat: *Emi Cristea*, Mont Blanc Massif (France). Head ♂: *Lucio Tolar*, Julian Alps (Slovenia). Young: *Dominique Fehr*, Alps (France).

Tatra Chamois

RUPICAPRA RUPICAPRA TATRICA

BL: 110-130 cm. SH: 78-90 cm. TL: 8-15 cm. W: 24-36 kg. HL: 17-26 cm (♂). Similar to the Alpine Chamois. Body pelage is dark brown in winter and rust yellow to reddish in summer. Dark middorsal stripe extending from the withers to the root of the dark tail, which is also clearly visible in the winter coat. Head mask with a white-yellowish coloration, more contrasting in winter. Underparts pale. Legs usually darker. Horns of males are larger in girth than those of females, with tips curving sharply backward and downward. Horns in females can be longer, but are slimmer and sometimes lack the hooks. Little sexual dimorphism.

♀

Juvenile ♂

♂ winter coat

summer coat

Rupicapra rupicapra tatrica

OTHER NAMES *French*: Chamois des Tatras. *German*: Tatragams. *Spanish*: Rebeco de Tatra. *Russian*: Татринская серна. *Slovak*: Kamzík vrchovský tatranský. *Polish*: Kozica tatrzanska.

SUBSPECIES Considered as a subspecies of *R. rupicapra* (Alpine Chamois): *R. r. rupicapra* (Alpine Chamois), *R. r. tatrica* (Tatra Chamois), *R. r. balcanica* (Balkan Chamois), *R. r. cartusiana* (Chartreuse Chamois). *R. r. carpatica* (Carpathian Chamois) has been elevated to full species. *R. a. asiatica* (Anatolian or Turkish Chamois) and *R. a. caucasica* (Caucasian Chamois) are now considered subspecies of *R. asiatica* (Asia Minor Chamois).

REPRODUCTION *Gestation*: 170 days. *Young per Birth*: 1, rarely 2. *Weaning*: 6 months. *Sexual Maturity*: 2.5 years (♀), 3.5-4 years (♂). *Life Span*: 14-22 years. No specific information is available for this subspecies, but probably like other Alpine Chamois, with rut beginning in the middle of October and ending in December. ♂ hardly eat during this time and live on accumulated fat reserves. During this season ♂ join ♀ herds and try to drive away other ♂. The risk of getting injured during fights is quite high and can lead to the death of one of the opponents.

BEHAVIOR *Family Group*: ♀ and young in small flocks of 5-30 animals, adult ♂ solitary. *Diet*: Both a browser and a grazer: grasses, leaves, buds, shoots, fungi. *Main Predators*: Lynx, wolf, bear, fox. No specific information is available for this subspecies, but probably like other Alpine Chamois. Diurnal, feeding early and late, with the middle part of the day spent resting.

DISTRIBUTION *Native*: Poland, Slovakia. Found in W Tatras (Slovakia and Poland) and E Tatras, which consist of the High Tatras (Slovakia and Poland) and the Belianske Tatras (Slovakia), all protected by national parks in both countries. The two distribution areas are separated by a populated valley both deep and wide.

HABITAT Open and semi-open alpine habitat, including alpine meadows, cliffs, boulder fields, and dwarf pine. The use of alpine habitat above timberline is a distinctive behavioral feature of this subspecies. They have never been observed in forest habitats.

STATUS Critically Endangered. Estimated population was 800 individuals (513 in Slovakia and 207 in Poland) in 2010. Because of concerns of survivability of this subspecies in its native range, it was also artificially introduced in the Low Tatras, situated S of Tatras, from 1969 to 1976. Current population living in Low Tatras NP is about 100. Fluctuation in the number of these animals is attributed to avalanches, predation, poaching, and an uncontrolled influx of tourists.

PHOTO CREDITS ♂: *Peter Erzvo Zvonar*, Lomnicky Peak, High Tatras (Slovakia). ♀: *Juraj Kovacik*, Low Tatras, Nizke Tatry (Slovakia). Head ♀: *Marcin Białek*, Tatra Mountains (Slovakia). Head ♂: *Wesss17*, Tatra Mountains (Slovakia). Young: *Sabina Kłosowska*, Tatra Mountains (Poland).

Balkan Chamois

RUPICAPRA RUPICAPRA BALCANICA

BL: 110-130 cm. SH: 70-85 cm. TL: 8 cm. W: 30-45 kg. HL: 17-30 cm (♂). Somewhat larger than the Alpine Chamois, with longer horns, and lighter in color. Short, smooth summer coat, overall tawny or reddish brown, while in winter it becomes a chocolate brown, with long guard hairs covering a woolly underlayer, with a yellowish tint. Dark dorsal stripe extending from the occiput down to the root of the tail. Underparts pale. Legs darker than flanks and neck. Slight mane on the throat. Jaw, cheeks, and nose bridge strikingly white. Black stripe running from the eye to the muzzle. Hooves with hard, sharp edges, and rubbery soles. Slender, black horns, found in both sexes, round in cross section, rising vertically from the forehead, curve sharply backward on their top third like hooks. The female's horns can be longer than the male's, but are slimmer and sometimes lack the hooks. Little sexual dimorphism.

♀

winter coat

summer coat

♂

winter coat

Rupicapra rupicapra balcanica

OTHER NAMES *French*: Chamois des balkans. *German*: Balkangemse. *Spanish*: Rebeco de los Balcanes. *Russian*: Балканская серна. *Albanian*: Dhija, egér. *Bulgarian*: Diwa kosa. *Czech*: Kamzici zver. *Croatian*: Divokoza. *Greek*: Agriogido. *Montenegrin*: Dovikoza. *Serb*: Divokoza.

SUBSPECIES Considered as a subspecies of *R. rupicapra* (Alpine Chamois): *R. r. rupicapra* (Alpine Chamois), *R. r. tatrica* (Tatra Chamois), *R. r. balcanica* (Balkan Chamois), *R. r. cartusiana* (Chartreuse Chamois).

REPRODUCTION *Gestation*: 170 days. *Young per Birth*: 1, rarely 2. *Weaning*: 6 months. *Sexual Maturity*: 1.5 years (♀), 4 years (♂). *Life Span*: 15 years. Mating period usually in November.

BEHAVIOR *Family Group*: ♀ and young in small flocks of 5-15 animals, smaller in winter; ♂ older than 5 years usually solitary, except during the breeding season. *Diet*: Both a browser and a grazer: grasses, leaves, buds, shoots, fungi. *Main Predators*: Feral dog, gray wolf, golden eagle, bear, fox, wild cat. Gregarious. The older ♀ in the herd have a clearly expressed hierarchy and higher ranks, while the young, 1- to 3-year-olds are subordinates. In populations with higher density and larger size, the level of social stress is higher, and younger ♀ may eat less food. From July to December they spend more time in the alpine zone than in the forests. From January to June most of the herds stay under the upper border of the forest. The herds are largest in the warmer months, with the maximum in August-September. Grazing is more intense in the morning and during the late afternoon hours. Except for food, the factor in choosing habitat is the temperature regime. In the winter they prefer warm and sunny places and in the summer, windy and shady ones. In foggy and cloudy weather they graze longer and at night they are not active.

DISTRIBUTION *Native*: Albania, Bosnia and Herzegovina, Bulgaria, Croatia, Greece, Kosovo, Macedonia, Montenegro, Serbia, Voivodina. Found in isolated habitats in the mountains of the Balkan Peninsula. In Greece it is found in the Rhodopes and the mountain ranges from Epirus to NW Parnassos. In Albania, in the Albanian part of the Alps in the N, in the E in Dibra highlands, the Librazhd region and Puke, the Mirdite and Mat, in central Albania in Barat and Skrapar, and in the S in Kolonje and Permett. In former Yugoslavia it is found in the mountain ranges of Bosnia and Herzegovina, Montenegro, Serbia, Kosovo, and Macedonia. In Bulgaria it is found on the steep slopes of rocky complexes in the Rila, Pirin, Stara Planina, and Rhodopes mountain ranges.

HABITAT Subalpine meadows, in proximity to cliffs and rocky formations during summer, whereas it moves to lower altitudes in forested zones in winter.

STATUS Least Concern. Estimated population exceeding 17,000 individuals. The status of the species is safe in the countries of former Yugoslavia (Bosnia-Herzegovina, Croatia, Macedonia, Slovenia, Federal Republic of Yugoslavia), vulnerable in Albania, rare in Bulgaria, and endangered in Greece. Major threats include poaching, disturbance by tourists, and livestock grazing.

PHOTO CREDITS ♂: *Savvas Vasileiadis,* Mount Olympus NP (Greece). ♀: *Josef Lubomir Hlasek* and *Xristos Dimadis*, Mount Olympus NP (Greece). Head ♀: *Boris Belchev* (Bulgaria). Head ♂: Mount Olympus NP (Greece).

Chartreuse Chamois

RUPICAPRA RUPICAPRA CARTUSIANA

BL: 115-125 cm. SH: 75-90 cm. TL: 3-4 cm. W: 30 kg (♂), 22 kg (♀). HL: 23-27 cm (♂). Intermediate in characteristics between the Pyrenean and Alpine Chamois. One of the stockiest Chamois subspecies, just under Carpathian Chamois. Winter coat is almost black, with the summer coat pale brown, very similar to that of the Alpine Chamois. Head is very dark colored with a white facial mask and clearly visible dark bands. Underparts pale. Black stripe running from the eye to the muzzle. Legs usually darker. Slender, black horns, found in both sexes, round in cross section, rising vertically from the forehead, with large circumferences. Little sexual dimorphism.

♀

Young

winter coat

summer coat

♂

winter coat

Rupicapra rupicapra cartusiana

OTHER NAMES *French*: Chamois Chartreuse. *German*: Chartreuse-Gämse. *Spanish*: Rebeco de la Cartuja. *Russian*: Шартрская серна.

SUBSPECIES Considered as a subspecies of *R. rupicapra* (Alpine Chamois): *R. r. rupicapra* (Alpine Chamois), *R. r. tatrica* (Tatra Chamois), *R. r. balcanica* (Balkan Chamois), *R. r. cartusiana* (Chartreuse Chamois). *R. r. carpatica* (Carpathian Chamois) has been elevated to full species. *R. a. asiatica* (Anatolian or Turkish Chamois) and *R. a. caucasica* (Caucasian Chamois) are now considered subspecies of *R. asiatica* (Asia Minor Chamois). This subspecies is not recognized by some authors.

REPRODUCTION *Gestation*: 170 days. *Young per Birth*: 1, rarely 2. *Weaning*: 6 months. *Sexual Maturity*: 2.5 years (♀), 3.5-4 years (♂). *Life Span*: 14-22 years. No specific information is available for this subspecies, but probably similar to other subspecies of Alpine Chamois.

BEHAVIOR *Family Group*: ♀ and young in small flocks of 5-30 animals, adult ♂ solitary. *Diet*: Both a browser and a grazer: grasses, leaves, buds, shoots, fungi. *Main Predators*: Lynx, wolf, fox. Diurnal, feeding early and late, with the middle part of the day spent resting. It occupies mostly forest and usually spends the winter at low altitude in thickets of large coniferous forests and wooded canyons where it typically moves very little. During the summer, it is usually on the rocks and in the highest part of the mountains. Average home range sizes of 8,000 ha for ♂ and 2,000 ha for ♀. Oldest animals have a tendency to occupy larger home ranges than younger ones.

DISTRIBUTION *Native*: France. Found only in Massif of the Chartreuse, which forms part of the pre-Alps between Grenoble and Chambery at the W edge of the French Alps.

HABITAT Heavily forested limestone massif of the Chartreuse, covered by a mixed conifer and deciduous forest, between 600 and 2,000 m elevation.

STATUS Vulnerable. Restricted to a 280 km^2 area of state forest. Total estimated population is about 2,000 individuals. Alpine Chamois (*R. r. rupicapra*) was introduced in 1974 at the N end of the mountain massif, so there is a possibility of hybridization of this subspecies. Other threats include food competition with poorly controlled Red Deer, Roe Deer, and Mouflon.

PHOTO CREDITS Summer coat ♂: *Punasotka,* Chartreuse Mountains (France). Head ♂: *Vivien Martin,* Chartreuse Mountains (France). ♀: *Ollivier Daeye*, Chartreuse Mountains (France). Young: *Yves Lesquer*, Chartreuse Mountains (France).

Carpathian Chamois

RUPICAPRA CARPATICA

BL: 115-125 cm. SH: 75-90 cm. TL: 3-4 cm. W: 50-62 kg (♂), 35-36 kg (♀). HL: 23-30 cm (♂). Largest species of Chamois, with longer horns and darker winter and summer coat. Short, smooth summer coat, overall tawny or reddish brown, while in winter it becomes a chocolate brown, with guard hairs measuring 10-20 cm long covering a woolly underlayer. Underparts pale. Legs usually darker. Slight mane on the throat. Jaw, cheeks, and nose bridge strikingly white. Black stripe running from the eye to the muzzle. Hooves with hard, sharp edges, and rubbery soles. Slender, black horns, found in both sexes, round in cross section, rising vertically from the forehead, curve sharply backward on their top third like hooks. The female's horns can be longer than the male's, but are slimmer and sometimes lack the hooks. Little sexual dimorphism.

summer coat   winter coat

♀

summer coat

♂

winter coat

summer coat

Young

422

Rupicapra carpatica

OTHER NAMES *French*: Chamois des Carpathes. *German*: Karpaten-Gämse. *Spanish*: Rebeco de los Cárpatos. *Russian*: Карпатская серна. *Romanian*: Capra neagra.

SUBSPECIES Monotypic. Formerly considered a subspecies of *R. rupicapra* (Alpine Chamois).

REPRODUCTION *Gestation*: 165-175 days. *Young per Birth*: 1, rarely 2. *Weaning:* 6 months. *Sexual Maturity*: 2.5 years (♀), 3.5-4 years (♂). *Life Span:* 14-22 years. Mating season in November-December. Births occur in May-June.

BEHAVIOR *Family Group*: ♀ and young in small flocks of 5-30 animals, adult ♂ solitary. *Diet*: Both a browser and a grazer: grasses, leaves, buds, shoots, fungi. *Main Predators*: Gray wolf, Eurasian lynx. Similar to other Chamois. In warm season, graze early in morning and seek shade during warmest period of the day, and resume grazing in late afternoon when temperatures are cooler. Seasonal migrations occur between lower-elevation forests in winter and subalpine grasslands in the spring. The seasonal grazing of sheep on alpine pastures provides significant competition for food, and Chamois tend to select meadow areas that are hard for sheep to get to, although these tend to be of inferior quality. ♂, which lose condition during the intense mating period, are especially susceptible to harsh environments.

DISTRIBUTION *Native*: Romania. Found only in Carpathian Mountains, Romania. The largest populations occur in the Southern Carpathians, in the Fagaras, and the Retezat Mountains. Lower-density populations are found in the Buzau and Hasmas mountains, Vrancea Mountains, and also in the Ceahlau Mountains and the Rodnei Mountains, in the Eastern Carpathians, and in the Piatra Craiului Mountains, in the Southern Carpathians.

HABITAT Alpine habitats in summer and lower ecotone areas of grasslands and forest in winter.

STATUS Vulnerable. In 2010, the total population was estimated to be around 6,400 animals. Major concerns are small, fragmented populations that could be extirpated, disturbance by shepherds and dogs, competition with domestic livestock, and poaching.

PHOTO CREDITS ♂: *Christian Schoissingeyer* (Romania). ♀: *Octavian si Viorica*, Poiana (Romania). Head ♀: *Eduard Wichner*, Piatra Craiului Mountains (Romania) and *Cristian Vidrascu*, Caltun, Fagaras Mountains (Romania). Young: *Cristian Vidrascu*, Caltun, Fagaras Mountains (Romania).

Anatolian Chamois

RUPICAPRA ASIATICA ASIATICA

BL: 115-125 cm. SH: 70-75 cm. TL: 3-4 cm. W: 40 kg (♂), 22 kg (♀). HL: 23-25 cm (♂). General color in winter is dark, smoky brown to black. Summer pelage color is brown with a broad darkish dorsal stripe. Neck and legs are blackish brown, usually darker than in Alpine Chamois. Underparts are pale. Rump patch is white. Throat, lower jaw, and front of face are yellowish white, and there are dark stripes across the eyes to the muzzle. Immature specimens are light brown in color, with a narrow distinct dorsal stripe. Horns, found in both sexes, are relatively short and thin, not as heavy and long as in other subspecies. Females are slightly smaller than males.

Rupicapra asiatica asiatica

OTHER NAMES Turkish Chamois, Asia Minor Chamois. *French*: Chamois d´Anatolie. *German*: Anatolischer-Gämse. *Spanish*: Rebeco de Anatolia, gamuza turca. *Russian*: Анатолийская (турецкая) серна. *Turkish*: Cengel boynuzlu, dag kecisi, samua. *Georgian*: Archvi, psiti.

SUBSPECIES Formerly considered a subspecies of *R. rupicapra* (Alpine Chamois). Considered as a full species, under *R. caucasica,* by some authors. The justification for the separation of subspecies *asiatica* and *caucasica* has been questioned for a long time.

REPRODUCTION *Gestation*: 165-175 days. *Young per Birth*: 1, rarely 2. *Weaning*: 6 months. *Sexual Maturity*: 2.5 years (♀), 3.5-4 years (♂). *Life Span*: 14-22 years. Mating season is from late October to early December, and births occur from late April to mid-June.

BEHAVIOR *Family Group*: ♀ and young in small flocks of 5-30 animals, adult ♂ solitary. *Diet*: Both a browser and a grazer: grasses, leaves, buds, shoots, fungi. *Main Predators*: Lynx, wolf, domestic dog. No specific information is available for this subspecies, but probably similar to the Alpine Chamois. Mostly diurnal, but known to forage at night. Seasonal migrations occur between alpine areas occupied in summer and lower-elevation forested areas in winter.

DISTRIBUTION *Native*: Turkey, Georgia. *Regionally Extinct:* Armenia. Endemic to the NE parts of Anatolia and Turkey, and extends into Georgia along a small strip parallel to the border. The largest populations occur in the Kackar Mountains in Artvin Province, and in W extensions of the Lesser Caucasus like the Karcal Mountains, and the Yalnizcam and Meskheti ranges.

HABITAT Heavily forested limestone massif of the Chartreuse, covered by a mixed conifer and deciduous forest, between 600 and 2,000 m elevation.

STATUS Least Concern. Estimated population does not exceed 600-700 individuals in Turkey, and 200 in Georgia. Main threats include poaching, high legal harvest quotas, and small fragmented populations with habitat loss and degradation.

Caucasian Chamois
RUPICAPRA ASIATICA CAUCASICA

BL: 125-135 cm (♂), 96 cm (♀). SH: 78-86 cm. TL: 8-15 cm. W: 30-50 kg (♂), 25-42 kg (♀). HL: 17-25 cm (♂). Slightly larger than the Alpine Chamois, with shorter and more compact horns. Summer coat is a smooth tawny or reddish brown to fox red, with a dark stripe running along the spine. Winter pelage is chocolate brown, with fairly long guard hairs, over a dense, woolly underfur. Longer hair also present on the throat. Underparts are pale. Legs usually darker than body. Facial mask reaches up to the back of the neck. Coloration at the base of the horns is paler than in Carpathian Chamois. Throat patch is large, whitish above and orange below. Horns, found in both sexes, short and stout, rising nearly vertically, with a relatively narrow spread. Female horns are slightly shorter, less hooked, and thinner.

Rupicapra asiatica caucasica

OTHER NAMES Asia Minor Chamois. *French*: Chamois du Caucase. *German*: Kaukasus-Gämse, Kleinasien-Gämse. *Spanish*: Rebeco caucásico, rebeco de Asia Menor. *Russian*: Кавказская серна. *Armenian*: Kovkasyan lernayts. *Azeri*: Köpkör, garapacha. *Ossete*: Archvi, psiti. *Georgian*: Shychʻi.

SUBSPECIES Formerly considered a subspecies of *R. rupicapra* (Alpine Chamois). Considered as a full species, under *R. caucasica,* by some authors. The justification for the separation of subspecies *asiatica* and *caucasica* has been questioned for a long time.

REPRODUCTION *Gestation*: 165-175 days. *Young per Birth*: 1, rarely 2. *Weaning*: 6 months. *Sexual Maturity*: 2.5 years (♀), 3.5-4 years (♂). *Life Span:* 14-22 years. The main rut extends from November into mid-December, with most births occurring in May-early June.

BEHAVIOR *Family Group:* ♀ and young in small flocks of 5-30 animals, adult ♂ solitary. *Diet:* Both a browser and a grazer: grasses, leaves, buds, shoots, fungi. *Main Predators*: Lynx, wolf, domestic dog. In summer they graze in forest and alpine areas, while in winter they remain in forest where there is less snow. Mostly diurnal, but known to forage at night. This very agile animal, when alarmed, will run to the most inaccessible places, making leaps as high as 2 m and spanning as much as 6 m, reaching speeds of up to 50 kmph over steep and uneven ground.

DISTRIBUTION *Native*: Azerbaijan, Georgia, Russia. The largest population is found in the Kavkazsky Biosphere Reserve, in the Russian Federation. Smaller populations are found in a number of national parks and Zapovedniks in the Greater Caucasus of several jurisdictions of the Russian Federation. In Georgia, it occurs in Tusheti NP and Lagodekhi State Reserve, and probably in the Lesser Caucasus near the Turkish border. In Azerbaijan, in the Zafgatala and Ilusu State reserves and the W part of Shakhdag NP.

HABITAT Subalpine upper and high-mountain forest zones of the Greater Caucasus, except the S, dry part of the region. Alpine rocky areas and alpine as well as subalpine meadows. They have been forced into the alpine belt due to human development on the lower mountain slopes.

STATUS Least Concern. Estimated population was 8,000 animals in 2010, and declining. Major threats include poaching outside protected areas, habitat loss to pastures for domestic livestock, and competition with Tur, Red Deer, and Roe Deer.

Mountain Goat

OREAMNOS AMERICANUS

BL: 155-180 cm (♂), 140-170 cm (♀). SH: 80-110 cm. TL: 10-20 cm. W: 95-130 kg (♂), 60-90 kg (♀). HL: 21-30 cm. Medium-sized animal. Short, white woolly summer coat, replaced in winter by shaggy dense yellowish pelage. During spring, the molt makes these animals look extremely ragged. Small ridge of long, soft hair on the neck, forming a hump. Beard present on the chin in both sexes. Bear-like body, supported by muscular legs, ending with hooves specially configured for mountain life. Black eyes and nose contrasting greatly with the otherwise white head. Black, slightly curved horns found in both sexes. Females smaller than males, with slimmer, straighter horns, less divergent at the tips, and can be longer as well; otherwise very similar to males.

♀

winter coat

Juvenile

Young

♂

summer coat

Oreamnos americanus

OTHER NAMES Rocky Mountain Goat. *French*: Chèvre des montagnes Rocheuses. *German*: Schneeziege, Bergziege. *Spanish*: Cabra blanca, cabra de las Rocosas. *Russian*: Американская снежная коза. *Cree*: Mathateke. *Dogrip*: Sahzhoa. *Navajo*: Tse-Ta Dz.

SUBSPECIES Monotypic. Includes *kennedyi*, *missoulae*, and *columbiae*. Phylogenetic relationships to other genera in Caprini are unclear. Despite its name, it is not a true goat, being more closely allied with the Chamois and Gorals than to the genus *Capra*.

SIMILAR SPECIES The only other North American Bovid with white pelage is the Dal's sheep (*Ovis dalli*), which has large spiral horns. May be confused with ewes of Bighorn Sheep (*Ovis canadensis*), but the sheep can be distinguished by their tan-colored horns and brown coat.

REPRODUCTION *Gestation*: 175-180 days. *Young per Birth*: 1, rarely 2. *Weaning*: 3 months. *Sexual Maturity*: 30 months. *Life Span:* 18 years. Mating occurs from November to January, with the births taking place in late May and early June. Kids are able to follow their mothers within a week, and, once weaned, are driven away by their mothers as the next young is born.

BEHAVIOR *Family Group*: During the warmer months, groups of fewer than 4 animals are normal, while adult ♂ are frequently solitary. However, during the winter these groups join together to form large herds. *Diet*: Grasses, leaves, coniferous trees. *Main Predators*: Cougar, brown bear. Most active in the late afternoon and early morning, and frequently continue grazing throughout the night. Movements throughout the 24-hour day generally cover several hundred meters. Resting spots are often shallow depressions excavated using the front feet, which they also use when searching for salt. They have exceptional speed and agility on steep terrain. Home ranges average about 23 km² in size, although in winter, these become much smaller. Population densities vary widely (up to 14 animals per km²), although the average figure is thought to be between 1 and 2 animals per km². The rare fights between rival ♂ are extremely violent, often causing serious injury or death. Opponents thrust their sharp horns at each other's flanks and rump in an attempt to gore the soft flesh.

DISTRIBUTION *Native*: Canada, United States. Found in SE Alaska (USA), S Yukon, and SW Northwest Territories (Canada) to N-central Oregon, central Idaho, and Montana (USA). Introduced to Kodiak, Chichagof, and Baranof islands (Alaska), Olympic Peninsula (Washington), central Montana, Black Hills (South Dakota), and to Colorado, Utah, and NE Nevada (USA).

HABITAT Mountainous regions in W Canada and the NW United States.

STATUS Least Concern. Due to its inaccessible habitat, it has been less affected by human activity than any other large North American game animal. Estimated numbers: Alaska: 12,000, Yukon and Mackenzie: no records, Montana: 4,500, Idaho: 2,800, Washington: 5,000, South Dakota: 4,000, Colorado: 400.

PHOTO CREDITS ♂: *Greg Boreham*, Mount Evans (USA). ♀: *Iakov Filimonov*. Head ♂: *Andrey Kotkin*, Moscow Zoo (Russia). Head ♀: *Sandra Leidholdt*, Mount Evans (USA). Young: *Carl Neufelder*, Mount Evans (USA) and *James E. Butler*, Glacier NP (USA). Juvenile: *Erin Willett*, Siyeh Bend (USA), *Randall Runtsch*, Mount Evans (USA). 427

Sumatran Serow

CAPRICORNIS SUMATRAENSIS

BL: 140-155 cm. SH: 91 cm. TL: 8-16 cm. W: 85-140 kg. HL: To 23 cm. Small-bodied goat-antelope. General color black or dark gray, with weak brownish demarcations on the fetlocks. The hair of the coat is long and coarse, and a long mane of hoary gray to black, mixed with white, occurs on the neck. Legs and body dark black. Long ears are narrow and pointed. Face bearing large scent glands below the eyes. Lower jaw is whitish. A small light patch is visible at the junction of the jaw and throat. Neck is short and broad. Tail is black, fairly bushy. Horns are black, short and conical, sharply pointed, and directed backward. Little sexual dimorphism.

Capricornis sumatraensis

OTHER NAMES Southern Serow. *French*: Serow de Sumatra. *German*: Südlicher Serau. *Spanish*: Serau común, serau de Sumatra. *Russian*: Суматранский серау. *Bothias*: Gya. *Burmese*: Tau-tshiek. *Chinese*: Lie-lin. *Hindi*: Sarao. *Kashmiri*: Tamu, halij, salabhir. *Lepchas*: Sichi. *Malayan*: Kambing-utan. *Nepali*: Thar, ther. *Sikkim:* Gya. *Thai*: Liang-pa. *Tibetan*: Kha sya.

SUBSPECIES Monotypic. A number of subspecies were previously recognized, but are now considered full species. Includes *sumatraensis* (Sumatra), *swettenhami* (Malay Peninsula), and *robinsoni*, with *sumatraensis* having precedence. The taxonomy of Serows is not resolved and further research is needed.

SIMILAR SPECIES Smaller than the Himalayan and Chinese Serows and with smaller horns.

REPRODUCTION *Gestation*: 210 days. *Young per Birth*: 1, rarely 2. *Weaning*: 12 months. *Sexual Maturity*: 30 months (♀), 30-36 months (♂). *Life Span*: 10 years. Serows are thought to mate primarily between October and November.

BEHAVIOR *Family Group*: Solitary or in small groups. *Diet*: Predominantly a browser. *Main Predators*: Leopard, tiger. Generally a solitary animal, although it may sometimes move about in groups of several individuals. Each Serow inhabits a small area which is well marked with trails, dung heaps, and scents. This small area of habitat is selected so it can provide all the needs of the Serow, such as sufficient grass, shoots, and leaves on which to feed during the early morning and late evening, and suitable sheltered resting places in caves or under overhanging rocks and cliffs. This home range is defended against any intruding Serows by using their dagger-like horns, which are also used by these rather aggressive goat-antelopes to fight off predators. Although less specialized for climbing rugged mountains than some of its relatives, and with a somewhat slow and clumsy gait, the Serow is nevertheless adept at descending steep, rocky slopes, and is also even known to swim between small islands in Malaysia.

DISTRIBUTION *Native*: Indonesia, Malaysia, Thailand. Found in Indonesia (Sumatra), Malaysia (peninsular Malaya), and Thailand. In Indonesia (Sumatra), limited almost entirely to the volcanic mountain chain of the Barisan Mountains which run along the W spine of Sumatra from Aceh in the N to Lampung in the S. Although suitable habitat is more extensive within these mountains, there are only three known major concentrations: the Aceh highlands in the N, the Kerinci highlands in the center, and the Barisan Seletan highlands in the S. It is also found scattered through peninsular W Malaysia, but concentrated in the N states, especially Kelantan, Perlis, and Perak.

HABITAT It inhabits steep mountain slopes between 200 and 3,000 m, covered by both primary and secondary forests.

STATUS Vulnerable. No population estimates have been made in Indonesia. The estimated population for peninsular Malaysia is 500-750 animals, scattered through many very small, isolated populations. Its numbers have been severely reduced by persistent poaching by locals.

PHOTO CREDITS ♀: *Alex Kantorovich*, Dusit Zoo (Thailand). Head ♀: *Maxime Thué*, Zoo Melaka (Malaysia). ♂: *Jonas Livet*, Zoo Melaka (Malaysia).

Chinese Serow

CAPRICORNIS MILNEEDWARDSII

BL: 140-180 cm. SH: 100-112 cm. TL: 8-16 cm. W: 85-140 kg. HL: To 26.7 cm. Tall, long-legged, dark goat-antelope. Large head and thick neck, with a relatively short body, covered by long hair. Pelage is generally black, grading to reddish on flanks, rump, and tail. Middorsal black stripe. Extremely long, shaggy mane silvery to white, mixed with black, hanging down the neck. Tail is short and bushy, tipped with black. Head is browner. Lower lips are white. Prominent preorbital glands. Ears are large. Undersides are often paler. Lower legs are a rust color. Horns, found in both sexes, are short and recurved. Little sexual dimorphism.

Capricornis milneedwardsii

OTHER NAMES White-maned Serow, Mainland Serow, Southwest China Serow. *French*: Saro de Chine. *German*: Chinesischer Serau. *Spanish*: Serau chino. *Russian*: Китайский серау. *Tibetan*: Kha sya.

SUBSPECIES Monotypic. The name *C. milneedwardsii* formerly included *C. m. milneedwardsii* (Chinese Serow), and *C. m. maritimus* (Indochinese Serow) as subspecies: these are all elevated to full species here. Includes *argyrochaetes* (Hengduan Shan), *brachyrhinus, chrysochaetes, cornutus, erythropygius, fargesianus, longicornis, maxillaris, microdontus, montinus* (S Yunnan, SW Sichuan), *osborni, platyrhinus, pugnax, ungulosus,* and *vidianus*.

SIMILAR SPECIES Much larger than a Goral and much smaller than a Takin. Slightly larger than the Sumatran Serow, with longer horns.

REPRODUCTION *Gestation*: 240 days. *Young per Birth*: 1, rarely 2. Births usually in September or October.

BEHAVIOR *Family Group*: Alone or in small groups. *Diet*: Feeds on a wide range of leaves and shoots, and visits salt licks. It is territorial. It usually stays in a small area of only a few square kilometers where it grazes on grass, shoots, and leaves from along beaten paths. It marks its territory with droppings and scent markings. It is most active at dawn and dusk, and spends the rest of the day in thick vegetation. In summer, it inhabits steep areas with forested cliffs, and apparently descends into the forest belt in winter.

DISTRIBUTION *Native*: China. It is widely distributed through much of central and SE China. The general distribution range may be taken to include all the area of SW China from S Gansu southward through Sichuan and most of Yunnan, and beyond into Myanmar. Records show a more or less continuous distribution along the ranges of the Hengduan mountain system. E of this region, populations occur in adjacent mountain areas of Qinling, Shaanxi, and Guizhou. A few populations exist in the NW Hengduan Mountains of Yushu and Nangqen (Qinghai). The species has a comparatively widespread distribution through W and S Zhejiang, N Fujian, most of Jiangxi, E Guizhou, N Guangdong, E and SW Guangxi, E and S Yunnan, where it inhabits low mountains and foothills, and SW Sichuan. There may be zones of overlap or intergrading with the Himalayan Serow in the SW and with the Indochinese Serow in the S areas of the range.

HABITAT Rugged, steep terrain, but also in lowland forest. In Sichuan it occurs at elevations of 1,500-2,200 m, in habitats not far from tall shrubs.

STATUS Near Threatened. No total estimates of numbers have been made. Main threats include habitat degradation and fragmentation, and illegal hunting.

PHOTO CREDITS ♀: *ZhongYing Koay*, Zoo Taiping (Malaysia). ♂: Based on photos from Wolong National Nature Reserve (China).

Indochinese Serow
CAPRICORNIS MARITIMUS

BL: 140-155 cm. SH: 85-94 cm. TL: 11-16 cm. W: 85-140 kg. HL: To 16 cm. Tall, long-legged, dark goat-antelope, smaller than the Chinese Serow. Pelage is blackish with grayish or reddish grizzling, especially on the long mane and legs. Hair is coarse and rather thin. Shaggy mane down back of neck extending as ridge of coarse hair down back. White collar on the neck below the jaws and a distinct white patch around the corners of the mouth. Ears are large, whitish to tawny inside. Prominent glands in front of eye. Tail is short and bushy. Lower legs are brownish red, turning whitish above the hooves. Underparts are darkish. Horns, found in both sexes, are longer, stouter, and more heavily annulated than those of any Goral. Little sexual dimorphism.

♀

Young

♂

Capricornis maritimus

OTHER NAMES Tonkin Serow, Maned Serow, Mainland Serow. *French*: Saro d'Indochine. *German*: Indochinesischer Serau. *Spanish*: Serau de indochina. *Russian*: Индокитайский серау. *Thai*: Lieng pha, yurng, korum.

SUBSPECIES Monotypic. Formerly considered a subspecies of *C. milneedwardsii*. It was also previously considered as a subspecies of Sumatran Serow *(C. sumatraensis)*. Includes *annectens*, *benetianus*, *berthetianus*, *gendrelianus*, and *rocherianus*.

SIMILAR SPECIES Much larger than a Goral and much smaller than a Takin. Slightly larger than the Sumatran Serow, with longer horns.

REPRODUCTION *Gestation*: 210 days. *Young per Birth*: 1, rarely 2. Births usually in September or October.

BEHAVIOR *Family Group*: Alone or in small groups. *Diet*: Feeds on a wide range of leaves and shoots, and visits salt licks. It is territorial. It usually stays in a small area of only a few square kilometers where it grazes on grass, shoots, and leaves from along beaten paths. It marks its territory with droppings and scent markings. It is most active at dawn and dusk, and spends the rest of the day in thick vegetation.

DISTRIBUTION *Native*: Cambodia, Laos, Myanmar, Thailand, Vietnam. In Laos it is still widespread, especially along the Annamite mountain range of E-central and S Laos. In Cambodia it is probably naturally restricted to the hilly and mountainous terrain that surrounds the Mekong and Tonle Sap central plains. In Vietnam the species is likely widespread, except perhaps for the far S Mekong Delta region. The distribution in Myanmar appears to follow the forested mountain ranges surrounding the central plains. A larger distribution area occurs in the mountains in the N (Kachin state) and in the mountains E, to Myanmar's borders with China, Laos, and Thailand. In Thailand it is confined to the mountainous areas of the N and W, with isolated populations in hilly areas in the E and SE. The narrow isthmus is apparently a clear barrier between the distribution ranges of *C. maritimus* and *C. sumatraensis*.

HABITAT Rugged, steep hills and rocky places, especially limestone regions up to 4,500 m, in hill and mountain forest areas with gentler terrain, and in flatter areas marginally. Also on small offshore islands; has been reported swimming between them, and in Cambodia appears to occupy small, very naturally isolated karst limestone outcrops in the level lowlands of the Mekong plains.

STATUS Near Threatened. No total estimates of numbers have been made, but it is probably declining. Main threats include poaching by locals for food and traditional medicine, and habitat destruction.

PHOTO CREDITS ♂: *VPC Animals Photo*, Dusit Zoo (Thailand). Head ♂: *Anan Kaewkhammul* (Thailand). Head ♀: *Jatesada Natayo* (Thailand). Young: *Jonas Livet*, Phnom Tamao Zoo (Cambodia) and *TontanTravel.com*, Khao Yai NP (Thailand). ♀: *Phil Collet* (Thailand).

Himalayan Serow

CAPRICORNIS THAR

BL: 140-170 cm. SH: 90-110 cm. TL: 11-16 cm. W: 85-140 kg. HL: 16-34 cm. Similar to the Chinese Serow. General body color grizzled black or dark gray above, turning to rusty red on throat, chest, flanks, hindquarters, and upper legs. A darker black dorsal line is sometimes visible. Coarse hair, a long mane mixed with black and white hairs. Underparts and lower legs are dirty white. Chin and inside of ears white. Head comparatively large, reddish brown in Kashmir populations. Lower legs are a mixture of red and white in the northern Bengal race. The Punjab race has a woolly undercoat. Prominent long ears, with creamy-white hairs inside. Large preorbital gland. Tail short and bushy. Horns are black, conical, sharply pointed, and directed backward. Both sexes are similar, but female horns are thinner.

Capricornis thar

OTHER NAMES Nepalese Serow, Western Serow. *French*: Saro de l'Himalaya. *German*: Nepal-Serau, Himalaya-Serau. *Spanish*: Serau del Himalaya. *Russian*: Гималайский серау. *Assamese*: Deo sagoli. *Bengali*: Jongli chagol. *Hindi*: Sarao. *Naga*: Tellu. *Bhotia*: Gya. *Kashmiri*: Halj. *Mizo*: Saza.

SUBSPECIES Monotypic. Formerly considered a subspecies of *C. sumatraensis*. Includes *bubalina* (Nepal), *humei* (Kashmir), *rodoni* (Punjab), *thar* (Nepal and Sikkim), and *jamrachi* (N Bengal), with *thar* having priority. It is now believed that the Red Serow of the Garo, Naga, and Mishmi Hills (India) is more closely related to the Himalayan Serow (*C. thar*) than the Burmese Red Serow (*C. rubidis*).

REPRODUCTION *Gestation*: 210 days. *Young per Birth*: 1. In the Himalayas, rut commences at the end of October, and 1 or sometimes 2 young are born in May or June.

BEHAVIOR *Family Group*: Likely solitary or in small groups of 2-5 individuals. *Diet*: Browser. *Main Predators*: Leopard, dhole, eagles. Usually diurnal. The Himalayan Serow is more or less a solitary creature, though 4 or 5 individuals may be seen feeding on the same hill. It shelters in thickly wooded gorges and shallow caves, and comes out to feed in the mornings and evenings on open slopes. Its movements belie its awkward appearance on rocks as well as on flat ground. When alarmed, it bounds away with a hissing snort or a whistling scream.

DISTRIBUTION *Native*: Bangladesh, Bhutan, China, India, Nepal. The Himalayan Serow is widespread but sparsely distributed throughout the forested southern slopes of the Himalaya in N India, from Jammu and Kashmir to the Mishmi Hills in Arunachal Pradesh, and in the hill states of NE India. It is known to be locally present between 300 and 3,000 m as in all Himalayan states, and is found extensively in the Sutlej and Beas River catchments (Himachal Pradesh). Almost nothing is known of its distribution in Bhutan, other than it can exist in subtropical and temperate zones, and has been recorded in Royal Manas and Black Mountain NP. This Serow is probably widespread throughout the forested mountain slopes of Nepal. In China, it occurs in the forest belt between 2,000 and 3,000 m only in the narrow area on S slope of Qomolangma on the border with Nepal. A population is found in the narrow area E of the Big Bend of the Yarlung Zangbo River, where it inhabits sub-alpine forests.

HABITAT It inhabits rugged steep hills and rocky places, especially limestone regions up to 3,000 m above sea level, and also hill and mountain forest areas with gentler terrain.

STATUS Near Threatened. No estimates of population size are available. Main threats include poaching by locals for meat and traditional medicine, and habitat disturbance and fragmentation.

PHOTO CREDITS *Mel Lewis*, Nainital-Mussoorie (India). Head: *Tobias Schmid*, Phajoding (Bhutan).

Red Serow

CAPRICORNIS RUBIDUS

BL: 140-155 cm. SH: 85-95 cm. TL: 8-16 cm. W: 110-160 kg. HL: 15-21 cm. Small-bodied goat-antelope. Coarse pelage reddish brown, with a black hair base rather than white. Undersides whitish. A thin dark dorsal stripe runs along the spine from the shoulders to the tail. The top of the neck has a mane of longer hairs which can be erected when excited. Face has no distinctive markings, but large preorbital glands are present in front of the eyes. White patch beneath the jaw extending to a white bib at the top of the throat. Ears long and pointed. White hair on the fetlocks. Tail is bushy. Conical, short, backward-curving horns are found in both sexes. Horns are longer and thicker in males.

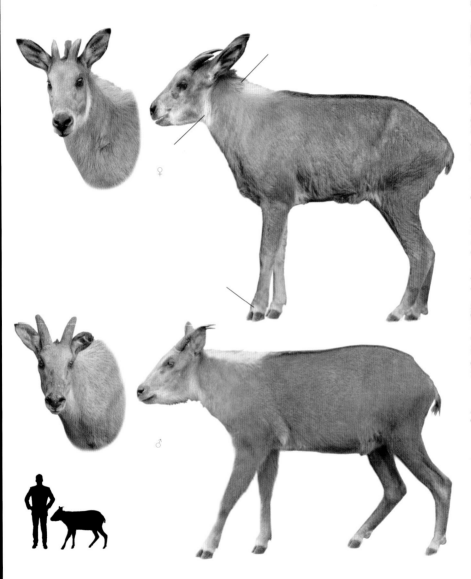

Capricornis rubidus

OTHER NAMES Burmese Red Serow, Arakan Serow. *French*: Saro carmin, saro rouge. *German*: Roter Serau. *Spanish*: Serau rojo, serau de Birmania. *Russian*: Красный серау.

SUBSPECIES Monotypic. Formerly considered a subspecies of *C. sumatraensis.*

SIMILAR SPECIES The reddish color of this species readily distinguishes it from the other black, gray, or dark brown *Capricornis* species. Some authors, however, suggest that Indian populations of red-colored Serow actually belong to *C. thar*; this situation has not been resolved. The smaller Red Goral is found in the same region as the Red Serow, but it is much smaller and more compact, and lacks the Serow's neck mane. Gorals also have smaller horns and lack a neck mane.

REPRODUCTION *Gestation:* 210 days. *Young per Birth*: 1. *Weaning*: 5-6 months. *Sexual Maturity*: 30 months (♀), 30-36 months (♂). *Life Span*: 10-20 years.

BEHAVIOR *Family Group*: Likely solitary or in small groups of 2-5 individuals. *Diet*: Grass, shoots, and leaves. *Main Predators*: Leopard, dhole, eagles. Nothing is known specifically about the ecology of the Red Serow, but it is likely similar to other Serow species. Serows tend to be most active in the morning and late afternoon or early evening. Caves and overhanging cliffs may be used for shelter. Serows are generally sedentary, and the preorbital glands may play a role in territorial marking. When alarmed, they vocalize with a loud whistle or a snort.

DISTRIBUTION *Native*: Myanmar. This species is known from N, and perhaps W, Myanmar. Its range is not well known, partly because of confusion with another Red Serow form in adjacent territories to the W in Assam and Bangladesh, and the fact that all Serows can show varying amounts of red and black coloration. True *rubidus* specimens have a black hair base rather than white. The species may overlap in some locations with *C. milneedwardsii* which extends through most of the Shan States and Pegu (Bago) Yoma at least as far W as the Ayeyarwady River. In NE India, Serows attributed to *C. rubidus* are considered to be *C. thar*.

HABITAT Hilly tropical forests in NE India (S of the Brahmaputra River), Bangladesh (E of the Jumuna River), and N Myanmar. Populations from India and Bangladesh, although reddish in color, may belong to either *C. rubidus* or *C. thar.*

STATUS Near Threatened. There are no current estimates for the wild population of Red Serow, but it is probably declining, due to poaching and logging.

PHOTO CREDITS *Brent Huffman, Elias Sadalla,* and *KASA (Kouprey Amigos dos Santuarios dos Animales)*, Assam State Zoo (India); this may be a distinct (but unnamed) species or subspecies of Serow.

Japanese Serow

CAPRICORNIS CRISPUS

BL: 95-102 cm. SH: 67-74 cm. TL: 6-7.5 cm. W: 31-48 kg. HL: 8-15 cm. Small-sized goat-antelope. Upper coat is not uniform in color, unlike in other Serows, being mottled, made of long hairs varying from white to purplish black in color. Four pelage color variations: black, black with a dorsal white spot, dark brown, and whitish. Underparts are light. Legs dark brown or black in color. There may be a dark collar encircling the lower neck. White beard under the chin extends down the throat and up along the jowls. Long ears pointed and covered in brown hair. Bridge of the nose is dark and naked. Preorbital glands are well developed. Tail moderately bushy. Both sexes carry the slightly curved horns, which are ridged on their lower two-thirds. Sexual dimorphism is minimal.

♂

Young

♀

438

Capricornis crispus

OTHER NAMES *French*: Serow du Japon. *German*: Japanischer Serau. *Spanish*: Serau japonés. *Russian*: Японский серау. *Japanese*: Nihon kamoshika. *Chinese*: Lie-lin.

SUBSPECIES Monotypic. Formerly included the Formosan Serow (*C. swinhoei*) as a subspecies. Includes *pryerianus, pryeri,* and *saxicola.*

SIMILAR SPECIES Smaller and with relatively shorter ears compared with Sumatran Serow. Larger and shaggier than the Formosan Serow. Serows have larger preorbital glands and a straighter facial profile than Gorals.

REPRODUCTION *Gestation*: 215 days. *Young per Birth*: 1, rarely 2. *Weaning*: 5-6 months. *Sexual Maturity*: 2.5 years (♀), 2.5-3 years (♂). *Life Span*: 20 years. The breeding season ranges from September to January, with peak conception from late October to early November. Newborn Japanese Serows are followers, although hiding behavior has been observed. Mothers are often intolerant of yearlings if a newborn is present. Horns begin to develop at 4 months old in both sexes. As adulthood is reached, the thicker transverse rings are forced upward by development of thinner horn rings at the base.

BEHAVIOR *Family Group*: Solitary, in pairs, or small family groups. *Diet*: Fleshy leaves, evergreen leaves, shoots, acorns. They feed during the early morning and late afternoon, sheltering in caves and under rock ledges during the rest of the day. While they move with a slow, clumsy gait, they are sure footed and steady, negotiating steep rocky slopes with ease. Mostly monogamous, but 20% of territorial ♂ may be polygynous, with 2 territorial ♀. Monogamous pairs are maintained by overlap between home ranges of solitary ♂ and solitary ♀. Young and mature offspring occur within the home range of an adult pair, although offspring will eventually disperse or establish their own territories within the home range of an adult. For most of the year, they live in small, discrete home ranges (from 1.3 to 22 ha). These may constitute exclusive territories, defended against members of the same sex. Both sexes mark their home ranges with the secretion from their preorbital glands. Regular paths are established within these ranges, leading to specific defecation and resting spots. During conflicts, the opponents chase each other, inflicting serious injuries by stabbing with their sharp horns. The behavioral repertoire includes head butting, chasing, putting head down or up, hooking, hopping, horning, kicking, lip curling, low stretching, marking, nasogenital contact, and nasonasal contact. Japanese Serows will stand on tree stumps and rocks.

DISTRIBUTION *Native*: Japan. Endemic to Japan on three of the main islands: Honshu, Shikoku, and Kyushu. Widespread in appropriate habitat on Honshu, but is absent from lowland cultivated areas and areas around human settlements. On Shikoku and Kyushu, their distribution is more limited. Extinct in W Honshu and greatly reduced in other areas before the early 20th century. Since the 1960s, their range has been expanding.

HABITAT Densely wooded hillsides and conifer forests in Japan.

STATUS Least Concern. Total population is 100,000 animals, stable or increasing.

PHOTO CREDITS ♀: *Windfuchs*, Zoo Schönbrunn (Austria). ♂ and heads: *Sergey Chichagov*, Zoo Schönbrunn (Austria). Young: *Yumi* (Japan) and *Tomoko Ichishima*, Inokashira Park Zoo (Japan). 439

Formosan Serow

CAPRICORNIS SWINHOEI

BL: 95-102 cm. SH: 50-70 cm. TL: 6-7.5 cm. W: 18-30 kg. HL: 7.4-11.2 cm. Small-sized animal, resembling a Goral more than other Serows, being relatively small. Short, relatively smooth and curly coat. Body dark brown to reddish. A narrow dorsal line is present. Underside of the chin and throat are pale yellowish to reddish brown. Legs noticeably darker than the body. Large ears. Unlike in other Serows, there is not an extensive mane on the neck. Ears are relatively large, brown externally and paler internally. Both males and females have horns, which are sharply pointed and have only a slight backward curve. Horns in males usually show greater wear than those of females. The bottom portion of the horns is ridged. Very little sexual dimorphism.

Juvenile

Young

440

Capricornis swinhoei

OTHER NAMES Taiwan Serow. *French*: Saro de Formose. *German*: Formosa Serau, Taiwan-Serau. *Spanish*: Serau de Formosa. *Russian*: Формозский (тайваньский) серау.

SUBSPECIES Monotypic. Formerly considered as a subspecies of the Japanese Serow (*C. crispus swinhoei*).

SIMILAR SPECIES In the wild, no similar species share the range of the Formosan Serow. The closely related Japanese Serow (*C. crispus*) is much shaggier and has a larger body size and shorter ears. All other Serow species are much larger and have a shaggy mane on the nape of the neck. Gorals (*Nemorhaedus*) also have a light throat bib, but are generally grayer and not as rich brown in color. Unlike the Formosan Serow, Gorals do not have preorbital glands in front of their eyes.

REPRODUCTION *Gestation*: 210 days. *Young per Birth*: 1, rarely 2. *Sexual Maturity*: As early as 16 months. *Life Span*: 15 years. During courtship, the ♂ will pursue the ♀, gently touching her with his horns or using his front legs to intermittently touch the ♀'s belly and hips. Aggressive encounters involve individuals facing each other with horns lowered. Breeding usually occurs between September and January, and the young are born after March. Young can stand and walk the day they are born, and usually follow their mothers closely. They will start to test solid food around 1 month after birth. From 6 to 12 months old, calves gradually separate from mothers and live independently.

BEHAVIOR *Family Group*: Solitary, but pairs may occur temporarily. *Diet*: Young shoots, leaves, and grasses. *Main Predators*: Formerly the clouded leopard. It may compete with Formosan Sambar (*Cervus unicolor swinhoei*) and Formosan Muntjac (*Muntiacus reevesi micrurus*), the two other large herbivores on Taiwan, although such competition may be mitigated by habitat segregation. In undisturbed areas, Formosan Serows are most active during the few hours after sunrise and again before sunset. However, in regions with human presence they may become more nocturnal. They are strong mountain climbers and can easily jump at least 2 m high, and some animals have even been known to climb up into trees. Their hooves separate into two halves that can easily hold on to rocks on steep slopes. It appears that this species is territorial: marking of trees using the horns and scent marking with the preorbital glands may define territorial boundaries. When irritated or alarmed, this species stamps its forefeet and may whistle at the same time.

DISTRIBUTION *Native:* Taiwan. Endemic to Taiwan and widely distributed in the mountainous regions throughout the island. It occupies elevations from 50 m to greater than 3,900 m just below the peak of Yu-shan, the highest mountain in the country. However, most populations today occupy regions higher than 1,000 m because most lowlands are encroached upon by humans.

HABITAT Mountainous region on the E half of Taiwan. It can be found in coniferous and mixed deciduous forests, as well as in alpine grasslands and on cliff tops.

STATUS Least Concern. There is no estimate of total population size. Main threats include habitat destruction and poaching.

PHOTO CREDITS *Chan Te Chuan*, Taipei Zoo (Taiwan). Juvenile: *Pierre de Chabannes*, Taipei Zoo (Taiwan).

Red Goral
NEMORHAEDUS BAILEYI

BL: 93-103 cm. SH: 57-61 cm. TL: 7-10 cm. W: 20-30 kg. HL: 9-16 cm (♂), 7.5-13 cm (♀). One of the smallest Goral species. Bright reddish-brown to fox-red color with long, soft, shaggy hair. A thin dark stripe runs along the spine from the head to the tip of the tail. Legs are the same rich red as the body, while the undersides are a lighter buff color. Black-colored tail is very short for a Goral, but a long tuft of dark hair at the end may double its apparent length. Face slightly lighter in color than the body, with a dark patch just above the nose. Margin of upper and lower lips white. Light throat bib is less defined than in other Gorals. Ears relatively short, whitish on the inside. Both males and females have a pair of black, short, arcing horns. Horns of males tend to be longer and thicker than those of females. Females slightly larger than males, otherwise very similar.

Nemorhaedus baileyi

OTHER NAMES Brown Goral. *French*: Goral roux, bouquetin du Népal. *German*: Roter Goral, Tibetanischer Goral. *Spanish*: Goral rojo. *Russian*: Красный горал. *Burmese*: Taung hseik. *Mizo*: Sathar. *Tibetan*: Ra-mar.

SUBSPECIES *N. b. baileyi* (Tibetan Red Goral): Chinese Tibet. *N. b. cranbrooki* (Burmese Red Goral): Assam and upper Myanmar. The validity of these subspecies is uncertain.

SIMILAR SPECIES Easily distinguished from other members of the genus *Nemorhaedus* by its reddish coat; all other Gorals are grayish brown with grizzled hairs. It is also the smallest Goral, and has a greater curvature to its horns. The similarly colored Red Serow (*Capricornis rubidus*) is much larger, with longer horns, coarser hair, and a distinct white throat bib.

REPRODUCTION *Gestation*: 180 days. *Young per Birth*: 1. *Weaning*: 3.5 months. *Sexual Maturity*: 1.5 years (♀), 3 years (♂). *Life Span*: Up to 15 years. Red Goral tend to breed in late autumn and early winter (September to December). During the rut, ♂ will follow ♀ closely, being in frequent nasogenital contact, often accompanied by smelling and licking, in order to determine the onset of estrus. Non-receptive ♀ will either flee from the advances of ♂ or threaten them by butting the body of the ♂ with their head. Receptive ♀ tend to stand still as the ♂ approaches, signaling their estrus by raising the tail. Flehmen has been observed during the majority of encounters. Births tend to occur in June and July, although some infants have been seen as early as April.

BEHAVIOR *Family Group*: Mostly solitary, sometimes in groups of up to 3 animals (usually a mother and her offspring). *Diet*: Lichens, also grasses, stems, and leaves. *Main Predators*: Leopard, jackal. Most active during the day, and tend to retreat to inaccessible cliffs at night, where they sleep on sheltered ledges. They are strong climbers and jumpers, and seek safety from predators by fleeing up cliffs. They can clear obstacles over 1.8 m high from a standing start. Although generally quiet, ♂ make a call which sounds like "zer-zer" during the breeding season; ♀ Red Goral also whistle as ♂ approach. Red Goral typically inhabit a home range of around 40 ha. In summer, they move up in elevation, often above timberline to alpine meadows and thickets. From November through March, they move downslope to avoid snow, returning to higher elevations in April. ♂ are territorial during the breeding season.

DISTRIBUTION *Native*: China, India, Myanmar. This species is found in N Myanmar, China (SE Tibet and Yunnan), and NE India (Arunachal Pradesh).

HABITAT Red Goral inhabit coniferous montane woodlands at high elevations (2,000-4,500 m above sea level), utilizing meadows, cliffs, forests, and areas of scrub within this habitat. In the summer, they are found at higher altitudes, occasionally above the treeline. As winter snows arrive, the goral moves to lower elevations where the forests become mixed with deciduous trees.

STATUS Vulnerable. Fewer than 10,000 Red Goral are believed to survive today. The actual number may be quite a bit lower.

PHOTO CREDITS ♀: *Alex Kantorovich*, Beijing Zoo (China). Head ♀: *traaaaaaaav*, Shanghai Zoo (China). Head ♂: *Sergey Chichagov*, Beijing Zoo (China). Animals from Beijing Zoo may be hybrids with Chinese Goral.

Himalayan Brown Goral
NEMORHAEDUS GORAL

BL: 82-120 cm. SH: 60-71 cm. TL: 7.5-20 cm. W: 35-42 kg. HL: 15-18 cm (♂). Large Goral. Back slightly arched, and the facial profile is concave. Coat is medium brown in color with black-tipped hairs, rufous brown above and paler below. Pelage is shaggy in winter. White patch on throat and chin. Black dorsal stripe and tail. Slender legs light tan in color. Black stripe down the front of the legs. Old males have a short, semi-erect mane on the neck. Distal half of tail is black and not bushy. Both sexes have black, short, pointed horns which curve backward, with small, irregular ridges. Horns comparatively straight and not heavily ringed. Females have more slender horns than males.

♀

♂

Young

Nemorhaedus goral

OTHER NAMES Eastern Gray Goral. *French*: Goral de l'Himalaya, bouquetin du Népal, Goral à queue courte. *German*: Grauer Goral, Osthimalaja-Goral. *Spanish*: Goral marrón del Himalaya. *Russian*: Гималайский бурый горал. *Assamese*: Deo sagoli. *Bengali*: Ram chhagol. *Bothia*: Ra giyu. *Hindi*: Ghoral. *Kashmiri*: Pij, pijur, rai, ran. *Lepchas*: Suh-ging. *Nepali*: Ghoral. *Tamil*: Koral atu. *Thai*: Kwangpa. *Tibetan*: Nawa.

SUBSPECIES Monotypic. The name *N. goral* (Himalayan Goral) formerly included *N. goral* (Himalayan Brown Goral), and *N. bedfordi* (Himalayan Gray Goral) as subspecies: these are elevated to full species here. Includes *hodgsoni*.

SIMILAR SPECIES Somewhat resembles a Serow, differing by its smaller size, shorter horns, lack of facial glands, and certain details of the skull.

REPRODUCTION *Gestation*: 170-218 days. *Young per Birth*: 1, rarely up to 3. *Weaning*: 7-8 months. *Sexual Maturity*: About 3 years. *Life Span*: 17 years. Rut begins in the period from late September to November in the far N and from early November into December in the S. ♀ when accompanied by young tend to aggregate. Kids are born between April and May and stay with the mother for about 1 year.

BEHAVIOR *Family Group*: Old ♂ are usually solitary; otherwise they live in small groups of 4-5, rarely more than 10. *Diet*: Grasses, leaves, twigs, nuts; they drink water daily, particularly after morning feeding. *Main Predators:* Dhole, leopard, lynx, tiger, marten, wolf. Most active in the early morning and late evening, but on cloudy days roam throughout the day. They become nocturnal when confronted with persistent human disturbance. They often drink after eating in the morning, thereafter retiring to a rock ledge on which to rest until evening. They never feed far from escape cover. Extremely nimble, they can move at high speeds across formidable terrain. Their remarkable camouflage is extremely effective, along with the fact that they lie motionless, Gorals are extremely difficult to spot, even when in plain sight. Alarm vocalizations consist of hissing or a sneezing noise. ♂ are territorial. Groups inhabit an area of about 40 ha. During the mating season, ♂ may occupy and mark territories of 22-25 ha.

DISTRIBUTION *Native*: Bhutan, China, India, Nepal. It has a narrow distribution zone in China that is located in the border area of Tibet. In Bhutan, it occurs throughout the N third of the country. It is also found across most of the S slopes of the Himalayas of N India from Jammu and Kashmir to E Arunachal Pradesh, as far as the Brahmaputra. The Sutlej River is the probable distributional boundary between the Himalayan Brown and Gray Goral.

HABITAT Wooded mountain slopes at elevations of 1,000-4,000 m in the Himalayas, using precipitous cliffs and rough rocky terrain, with a fairly dense cover of thorny shrubs and trees.

STATUS Near Threatened. No estimate of population size is available in China, but numbers are thought to be small. Main threats include habitat destruction and fragmentation.

PHOTO CREDITS ♂: Kyoto City Zoo (Japan). Head ♂: *Alex Meyer*, Delhi Zoo (India). ♀ and head: *Avadhesh Malik*, Uttarakhand (India) and *Manjot Singh* (India). Young: *Ali Arsh,* National Zoological Park, New Delhi (India).

Himalayan Gray Goral

NEMORHAEDUS BEDFORDI

BL: 95-130 cm. SH: 60-80 cm. TL: 7.5-18 cm. W: 35-42 kg. HL: 13-23 cm. Large Goral. Back slightly arched, Facial profile concave. Coat is gray-brown to yellowish-gray color, suffused with black. Dorsal stripe barely visible. White throat patch extending to the chin, upper lip, jaws, and cheeks. Dark streak on the muzzle. Tail is relatively short, and the base is blackish. Legs are paler than the body, white to fawn in color, with a dark brown line on the front. Underside is whitish. Both sexes have black, short, pointed horns which curve backward, more curved and with heavier rings than those of Himalayan Brown Goral. Females have more slender horns than males.

Nemorhaedus bedfordi

OTHER NAMES Western Gray Goral. *French*: Goral de Bedford. *German*: Westhimalaja-Goral. *Spanish*: Goral gris del Himalaya. *Russian*: Гималайский серый горал. *Annamese*: Deo chagal. *Bothia*: Ra giyu. *Hindi*: Goral. *Kashmiri*: Pij, pijur, rai, rom. *Korean*: San yang. *Lepchas*: Suh-ging. *Nepali*: Ghoral. *Tamil*: Koral atu. *Thai*: Kwang-pa. *Tibetan*: Nawa.

SUBSPECIES Monotypic. Formerly considered a subspecies of *N. goral* (Himalayan Goral).

REPRODUCTION *Gestation*: 170-218 days. *Young per Birth*: 1, rarely up to 3. *Weaning*: 7-8 months. *Sexual Maturity*: About 3 years. *Life Span*: 15 years. Mating occurs in November-December, and young are born in April-May and stay with the mother for about 1 year.

BEHAVIOR *Family Group*: ♂ are usually solitary; otherwise they live in small groups of 2-9. ♂ join ♀ herds only during the mating season; mating-season mixed herds consist of a single adult ♂, adult ♀ and their young, and subadult ♀. *Diet*: Grass, shrubs, leaves. *Main Predators*: Dhole, leopard, lynx, tiger, marten, wolf. Primarily diurnal. They avoid open areas during warmer days. They seek security cover in dense, tall vegetation in steep, rocky terrain. They have a matriarchal society, consisting of a basic family group of an adult female with 1 or 2 young of the year and other offspring 1-3 years old.

DISTRIBUTION *Native*: India, Pakistan. Found in Pakistan (Kashmir) and NW India (Chamba, Kulu). The Sutlej River is the probable distributional boundary between the Himalayan Brown and Gray Goral.

HABITAT Wooded mountain slopes at elevations of 350-3,000 m. In Pakistan, they occur in Himalayan foothills in diverse plant communities, including scattered pine and thorny shrub habitats. They prefer open vegetation with good grass cover and avoid shrub-rich patches, especially areas where the shrub height exceeds their shoulder height.

STATUS Near Threatened. In Pakistan, estimated population is fewer than 1,000 individuals, extending into adjacent areas of India. Main threats include habitat alteration and disturbance, poaching, and livestock grazing.

PHOTO CREDITS ♂: Based on photos from Rajaji NP (Pakistan) and *Paul Snook*, Patikka, Kashmir (Pakistan). ♀: *Scott Christian*, Marghazar Zoo (Pakistan). Head ♂: *Sanjay Shrishrimal*. Head ♀: *Ali Arsh*.

South Chinese Goral

NEMORHAEDUS GRISEUS

BL: 82-130 cm. SH: 50-78 cm. TL: 8-20 cm. W: 20-35 kg. HL: 23 cm (♂), 18 cm (♀). Coat consisting of dense hairs, comparatively short, and not woolly. Pale grayish brown to brown, with a varying black overlay, a dark dorsal stripe, and dark brown forehead. Pale patch in throat is edged orange, chin dark. Woolly undercoat with long, coarse guard hairs. Summer coat shorter and thinner. Tail is dark and bushy, relatively long, black on the upper and lower surfaces. Lower parts of the legs, above the hooves, are light cream. Forelegs sometimes reddish with black stripe. Males have a short, semi-erect mane and longer conical horns than those seen in females, otherwise very similar.

♀

Young

Juvenile

♂

Nemorhaedus griseus

OTHER NAMES Chinese Long-tailed Goral, Gray Goral, Gray Long-tailed Goral, Central Chinese Goral. *French*: Goral gris, goral chinois. *German*: Chinesischer Goral. *Spanish*: Goral chino, goral gris. *Russian*: Китайский серый горал.

SUBSPECIES Monotypic. The name *N. griseus* (Chinese Goral) formerly included *N. evansi* (Burmese Goral), and *N. griseus* (South Chinese Goral) as subspecies: these are elevated to full species here. Previously considered as a subspecies of *N. goral* (*N. g. arnouxianus*). Includes *cinerea, arnouxianus, curvicornis, fantozatianus, fargesianus, galeanus, initialis, iodinus, niger, pinchonianus, versicolor, vidianus, xanthodeiros,* and *henryanus*.

SIMILAR SPECIES Serows are much larger and have darker fur with long coarse hairs, and a thicker neck and larger head. Differs from the Himalayan Goral by usually having a longer coat and a long, tufted tail.

REPRODUCTION *Gestation*: 170-218 days. *Young per Birth*: 1, rarely 2. *Sexual Maturity*: 1.5 years. *Life Span*: 22 years. Rut begins from late September to November in the far N and from early November into December in the S. ♀ when accompanied by young tend to aggregate. Kids are born between April and May and stay with the mother for about 1 year.

BEHAVIOR *Family Group*: Small groups of 4-12 individuals; older ♂ probably solitary. *Diet*: Grasses, leaves, twigs, and nuts. *Main Predators*: Dhole, leopard, lynx, tiger. Gorals are diurnal, and are most active in the early morning and late evening, but can be active throughout on overcast days. Group home range size is typically around 40 ha, with ♂ occupying marked territories of 22-25 ha during the mating season.

DISTRIBUTION *Native*: China. Found in central and SE China, Sichuan NE to Shanxi, Henan, Hubei, and E to Fujian, and in the mountainous S of China, as far as W Xizang and Yunnan.

HABITAT Steep areas and plateaus in mountainous areas and will sometimes use subtropical mixed forests and evergreen-deciduous forests near cliffs, but primarily stays within rugged rocky terrain.

STATUS Vulnerable. No estimate of total population, but numbers are believed to be declining due to hunting.

PHOTO CREDITS *Sergey Chichagov,* Shanghai Zoo (China) and Tallinn Zoo (Estonia).

Burmese Goral

NEMORHAEDUS EVANSI

BL: 50-70 cm. SH: 50-70 cm. TL: 12-18 cm. W: 20-30 kg. HL: 15-18 cm. Smaller than the Chinese Goral. Coat consisting of dense hairs, comparatively short, and not woolly. General color is pale grayish to brown, underside is pale gray fawn. Legs are golden to creamy gold or browner. Dark dorsal stripe. Small yellow to white throat patch. Tail is dark brown. Summer coat shorter and thinner. Horns, present in both sexes, are very small. Males have longer conical horns that those seen in females, otherwise very similar.

♂

♀

Nemorhaedus evansi

OTHER NAMES Evans's Long-tailed Goral, Burmese Long-tailed Goral, Thai Goral, Gray Long-tailed Goral. *French*: Goral d'Evans. *German*: Burma-Goral. *Spanish*: Goral de Birmania. *Russian*: Бирманский серый горал.

SUBSPECIES Monotypic. Formerly considered a subspecies of *N. griseus* (Chinese Goral). Previously considered as a subspecies of *N. caudatus* (*N. c. evansi*).

SIMILAR SPECIES Serows are much larger and have darker fur with long coarse hairs, and a thicker neck and larger head.

REPRODUCTION *Gestation*: 180 days. *Young per Birth*: 1, rarely 2. *Sexual Maturity*: 3 years. *Life Span*: 15 years. Rut begins from early November into December. ♀ when accompanied by young tend to aggregate. Kids are born between April and May and stay with the mother for about 1 year.

BEHAVIOR *Family Group*: Small groups of 1-6 individuals; older ♂ probably solitary. *Diet*: Mainly a browser; grasses, forbs, low shrubs, twigs of leaves of larger trees. *Main Predators*: Dhole, leopard, lynx, tiger. Most active in the early morning and late evening, but can be active throughout on overcast days. Population density of about 5 individuals per km². Their attachment to a small home range makes them vulnerable to human predation. They have good vision, rapid escape responses, and a pelage that disguises them well. Their horns are used when defending themselves from predators or other competing ♂, but can also be used when carrying out various different courtship or dominance behaviors.

DISTRIBUTION *Native*: China, Myanmar, Thailand. Found in central and S Myanmar and Thailand, E to Chiang Mai District and S to Raheng, N into Yunnan, China.

HABITAT Rocky, steep terrain with tall vegetation cover, often on slopes over 60 degrees. In some areas found at elevations of 1,600-1,970 m.

STATUS Vulnerable. Poaching, deforestation, and agricultural development are major causes of declines and fragmentation of Burmese Goral populations. In Thailand, they have been hunted for their meat, horns, and the oil that comes from boiling the head and bones, bringing them close to extinction.

PHOTO CREDITS ♂, ♀: *Anan Kaewkhammul,* Chiang Mai Night Safari (Thailand). Head ♂: *Jonas Livet*, Chiang Mai Night Safari (Thailand).

Long-tailed Goral
NEMORHAEDUS CAUDATUS

BL: 81-129 cm. SH: 51-81 cm. TL: 14-18 cm. W: 28-47 kg (♂), 22-45 kg (♀). HL: 14-21 cm (♂). Long-haired Goral. Grayish yellowish brown in color, with a dark dorsal stripe. Throat patch is small and white, not yellowish. Face is black in front, grayish yellow on the sides. Chin is black. Front of lower legs is a light gray brown, contrasting with the white feet. Upper side of tail is similar in color to the back; a broad white fringe borders the tail below. Inconspicuous glands in front of the eyes. The tips of the horns curve back and are basally annulated. Females usually are lighter in shade, with smaller horns.

♂

♀

Young

Nemorhaedus caudatus caudatus

Nemorhaedus caudatus raddeanus

OTHER NAMES Korean Long-tailed Goral, North Chinese Goral, Chinese Gray Goral, Amur Goral. *French*: Goral à queue longue. *German*: Langschwanzgoral. *Spanish*: Goral de cola larga. *Russian*: Северо-восточный длиннохвостый горал *(caudatus),* Амурский длиннохвостый горал *(raddeanus).*

SUBSPECIES *N. c. caudatus* (North Chinese Long-tailed Goral): N China, Hebei, Neimenggu, Shansi; shaggy, somewhat woolly coat, tail tuft long, bushy, and black, much darker than base of tail and middle of back, narrow white fringe borders the tail below, color from pale buffy gray to dark grayish brown, dark dorsal stripe, white throat patch. *N. c. raddeanus* (Amur or Korean Long-tailed Goral): China, North Korea, Asian Russia, South Korea; long-haired race, grayish yellowish brown in color, dark dorsal stripe, large white throat patch, face black in front, grayish yellow on the sides, front of lower legs light gray brown, contrasting with the white feet, upper side of tail is similar in color to the back; a broad white fringe borders the tail below. Previously considered as a subspecies of *N. goral*. Validity of these subspecies is uncertain.

SIMILAR SPECIES Differs from the Himalayan Goral by usually having a longer coat, a long, tufted tail, black stripes on forelegs passing to outer leg below knee rather than down median, and shorter horns. Chinese Goral has more black fur on its tail, more contrast between the color of lower legs and body, and the throat patch is surrounded by a darker-colored border (light orange or light brown). Alpine Chamois has a thinner body, with longer neck and legs, and horns have a hook-like shape.

REPRODUCTION *Gestation*: 180-260 days. *Young per Birth*: 1-2. *Sexual Maturity*: 3 years. *Life Span:* 15 years. Mating takes place in early winter, and 1, or rarely 2-3, kids born about 6 months later. ♀ when accompanied by young tend to aggregate.

BEHAVIOR *Family Group*: Small groups of 4-12 individuals, with older ♂ usually solitary. *Diet*: A wide range of plant material: grass, herbs and shoots, leaves of small trees, nuts, and even some fruit. Group home range size is typically around 40 hectares, with ♂ occupying marked territories of 22-25 ha during the mating season. Diurnal, and most active in the early morning and late evening, but can be active throughout on overcast days. It keeps to steeper slopes where it is very agile over rocky crags and cliffs. Visits salt licks. Gives hissing sneeze call when alarmed.

DISTRIBUTION *Native*: China, North Korea, South Korea, Russian Federation. E Russia (Primorsky and Khabarovsk Territories), NE China, North Korea, and South Korea. Its distribution is patchy because Goral are confined to specific habitat.

HABITAT Steep mountainous areas and will sometimes use evergreen forests near cliffs, but primarily stays within rugged, rocky terrain. It inhabits steep and rocky terrain in evergreen and deciduous forests, especially with exposed grassy ridges from about 500 to 2,000 m.

STATUS Vulnerable. There are no reliable total population estimates. Estimated population in Russia up to 500, and 700 in South Korea. Main threats are poaching, habitat degradation, and grazing competition.

PHOTO CREDITS *Sergey Chichagov*, Tallinn Zoo (Estonia).

White-faced Muskox

OVIBOS MOSCHATUS WARDI

BL: 190-245 cm. SH: 120-151 cm. TL: 9-14 cm. W: 270-340 kg. Long, shaggy guard hairs, dark brown in color, almost reaching the ground. Hidden beneath these guard hairs is an insulating layer of light gray underwool. Lower legs pale, as is a patch in the center of the back. Body massive, and seems even more so due to the long hair and short legs. Hump on the shoulders. Head carried low with no neck. Large hooves. Hook-like horns, found in both sexes, pale yellow in color, forming a large boss on the skull, thinning as they sweep down and away from the head, ending with the sharp tips curving upward. Horns significantly thicker and form a larger boss in males. Females smaller than males, with much less massive horns.

♀

♂ Juvenile

♂

Young

Ovibos moschatus wardi

OTHER NAMES Greenland Muskox. *French*: Boeuf musqué. *German*: Moschusochse, Bisamochse, Schafsochse. *Spanish*: Buey almizclero, toro almizclero. *Greenlandic*: Umimmak. *Icelandic*: Saudnaut, moskusuxi. *Navajo*: Tse'Ta Dibé. *Norwegian*: Moskusfé. *Russian*: Гренландский (белоголовый) овцебык.

SUBSPECIES Considered as a subspecies of *O. moschatus* (Muskox): *O. m. moschatus* (Barren Ground Muskox), *O. m. wardi* (White-faced or Greenland Muskox). The validity of these subspecies has been questioned by some authors.

REPRODUCTION *Gestation*: 255 days. *Young per Birth*: 1, rarely 2. *Weaning*: 10-18 months. *Sexual Maturity*: 3-4 years (♀), 5-6 years (♂). *Life Span*: 24 years. ♀ give birth between April and June, and do so among the herd.

BEHAVIOR *Family Group*: Herds of 10-20 animals with an adult ♂ and several ♀ with their offspring. ♂ not belonging to one of these herds may form bachelor groups. *Diet*: Grasses, sedges, flowering plants, leaves of shrubs. *Main Predators*: Wolf, rarely polar bear. Nomadic, perpetually wandering the Arctic tundra, moving an average of 2 km daily between feeding sites. Periods of grazing are alternated with rest periods, each about 2.5 hours long. Muskox migrates from sheltered, moist lowlands in the summer to higher, barren plateaus in winter. The primary reason for this is food, as the exposed plateaus do not accumulate snow due to the high winds, therefore making food easier to find. The distance traveled between summer and winter areas generally does not exceed 80 km. The characteristic defense pattern of this species is a ring, with the young hidden in the center and the adults facing outward. Conflicts between ♂ occur throughout the year, although the frequency is expectedly higher during the breeding season. Confrontations generally consist of two rivals rushing toward each other at up to 40 kmph, clashing their horns together. This may occur up to 20 times in a row over a course of 50 minutes. Accompanied by these charges are lion-like roars. These fights merely determine dominance, with the loser remaining part of the herd.

DISTRIBUTION *Native*: Canada, Greenland. *Reintroduced*: United States (Alaska). *Introduced*: Russia, Norway, Sweden. Naturally distributed throughout the Canadian Arctic islands (except King William Island, whose Muskoxen are treated as Barren Ground Muskoxen, and Baffin Island, which has no Muskoxen), and on the N and E coasts of Greenland. From E Greenland, it has been introduced and transplanted to a number of locations: Fairbanks, Nunivak Island, and Unalakleet, Nelson Island, the Seward Peninsula, Cape Thompson, and the Arctic National Wildlife Refuge (Alaska), on the Taimyr Peninsula and Wrangel Island (Russia), near Fort Chimo (Canada), and in W Greenland, Svalbard, mainland Norway, and Sweden. Probably all introductions and transplants of Muskoxen throughout the world have been of the Greenland subspecies, with no Barren Ground Muskoxen having been transplanted anywhere.

HABITAT Arctic tundra.

STATUS Least Concern. Estimated population around 75,000.

PHOTO CREDITS ♂: *Greg Lasley*, Nome, Alaska (USA), *Stephen Chase*, Girdwood, Alaska (USA). ♀: *John Hoyt*. Head ♀: *Ben Hattenbach,* Arctic National Wildlife Refuge, Alaska (USA). Young: *Evan E. Fusco, MD*, Alaska (USA). Juvenile: *Sergey Chichagov*, Tallinn Zoo (Estonia).

Barren Ground Muskox

OVIBOS MOSCHATUS MOSCHATUS

BL: 190-250 cm. SH: 120-151 cm. TL: 9-14 cm. W: 180-410 kg. Larger body and horns than the White-faced Muskox, with a darker face, saddle, and lower legs. Long, shaggy guard hairs, dark brown in color, almost reaching the ground. Hidden beneath these guard hairs is an insulating layer of light gray underwool. Lower legs pale. The body is massive, and seems even more so due to the long hair and short legs. Hump on the shoulders. Head carried low with no neck. Hook-like horns are found in both sexes, pale yellow in color, forming a large boss on the skull, thinning as they sweep down and away from the head, ending with the sharp tips curving upward. Horns significantly thicker and form a larger boss in males. Males larger than females.

♀

Young

♂

Ovibos moschatus moschatus

OTHER NAMES Mainland Muskox, Black-faced Muskox. *French*: Boeuf musqué. *German*: Moschusochse, Bisamochse, Schafsochse. *Spanish*: Buey almizclero, toro almizclero. *Greenlandic*: Umimmak. *Icelandic*: Saudnaut, moskusuxi. *Navajo*: Tse'Ta Dibé. *Norwegian*: Moskusfé. *Russian*: Канадский (черноголовый, или тундровый) овцебык.

SUBSPECIES Considered as a subspecies of *O. moschatus* (Muskox): *O. m. moschatus* (Barren Ground Muskox), *O. m. wardi* (White-faced or Greenland Muskox). Includes *niphoecus* (Hudson Bay or Wager Muskox) from King William Island, the Boothia and Melville peninsulas, and the area bordered on the W by the Back River and on the S by Baker Lake and Chesterfield Inlet.

SIMILAR SPECIES White-faced Muskox is smaller in body and horns, and tends to have a lighter face, saddle, and lower legs, but distinction between the two is based mostly on location of the animal, and the two subspecies can interbreed.

REPRODUCTION *Gestation*: 255 days. *Young per Birth*: 1, rarely 2. *Weaning*: 10-18 months. *Sexual Maturity*: 3-4 years (♀), 5-6 years (♂). *Life Span*: 24 years. Similar to White-faced Muskox. Breeding season from late August into September. Births between April and June. Calves are born with very short guard hair and nubs where the horns will begin growing soon after; they are also born with a layer of baby qiviut and over the harsh winter are dependent on the cows for both additional body warmth and protection from the elements by standing in the skirt.

BEHAVIOR *Family Group*: Herds as small as 5 animals during the summer, and may join with other small groups to form herds as large as 60 individuals in the winter. Most herds average between 10 and 20 animals. *Diet*: Grasses, sedges, flowering plants, leaves of shrubs. *Main Predators*: Wolf, rarely polar bear. Similar to White-faced Muskox. Social species, with a harem breeding system. Dominance among ♂ is determined during the breeding season, through head butting and chasing, as well as grunting and bellowing. Among ♀, dominance is determined by age and size, through pushing, shoving, and chasing. They can run as fast as 40 kmph, but they can easily overheat; for this reason, they are generally slow moving and have very short migrations within the home range. However, under certain conditions (weather permitting), Muskoxen calves as well as adults will play.

DISTRIBUTION *Native*: Canada. Formerly found from Point Barrow (Alaska), eastward across the N slope of Alaska and Canada to Port Nelson, Manitoba, on Hudson Bay, and northward to include King William Island and the Boothia and Melville peninsulas. Today, it is found only in Canada, on the N slope of the mainland from about Cape Bathurst on the Beaufort Sea eastward to about Chesterfield Inlet on Hudson Bay, and southward to latitude 63°N between Artillery and Dubawnt lakes. Muskoxen on King William Island are considered to be of this subspecies.

HABITAT Arctic tundra. Moist habitats in the summer. In winter, stays on hilltops or slopes where winds minimize the snow depth.

STATUS Least Concern. Estimated population around 5,300 animals.

PHOTO CREDITS ♂: *John Strother* (Canada) and Moscow Zoo (Russia). ♀: *Mirek Heran,* Plzen Zoo (Czech Republic). Young: *Ailis Vann.*

Mishmi Takin
BUDORCAS TAXICOLOR

BL: 170-220 cm. SH: 100-130 cm. TL: 7-20 cm. W: 150-350 kg. HL: 25-64 cm (♂). Large and stocky goat-antelope. Bovine-like body covered with dense hair. Less colorful than other subspecies, being an overall smoky brown color, suffused with grayish yellow, darker on the legs and face, and lighter on the back. A dark dorsal stripe may be apparent, from the occiput to the root of the tail. Short, stocky legs with broad hooves and strong dewclaws. Body stocky and chest deep. In profile, face convex with the nasal ridge arching outwards. Both sexes carry strong horns that curve out, backward, and upward at the tips. The bases of the horns may have transverse ridges. Rather than localized scent glands, the takin has an oily, strong-smelling substance secreted over the whole body. Females significantly smaller than males.

Juvenile

Young

Budorcas taxicolor

OTHER NAMES Himalayan Takin. *French*: Takin des Mishmi. *German*: Mishmi-Takin, Rindergemse, Gnuziege. *Spanish*: Takín de Mishmi. *Russian*: Бирманский такин. *Burmese*: Tha Min. *Rawan*: Shafight. *Tibetan*: Ri-ka, ye-more, shing-na.

SUBSPECIES Monotypic. The name *B. taxicolor* (Takin) formerly included *B. taxicolor* (Mishmi Takin), *B. bedfordi* (Golden Takin), *B. tibetana* (Sichuan Takin), and *B. whitei* (Bhutan Takin) as subspecies: these are all elevated to full species here.

SIMILAR SPECIES Similar in size to the Bhutan Takin, but with larger and more massive horns. Smaller and much darker than the Sichuan and Golden Takin.

REPRODUCTION *Gestation*: 7-8 months. *Young per Birth*: 1, rarely 2. *Weaning*: 9 months. *Sexual Maturity*: At 2.5 years. *Life Span*: 15 years. Mating takes place between July and August. Adult ♂ compete for dominance by sparring head-to-head with opponents, and both sexes appear to use the scent of their own urine to indicate dominance.

BEHAVIOR *Family Group*: Small mixed herds in winter, herds of over 100 have been seen in summer, old ♂ often solitary. *Diet*: Grasses, leaves, buds, shoots. *Main Predators*: Bear, wolf. Takin feed in early morning and late afternoon, although on overcast days they may remain active throughout the day. Takin use narrow trails through the dense growth, which they regularly pass through in traveling between feeding and resting places. When threatened, they retreat into dense bamboo thickets, where they lie down. In the summer they eat forbs and leaves. In the winter, twigs and evergreen leaves. They may travel many km to find a salt lick. Many of them will gather at the salt lick and stay for several days. Adult ♂ have been recorded pressing their bodies close to the ground with their necks stretched out in a very successful use of camouflage. The alarm call resembles a cough, and when uttered by one member of a herd, causes the whole group to flee. They have very keen senses of smell, hearing, and sight.

DISTRIBUTION *Native*: Bhutan, China, India, Myanmar. Found in the SE of Tibet and NW Yunnan, but its distribution in China is split into two sections by the extreme NE tip of India and N Myanmar. Geographic boundary between the ranges of Bhutan and Mishmi Takin is uncertain, and there may be areas of intergradation in the Mishmi Hills (India) and adjacent areas.

HABITAT Steep rugged terrain, primeval forests, bamboo or rhododendron jungles, or open meadows.

STATUS Endangered. Estimated population about 3,500, mostly in Tibet. In Myanmar populations are decreasing because of hunting for bushmeat, and it is now rare. Habitat destruction and poaching are also threatening Mishmi Takin populations in China.

PHOTO CREDITS ♀: *Sergey Chichagov*, Tallinn Zoo (Estonia). ♂ and juvenile: *Sergey Chichagov*, Riga Zoo (Latvia). Head ♂: *Noemi Dalma Soos*, Sóstó Zoo (Hungary). Young: *Tom Van Deuren*, Antwerpen Zoo (Belgium) and *Sergey Chichagov*, Riga Zoo (Latvia).

Golden Takin
BUDORCAS BEDFORDI

BL: 170-220 cm. SH: 100-140 cm. TL: 7-20 cm. W: 150-350 kg. HL: 45-58 cm (♂). Large and stocky goat-antelope. Bovine-like body covered with dense hair. Body hairs white or off-white, with the gold being somewhat darker in males and creamy in females. Usually there is no dorsal stripe. There may be scattered dark hairs on the knees, hocks, and tip of tail. In adult males, hairs in neck and forechest are golden. Calves have brown hair. Short, stocky legs with broad hooves and strong dewclaws. Body stocky and chest deep. In profile, face convex with the nasal ridge arching outward. Both sexes carry strong twisted horns that curve out, backward, and upward at the tips. The bases of the horns may have transverse ridges. Horns are less massive in females. Females significantly smaller and darker than males.

♀

Juvenile

Young

♂

Budorcas bedfordi

OTHER NAMES Shaanxi Takin. *French*: Takin doré. *German*: Goldentakin. *Spanish*: Takín dorado. *Russian*: Золотой такин. *Tibetan*: Ri-ka, ye-more.

SUBSPECIES Monotypic. Formerly considered a subspecies of *B. taxicolor* (Takin).

SIMILAR SPECIES Golden Takin is slightly smaller than the Sichuan Takin, and has a brighter color. It is larger than the Bhutan Takin.

REPRODUCTION *Gestation*: 7-8 months. *Young per Birth*: 1, rarely 2. *Weaning*: 9 months. *Sexual Maturity*: At 2.5 years. *Life Span*: 15 years. Mating takes place between early June and the end of July. Adult ♂ compete for dominance by sparring head-to-head with opponents, and both sexes appear to use the scent of their own urine to indicate dominance. The birth season takes place from early February to late March. Mother-infant relationship is very close when calf is less than 7 days old, but the attention of mother to her calf declines afterward.

BEHAVIOR *Family Group*: Small groups of 15-20 individuals, sometimes up to 50-60 individuals, although older ♂ will become more solitary. *Diet*: Grasses, leaves, buds, shoots. *Main Predators*: Bear, wolf. During the winter months they descend the mountains to escape the cold of winter and to browse on more nutritious vegetation. During the day Takin generally rest, choosing to spend their mornings and late afternoons moving around and grazing. They are agile climbers. They deliberately seek out sunlight during the cold winter months, trekking farther up the mountain in search of warmth. On higher ground, they enjoy greater exposure to the sun's rays. When disturbed, they will give a "cough" alarm and the herd will retreat and lie on the ground for camouflage. They use the same path through thickets on regular visits to salt licks and grazing areas. Rearing up, they can balance on their hind legs to nip off branch tips 2.5 m above ground. They may prop their forelegs or just their chest against a tree trunk and then lean forward until the trunk snaps. They can be aggressive if cornered or frightened.

DISTRIBUTION *Native*: China. Found only in the Qinling Mountains in Shaanxi Province of W China.

HABITAT Subalpine forests at elevations ranging from 1,500 to 3,700 m. They inhabit mixed coniferous and broad-leaved deciduous forest and subalpine coniferous forest.

STATUS Endangered. Estimated total population estimated as 5,000 in 2001. The main threats are habitat loss and degradation, hunting and changes in native species dynamics. Numbers seem to have increased in recent years, probably due to the protection given to Giant Panda populations in reserves in the distribution range.

PHOTO CREDITS ♂: *Sergey Chichagov*, Beijing Zoo. Head ♂: *Yasuki Ichishima*, Tama Zoo (Japan). ♀: *Sergey Chichagov*, Shanghai Zoo (China). Head ♀: *Sergey Chichagov*, Suzhou Zoo (China). Juvenile: *Tomoko Ichishima*, Tama Zoo (Japan) and *Sergey Chichagov*, Beijing Zoo (China). Young: *Joe Motohashi*, Yokohama Zoo (Japan).

Sichuan Takin

BUDORCAS TIBETANA

BL: 170-220 cm. SH: 100-130 cm. TL: 10-22 cm. W: 150-350 kg. HL: 25-64 cm (♂). Large and stocky goat-antelope, largest subspecies of Takin. Long, shaggy coat. In summer the head, neck, and shoulders are golden yellow washed with gray, gradually passing into gray or blackish on hindquarters and legs. Nose black. Ears black and white. Tail black with some whitish hairs. Lower legs black in front and white behind. Black dorsal stripe is well defined, extending from shoulders to tail. In winter, the yellow areas become gray. Horns thinner, more arched, and less distinctly ridged at the base than those of the Mishmi Takin. Males have thicker horns and a darker face than females. Females are much more brown than males at all seasons.

Juvenile

Young

♀

♂

Budorcas tibetana

OTHER NAMES Tibetan Takin, Moupin Takin. *French*: Takin du Sichuan. *German*: Sichuan-Takin. *Spanish*: Takín de Sichuan. *Russian*: Сычуанский такин.

SUBSPECIES Monotypic. Formerly considered a subspecies of *B. taxicolor* (Takin).

SIMILAR SPECIES Sichuan Takin is the largest Takin. It has a duller and darker color than the Golden Takin, in addition to a different range of habitat.

REPRODUCTION *Gestation*: 200-220 days. *Young per Birth*: 1, rarely 2. *Weaning*: 9 months. *Sexual Maturity*: At 2.5 years. *Life Span*: 19 years. Mating season occurs from July through August. Within 3 days of its birth, a Takin kid is able to follow its mother through most types of terrain.

BEHAVIOR *Family Group*: Groups of up to 30 individuals; old ♂ often solitary. *Diet*: Leaves of rhododendrons, oaks, and bamboo, grasses, shrubs, bark, and herbs. *Main Predators*: Bear, wolf. Takins have adaptations that help them stay warm and dry during the bitter cold of winter in the Himalayas. A thick secondary coat is grown to keep out the chill. The large, moose-like snout has large sinus cavities to warm up the air a Takin inhales before it gets to the lungs. Yet another protection is their oily skin. Although they have no skin glands, their skin secretes an oily, bitter-tasting substance that acts as a natural raincoat in storms and fog. Streaks of this oily stuff can be seen where Takins rub. They also have an odor that smells like a strange combination of horse and musk. Takins eat in the early morning and again in the late afternoon, and they rest when they are not feeding. Since they live at altitudes above 4,300 m, they feed on many kinds of alpine and deciduous plants and evergreens. When it comes to food, Takins eat almost any vegetation within reach. They can easily stand on their hind legs, front legs propped against a tree, to reach for higher vegetation if they need to. Each spring, Takins gather in large herds and migrate up the mountains to the tree line. As cooler weather approaches and food becomes scarce, the Takins move down to forested valleys. As they move up, down, or across the mountains, Takins use the same routes over and over. This creates a series of well-worn paths through the dense growth of bamboo and rhododendrons that lead to their natural salt licks and grazing areas.

DISTRIBUTION *Native*: China. Found along the E margin of the Tibetan Plateau. Here, its distribution runs from the Min Mountains along the Sichuan-Gansu provincial border, S through the Qionglai Mountains W of Chengdu to the border with Yunnan Province.

HABITAT Dense bamboo forests.

STATUS Vulnerable. No total population estimate, but several thousand animals are believed to inhabit the Qionglai and Min mountains. Threatened by ongoing poaching and habitat destruction.

PHOTO CREDITS ♂ and ♀: *Andrey Kotkin*, Moscow Zoo (Russia). Juvenile and young: *Fr. Theodore Bobosh* and *David Valenzuela*, San Diego Zoo (USA). Head ♂: *Joanne Vujnovich,* San Diego Zoo (USA). Head ♀: *Klaus Rudloff*, Tierpark Berlin (Germany). Young: *Pamela Schreckengost,* San Diego Zoo (USA).

Bhutan Takin

BUDORCAS WHITEI

BL: 170-220 cm. SH: 107-140 cm. TL: 7-20 cm. W: 150-350 kg. HL: 25-37 cm (♂). The smallest Takin. Body covered with dense hair, including long hair on the jaws and chin, stout legs, prominent dewclaws, and a greater height at the shoulder than at the hindquarters, as the other species of Takin. Dark brown color, on average somewhat darker than the Mishmi Takin, with paler back and a middorsal stripe. Underparts and limbs almost black. Front part of head and sides also black. Horns grow slightly upward, then turn outward and backward, with the horn tips upward. Horns shorter and less massive than in other Takins, and less widely spread, with tips less turned inward than in the Sichuan Takin. Males significantly larger than females in horn and body measurements.

Young

♀

♂

Budorcas whitei

OTHER NAMES *French*: Takin de Bhoutan. *German*: Bhutan-Takin. *Spanish*: Takín de Bhutan. *Russian*: Бутанский такин. *Burmese*: Tha Mi. *Rawan*: Shafight. *Tibetan*: Ri-ka, ye-more, shing-na.

SUBSPECIES Monotypic. Formerly considered as a synonym of *B. taxicolor taxicolor* by some authors. Formerly considered a subspecies of *B. taxicolor* (Takin).

REPRODUCTION *Gestation*: 210 days. *Young per Birth*: 1, rarely 2. *Weaning*: 9 months. *Sexual Maturity*: 2.5-3.5 years. *Life Span*: 15 years. Mating takes place between August and September and births occur in March-April. Adult ♂ compete for dominance by sparring head-to-head with opponents, and both sexes appear to use the scent of their own urine to indicate dominance.

BEHAVIOR *Family Group*: Small mixed herds in winter, herds of over 100 have been seen in summer, old ♂ often solitary. *Diet*: Mostly a browser, it feeds on leaves found on deciduous trees or shrubs, but also on grasses, bamboo, and herbs. *Main Predators*: Bear, wolf, snow leopard. Diurnal, active in the day, resting in the heat on particularly sunny days. Takin gather in small herds in winter and herds of up to 100 individuals in the summer; in winter, they move to lower elevations and split into smaller herds of 10-50 individuals, mostly in the Gasa District. As is often seen in Bison, old ♂ are often solitary. Takin feed in the early morning and late afternoon, although on overcast days they may remain active throughout the day. Takin use narrow trails through the dense growth, which they regularly pass through in traveling between feeding and resting places. When threatened, they retreat into dense bamboo thickets, where they lie down. Adult ♂ have been recorded pressing their bodies close to the ground with their necks stretched out in a very successful use of camouflage. The alarm call resembles a cough, and when uttered by one member of a herd, causes the whole group to flee.

DISTRIBUTION *Native*: Bhutan, China, India. In Tibet, China, this species is known to occur S of the Yarlung Zangbo River, from Gyaca, Nangxian, Mainling, Myingchi, Cona, and Lhunze, on the S flank of the E Himalaya, to the W side of the big bend of the Yarlung Zangbo River. In Bhutan it is believed the species occurs in scattered populations throughout the forested and unforested mountain slopes along Bhutan's N border. In India it occurs in Arunachal Pradesh and Sikkim.

HABITAT Subtropical to subalpine forests, mainly between 2,000 and 3,500 m, but sometimes going as low as 1,500 m, or up to areas above timberline.

STATUS Vulnerable. There is no known estimate of population size within China, Bhutan, or India. Within Tibet, about 500 animals may survive. Threats include competition and disease transmission from domestic livestock, habitat loss, and loss or disruption of migration routes.

PHOTO CREDITS ♀: *Hartfried Schmid*, Thimphu (Bhutan). ♂: *Mark Fischer*, Thimphu (Bhutan). Head ♂: *Craig Adams,* Thimphu (Bhutan). Young: *Edwin de Jongh* (Bhutan).

Southern Sable
HIPPOTRAGUS NIGER NIGER

BL: 190-255 cm. SH: 117-143 cm. TL: 40-75 cm. W: 190-250 kg (♂), 160-180 kg (♀). HL: 80-165 cm (♂), 60-100 cm (♀). Large antelope, with shoulders higher than hindquarters. This is the only subspecies in which females become nearly black, though they tend to be lighter than males. Mature males are chestnut to jet black. The white belly contrasts greatly with the back and sides. Face is white with a black facial mask consisting of a wide black stripe on the bridge of the nose, and stripes running from the eyes to the nose. Thick neck enhanced by a mane of stiff hair. Ears long and narrow, light chestnut outside, white inside, not tufted at the tips. Tail is tufted. Semi-circular, scimitar-shaped, ringed horns, found in both sexes. Females are slightly smaller, and have smaller, less curved horns. Young turn dark as yearlings.

♀

Young

♂
Juvenile

♂

Hippotragus niger niger

OTHER NAMES Black Sable, Common Sable. *French*: Hippotrague noir. *German*: Südafrikanische Rappenantilope. *Spanish*: Antílope sable sudafricano, antílope caballo, hipotrago negro. *Russian*: Обыкновенная (Южная) чёрная антилопа. *Afrikaans*: Swartwitpens. *Swahili*: Palahala, mbarapi. *Sepedi*: Phalafala.

SUBSPECIES Considered as a subspecies of *H. niger* (Sable Antelope): *H. n. niger* (Southern Sable), *H. n. kirkii* (Western Zambian Sable), *H. n. anselli* (Ansell's Sable). Includes *harrisi* and *kaufmanni*. *H. roosevelti* (Roosevelt's Sable) and *H. variani* (Giant Sable) are now considered as separate species.

REPRODUCTION *Gestation*: 240-280 days. *Young per Birth*: 1. *Weaning*: 6-8 months. *Sexual Maturity*: 2-3 years. *Life Span*: 17 years. Breeding is seasonal, with births coinciding with the region's rainy season. After birth, the calf lies concealed for at least 10 days.

BEHAVIOR *Family Group*: Maternal herds of 10-30 animals led by an adult ♂. ♂ form small bachelor herds. Larger mixed herds of over 100 animals have been recorded. *Diet*: Medium-high grasses, leaves. *Main Predators*: Lion, leopard, spotted hyena. Most active during the early morning and late afternoon. Where not persecuted, they are not excessively wary, often running a short distance when startled, then stopping and looking back. When closely pursued, they can run as fast as 57 kmph for considerable distances. When wounded or cornered, they viciously defend themselves with their horns. The distance at which an animal defends itself instead of fleeing seems to be smaller than that of comparable species. Old ♂ are territorial. When fighting, ♂ drop to their "knees" and engage in horn wrestling. Fatalities from these combats are rare. Maternal herds are led by a dominant ♂, who defends an area of 300-500 m extending outward from the herd. Population densities vary between 0.4 and 9.2 per km^2. Extremely susceptible to droughts with a severe, rapid depletion of forage quality. These often result in high mortalities. As they are intolerant of severe cold spells, it is essential that the habitat include patches of thicket vegetation that allow refuge from cold and winds. However, if not confined by a lack of space or game fencing, they may migrate away from these conditions.

DISTRIBUTION *Native*: Angola, Botswana, Mozambique, Namibia, South Africa, Zambia, Zimbabwe. *Introduced:* Swaziland. Formerly occurred widely in the savanna woodlands of S and E Africa. They have been eliminated from large areas of their former range. Found S of the Zambezi River, in Mozambique, Zimbabwe, NE South Africa (N Transvaal), N Botswana, Caprivi Strip (NE Namibia), Zambia W of the Zambezi, and SE Angola.

HABITAT Savanna woodland. It spends the wet season in woods open enough to support an understory of grasses no more than 30 cm high on well-drained soils, and in the dry season emerges onto the grasslands in search of green grass and forbs. Rarely found more than 3 km away from grasslands. Very widely translocated.

STATUS Least Concern.

PHOTO CREDITS ♂: *Fr. Marek Marciniakss* (Botswana). Head ♂: *Dr. Bruce Campbell,* Mopani (Zimbabwe). ♀: *Adrian Storm,* Shona Langa Game Breeders (South Africa). Head ♀: *Charles Pence*, Fossil Rim Wildlife Center (USA). Young: *Vladimir Romanovskiy*, Moscow Zoo (Russia). Juvenile: *Thomas Kalcher*, Chobe NP (Botswana).

Western Zambian Sable

HIPPOTRAGUS NIGER KIRKII

BL: 190-255 cm. SH: 117-143 cm. TL: 40-75 cm. W: 190-250 kg (♂), 160-180 kg (♀). HL: 110-165 cm (♂), 60-100 cm (♀). Sexual dimorphism present: females and young are chestnut brown to chocolate brown, mature males are jet black to dark brown. White belly. Face is white with a black facial mask consisting of a wide black stripe on the bridge of the nose, and stripes running from the eyes to the nose. In some adult males, the white side facial stripes are abbreviated as in the Giant Sable. Thick neck enhanced by a mane of stiff hair. Ears long and narrow, light chestnut outside, white inside, not tufted at the tips. Tail is tufted. Semi-circular, scimitar-shaped, ringed horns, found in both sexes. Females are slightly smaller, and have smaller, less curved horns.

Juvenile ♂

♀

Young

face variation

♂

Hippotragus niger kirkii

OTHER NAMES Kirk's Sable. *French*: Hippotrague noir. *German*: Kirk-Rappenantilope. *Spanish*: Antílope sable de Zambia. *Russian*: Замбийская чёрная антилопа. *Swahili*: Palahala, mbarapi. *Ndebele*: Umtjwayeli, ingwalathi. *Xhosa*: Iliza. *Sepedi*: Phalafala. *Setswana*: Kwalata. *Swati*: Impalampala.

SUBSPECIES Considered as a subspecies of *H. niger* (Sable Antelope): *H. n. niger* (Southern Sable), *H. n. kirkii* (Western Zambian Sable), *H. n. anselli* (Ansell's Sable). *H. roosevelti* (Roosevelt's Sable) and *H. variani* (Giant Sable) are now considered as separate species.

SIMILAR SPECIES May be distinguished from Roan Antelope by its black color, the strong contrast between dark sides and snowy belly, the different pattern of the head, the absence of tufts at the tips of the ears, and the longer, more robust horns. Similar to the Southern Sable, ♀ are lighter in color.

REPRODUCTION *Gestation*: 240-280 days. *Young per Birth*: 1. *Weaning*: 6-8 months. *Sexual Maturity*: 2-3 years. *Life Span*: 17 years. Breeding season lasts from May to July, with a peak mating in June. Births occur at the end of rains. Normally 1 calf is born during the end of the rainy season when long grass is available for cover. The mother stays concealed for the first week of the calf's 3-week hiding phase. After the first week, the mother joins a maternal group that the calf will eventually join. Yet, the calf will seek out the mother only for nursing.

BEHAVIOR *Family Group*: Maternal herds of 10-30 animals led by an adult ♂. ♂ form small bachelor herds. Larger mixed herds of over 100 animals have been recorded. *Diet*: Both graminivorous and folivorous, although grass makes up the bulk of their diet. *Main Predators*: Lion, leopard, spotted hyena. Diurnal. Most active during the early morning and late afternoon. Gregarious, forming stable family groups of 6-40 individuals, consisting of several adult ♀, their young offspring, and usually, 1 dominant adult ♂. The young often form a crèche and are accompanied and guarded by 1-2 ♀. Bachelor herds are unstable and consist of 2-10 ♂ aged between 3 and 6 years. Post-mature and non-dominant adult ♂ tend to become solitary nomads. Territorial ♂ are single during the rut but outside it, they abandon their territories and join a family group. Dominant ♂ defend harems of ♀ and their immediate foraging territory extending 300 to 500 m out from the herd. These dominant ♂ mate with ♀ in their harem and vigorously defend them against intruding ♂. ♂ may drop to their knees and engage in horn wrestling in fights. Fatalities from these fights are rare.

DISTRIBUTION *Native*: Angola, DR Congo, Zambia. *Introduced*: South Africa. Found N of the Zambezi, in Katanga W of the Luanga, Zambia, SE DR Congo, and E Angola.

HABITAT Wooded savannas.

STATUS Vulnerable. Sable Antelope have been eliminated from large areas of their former range due to a combination of disease, drought-caused food shortages, and habitat loss and degradation, compounded by interspecific competition.

PHOTO CREDITS ♂, ♀, juvenile and young: *Adrian Storm,* Shona Langa Game Breeders (South Africa). Head ♂: *Ryno Verwey,* Ryno Rare Game (South Africa). Head ♀: *Dries Visser,* Dries Visser Pure-Bred Game (South Africa).

Ansell's Sable

HIPPOTRAGUS NIGER ANSELLI

BL: 190-255 cm. SH: 117-143 cm. TL: 40-75 cm. W: 190-250 kg (♂), 160-180 kg (♀). HL: 110-165 cm (♂), 60-100 cm (♀). Similar to the Western Zambian Sable. Mature males are deep brown. Females and young are chestnut brown to chocolate brown. White belly. White face stripes are broader than in other subspecies. Thick neck enhanced by a mane of stiff hair. Ears long and narrow, light chestnut outside, white inside, not tufted at the tips. Tail is tufted. Semi-circular, scimitar-shaped, ringed horns, found in both sexes. Females are slightly smaller, and have smaller, less curved horns.

♂

♂

Juvenile

♀

Hippotragus niger anselli

OTHER NAMES Eastern Zambian Sable. *French*: Hippotrague noir. *German*: Kirk-Rappenantilope. *Spanish*: Antílope sable de Ansell. *Russian*: Черная антилопа Анселла.

SUBSPECIES Considered as a subspecies of *H. niger* (Sable Antelope): *H. n. niger* (Southern Sable), *H. n. kirkii* (Western Zambian Sable), *H. n. anselli* (Ansell's Sable). This subspecies is considered as a synonym of *kirkii* by some authors. *H. roosevelti* (Roosevelt's Sable) and *H. variani* (Giant Sable) are now considered as separate species.

SIMILAR SPECIES Similar to the Western Zambian Sable.

REPRODUCTION *Gestation*: 240-280 days. *Young per Birth*: 1. *Weaning*: 6-8 months. *Sexual Maturity*: 2-3 years. *Life Span*: 17 years. There is no specific information for this subspecies, but probably similar to the Western Zambian Sable. They breed seasonally, so that offspring births coincide with high food abundance.

BEHAVIOR *Family Group*: Maternal herds of 10-30 animals led by an adult ♂. Younger ♂ are allowed to stay with their herd until they are about 3 years old. Young ♂ typically band together to form bachelor groups. Larger mixed herds of over 100 animals have been recorded. *Diet*: Both graminivorous and folivorous, although grass makes up the bulk of their diet. *Main Predators*: Lion, leopard, spotted hyena. There is no specific information for this subspecies, but probably similar to the Western Zambian Sable. Diurnal. Most active during the early morning and late afternoon. Gregarious, forming stable family groups, consisting of several adult ♀, their young offspring, and usually, 1 dominant adult. Territorial ♂ uses urination and defecation scent markings along his territory's perimeter to warn all other rival ♂. Fights start by the rival ♂ slowly circling each other, shaking their heads, dropping to their knees, and finally clashing horns, with more pushing than slashing. Fatalities from these fights are rare.

DISTRIBUTION *Native*: Malawi, Mozambique, Tanzania, Zambia. Found in Zambia E of the Luangwa, Malawi, N Mozambique, and SE Tanzania in Tendaguru region. In Malawi they are confined to protected areas, with the two largest populations in Liwonde and Nkhotakota Game Reserve. In Mozambique, the largest population is in the Niassa Game Reserve.

HABITAT Wooded savannas. They generally avoid dense woodlands and short-grass savannas.

STATUS Least Concern. It has been eliminated from large areas of its former range by meat hunting and loss of habitat to the expansion of agricultural settlement and livestock. Poaching and armed conflict have been a major threat, especially in Mozambique. Its horns have contributed to its sharp decline, being a highly prized hunting trophy.

PHOTO CREDITS ♂: *Robin Pope Safaris*, Majete Game Reserve (Malawi). ♀: cuatrok77. Head ♂: *Gualtiero Boffi* (Malawi). Juvenile: *Lubomír Prause*, Liwonde NP (Malawi) and Game Haven (Malawi).

Giant Sable

HIPPOTRAGUS VARIANI

BL: 190-255 cm. SH: 117-143 cm. TL: 40-75 cm. W: 190-250 kg (♂), 160-180 kg (♀). HL: 110-165 cm (♂), 60-100 cm (♀). Slightly smaller in body size than the Southern Sable, but with much larger horns, often widely spread at the tips. Male has the same glossy black coat as the typical Sable, but its face differs by being mostly black, with white restricted to a white oblong in front of the eye, or very vaguely continuing to the snout. Female coat is bright chestnut red. White belly. Thick neck enhanced by a mane of stiff hair. Ears long and narrow, light chestnut outside, white inside. Tail is tufted. Semi-circular, scimitar-shaped, ringed horns, found in both sexes, much larger than in other subspecies. Females are slightly smaller, and have smaller, less curved horns.

Hippotragus variani

OTHER NAMES Angolan Sable, Royal Sable. *French*: Hippotrague déant de l'Angola, hippotrague noir géant. *German*: Riesenrappenantilope. *Spanish*: Antílope sable gigante. *Russian*: Гигантская чёрная антилопа. *Angolan*: Palanca negra gigante.

SUBSPECIES Monotypic. Formerly considered a subspecies of *H. niger* (Sable Antelope). This subspecies may hybridize with Roan Antelope; these hybrids may be able to reproduce.

SIMILAR SPECIES The body size, weight, and spoor are similar to those of the typical Sable; the horns are much longer, however, and the facial markings are quite different.

REPRODUCTION *Gestation*: 240-280 days. *Young per Birth*: 1. *Weaning*: 8 months. *Sexual Maturity*: 2-3 years. *Life Span*: 17 years. Breeding is seasonal, with births coinciding with the region's rainy season. After birth, the calf lies concealed for at least 10 days.

BEHAVIOR *Family Group*: Maternal herds of 10-30 animals led by an adult ♂. ♂ form small bachelor herds. Larger mixed herds of over 100 animals have been recorded. *Diet*: Medium-high grasses, leaves. *Main Predators*: Lion, leopard, spotted hyena. Little is known about its biology or ecology.

DISTRIBUTION *Native*: Angola. Found only in N-central Angola in a limited area between the Cuanza and Luando rivers, mainly in and around the Luando Reserve and Kangandala NP.

HABITAT Wooded savannas, within the Angolan miombo ecosystem associated with natural salt licks that are found around the natural parks. As these woodlands are nutrient poor, these licks are of vital importance as nutrient hotspots.

STATUS Critically Endangered. It has a very restricted range in Angola and has suffered from the effects of many years of military conflict in its area of distribution. Total numbers surviving were estimated at 200-400 individuals in 2007, and no known subpopulation currently contains more than 50 mature individuals. Although the situation in Angola has stabilized to some extent, populations are still declining and Giant Sable faces several threats, including hybridization with Roan Antelope.

PHOTO CREDITS Based on photos from *Pedro vaz Pinto* (Angola Field Group), Kangandala NP, and Luando Special Reserve (Angola).

Roosevelt's Sable
HIPPOTRAGUS ROOSEVELTI

BL: 175-182 cm. SH: 128 cm. TL: 52 cm. W: 190-250 kg (♂), 160-180 kg (♀). HL: 81-165 cm (♂), 61-102 (♀). Similar to the Southern Sable, but noticeably smaller in size, average horn length much smaller, and usually lighter in color, from seal brown to reddish black; even at full maturity most males show reddish highlights in their coats. Sexual dimorphism present: females are bright rufous to pale golden red, contrasting with the nearly black color of mature males. The white belly contrasts greatly with the back and sides. Face similar to that of the Southern Sable. Ringed horns found in both sexes, smaller and less curved in females. Young under 2 months typically are light brown.

Young

♂ Juvenile

♀

♂

Hippotragus roosevelti

OTHER NAMES Shimba Sable, East African Sable. *French*: Hippotrague de Roosevelt. *German*: Ostafrika-Rappenantilope. *Spanish*: Antílope sable de Roosevelt, hipotrago sable oriental. *Russian*: Шимбская чёрная антилопа (Чёрная антилопа Рузвельта). *Swahili*: Palahala.

SUBSPECIES Monotypic. Formerly considered a subspecies of *H. niger* (Sable Antelope).

SIMILAR SPECIES Slightly smaller, lighter in color (no jet black color) and with shorter horns than other species of Sable Antelope. May be distinguished from Roan Antelope by its black color, the strong contrast between dark sides and snowy belly, the different pattern of the head, the absence of tufts at the tips of the ears, and the longer, more robust horns.

REPRODUCTION *Gestation*: 240-280 days. *Young per Birth*: 1. *Weaning*: 6 months. *Sexual Maturity*: 2.5 years (♀). Most births occur during the end of the rainy season when long grass is available for cover. The mother stays concealed for the first week of the calf's 3-week hiding phase. After the first week, the mother joins a maternal group. ♀ care for their young primarily by nursing them and hiding them from predators. Young are weaned at 6 months of age, usually toward the end of the dry season when the vegetation is lowest in protein and other nutrients.

BEHAVIOR *Family Group*: Maternal herds of 10-30 animals led by an adult ♂. ♂ form small bachelor herds. *Diet*: Specialized grazers but occasionally feed on foliage and herbs particularly during dry season; during wet season, they select leafy and palatable grasses. *Main Predators*: Lion, leopard, spotted hyena. Most active during the early morning and late afternoon. Home ranges of herds are 10-25 km². A herd's home range will include territories of 2-5 ♂, with territories of 4-9 km². The social organization is similar to that of the Southern Sable. The oldest, most dominant ♀ remains vigilant at a certain distance from the other members of the herd. Two ♀ may dispute dominance, and a herd may divide into two smaller herds, each with its own home range.

DISTRIBUTION *Native*: SE Kenya, E Tanzania. From the Shimba Hills near the SE coast of Kenya, S discontinuously in coastal Tanzania to the Selous Reserve in S Tanzania; throughout the Selous Reserve; in the Kilombero Valley to the W of the Selous; and S and SE of the Selous; and S to the Ruvuma River along the Tanzania-Mozambique border. Sable species below the Ruvuma River have shown evidence of hybridization.

HABITAT Open grasslands. Prefer fairly sparse open woodland with dense to medium-tall grass, but generally avoid areas of heavy grazing pressure.

STATUS Classed as Endangered in Kenya. The Shimba Hills population of about 120 animals is protected. So are the small, scattered populations along the Tanzania coast, though they suffer from local poaching. But a 1998 aerial survey counted 3,900 Sable Antelopes in the Selous and another 6,700 outside it.

PHOTO CREDITS ♂: *Charles Tomalin* (wildviews.com). Head ♂: *Tim Lake*. ♀: *Rick Edwards*. Young: *Annielina*. Juvenile: *Luke Berman*. All photos from Shimba Hills Reserve (Kenya).

Southern Roan Antelope

HIPPOTRAGUS EQUINUS EQUINUS

BL: 200-265 cm. SH: 126-160 cm. TL: 60-75 cm. W: 235-300 kg (♂), 215-280 kg (♀). HL: 60-100 cm. Large antelope, with shoulders higher than hindquarters. Upper body grayish brown in color with the legs darker. Forelegs of males more darkly marked than those of females, which show fairly consistent coloration. Underparts white. Face with a black-brown and white facial mask, slightly lighter in females, consisting of a white spot on either side of the eye and a white muzzle. In some subspecies, while females have only a black muzzle and a roan-colored forehead, the muzzle and forehead of males are uniformly emblazoned with black. Erect, dark-tipped mane on the neck and withers. Light beard present on the throat. Long tuft of dark hair present on the tips of the ears. Tail has a black tassel. Arched, ringed horns found in both sexes. Females are similar to males, but slightly smaller and with smaller and less heavily ringed horns.

♀

Young

Juvenile

♂

476

Hippotragus equinus equinus

OTHER NAMES *French*: Antilope rouanne, antilope cheval, hippotrague. *German*: Pferdeantilope. *Spanish*: Hipótrago equino, antílope ruano. *Russian*: Южная лошадиная антилопа. *Afrikaans*: Bastergemsbok. *Swahili*: Korongo. *Ndebele*: Ithaka.

SUBSPECIES Six subspecies have been described, but their validity is in doubt, and only Western Roan subspecies (*koba*) constitute a genetically separate group from those in the rest of Africa. Includes *langheldi* (Eastern Roan, from S Uganda, Kenya, Rwanda, Burundi, Tanzania), *equinus* (Southern Roan, from Zimbabwe, South Africa, Mozambique), and *cottoni* (Angolan Roan, from Angola, Zambia, Zimbabwe, parts of Congo, Namibia, Botswana, and Malawi).

SIMILAR SPECIES Larger than the Sable, but has smaller horns, a different pattern on the head, tufts at the tips of the ears, and a different color. Roan from N-central Angola are redder than other specimens.

REPRODUCTION *Gestation*: 268-280 days. *Young per Birth*: 1. *Weaning*: 4-6 months. *Sexual Maturity*: 2.5-3 years. *Life Span*: 17 years. No specific breeding season for this species. ♀ are capable of reproducing every 10-10.5 months. A pregnant ♀ will separate from her herd prior to giving birth, and remain with her new calf for about 5 days afterward. After the ♀ has rejoined the herd, the young calf remains concealed for 5 more weeks, subsequently joining a crèche with other youngsters in the herd.

BEHAVIOR *Family Group*: Harem groups with a single dominant ♂ with 6-35 animals. ♂ associate in bachelor herds of 2-5 animals. *Diet*: Medium-high grasses, rarely leaves. *Main Predators*: Lion, leopard, spotted hyena, Cape hunting dog. Most active in the morning, late afternoon, and evening. Relatively unwary, running away from a potential source of danger for a short distance, then stopping to look back. When pressured, they can run up to 57 kmph. If cornered, they are formidable opponents, charging and brandishing their horns with skill. They never move far from water (4 km at most), and overall have localized movements, using 200-400 ha at any given time, with a home range of no more than 10,000 ha throughout the year. Neighboring herds rarely share territory. ♀ herds are accompanied by a single adult ♂, who defends a wide swath (300-500 m) around his herd against potential rivals. Young ♂ are driven from their natal herds when they reach 2.5 years of age. Fighting for dominance is prevalent among both ♂ and ♀, with the most dominant initiating herd movements. Fights occur with both animals on their "knees" (carpal joints) and are almost exclusively horn against horn.

DISTRIBUTION *Native*: Angola, Benin, Botswana, Burkina Faso, Cameroon, Central African Republic, Chad, DR Congo, Côte d'Ivoire, Ethiopia, Ghana, Guinea, Guinea-Bissau, Kenya, Malawi, Mali, Mauritania, Mozambique, Namibia, Niger, Nigeria, Rwanda, Senegal, South Africa, Sudan, Tanzania, Togo, Uganda, Zambia, Zimbabwe. *Reintroduced:* Swaziland.

HABITAT Lightly wooded savanna with open areas.

STATUS Least Concern.

PHOTO CREDITS ♂: *Kenneth Coe*, Kafue NP (Zambia). Young: *Janet M. Horsman*, Chester Zoo (UK). Head ♀: *Jeff Buck*, Chester Zoo (UK). Head ♂: *John Davies*, Port Lympne Wild Animal Park (UK). Juvenile: *Tambako the Jaguar*, Chester Zoo (UK) and *Adam Fink*.

Western Roan Antelope

HIPPOTRAGUS EQUINUS KOBA

BL: 200-320 cm. SH: 130-150 cm. TL: 60-75 cm. W: 230-300 kg (♂), 215-280 kg (♀). HL: 60-100 cm. General color is pale tawny to reddish. Face with a black and white facial mask, slightly lighter in females, consisting of a white spot on either side of the eye and a white muzzle. In some males, the black may extend to the throat. Forehead is chestnut to reddish brown in females, and may be black in males. Forelegs of males more darkly marked than those of females, which show fairly consistent coloration. Underparts white. Erect, dark-tipped mane on the neck and withers. Light beard present on the throat, darker in males. Tuft of dark hair present on the tips of the ears. Tail has a black tassel. Arched, ringed horns found in both sexes. Females are similar to males, but slightly smaller and with smaller and less heavily ringed horns.

Young

♀

♂

Juvenile

♂

Hippotragus equinus koba

OTHER NAMES *French*: Antilope rouanne, antilope cheval, hippotrague. *German*: Pferdeantilope. *Spanish*: Hipótrago equino, antílope ruano. *Russian*: Западная лошадиная антилопа. *Afrikaans*: Bastergemsbok. *Swahili*: Korongo. *Ndebele*: Ithaka.

SUBSPECIES Six subspecies have been described, but their validity is in doubt, and only Western Roan subspecies (*koba*) constitute a genetically separate group from those in the rest of Africa. Includes *charicus* (E Nigeria, Cameroon, Chad, and Central African Republic), *bakeri* (S and E Sudan, extreme W Ethiopia, NE DR Congo, and N Uganda), and *koba* (Senegal to W Nigeria), with *koba* having priority.

SIMILAR SPECIES Southern Roan is grayish roan. Angolan and East African Roan are redder.

REPRODUCTION *Gestation*: 276-287 days. *Young per Birth*: 1. *Weaning*: 4-8 months. *Sexual Maturity*: 20-24 months (♀), 30-36 months (♂). *Life Span*: 17 years. Breeding season in January-February. The ♀ leaves the herd a few days before giving birth to seek cover for the concealment of her calf. The calf remains hidden for 6-8 weeks, suckling in the morning and evening, and starts to move around with the herd when it is 2 months old. Nursery herds of up to 20 calves form during the day.

BEHAVIOR *Family Group*: Harem groups with a single dominant ♂ with 6-35 animals. *Diet*: Medium-high grasses, rarely leaves. *Main Predators*: Lion, leopard, spotted hyena, Cape hunting dog. Active from sunrise to midmorning and again late in the afternoon. It forms small breeding herds of 5-12 but sometimes up to 80 individuals. Other social groupings include a herd ♂ that defends the breeding herd against intruding ♂, bachelor herds, and nursery herds. Breeding herds occupy the same ranges for many years. Pedal glands, bush and grass horning, urination, and dung heaps all form part of the demarcation of the ranges. Within a breeding herd the individuals are spaced some 5 to 10 m apart. The breeding herd has a strict social hierarchy with a dominant ♀ who leads the herd to feeding sites and water. The herd ♂ evicts the young ♂ from the breeding herd when they become 2 years old and they then join a bachelor herd. Herd ♂ only take over a breeding herd when they are 5-6 years old, and their prime breeding age is 6-7 years.

DISTRIBUTION *Native*: Benin, Burkina Faso, Cameroon, Central African Republic, Chad, DR Congo, Côte d'Ivoire, Ethiopia, Ghana, Guinea, Guinea-Bissau, Mali, Mauritania, Niger, Nigeria, Senegal, Sudan, Togo, Uganda. *Regionally Extinct*: Eritrea, Gambia. Found from Senegal eastward to Nigeria, N Cameroon, S Chad, Central African Republic, S and E Sudan, the Gambella region of extreme W Ethiopia, NE DR Congo, and N Uganda.

HABITAT Woody savannas, never dense vegetation, in grassy plains and hills up to 2,000 m. Found near permanent water points.

STATUS Least Concern. The largest populations are found in Burkina Faso (7,500) and Cameroon (6,000). However, large numbers are also believed to survive in S Sudan.

PHOTO CREDITS ♂ and juvenile: *Philippe Boissel,* Toubacouta (Senegal). ♀: Bandits National Reserve (Senegal). Young: *Jonas Van del Voord*, Pendjari NP (Benin). Head ♀: *Ignacio Yúfera* (Senegal). Juvenile head: *Emmanuelle Dagniaux*, Pendjari NP (Benin). Head ♂: *Filippo Tafi*, Bandia Reserve (Senegal).

Kalahari Gemsbok

ORYX GAZELLA GAZELLA

BL: 180-200 cm. SH: 120-125 cm (♂), 112 cm (♀). TL: 45-90 cm. W: 200-275 kg (♂), 180-210 kg (♀). HL: 70-150 cm. A heavily built large antelope, with the appearance of having no neck. Light brownish gray to tan in color, with lighter patches toward the bottom rear of the rump. Tail long and black in color. A blackish stripe extends from the chin down the lower edge of the neck, through the juncture of the shoulder and leg along the lower flank of each side to the blackish section of the rear leg. Muscular neck and shoulder. Ears large and rounded. Legs have white socks with a black patch on the front of both the front legs. Long, straight horns, found in both sexes, ringed for about one-third of the length. In males, these horns are perfectly straight, extending from the base of the skull to a slight outward and rearward angle. Females slightly smaller than males, with longer, thinner, more parallel horns with a slight outward and rearward curve in addition to their angle.

Juvenile

♂

Young

♀

Oryx gazella gazella

OTHER NAMES Gemsbuck, Southern Oryx. *French*: Oryx gazelle. *German*: Südafrikanischer Spiessbok. *Spanish*: Órice de El Cabo, órice gacela, órice gris, pasán. *Russian*: Гемсбок (Калахарский или южноафриканский орикс). *Afrikaans*: Gensbok. *Ndebele*: Inkukhama. *Setswana*: Kukama. *Swati*: Inyamatane. *Xitonga*: Mhala.

SUBSPECIES *O. g. gazella* (Kalahari Gemsbok), *O. g. blainei* (Angolan Gemsbok). Some authors consider these subspecies invalid. Includes *aschenborni* (Kalahari Desert, Namibia), *capensis* (Cape Province, South Africa), and *pasan* (Cape of Good Hope, Western Cape Province, South Africa).

SIMILAR SPECIES Beisa Oryx lacks a dark patch at the base of the tail, has less black on the legs (none on the hind legs), and less black on the lower flanks.

REPRODUCTION *Gestation*: 255 days. *Young per Birth*: 1, rarely 2. *Weaning*: 4.5 months. *Sexual Maturity*: 1.5-2 years. *Life Span*: 20 years. At birth, calves are an inconspicuous brown color. Young do not join their herd after birth. Instead, they lie still, camouflaged against dark brown grasses. Calves nurse up until 4.5 months old, and the mother returns 2-3 times a day to nurse her calf. Distinctive markings appear when weaning is complete, signifying the calf is ready to join the herd. ♂ calves leave the herd to form groups with other juvenile ♂, whereas ♀ become integrated with their mother's herd.

BEHAVIOR *Family Group*: Herds of about 10-40 animals, which consist of a dominant ♂, a few non-dominant ♂, and ♀. *Diet*: Predominantly grazers, although they broaden their diets in the dry season to include a greater proportion of browse, ephemerals, and acacia pods. They drink water regularly when available, but can get by on water-storing melons, roots, bulbs, and tubers, for which they dig assiduously. *Main Predators*: Lion, wild dog, hyena. Gemsbok are mainly desert dwelling and do not depend on drinking to supply their physiological water needs. They can reach running speeds of up to 60 kmph. ♀ use their horns to defend themselves and their offspring from predators, while ♂ primarily use their horns to defend their territories from other ♂.

DISTRIBUTION *Native*: Botswana, Namibia, South Africa, Zimbabwe. *Possibly Extinct:* Angola. They remain widely, albeit patchily, distributed in SW southern Africa, although populations in Angola are now considered extirpated. They have also been introduced in small numbers to areas outside their natural range, such as private game ranches in Zimbabwe.

HABITAT Adapted to waterless wastelands uninhabitable for most large mammals, Gemsboks inhabit semi-arid and arid bushland and grassland of the Kalahari and Karoo and adjoining regions of S Africa. They are equally at home on sandy and stony plains and alkaline flats. They range over high sand dunes and climb mountains to visit springs and salt licks.

STATUS Least Concern. Estimated population of 373,000 animals.

PHOTO CREDITS ♂: *Arthur Ramos*, Lion Country Safari (USA). Head ♂: *Leigh Thomson*, Sossusvlei (Namibia). ♀: *Alex Meyer,* Berlin Zoo (Germany). Head ♀: *Alexander Mitrofanov*. ♀: *Chris Kruger*, Kgalagadi Transfrontier Park (South Africa, Botswana). Young: *Sergey Chichagov*, Lisbon Zoo (Portugal).

Angolan Gemsbok

ORYX GAZELLA BLAINEI

BL: 180-200 cm. SH: 120-125 cm (♂), 112 cm (♀). TL: 45-90 cm. W: 200-275 kg (♂), 180-210 kg (♀). HL: 70-150 cm. Identical to the Kalahari Gemsbok, except that it is somewhat paler and grayer, with narrower black markings, and has slightly smaller horns. Light gray to brownish gray in color, with lighter patches toward the bottom rear of the rump. Tail long and black in color. A blackish stripe extends from the chin down the lower edge of the neck, through the juncture of the shoulder and leg along the lower flank of each side to the blackish section of the rear leg. Muscular neck and shoulders. Ears large and rounded. Legs have white socks with a black patch on the front of both the front legs. Long, straight horns, found in both sexes, ringed for about one-third of the length. Females slightly smaller than males, with longer, thinner, more parallel horns.

Oryx gazella blainei

OTHER NAMES *French*: Oryx angolais. *German*: Angola-Spiessbock. *Spanish*: Órix de Angola. *Russian*: Ангольский орикс.

SUBSPECIES *O. g. gazella* (Kalahari Gemsbok), *O. g. blainei* (Angolan Gemsbok). Some authors consider these subspecies invalid.

REPRODUCTION *Gestation*: 255 days. *Young per Birth*: 1. *Weaning*: 3.5 months. *Sexual Maturity*: 1.5-2 years. *Life Span:* 20 years. Gemsbok are polygynous. The resident ♂ of the herd mates with receptive ♀. Solitary territorial ♂ are known to attempt to herd mixed or nursery herds onto their territories, thereby securing exclusive mating access to the ♀. There is no specific information available for this subspecies, but probably similar to the Kalahari Gemsbok. No specific birth period, but breeding is probably year-round. Calves are born throughout the year with a peak in August and September. ♀ leave the herd to give birth to a single calf. Calves stay hidden for a period of 3-6 weeks before the mother and calf rejoin the herd. The black markings begin to appear and the horns are already developed when the calf joins the herd. The ♀ comes into heat again shortly after giving birth.

BEHAVIOR *Family Group*: Herds of about 10-40 animals, which consist of a dominant ♂, a few non-dominant ♂, and ♀. *Diet*: Grass, sometimes also tsammas, succulent rhizomes and tubers; dig for water in sand at times, but can go for days without drinking and may be encountered very far from water. *Main Predators*: Lion, wild dog, hyena. There is no specific information available for this subspecies, but probably similar to the Kalahari Gemsbok. They spend more than half of the day inactive, in shade if possible, to avoid overheating. Body temperature can be raised during the day and excess heat is dissipated at night. They graze for long periods at night when the moisture content of the vegetation is higher. Dominance hierarchy in both ♂ and ♀ in a herd. In fights between ♂, they stand alongside one another and stab backward and sideways over their shoulders. Dominant ♂ are recognizable by their head-high stance, they have a larger scrotum, and only territorial ♂ are sexually active. Territories are marked with small, neat dung piles, deposited in a very low crouch so that the pellets do not scatter. Secretion from glands between the hooves of all four feet is deposited by pawing the ground or while walking around. They also thrash the leaves, bark, and branches of bushes. Herds bunch around calves if spotted hyenas are detected, and the adults use their horns in defense. Groups of hyenas are usually unsuccessful in hunting adult Gemsbok, which defend themselves against predators by slashing with their horns while covering their rear by backing into a thorny bush. Gemsbok love salty mineral deposits and lick them, often making substantial holes in the process, and visit them frequently.

DISTRIBUTION *Native*: Angola. Found only in the Mocâmedes Desert region of SW Angola.

HABITAT Prefers open dry landscape as well as open grassveld in semi-desert areas and open savanna. May even penetrate open woodland in search of new grazing areas.

STATUS Unknown. This subspecies may be extinct.

PHOTO CREDITS Based on photos from Angola.

Beisa Oryx
ORYX BEISA

BL: 153-170 cm. SH: 110-120 cm. TL: 45-50 cm. W: 167-209 kg (♂), 116-188 kg (♀). HL: 74-90 cm. A compact and muscular animal, with relatively long body, short and slender legs, and broad neck. Coat ocher gray with a pinkish wash, with a black flank band that forms a boundary between the body color and the white belly, wider than in Fringe-eared Oryx, but narrower than in Gemsbok. Black bands above the knees of the front legs. No dark patch on the rump and thighs. Conspicuous black facial markings including a thick stripe running from the base of the horns, through the eye, to the lower cheek, usually not reaching down to the lower jaw, a bell-shaped nose patch which does not touch the cheek stripes, and a patch on the forehead. Black dorsal stripe runs into the black, long, tufted tail. Long and narrow ears, with a black tip but without a hair fringe. Horns are long, narrow, and virtually parallel, ringed on the lower half, with 15-25 rings. Females have longer and thinner horns.

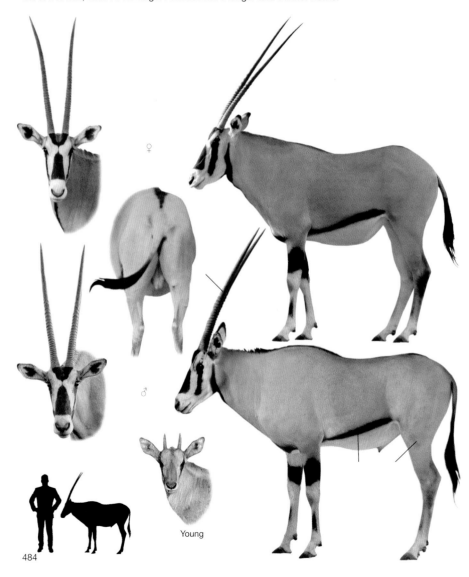

♀

♂

Young

Oryx beisa

OTHER NAMES East African Oryx, Beisa, Ethiopian Oryx. *French*: Oryx beïsa, oryx d'Afrique de l'Est. *German*: Ostafrikanische Oryx, Beisa-Antilope. *Spanish*: Órice beisa. *Russian*: Восточноафриканский орикс (бейза).

SUBSPECIES Monotypic. The name *O. beisa* (Beisa Oryx) formerly included *O. beisa* (Beisa Oryx), *O. callotis* (Fringe-eared Oryx), and *O. gallarum* (Galla Oryx) as subspecies: these are all elevated to full species here. *O. beisa* was also formerly considered a subspecies of *O. gazella*.

SIMILAR SPECIES May be confused with the Roan Antelope with which it shares some similarities in head markings; but horns are quite different. Fringe-eared Oryx is somewhat smaller, has a tuft of hair in the ears, a longer eye stripe, and heavier horns. Galla Oryx has a paler gray color, extending below the black flank band, a longer eye stripe, and usually has narrower dorsal and flank bands; otherwise very similar. Gemsbok has longer and more divergent horns, and a wider black flank band.

REPRODUCTION *Gestation*: 240-280 days. *Young per Birth*: 1. *Weaning*: 3.5 months. *Sexual Maturity*: 1.5-2 years (♀), 5 years (♂). *Life Span*: 18 years. ♂ rest the chin on the ♀'s crop as a prelude to mounting, and the ♀ responds by circling with her head low, like other Hippotragini. In mating, the ♂ rears upright, firmly grasping the ♀'s loin. Breeding occurs probably throughout the year.

BEHAVIOR *Family Group*: Mixed herds of 7-30 animals. Old ♂ usually solitary. *Diet*: Dry-desert vegetation, independent of standing water. *Main Predators*: Lion, leopard, hyena, Cape hunting dog. Beisa Oryxes amble, nodding their heads when walking fast, and have a flowing trot. They rest like other Oryxes in the heat of the day, either standing or lying, usually under shade. Herds have a hierarchy, with a ♀ leading the herd and a dominant ♂ bringing up the rear. When threatened, they usually flee, although when cornered they present a spirited defense, sometimes inflicting fatal injuries with their spear-like horns.

DISTRIBUTION *Native*: Somalia, Ethiopia, Djibouti. *Possibly Extinct*: Eritrea, Sudan. Found in N and central Somalia, and the Ogaden region of Ethiopia, N to Berbera (Somalia), W to Eritrea, and S into the Awash Valley.

HABITAT Desert country, arid grassland, and thornscrub.

STATUS Near Threatened. Total population in Ethiopia reaches at least 4,000-5,000 (mostly in Awash NP), with numbers generally in decline. It is a rare species in the Ogaden. The small population of Grand Gammareh in Djibouti is considered to be small and slightly increasing.

PHOTO CREDITS ♂: *Tommy Pedersen,* Awash NP (Ethiopia). ♀ and ♀ head: *James Middleton,* Awash NP (Ethiopia). Head ♂: *Ignacio Yufera,* Awash NP (Ethiopia). Young: *Volker Sthamer* (Ethiopia).

Fringe-eared Oryx

ORYX CALLOTIS

BL: 153-170 cm. SH: 110-120 cm. TL: 45-50 cm. W: 167-210 kg (♂), 116-188 kg (♀). HL: 76-81 cm (♀). Large, long-bodied animal. Fawn colored, browner and darker than the Beisa Oryx. Ears long and pointed, with a distinctive tuft of long hairs at the tips. Black flank bands are narrow, 3-4.5 cm wide (narrowest of any common Oryx), and there are no black markings on rump or hind legs. Black bands above the knees of the front legs. Dorsal black stripe is much reduced, usually confined to the rump. Face is deep ocher, except for the white muzzle stripes. Black facial stripes do not join to form a band above the muzzle, and the white stripes are continuous from above the eyes to the muzzle in most individuals. Short, stiff, chestnut-brown mane. Horns shorter and less divergent than in Gemsboks, being similar to those of Beisa Oryx but heavier, with parallel rings on the lower half. Little sexual dimorphism, with females having longer, straighter, and thinner horns.

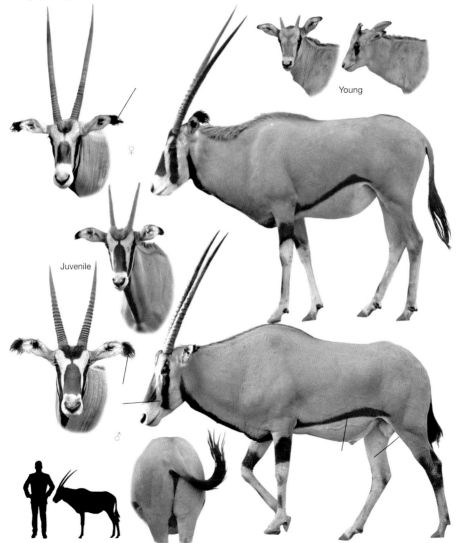

Young

♀

Juvenile

♂

Oryx callotis

OTHER NAMES Burton's Fringe-eared Oryx. *French*: Oryx frangé, oryx à oreilles frangées. *German:* Büschelor-Oryx, Büschelohr Spiessbok. *Spanish*: Órice de Kenia, órice empenachado. *Russian*: Кистеухий орикс.

SUBSPECIES Monotypic. Formerly considered a subspecies of *O. beisa* (Beisa Oryx).

REPRODUCTION *Gestation*: 255-270 days. *Young per Birth*: 1. *Weaning*: 5 months. *Sexual Maturity*: 2 years (♀), 18-24 months (♂). *Life Span*: 18 years. ♀ can breed throughout the year, but young are often more numerous early in the dry season from June to August. When ready to give birth, they will leave the herd to find a safe place from predators such as lions and hyenas. The calf is hidden for 2-3 weeks, with the ♀ returning to nurse the young several times a day. Once the calf is strong enough, it joins the herd and continues to suckle for another 5 months.

BEHAVIOR *Family Group*: Mixed herds of 30-40 animals, but much larger herds have been observed during the wet season. *Diet*: Grasses, leaves, buds, fruit. This species can be found far from water and can go for days without drinking, as it obtains moisture from the plants it eats. *Main Predators*: Lion, leopard, hyena, Cape hunting dog. It uses water holes during daylight hours in association with other species to enhance predator detection; if individuals of another prey species are alarmed or flee, it will follow. Individuals might give alarm snorts and watch intently if lions or cheetahs are nearby, but they usually pay no attention to golden jackals or spotted hyenas. They alternate feeding and resting throughout the day and night. They are nomadic, apparently more than the Gemsbok. Their movements are driven by rainfall and availability of green vegetation. Home ranges are typically less than 400 km². They move in herds of 30-40 animals. Herds consist mainly of ♀ and their young, with 10-12 dominant ♂ that compete for ♀. In the wet season, groups can be as large as several hundred animals. Fights among ♂ are of low to medium intensity. The ♂ clash their horns frontally, parallel, or at an acute angle, but do not attempt to gore each other. Fighting techniques include simple head butting, horn pressing, clash fighting, push fighting, and forehead pressing, with fencing and whirling the most common fighting tactics. While marching, the herd is usually led by a ♀, but not always the same individual, and the dominant ♂ brings up the rear.

DISTRIBUTION *Native:* Kenya, Tanzania. Distributed entirely S of the Tana River in E Kenya and NE Tanzania, with a major center of distribution in Tsavo (E) and the Galana Ranch region, spreading W and S to Mkomazi, Amboseli, and sporadically appearing in Serengeti. The Tana River forms the boundary between the Fringe-eared and Beisa Oryxes.

HABITAT Dry open grasslands and woodlands of semi-desert areas and savanna in eastern Africa.

STATUS Vulnerable. Estimated population is 17,000 animals, 60% in protected areas.

PHOTO CREDITS ♀: *Peter Steward*, Tsavo East NP (Kenya) and *Cheryl Hyde* and *Eric Wortman*, The Wilds, Cumberland, OH (USA). ♂: *Kenneth Coe,* Tsavo West NP (Kenya). Head ♂: *Steve Garvie*, Tsavo West NP (Kenya). Head ♀: *Lee Ann Fisher*, Tsavo West NP (Kenya). Young: *Fr. Theodore Bobosh*, The Wilds, Cumberland, OH (USA). Juvenile: *Ingmar Sörgens*, Tsavo West NP (Kenya).

Galla Oryx

ORYX GALLARUM

BL: 169 cm. SH: 110-120 cm. TL: 46 cm. W: 167-209 kg (♂), 116-188 kg (♀). HL: 65-86 cm. Pale gray coat extending below the black flank band, which is therefore not a boundary between the body color and the white underside. Face is paler than the neck, sometimes even whitish, with black facial markings including a thick stripe running from the base of the horns, through the eye, to the lower cheek, usually reaching down to the lower jaw, a bell-shaped nose patch which sometimes touches the cheek stripes, and a patch on the forehead. Forelegs are white with black bands above the knees. No dark patch on the rump and thighs. Very thin black dorsal stripe, which may be absent, runs into the black, long, tufted tail. Ears are long and narrow, with a black tip. Horns are long, narrow, and virtually parallel, ringed on the lower half, slightly shorter than in Beisa Oryx. Females have longer and thinner horns.

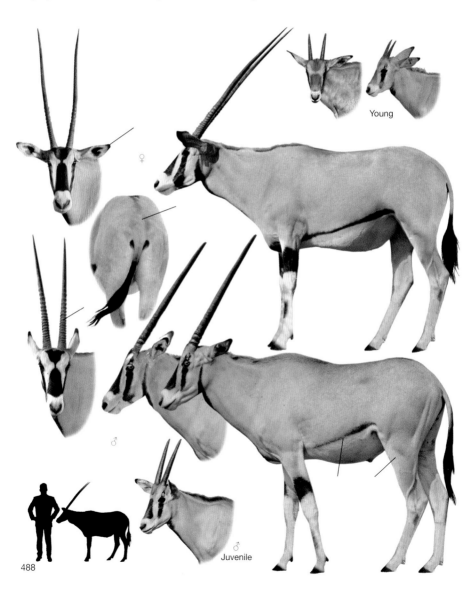

Young

♀

♂

♂
Juvenile

Oryx gallarum

OTHER NAMES East African Oryx. *French:* Oryx d'Éhiopie. *German*: Galla-Oryx. *Spanish*: Órice de Etiopía. *Russian*: Бейза Галла. *Swahili*: Choroa, bara bara.

SUBSPECIES Monotypic. Formerly considered a subspecies of *O. beisa* (Beisa Oryx). Includes *annectens* (Laipikia Oryx, central Kenya and E Uganda).

SIMILAR SPECIES May be confused with the Roan Antelope with which it shares some similarities in head markings; but horns are quite different. The Fringe-eared Oryx is somewhat smaller, has a tuft of hair in the ears, and a longer eye stripe. The Beisa Oryx has an ocher-gray color, a wider black flank band forms a boundary between the body color and the white belly, and it has a shorter eye stripe; otherwise very similar.

REPRODUCTION *Gestation*: 265-300 days. *Young per Birth*: 1. *Weaning*: 3.5 months. *Sexual Maturity*: 1.5-2 years (♀), 5 years (♂). *Life Span*: 18 years. ♂ rest the chin on the ♀'s croup as a prelude to mounting, and the ♀ responds by circling with her head low, like other Hippotragini. Breeding occurs throughout the year, though synchronized calving has been reported. After birth, calves lie up for 2-6 weeks, after which they join the herd.

BEHAVIOR *Family Group*: Mixed herds of 6-40 animals. Old ♂ usually solitary. *Diet*: Grasses, leaves, buds, fruit. *Main Predators*: Lion, leopard, hyena, Cape hunting dog. It has a number of physiological adaptations which allow it to conserve water. Under conditions of extreme heat and low water, the Oryx can raise its body temperature to 46.5° C. Up to this temperature, there is a normal flow of heat from the body to the environment without a loss of water. Only after this point does it start to perspire. Herds have a definite hierarchy, with a ♀ leading the herd and a dominant ♂ bringing up the rear. However, if the lead ♀ strays off the set course, the ♂ hurries to the front to redirect the march. When threatened, they usually flee, although when cornered they present a spirited defense, sometimes inflicting fatal injuries with their spear-like horns.

DISTRIBUTION Found in N Kenya, N of the Tana River and in the Lake Turkana district, and in NE Uganda (Karamoja); its range probably extends an unknown distance into S Somalia and SE Ethiopia.

HABITAT Short-grass steppes, semi-deserts, and brush savannas in eastern Africa.

STATUS Near Threatened. Their numbers and distribution have declined markedly, especially at the margins of their range (Uganda and Somalia), but still occur quite widely in areas of N and E Kenya, where human and livestock densities are low (Samburu region and elsewhere in N Kenya).

PHOTO CREDITS ♀: *Chris Hodges*. ♂: *Robbin Merritt*. Head ♂: *Adam Brin*. Head ♀: *Lawrence Bizzarro*. Juvenile: *Juergen Ritterbach*. Young: *John Paramore* and *Frederic Salein*. All photos at Samburu National Reserve (Kenya).

Arabian Oryx

ORYX LEUCORYX

BL: 140-235 cm. SH: 81-102 cm. TL: 45-60 cm. W: 65-75 kg (♂), 54-70 kg (♀). HL: 50-68 cm. The smallest Oryx, moderately heavy, with a hump over the withers. Coat is bright white in color, with no color washes as in the other Oryx species. Legs are brown to black, except for white ankle bands. Face is marked with dark splotches running from the eyes down the cheeks and under the jowls, and dark triangles of hair on the forehead and down the bridge of the nose. Neck has a sparse mane. Fringed tail is dark brown to black on the lower half. Long, straight, ringed horns, found in both sexes. Female horns are slightly thinner and longer than male horns. Young Oryxes only have tail and knee markings and are generally various shades of brown.

Young

♂

Juvenile

♂

♀

Oryx leucoryx

OTHER NAMES White Oryx. *French*: Oryx d'Arabie. *German*: Arabische Oryx, Weiße Oryx. *Spanish*: Órice de Arabia, órice blanco. *Russian*: Аравийский (белый) орикс. *Arabic*: Ouach.

SUBSPECIES Monotypic. Includes *beatrix*, *latipes,* and *leucoryx*.

SIMILAR SPECIES Scimitar-horned Oryx has also a white coat, but the neck and chest are bright russet, horns scimitar shaped. Addax has spirally twisted horns.

REPRODUCTION *Gestation*: 255-270 days. *Young per Birth*: 1. *Weaning*: 3.5 months. *Sexual Maturity*: 13 months (♀). *Life Span*: 20 years. There is no fixed rutting season. Under captive breeding conditions, births occur throughout the year. ♂ spar when competing for ♀ and these fights may end in injury or death. Calves can join the herd a few hours after birth.

BEHAVIOR *Family Group*: Mixed herds of 2-15 individuals. *Diet*: Grasses, leaves, buds. *Main Predators*: Only jackals, which prey on calves, remain in native area. Shallow depressions are excavated in the soft earth under trees and bushes, and are used to rest in during the heat of the day. The bright white coat is extremely reflective, acting as a cooling mechanism in the parching desert. These Oryxes have the amazing ability to detect rainfall, and will subsequently move in its direction to intercept the new, lush growth. These erratic movements may span hundreds of kilometers. One of the introduced herds in Oman utilizes home ranges of about 3,000 km^2. This area is broken into several smaller patches (100-300 km^2 in area), each of which is used for 1-18 months before moving on. Population density is low, about 0.035 animals per km^2.

DISTRIBUTION *Regionally Extinct*: Egypt (Sinai), Iraq, Kuwait, Syria, Yemen. *Reintroduced*: Israel, Oman, Saudi Arabia, United Arab Emirates. *Introduced*: Bahrain, Qatar. Formerly occurred through most of the Arabian Peninsula, N to Kuwait and Iraq. Range had already contracted by the early years of the 20th century and the decline accelerated thereafter. The last wild individuals were probably shot in 1972 on the Jiddat al Harasis. They have been reintroduced to Oman (Arabian Oryx Sanctuary), Saudi Arabia (Mahazat as-Sayd Reserve, Uruq Bani Ma'arid Reserve), Israel (three sites in the N Arava and Negev Desert), United Arab Emirates (Arabian Oryx Reserve), and Jordan (Wadi Rum). There is a small introduced population on Hawar Island, Bahrain, and large semi-managed populations at several sites in Qatar and United Arab Emirates.

HABITAT Formerly barren steppes, semi-deserts, and deserts of the Arabian Peninsula.

STATUS Vulnerable. Hunted to the brink of extinction, this Oryx has been saved by captive breeding. By 1965, fewer than 500 animals were thought to remain in existence. Thankfully, in the 1950s, efforts to establish captive herds in Arabia were made, and in 1962, several were exported to the United States. Along with individuals from a few European zoos, these Oryxes were placed in a breeding facility in the Phoenix Zoo (Arizona), where they successfully bred. Today, over 100 Arabian Oryxes have been returned to the wild in Oman and Jordan, while the captive population is over 600 animals.

PHOTO CREDITS ♀: *Laura Anglin*, San Diego Zoo (USA). ♂: *A. Rahman AlKhulaifi* (Qatar). Head ♀: *Valerie Abbott*, Miami Metro Zoo (USA). Head ♂: *Adriano Spiccia*, Zürich Zoologischer Garten (Switzerland). Young: *Christopher John Holland,* Marwell Wildlife (UK). Juvenile: *Jose R. Castello*, Jerez Zoo (Spain).

Scimitar-horned Oryx

ORYX DAMMAH

BL: 160-175 cm. SH: 110-125 cm. TL: 37-60 cm. W: 180-200 kg (♂). HL: 82-150 cm. A large, heavily built antelope. Coat white, neck and chest reddish brown. There may be a light wash of russet over the flanks and thighs. Facial mask consisting of vertical russet stripes which pass through the eyes, and a wide reddish nose stripe. Faint ruddy flank stripe. Long, tufted tail dark brown on the outer half. Thin, scimitar- or sickle-shaped horns, found in both sexes, virtually ringless, curving up and over the back. Horns are fairly fragile and are prone to breaking. Calves are light brown, with a white abdomen and a black-tipped tail, changing to adult coloration when the animals are 3-12 months old. Female similar to the male, slightly smaller and horns more slender.

Juvenile

♀

♂

Young

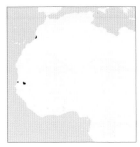

Oryx dammah

OTHER NAMES Scimitar Oryx, Sahara Oryx, White Oryx. *French*: Oryx algazelle, oryx de Libye, oryx blanc, oryx à cou roux, oryx à cornes. *German*: Säbelantilope. *Spanish*: Órice de cuernos de cimitarra, órice blanco. *Russian*: Саблерогая антилопа, или сахарский орикс. *Arabic*: Maha, abu hirab, ouach. *Hausa*: Walwaji. *Peulh*: Dieri kari.

SUBSPECIES Monotypic. Includes *algazel* (Western White Oryx, Sudan) and *dammah*.

REPRODUCTION *Gestation*: 240-255 days. *Young per Birth*: 1. *Weaning*: 3.5 months. *Sexual Maturity*: 11-30 months (♀), 10-30 months (♂). *Life Span*: 20 years. ♂ fight by butting their heads; injuries may occur, but they are usually not fatal. While the Scimitar-horned Oryx is an opportunistic breeder, births peak in March and October. Within hours after birth, both mothers and calves return to the main herd. Maternal attention is minimal.

BEHAVIOR *Family Group*: Mixed herds of 10-40, sometimes more. Formerly thousands of animals would group for migration. Seldom solitary. At times old ♂ would join herds of Dama Gazelles. *Diet*: Grasses, legumes, succulent plants, acacia pods, fruits. *Main Predators*: Lion, leopard, hyena, Cape hunting dog. Extremely gregarious, and there is a distinct reluctance in individuals to remain solitary. During the wet season, herds migrate N into the Sahara, returning S as the dry season approaches. They have numerous physiological adaptations to desert life which allow them to go without drinking water for weeks, or possibly even months. Specialized kidneys prevent excess loss of water through urine, while perspiration is minimized by raising body temperature to a maximum of 46.5° C. Up to this temperature, there is a normal flow of heat from the body to the environment without a loss of water. Only after this point does it start to perspire. Long-distance movements mainly occur at night. Scimitar-horned Oryxes amble, nodding their heads when walking fast; they have a flowing trot.

DISTRIBUTION *Regionally Extinct*: Algeria, Burkina Faso, Chad, Egypt, Libya, Mali, Mauritania, Morocco, Niger, Nigeria, Senegal, Sudan, Tunisia, Western Sahara. May formerly have been widespread across N Africa, at least in arid and Saharan areas, but now Extinct in the Wild over all its range. Captive herds are kept in fenced protected areas in Tunisia, Senegal, and Morocco (Sous Massa NP).

HABITAT Grassy steppes, semi-deserts, and deserts in a narrow strip of central N Africa.

STATUS Extinct in the Wild. In United Arab Emirates, more than 4,000 occur in a private collection, and as many as 2,000 occur in private ranches in Texas (USA). Reintroduced in Tunisia and introduced in Israel.

PHOTO CREDITS ♂: *Alex Meyer*, Chapultepec Zoo (Mexico). ♀: *Jose R. Castello*, Vigo Zoo (Spain). Head ♀: *Daniel Mac Alister*, Biblical Zoo, Jerusalem (Israel). Head ♂: *Daniel Holmes*, Pamandan Ranch, TX (USA). Young: *Nick Karpov*, Berlin Tierpark (Germany). Juvenile: *Ulrike Joerres*, Aalborg Zoo (Denmark).

Addax

ADDAX NASOMACULATUS

BL: 110-130 cm. SH: 95-115 cm. TL: 25-35 cm. W: 100-125 kg (♂), 60-90 kg (♀). HL: 60-109 cm (♂), 55-80 cm (♀). Medium-sized antelope. Short, glossy coat off-white to pale grayish brown in color, lighter in the summer and darker in the winter. Rump, underparts, limbs, and lips are pure white. White X-shaped blaze on the face, and a mat of dense, dark hair on the forehead. Chin, lips, and inside of the ears pure white. Long hairs on the throat form a scraggly beard. Tail rather long, but not reaching to the hocks, with a white to black tuft at tip. Horns long, rather thin, diverging and spirally twisted, up to almost 3 turns, ringed on the basal half. Hooves considerably enlarged, adapted to walking on soft, sandy soil. Females similar to males, slightly smaller and with thinner, shorter horns, but are otherwise similar. Calves are reddish brown.

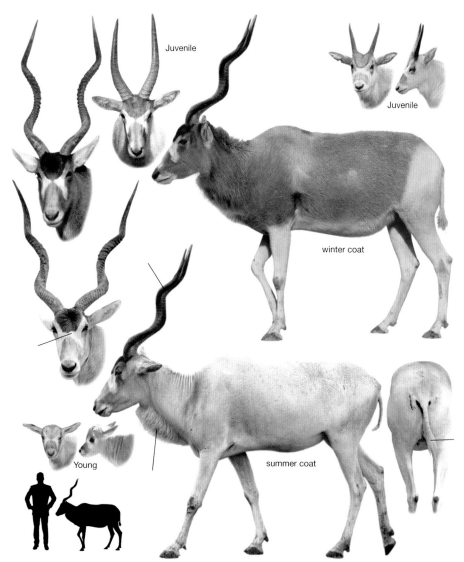

Juvenile

Juvenile

winter coat

Young

summer coat

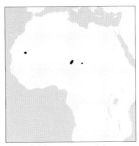

Addax nasomaculatus

OTHER NAMES *French*: Antilope à nez tacheté, antilope blanche. *German*: Mendesantilope. *Spanish*: Adax. *Russian*: Аддакс. *Arabic*: Berger el Ouach, Achach, Mahe, Adaks. *Hausa*: Warwaji, mariri.

SUBSPECIES Monotypic.

REPRODUCTION *Gestation*: 255 days. *Young per Birth*: 1. *Weaning*: 3.5 months. *Sexual Maturity*: 1.5 years (♀), 3 years (♂). *Life Span*: 19 years. Courtship includes ritualized foreleg kicking (laufschlag). The ♂ rests his chin on the ♀'s croup as a prelude to mounting. The ♀ responds by circling, her head low, like other Hippotragini. While mating, the ♂ rears upright, firmly grasping the ♀'s loin. ♀ leave the herd a few days prior to birth of a calf and are typically accompanied by an adult ♂, which remains with the ♀ and calf for some time after birth. Births occur primarily in winter and spring, although captive observations indicate that births may occur throughout the year. Neonates are hiders, rejoining the herd, but forming a crèche with other calves, after about 2 weeks.

BEHAVIOR *Family Group*: Mixed herds with 2-20 individuals (formerly more), led by an old ♂. *Diet*: Grasses, herbs, leaves on small bushes. *Main Predators*: Formerly lion, leopard, hyena (exterminated). Most active from dusk until dawn, the coolest time (night) in the Sahara. To protect themselves from strong winds and the glaring sun during the day, Addax dig "beds" into the sand with their forefeet in which they rest, often in the shade of boulders or bushes. A nomadic species, this antelope wanders the dunes of the Sahara searching for the scant vegetation which grows there. It is able to obtain all needed moisture from its food, and rarely, if ever, drinks water. ♂ leave small piles of fecal matter, while ♀ reportedly scatter their dung. Addax live in small herds with a distinct social hierarchy, seemingly based on age. The most desert-adapted of antelopes, Addax apparently are able to sense changes in humidity and find places where rain has fallen or vegetation is sprouting. Their senses of sight, smell, and hearing are very good.

DISTRIBUTION *Native*: Chad, Mauritania, Niger. *Regionally Extinct*: Algeria, Egypt, Libya, Sudan, Western Sahara. *Reintroduced*: Morocco, Tunisia. Formerly widespread in the Sahelo-Saharan region of Africa, W of the Nile Valley, and present in suitable habitats in all countries sharing the Sahara Desert. As with other ungulates of the Sahelo-Saharan fauna, the Addax has undergone an unprecedented reduction in geographical range over the past century. Today, the only known remaining population survives in the Termit-Tin Toumma region of Niger. There are sporadic records of small isolated groups and individuals from E Air Mountains and Western Ténéré Desert in Niger, and from the Equey region of W Chad. Possible rare vagrants from these areas may be seen in N Niger, S Algeria, and Libya. The Addax breeds well in captivity and has been introduced into some ranches in Texas and New Mexico (USA).

HABITAT Deserts with little vegetation.

STATUS Critically Endangered. Almost extinct in the wild, with a maximum of only about 500 animals over its former range. There are about 1,700 animals in captivity.

PHOTO CREDITS Summer coat: *Ulrike Joerres*, Safari de Peaugres (France). Winter coat and head: *Alex Meyer*, San Antonio Zoo (USA). Young: *Alex Kantorovich* and *Nick Karpov*, Berlin Tierpark (Germany). Juvenile: *Sergey Chichagov*, Nahariya Zoo (Israel).

Blue Wildebeest
CONNOCHAETES TAURINUS

BL: 180-240 cm (♂), 170-230 cm (♀). SH: 141-156 cm (♂), 129-144 cm (♀). TL: 60-100 cm. W: 232-295 kg (♂), 165-216 kg (♀). HL: To 83 cm (♂), 30-40 cm (♀). Large antelope. Coloration dark blue gray with a tinge of brown and a silvery sheen. Lower segments of limbs tan colored. Underparts slightly darker. Series of short black stripes on the neck and shoulders. Slight hump above the shoulders, with a slight slope toward the rear. Long, horse-like tail is black. Convex face black from crown to nostrils, with a reddish tinge on the forehead; side of face paler gray, often reddish tinged. Black beard. Mane along the upper side of the neck black and erect. Horns without rings in both sexes, arise from swollen bosses and go out and somewhat down, then rise up; tips curve inward and slightly backward. Female similar to male, smaller, with thinner horns.

♀

♂

Young

Juvenile

Connochaetes taurinus

OTHER NAMES Brindled Gnu, Black-bearded Wildebeest. *French*: Gnou à queue noire, gnou bleu à barbe noire. *German*: Südliches Streifengnu, Weissbartgnu. *Spanish*: Ñu azul, ñu gorgón. *Russian*: Голубой (чернобородый) гну. *Afrikaans*: Blouwildebees.

SUBSPECIES Monotypic. The name *C. taurinus* (Wildebeest) formerly included *C. taurinus* (Blue Wildebeest), *C. mearnsi* (Western White-bearded Wildebeest), *C. albojubatus* (Eastern White-bearded Wildebeest), and *C. johnstoni* (Johnston's Wildebeest) as subspecies: these are all elevated to full species here. Includes *reichei*, *mattosi* (Angola Wildebeest), and *borlei*.

SIMILAR SPECIES Black Wildebeest is smaller, has a brush-like tuft on the muzzle, tufts on the throat and between the legs, a white tail, and differently shaped horns.

REPRODUCTION *Gestation*: 250 days. *Young per Birth*: 1. *Weaning*: 4-8 months, some suckling may occur until 1 year of age. *Sexual Maturity*: 2 years (♀), 3-4 years (♂). *Life Span*: 20 years. Rut is between April and early June in South Africa. Births are extremely seasonal, with all births occurring in a period of 2-3 weeks before the rains. This flood of youngsters prevents predators from decimating the new population, as they might if births were spread out over a longer period of time. A young Wildebeest can stand just 15 minutes after birth, and can follow its mother shortly thereafter.

BEHAVIOR *Family Group*: ♀ and young in groups of 10-1,000 animals. Young ♂ form small bachelor groups, while mature ♂ are generally solitary. *Diet*: Grazers; short green grasses; they need to drink every day. *Main Predators*: Lion, spotted hyena, Cape hunting dog, leopard, cheetah, crocodile. Activity is concentrated in the morning and late afternoon, with the hot middle hours of the day being spent resting. Extremely agile. When alarmed, they will prance about, waving their tails and pawing the ground. If a potential threat approaches close enough, they will run for a short distance and then turn back to reassess the situation, repeating the action as needed. Large, mixed migratory herds, with thousands of animals making long treks, but sedentary herds are also found, with a home range of about 1 km². Adult ♂ are territorial, and may occupy their territories for a few weeks or for the entire year. Size of territory varies from about 1 to 1.6 ha, and the boundaries are marked with dung heaps, preorbital gland secretions, and the pawing of the earth. The average distance between these ♂ averages 100-140 m. Competition between ♂ comprises displays, loud grunting calls, and shoving with the horns, although rarely are these serious fights. Only ♂ with a territory may mate. Unusual for most Bovids, with the exception of cattle, Wildebeest enjoy rolling in sand and dirt. When possible, they will drink twice daily. They are often seen grazing with Burchell's zebra.

DISTRIBUTION *Native:* Angola, Botswana, Mozambique, Namibia, South Africa, Swaziland, Zambia, Zimbabwe.

HABITAT Savanna woodland areas, especially acacia savanna, with plenty of shade and water. Short-grass areas on riverbanks in the dry season.

STATUS Least Concern. Estimated population in 1998 was 128,000 animals, mostly in protected areas and private farms.

PHOTO CREDITS ♀: *Gerrit De Vries*. ♂: *Davide Martini*, Kruger NP (South Africa). Young, juvenile, and ♀ head: *Sergey Chichagov*, Kaunas Zoo (Lithuania).

Johnston's Wildebeest
CONNOCHAETES JOHNSTONI

BL: 170-230 cm. SH: 106-114 cm. TL: 60. W: 160-180 kg. HL: To 83 cm. Pelage brownish gray, browner than that of other species, pale legs, and short black tail. The front of the convex face is covered with bristly black hair and, rarely, a white band across the face in front of the eyes. Slight hump above the shoulders, with a slight slope in the body toward the rear. Mane stands up as it does in *taurinus*. Black flowing beard is present in both sexes, appearing almost like a dewlap. Both sexes possess horns without rings. Males have a very wide horn span, as in *taurinus*, but otherwise rather different in appearance. The horns do not curve so far downward. The horn span in the female is much shorter than in *taurinus*. Female similar to male, but smaller and with thinner horns.

Young

Juvenile

Connochaetes johnstoni

OTHER NAMES Nyassa Wildebeest, Cookson's Wildebeest, White-banded Wildebeest. *French*: Gnou de Johnston, gnou du Selous. *German*: Njassa-Gnu, Weissbartgnu. *Spanish*: Ñu de Johnston. *Russian*: Ньясский гну *(johnstoni),* включает подвид Гну Куксона *(cooksoni).*

SUBSPECIES Monotypic. Formerly considered a subspecies of *C. taurinus* (Wildebeest). Includes *cooksoni* (Cookson's Wildebeest), which is considered as a different subspecies by some authors, and *rufijianus* (Rufigi Vvalley, Tanzania).

SIMILAR SPECIES Nyassa Wildebeest has a small body and horns, and is browner than other races, and is sometimes referred to as the White-banded Wildebeest for the pale chevron between the eyes (often absent in the Tanzania population). Cookson's Wildebeest has the largest body and horns of any Wildebeest, and is usually browner. Blue Wildebeest has also a black beard, but is darker. Eastern and Western White-bearded Wildebeest have a white beard.

REPRODUCTION *Gestation*: 240-255 days. *Young per Birth*: 1. *Weaning*: 4 months, although some suckling may occur until 1 year of age. *Sexual Maturity*: 1.5-2.5 years (♀), 3 years (♂). *Life Span*: 20 years. The rut is in March-April, and at this time the number of territorial ♂ increases greatly. Young ♂ are expelled from the breeding herds in August-September, 2 months before calving begins.

BEHAVIOR *Family Group*: ♀ and young in groups of 9-20 animals. Young ♂ (under 3 years of age) form small bachelor groups, while mature ♂ are generally solitary. *Diet*: Predominantly a grazer; grasses. *Main Predators*: Lion, spotted hyena, Cape hunting dog, leopard, cheetah, crocodile. There is no specific information for this species, but probably similar to other Wildebeest. Most Wildebeest feed off and on throughout the day and night, depending on the season and availability of forage.

DISTRIBUTION *Native*: Mozambique, Tanzania, Zambia. *Regionally Extinct*: Malawi. Found N of Zambezi River in Mozambique to E-central Tanzania, and formerly as far N as the Wami River, SE Malawi, where now it is extinct (Nyassa Wildebeest). Cookson's Wildebeest is restricted to the Luangwa Valley, Zambia, with vagrants occasionally ranging onto the adjacent plateau and into W Malawi.

HABITAT Savanna, interspersed with miombo woodland.

STATUS Least Concern. Estimated population of 88,000 animals, two-thirds in protected areas (70,000 in the E part of the Selous Game Reserve, 12,000 in Mikumi NP, 6,000 in the Luangwa Valley in Zambia and in SE Tanzania).

PHOTO CREDITS ♀: *Dominique Mignard*, Selous Reserve (Tanzania). ♂: *Adam Rees*, Mikumi NP (Tanzania). Young: *Juraj Ujhazy* (Zambia). Juvenile: *Mirko Eggert*, Mikumi NP (Tanzania).

Western White-bearded Wildebeest
CONNOCHAETES MEARNSI

BL: 180-240 cm (♂), 170-230 cm (♀). SH: 100-123 cm (♂), 117 cm (♀). TL: 70-100 cm. W: 208 kg (♂), 163 kg (♀). HL: To 83 cm. Smallest and darkest-hued species, with darker legs that contrast less with the general body color. Pelage blackish on the chest and flanks. Black tail, longer than that of other species. Underparts slightly darker than the main coat. Mane hangs limp, as in *albojubatus*. Flowing conspicuous white beard, appearing almost like a dewlap. Slight hump above the shoulders, with a slight slope in the body toward the rear. Front of the convex face covered with bristly black hair. Both sexes posses non-ringed horns; without such a wide spread as in other species, and the tips do not turn inward as much, but they have a more pronounced frontal boss. Female similar to male, smaller, with thinner horns.

♀

Juvenile

♂

Young

Connochaetes mearnsi

OTHER NAMES Serengeti White-bearded Wildebeest. *French*: Gnou de Mearns. *German*: Serengeti-Weissbartgnu, Westliches-Weissbartgnu. *Spanish*: Ñu barbiblanco del Serengeti. *Russian*: Западный белобородый гну. *Swahili*: Nyumbu Magharibi.

SUBSPECIES Monotypic. Formerly considered a subspecies of *C. taurinus* (Wildebeest). Includes *henrici* (Serengeti, Tanzania), *lorenzi* (N Ngorongoro Crater, Tanzania), and *schulzi* (S Ngorongoro Crater, Tanzania).

SIMILAR SPECIES Smallest and darkest-hued species, with a longer tail. It also features the shortest horns, but with more developed boss in ♂.

REPRODUCTION *Gestation*: 240-255 days. *Young per Birth*: 1. *Weaning*: 4 months, although some suckling may occur until 1 year of age. *Sexual Maturity*: 1.5-2.5 years (♀), 3 years (♂). *Life Span*: 20 years. Rutting occurs at the end of the rains. There is no ritualization of behavior. The birth period lasts only 3 weeks, starting up about 1 month before the rainy season, around February. Newborns can gain their feet in as little as a few minutes. Pregnant Wildebeests in migratory populations gather together on calving grounds and drop calves by the dozens between dawn and midday. Once the newborns have gained their feet and have suckled for the first time, they are led into the nearest nursery herd.

BEHAVIOR *Family Group*: ♀ and young in groups of 10-1,000 animals. Young ♂ (under 3 years of age) form small bachelor groups, while mature ♂ are generally solitary. *Diet*: Completely grazers, 100% on grass. *Main Predators*: Lion, spotted hyena, Cape hunting dog, leopard, cheetah, crocodile. Activity is concentrated in the morning and late afternoon, with the hot middle hours of the day being spent resting. Extremely agile. When alarmed, they will prance about, waving their tails and pawing the ground. They migrate throughout the year, constantly seeking fresh grazing and better-quality water. The precise timing is dependent upon the rainfall patterns each year. In late November and December, the herds arrive on the short-grass plains of the Serengeti. By May all seem to be moving N, with a series of moving columns, often containing hundreds of thousands of animals, joined by many zebra, and a scattering of Thomson's and Grant's Gazelles. September sees the herds spread out across the N Serengeti, where the Mara River provides the migration with its most serious obstacle. By October the herds are migrating again with more accord: all are heading S, returning to the green shoots which follow the rains on the short-grass plains of the S Serengeti in November.

DISTRIBUTION *Native:* Kenya, Tanzania. Serengeti-Mara ecosystem: N Tanzania and S Kenya west of the Gregory Rift Valley, reaching Lake Victoria at Speke Bay.

HABITAT Short-grass plains, never too far from water, and migrate when growth stops in the dry season.

STATUS Least Concern. Estimated population in 1998 was 942,000 animals (98% in and around protected areas).

PHOTO CREDITS ♂: *Maurizio Bersanelli*. ♀: *Richard Mortel*, Ngorongoro (Tanzania). Head ♀: *Simon English*, Ngorongoro (Tanzania). Head ♂: *Lincol Lin*, Serengeti (Tanzania). Young: *Xinyi Xu*, Serengeti (Tanzania). Juvenile: *Sergei Golyshev*, Serengeti (Tanzania).

Eastern White-bearded Wildebeest
CONNOCHAETES ALBOJUBATUS

BL: 195 cm. SH: 125-145 cm (♂), 115-142 cm (♀). TL: 60 cm. W: 222-271 kg (♂), 179-208 kg (♀). HL: To 83 cm. Palest species in coloration. Body color pale grayish, frequently darker in the foreparts; bridled striping subdued. Beard and throat fringe creamy white with black hairs intermixed, occasionally all-black fringes. Mane does not stand erect, as in *taurinus*, but hangs limp. Slight hump above the shoulders, with a slight slope in the body toward the rear. Front of the convex face covered with bristly black hair. White facial band below the eyes may be present in some individuals. Long, horse-like tail black, shorter than in *mearnsi*. Both sexes possess horns, slightly broadened at the base, without rings. The horns are not strongly down-curved. Female similar to male, smaller, with thinner horns.

♀

Juvenile

Young

♂

Connochaetes albojubatus

OTHER NAMES *French*: Gnou à barbe blanche. *German*: Östliches-Weissbartgnu. *Spanish*: Ñu barbiblanco oriental, Ñu de barba blanca. *Russian*: Восточный белобородый гну. *Swahili*: Nyumbu masharikimash ariki.

SUBSPECIES Monotypic. Formerly considered a subspecies of *C. taurinus* (Wildebeest). Includes *hecki* (Heck's Wildebeest) and *babaulti*.

SIMILAR SPECIES The lightest-colored species, beard white to tan, with darker stripes than in other species.

REPRODUCTION *Gestation*: 240-255 days. *Young per Birth*: 1. *Weaning*: 4-9 months. *Sexual Maturity*: 1.5-2.5 years (♀), 3 years (♂). *Life Span*: 20 years. No specific information available for this species, but probably similar to *C. mearnsi*.

BEHAVIOR *Family Group*: ♀ and young in groups of 10-1,000 animals. Young ♂ form small bachelor groups, while mature ♂ are generally solitary. *Diet*: Grazers; prefer short grasses, but will eat taller grasses during the dry season; generally drink twice a day. *Main Predators*: Lion, spotted hyena, Cape hunting dog, leopard, cheetah, crocodile. Activity is concentrated in the morning and late afternoon, with the hot middle hours of the day being spent resting. Extremely agile. When alarmed, they will prance about, waving their tails and pawing the ground. If a potential threat approaches close enough, they will run for a short distance and then turn back to reassess the situation, repeating the action as needed. When pressed they have been clocked running over 80 kmph. Three main migrations: from Nairobi NP in the dry season to the Athi-Kapiti Plains in the wet season; from Amboseli NP in the dry season S across the Tanzanian border to the Rift Valley between Lakes Netron and Magadi in the wet season; and from the Tarangire and Lake Manyara in the dry season eastward to the Simanjiro Plains in the wet season.

DISTRIBUTION *Native:* Kenya, Tanzania. N Tanzania to central Kenya just S of the equator, W to the Gregory Rift Valley. The Eastern White-bearded (*albojubatus*) and Western White-bearded (*mearnsi*) Wildebeests are separated by the W wall of the Gregory Rift.

HABITAT Alkaline, seasonally flooded grasslands with swamps and wooded bushland.

STATUS Least Concern. Estimated population is 94,000 animals, about two-thirds in and around protected areas (35,000 in Tanzania, in Tarangire NP, Lake Manyara region, and Amboseli NP, and 20,000 in Kenya, migrating between Nairobi NP and the Athi-Kapiti Plains).

PHOTO CREDITS ♂: *Son of Groucho*, Amboseli NP (Kenya). Head: *Steve Riall*, Amboseli NP (Kenya). ♀: *Steve Riall,* Amboseli NP (Kenya). Juvenile: *Ellen Olson,* Amboseli NP (Kenya). Young: *James Bailey*, Amboseli NP (Kenya).

Black Wildebeest

CONNOCHAETES GNOU

BL: 185-220 cm (♂), 170-205 cm (♀). SH: 110-120 cm (♂), 90-105 (♀). TL: 85-100 cm. W: 140-180 kg (♂), 110-160 kg (♀). HL: 45-78 cm. Large antelope. Chocolate-brown to black coat, short and glossy in summer, becoming shaggier in winter. Tufts of long, brush-like blackish hair on face, and a beard on the neck which extends to the chest. Light patch on the nape of the neck, topped by a dark-tipped mane. The back is nearly level, and the neck is quite thick. Long, horse-like tail, bright white. Eyes small and beady, which, along with bristly hair on the face, create a very strange look. Hook-like, smooth horns curve downward, forward, and then upward; found in both sexes, they expand into a hard shield-like base in males. Female similar to male, but somewhat smaller, with thinner horns.

♂

Young

Juvenile

♂

♀

504

Connochaetes gnou

OTHER NAMES White-tailed Gnu, White-tailed Wildebeest. *French*: Gnou à queue blanche. *German*: Weissschwanzgnu. *Spanish*: Ñu negro. *Russian*: Белохвостый гну. *Afrikaans*: Swartwildebees. *Ndebele*: Imbudumo. *Xhosa*: Inqu, imbuthuma. *Zulu*: Inkonkoni. *Sepedi*: Podumô. *Sesotho*: Mmamononwane. *Swati*: Ingongoni. *Xitsonga*: Mbutuma. *Tshivenda*: Khongoni.

SUBSPECIES Monotypic. It may hybridize with *C. taurinus*, which can occur when the two species are mixed unnaturally on fenced land; hybrids are known to be fertile.

SIMILAR SPECIES Could be confused with the Blue Wildebeest, but the brush-like tuft on the muzzle, the tufts on the throat and between the legs, the color of the tail, and the shape of the horns are, with the smaller size, characteristics for identification.

REPRODUCTION *Gestation*: 253 days. *Young per Birth*: 1. *Weaning*: 6 months. *Sexual Maturity*: 16 months (♀), 3 years (♂). *Life Span*: 20 years. Breeding season is from February to April, with the subsequent calves being born between November and December. The single calf stays with the mother until the birth of the next one.

BEHAVIOR *Family Group*: ♀ and young in closed herds of 11-50 animals, ♂ in bachelor groups. *Diet*: Short grasses. *Main Predators*: Lion, spotted hyena, Cape hunting dog, leopard, cheetah, crocodile. Active morning and late afternoon, resting in the open during the day and not seeking shade. Mainly a grazer, often kneeling to do so. Will browse on bushes in winter. Dependent on water. Eyesight and hearing are excellent, sense of smell is good. Can run at a good speed. Defend themselves bravely when attacked. They have the reputation of being untrustworthy and dangerous in captivity. Maternal herds have a distinct hierarchy, and ♀ have been seen attacking and fighting with strangers. Bachelor herds rarely display any aggressive symptoms. Herds of ♀ and their young wander in home ranges averaging 100 ha in size, passing through territories of breeding ♂. These territories are set up by ♂ over 4 years of age, and are marked in the center with dung middens, in which the owner urinates, scrapes, and rolls. Territorial conflicts involve ritualized posturing and horn wrestling, accompanied by a blaring, two-part call, "genu." It is quite vocal, including a loud, high-pitched "ge-nu" and a resonant "hick" accompanied by an upward jerk of the chin, which gives the impression of constant hiccups.

DISTRIBUTION *Native*: South Africa. *Reintroduced:* Lesotho; Swaziland. *Introduced:* Namibia. No truly wild individuals survive today; all are descended from captive individuals, and those in their native habitat are kept on game farms. By the end of the 19th century, excessive hunting reduced the formerly vast population to a few individuals surviving on two farms in South Africa; protection has allowed the species to recover. It has now been reintroduced to parts of its former range (W Swaziland and W Lesotho) and into farmland areas outside of its natural range (Namibia).

HABITAT Open plains and grassland where water is available. Areas of short-grass feeding and good visibility are preferred.

STATUS Least Concern. Estimated population is 20,000 animals.

PHOTO CREDITS ♀: *Alex Meyer,* Madrid Zoo (Spain), ♂: *Dominique Pipet*, Réserve Africaine de Sigean (France). Head ♂: *Sarah Cotton,* Marwell Wildlife, Owslebury (UK). Juvenile: *Dmitry Osipov*. Young: *Andrey Kotkin*, Moscow Zoo (Russia).

Hirola
BEATRAGUS HUNTERI

BL: 120-200 cm. SH: 95-100 cm. TL: 30-45 cm. W: 80-118 kg. HL: 45-60 cm (♂), 35-49 cm (♀). Medium-sized antelope. Coat is light sandy brown, which turns more gray in adult males. Two white lines form a chevron between the eyes. These chevron lines encircle each eye, emphasizing their position. Dark-colored preorbital glands, which are enlarged when excited. Long, thick tail is white, as are the ears, which are tipped with black. Skin on the nape of the neck thickens considerably in mature males, and folds up behind the horns in a conspicuous ridge when the ears are pricked. Lyrate horns found in both sexes, much more like those of an Impala than a Topi or Hartebeest, but shorter and sturdier, with heavy rings along most of their length. Female similar to male, but smaller and with lighter horns.

Juvenile

♀

♂

Beatragus hunteri

OTHER NAMES Hunter's Hartebeest, Herola, Four-eyed Antelope. *French*: Hirola, damalisque de Hunter. *German*: Hunters Leireantilope. *Spanish*: Hirola, antilope de Hunter, damalisco de Hunter. *Russian*: Антилопа Хантера (Хирола). *Bambara*: Tankòu. *Galla*: Blanketta. *Kirundi*: Inyemera. *Swahili*: Nyamera. *Somali*: Aholi, hirola.

SUBSPECIES Monotypic. This species is thought to be the evolutionary link between true Hartebeests and Topis and Tsessebes (*Damaliscus*); as such it is a relict species, and only exists today due to its unique habitat requirements.

SIMILAR SPECIES Cannot be confused with any other Hartebeest owing to its general features, the shape of the horns, and the conspicuous white chevron between the eyes. Topi is much darker and larger, with shorter horns.

REPRODUCTION *Gestation*: 7.5-8 months. *Young per Birth*: 1. Breeding occurs at the onset of the long rainy season in March and April, with the majority of births occurring just prior to the short rains in October and November. Young go through a brief "lying up" phase, hiding away from their mothers.

BEHAVIOR *Family Group*: ♀ and their young in herds of 5-40 animals, generally led by a single territorial ♂. All-♂ groups are common, and may be associated with Topi bachelor herds. *Diet*: Grasses. Drinks when water is available, but can exist for long periods without it. *Main Predators*: Lion, hyena, cheetah. Most feeding activity occurs in the early morning and evening. Hirola are very good at storing fat, which, along with a low activity level, helps this species to survive droughts. Herds are fairly sedentary, adult ♂ especially so. ♂ holding territories often posture on "stamping grounds" created by scraping at the dirt with their hooves and marked with dung heaps, in which head bobbing, made more conspicuous by the white ears and facial mask, plays a large part. Scent marking of grasses with secretions from the preorbital gland is also common. When fighting in earnest, ♂ generally kneel in front of their opponent, while wrestling and sparring occur in an upright position.

DISTRIBUTION *Native:* Kenya, Somalia. Endemic to NE Kenya and SW Somalia. In Kenya, Hirola currently occur between Garsen, Bura, and Galma Galla/Kolbio. Current status in SW Somalia is not known, but its former range has been badly affected by prolonged civil and military conflicts. There is a small translocated population in Tsavo East NP, outside the species' natural range.

HABITAT Arid, grassy plains bound by semi-desert inland and coastal forests.

STATUS Critically Endangered. This antelope has recently become very rare, with current censuses reporting fewer than 400 individuals. Threatened by competition from domestic livestock within its very limited range, poaching, loss of habitat, drought, and rinderpest.

PHOTO CREDITS ♀: *Steve Garvie*, Tsavo East NP (Kenya) and *Abdullahi Hussein Ali* (Kenya). ♂: *Andrew Woodley*, Tsavo East NP (Kenya).

Korrigum
DAMALISCUS KORRIGUM

BL: 150-205 cm. SH: 127-132 cm. TL: 40-60 cm. W: 122-136 kg. HL: To 84 cm. The largest of the Topis, with the largest horns. Color bright reddish orange. Bluish-black patches on shoulders, hips, and upper legs less extensive than in the Tiang or Topis, and the lower legs are much the same color as the body. Bluish-black face blaze has a narrow streak running from it below and behind the eye. Tail fairly short, barely reaching the hocks, with a crest of black hairs on the lower third. Horns in both sexes thick, rather short, strongly ringed, and lyrate. They rise in a gentle backward curve, diverging slightly, then turning slightly upward at the tips. Females slightly smaller than males; otherwise very similar. Young are sandy colored for the first 2 months.

Damaliscus korrigum

OTHER NAMES Senegal Hartebeest, West African Korrigum, Darfur Tiang, Western Topi. *French*: Damalisque. *German*: Leriantilope. *Spanish*: Bubalo de Senegal. *Russian*: Корригиум.

SUBSPECIES Monotypic. The name *D. korrigum* formerly included *D. korrigum* (Korrigum), *D. tiang* (Tiang), *D. ugandae* (Uganda Topi), *D. eurus* (Ruaha Topi), *D. topi* (Coastal Topi), *D. jimela* (Serengeti Topi) as subspecies: these are all elevated to full species here. Includes *korrigum* (Senegal to N Nigeria) and *purpurescens* (Purple Hartebeest, E and N Nigeria and N Cameroon).

SIMILAR SPECIES Korrigum and Tiang are relatively larger Topis, very bright reddish-orange color; they are generally distinguished from the other Topis by the concave profile of the head and the flatter (backward-slanting) but more curving horns. Tiang is more reddish than Korrigum, the iridescence of the coat has a purplish tinge, and dark patches on shoulders, hindquarters, and upper legs are more extensive. Ruaha Topi is very similar, but paler. Serengeti Topi has smaller, shorter horns, and shoulder patches are larger.

REPRODUCTION *Gestation*: 210 days. *Young per Birth*: 1. *Weaning*: After 4 months. *Sexual Maturity*: 1.5-2 years (♀), 3-4 years (♂). *Life Span*: 14 years. Breeding is seasonal; calving occurs at the end of the dry season, in March. The calf usually remains hidden until it is strong enough to follow the herd.

BEHAVIOR *Family Group*: Herds of 15-30, sometimes hundreds during seasonal migrations in search of new grass during the early rains. *Diet*: Grasses, avoiding very short grass, and eating very few forbs; drinks water, but is able to go without it for long periods. *Main Predators*: Lion, leopard, cheetah, Cape hunting dog. Often mingles with other species such as zebra, Wildebeest, and Hartebeest. Breeding ♂ are territorial during the rut, each defending a well-marked stamping ground against other ♂, through which ♀ and juveniles wander freely. After the rut the herds split, with ♂ and ♀ forming groups by themselves. Exclusively a grazer, able to thrive on dry grasses not eaten by other antelopes. Eyesight, hearing, and sense of smell are good. A very fast runner, probably as swift as the Tsessebe.

DISTRIBUTION *Native:* Benin, Burkina Faso, Cameroon, Ghana, Niger, Nigeria. *Regionally Extinct*: Gambia, Guinea-Bissau, Mauritania, Mali, Senegal. An important population survives in W Arly-Pendjari complex, on the borders of Benin, Burkina Faso, and Niger; smaller populations have been reported from N Cameroon (Waza and Bouba Ndida NP), NE Nigeria, Red Volta River valley in NE Ghana, and probably N Togo.

HABITAT Grasslands and savanna woodlands, sometimes in arid country, usually below elevations of 1,500 m. Although they are usually found in extensive floodplains, they can go without water for long periods, as long as green pastures are available.

STATUS Vulnerable. Population estimate of 1,850-2,650 animals, nearly all entirely confined to protected areas. Its survival is threatened by illegal hunting and the expansion of cattle into the limited are of suitable habitat remaining.

PHOTO CREDITS *Mark Piazzi,* Waza NP (Cameroon).

Tiang
DAMALISCUS TIANG

BL: 150-205 cm. SH: 127 cm. TL: 40-60 cm. W: 122 kg. HL: To 72 cm. A large Topi, intermediate in body and horn size between the Korrigum and Topis. Coat color is a rich reddish bay suffused with an iridescent purplish tinge. Ash-gray patches on shoulders, hips, and upper legs, with reddish tinge more extensive than in the Korrigum. Lower legs are bright cinnamon, unlike in the Korrigum. Blackish-gray face blaze with a reddish-purple tinge. Tail fairly short, barely reaching the hocks, with a crest of black hairs on the lower third. Horns in both sexes thick, rather short, strongly ringed, and lyrate. Horns are shorter and a little slimmer than in Korrigum, and not as sharply turned up at the tips. Difference in horn size between males and females is greater than in other Topis.

Damaliscus tiang

OTHER NAMES *French*: Tiang. *German*: Tiang. *Spanish*: Tiang. *Russian*: Тианг *(tiang)*.

SUBSPECIES Monotypic. Formerly considered a subspecies of *D. korrigum* (Topi). Considered as a synonym of *D. korrigum* by some authors. Includes *floweri* (Blue Nile in Sudan), *jonesi* (Jones's Hartebeest, Kordufan in Sudan), *lyra* (Central African Topi, S Chad and N Central African Republic).

SIMILAR SPECIES Korrigum and Tiang are relatively larger, very bright reddish-orange color; they are generally distinguished from the other Topis by the concave profile of the head and the flatter (backward-slanting) but more curving horns. Ruaha Topi is very similar, but paler. Serengeti Topi has smaller, shorter horns, and shoulder patches are larger.

REPRODUCTION *Gestation*: 210 days. *Young per Birth*: 1. *Weaning*: After 4 months. *Sexual Maturity*: 1.5-2 years (♀), 3-4 years (♂). *Life Span*: 14 years. Breeding is seasonal; calving occurs at the end of the dry season (end of March). The calf usually remains hidden until it is strong enough to follow the herd.

BEHAVIOR *Family Group*: Herds of 15-30, sometimes hundreds, or even thousands during seasonal migrations in search of new grass during the early rains. *Diet*: Grasses, avoiding very short grass, and eating very few forbs. *Main Predators*: Lion, leopard, cheetah, Cape hunting dog. Highly gregarious. Often mingles with other species such as zebra, Wildebeest, and Hartebeest. Breeding ♂ are territorial during the rut, each defending a well-marked "stamping ground" against other ♂, through which ♀ and juveniles wander freely. After the rut the herds split, with ♂ and ♀ forming groups by themselves. Exclusively a grazer, able to thrive on dry grasses not eaten by other antelopes. Drinks water, but is able to go without it for long periods. Eyesight, hearing, and sense of smell are good. A very fast runner, probably as swift as the Tsessebe. Tiang and Kob migrate N and S on the plains E of the Nile, the Tiang from the Duk Ridge to and from the floodplains of the Kidepo River, the Kob from the Guom Swamps past the Boma Plateau and back. The meeting of these two species with the Reedbuck and Mongalla Gazelle, at the turning point of their respective seasonal movements, is a spectacular event. There are indications that the paths of migrations are changing in response to human activity.

DISTRIBUTION *Native:* Central African Republic, Chad, Ethiopia, Kenya, Sudan. Found in Sudan, E of the Nile, extending into Ethiopia. Individuals E of Cameroon are also considered as Tiang by many authors: S Chad, N Central African Republic, Sudan, SW Ethiopia, and extreme NW Kenya.

HABITAT Savanna and floodplain grasslands, also woodlands.

STATUS Least Concern. Estimated population of 160,000 in S Sudan in 2007. The population may be decreasing mainly due to hunting. One-quarter occur in protected areas: Zakouma NP, Salamat and Aouk Reserves (Chad), Manovo-Gounda-St Floris NP (CAR), Dinder and Boma NP (Sudan), Omo and Mago NP (Ethiopia), and Sibiloi NP (Kenya).

PHOTO CREDITS Reconstruction based on photos from *Prill*, *Volodymyr Byrdyak*, Boma NP (Sudan) and Zakouma NP (Chad).

Uganda Topi
DAMALISCUS UGANDAE

BL: 240-268 cm (♂), 230-249 kg (♀). SH: 100-130 cm. TL: 40-60 cm. W: 136-168 kg (♂), 120-140 kg (♀). HL: To 72 cm. Medium-large antelope. Coat maroon suffused with an ashy sheen, glossy, almost iridescent, much darker than in Korrigum and Tiang. Slender legs light tan on the lower half, black on the upper half, extending upward onto the shoulders and lower haunches, often appearing gray under strong sunlight. Hump above the shoulders. The back slopes downward from the shoulders toward the rump. Rump and tail lighter in color, tail ends in a brush-like black tuft. Face elongated and fairly narrow, on a relatively short neck. Front of the face black, in a stripe with considerable spread across the nose bridge, tan-colored lips. Ears very slender. Lyre-shaped horns in both sexes, strongly ringed for their entire length, with the exception of the very tips. Female similar to the male, but usually lighter in color, with horns shorter and less deeply ringed. Young have sandy-brown coat.

♀

Young

Juvenile

♂

Damaliscus ugandae

OTHER NAMES Ankole Topi. *French*: Topi, damalisque. *German*: Topi, Leriantilope, Tiang. *Spanish*: Topi. *Swahili*: Nyamera. *Afrikaans*: Basterhartebees. *Russian*: Угандский Топи.

SUBSPECIES Monotypic. Formerly considered a subspecies of *D. korrigum* (Topi).

SIMILAR SPECIES Tsessebe have crescent horns instead of lyre-shaped horns. Coke's and Lichtenstein's Hartebeests are a similar shape and size but are a lighter color and lack black markings on their thighs. Korrigum is larger, a very bright reddish-orange color, with larger horns, and lower legs the same color as the body. Tiang is intermediate in body and horn size between Korrigum and Topis, rich reddish bay with an iridescent purplish tinge. Coastal Topi has a darker and richer color, heavily suffused with a mauve bloom, showing also great sexual dimorphism. Serengeti Topi is slightly smaller, with shorter horns, and shoulder patches are larger.

REPRODUCTION *Gestation*: 225-240 days. *Young per Birth*: 1. *Weaning:* 4 months. *Sexual Maturity*: 1.5-2 years (♀), 3-4 years (♂). *Life Span*: 14 years. Two calving peaks in the year, unlike other *Damaliscus*, but mating takes place sporadically throughout the year as ♀ groups happen to move through high-density territory areas. Most ♀ enter the lek individually or in small groups when in estrus, and they compete with each other fiercely for the attention of the best ♂.

BEHAVIOR *Family Group*: ♂ are clustered into territorial leks. ♀ and young live in herds of 200-300, even up to 1,000, moving around the lek accompanied by hundreds of bachelor ♂. *Diet*: Grasses, avoiding very short grass, and eating very few forbs. *Main Predators*: Lion, leopard, cheetah, Cape hunting dog. Gregarious, with a remarkable social organization, linked to the geographic and seasonal distribution of food. ♀ form large herds that move across the territories of many different ♂. ♂ defines his territory by depositing dung in a series of places, marking grass stems with the scent from his preorbital face glands, and standing for long periods in a prominent place. If another ♂ intrudes upon his territory, the two go down on their knees and fight with their horns. Most active in the morning and evening.

DISTRIBUTION *Native:* DR Congo, Rwanda, Uganda. Found in the Ankole region of SW Uganda, extending to Rutshuru Plains in DR Congo, and to Akagera NP in Rwanda.

HABITAT Prefers grassland habitats, including large treeless plains, to areas with little bush and tree savannas. May sometimes be found in uplands, but usually found in the lowlands.

STATUS Least Concern. Estimated population was 5,000 in Queen Elizabeth NP in the late 1970s.

PHOTO CREDITS ♂ and head: *Martha de Jong-Lantink,* Queen Elizabeth NP (Uganda). ♀: *Scott Lamont*, Ishasha area, Queen Elizabeth NP (Uganda). Head ♀: *Tore Berg*, Lake Mburo NP (Uganda). Young: *François-Olivier Dommergues,* Akagera NP (Rwanda) and *David Beadle*, Queen Elizabeth NP (Uganda).

Ruaha Topi
DAMALISCUS EURUS

BL: 195-223 cm (♂), 185-204 cm (♀). SH: 100-130 cm. TL: 45 cm. W: 136-168 kg (♂), 120-139 kg (♀). HL: To 72 cm. Medium-large antelope. Size and color similar to that of the Uganda Topi, but noticeably paler, bright reddish bay in the posterior dorsal region. Slender legs light tan on their lower half. Black on the upper half of the forelegs and shoulders larger than in other Topis. Rump and tail lighter in color, tail ends in a brush-like black tuft. Face elongated and fairly narrow, on a relatively short neck. Front of the face black, in a stripe with considerable spread across the nose bridge, tan-colored lips. Dark eye stripe extending to the subauricular spot. Ears very slender. Lyre-shaped horns in both sexes, strongly ringed for their entire length, with the exception of the very tips. Female similar to the male, but usually lighter in color, with horns shorter and less deeply ringed. Young have sandy-brown coat.

Damaliscus eurus

OTHER NAMES Usangu Topi. *French*: Topi du Ruaha. *German*: Ruaha-Topi. *Spanish*: Topi de Ruaha. *Russian*: Танзанийский Топи. *Swahili*: Nyamera usangu.

SUBSPECIES Monotypic. Formerly considered a subspecies of *D. korrigum* (Topi). Considered by some authors as a synonym of *D. jimela*.

REPRODUCTION *Gestation*: 225-240 days. *Young per Birth*: 1. *Weaning*: 4 months. *Sexual Maturity*: 1.5-2 years (♀), 3-4 years (♂). *Life Span*: 14 years. Seasonal. Calving occurs at the end of the dry season.

BEHAVIOR *Family Group*: ♂ are clustered into territorial leks; the number may vary greatly according to the water level of Lake Rukwa. *Diet*: Grasses, especially floodplain grasses, following the flooding of Lake Rukwa. *Main Predators*: Lion, leopard, cheetah, Cape hunting dog. Sedentary, requiring green grass and water throughout the year. Naturally, they are found close to water. Ruaha Topi move back and forth according to the fluctuations of the lake. Moderate droughts can help them, as receding water exposes green grass. When conditions are ideal, they are extremely fecund. They suffer under extreme droughts and extreme floods. When the lake level is high, the population is concentrated on two small areas of high ground; when most of the grazing areas are inundated, there is high morbidity. When conditions are poor, they do not breed.

DISTRIBUTION *Native:* Tanzania. Found in the Upper Ruaha and Lake Rukwa ecosystem in SE Tanzania. It is not known whether there are any populations between this area and the Serengeti ecosystem where the Serengeti Topi occurs.

HABITAT Valley grasslands, extending into parklands and occasionally open woods, in periodically flooded country. Prefers grassland habitats, including large treeless plains, to areas with little bush and tree savannas. May sometimes be found in uplands, but usually found in the lowlands.

STATUS Least Concern. Estimated population is 12,000 individuals: 5,500 in the Katawi-Rukwa ecosystem (although by 2009 only 560 were counted), 4,500 in the Moyowosi-Kigosi Game Reserve, 1,500 in the Ugalla Game Reserve. There is little information on the population in Mahale NP and Usanga, although it is now rare. Threats include habitat loss and illegal hunting. Part of the habitat is protected by Katavi NP and Rukwa Game Reserve.

PHOTO CREDITS *Helmut Spudich,* Katavi NP (Tanzania).

Serengeti Topi
DAMALISCUS JIMELA

BL: 150-205 cm. SH: 104-126 cm. TL: 40-60 cm. W: 111-147 kg (♂), 90-130 kg (♀). HL: To 72 cm. Smaller than other Topis. Coat deep reddish or purple brown, glossy. Slender legs light tan on the lower half, black on the upper half, extending upward onto the shoulders and lower haunches. Shoulder patches larger than in other Topis. Hump above the shoulders. Rump and tail lighter in color, tail ends in a brush-like black tuft. Front of the face black. Ears very slender. Lyre-shaped horns in both sexes, shorter than in other Topis, strongly ringed for their entire length, with the exception of the very tips. Female similar to the male, usually lighter in color, with horns shorter and less deeply ringed. Young have sandy-brown coat.

♀

Young

Juvenile

♂

Damaliscus jimela

OTHER NAMES Unyamwezi Topi. *French*: Topi du Serengeti, damalisque. *German*: Serengeti-Topi, Leriantilope. *Spanish*: Topi del Serengeti. *Russian*: Топи, Топи Серенгети. *Swahili*: Nyamera.

SUBSPECIES Monotypic. Formerly considered a subspecies of *D. korrigum* (Topi).

SIMILAR SPECIES Smallest species of Topi, with shorter horns, and larger shoulder patches. Korrigum and Tiang are larger, very bright reddish-orange color. Uganda and Ruaha Topi are darker, with larger and more diverging horns.

REPRODUCTION *Gestation*: 225-240 days. *Young per Birth*: 1. *Weaning*: 4 months. *Sexual Maturity*: 1.5-2 years (♀), 3-4 years (♂). *Life Span*: 14 years. Births occur generally between July and December. They are able to stall the labor process in the event of a threat. Young lie hidden for a few days before following their mothers, but will rest more frequently than adults. Similarly aged calves will form a kindergarten, which may be guarded by a single ♀ while the other mothers spread out to graze.

BEHAVIOR *Family Group*: Mature ♂ solitary, or loosely associated with a group of 8-20 ♀ and their young. Bachelor ♂ between 1 and 4 years of age form small bachelor herds. Large migratory herds of several thousand animals also form among certain populations. *Diet*: Grasses, very rarely leaves; drink daily if possible, but can go for long periods without water. *Main Predators*: Lion, leopard, cheetah, Cape hunting dog. Typical sentry position, in which a single animal will stand on a termite mound for hours surveying the surrounding territory; termite mounds are also a favorite resting area, and they may even doze off while lying on these raised platforms. Adult ♂ hold territories which vary dramatically from 1 to 400 ha; smaller territories are only held briefly during the breeding season. A ♂ will mark his personal range with urine, dung piles, digging up the soil with his horns, and by smearing secretions from his preorbital glands on vegetation. Competition between rival ♂ consists of posturing and ritualistic sparring with the horns, which involves crashing their horns together as both lunge forward to their knees. During the breeding season, a territorial ♂ is readily recognized by his erect posture, with his head held high above his body. If alarmed suddenly, they may actually jump over one another in their haste to flee the area. While they generally run at a jog, if pressed they may reach speeds in excess of 70 kmph. While on the move, Topi have the odd habit of bobbing their heads.

DISTRIBUTION *Native:* Kenya, Tanzania. Restricted to the Serengeti-Mara ecosystem.

HABITAT Prefers grassland habitats, including large treeless plains, to areas with little bush and tree savannas.

STATUS Least Concern. Estimated population is 93,000 animals (55,000 in Serengeti NP, and 33,000 in Maasai Mara National Reserve).

PHOTO CREDITS ♂: *Matt Plummer,* Serengeti (Tanzania). Head ♂: *Erick Tseng,* Serengeti (Tanzania). ♀: *Andrea Negro,* Maasai Mara (Kenya). Head ♀: *Roger Smith (rogersmithpix)*, Maasai Mara (Kenya). Young: *Joe Pyrek*, Serengeti (Tanzania). Juvenile: *Johannes Dag Mayer* and *C. E. Timothy Paine* (Tanzania).

Coastal Topi

DAMALISCUS TOPI

BL: 200 cm. SH: 100-130 cm. TL: 43 cm. W: 110-130 kg. HL: To 72 cm. The smallest species of Topi. Similar in color to the Serengeti Topi, but darker and richer, heavily suffused with a mauve bloom, becoming paler in the belly. Rump and tail lighter in color, tail ends in a brush-like black tuft. Hump above the shoulders. The back slopes downward from the shoulders toward the rump. Facial blaze is blackish gray, with a reddish tinge, sprinkled with white hairs. Horns, found in both sexes, are slender, bend backward very slightly, and are longer than in other East African Topi. Female similar to the male, with horns significantly shorter and less deeply ringed. Sexual dimorphism in size is greater than in other East African Topi.

Damaliscus topi

OTHER NAMES *French*: Topi cotier. *German*: Küsten-Topi. *Spanish*: Topi de costa. *Russian*: Прибрежный (сомалийский) Топи.

SUBSPECIES Monotypic. Formerly considered a subspecies of *D. korrigum* (Topi). Considered by some authors as a synonym of *D. jimela*.

SIMILAR SPECIES Tsessebe have crescent horns instead of lyre-shaped horns. Coke's and Lichtenstein's Hartebeests are a similar shape and size but are a lighter color and lack black markings on their thighs. Very little morphological difference from Serengeti Topi (*D. jimela*), though geographically separated.

REPRODUCTION *Gestation*: 225-240 days. *Young per Birth*: 1. *Weaning*: 4 months. *Sexual Maturity*: 1.5-2 years (♀), 3-4 years (♂). *Life Span*: 14 years. No specific information is available for this species, but apparently breeding is year-round, not seasonal as in most Topi.

BEHAVIOR *Family Group*: ♂ are clustered into territorial leks. ♀ and young live in herds of 200-300, even up to 1,000, moving around the lek accompanied by hundreds of bachelor ♂. *Diet*: Grasses, avoiding very short grass, and eating very few forbs. *Main Predators:* Lion, leopard, cheetah, Cape hunting dog. No specific information is available for this species, but probably similar to other Topi. Appear to emerge from cover at dawn to graze, retire to light woodland in the middle of the day, and reemerge toward dusk.

DISTRIBUTION *Native:* Kenya, Somalia. Found in coastal E Africa, from the Shebelle River in Juba region of Somalia S at least to Malindi, Kenya, being isolated from other Topis. There is a tiny population in Tsavo East (Kenya), which likely originated from the coastal areas and followed the Galana River and artificial water holes to end up in the middle of Tsavo East. Its current distribution in Somalia is not known, but formerly occurred in S Somalia in riverine grasslands on the lower Shebelle and Juba rivers.

HABITAT Floodplain grasslands of Kenya and Somalia.

STATUS Near Threatened. Estimated population is 83,000 animals on the Kenya coast, with smaller populations remaining in S Somalia, mostly outside protected areas. Main threats include hunting and expansion of livestock grazing.

PHOTO CREDITS Based on photos from Lamu Conservation Trust (Kenya) and *Simon J. Tonge*, Tsavo East NP (Kenya).

Western Tsessebe
DAMALISCUS LUNATUS

BL: 150-230 cm. SH: 119-122 cm. TL: 40-60 cm. W: 120-140 kg. HL: To 40 cm (♂), to 37 cm (♀).
Medium-large antelope with shoulders higher than hindquarters, and back sloping downward.
Overall color chestnut brown, front of face black, forelimbs and thighs grayish or bluish black,
hind limbs brownish yellow to yellow. Belly reddish in front, becoming yellowish white in back.
Their darker pelage is evident overall, notably in the black patches on the shoulders and rump.
The dominant color of the pelage (on the neck and back) is dark brown. Tail somewhat shorter
than in the Topi, and has a crest of long, dark hairs on the lower half. Horns are long and lyrate,
with narrow pedicels, lunate or crescent shaped when viewed from the front, ringed for almost
the entire length, and thicker at the base in males. Female similar, but smaller, with thinner
horns.

♂

Young

Juvenile

♀

Damaliscus lunatus

OTHER NAMES Common Tsessebe, Tsessebe, Sassaby. *French*: Sassabi. *German*: Leierantilope, Halbmondantilope. *Spanish*: Tsessebe común, sasabi. *Russian*: Западный сассаби. *Afrikaans*: Basterhartbees. *Ndebele*: Inkolome. *Swati*: Mzanxi.

SUBSPECIES Monotypic. The name *D. lunatus* formerly included *D. lunatus* (Western Tsessebe), and *D. superstes* (Bangweulu Tsessebe) as subspecies: these are elevated to full species here.

SIMILAR SPECIES Topis have a slight variation in horn structure and coat shade is darker; herd structures of female topis are larger. Bangweulu Tsessebe is larger, darker with horns thicker and wider spread.

REPRODUCTION *Gestation*: 210 days. *Young per Birth*: 1. *Weaning*: 24-40 months. *Sexual Maturity*: 1.5-2 years (♀), 3 years (♂). *Life Span*: 15 years. The rut starts in mid-February and stretches through March. The ♀ estrous cycle is shorter, but happens in this time. The breeding process starts with the development of a lek. Leks are established by the congregation of adult ♂ in an area which ♀ visit only for the purpose of mating. Dominant ♂ occupy the center of the leks, so ♀ are more likely to mate at the center than at the periphery of the lek.

BEHAVIOR *Family Group*: ♀ form herds of 6-10, with their young. After ♂ turn 1 year of age, they are ejected from the herd and form bachelor herds that can be as large as 30 young ♂. Territorial adult ♂ form herds the same size as those of young ♂, although the formation of adult ♂ herds is mainly seen in the formation of a lek. *Diet*: Grazers which utilize a wide range of grass species. They select leaves over the stems. They prefer fresh growth, and are attracted to burned areas. Drink water regularly when available, but able to do without it for long periods. *Main Predators*: Lion, leopard. Active mainly morning and evening. Eyesight and hearing are very good, sense of smell is good. A highly curious animal. Social animals, not as gregarious as members of the Topi group. Territorial behavior includes moving in erect posture, high stepping, defecating in a crouch stance, ground horning, mud packing, shoulder wiping, and grunting. The most important aggressive display of territorial dominance is in the horning of the ground. Another form of territorial marking is through the anointing of their foreheads and horns with secretions from glands near their eyes, accomplished by inserting grass stems into their preorbital glands to coat them with secretion, then waving them around, letting the secretions fall onto their heads and horns. They can run at a maximum of 80 kmph. For ♂, horn size plays an important role in territory defense and mate attraction, although horn size is not positively correlated with territorial factors of mate selection.

DISTRIBUTION *Native*: Angola, Zambia, Namibia, Botswana, Zimbabwe, South Africa.

HABITAT Grasslands, open plains, and lightly wooded savannas, but they are also found in rolling uplands and very rarely in flat plains below 1,500 m above sea level.

STATUS Least Concern.

521

Bangweulu Tsessebe
DAMALISCUS SUPERSTES

BL: 150-230 cm. SH: 120 cm. TL: 40-60 cm. W: 120-137 kg. HL: To 35-40 cm (♂), 30-39.5 cm (♀). Medium-large antelope. Body is chocolate brown, darker than in Western Tsessebe. Front of the face black. Ears particularly dark brown. Shoulder and haunch patches mostly dark blackish gray, while limbs are brownish yellow and the bellies are lighter. Tail tuft black. Horns are thicker and more widely spread, with a broader pedicel than in Western Tsessebe. They grow symmetrically outward, with the tips curving inward to form a sphere, ringed for almost the entire length, and thicker at the base in males. Female similar, but smaller, with thinner horns.

Damaliscus superstes

OTHER NAMES *French*: Sassabi du Bangweulu. *German*: Bangweulu-Sassaby *Spanish*: Tsessebe del Bangweulu. *Russian*: Сассаби Бангвеулу.

SUBSPECIES Monotypic. Formerly considered a subspecies of *D. lunatus* (Tsessebe).

SIMILAR SPECIES Western Tsessebe is smaller and lighter, with relatively thinner horns, otherwise very similar. Topis have a slight variation in horn structure and coat shade is darker; herd structures of ♀ Topis are larger.

REPRODUCTION *Gestation*: 210 days. *Young per Birth*: 1. *Weaning*: 24-40 months. *Sexual Maturity*: 1.5-2 years (♀), 3 years (♂). *Life Span*: 15 years. There is no specific data for this species, but probably similar to the Western Tsessebe.

BEHAVIOR There is little specific information available for this species, but presumably very similar to the Common Tsessebe. Sedentary, requiring green grass and water throughout the year. Naturally, they are found close to water. Moderate droughts can help them, as receding water exposes green grass. They suffer under extreme droughts and extreme floods. When conditions are ideal, they are extremely fecund. When conditions are poor, they may not breed.

DISTRIBUTION *Native*: Zambia. *Regionally Extinct*: DR Congo. Found in SW Bangweulu Flats restricted within the E catchment of the Luombwa River (a tributary of the Luapula) and bordered by the Lukulu River in the E. It is extinct in Futwe Plain in Katanga (DR Congo).

HABITAT Grasslands, open plains, and lightly wooded savannas, like other large species of *Damaliscus*.

STATUS Least Concern. May be extinct in Katanga, and the range in Zambia has shrunk, but there are still good populations on the southern half of the Bangweulu Flats. The current population is estimated at around 3,500 individuals and increasing, with animals having been translocated to private land.

PHOTO CREDITS ♂: *Kenneth K. Coe*, Bangweulu Wetlands (Zambia). ♀: *Nigel Voaden,* Bangweulu Wetlands (Zambia).

Bontebok

DAMALISCUS PYGARGUS

BL: 140-160 cm. SH: 90-102 cm. TL: 30-45 cm. W: 86 kg (♂), 56 kg (♀). HL: 32-36 cm (♂), 29-33 (♀). Medium-sized antelope. Rich dark brown, short, glossy coat, with a purple gloss on the sides of the head, flanks, and upper part of the limbs. Underparts, insides of the legs, and lower legs white. White patch on the rump surrounding the tail. White blaze on the face, consisting of a slender patch on the forehead, and a wider, longer stripe down the nose; these 2 patches are continuous from base of horns to the nose, narrower between the eyes. Calves are light yellowish brown with dark faces, and have none of the markings of adults. Both sexes carry strongly ringed, black, lyre-shaped horns; the horns are initially upright, then curve backward and outward, and then curve slightly forward toward the tips. Females similar to males, with less robust horns.

♀

Young

Juvenile
(5 mo)

♂

Juvenile

Damaliscus pygargus

OTHER NAMES *French*: Bontebok, damalisque à front blanc. *German*: Buntbok. *Spanish*: Bontebok. *Russian*: бонтбок. *Afrikaans*: Bontebok. *Sepedi*: Pitsi ya maronthonthwane. *Swati*: Inyamatane.

SUBSPECIES Monotypic. The name *D. pygargus* formerly included *D. pygargus* (Bontebok), and *D. phillipsi* (Blesbok) as subspecies: these are elevated to full species here. The valid name of this species is *D. pygargus*, not *D. dorcas*.

SIMILAR SPECIES Blesbok has a white facial band usually interrupted by a dark narrow band between the eyes, an inconspicuous pale brown patch on rump, with only base of tail pure white, and the lower part of legs is not fully white. Tsessebe and Topi are similar in shape, but larger and with the back much more sloping.

REPRODUCTION *Gestation*: 238-256 days. *Young per Birth*: 1. *Weaning*: 4 months. *Sexual Maturity*: 2.5 years. *Life Span*: 17 years. The rut occurs from January to the middle of March. The ♀ does not leave the herd to give birth, and calves have a strong instinct to follow their mothers.

BEHAVIOR *Family Group*: ♂, ♀, and mixed herds are found, rarely exceeding 40 animals. *Diet*: Short grasses. *Main Predators*: Lion, leopard, cheetah, hyena, Cape hunting dog. Primarily diurnal, although there is a lull in activity during the hottest part of the day, spent resting in sheltered areas. Unlike other antelopes, they are not good jumpers, with a 135 cm high fence being tall enough to enclose a herd. They are adept at crawling under objects. When water is available, they drink at least once a day, although they can survive without water for several days. In the past, herds would migrate between seasonal pastures, congregating in large numbers during the fall and winter. As ♂ approach maturity, they form territories 10-40 ha in size, while the territories of Blesbok are significantly smaller. Old ♂ are territorial, and mark their ranges prominently with dung heaps, on which they often rest, and also with scrapes in the ground as well as secretions from the preorbital glands. A ♂ generally remains on his territory year-round. Conflicts between neighboring ♂ over territorial boundaries are rare, consisting primarily of ritualized parallel displays. Small herds of ♀ and their young circulate through several individual territories during the breeding season. A ♀ dominance hierarchy exists which is maintained by horn clashing. Marking of plant stalks with preorbital gland secretions is seen in both sexes.

DISTRIBUTION *Native*: South Africa. Coastal plains in the Western Cape Province in S South Africa.

HABITAT A mixture of grassland and low scrub in the fynbos zone. Needs grass, shelter, and permanent water.

STATUS Near Threatened. It was once hunted to the brink of extinction, and reduced to just 17 wild individuals, but the population has since grown, and over 1,000 animals now live in Bontebok NP near Swellendam, and on a number of private ranches in South Africa. Nearly all of these introductions have been outside the Bontebok's natural historic range.

PHOTO CREDITS ♂: *Nico Smit* (South Africa). Head ♂: *Pierre de Chabannes*, Ellen Trout Zoo (USA). Young: *Les Catchick*. ♀: *Brian James Manson*, San Diego Zoo (USA). Juvenile: *Arthur Chapman*, Bontebok NP (South Africa) and *Sergey Chichagov*, San Diego Zoo (USA).

Blesbok

DAMALISCUS PHILLIPSI

BL: 140-160 cm. SH: 85-100 cm. TL: 30-45 cm. W: 65-80 kg (♂), 55-70 (♀). HL: 50 cm (♂). Medium-sized antelope, slightly smaller than Bontebok. Body color is reddish brown, without the purple gloss of the Bontebok, with a lighter-colored saddle on the back, and the rump an even lighter shade. Legs are brown with a white patch behind the top part of the front legs. Lower legs are dark brown. Underparts and insides of legs are white, with the outsides being the same color as the body. Rump is the same color as the back, and the white at the base of the tail does not extend onto the back of the rump. Prominent white blaze on the face and a horizontal brown stripe which usually divides this blaze above the eyes. Both sexes carry straw-colored horns, ringed almost to the tip. Females are similar to males, with slightly more slender horns.

Young

Juvenile

♀

♂

Damaliscus phillipsi

OTHER NAMES *French*: Blesbok, damalisque à front blanc. *German*: Blessbok. *Spanish*: Blesbok. *Russian*: Блесбок. *Zulu*: Inoni. *Xhosa*: Ilinqa.

SUBSPECIES Monotypic. Formerly considered a subspecies of *D. pygargus*.

SIMILAR SPECIES Bontebok is slightly larger, generally darker and more richly colored, with a white facial band usually continuous from base of horns to the nose, a white patch on rump, and lower parts of legs mostly white. Although Blesbok and Bontebok can interbreed, the offspring being known as the Bontebles or Baster Blesbok, the two species do not share the same habitat in the wild.

REPRODUCTION *Gestation*: 240-246 days. *Young per Birth*: 1. *Weaning*: 4 months. *Sexual Maturity*: 2.5 years (♀). *Life Span*: 13 years. Seasonal breeder, with rutting from March to May. Births peak during November and December. The ♀ does not leave the herd to give birth, and calves have a strong instinct to follow their mothers. Mothers chase other Blesbok away and will only suckle their own calf.

BEHAVIOR *Family Group*: ♂, ♀, and mixed herds of 5-30 animals, sometimes many more, rarely exceeding 70. *Diet*: Short grasses. When water is available, they drink at least once a day, although they can survive without water for several days. *Main Predators*: Cheetah, lion, leopard, wild dog, hyena, python, jackal, eagles (young). Shy and alert, they rely on speed and endurance to escape predators, but, like other white-fronted *Damaliscus*, they are not good jumpers. Primarily diurnal, although there is a lull in activity during the hottest part of the day, spent resting in sheltered areas. In the past, herds would migrate between seasonal pastures, congregating in large numbers during the fall and winter. As ♂ approach maturity, they form territories about 2-4 ha in size, while the territories of Bontebok are significantly larger. Old ♂ are territorial, and mark their ranges prominently with dung heaps, on which they often rest. Other territorial marking includes scrapes in the ground as well as secretions from the preorbital glands. A ♂ generally remains on his territory year-round. Conflicts between neighboring ♂ over territorial boundaries are rare, consisting primarily of ritualized parallel displays. Small herds of ♀ and their young circulate through several individual territories during the breeding season. Marking of plant stalks with preorbital gland secretions is seen in both sexes.

DISTRIBUTION *Native*: South Africa. *Introduced*: Zimbabwe, Namibia, Botswana.

HABITAT Open veld or plains of South Africa. Preferred habitat is open grassland with water. Plains species, dislikes wooded areas. Very widely translocated.

STATUS Least Concern. It was hunted nearly to extinction, but having been protected, it has proliferated, largely because of the commercial value to private land owners, and because it is one of the few medium-sized antelopes that can be contained by normal stock fencing. Estimated population is around 240,000, 97% of which live outside reserves, and only 3% in national parks.

PHOTO CREDITS ♂: *Alessandro Zocchi* (South Africa). Young: Belfast Zoo (UK). ♀: Copenhagen Zoo (Denmark). Head: *Alex Meyer,* Berlin Zoo (Germany), *Sheila Bradford* (South Africa). Juvenile: *Stefan Selle* and *Anastasia Smith* (South Africa). 527

Swayne's Hartebeest
ALCELAPHUS SWAYNEI

BL: 175-250 cm. SH: 119 cm. TL: 45-70 cm. W: 135-200 kg (♂), 120-180 kg (♀). HL: 45-70 cm. Medium-sized Hartebeest. Coloration is a deep red chocolate brown or chestnut, with a fawn or cinnamon-colored rump, tail, and lower half of legs. Tail tuft is black. Face and upper parts of body have dark blackish markings: a black stripe from the shoulder to the knee, a black smudge on the flanks, and black markings on the outside of the hind limbs (on the darkest individuals these black markings do not show clearly in the field). Strongly ringed horns curve outward and slightly downward from the top of the head and then sweep upward at the tips, and usually, but not always, hook backward, and may or may not turn inward (seen from the front they are between a V and U shape). Females similar to males, but with slender horns, and usually paler in color.

♂

Young

♀

Juvenile

Alcelaphus swaynei

OTHER NAMES Korkay. *French*: Bubale de Swayne, bubale de Swain. *German*: Somalia-Kuhantilope. *Spanish*: Búbalo de Swayne, alcélafo de Swayne. *Russian*: Конгони Суэйни.

SUBSPECIES Monotypic. The name *A. buselaphus* (Hartebeest) formerly included *A. caama* (Red Hartebeest), *A. cokii* (Coke's Hartebeest), *A. lelwel* (Lelwel Hartebeest), *A. lichtensteinii* (Lichtenstein's Hartebeest), *A. major* (Western Hartebeest), *A. tora* (Tora Hartebeest), and *A. swaynei* (Swayne's Hartebeest) as subspecies: these are all elevated to full species here. At one time *swaynei* was regarded as a subspecies of *tora*.

SIMILAR SPECIES Swayne's Hartebeest belongs to the "lightly armed" group of Hartebeest. Swayne's Hartebeest is the E race of Tora Hartebeest, to which it is closely related, but it is distinguished by its considerably darker body color.

REPRODUCTION *Gestation*: 240 days. *Young per Birth*: 1. *Weaning*: 4 months. *Sexual Maturity*: 1.5-2.5 years. *Life Span*: 19 years. Breeding takes place throughout the year, although local populations may have seasonal peaks.

BEHAVIOR *Family Group*: Single-sex and mixed groups of 4-30 individuals. *Diet*: Grasses, rarely leaves. *Main Predators*: Lion, leopard, cheetah, spotted hyena, Cape hunting dog. It lives in open country, light bush, sometimes in tall savanna woodland. These are social animals and are normally seen in small herds. Each herd is under the leadership of the master ♂ which leads the ♀ with their young. The territory is defended by the ♂. The home range is 9-12 km² in size, greater during the wet season because of the availability of palatable grasses during this season. They usually graze peacefully, with the ♂ on slightly higher ground acting as sentinel for his herd. ♀ and ♂ alike are generally non-aggressive, although both sexes will fight vigorously in defense of their offspring or territory. They are primarily diurnal, grazing in the early morning and late afternoon, and resting in a shaded area during the hottest part of the day. They are often observed to move in a circle, usually returning in the evening to the point from where they started in the morning. They often remain in the same general area for prolonged periods. For the most part, they move slowly, feeding as they walk. Only occasionally do they walk in a deliberate fashion. During the dry season, the Hartebeests spend less time grazing, and they move shorter distances compared to the wet season. When fleeing, the herd runs in single file, and can reach speeds of up to 80 kmph.

DISTRIBUTION *Native*: Ethiopia. Swayne's Hartebeest survive in four isolated localities: Senkele Wildlife Sanctuary, Nechisar NP, Awash NP and Mazie NP. Otherwise extinct outside Ethiopia.

HABITAT Open grassland and bush regions. They are absent only from desert and forest, notably the Sahara and the W rainforest.

STATUS Endangered. Total population is estimated at 600 individuals; the small size of the population makes it close to qualifying as Critically Endangered. The ever-diminishing range of this species is threatened by loss of habitat to subsistence agriculture and livestock overgrazing. Poaching is still one of the main threats to its survival.

PHOTO CREDITS ♀: *Michel Le Mell* and *Tim Melling*. ♂: *Kenneth Coe* and *Coke and Som Smith*. Young: *Volker Sthamer*. All photos from Senkele Wildlife Sanctuary (Ethiopia).

Tora Hartebeest
ALCELAPHUS TORA

BL: 200 cm. SH: 130 cm. TL: 50 cm. W: 160 kg. HL: 48 cm. A large Hartebeest. Coloration is pale tawny to pale red brown, but may have a great deal of color variation. Hind legs and belly whitish to yellowish, rump patch dirty white. Tail tuft and front of forelegs black. Horns thinner and spreading more widely and sideways than in other Hartebeests, turning slightly up, then outward and upward, and finally upward again (seen from the front they are between a V and U shape). Relative lack of sexual dimorphism. Females similar to males, but with slender horns.

Alcelaphus tora

OTHER NAMES *French*: Bubale tora. *German*: Tora-Kuhantilope. *Spanish:* Búbalo de Etiopía, alcélafo de Etiopía. *Russian*: Topa.

SUBSPECIES Monotypic. Formerly considered a subspecies of *A. buselaphus* (Hartebeest).

SIMILAR SPECIES This species, like the Swayne's and Coke's Hartebeest, can be regarded as part of the "lightly armed" group. Swayne's Hartebeest is the E race of Tora Hartebeest, to which it is closely related, but it is distinguished by its considerably darker body color.

REPRODUCTION *Gestation*: 240 days. *Young per Birth*: 1. *Weaning*: 4 months. *Sexual Maturity*: 1.5-2.5 years. *Life Span*: 19 years. No specific information available for this species, but probably less intense seasonality in breeding, and less inter-male fighting than in other Hartebeest.

BEHAVIOR *Family Group*: Single-sex and mixed groups of 20 individuals. *Diet*: Grasses; their narrow head is well suited to selecting tender grass leaves from among the poorer quality stems and stalks. *Main Predators*: Lion, leopard, cheetah, spotted hyena. No specific information is available for this species, but probably similar to other Hartebeest. Active in the morning and late afternoon, resting in shade during the midday. Gregarious, with adult ♂ being territorial. At 3-4 years of age, the ♂ will establish a territory which will be defended by both sexes. In most regions, ♂ defend territories year-round, as ♀ breed within weeks of calving.

DISTRIBUTION *Native*: Eritrea, Ethiopia. *Regionally Extinct*: Sudan. May survive in low numbers in the savannas of Eritrea and some inaccessible parts of NW Ethiopia, but are probably extinct in Sudan.

HABITAT Tropical and subtropical dry savannas and grasslands.

STATUS Critically Endangered. Total population fewer than 250 mature individuals; it is still declining and no subpopulation contains 50 or more mature individuals. No individuals are held in captivity. This species may even be extinct. Habitat loss, overhunting, and competition with livestock are thought to be important causes of population decline.

PHOTO CREDITS Reconstruction by *José R. Castelló* (there are no photos or recent sightings of living specimens).

Red Hartebeest
ALCELAPHUS CAAMA

BL: 207-220 cm. SH: 122-133 cm. TL: 40-50 cm. W: 131-165 kg (♂), 105-136 kg (♀). HL: 45-67 cm. A large Hartebeest. General color is some shade of bright reddish brown. Forehead is black, with a dark facial blaze that is interrupted by a lighter band between the eyes. Blackish markings on back of neck, chin, shoulders, hips, and legs, and a wide, yellowish-white patch on sides and lower part of the rump. Long face and high frontal pedicel. Horns, found in both sexes, thick and V-shaped when viewed from the front. They grow slightly out and back from the pedicel, then up and forward, and finally bend sharply backward. Female similar to the male, but slightly smaller in size, with more slender horns and less richly colored.

♀

Young

Juvenile

♂

Alcelaphus caama

OTHER NAMES Cape Hartebeest, Khama's Hartebeest. *French*: Bubale caama. *German*: Kuhantilope, Kaama. *Spanish*: Búbalo rojo, alcélafo del Cabo. *Russian*: Каама (Капский или рыжий конгони). *Afrikaans*: Rooihartbees. *Ndebele*: Indluzele, iqhama, ihlezu. *Xhosa*: Ixhama. *Zulu*: Indluzele, inkolongwane. *Sepedi*: Thetele. *Sesotho*: Khama, lethodile, tlohela. *Swati*: Inkologwane, umzansi. *Xitsonga*: Nondzo. *Tshivenda*: Thendele. *Damara*: Khamab.

SUBSPECIES Monotypic. Formerly considered a subspecies of *A. buselaphus* (Hartebeest). Some confusion still exists among taxonomists as to whether it should remain in the genus *Alcelaphus* or be moved to its own.

REPRODUCTION *Gestation*: 240 days. *Young per Birth*: 1. *Weaning*: 7-8 months. *Sexual Maturity*: 24 months. *Life Span*: 16 years. Breading is seasonal, and estrus apparently lasts just 1 day. ♀ leaves the herd to give birth. Single calves are normally born before summer rains. For a short period after being born, calves are hidden in tall grass before joining the herd.

BEHAVIOR *Family Group*: Small herds of 10-30 animals. *Diet*: Selective grazer and browser; selecting specific plant species and prefers leaves; may eat melons and dig for tubers for moisture. Independent of water but will drink if it is available. *Main Predators*: Lion, leopard, cheetah, spotted hyena, Cape hunting dog. Territorial ♂ often present themselves on prominent mounds and mark their territories with dung piles. It is swift on foot and gregarious, occurring in herds of up to 30. It is primarily diurnal, grazing in the early morning and late afternoon, and resting in a shaded area during the hottest part of the day. During feeding periods, a sentry watches for potential sources of danger, and can often be seen standing on a termite mound in order to increase the range of visibility. When fleeing, the herd runs in single file, and can reach speeds of up to 75 kmph. At 3-4 years of age, ♂ attempt to hold a territory. Marked with dung piles, these defended regions average 31 ha in area, and are generally taken over by another ♂ after 4-5 years. ♀ and ♂ alike are generally non-aggressive, although both sexes will fight vigorously in defense of their offspring or territory. Population densities average 1.4 animals per km².

DISTRIBUTION *Native*: Namibia, Botswana, Zimbabwe, South Africa. Found in much of Namibia, extending into S Angola between the Cunene and Cubango rivers, and throughout the Kalahari region of Botswana. Vagrants occasionally wander into W Zimbabwe. In South Africa it formerly occurred in the W Transvaal, in parts of the Orange Free State and Natal, and throughout Cape Province; however, it was exterminated by early European settlers except for a narrow strip in the Northern Cape near Botswana. Now widely reintroduced on government reserves and private ranches, especially in the drier regions. Once again a common species, with its numbers increasing.

HABITAT Semi-arid bush savanna and open woodland. Very widely translocated.

STATUS Least Concern. Estimated population is 130,000 animals and increasing.

PHOTO CREDITS ♂: *Nico Smit*, Kalahari Desert (South Africa). Young: *Arthur Chapman* (South Africa). Head ♂: *Valerie Wexler*, Sidbury, Eastern Cape (South Africa). ♀: *Anilegna* (Namibia). Head ♀: *Colin Michaelis* (South Africa). Juvenile: *Rogeli González*, Etosha (Namibia).   533

Lichtenstein's Hartebeest
ALCELAPHUS LICHTENSTEINII

BL: 160-200 cm. SH: 120-136 cm (♂), 119-130 cm (♀). TL: 40-50 cm. W: 157-205 kg (♂), 160-181 (♀). HL: 40-60 cm. Overall color sandy yellow, with no appreciable lightening on the undersides. On the back is a faint reddish saddle which is fairly indistinct with the exception of where it meets the white rump in a crisp horizontal line. Brush-like tuft of hair at the base of the tail is black, as are the fronts of the lower forelegs. Shoulders are humped, body slopes downward toward the rear. Shoulders typically streaked with black, because of the shoulder-wiping ritual. Head elongated and slender. Tip of the muzzle dark brown or black, and lighter eyebrows. Preorbital secretion black. Broad and short frontal pedicel with slightly ringed horns in both sexes. Growing up and slightly out before turning toward each other, the tips of the horns turn sharply toward the rear. Females are slightly smaller than males.

Young

♀

♂

Alcelaphus lichtensteinii

OTHER NAMES Nkonzi. *French*: Bubale de Lichtenstein. *German*: Lichtensteins, Kuhantilope, Konzi. *Spanish*: Búbalo de Lichtenstein. *Russian*: Бубал Лихтенштейна. *Afrikaans*: Morfhartbees, Lichtenstein se hartbees. *Swahili*: Kongoni Kusi.

SUBSPECIES Monotypic. Formerly considered a subspecies of *A. buselaphus* (Hartebeest).

SIMILAR SPECIES This species, like the Western, Lelwel, and Red Hartebeest, can be regarded as part of the "heavily armed" group. Coke's Hartebeest is a lighter color and has horns that expand outward at the base and then taper upward and backward.

REPRODUCTION *Gestation*: 240 days. *Young per Birth*: 1. *Weaning*: 12 months. *Sexual Maturity*: 24 months. *Life Span:* 20 years. Breeding generally between December and February, with most calves being born during the July-September dry season. Within herds calves are born at the same time, which is an anti-predator mechanism. Calves are mobile shortly after birth, but usually lie in the open while the mother grazes in close proximity. Young ♂ are expelled from the herd at the age of 10-12 months and young ♀ leave the group at 15-18 months.

BEHAVIOR *Family Group*: Groups of 3-16 ♀ and young led by an adult ♂, bachelor ♂ in small groups or solitary. *Diet*: Selective grazers, prefer fresh growth. They prefer new growth in burned areas, for their mineral content. *Main Predators:* Lion, leopard, cheetah, spotted hyena, Cape hunting dog. They forage primarily in the early morning and late afternoon and evening, seeking refuge from the daytime heat by resting in shade. A herd is generally led by an adult ♂, who often takes up watch on a termite mound or other patch of elevated ground, and who will bring up the rear of the herd when in flight. This ♂ defends a territory of about 250 ha year-round, which is marked by "horning" the ground. This horning behavior is seen in both sexes, after which the animal may rub its horns on its sides, leaving dark patches of dirt just behind the shoulders. During the rut, a ♂ with a territory will try to collect as many ♀ as possible, whether from his herd or not. At this time, fights between rival ♂ are common, and can last for extended periods of time. The sense of sight is well developed, and is this antelope's main defense in the open territory which it frequents. The sense of smell is not especially keen. The primary vocalizations are a bellow and an odd sneeze-like snort. A very fast runner.

DISTRIBUTION *Native*: Tanzania, DR Congo, Angola, Zambia, Mozambique, Zimbabwe, South Africa. *Regionally Extinct*: Burundi. They formerly occurred widely in the miombo woodlands of S-central Africa (probably as far S as KwaZulu-Natal), but now occur mainly in wildlife areas in Tanzania, Mozambique, and Zambia. In South Africa, they have been recently reintroduced in Kruger NP and on private land in the Transvaal.

HABITAT Desert and semi-desert, with sand dunes, hard-packed terrain, and scant vegetation.

STATUS Least Concern. Highly vulnerable to poaching; its long-term survival is closely linked to the continuation of protection of its populations in areas such as Selous Game Reserve and the other key areas for this species in W and S Tanzania and Zambia.

PHOTO CREDITS *Kim Wolhuter*, Malilangwe (Zimbabwe) and *Andrew*, Kruger NP (South Africa). Young and head ♀: *Grant Edmondson*, Kafue NP (Zambia).

535

Lelwel Hartebeest
ALCELAPHUS LELWEL

BL: 182-200 cm. SH: 108-150 cm. TL: 46-57 cm. W: 175-218 kg (♂), 150-185 kg (♀). HL: To 70 cm. Large Hartebeest. Pelage color more reddish tan than neighboring species, with poorly expressed dark marking on the face, middorsal region, and front of the forelegs. Rump noticeably pale to whitish. The body slopes from the high shoulders down to the hindquarters, terminating with a black-tasseled tail. Legs proportionately long and built for speed. Preorbital secretion is colorless. Long and narrow head, a shape emphasized by the high placement of the eyes and the high horn pedicel. Relatively longer pedicels than in any other Hartebeest. Strongly ringed horns, found in both sexes, forming a narrow upright V when seen from the front, growing slightly outward and backward, then upward and forward, and finally bending sharply backward. Females have shorter and thinner horns.

♀

Juvenile

♂

Young

Alcelaphus lelwel

OTHER NAMES Jackson's Hartebeest. *French*: Bubale lelwel. *German*: Lelwel-Kuhantilope. *Spanish*: Búbalo de Lelwel, alcélafo de Lelwel. *Russian*: Лелвел.

SUBSPECIES Monotypic. Formerly considered a subspecies of *A. buselaphus* (Hartebeest). The Lelwel Hartebeest can hybridize with Coke's Hartebeest to make the Kenya Highland or Laikipia Hartebeest, or with Swayne's Hartebeest to make the Neumann Hartebeest. Includes *jacksoni* (N and W Uganda, N Rwanda, the Bukoba District of NW Tanzania, and W Kenya), *lelwel* (NE Congo, S Sudan, and SW Ethiopia S of the Blue Nile and W of the Omo River), *modestus* (Central African Republic) and *tschadensis* (S Chad), with *lelwel* having priority.

REPRODUCTION *Gestation*: 202 days. *Young per Birth*: 1. *Weaning*: 4 months. *Sexual Maturity*: 2 years (♀), 1 year (♂). *Life Span*: 20 years. The duration of the mating season is very short, so that competition between ♂ is intense. Like all Hartebeest, they fight by dropping to their front knees and pushing with their foreheads and horn pedicels, their horns interlocking to some extent, and the long pedicels in this species give extensive leverage. A ♀ indicates mating readiness by stretching her rump, with hind legs flexed, emphasizing the pale tone of the rump. The calves tend to be hiders for the first week and associate in loose neonatal groups after this point.

BEHAVIOR *Family Group*: Small herds consisting of ♀ and young, but sometimes larger herds up to 100 individuals. *Diet*: Grasses. *Main Predators*: Lion, leopard, cheetah, spotted hyena, Cape hunting dog. Found in large groups in wide grassy valleys. They move to higher ground and split up into small herds consisting of ♀ and young in the later part of the rainy season, from late April to June, and at this time the ♂ set up territories and compete for the ♀ herds. Each herd remains within one territory, restricting its movements to some 200-300 ha. The main feeding peak is late in the day. Members of a herd rest intermittently, sleeping for only a few minutes at a time, curled up or resting their chin on the ground. Territorial ♂ spend long periods standing on termite mounds. ♂ form defecation sites that mark the boundaries of their territories. ♀ form small herds that pass through these contiguous ♂ territories. ♀ herds show a form of hierarchy by aggressive posturing with their horns. Young ♂ tend to form bachelor herds and are also tolerated by the territorial ♂. ♀ are known to be very aggressive in the defense of their offspring. In captivity, ♀ show a dominance hierarchy in herd situations; aggression has been the major concern in captivity. ♂ introductions to the ♀ herd tend to be extremely combative. Sparring between ♀ and ♂ is common; the sparring does not usually escalate to a full fight.

DISTRIBUTION *Native:* Central African Republic, Chad, DR Congo, Ethiopia, Kenya, Sudan, Tanzania, Uganda.

HABITAT Open grassland and bush regions.

STATUS Endangered. Estimated population is fewer than 70,000 animals.

PHOTO CREDITS ♂: *Sam D'Cruz*, Murchison Falls (Uganda). Head ♂: *Erin Huber*, Murchison Falls (Uganda). Head ♀: *Mitchell Lea* (Uganda). Young: *J. A. Kok,* Murchison Falls (Uganda). Juvenile: *Wade Strickland*, Murchison Falls (Uganda).

Coke's Hartebeest
ALCELAPHUS COKII

BL: 177-200 cm. SH: 117-124 cm (♂), 112 cm (♀). TL: 45-70 cm. W: 129-171 kg (♂), 116-148 kg (♀). HL: To 70 cm. Medium-sized Hartebeest. Color sandy fawn, with the rump patch only slightly paler. Only the tail tuft is black. The body slopes from the high shoulders down to the hindquarters. Legs proportionately long and built for speed. Head shorter than in other subspecies, with a relatively lower frontal pedicel. Preorbital secretion black and sticky. Ringed horns, present in both sexes, short, rather thick, and bracket shaped, growing outward from the pedicel, then upward and backward. Less sexually dimorphic than any other Hartebeest.

♀

Young

Juvenile

♂

Alcelaphus cokii

OTHER NAMES Kongoni. *French*: Bubale kongoni. *German*: Kongoni-Kuhantilope, Cokes Kuhantilope. *Spanish*: Búbalo de Coke, alcélafo de Coke. *Russian*: Конгони Коука. *Swahili*: Kongoni Kaskazi.

SUBSPECIES Monotypic. Formerly considered a subspecies of *A. buselaphus* (Hartebeest). It can hybridize with Lelwel Hartebeest to make the Kenya Highland or Laikipia Hartebeest.

SIMILAR SPECIES This species, like the Tora and Swayne's Hartebeest, can be regarded as part of the "lightly armed" group. Horns are more widespread than in the Tora and Swayne's Hartebeest, resembling a curly bracket in shape, and are relatively short and more slender than in other Hartebeest, except for the Tora and Swayne's Hartebeest. Head shorter than in other subspecies, with a lower frontal pedicel, and the preorbital secretion is black and sticky, quite different from the secretion of the Lelwel and Swayne's Hartebeest.

REPRODUCTION *Gestation*: 240 days. *Young per Birth*: 1. *Weaning*: 4 months. *Sexual Maturity*: 3 years (♀). *Life Span*: 15 years. A territorial ♂ greets a ♀ with a head-up display and stands blocking her with his ears lowered, then turns slowly to sniff her genitals. Receptive ♀ stand with hind legs slightly spread, the tail to one side. The ♀ is continuously breeding, and frequently has two calves of different ages accompanying her. Hartebeest give birth throughout the year with peaks during the dry season. ♀ leave the herd and seek cover when giving birth, and calves hide for the first 2 weeks, and suckle for up to 4 months. ♂ calves may accompany their mothers for up to 2.5 years, then they join bachelor herds.

BEHAVIOR *Family Group*: Single-sex and mixed groups of 5-15 individuals. *Diet*: Medium-length grasses; they have to drink when the grass is dry; they are among the purest grazers. *Main Predators*: Lion, spotted hyena, Cape hunting dog. Mostly active early and late in day, but also by night. Harem herds occupy the most suitable places, but bachelor groups are also a common sight. They tend to migrate between short-grass, well-drained pastures in the rains and long grasses in the dry season. During the dry season, the ♀ and territory holders often form larger herds in areas of good grazing, dispersing again with the onset of the rains. Habitable areas are partitioned into permanent or semi-permanent territories, among which move herds of 6-15 ♀ and young.

DISTRIBUTION *Native:* Kenya, Tanzania. Found in S Kenya and N Tanzania. They have lost much of their range, but populations still occur in the Serengeti and Tarangire in Tanzania and Tsavo, and the Mara in Kenya.

HABITAT Grassy plains, open woodlands, dry scrub bush, and hills up to 2,000 m.

STATUS Least Concern. Population size estimated at 42,000, nearly three-quarters of which occur in protected areas. It has probably suffered the greatest reduction in range of all African ruminants. This is both because it is easily hunted, being relatively sedentary, and because its diet is almost equivalent to that of domestic cattle, leading to competition for food resources.

PHOTO CREDITS ♀: *Xinyi Xu*, Serengeti (Tanzania). ♂: *Sabra Phillips*, Serengeti (Tanzania). Juvenile: *Ken Wewerka*, Maasai Mara (Kenya) and *Peter Koppers*, Serengeti (Tanzania). Young: *Ken Wewerka*, Maasai Mara (Kenya).

Western Hartebeest
ALCELAPHUS MAJOR

BL: 200-250 cm. SH: 120-143 cm. TL: 50-57 cm. W: 120-200 kg. HL: 45-70 cm. The largest Hartebeest. Pelage color uniform tan brown, with no dark markings except on the lower forelegs and a black tail tuft. The body slopes from the high shoulders down to the hindquarters. The legs are proportionally long and built for speed. Head is extremely elongated and narrow, with a high frontal pedicel. Some individuals have a thin white band between the eyes. Horns, found in both sexes, are thick and massive, strongly twisted, U-shaped when viewed from in front, with the tips turned sharply backward. There is a low degree of sexual dimorphism.

Alcelaphus major

OTHER NAMES Kanki. *French*: Bubale kanki. *German*: Westafrika-Kuhantilope. *Spanish*: Búbalo occidental, alcélafo occidental. *Russian*: Западный конгони.

SUBSPECIES Monotypic. Formerly considered a subspecies of *A. buselaphus* (Hartebeest). Includes *invadens* (NE Nigeria to N Cameroon), *major* (Senegal and Guinea), and *matschiei* (Côte d'Ivoire to central Nigeria), with *major* having priority.

REPRODUCTION *Gestation*: 240 days. *Young per Birth*: 1. *Weaning*: 4 months. *Sexual Maturity*: 1.5-2.5 years. *Life Span:* 19 years. The breeding season is longer than in any other species, more than 3 months, except for the Coke's Hartebeest. Fighting is not as intense as in species with a short breeding season.

BEHAVIOR *Family Group*: Single-sex and mixed groups of 5-12 individuals. *Diet*: Grasses, rarely leaves. *Main Predators*: Lion, leopard, cheetah, spotted hyena, Cape hunting dog. Mainly active during the day. It grazes during the cooler morning and afternoon periods, resting in shaded areas during the hot daytime. ♀ form herds of 5-12 members, while ♂ generally remain solitary. While the herd is feeding, one member will act as a sentry, watching for possible predators. If threatened, the herd flees as a single-file group, reaching speeds of up to 80 kmph. Herds are generally sedentary; animals spend much of their day resting in shade to escape high noon-time heat. They will move as a herd to find water. In particularly dry seasons, or in times of drought, herds of ♀ will migrate together seeking water or better grazing. Western Hartebeest are generally not aggressive, but they will fight to protect their young or their claimed area. ♂ claim areas of plains averaging 31 ha, for periods of 4–5 years. ♂ protect their claimed area fiercely. ♂ have been known to go without water to protect their territory. If a ♂ leaves his territory to find water, another ♂ may usurp the territory.

DISTRIBUTION *Native*: Senegal, Mali, Guinea, Burkina Faso, Niger, Côte d'Ivoire, Ghana, Togo, Benin, Nigeria, Cameroon, Central African Republic, Chad. *Regionally Extinct*: Gambia. From Senegal E to W Central African Republic and SW Chad, although they have always been marginal in these last two countries. They have disappeared from much of their former range in this region, surviving mainly in and around protected areas; they no longer occur in Gambia (though migrants may enter from Senegal).

HABITAT Savanna bushland with open woodland. They are absent only from desert and forest, notably the Sahara and the W rainforest.

STATUS Near Threatened. Reported numbers were around 36,000 animals in 1999, with more than 95% surviving in and around protected areas.

PHOTO CREDITS *Jonas Van de Voorde*, Parc National de la Pendjari (Benin) and *Sylvain Gatti*.

Nilgai
BOSELAPHUS TRAGOCAMELUS

BL: 180-210 cm (♂), 170 cm (♀). SH: 120-150 cm. TL: 40-45 cm. W: 200-290 kg (♂), 120-212 kg (♀). HL: 15-25 cm (♂). Large Bovid, equine in appearance. Short coat yellow brown in females, gradually turns blue gray in males as they mature. Erectile mane on the nape and back and a hair pennant in the middle of the underside of the neck. White markings in the form of cheek spots, edges of the lips, ears, fetlocks, and a throat bib. Preorbital glands are small. Slender legs supporting a stocky body, which slopes downward toward the rear. Head long and slender. Tufted tail reaching the hocks. Only males have short, black, sharp horns which are straight and tilted slightly forward.

♀

♂
Juvenile

♂

Young

Boselaphus tragocamelus

OTHER NAMES Blue Bull. *French*: Antilope Nilgaut. *German*: Nilgauantilope. *Spanish*: Nilgó, toro azul. *Russian*: Нильгау. *Marathi*: Rohu. *Hindi*: Roz, rojra.

SUBSPECIES Monotypic.

REPRODUCTION *Gestation*: 243-247 days. *Young per Birth*: Generally 2, sometimes 1 or 3. *Weaning*: 10 months. *Sexual Maturity*: 18 months. *Life Span*: 21 years. Breeding occurs throughout the year, but the peak of mating is December-March, with the resulting calves born in September and October. Courtship is simple and may last only 45 minutes; a breeding ♂ will approach a ♀ stiffly, body stretched lengthwise and tail erect, with the tuft at a right-angle kink; the ♀ typically holds her head close to the ground and meanders forward; the ♂ then licks and nuzzles the ♀'s perineum. If she is receptive, the ♀ will raise her tail and elicit a flehmen response from the ♂, who then rests his chin on her rump, pushes his chest forward to touch her, and mounts. Pregnant ♀ become solitary as parturition approaches and keep neonates hidden from other conspecifics for about 1 month.

BEHAVIOR *Family Group*: Single-sex or mixed herds of 4-20 individuals, old ♂ may be solitary. *Diet*: Leaves, buds, grasses, fruit. *Main Predators*: Tiger, leopard, wolf, dhole. Mainly diurnal, with peaks in activity in the early morning and late afternoon. The sense of sight is well developed in this wary species. When chased, Nilgai can run up to 48 kmph. ♂ have been observed to establish territories during the breeding season, attempting to gather and keep small herds of ♀ (up to 10) within their area. ♂ compete with each other with threatening posture displays and neck wrestling, rarely leading to both rivals kneeling and lunging at each other with their horns. Normally silent, Nilgai have been recorded making a roaring vocalization. Senses of smell and eyesight are very good. The population density in central India is about 0.07 animals per km^2.

DISTRIBUTION *Native*: India, Nepal, Pakistan. *Regionally Extinct*: Bangladesh. *Introduced:* United States. Widely distributed in India and in the lowland zone of Nepal, extending into border areas of Pakistan where it is rare. Like the Blackbuck, there are currently more Nilgai living in a semi-wild state in Texas than in their native India.

HABITAT Grassy steppe and woodlands throughout India.

STATUS Least Concern. Indian population could exceed 100,000. Locally common to abundant in agricultural areas in the states of Haryana, Uttar Pradesh, Rajasthan, and Gujarat. No figures are available for Nepal. Numbers are very low in Pakistan. About 37,000 feral Nilgai are established on Texas ranches. Because its horns are not impressive and its meat is poor tasting, the Nilgai is not much sought after by hunters. Moreover, it is regarded as a close relative of the sacred cow by the Hindu religion, enjoying immunity from molestation; sometimes displays remarkably little concern in the presence of humans.

PHOTO CREDITS ♂ and ♀: *Alex Meyer,* Lion Country Safari (USA). Young: *Arjan Haverkamp*, Amsterdam Zoo (Netherlands). Head ♂: *Bob Thomson*, India Himalayan Foothills (India). Head ♀: *Ema W.*, Knowsley Safari Park (UK). Juvenile: *Neil Parker*, Ranthambore NP (India).

Four-horned Antelope
TETRACERUS QUADRICORNIS

BL: 90-110 cm. SH: 55-65 cm. TL: 10-15 cm. W: 15-25 kg. HL: 5-12 cm (♂). A small animal. Short, coarse coat yellow brown to dark reddish brown in color, with the undersides and inside surfaces of the legs whitish. Muzzle, back of ears, and stripes down the front of the legs are blackish. Large elongated preorbital glands and well-developed unguicular glands above false hooves on the rear legs. Legs slender. Rump is higher than the rest of the body. Smooth, conical horns, found only in the male, nearly straight and point upward. The main pair, found just in front of the ears, grow 5-12 cm long. Usually there is a second, shorter pair of horns on the foremost part of the forehead, reaching a length of only 2-4 cm. These secondary horns may fall off in older animals, or may merely be represented by nodules of black, hairless skin. Female similar to the male, but hornless.

♂

two-horned

♀

♂
Juvenile

Tetracerus quadricornis iodes

Tetracerus quadricornis quadricornis

Tetracerus quadricornis
subquadricornis

OTHER NAMES Chowsingha. *French*: Antilope tétracère, antilope a quatre cornes. *German*: Vierhornantilope. *Spanish*: Antílope de cuatro cuernos, antílope cuadricorne. *Russian*: Четырёхрогая антилопа, или чузинга. *Bhils*: Bhirul, chutia nagpur, kotari. *Deccan*: Jagli-bakri. *Gonds*: Bhir, kurus. *Guzrati*: Bhokra, phocra. *Hindi*: Chousingha, chouka, poda. *Nepali*: Chowsinghe, chowka. *Telegu*: Konda-gori. *Tamil*: Kapilaman.

SUBSPECIES *T. q. quadricornis*: Central and N India; largest subspecies, ♂ almost always have four horns. *T. q. iodes:* Sub-Himalayan region in N India and S Nepal; nearly as large, but have shorter horns, ♂ tend to have four horns. *T. q. subquadricornis:* S India; smallest subspecies, ♂ have only two horns.

SIMILAR SPECIES May be confused with the Indian Muntjac (*Muntiacus muntjak*) and Hog Deer (*Axis porcinus*), but ♂ of the latter two species have antlers that are shed annually, and both sexes have upper canines. ♂ Indian Muntjac is distinguished further by bony facial ridges that give rise to pedicels to support small antlers. Jerky movements of Four-horned Antelope distinguish it from other comparably sized ungulates in its native range. May be confused with the Indian Gazelle (*Gazella bennettii*), which has a similar size, but can be distinguished by the white and brown patterning of its pelage and large ringed horns.

REPRODUCTION *Gestation*: 225-240 days. *Young per Birth*: 1-3. *Life Span*: 10 years. Breeding peaks in June-July when the chance of seeing pairs of ♀ and ♂ is highest. Courtship behavior consists of the ♂ and ♀ kneeling and pushing at each other with intertwined necks, followed by ritual strutting by the ♂. Parturition can occur throughout the year in the wild, but newborns are noted most often in October-November in India. Offspring remain with their mothers for about 1 year, and an adult ♀ can be seen with her young-of-the-year and a juvenile.

BEHAVIOR *Family Group*: Usually solitary or in pairs. *Diet*: Leaves, grasses, shoots, fruit, not as dependent on water as previously suggested. *Main Predators*: Tiger, leopard, wolf, dhole, small cats. A shy, wary antelope, it dashes swiftly for cover at the first sign of danger. The gait of this antelope when walking or running is jerky. It is rarely found far from water, and must drink regularly in order to survive. Sedentary, inhabiting more or less the same region throughout it life. Whether territories are formed and defended has yet to be discovered. In the rut, ♂ can be extremely aggressive to members of the same sex. Easily tamed when young, it is very delicate in captivity.

DISTRIBUTION *Native*: India, Nepal. Distributed widely, but in scattered populations, over most of India, from the Himalayan foothills to peninsular India. A few may remain in Nepal.

HABITAT Tree-savanna deciduous and open habitats with lower tree density and high degree of deciduousness.

STATUS Vulnerable. Estimated population is fewer than 10,000 mature individuals.

PHOTO CREDITS ♂: *Alex Meyer*, Delhi Zoo (India) and *Sahana Chattopadhyay*, Rajiv Gandhi NP (India). Head ♂: *Atul Dhamankar*, Tadoba-Andhari Reserve (India) and *B. N. Singh*, Bandhavgarh NP (India). ♀: *Sanjay Shrishrimal*, Tadoba-Andhari Reserve (India). Young: *Manjeet and Yograj Jadeja,* Gir NP (India).

Eastern Giant Eland
TAUROTRAGUS DERBIANUS GIGAS

BL: 220-290 cm. SH: 150-175 cm. TL: 90 cm. W: 440-900 kg. HL: 120 cm. A very large antelope. Sandy-colored ground coat, with around 12 vertical white stripes on the torso. Short-haired black spinal crest down the neck to the middle of the back. Slender legs, with black and white markings just above the hooves and large black spots on the upper forelegs. Bridge of the nose charcoal black in color; thin, indistinct tan-colored chevron between the eyes. Lips white, along with several dots along the jawline. Pendulous dewlap, larger in males, from between the jowls hanging to the upper chest, with a fringe of hair on its edge. Amorphous band of black almost completely encircling the lower neck, extending onto the dewlap. Tail long, with a dark tuft of hair. Tightly spiraled horns, relatively straight, diverging from the base, in both sexes. Female more lightly built and smaller, with no mat of hairs on the forehead; horns smaller.

Young

Juvenile

♂

♀

Taurotragus derbianus gigas

OTHER NAMES Central African Giant Eland, Eastern Derby Eland. *French*: Éland de Derby. *German*: Riesen-Elenantilope. *Spanish*: Eland gigante oriental, eland de Lord Derby oriental. *Russian*: Центральноафриканская гигантская канна. *Azande*: Boja. *Ful*: Kemmba. *Kakwa*: Bobo. *Madi*: Matiko. *Yoruba*: Otolo.

SUBSPECIES Considered as a subspecies of *T. derbianus* (Giant Eland): *T. d. derbianus* (Western Giant Eland), *T. d. gigas* (Eastern Giant Eland). The validity of these subspecies is questioned by some authors. Includes *cameroonensis* (Cameroon), *congolanus* (Ubangi/Chari) and *gigas* (Bahr-el-Ghazal), with *gigas* having priority.

SIMILAR SPECIES The name Giant Eland is misleading, because it is generally smaller in size than the East African Eland. Rather, the Giant Eland has much larger, diverging horns.

REPRODUCTION *Gestation*: 270 days. *Young per Birth*: 1. *Weaning*: 6 months. *Sexual Maturity*: 15-36 months (♀), 4-5 years (♂). *Life Span*: 20 years. Mating occurs throughout the year, but peaks in the wet season. As in all antelopes, mating occurs at a time of food abundance. Fights occur for dominance, in which ♂ lock horns and try to twist the necks of their opponents. As an act during rut, the ♂ rub their foreheads in fresh urine or mud. They also use their horns to thresh and throw loose earth on themselves. The horns of older ♂ get worn out due to rubbing them on tree bark.

BEHAVIOR *Family Group*: Herds containing up to 60 animals of both sexes have been reported, though groups of 15-25 are more usual. ♂ often solitary. *Diet*: Foraging on a large variety of plant species, predominantly trees and shrubs, generally leaves and some pods, and to a lesser extent forbs, but very rarely grasses. They drink regularly. *Main Predators*: Lion, spotted hyena. Primarily nocturnal, Giant Elands are highly nomadic, with large home ranges and seasonal migration patterns. During the day, herds often rest in sheltered areas. A gregarious species, animals form smaller groups during the dry season and cluster together during the wet season. There is no evidence of territoriality, and ♂ rarely display aggressive tendencies, even during the breeding season. Giant Eland are alert and wary, making them difficult to approach and observe. They can be quite fast and, despite their size, are exceptional jumpers, easily clearing heights of 1.5 m.

DISTRIBUTION *Native*: Cameroon, Central African Republic, Chad, DR Congo, Sudan. *Possibly Extinct*: Uganda. It occurs in the central African region, and now survives mainly in NE Central African Republic. A separate population lives in N Cameroon, with herds crossing the Chad border to the E; occasional vagrants may enter Nigerian territory. They still occur in SW Sudan (Southern NP), from which they may visit NE DR Congo and NW Uganda.

HABITAT Broad-leaved savannas and glades in two isolated pockets in central and western Africa.

STATUS Least Concern. Estimated total population is 14,000-20,000 animals. Population in Sudan is fewer than 200 animals.

PHOTO CREDITS *Nick Hadad*, Johannesburg Zoo (South Africa). Head ♂: *Theologos Sosonis*, San Francisco Zoo (USA). Head ♀: *Nick Hadad*, Johannesburg Zoo (South Africa). Young: Houston Zoo (USA). Juvenile: *Sergey Chichagov*, San Diego Safari Park (USA).

Western Giant Eland

TAUROTRAGUS DERBIANUS DERBIANUS

BL: 220-290 cm. SH: 150-175 cm. TL: 90 cm. W: 440-900 kg. HL: 80-120 cm. Smaller than Eastern Giant Eland. Smooth coat is a bright rufous ground color, with up to 17 well-defined vertical white stripes on the torso. Short-haired black spinal crest down the neck to the middle of the back, especially prominent on the shoulders. Slender legs slightly lighter on their inner surfaces, with black and white markings just above the hooves. Large black spots on the upper forelegs. Bridge of the nose charcoal black in color; thin, indistinct tan-colored chevron between the eyes. Lips white, along with several dots along the jawline. Pendulous dewlap, larger in males, with a fringe of hair on its edge. Amorphous band of black almost completely encircling the lower neck, extending onto the dewlap. Tightly spiraled horns, relatively straight, diverging from the base, in both sexes, smaller than in Eastern Giant Eland. Female more lightly built and smaller, with no mat of hairs on the forehead, and smaller horns.

♂

Young

♀

Juvenile

Taurotragus derbianus derbianus

OTHER NAMES Western Derby Eland. *French*: Éland de Derby. *German*: Riesen-Elenantilope. *Spanish*: Eland gigante occidental. *Russian*: Западная гигантская канна. *Shona*: Mhofu. *Swahili*: Pofu. *Tswana*: Phôhu. *Zulu*: Impofu.

SUBSPECIES Considered as a subspecies of *T. derbianus* (Giant Eland): *T. d. derbianus* (Western Giant Eland), *T. d. gigas* (Eastern Giant Eland).

SIMILAR SPECIES The name Giant Eland is misleading, because it is generally smaller in size than the East African Eland. Rather, the Giant Eland has much larger, diverging horns.

SIMILAR SPECIES Eastern Giant Eland is larger, with longer horns, a duller overall color, and usually fewer body stripes.

REPRODUCTION *Gestation*: 265 days. *Young per Birth*: 1. *Weaning*: 6 months. *Sexual Maturity*: 15-36 months (♀), 2-3 years (♂). *Life Span*: 16 years. Unlike in other antelopes, mating usually occurs during the dry season, at the beginning of March, with most births taking place at the beginning of the dry season (November-December). ♂ compete using their horns for dominance, and the dominant ♂ will mate with several ♀.

BEHAVIOR *Family Group*: Herds containing more than 75 animals of both sexes have been reported, though groups of 15-25 are more usual. ♂ often solitary. *Diet*: Generalist foraging on a large variety of plant species varying according to season, predominantly trees and shrubs, generally leaves and some types of fruits, namely pods, and to a lesser extent also forbs, but very rarely grasses. They drink regularly. *Main Predators*: Lion, spotted hyena, leopard. Nocturnal, they rest during the day to escape the heat, and feed at night or early in the morning on grass, leaves, and branches. Adult ♂ prefer to live alone while ♀ and their young form groups of 20 or more. Herds are known to migrate extensively. It seems that larger groups split into smaller ones in the early dry season and join together again in the early wet season. During dry seasons they are able to live for weeks without water. There is no evidence of territoriality, and ♂ rarely display aggressive tendencies, even during the breeding season. Alert and wary, making them difficult to approach and observe. They can be quite fast and, despite their size, are exceptional jumpers, easily clearing heights of 1.5 m.

DISTRIBUTION *Native*: Senegal. *Regionally Extinct*: Côte d'Ivoire, Gambia, Ghana, Guinea, Mali, Sudan, Togo. The only confirmed wild population occurs in E Senegal. The presence of a viable population of this antelope in the surrounding states of Mali, Guinea, and Guinea-Bissau has not been confirmed.

HABITAT Broad-leaved savannas and glades in Niokolo Koba NP.

STATUS Critically Endangered. Population estimates suggests a total of 170 animals in Senegal (Niokolo Koba NP). This low population count is a result of overharvesting for meat and habitat destruction caused by the expansion of human and livestock populations. It is not held in captivity in any zoo. There is a small semi-captive population at Bandia and Fathala Reserves (Senegal).

PHOTO CREDITS ♂: *Lenka Bartunková* and *Pavel Brandl*, Fathala Wildlife Reserve (Senegal). ♀ and head ♂: *Tom Junek*, Bandia Reserve (Senegal). Head ♀: Derbianus Czech Society for African Wildlife, Fathala Wildlife Reserve (Senegal).

East African Eland

TAUROTRAGUS ORYX PATTERSONIANUS

BL: 200-345 cm. SH: 130-180 cm. TL: 60-90 cm. W: 300-1,000 kg. HL: To 65 cm (♂), to 68 cm (♀). Largest African antelope. Smooth tan or fawn coat. Up to 12 white vertical stripes on flanks, less well defined on mature males. Dark dorsal crest. Dark band on the backs of the forelegs above the knees. Backs of the pasterns are brownish black. Ears narrow and pointed. Younger adult males have a dark, narrow forehead tuft flanked with orange, and an incomplete white chevron below the eyes. White face markings disappear in older bulls as the narrow frontal tuft grows into a broad, long-haired bush. Pendulous, black-tufted dewlap on the lower throat (not on the chin). Tail long, reaching to the hocks, with a terminal black tuft. Slightly diverging horns, found in both sexes, virtually straight, with 2 tight twists, smaller than horns of Cape or Livingstone's Elands. Female like the male but smaller and more slightly built; general color rufous fawn; no mat of hairs on the forehead, horns lighter but often longer.

♀

♂
Old

Young

♂

Taurotragus oryx pattersonianus

OTHER NAMES Patterson's Eland, Eland Antelope. *French*: Éland. *German*: Elenantilope. *Spanish*: Antílope eland común. *Russian*: Восточноафриканская канна. *Maasai*: O sirua. *Ndebele*: Impofu. *Ovambo*: Ongalangombe. *Sepedi*: Phokhu. *Shona*: Mhofu. *Swahili*: Pofu, mbunju. *Swati*: Impophi. *Wolof:* Yomoussa. *Yei*: Unshefu.

SUBSPECIES Considered as a subspecies of *T. oryx* (Common Eland): *T. o. pattersonianus* (East African Eland), *T. o. livingstonei* (Livingstone's Eland), *T. o. oryx* (Cape Eland). Includes *pattersonianus* (Kenya) and *billingae* (Tanzania), with *pattersonianus* having priority. Considered as the same subspecies as *livingstonei* by some authors. There are broad overlap areas where both subspecies blend.

SIMILAR SPECIES Somewhat darker and more rufous than other subspecies, with the ♀ more brightly colored, and the white body stripes plainly visible; smaller horns.

REPRODUCTION *Gestation*: 270 days. *Young per Birth*: 1. *Weaning*: 6 months. *Sexual Maturity*: 15-36 months (♀), 4-5 years (♂). *Life Span*: 25 years. After birth the young lie briefly in concealment before joining a crèche or nursery with other infants.

BEHAVIOR *Family Group*: Large mixed groups, usually containing 25-70 individuals (up to 400 have been observed). *Diet:* They browse by breaking branches with their horns to reach foliage and flowers, and will snap boughs of substantial thickness, up to at least 5 cm in diameter. *Main Predators:* Lion, Cape hunting dog, leopard, spotted hyena. Most active in the morning and late afternoon, lying sheltered in the heat of the day. A very gregarious species, it is always found in large herds, with no dispersion during the rainy season. A possible explanation for this is the strong mutual attraction by calves, and a "safety-in-numbers" strategy. Elands are remarkably fast and have been recorded running over 70 kmph. Despite their size, they are exceptional jumpers, easily clearing heights of 1.5 m. Home range sizes vary dramatically with respect to sex and season. In the dry season, ♂ use an average of 12 km² out of their 41 km² total range. ♀ herds have a dry season range of 26 km², while in the wet season this expands to 220 km². There is no exclusive use of space or evidence for territoriality, but adult ♂ within a maternal herd have a distinct social hierarchy.

DISTRIBUTION *Native*: Ethiopia, Kenya, Rwanda, Sudan, Tanzania, Uganda. *Possibly Extinct*: Burundi. Found in SE Sudan, SE Ethiopia, SE and NE Uganda, S and W Kenya, and Tanzania. Some believe that the Elands of S Tanzania should be classified as Livingstone 's Eland because their horns are larger than those of other Eland in East Africa, and the white facial chevron is minimal or missing altogether in most individuals.

HABITAT Most savanna and open woodland types, from low to high rainfall areas. Occur from sea level to high mountain areas, including to 5,000 m on Mount Kilimanjaro, where they visit natural mineral licks.

STATUS Least Concern. Estimated population of 36,000 in Tanzania. Although they still occur widely they have been hunted to extinction, or near extinction, in many parts of their former range.

PHOTO CREDITS ♂: *Adit Ganguly* (Kenya). Head ♂: *Arjan Haverkamp*, Dierenpark Amersfoort (Netherlands). ♀: *Dellfoto*. Head ♀: *Tom Horton*, Rift Valley (Kenya). Young: *Ashley*, Maasai Mara (Kenya). Old ♂: *Herbie Pearthree,* Maasai Mara (Kenya). 551

Livingstone's Eland
TAUROTRAGUS ORYX LIVINGSTONEI

BL: 200-345 cm. SH: 170 cm (♂), 150 cm (♀). TL: 60-90 cm. W: 650-910 kg (♂), 400-600 kg (♀). HL: To 65 cm (♂), to 68 cm (♀). Slightly darker than the Cape Eland, gray to brown in color. Typically with 6 to 10 thin white stripes on its sides, less well defined on older males. Dark brown band on the rear surfaces of the forelegs above the knees, less pronounced than in East African Eland. The backs of the pasterns are whitish. The forehead hair mat is well developed and chocolate brown in color. Some populations have white streaks below the eyes. Males usually darker, gray or bluish gray with age. Pendulous, black-tufted dewlap on the lower throat (not on the chin). Tail with a terminal black tuft. Slightly diverging horns, found in both sexes, virtually straight, with 2 tight twists. Female like the male but smaller and more slightly built; general color fawn; no mat of hairs on the forehead, horns lighter but often longer.

♀

Juvenile

♂

Taurotragus oryx livingstonei

OTHER NAMES *French*: Éland du Livingstone. *German*: Elenantilope. *Spanish*: Antílope eland de Livingstone. *Russian*: Канна Ливингстона. *Swahili:* Pofu.

SUBSPECIES Considered as a subspecies of *T. oryx* (Common Eland): *T. o. pattersonianus* (East African Eland), *T. o. livingstonei* (Livingstone's Eland), *T. o. oryx* (Cape Eland). Includes *kaufmanni* (Caprivi), *livingstonei* (W Zambia), *niediecki* (Kafue River), *selousi* (Mashonaland) and *triangularis* (Zambezi), with *livingstonei* having priority. Cape and Livingstone's subspecies may interbreed and mixed specimens are frequent, having only 1-5 vertical body stripes.

SIMILAR SPECIES Cape Eland is slightly lighter in color and lacks the white stripes on its sides and the dark brown band on the rear surfaces of the forelegs. East African Eland is more rufous, the dark bands on the forelegs are darker, the backs of the pasterns are brownish black, and it has smaller horns.

REPRODUCTION *Gestation*: 271-279 days. *Young per Birth*: 1. *Weaning*: 5-6 months. *Sexual Maturity*: 15-36 months (♀), 4-5 years (♂). *Life Span*: 24 years. A single calf can be born throughout the year, but calving reaches its peak during the wet summer months (October - January).

BEHAVIOR *Family Group*: Large mixed groups, usually containing 25-70 individuals. *Diet*: Browsers, adapted to grazing: they may graze during the rainy season when grasses are plentiful, but browse more during the drier winter months. Although they drink water when it is plentiful, they obtain most of their water from their diet. *Main Predators*: Lion, Cape hunting dog, leopard, spotted hyena. Crepuscular, feeding in the early morning and in the evening. They spend more time in the shade on hot days and more time in sunny areas on windy days. Superb jumpers. Gregarious, but have a fluid and open system. Non-territorial and nomadic, with large home ranges, between 174 and 422 km². Form larger herds than most Bovids, with groups of 100 being common. Membership within a herd is variable. Individuals stay in a herd for several hours to several months. ♀ and juveniles tend to stay close together, whereas ♂ form smaller herds or wander individually. Unlike many antelope, Eland lack territorial behavior. The shorter and thicker horns of ♂ tend to be more effective during fights between ♂ in rut, where ♂ wrestle with their horns and ram heads. ♀ use their long, thin horns to deliver quick stabs at predators. Eland communicate by visual displays, olfactory cues, and auditory signals.

DISTRIBUTION *Native*: Botswana, DR Congo, Malawi, Mozambique, Namibia, Zambia, Zimbabwe. *Possibly Extinct*: Angola. *Introduced*: South Africa. Found in the extreme N and the Caprivi Strip in Namibia, Botswana N of the Kalahari, Zambia, Katanga Province in SE DR Congo, Malawi, Zimbabwe, and Mozambique except in the extreme S. It is probably extinct in Angola. It has been transplanted into South Africa, and can often be found right alongside the Cape Eland.

HABITAT From mountainous areas to semi-desert regions. They prefer open plains with wooded areas for cover. Widely translocated, thrive on cattle farms.

STATUS Least Concern.

PHOTO CREDITS ♂: *Thomas Retterat*, Mana Pools (Zimbabwe). ♀: *Dellfoto*. Juvenile: *Brian Gratwicke*, Harare (Zimbabwe).

Cape Eland
TAUROTRAGUS ORYX ORYX

BL: 200-345 cm. SH: 170 cm (♂), 150 cm (♀). TL: 60-90 cm. W: 700 kg (♂), 450 kg (♀). HL: To 65 cm (♂), to 68 cm (♀). Slightly smaller than northern subspecies. Body color is a uniform, dull fawn. Adults lack body stripes, though juveniles may be lightly striped. Typically, this subspecies does not have white streaks below the eyes or dark bands behind the knees. Backs of the pasterns are whitish. Males usually grayer or gray blue with age, with a distinctive dark mat of hair on the forehead. Pendulous, black-tufted dewlap on the lower throat (not on the chin), smaller in females. Tail somewhat shorter than in other subspecies, with a terminal black tuft. Slightly diverging horns, longer than in other subspecies, found in both sexes, thicker and much more prominently ringed in males. Female like the male but smaller and more slightly built, less brightly colored than in other subspecies; no mat of hairs on the forehead, horns lighter but often longer.

♀

Young

♂

Taurotragus oryx oryx

OTHER NAMES Southern Eland. *French:* Éland du Cap. *German:* Elenantilope. *Spanish*: Eland de El Cabo. *Russian*: Капская канна.

SUBSPECIES Considered as a subspecies of *T. oryx* (Common Eland): *T. o. pattersonianus* (East African Eland), *T. o. livingstonei* (Livingstone's Eland), *T. o. oryx* (Cape Eland). Includes *alces*, *barbatus*, *canna*, *oreas*, *oryx,* and *typicus*, with *oryx* having priority.

SIMILAR SPECIES East African Eland is darker and more rufous, ♀ more brightly colored, coat with up to 12 stripes plainly visible, smaller horns. Livingstone's Eland has brown pelt with 6-10 distinct vertical stripes on the flanks. In contrast, adult Cape Eland loses its stripes, does not have white streaks below the eyes or dark bands behind the knees.

REPRODUCTION *Gestation*: 273-280 days. *Young per Birth*: 1. *Weaning*: 6 months. *Sexual Maturity*: 18 months (♀), 4-5 years (♂). *Life Span*: 25 years. Calving season from October to January; during this time the ♂ leave the breeding herds to form bachelor groups.

BEHAVIOR *Family Group*: Small herds of 4-12 animals. *Diet*: Predominantly browsers; they graze on green grass, which is the bulk of the diet in summer; they prefer grass burned within the past year. Also eat leaves, twigs, fruit and berries, and dry fallen leaves. *Main Predators*: Lion, Cape hunting dog, leopard, spotted hyena. Gregarious, usually occurs in small herds but can form aggregations of more than 700 animals with a strict linear dominance hierarchy. It has a unique social organization and also forms nursery and bachelor herds. The large herds break up into small herds of 4-10 animals of either sex and all age classes when autumn starts, occurring at low densities in the winter. Feeding mainly occurs in the early morning and night, when vegetation contains more water. They break down branches by twisting them between their horns or hooking the horns over them. For thermoregulation they rest in shade when it is hot but will remain in the sun when it is cold. Not territorial and movements are generally determined by food preferences and availability. The range size of a herd in the wet season can vary from 174 to 422 km^2 but it reduces to 9-58 km^2 in the dry season.

DISTRIBUTION *Native*: Botswana, Lesotho, Namibia, South Africa, Swaziland. Namibia, except in the far N and the Caprivi Strip; the Kalahari region in S Botswana; South Africa; and the extreme S of Mozambique. Formerly widely distributed throughout South Africa, even as far SW as the present site of Cape Town; widely reintroduced on private ranches in South Africa. In Namibia, those found S of the game fence that extends from the Atlantic Ocean, S of Etosha Game Park, to Botswana, are considered as Cape Elands.

HABITAT Highly versatile in habitat choice and formerly occurred in the greater part of the Nama Karoo, the Succulent Karoo, the fynbos, and the more arid grasslands and savannas of South Africa. It can occur at high elevations and has the widest habitat tolerance of all the antelopes. Widely translocated, thrives on cattle farms.

STATUS Least Concern.

PHOTO CREDITS ♂: *Duncan Forrest,* Aquila Game Reserve (South Africa). Head ♂: *Marie and Alistair Knock*, Kgalagadi Transfrontier Park (South Africa). ♀: *Mark Shobbrook* (South Africa). Head ♀: *Arthur Chapman*, West Coast NP (South Africa). Young: *Sergey Chichagov*, Antelope Ranch (Israel).

Northern Lesser Kudu

AMMELAPHUS IMBERBIS

BL: 160-180 cm (♂), 140 cm (♀). SH: 95-120 cm (♂), 100 cm (♀). TL: 38-46 cm. W: 56-105 kg. HL: 60-90 cm (♂). Males paler gray, with less contrasting white markings than Southern Lesser Kudu. Two white spots on the posterior jawline. Incomplete white chevron between the eyes. Well-defined small white upper throat patch. White lower neck patch, less pronounced than in Southern Lesser Kudu. No throat beard. Distinctive 10-14 vertical body stripes, beginning farther back on the shoulders than in Southern Lesser Kudu. Last 2-3 stripes wrapping across the haunch converging near the front of the knee, becoming oblique. Lower legs tawny orange. Hind pasterns generally completely black but occasionally white. Tail dark. Small mane on the nape of the neck and along the spine in males. Horns, found in males, widely spiraled, dark, can be white tipped. Females and young bright reddish brown. Females slightly smaller.

Ammelaphus imberbis

OTHER NAMES *French*: Petit koudou. *German*: Kleiner Kudu. *Spanish*: Kudú menor septentrional, pequeño kudú septentrional. *Russian*: Северный малый куду. *Swahili*: Tandala ndogo. *Acholi*: Nyamugata. *Amharic*: Ambarayelle, sara. *Dborobo*: Chaihoo. *Galla*: Gadams. *Maasai*: Emato enhatu. *Somah*: Anderio, gdoir.

SUBSPECIES Monotypic. The name *A. imberbis* (Lesser Kudu) formerly included *A. imberbis* (Northern Lesser Kudu), and *A. australis* (Southern Lesser Kudu) as subspecies: these are all elevated to full species here. Often placed under the genus *Tragelaphus*.

SIMILAR SPECIES Southern Lesser Kudu is usually darker, bright tawny ocher, has more contrasting white markings, beginning farther up on the shoulders, and white areas anteriorly just above the hooves on all four legs.

REPRODUCTION *Gestation*: 240 days. *Young per Birth*: 1. *Weaning*: 6 months. *Sexual Maturity*: 15 months (♀), 4-5 years (♂). *Life Span*: 15 years. There is no fixed breeding season, so calves are born throughout the year. After birth, the young lie concealed away from their mother.

BEHAVIOR *Family Group*: Lives singly, in pairs, or in small family groups. Adult ♂ associate with ♀ only when breeding. *Diet*: Primarily leaves, sometimes grasses and fruit. Rarely drink. *Main Predators*: Leopard, Cape hunting dog, lion. They may be solitary, especially ♂, in pairs, or in small groups of related ♀ and their young. Fixed home ranges are occupied and most animals are sedentary, but in some areas seasonal movements are undertaken. Home ranges tend to be smallest in the dry season, expanding during the rains. ♂ ranges average 2-3 km^2 in size, whereas those of ♀ tend to be somewhat smaller at under 2 km^2. There is no territorial behavior by either sex. Most feeding takes place at night or during the cooler early morning hours. ♂ rely mainly on displays during rutting, and fighting is said to be rare. The alarm call is a sharp bark. A better runner than the Greater Kudu, and a good jumper. Extreme alertness and shyness protect this species from predators.

DISTRIBUTION *Native*: Ethiopia, Somalia. *Regionally Extinct*: Djibouti. Lowlands of E-central Ethiopia (Awash area) and NW Somalia.

HABITAT Semi-arid thornbrush lowlands within the northern reaches of the Somali-Maasai arid zone in the N Horn of Africa. It remains close to protective cover.

STATUS Near Threatened. The Northern Lesser Kudu is the rarer of the two species, and current population levels are unknown. Awash NP in the Great Rift Valley (Ethiopia) sustains a substantial protected population. It is not known if any survive in Somalia. Main threats include excessive hunting and competition with domestic livestock.

PHOTO CREDITS ♂: *Paul Cottis* and *Tim Melling*, Awash (Ethiopia). Head ♂: *Lars Petersson* (Ethiopia).

Southern Lesser Kudu
AMMELAPHUS AUSTRALIS

BL: 110-170 cm. SH: 90-110 cm. TL: 25-43 cm. W: 56-105 kg. HL: 60-90 cm (♂). A medium-sized, slender antelope. Color ranging among males and females from bright tawny ocher to reddish brown, chocolate brown with gray white on the neck, or grayish chocolate brown, to predominantly gray. Seven to 14 very distinctive white stripes on the sides, a white patch on both the upper and lower throat, 2 white cheek spots, and an incomplete white chevron between the eyes. Slender legs are tawny with black-and-white markings. Males have a small mane on the nape of the neck and along the spine. There is no beard on the throat. Tail not reaching the hocks, bushy, with white underside and black tip. Long spiraling horns, moderately diverging, found only in males, having 2-3 close twists. Female slightly smaller, without horns.

♀

Young

♂
Juvenile

♂

Ammelaphus australis

OTHER NAMES *French*: Petit koudou. *German*: Kleiner Kudu. *Spanish*: Kudú menor meridional, pequeño kudú meridional. *Russian*: Южный малый куду. *Swahili*: Tandala ndogo. *Acholi*: Nyamugata. *Amharic*: Ambarayelle, sara. *Dborobo*: Chaihoo. *Galla*: Gadams. *Maasai*: Emato enhatu. *Somah*: Anderio, gdoir.

SUBSPECIES Monotypic. Formerly considered a subspecies of *A. imberbis* (Lesser Kudu). Often placed in the genus *Tragelaphus*.

SIMILAR SPECIES Smaller than the Greater Kudu, more graceful, and the throat has two well-defined white patches and no fringe of hairs; stripes are more numerous and contrasting; horns smaller, forming a closer spiral and less diverging. Northern Lesser Kudu is paler gray, with less contrasting white markings, beginning farther back on the shoulder, and the last 2-3 white stripes converging near the front of the knee, and sometimes lacking the white areas anteriorly just above the hooves on the forelegs. ♀ Lowland Nyala has similar striping and body markings, but legs and neck are shorter.

REPRODUCTION *Gestation*: 240 days. *Young per Birth*: 1. *Weaning*: 6 months. *Sexual Maturity*: 15 months (♀), 4-5 years (♂). *Life Span*: 15 years. There is no fixed breeding season, so calves are born throughout the year. ♂ perform a shoving match, where they press their heads and horns together and attempt to force their horns down onto the nape of their opponent. ♂ and ♀ also perform a superiority contest, where the ♂ and ♀ stand fully erect on their hind legs and attempt to push each other over. The ♂ show restraint and are never aggressive toward ♀, though ♀ have been observed to butt their heads against the ♂. When the ♂ mount, they lay their neck and head down and onto the ♀'s back. After birth, the young lie concealed away from their mother.

BEHAVIOR *Family Group*: Mixed or single-sex troops of 2-5 individuals, rarely up to 24. Old ♂ are solitary. *Diet*: Primarily leaves, sometimes grasses and fruit; rarely drink. *Main Predators*: Leopard, Cape hunting dog, lion. Primarily active at night and in the early morning, seeking shelter shortly after sunrise. The alarm call is a sharp bark. Shy and wary, and when startled flees with the tail held up, revealing the white underside. A better runner than the Greater Kudu, and a good jumper. Leaps of up to 2 m have been recorded, though these are not common. Individual home ranges average 2.2 km² for ♂ and 1.8 km² for ♀. These areas overlap extensively with no apparent territoriality, and different parts are used at different times of the year. Population density rarely exceeds 1 per km².

DISTRIBUTION *Native*: Ethiopia, Kenya, Somalia, Sudan, Tanzania, Uganda. Lowlands of S Ethiopia, Somalia, extreme SE Sudan, extreme NE Uganda, N, central and S Kenya, and E Tanzania.

HABITAT Dry thornbrush and forests in E Africa. Can live in much drier habitat than the Greater Kudu.

STATUS Near Threatened. Estimated population in 1999 was 118,000 animals. In gradual decline over extensive areas of its range as human settlement expands.

PHOTO CREDITS ♂: *Steven Heap* and *Steve Garvie,* Tsavo West NP (Kenya). Head ♂: *Chris Matthews*, Bisanadi NR (Kenya). ♀: *Steven Heap,* Tsavo West NP (Kenya). Juvenile: *Tom Bauer,* Saint Louis Zoo (USA) and *Silvie "Akela Taka" Lišková*, Dvur Králové Zoo (Czech Republic). Young: *Bret Newton*, Fort Worth Zoo (USA) and *Lauren,* San Diego Zoo (USA).

Cape Greater Kudu
STREPSICEROS STREPSICEROS

BL: 185-245 cm. SH: 100-160 cm. TL: 30-55 cm. W: 120-315 kg. HL: 100-140 cm (♂). A large and slender antelope. Short, smooth coat from reddish fawn to pale blue gray, particularly in older males, darker than that of other subspecies. Sides of body conspicuously marked with 4-9 vertical white stripes. Neck and head darker than shoulders. Head with a white chevron between the eyes, 2-3 white cheek spots, and white lips. Ears large and round. No white markings on the throat. Abundant fringe of hairs from the chin to the neck, with 1-2 dark brown bands. Brownish mane and dorsal crest from neck and withers to the tail. Dark-tipped, bushy tail, white underneath. Belly is grayish, near black in the middle. Long spiraled horns, with 3 full turns, largely diverging as they slant back from the head. Female smaller and more slender, ground color fawn, with no horns. Young more reddish, with more pronounced white markings.

♀

♂
Juvenile

♂

Young

Strepsiceros strepsiceros

OTHER NAMES Eastern Cape Kudu. *French*: Grand koudou. *German*: Kap-Grosser Kudu. *Spanish*: Gran kudú meridional. *Russian*: Южный большой куду. *Afrikaans*: Koedoe. *Zulu*: Umgankla, igogo, imbodwane. *Shona*: Nhoro. *Swati*: Lishongololo.

SUBSPECIES Monotypic. The name *S. strepsiceros* (Greater Kudu) formerly included *S. strepsiceros* (Cape Greater Kudu), *S. zambeziensis* (Zambezi Greater Kudu), *S. chora* (Northern Greater Kudu), and *S. cottoni* (Western Greater Kudu) as subspecies: these are all elevated to full species here. Considered by some authors as the same species as *S. zambeziensis*, being a subpopulation that became isolated from the remaining S African population by human settlement. Often placed under the genus *Tragelaphus*.

SIMILAR SPECIES Identical to Zambezi Greater Kudu, except that the body is somewhat smaller and the horns are considerably shorter, though heavier in relation to their length.

REPRODUCTION *Gestation*: 255 days. *Young per Birth*: 1. *Weaning*: 6 months. *Sexual Maturity*: 18 months (♀), 21-24 months (♂). *Life Span*: 16 years. Breeding period seasonal, with rut in April-June and the majority of births in December-February, coinciding with rainfall peaks. Neonates remain hidden for some weeks. Young ♂ stay with their maternal group until they are 2 years old, then form loose all-♂ groups of mixed ages, establishing dominance hierarchies. For the rutting season the socially mature ♂ may leave their home ranges to become nomadic across a larger area, associating with ♀ herds of adjacent home ranges.

BEHAVIOR *Family Group*: Small matriarchal groups of up to several ♀ and their offspring; temporal congregations of 12 or more individuals are not uncommon. *Diet*: Non-selective browsers, feeding on leaves, shoots, pods, or fruits of a wide range of shrubs, trees, dicot forbs, and succulents. *Main Predators*: Lion, Cape hunting dog, leopard. Graze in the early mornings and late afternoons; rest in the shade during the hottest part of the day. Not migratory or territorial. They inhabit a static home range which is shared by various individuals of both genders, which may overlap by 80% with others. Home range is fixed and permanent, but the total area varies, from 90 to 350 ha during wet summer periods, expanding to 600 ha during droughts. When disturbed they will flee the area either to return immediately after or to establish a temporary additional home range some distance away. They repeatedly will flee to the same temporarily home range every time they are disturbed. Under normal circumstances, Kudu will sneak away and hide from potential enemies. When they run away their tail is turned upward so that the white underparts show.

DISTRIBUTION Coastal SE South Africa (Eastern Cape Province), with isolated populations in central South Africa.

HABITAT Dry semi-desert and thick valley bushveld areas with sufficient food and shrubs for shelter. Open woodland and rocky terrain with water nearby. Wooded areas along streams.

STATUS Least Concern.

PHOTO CREDITS ♂: *Sharon du Plessis,* Addo Elephant (South Africa). Head ♂: *Dr. Guillaume Emaresi,* Addo Elephant (South Africa). ♀: *Alun W.,* Addo Elephant (South Africa). Head ♀: *Daniel Mouton,* Addo Elephant (South Africa). Young and juvenile: *Sergey Chichagov,* Tallinn Zoo (Estonia).

Zambezi Greater Kudu
STREPSICEROS ZAMBEZIENSIS

BL: 185-245 cm. SH: 100-160 cm. TL: 30-55 cm. W: 120-315 kg. HL: 100-160 cm (♂).
Similar to the Cape Kudu. Coat from gray to pale ocher to reddish gray brown. Sides of body
conspicuously marked with 8-11 vertical white stripes, but this is variable. Males with a clear
white chevron on the face, often very short, and 2-3 white cheek spots. Ears large and round,
with white tips. Long throat mane, straw or pale red-brown colored, with blackish hair tips. No
white markings on the throat. Males with a short red-brown nuchal mane that becomes a white
dorsal stripe. Pasterns are brown and usually not black posteriorly. Lower legs are cinnamon.
Long spiraled horns, larger than in other subspecies. Female smaller and more slender, ocher
to bright grayish brown, with a poorly developed facial chevron, and ears do not have white
tips. Young grayish brown.

Juvenile

♀

♀

♀

♂

♂
Juvenile

Young

Strepsiceros zambeziensis

OTHER NAMES Greater Kudu, Southern Greater Kudu. *French*: Grand koudou de Zambèze. *German*: Sambesi-Grosser Kudu. *Spanish*: Gran kudú oriental. *Russian*: Замбезийский большой куду. *Afrikaans*: Koedoe. *Swahili*: Tandala kubwa.

SUBSPECIES Monotypic. Formerly considered a subspecies of *S. strepsiceros* (Greater Kudu). Considered by some authors as the same subspecies as *S. strepsiceros*. Includes *frommi* (Tanzania). Often placed under the genus *Tragelaphus*.

SIMILAR SPECIES Lesser Kudu ♂ are much smaller and have a dark gray coat, while ♀ generally have more white stripes on the body and have two white marks under the neck which are missing in Greater Kudu.

REPRODUCTION *Gestation*: 270 days. *Young per Birth*: 1. *Weaning*: 6 months. *Sexual Maturity*: 15-21 months (♀), 21-24 months (♂). *Life Span*: 15 years. Birthing season in January-April (N Zimbabwe), February-March (S Zimbabwe), and January-February (South Africa). Females separate themselves from the herd just before giving birth, leaving the calf lying in concealment. Neonates are hidden for 2 weeks, after which they join their mother's group during the day, but continue to hide for 4-5 weeks during the night.

BEHAVIOR *Family Group*: Small single-sex groups of up to 10 (congregations of 20-30 individuals have been recorded). *Diet*: Leaves and grasses. *Main Predators*: Spotted hyena, African wild dog, cheetah, leopard. Active throughout the 24-hour day. The large ears are extremely sensitive to noise, making these shy antelope difficult to approach. Under normal circumstances, Kudu will sneak away and hide from potential enemies. When startled, however, they flee with large jumps with their tails rolled upward and forwards. Kudu often stop and look back after a running for a short distance, a frequently fatal habit. Kudu are accomplished jumpers, with recorded heights of over 2.5 m. Herds disperse during the rainy season when food is plentiful, but as the dry season reaches its peak, they become concentrated in favorable areas. They are not territorial, although they do have home areas. Maternal herds have home ranges of approximately 4 km² which overlap with those of other groups. Home ranges of adult males are about 11 km², and generally encompass the ranges of 2-3 female groups. The spiral horns are so well developed for wrestling that they can sometimes become so severely interlocked that the 2 animals fighting cannot release each other. Wide repertoire of vocalizations, including barks, grunts, hooting bleats, and a strangulated whimper.

DISTRIBUTION Tanzania (except NW), S DR Congo, Malawi, Mozambique, Zambia, S Angola, Namibia, Botswana, Zimbabwe, Swaziland, N South Africa.

HABITAT Woodland thickets, often on rocky escarpments and hills. Flat savannas. They are capable of living near human settlement if adequate cover exists.

STATUS Least Concern.

PHOTO CREDITS ♂: *Gerrit De Vries* (South Africa). Heads: *Arjan Haverkamp*, Gaia Park Kerkrade Zoo (Netherlands). ♀: *Sally La Niece*, Sabi Sands Reserve (South Africa). Young: *Brian J. Smith*, Miami Zoo (USA). Juvenile ♂: *Neal Cooper*, Chobe NP (Botswana). Juvenile ♀: *Bruce James*, Chobe NP (Botswana).

Northern and Western Greater Kudu
STREPSICEROS CHORA AND STREPSICEROS COTTONI

BL: 236-245 cm (♂), 214 cm (♀). SH: 128-152 cm (♂), 128 cm (♀). TL: 32-51 cm. W: 280 kg. HL: 83-90 cm (♂). Smaller than other subspecies. Short, smooth, pale gray-brown coat, lighter than that of southern subspecies. Three to 7 vertical white flank stripes. White chevron between the eyes. Long pale nuchal mane with dark brown tips. Ears large and round, dark gray on the back. No white markings on the throat. Nape and throat manes may be very short and dark and restricted to the lower throat. Blackish-brown pasterns, with a whitish band above the hooves. Black-tipped, bushy tail, white underneath, not reaching the hocks. Long spiraled horns, with 3 full turns, largely diverging, smaller than those of southern subspecies. Female smaller and more slender, dull to pale fawn, with full facial chevrons, with no horns and no mane on nape and throat. Western Kudu is slightly smaller, with shorter horns, white chevron poorly expressed, and little black around the hooves; otherwise similar.

♀

♂

Juvenile

♂

Strepsiceros chora

Strepsiceros chora

Strepsiceros cottoni

OTHER NAMES Abyssinian Greater Kudu, Sudan Greater Kudu, East African Kudu. *French*: Grand koudou d'Abyssinie. *German*: Nördlicher Grosser Kudu. *Spanish*: Gran kudú septentrional. *Russian:* Абиссинский большой куду *(chora),* Западный большой куду *(cottoni).*

SUBSPECIES Monotypic. Formerly considered as subspecies of *S. strepsiceros* (Greater Kudu). Synonyms of *chora* includes *abyssinicus* (Kordofan to Somalia) and *bea* (Kenya). Western or Uele Kudu includes *burlacei, uellensis,* and *cottoni,* with *cottoni* having priority. Often placed under the genus *Tragelaphus.*

SIMILAR SPECIES Northern Greater Kudu has a smaller, paler body, and horns that are usually much smaller than in the E African or S subspecies, with usually only 4-6 vertical stripes on each side. Western Kudu is the smallest subspecies, with 4-8 vertical stripes.

REPRODUCTION *Gestation*: 210-240 days. *Young per Birth*: 1. *Weaning*: 6 months. *Sexual Maturity*: 15-21 months (♀), 21-24 months (♂). *Life Span*: 15 years. The pregnant ♀ departs from her group to give birth in tall grass or any other sufficiently dense cover, where the calf remains concealed for up to 2 months. The mothers visit their hidden offspring on a daily basis until the youngsters are strong enough to join the ♀ herds.

BEHAVIOR *Family Group*: ♀, calves, and subadults form small family herds, usually with 6-12 members; adult ♂ live alone or in bachelor groups of 2-6, joining ♀ herds in the mating season. *Diet*: Leaves and grasses. *Main Predators*: Lion, Cape hunting dog, leopard. Active throughout the 24-hour day. Kudu rely on concealment and spend nearly all their time hidden in thick bush. When disturbed, they will usually stop and listen to assess the situation and then move away quietly or dash off after giving a loud, sharp alarm bark, which is regarded as the loudest of all the antelope species. In flight they run with heads level to the ground with their horns laid back to avoid tangling in branches. Kudu often stop and look back after running for a short distance, which is frequently a fatal habit. Hearing, sight, and scent are very well developed. They are tremendous jumpers. Social grooming occurs in both family and bachelor herds. During the mating season, ♂ compete for access to ♀ by displays and clashing horns. Dominance is usually quickly and peacefully determined by a lateral display in which one ♂ stands sideways in front of another and makes himself look as large as possible. ♂ of about the same size and age engage in sparring contests in which they approach one another slowly, lock horns, and push back and forth until one gives up. Fights are rare and combatants are very rarely injured.

DISTRIBUTION Found in Ethiopia, Eritrea, the Blue Nile region of E-central Sudan, N slopes of the Gaan Libah in N Somalia, NE Uganda, N and central Kenya to Tanzania border. *Cottoni* is found in SE Chad, W Sudan, and extreme N Central African Republic.

HABITAT Shrub woodlands with protective cover, scrub, and open forests up to 2,450 m.

STATUS Least Concern. Unknown population levels.

PHOTO CREDITS ♂: *Sawadee* (Kenya). Head ♂: *Nevin Chernick*, Samburu (Kenya). Head ♀: *Sue Earnshaw*, Samburu (Kenya). ♀: *Arturo Pardavila III*, Samburu (Kenya). Juvenile: *YC Chung*, Samburu (Kenya).

Mountain Bongo

TRAGELAPHUS EURYCERUS ISAACI

BL: 170-250 cm. SH: 110-130 cm. TL: 45-65 cm. W: 240-400 kg (♂), 150-235 kg (♀). HL: 75-100 cm. The largest African forest antelope. Short, glossy coat, rich red chestnut in color, becoming darker in older males, with 10-15 vertical white torso stripes. Muzzle black, topped by a white chevron between the eyes, and flanked by 2 white cheek spots. Ears large, edged with white on the inside. Lower neck with a distinct light yellowish crescent-shaped white band. Black and white dorsal crest of stiff hairs. The legs are patterned boldly with chestnut, black, and white. Tail long with a terminal tuft of black hairs. Yellow-tipped, lyre-shaped horns are found in both sexes, and have 1 turn. Female similar to the male, paler, horns more slender and parallel, sometimes deformed. Young lighter than the adult.

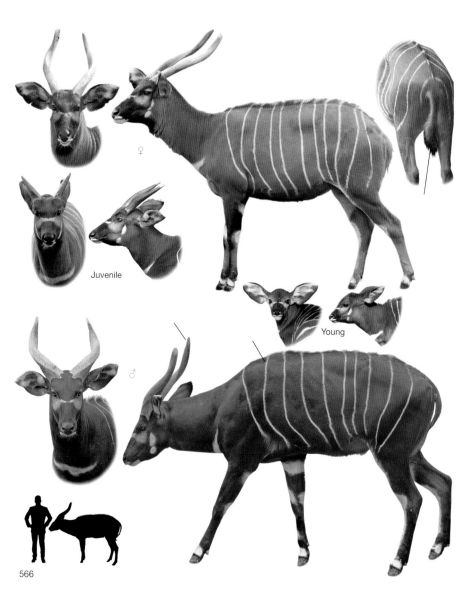

Juvenile

Young

Tragelaphus eurycerus isaaci

OTHER NAMES Eastern Bongo, Kenya Bongo. *French*: Bongo. *German*: Östlichen Bongo, Kenia-Bong. *Spanish*: Bongo de montaña, bongo oriental. *Russian*: Восточный (кенийский) бонго. *Bila*: Soli. *Kiladi*: Njiogika. *Lomongo*: Mongo, mpanga. *Yoruba*: Otolo.

SUBSPECIES *T. e. eurycerus* (Lowland or Western Bongo), *T. e. isaaci* (Mountain or Eastern Bongo). The validity of these subspecies is not recognized by some authors. Bongo it is the only spiral-horned antelope (Tragelaphid) in which both sexes have horns, and thus it was formerly placed under the genus *Taurotragus* (Elands), or under its own genus, *Boocercus*. However, most authors currently support the Bongo's position in the genus *Tragelaphus*.

SIMILAR SPECIES The Sitatunga is easily distinguished by its slender features, its darker, brown color, the less conspicuous stripes, and the greatly elongated hooves. Under captive conditions Bongo and Sitatunga may produce fertile offspring, called Bonxi. Mountain Bongo are somewhat larger and heavier than Lowland Bongo, old ♂ have a darker ground color and, supposedly, fewer stripes and thicker horns.

REPRODUCTION *Gestation*: 270 days. *Young per Birth*: 1. *Weaning*: 6 months. *Sexual Maturity*: 20 months. *Life Span*: 19 years. Mating season from October to January. Calves are left alone after birth, lying still in the undergrowth to avoid detection by predators. The mother returns to her calf to nurse throughout this period.

BEHAVIOR *Family Group*: Singly, in pairs, or in small groups of 9 or fewer ♀ and their young. *Diet:* Leaves, shoots, and grasses. *Main Predators:* Leopard, lion, hyena. Bongos are extremely shy and, when startled, disappear very quickly into the surrounding forest. When fleeing, they hold the horns against the back of the neck, so as not to tangle in the surrounding vegetation. This behavior is exhibited frequently, and most old animals have bare patches on their backs where the horns rest. Bongos wallow frequently in mud, afterward rubbing the mud against a tree, polishing their horns. Most active between dusk and early morning. The population density in S Sudan was found to be about 1.2 animals per km^2. Bongos have a wide range of vocalizations, including grunts, snorts, a weak mooing contact call, and a bleat-like alarm call.

DISTRIBUTION *Native*: Kenya. *Regionally Extinct*: Uganda. Confined to four completely isolated populations in patches of forest on Mount Kenya, the Mau and Eburu forests, and the Aberdares in Kenya.

HABITAT Mountain forest between 2,000 and 3,000 m above sea level in the Kenya highlands.

STATUS Critically Endangered. Estimated population was 100 individuals in 2007. All Bongos in captivity are from the isolated Aberdare Mountain portion of the species' range in central Kenya. The total number of Mountain Bongos held in captivity may exceed the total number remaining in the wild.

PHOTO CREDITS ♂: *José R. Castelló*, Madrid Zoo (Spain). ♀ and heads: *Ungulate Dave*, Marwell Zoo (UK). Young: Houston Zoo (USA). Juvenile: *Derek A. Young*, Taronga Zoo (Australia), *Ungulate Dave*, Marwell Zoo (UK).

Lowland Bongo

TRAGELAPHUS EURYCERUS EURYCERUS

BL: 170-250 cm. SH: 110-130 cm. TL: 45-65 cm. W: 240-400 kg. HL: 75-100 cm. A large antelope, somewhat smaller and lighter than the Mountain Bongo, and with more white stripes on the sides of the body. Short, glossy coat, rich red chestnut in color, becoming darker in older males, with 10-15 vertical white torso stripes. Muzzle black, topped by a white chevron between the eyes, and flanked by 2 white cheek spots. Ears large, edged with white on the inside. Lower neck with a distinct light yellowish crescent-shaped white band. Black and white dorsal crest of stiff hairs. The legs are patterned boldly with chestnut, black, and white. Tail long with a terminal tuft of black hairs. Yellow-tipped, lyre-shaped horns are found in both sexes, and have 1 turn. Female similar to the male, smaller, paler, horns more slender and parallel, sometimes deformed. Young lighter than the adult.

Tragelaphus eurycerus eurycerus

OTHER NAMES Western Bongo. *French*: Bongo. *German*: Westlichen Bongo. *Spanish*: Bongo occidental. *Russian*: Западный бонго. *Bila*: Soli. *Kiladi*: Njiogika. *Lomongo*: Mongo, mpanga. *Yoruba*: Otolo.

SUBSPECIES *T. e. eurycerus* (Lowland or Western Bongo), *T. e. isaaci* (Mountain or Eastern Bongo). The validity of these subspecies is not recognized by some authors. Includes *albovirgatus* (Sanaga River to Sudan), *cooperi* (Haut-Uele District in DR Congo), *eurycerus* (Sierra Leone to Togo), and *katanganus* (Katanga Province in DR Congo), with *eurycerus* having preference.

SIMILAR SPECIES Lowland Bongo is similar to the Mountain Bongo, except that old ♂ may have a lighter ground color, are slightly smaller, and may have more white stripes on the sides of the body. Sometimes the number of stripes on the animal varies from one side to the other.

REPRODUCTION *Gestation*: 270 days. *Young per Birth*: 1. *Weaning*: 6 months. *Sexual Maturity*: 24-27 months. *Life Span*: 19 years. Calves are left alone after birth, lying still in the undergrowth to avoid detection by predators. The mother returns to her calf to nurse throughout this period.

BEHAVIOR *Family Group*: Herds of 5-25 animals, usually with 1 mature ♂ and 1 or 2 younger ♂ within a matriarchal structure. Old ♂ tend to be solitary. *Diet*: Selective grazers, leaves, young shoots, bark, flowers, fruits, and roots; they use their horns as implements to dig or break branches; the mineral salts that they find among the ashes of burnt trees or at salt licks are an important part of their diet. *Main Predators*: Leopard. Like other Tragelaphine antelopes, adult ♂ are solitary and non-territorial. Most active during twilight hours and at night but move around during the day when it rains. Usually they spend the day ruminating in thick cover. They are shy, suspicious, and furtive by nature. They have a dorsal crest which they raise when roused and have a good turn of speed. When startled they can run away at a full gallop. In groups they appear less nervous and can be aggressive toward one another, probably to establish their rank. They produce several different sounds according to their mood. They grunt, make mooing noises and, like Bushbuck, Sitatunga, and Kudu, bark as well. Their senses of smell, hearing, and sight are highly developed. The population density was found to be about 0.2 to 1.2 animals per km^2.

DISTRIBUTION *Native*: Benin, Cameroon, Central African Republic, Congo, DR Congo, Côte d'Ivoire, Gabon, Ghana, Guinea, Liberia, Niger, Sierra Leone, Sudan, Togo. It ranges from Sierra Leone to Benin, being absent E of the Dahomey Gap, and then continues E of the Adamawa Highlands in Cameroon to S Sudan and Congo.

HABITAT Lowland rainforest from W Africa and the Congo basin to SW Sudan. Forest-savanna mosaic, clearings around water holes and mineral licks created by elephants.

STATUS Near Threatened. Estimated population may be fewer than 25,000 animals. It faces an ongoing population decline as habitat destruction and meat hunting pressures increase.

PHOTO CREDITS ♂: *Coke and Som Smith*, Dzanga Ndoki NP (Central African Republic). ♀: *Christophe Morio*, Dzanga Ndoki NP (Central African Republic).

Mountain Nyala
TRAGELAPHUS BUXTONI

BL: 240-260 cm (♂), 190-200 cm (♀). SH: 120-135 cm (♂), 90-110 cm (♀). TL: 20-25 cm. W: 180-300 kg (♂), 150-200 kg (♀). HL: 118 cm (♂). A large antelope. Generally gray brown color, but, since the coat is short and glossy in summer and shaggy in winter, the color can appear quite variable. Males tend to be darker, and young animals often have golden undertones to their coat. There is usually a pattern of white spots and a few stripes on the flanks. Distinctive white chevron between the eyes and 2 white spots on each cheek. Two patches of white on the underside of the neck, the upper very large, the lower crescent-like. Short dark brown mane on the neck continued on the spine as a brown and white crest. Tail not reaching to the hocks, bushy, with white underside and black tip. Horns long, heavy, and lyrate, usually with 1-1/2 or 2 twists, widely diverging. Females smaller than males, without horns. Young ocher colored.

♂
Juvenile

♀

♂

Young

Tragelaphus buxtoni

OTHER NAMES Gedemsa, Balbok. *French*: Gadamsa, nyala des montagnes. *German*: Bergnyala, Mittelkudu, Nördlichernyala. *Spanish*: Niala de montaña. *Russian*: Горная ньяла. *Amharic*: Yedega agazen.

SUBSPECIES Monotypic. Its common name is unfortunate, for this animal bears little resemblance to the common Nyala of SE Africa. It appears to be more closely related to the Greater Kudu.

SIMILAR SPECIES Greater Kudu ♂ have a shaggy fringe on the throat and much longer horns with a distinctive corkscrew spiral. Both sexes are lighter in color, with well-defined vertical stripes on the body.

REPRODUCTION *Gestation*: 8-9 months. *Young per Birth*: 1. *Weaning*: 3-4 months. *Sexual Maturity*: 2-3 years (♀), ♂ may be mature at this time, but cannot win breeding rights until 5-8 years. Birthing through the year, although there is usually a peak which coincides with climate (April to June in Bale, October to December in Arussi farther N). Calves lie up for a few weeks in dense cover, reducing the risk of predation in more open country. Once sure on their feet, the young will join their mother, continuing to nurse until 3-4 months of age. Calves remain closely attached to their mothers for as long as 2 years. Horns begin growing in ♂ at 6 months of age, and are of adult size by 6 years of age. It appears that a ♀ may not breed again as long as her previous offspring is still with her.

BEHAVIOR *Family Group*: Small groups of 2-13 animals, principally ♀ and young but often including a mature ♂. Old ♂ are solitary. *Diet*: Leaves of herbs and shrubs, sometimes grasses, ferns, and lichens. *Main Predators*: Leopard, possibly lion and hyena. Most active in the early mornings and late afternoons, although if undisturbed by humans they may be active at any time of the day or night. It is thought that this species may make seasonal migrations based on altitude, using the higher mountains in the dry season and the lowlands during the wet season. Not territorial. There are two main sounds that this species makes: a hoarse grunt, and a clear bark which acts as an alarm call. When fleeing from a predator, the tail is flipped up, showing off the white underside.

DISTRIBUTION *Native*: Ethiopia. Endemic to the highlands of Ethiopia, SE of the Rift Valley. Formerly occurred from Gara Muleta in the E to Shashamane and N Sidamo in the S, but has been eliminated from a large part of its former range. Currently, the main area of distribution is Bale Mountains NP and the E escarpments of the Bale massif. Smaller relict populations occur in Chercher Mountains, Arsi Mountains, and West Bale (Somkaro-Korduro ridge).

HABITAT Woodlands and grasslands between 2,000 and 4,000 m above sea level. Highest densities (up to 21/km²) have been recorded in the montane grasslands of Gaysay, Bale, where there is a combination of browse and grass with woodland cover to retreat to during the day. Forced into higher areas by human increase and livestock grazing.

STATUS Endangered. Estimated total population is 4,000 animals.

PHOTO CREDITS ♂ and head: *Rod Waddington*. ♀: *Ariadne Van Zandbergen*. Head ♀: *Jon Isaacs*. Young: *Ludwig Siege* and *Dominique Mignard*. Juvenile: *Vladimír Trailin*. All photos taken in Bale Mountains NP (Ethiopia).

East African Sitatunga
TRAGELAPHUS SPEKII

BL: 151-170 cm (♂), 135-144 cm (♀). SH: 88-125 cm (♂), 75-90 cm (♀). TL: 20-26 cm. W: 75-125 kg (♂), 50-57 kg (♀). HL: 55-90 cm (♂). Pelage is long, silky, shaggy, oily, and water repellent, grayish brown in color, with faint white stripes. May have white spots on the hindquarters. Males develop a scraggly mane as they age and have a prominent preorbital chevron and cheek spots. Females are a bright reddish brown, with faint or no preorbital markings. Hooves very elongated, with flexible toe joints and large false hooves. Tail not very bushy, merely tufted at the tip. The horns, found only on males, have 1 to 1-1/2 twists. Female smaller, more conspicuously striped.

Young

Tragelaphus spekii

Tragelaphus sylvestris

OTHER NAMES Northern Sitatunga, Speke's Sitatunga, Lake Victoria Sitatunga. *French*: Sitatunga de Speke. *German*: Ostafrika-Sitatunga. *Spanish*: Sitatunga del Lago Victoria. *Russian*: Восточноафриканская ситатунга. *Swahili*: Nzohe.

SUBSPECIES Monotypic. Formerly considered a subspecies of *T. spekii* (Sitatunga). It Includes *spekii* (W of Lake Victoria), *typicus*, *ugallae* (Ugalla, Tanzania) and *wilhelmi* (Ruhuhuma Swamp, Rwanda). Sitatunga can crossbreed with the Lesser Kudu, Bushbuck, and Bongo. Bongo hybrids are fertile and can reproduce.

SIMILAR SPECIES Nkosi Island Sitatunga (*T. sylvestris*) is controversial, as it is thought to be indistinguishable from the East African Sitatunga, which lives all around it; the main distinguishing factor for this species appears to be its smaller size, with shorter horns and much shorter, stronger hooves; it has not been studied much and very little information on it is available.

REPRODUCTION *Gestation*: 225-240 days. *Young per Birth*: 1. *Weaning*: 6 months. *Sexual Maturity*: 1-2 years (♀), 2-2.5 years (♂). *Life Span*: 20 years. Breeding occurs throughout the year. ♀ give birth on dry reed platforms that they create by trampling the vegetation, and they keep their neonates well concealed until the young can move through the dense swamp vegetation.

BEHAVIOR *Family Group*: Singly or in small, all-♀ groups. *Diet*: Leaves, buds, shoots, fruit, reeds, and grasses. *Main Predators*: Leopard, lion, python. Spend most of their time among boggy papyrus beds in swamps, so their elongated hooves and flexible toe joints are excellent adaptations, preventing them from sinking into the soft ground. Excellent swimmers, and, when threatened, flee into deep water. They may submerge themselves completely underwater, with only their nostrils above the waterline. ♂ have a loud, barking vocalization. They are most active at dawn and dusk, and may move onto marshy land at night.

DISTRIBUTION *Native*: Burundi, DR Congo, Ethiopia, Kenya, Rwanda, Sudan, Tanzania, Uganda. East African Sitatunga is found in swamps and marshes in the Bahr-el-Ghazal region of SE Sudan, Uganda, Rwanda, Burundi, and adjacent parts of Kivu Province in NE DR Congo, W Kenya surrounding Lake Victoria, NW Tanzania, and perhaps the Rift Valley in Ethiopia. Boundaries with the other Sitatunga species are unclear. *T. sylvestris* is found only on the Sesse Islands in the NW part of Lake Victoria in Uganda, specifically Bugalla, Bubembe, Fumve, and Nkosi islands; Nkosi Island is about 64 km offshore from the Ugandan mainland.

HABITAT It is semi-aquatic, and so specialized that it occurs only in swamps or permanent marshes. Partial to papyrus and phragmites within swamps, it may also occur in wetlands dominated by bulrushes, reeds, and sedges. It frequents the deepest parts of the swamp. Lake storms have forced the Nkosi Island Sitatunga to largely abandon its aquatic habitat and live mainly on dry land where it has adopted habits similar to those of a Bushbuck; a restricted diet probably accounts for its smaller size and shorter horns; living on dry land for its short, strong hooves.

STATUS Least Concern.

PHOTO CREDITS ♂: *Craig Fildes* and *Renee Gillett*, Maryland Zoo (USA). Head ♂: *Christine Metzgar*, Maryland Zoo (USA). ♀ and head: *Eric Haas*, Maryland Zoo (USA). Young: ZSL Whipsnade Zoo (UK) and Maryland Zoo (USA).

Western Sitatunga
TRAGELAPHUS GRATUS

BL: 115-170 cm. SH: 75-125 cm. TL: 30-35 cm. W: 40-120 kg. HL: 45-90 cm (♂). A large antelope, with amphibious habits. Long, shaggy, water-resistant coat, color from grayish brown to chocolate brown in males, with much variation in the white markings. Some individuals will exhibit the full complement of white facial markings, vertical white body stripes, white dorsal stripe, white neck bands, and white spots on the hips, while others will show little or no white except on the face. Coat shorter than in other Sitatungas. Hindquarters larger than the forequarters, giving a peculiar hunched appearance. Long and narrow hooves, up to 10 cm, with extended false hooves, an adaptation to the marshy environment. Tail not very bushy, merely tufted at the tip. Horns, found only on males, have 1 to 1-1/2 twists. Female reddish to reddish brown, smaller, without horns, more conspicuously striped.

Young

Juvenile

♀

♂

♂

coat variation

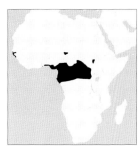

Tragelaphus gratus

Tragelaphus larkenii

OTHER NAMES Forest Sitatunga, Western Marshbuck. *French*: Sitatunga, guib d'eau, guib harnachée, limnotrague. *German*: Westliche Sitatunga, Wasserkudu, Sumpfbock. *Spanish*: Sitatunga occidental. *Russian*: Западная ситатунга *(gratus),* Лесная ситатунга *(larkenii).* Swahili: Nzohe. *Setswana*: Naakông. *Yei*: Unzunzu.

SUBSPECIES Monotypic. Formerly considered a subspecies of *T. spekii* (Sitatunga).

SIMILAR SPECIES Nile Sitatunga has a shorter, sparser, and less shaggy coat than other Sitatunga, rich dark brown in color, with 4 to 8 white stripes, sometimes faint, and a lateral strip of 12 to 15 spots, which may be reduced to 3-4 spots. Differs from the Bushbuck by its larger size and longer, more twisted horns.

REPRODUCTION *Gestation*: 7 months. *Young per Birth*: 1. *Weaning*: 6 months. *Sexual Maturity*: 1-2 years (♀), 2-2.5 years (♂). *Life Span*: 19 years. Breeding occurs throughout the year. Young lie in concealment on raised reed beds.

BEHAVIOR *Family Group*: Singly or in small, all-♀ groups. *Diet*: Leaves, buds, shoots, fruit, reeds, and grasses. *Main Predators*: Leopard, lion, python. Semi-social, non-territorial, and sedentary. ♀ tend to form herds and ♂ associate together or with ♀ until subadults. As adults, ♂ avoid one another. They move through the swamp along established pathways. Active both diurnally and nocturnally and may move into marshy land at night. They also lie on platforms of vegetation that each animal prepares for itself by repeated circling and trampling. They also stand and ruminate in the water. Slow and clumsy land runners, but their plunging run works well in water. Their broad and splayed hooves keep them from sinking in soft ground as deeply as other ungulates. ♂ often bark at night, sometimes as an alarm signal, or perhaps as a way of announcing their location. ♀ have a single higher-pitched bark.

DISTRIBUTION. Fragmented populations may be found in parts of Senegal, Gambia, Guinea-Bissau, possibly Guinea, N Sierra Leone, SW Côte d'Ivoire, SE Ghana, S Togo, S Benin, and S Nigeria. They are widespread in S Cameroon, Equatorial Guinea, Gabon, Congo, S Central African Republic, and nearly all of DR Congo. They also occur in the NE corner of Angola bordering Congo. The main population is centered in the Congo River basin. An isolated population is found along the S and E shores of Lake Chad in NE Nigeria, N Cameroon, and W Chad. Nile Sitatunga is found only in two areas of S Sudan: small swamps in SW Sudan near the DR Congo border, and the Sudd Swamps (Bahr-el-Ghazal) of the Upper White Nile.

HABITAT Swamp forests and marshes in central and W Africa.

STATUS Least Concern. Estimated population of Nile Sitatunga was 1,100 animals in the Sudd Swamps of S Sudan, in 1980. The main threat is loss of wetland habitats.

PHOTO CREDITS ♂: *Ellen van Yperen*, Fuengirola Zoo (Spain), *Xavier Bayod Farré*, Réserve Africaine de Sigean (France), and *Marek Velechovsky*. Head ♂: *Laurent Rzr*. ♀: *David L. Quayle*, Chester Zoo (UK). Head ♀: *Vagmak*, Attica Zoo (Greece). Young: *Michael Döring*, Zoom Experience Gelsenkirchen (Germany), *Michelle Bender*, NaturZoo Rheine (Germany). Juvenile: *nesihonsu*, Wroclaw Zoo (Poland) and *Adam Hobbs*, Chester Zoo (UK).

Zambezi Sitatunga
TRAGELAPHUS SELOUSI

BL: 115-170 cm. SH: 88-125 cm (♂), 75-90 cm (♀). TL: 30-35 cm. W: 75-125 kg (♂), 50-60 kg (♀). HL: 58-91 cm (♂). Shaggy, water-repellent pelage, uniformly drab brownish gray, without stripes and without spots on the hindquarters. Unlike females of other Sitatunga subspecies, females are darker brown, with faint or absent lateral lines and rump spots. Head with prominent preorbital spots in males and faint or obsolete preorbital spots in females. Hindquarters larger than the forequarters, giving a peculiar hunched appearance. Hooves long and extremely narrow, with extended false hooves. Tail not very bushy, merely tufted at the tip. Horns, found only on males, have 1 to 1-1/2 twists. Female smaller.

Tragelaphus selousi

OTHER NAMES Southern Sitatunga, Selous's Sitatunga, Zambezi Marshbuck. *French*: Sitatunga du Zambèze. *German*: Sambesi-Sitatunga. *Spanish*: Sitatunga del Zambeze. *Russian*: Замбезийская ситатунга (Ситатунга Селуса).

SUBSPECIES Monotypic. Formerly considered a subspecies of *T. spekii* (Sitatunga). Includes *inornatus* (NE Zambia) and *selousi* (Zambezi Valley). Some authors consider Sitatungas to be monotypic, as pelage color and presence of body stripes and spots are highly variable, even within the same population, and may change with age.

SIMILAR SPECIES Forest Sitatunga is slightly heavier, ♂ have numerous whitish spots and stripes, and ♀ are reddish brown. East African Sitatunga is slightly smaller, ♂ have few or no white stripes, and ♀ are bright chestnut.

REPRODUCTION *Gestation*: 210 days. *Young per Birth*: 1. *Weaning*: 6 months. *Sexual Maturity*: 1-2 years (♀), 2-2.5 years (♂). *Life Span:* 16 years. Peak birthing season in June-July, with most of the breeding in January-February, during the rainy season. Calves are born on reed platforms prepared by the mothers which return 2-4 times a day to suckle, and remain hidden longer than other Sitatunga species. Calves swim before they can walk properly.

BEHAVIOR *Family Group*: Singly or in small, all-♀ groups. *Diet*: Leaves, buds, shoots, fruit, reeds, and grasses. *Main Predators*: Leopard, lion, python. Feeding activities are most pronounced in the morning and evening, moving out of the reed beds and into woodland at night. Seasonal differences in diet occur relative to flooding regimes: during low-water periods, when they are confined to marshes, their diets are composed of little more than papyrus; during periods of high water, they spend more time in upland wooded areas and islands, where leaves of trees are browsed heavily, even to the point of being denuded. They appear to move little during seasonal flooding, which forces them into less preferred habitats of shallowly flooded grassland. They are not gregarious, and adult ♂ tend to occur alone, except during breeding. ♂ bark at each other throughout the year and avoid direct interactions. They are usually slow and inconspicuous, and are good swimmers.

DISTRIBUTION *Native*: Angola, Botswana, Congo, DR Congo, Mozambique, Namibia, Tanzania, Zambia, Zimbabwe. Its range is discontinuous and limited to wetland environments from S Congo through central DR Congo and Zambia northward to the S end of Lake Tanganyika, SW Tanzania, S to the Caprivi Strip in Namibia, Angola and N Botswana. Boundaries with the other Sitatunga subspecies are unclear.

HABITAT Swamp and marshes associated with rivers, lakes, and lowland forests of poor drainage that are scattered throughout their range. They make short seasonal migrations out of the reed beds during the annual flood.

STATUS Least Concern. Populations used to be stable in Botswana and Zambia (Bangweulu Swamps, Kafue NP, and Kasanka NP), but rare in Mozambique, Namibia, and Zimbabwe. Current populations are threatened by competition with livestock, loss of habitat, and altered hydrology in their critical wetland habitats.

PHOTO CREDITS Reconstruction from photos from Okavango Delta (Botswana).

Western Bushbuck

TRAGELAPHUS SCRIPTUS

BL: 100-150 cm. SH: 64-100 cm (♂), 61-85 cm (♀). TL: 19-24 cm. W: 40-80 kg (♂), 24-60 kg. (♀). HL: 25-55 cm (♂). The smallest species of Bushbuck, with the smallest horns. Bright chestnut-red coat, with a varied white pattern of up to 10 distinct transverse stripes, an upper and lower longitudinal flank band, and haunch spots. Black and white dorsal crest. Upper part of limbs darker, and the inner sides are white. Black line down the front of forelimbs. Underparts darker. Head and neck lighter, fawn color. The face has 2 white cheek spots, and a blackish band extending to the muzzle. Ears large and broad. Bushy tail, white underneath. Short horns, nearly straight, only diverging a little, strongly keeled, with 1 tight twist. Female smaller and without horns, lighter than the male and more conspicuously striped.

♀

♂

Juvenile

♂

578

Tragelaphus scriptus

OTHER NAMES Harnessed Antelope. Kewel, Senegal Bushbuck. *French*: Antilope harnaché, guib harnaché. *German*: Buschbock, Senegal-Schirrantilope. *Spanish*: Antílope jeroglífico, bushbuck septentrional. *Russian*: Пёстрый (западноафриканский) бушбок.

SUBSPECIES Monotypic. The name *T. scriptus* (Bushbuck) formerly included *T. scriptus* (Western Bushbuck), *T. phaleratus* (Central Bushbuck), *T. bor* (Nile Bushbuck), *T. decula* (Lake Tana Bushbuck), *T. meneliki* (Meneliki Bushbuck), *T. fasciatus* (Eastern Coastal Bushbuck), *T. ornatus* (Chobe Bushbuck), and *T. sylvaticus* (Cape Bushbuck) as subspecies: these are all elevated to full species here. Recent analysis has identified two major groups of Bushbucks: "scriptus" (including *scriptus, phaleratus, bor,* and *decula*) and "sylvaticus" (including *ornatus, fasciatus, meneliki,* and *sylvaticus*). Synonyms of *scriptus* include *leucophaeus, gratus,* and *obscurus.*

REPRODUCTION *Gestation*: 6 months. *Young per Birth*: 1. *Weaning*: 6 months. *Sexual Maturity*: 11-12 months. *Life Span*: 12 years. Breeding occurs throughout the year. The single young lies hidden away from its mother for the first few weeks of life.

BEHAVIOR *Family Group*: Usually solitary, although sometimes in pairs. *Diet*: Grasses as well as leaves, buds, and fruit. *Main Predators*: Leopard, lion, crocodile. Bushbuck are the least social of the African antelopes. They are often seen singly, although sometimes small groups of ♀ and their respective young are found. Bushbuck are not territorial, and except for disputes over ♀ in estrus they are not aggressive toward one another, so in areas with good-quality habitat there may be several animals in close proximity. Confrontations between ♂ are composed of displaying and charging, followed by the locking of horns and vigorous twisting in an attempt to throw the opponent off balance. Stabbing with the horns has also been noted. Active throughout the 24 hours of the day, although they tend to be nocturnal near human settlements. The daytime is spent concealed from predators in dense, bushy cover of the type that is usually found near rivers. They come out at night to feed in more open areas, but never venture far from some type of cover. Using trails through dense jungle, the Bushbuck ranges through a restricted home area, which may be only a few hundred meters across. These home ranges overlap extensively, and it has been noted that the greater the population density, the smaller these home ranges are. Bushbuck are very capable swimmers, and excellent jumpers. The call resembles the bark of a dog.

DISTRIBUTION S Mauritania, S Senegal, SW Mali, Gambia, Guinea-Bissau, Guinea, Sierra Leone, W Liberia. The boundary between the Central and Western Bushbuck has not been clearly established.

HABITAT Forests, and forest edges, found near free water.

STATUS Least Concern. Estimated population in the late 1990s in Senegal was more than 50,000 animals in protected areas.

PHOTO CREDITS *Johannes Pfleiderer* and *Bret Newton*, Gladys Porter Zoo, Brownsville (USA). ♂: *Pierre de Chabannes*, Gladys Porter Zoo, Brownsville (USA).

Central Bushbuck

TRAGELAPHUS PHALERATUS

BL: 114-165 cm (♂), 120-130 cm (♀). SH: 65-102 cm (♂), 75-85 cm (♀). TL: 21-30 cm. W: 32-115 kg (♂), 32-42 kg (♀). HL: 23 cm (♂). Very similar to Western Bushbuck. Reddish-brown coat, without any blackish suffusion except on the withers. Upper longitudinal band may be absent, especially on females. Lower longitudinal band present. Seven to 10 distinct transverse stripes. White dorsal crest. Several haunch spots, along with a white mark on the throat. White markings on the legs. Tail relatively short, long haired, and bushy, dorsally colored the same as the back, white underneath, and usually tipped in black. The keeled horns are short, nearly straight, only diverging a little, strongly keeled, with 1 or slightly more twists. Females smaller, a lighter shade, with more conspicuous stripes and spots, and without horns.

♀

Young

♂

Juvenile

Tragelaphus phaleratus

OTHER NAMES Harnessed Antelope, Kewel. *French*: Guib du Congo, antilope harnaché, guib. *German*: Kongo-Schirrantilope, Buschbock. *Spanish*: Bushbuck central, antílope jeroglífico. *Russian*: Центральноафриканский бушбок.

SUBSPECIES Monotypic. Belongs to the "scriptus" group. Formerly considered a subspecies of *T. scriptus* (Bushbuck). Includes *knutsoni, pictus, signatus,* and *punctatus.*

SIMILAR SPECIES Bongo is larger and stockier, dark russet red in color, with black legs with white patches.

REPRODUCTION *Gestation*: 180 days. *Young per Birth*: 1. *Weaning*: 4-6 months. *Sexual Maturity*: 11-12 months. *Life Span*: 12 years. Breeding occurs throughout the year. Non-territorial polygynous breeders.

BEHAVIOR *Family Group*: Usually solitary, sometimes in pairs. *Diet*: Grasses as well as leaves, buds, and fruit. Routinely drinks water. Considered as agricultural pests, eating various crops by night. *Main Predators*: Leopard, lion, spotted hyena. Active throughout the 24 hours of the day, although they can be nocturnal in some areas. While foraging, they remain close to shrubby cover. ♀ are organized in matrilineal clans, and ♂ are territorial, displaying agonistic behavior toward one another throughout the year. Lateral displays of varying intensity are the most common behavior, but overt aggression, threat displays, chasing, and escorting may be seen. ♀ also show aggressive behavior toward each other, most commonly with head butting, snout thrusting, neck winding, and jumping toward one another with raised head and ears held back. Mutual grooming is common among ♀. Savanna densities have been recorded at over 30 animals per km², while forest densities are much smaller, only 4 animals per km². ♂ compete fiercely for ♀ in estrus, but they are not territorial.

DISTRIBUTION *Native:* Benin, Burkina Faso, Cameroon, Central African Republic, Chad, Congo, DR Congo, Equatorial Guinea, Gabon, Ghana, Côte d'Ivoire, Mali, Niger, Nigeria, Togo. Found in S Mali, Côte d'Ivoire, central and S Burkina Faso, Ghana, Togo, Benin, extreme SW and SE Niger, Nigeria (except the extreme N), central and N Cameroon, S Chad, W and central Central African Republic, and probably extreme NW DR Congo, Equatorial Guinea, Gabon, S Congo, and extreme SW DR Congo (N of the Congo River). The boundary between the Central and Nile Bushbuck has not been clearly established.

HABITAT Riverine forest. More open savanna at night. Usually found near free water.

STATUS Least Concern.

PHOTO CREDITS ♂: *Bart Visser,* Mole NP (Ghana). Head ♂ and young: *Jonas Van de Voorde,* Parc National de la Pendjari (Benin). ♀: *Michael Lorentz,* Zakouma NP (Chad). Head ♀: *Marcin Bartosz Czarnoleski Trzaska,* Mole NP (Ghana). Juvenile: *Brendan van Son* and *AJ,* Mole NP (Ghana).

Nile Bushbuck
TRAGELAPHUS BOR

BL: 122-131 cm (♂), 118-126 cm (♀). SH: 68-91 cm (♂), 61-85 cm (♀). TL: 19-24 cm. W: 40-80 kg (♂), 24-60 kg (♀). HL: 23-25 cm (♂). Pale yellowish-brown coat, more ocher than in other Bushbucks, with little dark suffusion of the hairs on the neck and less red than in the Western and Central Bushbucks. Up to 10 transverse stripes, less distinct, especially on old individuals. Black dorsal crest. Only 1 longitudinal band, usually broken into spots and streaks. Several haunch spots, along with a white mark on the throat. White markings on the legs. Tail relatively short, long haired, and bushy, dorsally colored the same as the back, white underneath, and usually tipped in black. The horns are short, nearly straight, only diverging a little, strongly keeled, with 1 or slightly more twists. Female smaller and without horns.

♀

♂

♂
Juvenile

Tragelaphus bor

OTHER NAMES *French*: Guib du Nil. *German*: Sudan-Schirrantilope. *Spanish*: Bushbuck del Nilo. *Russian*: Нильский бушбок.

SUBSPECIES Monotypic. Belongs to the "scriptus" group. Formerly considered a subspecies of *T. scriptus* (Bushbuck). Includes *cottoni, dodingae, laticeps, locorinae, meridionalis,* and *uellensis*.

SIMILAR SPECIES Similar to the Central Bushbuck, but larger, with a lighter ground color and some stripes broken up into rows of spots.

REPRODUCTION *Gestation*: 180 days. *Young per Birth:* 1. *Weaning*: 4-6 months. *Sexual Maturity:* 11-12 months. *Life Span:* 12 years. Breeding occurs throughout the year. Courtship by the ♂ involves a form of lateral display without the dorsal crest or tail erect or the back arched, often while uttering an infant-like twittering call. ♂ will approach a ♀ rather quickly in a low-stretch position with the horns held back on the neck. Genital and urine testing, followed by lip curling of the ♂, are common. The ♂ rests his chin on the back and hindquarters of the ♀ before mounting. The single young lies hidden away from its mother for the first few weeks of life and selects its hiding places.

BEHAVIOR *Family Group*: Usually solitary, sometimes in pairs. *Diet*: Grasses as well as leaves, buds, and fruit. *Main Predators*: Leopard, lion, spotted hyena. Active throughout the 24 hours of the day, although they can be nocturnal in some areas. While foraging, they remain close to shrubby cover. ♀ are organized in matrilineal clans, and ♂ are territorial, displaying agonistic behavior toward one another throughout the year. Lateral displays of varying intensity are the most common behavior, but overt aggression, threat displays, chasing, and escorting may be seen. ♀ also show aggressive behavior toward each other, most commonly with head butting, snout thrusting, neck winding, and jumping toward one another with raised head and ears held back. Mutual grooming is common among ♀.

DISTRIBUTION *Native*: Central African Republic, DR Congo, Kenya, Rwanda, Sudan, Uganda. Nile Bushbuck is found in E Central African Republic, NE DR Congo, S Sudan, W Uganda, NW Kenya, and Rwanda; more research is needed to clearly establish the ranges of the Nile and the Central Bushbuck.

HABITAT Forest thickets and grasslands, but it may be found in a variety of habitats and at various elevations.

STATUS Least Concern.

PHOTO CREDITS Murchison Falls NP (Uganda). Juvenile: *David Cook*, Murchison Falls NP (Uganda). Head ♂: *Andrew Krohnberg*, Lake Mburo NP (Uganda).

Abyssinian Bushbuck
TRAGELAPHUS DECULA

BL: 109-145 cm (♂), 114-132 cm (♀). SH: 65-76 cm. TL: 19-24 cm. W: 35-45 kg. HL: 25 cm (♂). A smaller Bushbuck, ocher to yellow or sandy-brown colored, with a black dorsal crest. There usually is an upper horizontal white stripe and a lower row of spots, but sometimes these are diminished or lacking. Old animals may have only a few haunch spots and 2 white spots, 1 below the eye and the other on the lower jaw. Underparts are darker. Fully haired neck, with a white throat patch, and sometimes a white breast patch. Fronts of forelegs are white. Tail relatively short, long haired, and bushy, white underneath. Keeled horns, found only in males, nearly straight, with only 1 or slightly more twists. Female smaller and without horns.

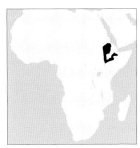

Tragelaphus decula

OTHER NAMES Lake Tana Bushbuck, Decula Antelope, Ethiopian Bushbuck. *French*: Guib decula. *German*: Äthiopien-Schirrantilope. *Spanish*: Bushbuck del Tana. *Russian*: Абиссинский бушбок.

SUBSPECIES Monotypic. Belongs to the "scriptus" group. Formerly considered a subspecies of *T. scriptus* (Bushbuck). Bushbucks that are thought to be hybrids between the lowland Abyssinian and montane Menelik forms are known to occur in the Rift Valley and perhaps elsewhere.

REPRODUCTION *Gestation*: 180 days. *Young per Birth*: 1. *Weaning*: 4-6 months. *Sexual Maturity*: 11-12 months. *Life Span*: 12 years. No specific information is available for this species, but probably similar to other Bushbuck. Breeding occurs throughout the year.

BEHAVIOR *Family Group*: Usually solitary, sometimes in pairs. *Diet*: Grasses as well as leaves, buds, and fruit. *Main Predators*: Leopard, lion, spotted hyena. No specific information is available for this species, but probably similar to other Bushbuck. Active throughout the 24 hours of the day, although they can be nocturnal in some areas. While foraging, they remain close to shrubby cover. ♀ are organized in matrilineal clans, and ♂ are territorial, displaying agonistic behavior toward one another throughout the year. Lateral displays of varying intensity are the most common behavior, but overt aggression, threat displays, chasing, and escorting may be seen. ♀ also show aggressive behavior toward each other, most commonly with head butting, snout thrusting, neck winding, and jumping toward one another with raised head and ears held back. Mutual grooming is common among ♀.

DISTRIBUTION *Native*: Djibouti, Eritrea, Ethiopia, Sudan. Found throughout Ethiopia, with the exception of the Gambella region in the extreme W, the montane habitat of the Menelik's Bushbuck, and the Juba and Webi Shebeli drainages in the SE. Also found in S Eritrea, SW Djibouti, extreme SE Sudan, and probably Somalia.

HABITAT Eritrean Sahelian Savanna and Somali Bushland and thicket ecoregions, usually near free water.

STATUS Least Concern. The Abyssinian Bushbuck is one of the least known species of Bushbuck.

PHOTO CREDITS Based on photos by *Jesús Gabán Bravo,* Mago NP, Omo Valley (Ethiopia).

Chobe Bushbuck

TRAGELAPHUS ORNATUS

BL: 117-145 (♂), 114-132 cm (♀). SH: 64-100 cm (♂), 61-85 cm (♀). TL: 19-24 cm. W: 40-80 kg (♂), 24-60 kg (♀). HL: 30 cm (♂). A medium-sized antelope, robustly built, slightly higher at the rump than at the shoulder. Males are brownish gray in color, have a rich dark rufous coat, becoming black on withers. Dorsal crest white. Six to 8 white transverse stripes and many haunch spots, but longitudinal bands are faint or represented by a row of spots. The outer sides of the legs are blackish above the knees and hocks and reddish below. The inner sides of the legs are white, with a broad black garter above the knees and hocks. There is a white stripe from the knees and hocks to the pasterns. The bushy tail is the same color as the back and white underneath, and usually has a black tip. The horns are short, nearly straight, only diverging a little, strongly keeled, with 1 tight twist. Females are pale red brown, have as few as 3 transverse stripes, and are smaller and without horns.

♀

Young

♂

Tragelaphus ornatus

OTHER NAMES *French*: Guib du Chobé. *German*: Sambia-Schirrantilope. *Spanish*: Bushbuck de Chobe. *Russian*: Чобский бушбок.

SUBSPECIES Monotypic. Belongs to the "sylvaticus" group. Formerly considered a subspecies of *T. scriptus* (Bushbuck).

SIMILAR SPECIES Western, Central, and Nile Bushbuck are more reddish with conspicuous white stripes and without any blackish suffusion except on the withers. Menelik and Cape Bushbuck are darker and less spotted. Nile and Lake Tana Bushbuck are more ocher.

REPRODUCTION *Gestation*: 180 days. *Young per Birth*: 1. *Weaning*: 6 months. *Sexual Maturity*: 11-12 months. *Life Span:* 12 years. Breeding peaks in April-May, at the end of the rainy season, and births are in October-November. The single young lies hidden away from its mother for the first few weeks of life.

BEHAVIOR *Family Group*: Usually solitary or in mother-offspring pairs. *Diet*: A variety of shrubs, legumes, and other plants. *Main Predators*: Leopard, lion, crocodile. Crepuscular and nocturnal, and spend much of the day resting and ruminating in forest cover. Using trails through dense jungle, the Bushbuck ranges through a restricted home area, which may be only a few hundred meters across. These home ranges overlap extensively, and it has been noted that the greater the population density, the smaller these home ranges are. ♂ compete fiercely for ♀ in estrus, but they are not territorial. Confrontations between ♂ are composed of displaying and charging, followed by the locking of horns and vigorous twisting in an attempt to throw the opponent off balance. Stabbing with the horns has also been noted. The Bushbuck is an excellent jumper, and swims well. The call resembles the bark of a dog.

DISTRIBUTION *Native*: Angola, Botswana, Burundi, DR Congo, Malawi, Mozambique, Namibia, Tanzania, Zambia, Zimbabwe. Found in S DR Congo, W Burundi, W Tanzania, Angola (except extreme SW), Zambia, Malawi, extreme NW and W-central Mozambique, NE Namibia (Caprivi Strip); N Botswana, and N Zimbabwe.

HABITAT Forest cover and forest edge, and areas that provide dense cover. Usually found near free water, which may be as much a reflection of their preferred forested habitats thriving near water as a physiological need.

STATUS Least Concern. It may be expanding in the equatorial forest zone as clearing for settlement and wood products opens the closed canopy, but numbers of the Chobe Bushbuck may be the lowest of any Bushbuck species, and poaching pressure may be a primary cause.

PHOTO CREDITS ♀: *Regine Mosimann,* Nyika NP (Malawi). Head ♀: *Berit Christophersen* (Zambia). ♂: *Syaolyao Cska*, South Luangwa (Zambia). Head ♂: *John Ramatsui* (Zambia). Young: *Robert Muckley*, South Luangwa (Zambia) and *John Leverton*, Kaingo (Zambia).

Cape Bushbuck
TRAGELAPHUS SYLVATICUS

BL: 117-145 cm (♂), 114-132 cm (♀). SH: 64-100 cm (♂), 61-85 cm (♀). TL: 19-24 cm. W: 40-80 kg (♂), 24-60 kg (♀). HL: 25-55 cm (♂). A medium-sized antelope, larger than other Bushbucks. Great variation in color and patterning: old males deep brown to blackish brown, with grayish sides and more chestnut above, with only a few spots on the hindquarters and perhaps the belly, and little or no trace of transverse or longitudinal stripes. Head lighter brown, with a dark brown forehead and the usual black nose stripe, with 2 white suborbital spots. White mark on the throat, and white spots, usually indistinct, on the face and haunches. Bushy tail, relatively short, white underneath. Horns short, nearly straight, only diverging a little, strongly keeled, with 1 tight twist. Female smaller and without horns, dark fawn color with similar white markings, tending to be paler on the shoulders and forelegs.

♀

Young

♂

Juvenile

♂

coat variation

Tragelaphus sylvaticus

OTHER NAMES Imbabala. *French*: Guib sylvain. *German*: Südliche Schirrantilope. *Spanish*: Bushbuck meridional. *Russian*: Капский бушбок. *Afrikaans*: Bosbok. *Swahili*: Mbawala, pongo. *Ndebele*: Imbabala. *Xhosa*: Ungece. *Shona*: Dsoma. *Sepedi*: Pabala. *Sesotho*: Pabala. *Setswana*: Serelebotlhoko kurunku. *Zulu*: Imbabala. *Yoruba*: Igala. *Zanda*: Gdodi. *Maasai*: Olpua.

SUBSPECIES Monotypic. Belongs to the "sylvaticus" group. Formerly considered a subspecies of *T. scriptus* (Bushbuck). Includes *barkeri* (Giant or Barker's Bushbuck), *brunneus* (W of Mount Kenya), *dama, delamerei* (Maasai Bushbuck, NW of Mount Kenya), *dianae, eldomae* (Mau Forest), *haywoodi* (Nyeri), *heterochrous, makalae, massaicus* (N Tanzania), *meruensis* (Mount Meru), *roualeynei* (Limpopo Bushbuck), *sassae, simplex,* and *tjaederi* (Nakuru). The Giant or Barker Bushbuck (*barkeri*) is a much larger animal with longer horns and may be a different subspecies.

SIMILAR SPECIES Somewhat similar to the Menelik's Bushbuck, except for the dark forehead. ♀ Bushbuck closely resemble ♀ Sitatunga, though the latter are a bit larger, have longer hair, and are found exclusively in swampy areas. ♀ Mountain Nyala are larger and have more well-developed vertical stripes, and tail is longer.

REPRODUCTION *Gestation*: 180 days. *Young per Birth*: 1. *Weaning*: 6 months. *Sexual Maturity*: 12 months (♀), 12-15 months (♂). *Life Span:* 12 years. Breeding occurs throughout the year, with a slight tendency to be concentrated around rainy periods in April-May and October-November.

BEHAVIOR *Family Group*: Usually solitary, although sometimes in pairs. *Diet*: Selective browser; eats leaves and shoots, buds, flowers, and fruit; may take dry fallen leaves in winter. May associate with baboons and monkeys to feed on fruit and leaves dropped from the trees. *Main Predators*: Leopard, lion, crocodile. Active throughout the 24 hours of the day, although they tend to be nocturnal near human settlements. Using trails through dense jungle, they range through a restricted home area (5 ha for ♂, 2.5 ha for ♀). ♂ will thrash the soil and bushes with their horns and rub their head and neck on bushes and trees. They cannot run very fast and avoid predators by hiding. They will enter water and are strong swimmers. Fights between ♂ can be fatal and they are very aggressive against predators and human hunters.

DISTRIBUTION *Native:* Botswana, Burundi, Kenya, Malawi, Mozambique, Rwanda, South Africa, Sudan, Swaziland, Tanzania, Uganda, Zimbabwe. Found in extreme S Sudan, E Uganda, W Kenya, E Rwanda, E Burundi, Tanzania, S Malawi, Mozambique, central and S Zimbabwe, E Botswana, Swaziland, and E and S South Africa. Barker Bushbuck is found in SE Sudan from Imatong Mountains, Mongalla (Equatoria Province) to Tanzania, and Kenya.

HABITAT Open forests, bush savannas, and dense woodlands, near permanent water. May make short seasonal movements away from permanent water when surface water is temporarily available. Not found in close proximity to Nyala as Nyala will always drive them away.

589

Eastern Coastal Bushbuck
TRAGELAPHUS FASCIATUS

BL: 117-150 cm (♂), 108-150 cm (♀). SH: 64-100 cm (♂), 55-85 cm (♀). TL: 19-24 cm. W: 40-80 kg (♂), 24-60 kg (♀). HL: To 35 cm (♂). Relatively large in body size. Coat color in males is dark gray brown on the back and gray on the sides, with 4-6 white stripes that are generally distinct, a broken longitudinal white flank band, and many white haunch spots. Head lighter brown, with little black on the crown and nose. Chevron between the eyes is usually absent. White mark on the throat. Dorsal neck hairs relatively short. Tail is short and bushy, dorsally colored the same as the back, white underneath. Horns, found only in males, nearly straight, with generally only 1 or slightly more twists. Female smaller and without horns, yellowish brown in color. Young are rufous.

♀

♂

♂
Juvenile

Tragelaphus fasciatus

OTHER NAMES Cumming's Striped Bushbuck, Somali Bushbuck. *French*: Guib côiter. *German*: Ostküsten-Schirrantilope. *Spanish*: Bushbuck de costa. *Russian*: Восточный (прибрежный) бушбок.

SUBSPECIES Monotypic. Belongs to the "sylvaticus" group. Formerly considered a subspecies of *T. scriptus* (Bushbuck). Includes *olivaceus* (SE Kenya) and *reidae* (Nakuru, NE Tanzania).

REPRODUCTION *Gestation*: 180 days. *Young per Birth*: 1. *Weaning*: 6 months. *Sexual Maturity*: 12 months (♀), 12-15 months (♂). *Life Span*: 12 years. There is no specific information available for this species, but probably breeding occurs throughout the year, as in other Bushbucks.

BEHAVIOR *Family Group*: Usually solitary, although sometimes in pairs. *Diet*: Grasses, shrubs, legumes, fruits. *Main Predators*: Leopard, lion, crocodile. Crepuscular and nocturnal. They spend most of the day resting and ruminating in forest cover, often alone, or in mother-offspring pairs. They do not range over a wide area. Home ranges are not exclusive, but individuals do have their exclusive place to rest during the day. Although they are not aggressive to one another, regular social interactions among Bushbucks are largely confined to mother-offspring pairs and ♂-♀ during the rut. They can be observed feeding on fallen fruits under trees where monkeys are foraging. In some locations, they are agricultural pests eating various crops by night.

DISTRIBUTION *Native*: Ethiopia, Kenya, Somalia, Tanzania. Found in SE Ethiopia, Somalia, E Kenya, and NE Tanzania. In Somalia Bushbuck are restricted to riverine habitats along the Jubba and Shabeelle rivers, Lak Bush Bush, and Lak Anole.

HABITAT Forested habitats, usually found near free water.

STATUS Least Concern. Subsistence hunting in SE Kenya reduced this species to very low levels by the mid-1990s. Habitat loss to agriculture and civil unrest has also reduced its numbers in Somalia.

PHOTO CREDITS ♂: *Ariadne Van Zandbergen,* Shimba Hills NP (Kenya). Head ♂: *Frédéric Salein,* coastal Kenya (Kenya). ♀: Shimba Hills NP (Kenya). ♀, Head ♀: *Charles Tomalin*, Mwaluganje Elephant Sanctuary (Kenya). Juvenile: *Joan Egert*, Shimba Hills NP (Kenya).

Menelik's Bushbuck

TRAGELAPHUS MENELIKI

BL: 117-145 (♂), 114-132 cm (♀). SH: 71-76 cm. TL: 19-24 cm. W: 40-80 kg (♂), 24-60 kg (♀). HL: 26-30 cm (♂). A medium-sized Bushbuck. Rather long coat of very dark brown to black hair. Contrasting white patches on throat, base of neck, and inside of legs, and a few white spots on the thighs. Head is reddish brown with a black nose stripe and an imperfect white chevron between the eyes. Dorsal crest is black, with some white. Bushy tail is the same color as the back and white underneath, and usually has a black tip. Short horns, nearly straight, only diverging a little, strongly keeled, with 1 tight twist, usually tipped in black. Females and immature males are reddish in color, with a tendency for the white markings to be more evident than on males.

♀

♂

♂
Juvenile

Tragelaphus meneliki

OTHER NAMES Arussi Bushbuck, Black Bushbuck, Ethiopian Highlands Bushbuck. *French*: Guib de Ménélik. *German*: Hochland-Schirrantilope. *Spanish*: Bushbuck de Menelik. *Russian*: Бушбок Менелика.

SUBSPECIES Monotypic. Belongs to the "sylvaticus" group. Formerly considered a subspecies of *T. scriptus* (Bushbuck). Includes *powelli* (Shoan Bushbuck), having similar white body markings to *meneliki* but a somewhat lighter general color; the ♀ is bright rufous, with a dark suffusion on neck and saddle. Bushbucks that are thought to be hybrids between the montane Menelik's and lowland Abyssinian forms (*T. decula*) are known to occur in the Rift Valley and possibly elsewhere.

SIMILAR SPECIES Coat darker and longer than in other subspecies. Menelik's Bushbuck is somewhat similar in appearance to the mountain races of East African Bushbuck in Kenya and the Cape Bushbuck in South Africa (*T. sylvaticus*). Mountain Nyala is larger, with longer horns, has several white spots on the hindquarters, and a short brown neck mane which continues as a brown and white dorsal crest.

REPRODUCTION *Gestation*: 6 months. *Young per Birth*: 1. *Weaning*: 6 months. *Sexual Maturity*: 11-12 months. *Life Span*: 12 years. Breeding occurs throughout the year. The single young lies hidden away from its mother for the first few weeks of life.

BEHAVIOR *Family Group*: Solitary, in pairs or small family parties of ♀ and young. *Diet*: Grasses as well as leaves, buds, and fruit. *Main Predators*: Leopard, lion, crocodile. They tend to spend the heat of the day lying up in dense bush. They have a loud barking alarm call, sometimes repeated, which can be heard from some distance away, and also a series of grunts. Peak activity is observed in early morning and late afternoon hours with resting peaking during midday. The Bushbuck ranges through a restricted home area, which may be only a few hundred meters across. These home ranges overlap extensively, and it has been noted that the greater the population density, the smaller these home ranges are. ♂ compete fiercely for ♀ in estrus, but they are not territorial. Confrontations between ♂ are composed of displaying and charging, followed by the locking of horns and vigorous twisting in an attempt to throw the opponent off balance. Stabbing with the horns has also been noted. The Bushbuck is an excellent jumper, and swims well.

DISTRIBUTION *Native:* Ethiopia. Endemic to Ethiopia in high-altitude forests of the Chercher, Din Din, Arussi, and Bale mountains, the mountains of W Shoa Province, and high areas in Illubabor Province.

HABITAT Ethiopia's highland forest up to the tree line at 4,000 m.

STATUS Least Concern. No accurate estimate has been made of their total population because of their nocturnal and furtive habits. They are protected within the area of Bale Mountains NP. They are numerous all over their range.

PHOTO CREDITS ♂: *David Beadle*, Dinsho (Ethiopia). ♀: *Graham Ekins* (Ethiopia). Head ♂: *Ariadne Van Zandbergen,* Dinsho, Bale Mountains NP (Ethiopia). Juvenile: *Jon Isaacs* (Ethiopia).

Lowland Nyala

NYALA ANGASII

BL: 135-195 cm. SH: 80-120 cm. TL: 40-55 cm. W: 55-140 kg. HL: 60-83 cm (♂). A large but slenderly built and very narrow antelope. Extreme sexual dimorphism. Females and immature males with short-haired, rufous-chestnut coat, with 10 or more vertical white stripes on the sides. White spots on the face, throat, flanks, and thighs. White chevron between the eyes. Bushy tail, white on the underside. Ears large. No horns on females, and no mane on the neck. Males larger, shaggy dark brown to charcoal-gray coat, often with a bluish tinge, enormously developed on the underside, differing in this respect from all other antelopes. The length of this coat generally obscures the torso stripes. Fewer and less conspicuous markings than on females, but there is a bold erectile white dorsal crest. Lower legs orange chestnut, contrasting strongly with the dark coat. Yellow-tipped horns, with 1 to 1-1/2 twists. Young similar to females.

♀

Young

♂

Juvenile

♂

Nyala angasii

OTHER NAMES Common Nyala. *French*: Nyala. *German*: Nyala, Flachlandnyala, Tiefland-Nyala. *Spanish*: Niala. *Russian*: Ньяла. *Afrikaans*: Nyalabosbok, inyala. *Swahili*: Litagayezi. *Ndebele*: Inyala. *Zulu*: Inyala inxala. *Setswana*: Tsama. *Swati*: Litagayezi, inyala. *Xitsonga*: Imbala-intendi, nyale.

SUBSPECIES Monotypic. Often placed in the genus *Tragelaphus*.

SIMILAR SPECIES Mountain Nyala was named for its similarity to the Nyala but is now considered a closer relative of the Kudu.

REPRODUCTION *Gestation*: 220 days. *Young per Birth*: 1, rarely 2. *Weaning*: 6 months. *Sexual Maturity*: 11-12 months (♀), 18 months (♂), although they are not socially mature until 5 years of age. *Life Span*: 16 years. Breeding is most frequent in the spring and autumn, with births occurring in the following autumn and spring. Mating opportunities for ♂ are decided through dominance behavior. Calves are left alone after birth, lying still in the grass to avoid detection by predators. The mother returns to her calf to nurse throughout this 3-week period.

BEHAVIOR *Family Group*: Single-sex and mixed troops of 2-10 individuals, old ♂ solitary. *Diet*: Leaves, fruits, and grasses. *Main Predators*: Leopard, lion, Cape hunting dog. Nyala are very shy, and are very cautious when approaching open spaces. Most sightings of this species are at water holes. Most active during the early morning and late afternoon, resting in thick brush during the hottest times of the day. The alarm call is a sharp, dog-like bark. Individual home ranges average 0.65 km² for ♂ and 0.83 km² for ♀. These individual areas overlap extensively, and there is no indication of territoriality. Juvenile ♂ look like ♀; this may protect them from the dominant ♂, and allow them to grow up under the protection of the herd. The alarm call is a deep bark.

DISTRIBUTION *Native*: Malawi, Mozambique, South Africa, Swaziland, Zimbabwe. *Introduced*: Botswana, Namibia. Its natural range comprises SE Africa from the Lower Shire Valley in Malawi through Mozambique and Zimbabwe to E South Africa and Swaziland. Introduced to Namibia in the N commercial farming districts. It does not occur naturally in Botswana, but some of the Tuli block farms in the E have been colonized as a result of the spread of Nyala from populations introduced to farms in the adjacent region of South Africa. In Swaziland, it was extinct by the 1950s, but has been successfully reintroduced.

HABITAT Thickets in savanna woodland and riverine bush, although not dependent on water. Widely translocated.

STATUS Least Concern. South Africa has at least 30,000 animals, with 25,000 in KwaZulu-Natal, more than 1,000 on protected areas and ranches in Swaziland, not more than 3,000 in Mozambique, and 1,000 in Zimbabwe, while numbers in Malawi have fallen to about 1,500. Namibia has the smallest population, about 250. Over 80% of the total population is protected, mostly in South African protected areas, and 10 to 15% occur on private land. They mostly occur in South Africa due to the high demand for adult ♂ as game trophies.

PHOTO CREDITS ♂: *Morten Dreier*, KwaZulu-Natal (South Africa). Head ♂: *Ruslou Koorts*, Zwartkloof Reserve (South Africa). ♀ and head ♀: *Nico Smit*, Mkuze Reserve (South Africa). Young: *Spacebirdy*, Tiergarten Schönbrunn (Austria). Juvenile: *Rowley Taylor*, Tomali (Malawi) and *Gary Meade*, Thanda Reserve (South Africa). 595

Asian Wild Water Buffalo

BUBALUS ARNEE

BL: 240-300 cm. SH: 150-190 cm. TL: 60-100 cm. W: 700-1,200 kg. A large, heavily built animal, without a pronounced hump. Skin color light gray to black, usually mud covered, with rather long hairs, but many parts are hairless, particularly with age. Neck large and thick, with a white V running across the front. Forehead narrow, ears large. No dewlap on the throat. Tail has a bushy end. The 4 legs have an off-white coloring that runs down from knees to hooves. Hooves large and splayed. Horns in both sexes, heavy at the base, triangular in cross section, and widely spreading along the outer edges, exceeding in size the horns of any other living Bovid. Horns curve like the crescent moon with a narrow tip. Wild Water Buffalo are larger and heavier than Domestic Buffalo, and have large horns with a larger curve. Females smaller than males, with horns rounder in cross section and lighter, but may be longer.

Juvenile

♂

spp. *fulvus*

♀

596

Bubalus arnee fulvus

Bubalus arnee arnee

Bubalus arnee theerapati

OTHER NAMES Asian Water Buffalo, Asiatic Buffalo, Arni. *French*: Buffle d´eau. *German*: Arni, Wasserbüffel. *Spanish*: Búfalo de agua. *Russian*: Азиатский водяной буйвол.

SUBSPECIES The wild forms of Water Buffalo are considered under *B. arnee*, reserving *B. bubalis* for the domestic and feral forms. Subspecies include: *B. a. arnee* (found in much of India and Nepal), *B. a. fulvus* (Assam and neighboring areas), *B. a. theerapati* (SE Asia), *B. a. migona* (Sri Lanka).

SIMILAR SPECIES *B. a. fulvus* is the largest subspecies. *B. a. arnee* is smaller, darker, with more contrasting white below the knees; the tail reaches the hocks, and the muzzle is white. *B. a. theerapati* is smaller and has a smaller horn span.

REPRODUCTION *Gestation*: 324 days. *Young per Birth*: 1, rarely 2. *Weaning*: 6-9 months. *Sexual Maturity*: 18 months (♂), 36 months (♀). *Life Span*: 25 years. Seasonal breeders in most of their range, typically in October and November. Some populations breed year-round. Dominant ♂ mate with the ♀ of a clan who subsequently drive them off.

BEHAVIOR *Family Group*: Herds with ♀ and young led by an old ♀; adult ♂ form bachelor groups of up to 10 individuals, with older ♂ often solitary, and spend the dry season apart from the female clans. ♂ move into ♀ areas during the breeding season. *Diet:* Grazers, feeding mainly on true grasses when available, such as scutch grass, and sedges, but they also eat herbs, fruits, and bark, as well as browsing on trees and shrubs. They also feed on crops, including rice, sugarcane, and jute, sometimes causing considerable damage. *Main Predators:* Tiger, Asian black bear. Both diurnal and nocturnal. Adult ♀ and their young form stable clans of as many as 30 individuals that have home ranges of 170-1,000 ha, including areas for resting, grazing, wallowing, and drinking. Several clans form a herd of 30-500 animals that gather at resting areas. During the day they usually bathe in the mud or sleep in the tall grasses. Caked mud on the skin helps to alleviate the heat and it also serves to protect the Wild Water Buffalo from insects.

DISTRIBUTION *Native*: Bhutan, Cambodia, India, Myanmar, Nepal, Thailand. *Possibly Extinct*: Vietnam. *Regionally Extinct*: Bangladesh, Indonesia, Laos. Formerly widespread from E parts of Nepal and India E throughout Indochina, including the Malayan Peninsula. It has become extinct over much of its original range from loss of habitat to agriculture and domestic cattle diseases, but a few herds, which are believed to be descended from native stock, are still found in reserves or remote areas of Nepal, NE India, and Indochina.

HABITAT Restricted to remnant and widely disjunct riverine areas and associated swamps, lowland grasslands, and lowland forests.

CONSERVATION STATUS Endangered. Estimated population of Wild Water Buffalo is 4,000 animals, but this may include feral and hybrid Buffalo. In fact, it is possible that no true wild specimens exist anymore. Crossbreeding with Domestic Buffalo as well as shrinkage and destruction of habitat are considered major threats.

PHOTO CREDITS ♂: *Susan Roehl*, Kaziranga NP (India). Head and juvenile: *Raghunandan Kulkarni*, Kaziranga NP (India). ♀: *Raymond J. C. Cannon,* Kaziranga NP (India).

Sri Lankan Wild Water Buffalo

BUBALUS ARNEE MIGONA

BL: 240-300 cm. SH: 150-190 cm. TL: 60-100 cm. W: 700-900 kg. A large, heavily built animal, with smaller horns than other subspecies. Skin color gray to black. Moderately long, coarse, and sparse hair directed forward from the haunches to the long and narrow head. Tuft on the forehead, and ears comparatively small. Neck large and thick, usually with no white markings across the front. Forehead narrow. Tail has a bushy end. Legs may have an off-white coloring that runs down from knees to hooves like socks. Hooves large and splayed. Horns in both sexes, thicker and usually shorter in males. In females horns are thin and wide set, with an up-curved crescent shape. Horn shape is very variable. Males larger and more muscular than the females. Calf is lighter brown in color, with its skin covered in soft hair.

Juvenile

♂

♀

horn variation

Bubalus arnee migona

OTHER NAMES Sri Lankan Asian Water Buffalo. *French*: Buffle du Sri Lanka. *German*: Sri Lanka Wasserbüffel. *Spanish*: Búfalo de agua de Sri Lanka. *Russian*: Цейлонский водяной буйвол.

SUBSPECIES The wild forms of Water Buffalo are considered under *B. arnee*, reserving *B. bubalis* for the domestic and feral forms. Subspecies include: *B. a. arnee* (found in much of India and Nepal), *B. a. fulvus* (Assam and neighboring areas), *B. a. theerapati* (SE Asia), *B. a. migona* (Sri Lanka). With the intrusion of the feral Buffalo into the deeper recesses of the jungle, crossbreeding may occur and the pure wild strain may gradually get diluted.

SIMILAR SPECIES Much darker, larger, and hairier than the Domestic Buffalo, horns stouter with the last third of their length curved forward, limbs and tail more elongated, and the stride longer and smoother than the shuffling waddle of the shorter-limbed domesticated animal, which is gray in color. ♂ with heavy forequarters with a prominent ridge extending backward from the high withers, neck with mane wrinkles. Wild calves and many hybrids are of a coppery hue, whereas the young of the domesticated animals are light gray. Hoof prints and mounds of dung are much larger than those of the domestic animal. Sri Lankan Wild Water Buffalo resembles the Indian Wild Water Buffalo, with a smaller horn span.

REPRODUCTION *Gestation*: 300-340 days. *Young per Birth*: 1, rarely 2. *Weaning*: 6-9 months. *Sexual Maturity*: 18 months (♂), 36 months (♀). *Life Span*: 25 years. ♀ gives birth in seclusion having left the herd temporarily. The mother looks after the calf for 6-9 months and will defend it aggressively. During this period the calf is weaned and then becomes a part of the herd.

BEHAVIOR *Family Group*: Herd with ♀ and their offspring; ♂ move out and either form ♂ groups or live alone; mature ♂ live alone. *Diet*: Grazers, feeding mainly on true grasses. *Main Predators*: Leopard, bear, tiger. They have a reputation of being dangerous, and will become aggressive if cornered or wounded. ♂ are highly territorial and mark out their areas distinctly. ♂ live a solitary life in their territories, and will fight when another ♂ invades their territories, by charging and butting it. Generally, one charge is sufficient to drive the intruder away. However, if the intrusion is during the mating season the two ♂ will continue to fight. The clatter of their horns when they meet at speed is quite loud. It is a strong swimmer and seems to prefer the muddier pools; it gets itself caked in mud to get rid of any ticks or parasites.

DISTRIBUTION *Native*: Sri Lanka. The bulk of the free-roaming Buffalo in Sri Lanka are feral domestic ones that live in large unstable herds.

HABITAT Restricted to jungles of the low-country dry zone. They can be seen serenely lying in any type of water body, such as reservoirs, rivers, streams, and canals.

CONSERVATION STATUS Endangered. Threatened by interbreeding with Domestic Buffalo.

PHOTO CREDITS ♂: *Peter Nijenhuis*, Udawalawe NP (Sri Lanka). Head ♂: *Gihan Kanchana*, Yala NP (Sri Lanka). Juvenile: *Elizabeth Young*, Bundala NP (Sri Lanka). ♀: *Jon Bower*, Yala NP (Sri Lanka). Head ♀: *Asiri Wanigarathne*, Yala NP (Sri Lanka) and *Shaanea Mendis*.

Domestic Swamp Buffalo
BUBALUS BUBALIS VAR. KERABAU

BL: 240-300 cm. SH: 127-137 cm (♂), 124-129 cm (♀). TL: 60-100 cm. W: 420-700 kg (♂), 400-425 kg (♀). A large, heavily built animal, with a deep, massive barrel-shaped body. Smaller than Domestic River Buffalo. Short, heavy-boned legs. Skin color is slate gray or brown with a dove-gray chevron on the chest and gray markings on the head and lower legs. Adults with very little hair on their bodies. Pink-skinned white individuals occur as well. Short face with flat forehead, prominent eyes, wide muzzle, and long neck. Horns present in both sexes, triangular in cross section, sweeping back in a wide crescent at forehead level. Tail has a bushy end. Females smaller than males. There are no clear differences between breeds except for body size.

Juvenile

Young

Bubalus bubalis var. *kerabau*

OOTHER NAMES Domestic Water Buffalo, Carabao. *French*: Buffle d'eau. *German*: Wasserbüffel, Sumpfbüffel. *Spanish*: Búfalo de agua. *Russian*: Домашний (болотный) буйвол. *Malay*: Kerbau. *Indonesian*: Kerbau, mahesa, moending. *Thai*: Kwai, marid. *Khmer*: Krabey, beng. *Lao*: Bahnar. *Filipino*: Carabao.

SUBSPECIES The wild forms of Water Buffalo are considered under *B. arnee*, reserving *B. bubalis* for the domestic and feral forms, although they are the same species. There are two general breed groups or subspecies of Domestic Buffalo: the River type (*bubalis*), and the Swamp type (*kerabau*). The River type has 50 chromosomes, while the Swamp type has only 48, but fertile offspring occur between the two. It does not hybridize with cattle, which have 60 chromosomes. The breeds of Swamp Buffalo are not as clearly defined as in the River Buffalo.

REPRODUCTION *Gestation*: 300-340 days. *Young per Birth*: 1, rarely 2. *Weaning*: 6-9 months. *Sexual Maturity*: 18 months (♂), 36 months (♀). *Life Span*: 25 years. Seasonal breeders in most of their range, typically in October and November. Some populations breed year-round. Dominant ♂ mate with the ♀ of a clan who subsequently drive them off.

BEHAVIOR *Family Group*: 10-30 individuals. *Diet*: Grazers, feeding mainly on true grasses when available, such as scutch grass, and sedges, but they also eat herbs, fruits, and bark, as well as browsing on trees and shrubs. They also feed on crops, including rice, sugarcane, and jute, sometimes causing considerable damage. *Main Predators*: Tiger, Asian black bear. Water Buffalo were domesticated approximately 5,000 years ago in the Indus Valley, in China, and in Mesopotamia. It is an integral component of traditional Asian agriculture through contributions to meat, draft power, and milk, and thus has a pivotal role in agriculture in several Asian countries. Docile and gentle creatures, rarely make any noise. Swamp Buffalo is mainly used as a draft animal and produces very little milk, so it is rarely kept strictly for dairy purposes. Swamp Buffalo is better adapted for work under humid conditions than River Buffalo. Swamp Buffalo prefers stagnant water pools and mud holes.

DISTRIBUTION Widespread in tropical and subtropical countries with hot and humid climates. River Buffalo are found more in the W and reside in Indochina, the Mediterranean, Egypt, and parts of South and Central America. Swamp Buffalo are more easterly in distribution and inhabit China, Indochina, and SE Asia, as well as Australia.

HABITAT Low-lying alluvial grasslands and their surrounds, with riparian forests and woodlands also used.

CONSERVATION STATUS Domesticated. Total Domestic Buffalo population can be estimated to be roughly 170 million animals, of which approximately 97% are in Asian countries.

PHOTO CREDITS ♂: *Alan Hill*, Port Lympne Zoo (UK). Head ♂: *Tomoko Ichishima*, Tama Zoo (Japan). Young: *Bela Lund (Mouseshadows)*, Yangshuo, Guangxi (China). ♀: West Midland Safari Park (UK). Juvenile: *Saifon Singsena*, Sakon Nakhon (Thailand).

Domestic River Buffalo

BUBALUS BUBALIS VAR. BUBALIS

BL: 240-300 cm. SH: 133-142 cm. TL: 60-100 cm. W: 450-1,000 kg. A large, heavily built animal, smaller than Wild Water Buffalo. Larger, longer bodied, longer legged, and darker than Swamp Buffalo. Skin color is black to dark brown, without white markings, with moderately long, coarse, and sparse hair. Sacrum more prominent than the withers. Tail has a bushy end. Horns present in both sexes, usually curving back from a strongly convex forehead and often tightly curled. Females smaller than males. Each breed may display unique characteristics. Murrah has tightly curved horns. Jafarabadi has heavy horns, inclined to droop at each side of the neck and then turning up at thepoints.

♀

Murrah breed

Jafarabadi breed

Juvenile

♂

Bubalus bubalis var. bubalis

OTHER NAMES Water Buffalo, River Buffalo. *French*: Buffle d'eau. *German*: Wasserbüffel, Sumpfbüffel. *Spanish*: Búfalo de agua. *Russian*: Домашний (речной) буйвол.

SUBSPECIES The wild forms of Water Buffalo are considered under *B. arnee*, reserving *B. bubalis* for the domestic and feral forms, although they are the same species. There are two general breed groups or subspecies of Domestic Buffalo: the River type (*bubalis*), and the Swamp type (*kerabau*). The River type has 50 chromosomes, while the Swamp type has only 48, but fertile offspring occur between the two. It does not hybridize with cattle, which have 60 chromosomes. River Buffalo has given rise to a number of highly specialized breeds such as the Murrah in India, and the Nili Ravi and Kundi in Pakistan.

REPRODUCTION *Gestation*: 300-340 days. *Young per Birth*: 1, rarely 2. *Weaning*: 6-9 months. *Sexual Maturity*: 18 months (♂), 36 months (♀). *Life Span*: 25 years. Seasonal breeders in most of their range, typically in October and November. Some populations breed year-round. Dominant ♂ mate with the ♀ of a clan who subsequently drive them off.

BEHAVIOR *Family Group*: 10-30 individuals. *Diet*: Grazers, feeding mainly on true grasses when available, such as scutch grass, and sedges, but they also eat herbs, fruits, and bark, as well as browsing on trees and shrubs. They also feed on crops, including rice, sugarcane, and jute, sometimes causing considerable damage. *Main Predators*: Tiger, Asian black bear. Water Buffalo were domesticated approximately 5,000 years ago in the Indus Valley, in China, and in Mesopotamia, from where it was introduced in Egypt and in Italy, as well as in the Balkans. River Buffalo is mainly used as a dairy animal, while Swamp Buffalo is a draft animal and a meat source. There is an increased interest in the exploitation of Buffalo as a resource for milk production, milk products, and meat; as a consequence, River Buffalo have been introduced in many European countries as well as in Swamp Buffalo–dominated areas. River Buffalo have a preference for clear running water for wallowing, while Swamp Buffalo prefer stagnant water pools and mud holes. They are traditionally managed in domestic conditions together with the calf. Water Buffalo utilize lower-grade roughage and graze a wider range of plants more efficiently than cattle do. Unlike in cattle, feeding concentrates like grain does not cause a Buffalo cow to produce more milk. Instead, intensive feeding tends to cause serious digestive problems for Buffalo that can translate into less, rather than more, milk.

DISTRIBUTION Widespread in tropical and subtropical countries with hot and humid climates. River Buffalo are found more in the W and reside in Indochina, the Mediterranean, Egypt, and parts of South and Central America. Swamp Buffalo are more easterly in distribution and inhabit China, Indochina, and SE Asia, as well as Australia.

HABITAT Low-lying alluvial grasslands and their surrounds, with riparian forests and woodlands also used.

CONSERVATION STATUS Domesticated.

PHOTO CREDITS Murrah: *Kleomarlo*, Philippine Carabao Center (The Philippines). ♀: Tiergarten Schönbrunn (Austria), Swierkocin Zoo (Poland), and *Eric Isselee*. Juvenile: *Chris Morriss* (UK).

Tamaraw
BUBALUS MINDORENSIS

BL: 220 cm. SH: 95-120 cm. TL: 60 cm. W: 200-274 kg. HL: 30-51 cm. A small, stocky Buffalo. Coat is short and rather dense. Adults are grayish black in color, with white markings on the insides of the forelegs, above the eyes, inner ears, and on the throat. Thin tail extending down to about the hocks. Horns, found in both sexes, are relatively straight, backward pointing, and extremely stout. Each horn is very wide and triangular at the base and remains very thick for most of the length; only toward the sharp tips do they become narrower and more rounded in cross section. Females very similar to males in color and horn size, with very little sexual dimorphism. Subadults and juveniles are reddish brown to gray, with a dark dorsal stripe. Calves are generally reddish in color.

Young

Juvenile

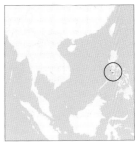

Bubalus mindorensis

OTHER NAMES Mindoro Dwarf Buffalo, Dwarf Water Buffalo. *French*: Tamarau. *German*: Tamarau, Tamaraw, Tamarao, Mindorobüffel. *Spanish*: Tamarao, búfalo de Mindoro. *Russian*: Тамарау, или филиппинский буйвол. *Filipino*: Tamarao, cimmaron, carabao, cabao, tanarau.

SUBSPECIES Monotypic.

SIMILAR SPECIES Within its range, Tamaraw is a distinctive native species. Domestic Water Buffalo tend to be less stocky; their horns grow from the sides of their heads and arc in a C-shape, whereas the horns of the Tamaraw are set close together at the top of the head and grow in a V-shape. Tamaraw may be confused with Anoa because of the whitish markings on the face, neck, and legs, but Tamaraw is larger and has short and thick horns with an outward initial direction, as opposed to the closely approximated and backward-directed horns of Anoa.

REPRODUCTION *Gestation*: 276-315 days. *Young per Birth*: 1. *Life Span*: 20-25 years. Tamaraw tend to give birth during or slightly after the rainy season, from June to November. December and January appear to be prime birthing months for one population. Babies are born reddish brown in color, and slowly darken over 3 or 4 years to the adult coloration. Most youngsters will stay with their mothers until they are between 2 and 4 years old.

BEHAVIOR *Family Group*: Solitary or in pairs rather than in herds. *Diet*: Grasses. *Main Predators*: None, apart from humans. Formerly diurnal and rather tame, but with increasing persecution has become nocturnal, concealed, and aggressive. Basically a forest animal, requiring dense vegetation for resting, water for drinking, and open grazing land. Captive animals tend to be most active in the early morning and late afternoon and evening. Mud wallowing appears to be an important activity, as in Water Buffalo. Although the species is reportedly fierce when cornered, its rarity makes this an unusual occurrence. Among themselves, conflict is usually in the form of animals chasing each other, sometimes over distances as long as a km. The head, especially the horns, is used to signal aggression, being lowered so that the horns are vertical and then shaken from side to side. Said to be exceptionally difficult to keep and breed in captivity.

DISTRIBUTION *Native*: Philippines. Endemic to the Philippine island of Mindoro, where it was formerly widespread. However, the current range is only two or three areas: Mount Iglit-Baco NP, Mount Aruyan/Sablayan, and Mount Calavite Tamaraw Preserve.

HABITAT Areas with mixed forest and grassland, at elevations up to 1,830 m.

STATUS Critically Endangered. In 2006, the total population was estimated at around 300 or fewer individuals, with 40 to 60% of these mature individuals. Legally protected, but heavily poached by farmers, cattle ranchers, and tribesmen.

PHOTO CREDITS ♂: based on photos from The Philippines. Head ♂: *Josef Suchomel* (The Philippines). ♀: *Gregg Yan/WWF* and Gene Pool Farm, Mount Iglit-Baco NP (The Philippines). Head ♂, young, and juvenile: *Tomas Junek,* Mount Iglit-Baco NP (The Philippines).

Lowland Anoa
BUBALUS DEPRESSICORNIS

BL: 122-188 cm. SH: 81-90 cm. TL: 41 cm. W: 200-250 kg. HL: 18-37 cm. A miniature form of Buffalo. Plump body, thick neck, short and stout legs, and long tail. Thick black hide is covered with short, dark brown or black hair, with males tending to be darker than females. Undersides may be light brown. White markings on the head, around the eyes, on the lower jaw, and on the inner surface of the ears. White markings also on lower legs, and a white crescent-shaped throat bib. Forelegs sometimes are white to yellowish white from knee to hoof. Horns short, triangular in cross section, flattened and keeled, found in both sexes; they begin at the edge of the forehead and point diagonally backward. Females with slightly smaller horns, lighter in color than males. Juveniles have a woolly brown to bright rufous-orange coat, but there is much variation.

Juvenile

♀

♂

Young

Bubalus depressicornis

OTHER NAMES Midget Buffalo, Sapiutan. *French*: Anoa de Malaisie. *German*: Anoa, Flachlandanoa, Gemsbüffel. *Spanish*: Anoa de llanura. *Russian*: Равнинный аноа. *Sulawesi*: Anoeang, sapi oetani, boeoeloe toetoe. *Filipino*: Tamaran.

SUBSPECIES Monotypic. The name *B. depressicornis* (Anoa) formerly included *B. depressicornis* (Lowland Anoa), and *B. quarlesi* (Mountain Anoa) as subspecies: these are elevated to full species here.

SIMILAR SPECIES Mountain Anoa is smaller, with longer, woollier hair that molts every February to April, showing faint spots on the head, neck, and limbs.

REPRODUCTION *Gestation*: 275-315 days. *Young per Birth*: 1, rarely 2. *Weaning*: 6-9 months. *Sexual Maturity*: 2-3 years. *Life Span*: 30 years. There does not appear to be an obvious breeding season.

BEHAVIOR *Family Group*: Solitary. *Diet*: Vegetation (aquatic plants, ferns, grasses, saplings, fallen fruit, palm, and ginger). They have been recorded to drink seawater which is thought to fulfill their mineral needs in areas that do not have salt licks or mineral spring water. *Main Predators*: Python, civet (infant). Shy and primarily nocturnal, feeding during the early morning, resting in shade through the hottest parts of the day. It is still unknown whether ♂ are territorial or not. ♂ have been seen marking trees with their horns and scratching the soil after they urinate. The preferred gait is a walk, though when fleeing, they are known to make clumsy leaps. Their bodies are very efficient at crashing through the forest undergrowth, with the short horns being held close to the back in order to avoid being tangled. If cornered or approached within a critical distance, Anoas will turn and attack violently. They are considered very excitable and dangerous to their opponents, as their sharp horns can be used as daggers, especially young ♂ in the breeding season, and ♀ with young. Several fatalities in zoos have resulted from attempts to keep these solitary animals in pairs or groups, with the larger animals disemboweling their counterparts with their horns.

DISTRIBUTION *Native:* Indonesia. Formerly throughout the lowlands of Sulawesi (Celebes). At present, it is found on Sulawesi Island. It remains uncertain whether the two species are sympatric or parapatric in their distribution. Across the island, local distribution of Anoa species remains unclear. Also present in the central and N of Buton Island.

HABITAT Swampy forests; damp, dense undergrowth on the island of Sulawesi.

STATUS Endangered. It occurs in a number of protected areas: Lore Lindu NP, Bogani Nani-Wartabone NP, Tanjung Peropa Nature Reserve on Sulawesi, and Lambu Sango Wildlife Reserve on Buton Island, with an estimated population of 2,500 mature individuals. The captive population was around 125 individuals in zoos as of 1998. Of these, a small number are thought to be Mountain Anoa, although their taxonomic status remains unconfirmed.

PHOTO CREDITS ♂: *The Land*, Marwell Zoo (UK). ♀ and young head: *Arjan Haverkamp*, Artis Zoo (Netherlands). Head ♂: *Arif Wijayanto*, Taman Safari (Indonesia). Head ♀: *Hans De Bisschop*, Antwerp Zoo (Belgium). Young: *Lukas Blazek*. Juvenile: *Richard Southwell*, Chester Zoo (UK).

Mountain Anoa
BUBALUS QUARLESI

BL: 122-153 cm. SH: 71 cm. TL: 20-27 cm. W: 56-150 kg. HL: 15-20 cm. Smallest of the world's wild cattle. Similar in form to the Lowland Anoa. Barrel-shaped body with slender legs. Dark brown or black coat, very woolly. Males usually darker in color than females. Very few markings on the body: on each leg, there are 2 faint light spots just above the hooves, and there are usually no markings on the face or throat. Underparts are lighter than the back, but never white. Ears small and relatively narrow. Tail relatively short, not reaching nearly to the hocks. Relatively short horns, similar in both sexes; smooth, straight, conical, rounded in cross section, and angled toward the rear. Calves are born with a very woolly coat, usually a golden-brown color; it gradually grows darker.

Bubalus quarlesi

OTHER NAMES *French*: Anoa de montagne, anoa de Quarle. *German*: Berganoa, Gebirgsanoa, Zwerganoa. *Spanish*: Anoa de montaña. *Russian*: Горный аноа.

SUBSPECIES Monotypic. Formerly considered a subspecies of *B. depressicornis* (Anoa). There is still debate about whether Lowland Anoa and Mountain Anoa are distinct species.

SIMILAR SPECIES Lowland Anoa is very similar in appearance and inhabits a similar range. Differences of the Mountain Anoa include a thick woolly coat in adults, faint or absent white markings, and round horns, not triangular in cross section.

REPRODUCTION *Gestation*: 276-315 days. *Young per Birth*: 1. *Weaning*: 6-9 months. *Sexual Maturity*: 2-3 years. *Life Span*: 25 years. Mating occurs year-round. ♂ test the receptiveness of ♀ to breeding by using flehmen (lip curl). After a continued sexual parade interspersed with testing the ♀'s urine, the ♂ places his chin on the rump of the ♀ and then mounts. Throughout courting, both ♂ and ♀ make short moos. Although usually solitary animals, they will form a herd when ♀ are about to give birth.

BEHAVIOR *Family Group*: Solitary or in pairs comprising a mother and her offspring, or an adult ♂ and ♀; never associate in larger groups. *Diet*: Leaves and grasses. *Main Predators*: No natural predators, although it is currently highly threatened by humans. Most active during the morning, retreating to sheltered areas during the midday hours. They may seek shelter under large fallen trees, under overhanging rocks, and in spaces beneath tree roots. Mud wallows and pools are used for bathing. The short horns are used in both displays (thrashing at bushes or digging up soil) and in physical altercations: a bump using the front surfaces of the horns is used to show dominance, while in fights sharp upward stabs are used in an attempt to wound the opponent's belly or sides. When excited, Mountain Anoa vocalize with a short "moo."

DISTRIBUTION *Native*: Indonesia. Found only on the islands of Sulawesi and Buton in Indonesia. It remains uncertain whether the two species, *B. depressicornis* and *B. quarlesi*, are sympatric or parapatric in their distribution. Across the island, local distribution of Anoa species remains unclear, as they may occur in forest patches at different altitudes or sympatrically. There are several key protected areas thought to hold significant populations of this species, including Lore Lindu NP, Bogani Nani-Wartabone NP, and Tanjung Peropa Nature Reserve on Sulawesi.

HABITAT Rainforest, areas with dense vegetation, permanent sources of water, and low human disturbance, at altitudes up to 2,000 m.

STATUS Endangered. It is unknown exactly how many Mountain Anoa remain in the wild, due to the challenges of seeing Anoa in dense forest and distinguishing from the similar Lowland Anoa. It is estimated that there are fewer than 2,500 adult Mountain Anoa in the wild.

PHOTO CREDITS ♂: *Pierre de Chabannes*, Ragunan Zoo, Java (Indonesia). Head ♂: *Mirek Heran*, Zoo Decin (Czech Republic). ♀: Zoo Decin (Czech Republic).

Cape Buffalo

SYNCERUS CAFFER

BL: 240-340 cm. SH: 148-175 cm. TL: 50-110 cm. W: 500-900 kg (♂), 350-620 kg (♀). HL: 66-160 cm. The largest of the African Buffalo. Body is heavy-set, with stocky legs, a large head, and short neck. Body sparsely covered with hairs in adults (well haired in younger individuals). Jet-black coat. No distinct markings on the body. Ears are large and tend to droop, and meagerly fringed. Tail long with a terminal tuft. Both male and female have heavy horns, hook shaped, curving first downward and then hooking up and inward. The horns of males are larger than those of females, and in males the bases of the horns expand into a convex boss. Calves black or dark reddish brown.

♀

Juvenile

Young

♂

Syncerus caffer

OTHER NAMES Southern Savanna Buffalo. *French*: Buffle d'Afrique. *German*: Afrikanischer Büffel, Kaffernbüffel. *Spanish*: Búfalo cafre. *Russian*: Капский, или южный буйвол. *Afrikaans:* Buffel. *Swahili*: Nyati, mbogo. *Zulu*: Inyathi. *Maasai*: Olaro. *Sesotho*: Nare. *Swati*: Inyatsi. *Xitsonga*: Nyarhi. *Tshivenda*: Nari. *Lozi*: Nali. *Yei*: Unyati.

SUBSPECIES Monotypic. The name *S. caffer* (African Buffalo) formerly included *S. caffer* (Cape Buffalo), *S. brachyceros* (West African Savanna Buffalo), *S. mathewsi* (Mountain or Virunga Buffalo), and *S. nanus* (Forest Buffalo) as subspecies: these are all elevated to full species here. The African Buffalo exhibits extreme morphological variability, which has led to controversies about the taxonomic status of the species.

REPRODUCTION *Gestation*: 330-346 days. *Young per Birth*: 1, rarely 2. *Weaning*: 6 months. *Sexual Maturity*: 3.5-5 years. *Life Span:* 15-29 years. Breeding from January to April in S Africa with the majority of births occurring in January and February. In E Africa where a double rainy season occurs, the seasonal pattern of breeding is less marked.

BEHAVIOR *Family Group:* Large herds of 50-500 animals, comprising smaller subgroups of bachelor ♂, ♀ and their young, or juveniles. Old ♂ may be solitary. *Diet*: They graze extensively on fresh grass, turning only to herbs, shrubs, and trees when there is a deficiency of grass. *Main Predators*: Lion, spotted hyena, crocodile. During dry seasons mass herds keep to drainage lines and rivers but during moist seasons the herds split into temporary, smaller herds that spread onto larger plains. Family Groups are relatively stable with fixed bonding between mothers and their offspring until an age of 3 years, and they have demarcated home ranges, although large herds may follow a seasonal cyclic movement of mini-migrations. They do not display any territorial behavior. Herds will stick together and may charge as a unit when threatened, a tactic which ensures that predators have difficulty preying on even young and feeble animals. Ox-peckers and cattle egrets are birds which frequently accompany them, feeding on insects flushed from the grass and also eating biting insects from their skin. Regular use of mud wallows also helps protect Buffalo from insects. They spend most of the day lying in the shade. They can often be found drinking water in the early morning and late afternoon, and most feeding takes place during the cooler night. They are very dangerous when cornered or injured, capable of inflicting considerable damage.

DISTRIBUTION S Ethiopia, extreme S Somalia, Kenya, S Uganda (Lake Mburo), Rwanda, Burundi, SE DR Congo, Tanzania, Malawi, Zambia, N Botswana, Zimbabwe, NE Namibia, Mozambique, NW Lesotho, South Africa. *Reintroduced:* Swaziland. It is now generally confined to protected areas, within which it is well represented, and other areas which are sparsely settled.

HABITAT Variety of habitats, including open savanna, woodlands, and rainforest. Prefers areas with lots of grass, preferably 5-80 cm tall, shade, and water. Does not occur where there is less than 250 mm rain of per year.

STATUS Least Concern. Estimated population is 550,000.

PHOTO CREDITS ♂: *Linda Strande*, Kruger (South Africa). ♀: *Arno Meintjes* and *Lucila de Avila Castilho,* Kruger (South Africa). Head ♀: *Peter Zurek*. Young: *Angie Cole*, Maasai Mara (Kenya). Juvenile: *Eduard Kyslynskyy*, Lake Nakuru NP (Kenya) and *Jenelle Flewellen Photography*, Aberdare (Kenya).

Mountain Buffalo
SYNCERUS MATHEWSI

BL: 200-245 cm. SH: 120-145 cm. TL: 55-70 cm. W: 300-500 kg (♂), 250-450 kg (♀). HL: 53-72 cm. A stockily built Buffalo, with relatively short legs, large head, and short neck, similar in size to the Savanna Buffalo. Dark brown to black smooth coat, usually only slightly reddish, especially on females. No distinct markings on the body. Body sparsely covered with hairs in adults. Tail long with a terminal tuft. Head convex in profile. Ears fringed with hairs. Horns found in both sexes. In males, horns are long, less widely spread laterally than those of Cape Buffalo, nearly meeting in the midline, with the base expanded and flattened. Boss more developed than in West Savanna Buffalo, but less than in Cape Buffalo. Horns of females smaller than in males.

Syncerus mathewsi

OTHER NAMES Virunga Buffalo, Sudanese Buffalo, Northwestern Buffalo. *French*: Buffle de Mathews. *German*: Virunga-Büffel. *Spanish*: Búfalo de montaña. *Russian*: Центральноафриканский горный буйвол.

SUBSPECIES Monotypic. Formerly considered a subspecies of *S. caffer* (African Buffalo). It is not universally recognized as a species, and considered as an intermediate between the Savanna Buffalo and the smaller Forest Buffalo. Intergrades may occur where the distributions of the Buffalo species meet. Synonyms of *mathewsi* include *cottoni*.

SIMILAR SPECIES On the basis of horn shape, Mountain Buffalo is intermediate between Cape and Forest Buffalo. Cape Buffalo is larger, darker, black rather than brownish, horns curve down to the level of the skull, so that when the skull is placed on the floor the horns touch the floor, and ♂ have frontal bosses. Forest Buffalo is smaller, more lightly built, reddish in color (old ♂ may be dark brown), face narrower and straighter, and ears have a heavy fringe of hairs.

REPRODUCTION *Gestation*: 340 days. *Young per Birth*: 1, rarely 2. *Weaning*: 6 months. *Sexual Maturity*: 3.5-5 years. *Life Span*: 23 years. There is no specific information available for this species, but probably similar to the Cape Buffalo.

BEHAVIOR *Family Group*: Herds probably smaller than those of Cape and Savanna Buffalo, given its mountainous habitat. *Diet*: Grass. *Main Predators*: Lion, crocodile. There is no specific information available for this species, but probably similar to Forest Buffalo. During the dry season they select habitats with high-quality food and water, and with low risk of predation. During the wet season, they prefer upland steppes due to the low abundance of tsetse flies, despite their higher risk of predation.

DISTRIBUTION SW Uganda, W Rwanda, E DR Congo. Restricted to a forested mountainous area from the Virunga volcanoes N along the W side of Lake Edward.

HABITAT Tropical montane forest, at elevations of 3,000-3,500 m. It is found in open montane meadows, bamboo stands, and less frequently in alpine areas.

STATUS Least Concern. Estimated population in Virunga NP (DR Congo) was 2,100 animals in 2010. The Rwanda civil war has decreased numbers in the W side of the Parc National des Volcans.

PHOTO CREDITS Reconstruction based on photos from Virunga NP (DR Congo).

West and Central Savanna Buffalo
SYNCERUS BRACHYCEROS

BL: 200-245 cm. SH: 120-145 cm. TL: 55-70 cm. W: 300-500 kg (♂), 250-450 kg (♀). HL: 53-95 cm. Smaller than the Cape Buffalo and bigger than the Forest Buffalo. Dark brown coat, usually only slightly reddish, apparently never quite black. No distinct markings on the body. The body is heavyset, with stocky legs, a large head, and short neck. Body sparsely covered with hairs in adults (well haired in younger individuals). Tail long with a terminal tuft. Both males and females have horns. Horns widely spread laterally, less curved than on the Cape Buffalo, nearly meeting in the midline, but not forming a convex boss. The horns of males are larger than those of females.

♀

♂

Young

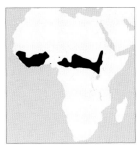

Syncerus brachyceros

OTHER NAMES Lake Chad Buffalo, Sudanese Buffalo, Northwestern Buffalo. *French*: Buffle du Tchad. *German:* Suda-Büffel. *Spanish*: Búfalo de sabana. *Russian*: Северо-западный (саванный) буйвол. *Swahili*: Mbogo. *Tswana*: Nare.

SUBSPECIES Monotypic. Formerly considered a subspecies of *S. caffer* (African Buffalo). Synonyms of *brachyceros* include *aequinoctialis* (Central African Savanna Buffalo or Nile Buffalo), *azrakensis, centralis, neumanii, planiceros,* and *solvayi*.

SIMILAR SPECIES Cape Buffalo is larger, darker, black rather than brownish, horns curve down to the level of the skull, so that when the skull is placed on the floor the horns touch the floor, and ♂ have frontal bosses. Forest Buffalo is smaller, more lightly built, reddish in color (old ♂ may be dark brown), face narrower and straighter, and ears have a heavy fringe of hairs. There are populations that appear to be intermediate in S Nigeria, Central African Republic, and N Cameroon. There are red forms that may be found from Guinea to Chad E to N Uganda in the Sahel Sudan savanna.

REPRODUCTION *Gestation*: 340 days. *Young per Birth*: 1, rarely 2. *Weaning*: 6 months. *Sexual Maturity*: 3.5-5 years. *Life Span*: 23 years. Similar to the Cape Buffalo.

BEHAVIOR *Family Group*: Large herds, comprising smaller subgroups of bachelor ♂, ♀ and their young, or juveniles. Old ♂ may be solitary. *Diet*: Grass; woody plant species are more important during the dry season than in the rainy season. *Main Predators*: Lion, crocodile. Regular, almost rhythmic, movement to feeding areas and watering sources occurrs during mornings and afternoons. Daily distances traveled are 5-7 km, and ranges include areas of 45-60 km^2. They graze more during daylight hours.

DISTRIBUTION SE Senegal, SW Mali, Guinea-Bissau, Guinea, NW Sierra Leone, Liberia, Côte d'Ivoire, S Burkina Faso, Ghana, Togo, Benin, W Niger, Nigeria, N Cameroon, S Chad, Central African Republic, Sudan, N DR Congo, W Ethiopia, Uganda, NW Kenya. *Extinct*: Gambia, Eritrea.

HABITAT They live in a variety of habitats ranging from typical Sahelian shrub savannas to Sudanian woodlands, across sub-Saharan Africa. They use open grasslands but are never far from shrub or forest cover and water. The availability of surface water and cover are the main constraints on habitat use, as they must drink at least every two days and are unable to survive on the moisture content of their food alone.

STATUS Least Concern. Estimated population for West African Savanna Buffalo about 20,000, with the largest numbers in Senegal, Côte d'Ivoire, Burkina Faso, Benin, and Cameroon. Central African population is some 60,000 with most in DR Congo and the Central African Republic. In decline over extensive areas because of meat hunting and continuing loss of habitat.

PHOTO CREDITS ♂: *Jonas Van de Voorde*, Parc National de la Pendjari (Benin) and *Tom Junek, Pavel Brandl, Paul Hejcmanová*, Niokolo-Koba NP (Senegal). ♀: *Jan Sevcik*, Bandia (Senegal). Young: *Magdalena Fischhuber* (Senegal). Heads: *Michael Lorentz*, Zakouma NP (Chad).

Forest Buffalo
SYNCERUS NANUS

BL: 180-220 cm. SH: 100-130 cm. TL: 70 cm. W: 320 kg (♂), 260 kg (♀). HL: To 40 cm. Smaller and less massive than the Cape Buffalo. Pale reddish-brown coat, with dark markings on the limbs, shoulders. Tend to darken with age and may thus have dark patches mingled with the red base color. Face narrower and straighter than in Savanna Buffalo. Ears are large and tend to droop, edged by a long fringe of hairs, including 2 white tufts. The tail is tufted. Both males and females have horns, which are relatively straight and which sweep backward in line with the forehead; they do not sweep down and do not form a convex boss, as in the Cape Buffalo. The horns of males are larger than those of females. Forest Buffalo have much shorter horns than Cape Buffalo.

Young

♀

Juvenile

♂

Syncerus nanus

OTHER NAMES Congo Buffalo, Dwarf Forest Buffalo, Red Buffalo. *French*: Buffle nain, buffle de forêt. *German*: Rotbüffel, Waldbüffel. *Spanish*: Búfalo rojo, búfalo enano, búfalo africano selvático. *Russian*: Карликовый лесной буйвол.

SUBSPECIES Monotypic. Formerly considered a subspecies of *S. caffer* (African Buffalo).

REPRODUCTION *Gestation*: 340 days. *Young per Birth*: 1, rarely 2. *Weaning*: 6 months. *Sexual Maturity*: 3.5-5 years. *Life Span*: 18-29 years. Forest Buffalo will breed year-round if conditions allow, but where water is scarce most births occur during the wet season. At birth, the calf is usually bright red.

BEHAVIOR *Family Group*: Small mixed herds of 8-20 animals. *Diet*: Principally grazers but some herbaceous plants and browse may be taken occasionally. *Main Predators*: Leopard. They have relatively small herds compared to those of the Cape Buffalo, as small as 3 and rarely over 30. If they are in a large group, they will spend more time grazing since there is less need to devote time to alert behavior. A herd typically consists of 1 or occasionally 2 ♂, and a harem of ♀, juveniles, and calves. Forest Buffalo ♂ remain with the herd continually, year-round, whereas Cape buffalo ♂ stay in bachelor herds until the wet season when young ♂ join the ♀, mate, help protect the young calves, and then leave. Animals usually remain in the same herd for their entire lives. Herds can split into 2 groups for a short period of time before merging back together. Home ranges of herds overlap extensively and there is no evidence of territories or territorial defense. Forest Buffalo are relatively unaffected by seasonal cycles. However, in the wet season, herds will be more spread out in the forest, and these animals tend to use resting places based on sand during the wet season but use dirt and leaves during the dry season. Moreover in open habitats such as clearings, groups are more aggregated when resting and more rounded in shape compared to groups in forest during the wet season. Savannas are where the Buffalo graze, while the marshes serve as wallows and help with the insects.

DISTRIBUTION *Native*: Angola, Cameroon, Central African Republic, Congo, DR Congo, Equatorial Guinea, Gabon, Nigeria. Lowland rainforest regions of W and central Africa, including S Nigeria, S and central Cameroon, S Central African Republic, Equatorial Guinea, Sao Tome and Principe, Gabon, Congo, central and N DR Congo, W and central Angola.

HABITAT Preference for open, grassy areas within the equatorial forest zone. In areas of extensive closed forest it occurs at much lower densities, whereas in secondary forest, densities may be higher.

STATUS Least Concern. Estimated total population is about 60,000. It has been greatly reduced in some areas by illegal hunting, especially in W Africa.

PHOTO CREDITS ♂: *Isaac Hsieh*, San Diego Zoo (USA) and Chester Zoo (UK). Head ♂: *David Meadows,* Chester Zoo (UK). ♀: *Richard Southwell*, Chester Zoo (UK) and *Andrew Short,* Marwell Zoo (UK). Head ♀: *Nigel Swales*, Chester Zoon (UK). Young: *Steve Wilson*, Chester Zoo (UK). Juvenile: Chester Zoo (UK) and *Maxime Thué,* Zoo du Bassin d'Arcachon (France).

European Bison
BOS BONASUS

BL: 210-350 cm. SH: 150-200 cm. TL: 30-80 cm. W: 350-1,000 kg. Largest ungulate in Europe. Coat dense and uniformly dark brown to golden brown in color. Neck short and thick, intensified by longer hair which forms a short mane on the underside. High hump on shoulders. Broad head that is carried relatively low, but higher than in American Bison. Body relatively narrow, especially in the hindquarters. Mane of coarse, woolly hair on shoulders and neck, short beard on the chin. Tasseled tail. Curly mop of hair on the forehead. Horns, found in both sexes, projecting outward and then curving upward and slightly forward. Females have slimmer horns, more bent inside, a thinner neck, and a smaller hump than males.

Young

Juvenile

Bos bonasus

OTHER NAMES Wisent. *French*: Bison d'Europe. *German*: Europäische Bison. *Spanish*: Bisonte europeo. *Russian*: Европейский зубр.

SUBSPECIES *B. b. bonasus* (Lowland Wisent): Poland, Belarus, Russia, Lithuania, Romania, Ukraine. *B. b. caucasicus* (Highland or Caucasian Wisent): It has been interbred with Lowland Bison, and no true line remains of this subspecies; about 2,200 survive.

SIMILAR SPECIES European Bison are taller than American Bison, have longer legs, nose is set farther forward than the forehead when the neck is in a neutral position, body is less hairy, though the tail is hairier, and horns point forward through the plane of their faces, making them more adept at fighting through the interlocking of horns in the same manner as Domestic Cattle, unlike the American Bison, which favors charging. European Bison are less tameable than the American Bison, and breed with Domestic Cattle less readily.

REPRODUCTION *Gestation*: 254-272 days. *Young per Birth*: 1, rarely 2. *Weaning*: 6-8 months. *Sexual Maturity*: 2 years (♀), 8 years (♂). *Life Span*: 27 years. During mating season, from August to October, a ♂ will move between groups looking for ♀ in estrus. ♂ will attend her for several days before mating, and will try to prevent any other ♂ from getting near her. Some ♂ are severely injured during these head-butting bouts. After mating, the ♂ will look for another ♀ ready to mate. The mother leaves the herd to give birth to her calf, which is able to run only hours after it is born.

BEHAVIOR *Family Group*: Maternal groups of around 20 individuals; ♂ are either solitary or in small groups. *Diet*: Grasses, leaves, bark, lichens, and mosses. *Main Predators*: Wolf, lynx (young animals). Active throughout the day, though the distribution of activity is affected by food supply. In the summer, feeding occurs primarily in the morning and evening, and rarely at night. In the winter, 2-5 feeding sessions per day have been recorded, mostly in the morning and evening before midnight. Although movements are generally slow, short gallops are rarely observed. Despite their size, European Bison can jump across 3 m wide streams and 2 m tall fences. They are dependent on water, knocking holes in the ice in winter with their hooves to reach the liquid. Vocalizations other than short grunts or snorts are rare.

DISTRIBUTION *Native*: Belarus, Lithuania, Poland, Romania, Russian Federation, Slovakia, Ukraine. *B. b. bonasus* was driven Extinct in the Wild in 1919, and *B. b. caucasicus* was extirpated by 1927. The species survived only in a few European zoos. As a result of reintroductions and introductions, it now occurs in free-ranging and semi-free herds in Poland, Lithuania, Belarus, Russian Federation, Ukraine, and Slovakia. The introduced Kyrgyzstan subpopulation has recently gone extinct.

HABITAT Mixed deciduous forests.

STATUS Vulnerable. Total population is 3,200 (43% in captivity).

PHOTO CREDITS ♂: *Olli A.* and *Pilot Micha*, Alpenzoo Innsbruck (Austria). ♀: *Anja Jonsson*, Borås Djurpark (Sweden). Young: *Peter Bolliger*, Wildpark Langenberg (Switzerland) and *Ulrike Joerres*, Tiergarten Mönchengladbach (Germany). Head ♀: *Neil McIntosh*, Whipsnade Wild Animal Park (UK). Head ♂: *Steve Johnson*, Highland Wildlife Park (UK). Juvenile: *Sergey Chichagov*, Tallinn Zoo (Estonia).

Wood Bison

BOS BISON ATHABASCAE

BL: 304-380 cm (♂), 210-350 cm (♀). SH: 167-195 cm (♂), 150-180 cm (♀). TL: 43-60 cm. W: 460-998 kg (♂), 360-544 kg (♀). Largest ungulate in North America. Larger, darker, and warier than Plains Bison. Dark brown to golden coat long and shaggy on the forequarters, including the front legs, the short neck, and shoulders. Large, woolly, bearded beneath the chin in both sexes. On the forehead, the hair is woolly and curly, giving the head a mop-like appearance between the horns. Massive forequarters and large shoulder hump, with the head carried low. Comparatively small hindquarters with shorter hair and a distinctive tasseled tail. Short black horns, present in both sexes, arch backward, outward, and then upward, curving slightly in at the blunt tips. Females smaller than males, with smaller horns that tend to curve inward at the top. Calves light reddish brown.

Young

♀

♂

Bos bison athabascae

OTHER NAMES Mountain Buffalo, Wood Buffalo, American Bison. *French*: Bison des bois. *German*: Waldbison. *Spanish:* Bisonte americano de bosque, bisonte de montaña, búfalo de montaña. *Russian*: Североамериканский лесной бизон. *Chipewyan*: Jejëre Junarejëre. *Cree*: Puscowmostus. *Dogrib*: Jehji. *South Slavey*: Dechitah goejide.

SUBSPECIES *B. b. athabascae* (Wood Bison), *B. b. bison* (Plains Bison). The validity of this subspecies is questioned by some authors. Previously included in the genus *Bison*.

SIMILAR SPECIES Wood Bison is much heavier than Plains Bison, has a taller hump, and coat has a shaggy appearance, shedding during the summer to make way for a lighter coat. In contrast, Plains Bison has a glossy coat with shorter hairs. The beard of Wood Bison is more pointed than that of Plains Bison. Wood Bison has short horns, and its horns extend sideways and back from its head. The Plains Bison has much larger horns. Compared with the European Bison, the Wood Bison is shorter and more massively built, but has slimmer hindquarters, has a longer and thicker mane, a shorter and less bushy tail, and horns that are more curved.

REPRODUCTION *Gestation*: 277-293 days. *Young per Birth*: 1, rarely 2. *Weaning*: 5-6 months. *Sexual Maturity*: 2-3 years. *Life Span*: 30 years. Birth season from April to August with most calves born in May. They generally have a single calf twice every 3 years. In order to evade predators, calves can stand within 30 minutes of birth and can run and kick within hours. After a week, calves will begin grazing but continue to nurse for several months. Calves are red in color; after 10 weeks, their coats begin to darken and become dark brown by about 15 weeks of age.

BEHAVIOR *Family Group*: Herds of ♀ and their young (generally less than 3 years old) with about 20-60 animals; ♂ are found in smaller bachelor herds or are solitary, except during the breeding season in late summer. They have strong social bonds and like to be near other Bison. *Diet*: Grasses, sedges, and forbs. They can use a variety of other plants (silverberry, willow leaves). *Main Predators*: Wolf, human. Generally remain within a home range but move between seasonal ranges, and move each day from meadow to meadow, where they graze and rest before moving on. Although they move slowly when feeding, they are capable of moving rapidly over long distances. The size of their year-round range tends to increase with population size, and also depends on habitat quality. In lower-quality habitats they will move over a larger home range.

DISTRIBUTION *Native*: Canada. Wood Bison once ranged across NW Canada and were also found in a large region in interior and S-central Alaska. Current range is restricted by wildlife and reportable disease management policies, and free-ranging Wood Bison are found only in Canada.

HABITAT Meadows, around lakes and rivers, and in recent burns.

STATUS Near Threatened. Considered at risk, and is currently on the Endangered Species list for Canada. There are currently only approximately 3,000 Wood Bison located in the wild.

PHOTO CREDITS ♂: *Woody Hayashi*, Wood Buffalo NP (Canada). ♀: *Cynthia Berry (cj berry)*, Calgary Zoo (Canada). Head ♂: *Brandon Smith*, Elk Island NP (Canada). Head ♀: *Steve Craig*. Young: *Frederick Colbourne PhD*, Elk Island NP (Canada).

Plains Bison

BOS BISON BISON

BL: 304-380 cm (♂), 210-350 cm (♀). SH: 167-195 cm (♂), 150-180 cm (♀). TL: 43-60 cm. W: 600-860 kg (♂), 360-544 kg (♀). Slightly smaller than Wood Bison. Dark brown to golden coat, lighter and woollier than in Wood Bison, with a longer beard, thicker mane, and shorter tail than in Wood Bison. Dorsal cape well defined, yellow ocher in color, with a sharp demarcation between it and the rest of the body. As winter progresses, the coat changes color and is lighter colored by spring. Older animals have more hair on their heads. Shoulder hump is lower and more centrally located than in Wood Bison. Horns present in both sexes, larger than in Wood Bison, arching backward, outward, and then upward, curving slightly in at the blunt tips. Female smaller than male, with slender horns, pointing upward. Calves are born a light reddish-brown color, but generally change to dark brown by 6 months of age.

♀

Juvenile

Young

♂

Bos bison bison

OTHER NAMES American Buffalo, Indian Buffalo. *French*: Bison des plaines. *German*: Präriebison. *Spanish*: Bisonte americano de llanura, búfalo. *Russian*: Североамериканский равнинный бизон.

SUBSPECIES *B. b. athabascae* (Wood Bison), *B. b. bison* (Plains Bison). The validity of this subspecies is questioned by some authors. Unfortunately, most modern populations of Plains Bison have been interbred with Domestic Cattle; only the Yellowstone and some Canadian populations, such as Elk Island, can be guaranteed to be free of cattle genes. Previously included in the genus *Bison*.

REPRODUCTION *Gestation*: 270-300 days. *Young per Birth*: 1, rarely 2. *Weaning*: 5-6 months. *Sexual Maturity*: 2-3 years. *Life Span*: 25 years. The breeding season is in July-August, when smaller herds join to form a group of up to 400 animals. ♀ are very protective of their young, and few predators are willing to face a protective mother Bison.

SIMILAR SPECIES See Wood Bison and European Bison.

BEHAVIOR *Family Group*: Herds of ♀ and their young (generally less than 3 years old) with about 60 animals; ♂ are found in smaller bachelor herds or are solitary. *Diet*: Prairie grasses, and in winter, lichens and mosses. *Main Predators*: Human. Due to their bulk and the climate in which they live, Bison may be active at any hour, although there appears to be a preference for daylight hours. Most feeding occurs in the early morning and around dusk. Daily movements of around 5 km are average, with a group circulating in a home range 30-100 km² in size depending on the season. In addition, certain populations make large-scale migrations, moving up to 250 km from higher, more N areas, to sheltered valleys and lowlands in the autumn, and back again in the spring. During winter, they will paw away deep snow to reach the dried shrubs hidden underneath. Grooming is a surprisingly frequent activity among Bison, with animals rubbing themselves on trees until all of the bark has been torn off, and the trunk left smooth. Dust baths in loose patches of soil are apparently a favorite activity, although the large hump on the shoulders generally means that the animal must get up and switch sides instead of rolling over. Despite their size, Bison are accomplished athletes, able to run at speeds of up to 50 kmph and swim rivers over 1 km wide.

DISTRIBUTION *Native*: United States. *Regionally Extinct*: Mexico. Plains Bison occurred from N Mexico to central Alberta. Current range is restricted by land use and wildlife management policies.

HABITAT Plains Bison prefer open habitats provided by meadows and grasslands.

CONSERVATION STATUS Near Threatened. The population underwent a drastic decline in the 19th century caused by overhunting but has since partially recovered.

PHOTO CREDITS ♂: *Travis Shinabarger*, Yellowstone NP, Wyoming (USA). ♀: *Tom Kelly*, Yellowstone NP, Wyoming (USA). Head ♀: *Ken McElroy*, Yellowstone NP, Wyoming (USA). Young: *D. L. Ashliman* and *Tearswept*, Yellowstone NP, Wyoming (USA). Juvenile: *Sergey Chichagov*, Tallinn Zoo (Estonia).

Indian Gaur
BOS GAURUS GAURUS

BL: 250-330 cm. SH: 170-220 cm. TL: 70-100 cm. W: 700-1,000 kg. HL: 32-80 cm. Massively built, with relatively short limbs. Dark brown to olive-black coat short and dense, with white stockings on all 4 legs, lacking a white rump patch as in the Banteng. Bulging gray-tan ridge connects the horns on the forehead. Absent or slightly developed dewlap, no throat fringe. Shoulder hump, very pronounced in adult males. Tail short, reaching but little if at all below the hocks. Horns in both sexes, growing from the sides of the head, curving upward, yellow at the base and turning black at the tips. Males considerably larger than females. Females are substantially smaller, with dorsal ridges, dewlaps, and horns less developed.

♀

Juvenile

Young

♂

Bos gaurus gaurus

OTHER NAMES Indian Bison. *French*: Gaur de l'Inde. *German*: Indischer Gaur. *Spanish*: Gaur indio. *Russian*: Индийский гаур. *Hindi*: Gaur, gauri-gai, gor *Tamil*: Katuerimai.

SUBSPECIES Considered as a subspecies of *B. gaurus* (Gaur): *B. g. gaurus* (Indian Gaur), *B. g. laosiensis* (Southeast Asian Gaur). The domestic Gaur, Gayal, or Mithun (*B. frontalis*) and the Gaur (*B. gaurus*) are considered a single species.

REPRODUCTION *Gestation*: 275 days. *Young per Birth*: 1, rarely 2. *Weaning*: 7-9 months. *Sexual Maturity*: 2-3 years. *Life Span*: 30 years. Breeding takes place throughout the year, though there is a peak between December and June.

BEHAVIOR *Family Group*: Small mixed herds of 2-40 individuals; adult males may be solitary. *Diet*: Grasses, shoots and fruit. *Main Predators*: Tiger, leopard, dhole, crocodile. Basically diurnal, but where populations have been disturbed by humans, they have become largely nocturnal, rarely seen in the open after 8:00 in the morning. During the dry season, herds congregate and remain in small areas, dispersing into the hills with the arrival of the monsoon. While Gaurs depend on water for drinking, they do not seem to bathe or wallow. When alarmed, Gaurs crash into the jungle at a surprising speed. Gaurs live in herds led by a single adult ♀. During the peak of the breeding season, unattached ♂ wander widely in search of receptive ♀. No serious fighting has been recorded between ♂, with size being the major factor in determining dominance. ♂ make a mating call of clear, resonant tones which may carry for more than 1.6 km. Gaurs have also been known to make a whistling snort as an alarm call, and a low, cow-like moo. The average population density is about 0.6 animals per km², with herds having home ranges of around 80 km². Domestic Gaurs live and forage in the vicinity of settlements, to which they come close to spend the night. They can be lured right up to a village with salt, an important element in the diet of all cattle. The clearings created by the hill tribes for growing crops provide food for Gaurs also; not only the crops but also the grass and forbs that colonize abandoned fields are undefended. When these factors are combined with the proximity of settlements to water and the protection from predators gained by sleeping close to people who tolerate, and even promote, the arrangement, all the conditions for self-domestication are met. The final stage of self-domestication is reached when animals have so lost their fear of humans that they can be used for food and trade. ♀ are usually aggressive when with calves, and there are instances known when people have been severely injured after being gored by one. ♂ are usually more docile.

DISTRIBUTION India, Nepal, and Bhutan. *Regionally Extinct*: Sri Lanka. Seriously fragmented within its range.

HABITAT Tropical woodlands.

STATUS Vulnerable. Estimated total population was 30,000 in 2000, with the largest populations found in India. The overall population is declining.

PHOTO CREDITS ♂: *Mayank Koshariya*, Kanha NP (India). ♀: *Gokulakrishnan G*, Vandular Zoo (India). Head ♂: *Dan Vermeer*, Kerala (india). Head ♀: *Alan Hill*, Whipsnade Wild Animal Park (UK). Juvenile: *Sandeep Gangadharan*, Kerala (India).

Southeast Asian Gaur

BOS GAURUS LAOSIENSIS

BL: 250-330 cm. SH: 170-220 cm. TL: 70-100 cm. W: 700-1,000 kg. HL: To 85 cm. Taller than Indian Gaur, massively built, with relatively short limbs. Nearly black coat short and dense, with white stockings on all 4 legs, lacking a white rump patch. Fringed ears. Bulging gray-tan ridge connects the horns on the forehead, extending farther down the face than in the Indian Gaur. Arch on top of the skull is less developed than in Indian Gaur. In some individuals, light-colored band just above the muzzle. Dewlap under the chin extends between the front legs, throat fringe. Shoulder hump, very pronounced in adult males. Tail short, reaching but little if at all below the hocks. Horns in both sexes, growing from the sides of the head, curving upward, yellow at the base and turning black at the tips. Males considerably larger than females. Females and young paler.

Bos gaurus laosiensis

OTHER NAMES Seladang, Mithun. *French*: Gaur malais, gaur de l'Indochine. *German*: Malaiengaur, Hinterindischer Gaur. *Spanish*: Gaur Malayo, gaur de Indochina. *Russian*: Индокитайский гаур. *Burmese*: Pyoung. *Thai*: Kra-ting.

SUBSPECIES *B. g. gaurus* (Indian Gaur), *B. g. laosiensis* (Southeast Asian Gaur), which includes *hubbacki* (Malayan Gaur, found in the Malay Peninsula S of the Isthmus of Kra; smaller), and *readei* (Indochinese Gaur; largest). The domestic Gaur, Gayal, or Mithun (*B. frontalis*) and the Gaur (*B. gaurus*) are considered a single species.

SIMILAR SPECIES Gayal lacks the massive shoulder hump, with thicker, but shorter horns; some Gayal are piebald, and even white, as the result of hybridizing with cattle. Indian Gaur has no throat fringe, the dewlap is only slightly developed, and the gray area of the forehead does not extends as far down the face.

REPRODUCTION *Gestation*: 270-314 days. *Young per Birth*: 1. *Weaning*: 7-9 months. *Sexual Maturity*: 2-3 years. *Life Span*: 30 years. Breeding takes place throughout the year, and young are born throughout the year, except October-December in Malaysia. During mating, the ♂ will emit a distance mating call that can be heard almost 1.5 km. Young are able to walk within minutes of being delivered.

BEHAVIOR *Family Group*: Small mixed herds of 2-40 individuals; adult ♂ may be solitary, but associate with ♀ at the breeding season. *Diet*: Fresh grasses, bamboo shoots, herbs, young sprouts of bushes, shrubs. It drinks water daily. *Main Predators*: Tiger, leopard, dhole. Diurnal, being most active in the morning and late afternoon, resting during the midday. In Thailand, they are mostly nocturnal, resting and sleeping almost the whole day long. Shy and rarely seen. Unless wounded, they do not attack people, preferring to run away. ♂ assert their dominance by posturing and parallel walking, showing off their profiles. Size is the major criterion determining the rank of an individual in a herd; 2 equally matched ♂ may lock horns in a head-to-head combat to assert dominance. Herds range widely and may cover several km daily. During the bamboo shoot season (August and September), large numbers congregate in the bamboo forests and follow elephant trails to eat young leaves of bamboo that grow beyond their reach and that the elephants have pulled down and left behind. Dust baths and wallows are rarely used. When alarmed, Gaurs snort and thump the ground with their forelegs. When alarmed they react by a harsh blowing of air through their nostrils and produce a snorting sound.

DISTRIBUTION Myanmar, Laos, Vietnam, Thailand, Cambodia, peninsular Malaysia (Taman Negara, Pahang, Kelantan), S China (S Yunnan). Seriously fragmented within its range.

HABITAT Tropical dry and evergreen forest, with adjacent open areas for grazing, from sea level to 2,600 m. Water holes and salt licks are essential, and are visited nightly.

STATUS Vulnerable. The global estimate was 13,000 to 30,000 in 2000, with 5,200 to 18,000 mature individuals. In Malaysia, the population was stated to be fewer than 500 individuals, and in Thailand fewer than 1,000. The overall population is declining.

PHOTO CREDITS ♂: *Lee Tennyson*, Zoo Negara (Malaysia). ♀: *David Gandy*, Khao Yai NP (Thailand). Head ♂: *Nadia Shazrin Asari*, Zoo Negara (Malaysia). Head ♀: *Steve Clifford* (Malaysia).

Gayal

BOS FRONTALIS

BL: 250 cm. SH: 120-170 cm (♂). TL: 70-100 cm. W: 400-560 kg (♂), 350-400 kg (♀). HL: To 85 cm. Smaller than the wild Gaur, with proportionally shorter limbs and lacking the massive shoulder hump. Color of head and body blackish brown in both sexes, but may be piebald, light brown, or even white (as the result of hybridizing with cattle). Lower portion of limbs white or yellowish. Fringed ears. Small dewlap under the throat. Relatively low dorsal hump. Head is shorter and broader than in Gaur, with a perfectly flat forehead and a straight line between the bases of the horns. Blackish horns in both sexes, thicker but shorter than in Gaur, extending almost directly outward from the sides of the head, and curving somewhat upward at the tips, but without any inward inclination. Females much smaller than males, with scarcely any dewlap on the throat. Most calves are brown.

Juvenile

Young

♀

♂

Bos frontalis

OTHER NAMES Mithun, Mithan, Domestic Gaur. *French*: Gayal. *Spanish*: Gayal. *Russian*: Гаял. *Adi*: Eso, hoho. *Nyishi*: Subu, sebe. *Sanskrit*: Gavaya. *Hindi*: Gavi, gayal. *Bengali*: Gvaya goru. *Assamese*: Mithun, mithan. *Apatani*: Seobo. *Mizos*: Shinl. *Naga*: Wei. *Tangkhul*: Seizang. *Manipuri*: Sandung. *Burmese*: Sia. *Chinese*: Dulong.

SUBSPECIES Gayal (*B. frontalis*) and Gaur (*B. gaurus*) are considered a single species. It is believed to be a semi-domesticated form derived from wild Gaur. They may interbreed freely with the Gaur, Banteng, Yak, and cattle of both the taurus and zebu types. Unlike most crosses between bovine species, those between Gayal and cattle result in fertile ♂ and ♀ offspring.

SIMILAR SPECIES Gaur is larger, and stands much higher at the withers, has a massive shoulder hump, and ♂ have a larger dewlap on the throat. The thick and massive horns are less flattened and much less curved than in the Gaur. In the hill ranges of Assam, where Gaur are still plentiful and interbreeding between Gayal and Gaur frequently occurs, Gayal are massive and Gaur-like. In the Chin Hills, where Gaur are scarce, the Gayal have lost their bulky proportions, probably by interbreeding with cattle.

REPRODUCTION *Gestation*: 281-296 days. *Young per Birth*: 1. *Weaning*: 7-9 months. *Sexual Maturity*: 2-3 years. *Life Span*: 30 years. Most calving occurs during the monsoon and autumn.

BEHAVIOR *Family Group*: Small mixed herds of 8-11 individuals; adult ♂ may be solitary, but associate with ♀ at the breeding season. *Diet*: Grasses, tree leaves, herbs, and shrubs. *Main Predators*: Tiger, leopard, dhole. Shy and timid, but unusually gentle, with a quiet disposition; normally even a stranger is safe to approach one. They come out for grazing in the morning and graze until the evening. They do not like warm temperatures and hot sun, and during the middle of the day they retire to the deep forest near small ponds, water springs, or streams. They can climb easily in sloppy, steep terrain, unlike Domestic Cattle or Buffalo. Many Gayals are not domesticated in the strict sense; herds live in a semi-tame state near jungle villages and come to settlements only in the evening to lick salt. In some regions of N India, they are used for field work and as draft animals. They are also important as a meat supply. To many tribes of N India and Burma, Gayals serve mainly as sacrificial animals.

DISTRIBUTION It occurs in India (Tripura, Mizoram, Assam, and Arunachal Pradesh), Bangladesh (Chittagong Hill Tracts), N Myanmar (Kachin State), and China (Yunnan Province in the Dulong and Nujiang River basins), as feral, semi-feral, and domestic animals.

HABITAT Feral animals live in the same habitat as Gaurs. Usually found at elevations from 300 to 3,000 m. In some areas, herds are allowed to browse freely in the woods; some return to the villages for protection at night, while others remain largely in the forests. The villagers keep the forest Gayals nearby by providing salt.

STATUS Domesticated. Estimated population is 50,000 feral animals in India. In Bhutan there are 60,000 animals that are hybrids with the local breed of cattle.

PHOTO CREDITS *Nick Karpov*, Tierpark Berlin (Germany).

Java Banteng
BOS JAVANICUS JAVANICUS

BL: 190-225 cm. SH: 160 cm. TL: 65-70 cm. W: 600-800 kg (♂), 400 kg (♀). HL: 60-75 cm (♂). Strong sexual dimorphism. Young males reddish brown, becoming blackish brown or black when fully mature, the blackish coloration progressing from front to back. Very old bulls may turn gray. Females chestnut-red color, with a dark dorsal stripe, smaller and slimmer than males. Large white rump patch, contrasting sharply with the color of the body. White stockings on lower legs. Hump on the back above the shoulders. Horns in males long and slim, round in cross section, more or less wrinkled near the base, but smooth for the rest of their length, growing widely outward from the top of the head, then curving smoothly upward and somewhat forward to sharp tips. Horn bases in old bulls are connected by a hairless, gristly shield. Horns of females very short and tightly curved, pointing inward at the tips. Borneo Banteng is smaller, with steeper horns, males chocolate brown.

♀

♂

Young

Bos javanicus javanicus

OTHER NAMES Scrub Bull, Red Bull. *French*: Tembadau, Banting de Java. *German*: Sunda-Ochse, Java Banteng. *Spanish*: Banteng de Java. *Russian*: Яванский бантенг.

SUBSPECIES *B. j. javanicus* (Java Banteng), *B. j. lowi* (Borneo Banteng), *B. j. birmanicus* (Burma Banteng). The domesticated form of Banteng, known as Bali cattle, is virtually identical in appearance to the wild Java Banteng.

REPRODUCTION *Gestation*: 285 days. *Young per Birth*: 1. *Weaning*: 6-9 months. *Sexual Maturity:* 2-3 years. *Life Span:* 20 years. While in captivity breeding has occurred throughout the year.

BEHAVIOR *Family Group*: Herds of 2-40 animals with a single mature ♂. Older ♂ live alone or with 1 or 2 other ♂. *Diet*: Grasses, leaves, and shoots. *Main Predators*: Dhole. Active during the night or day, but in areas with heavy human encroachment the herds are nocturnal. Herds feed throughout the night, pausing to rest and ruminate at intervals. Very shy and retiring, and due to their wariness they are hard to approach. Feeding in open clearings, Banteng depend on dense thickets in which to retire for shelter and safety. During the wet season, they may leave the valleys to forage, heading for forests at higher elevations. As the dry season takes hold, they return to the more open lowlands. Under favorable conditions they drink daily, preferring standing water. During droughts, they seem able to survive several days without water. In coastal areas where there are no mineral licks they can meet their need for salt by occasionally drinking seawater. Cows and dominant ♂ command the best pastures, and young and weaker bulls roam widely, rarely leaving the protection of the thick forest.

DISTRIBUTION *Native*: Java. Domestic Banteng has been introduced to several of the islands of E Indonesia including Sulawesi, Sumbawa, and Sumba, and in New Guinea and Australia (Cobourg Peninsula). Feral Banteng occurs in Kalimantan. Introduced Banteng occurs on the Indonesian islands of Enggano (off Sumatra) and Sangihe (off Sulawesi). Wild Banteng currently occurs on Java and possibly Bali, in Kalimantan (Indonesian Borneo), Sabah (part of Malaysian Borneo), Myanmar, Thailand, Laos, Vietnam, and Cambodia. On Borneo, it occurs in parts of E Sabah (Malaysia), including Tabin Wildlife Reserve, and in Kalimantan (Indonesia), it occurs along the border with Sarawak (Malaysia), as well as in the S-central region and two isolates in the E parts of the province (in and around Kutai NP and Hutan Kapur Sangkulirang Nature Reserve).

HABITAT Dense forest and bamboo jungles.

STATUS Endangered. Only a few thousand wild Banteng survive, and their numbers are decreasing. Most populations are endangered because their habitats are being encroached upon by the growing human population. Trophy hunting has been instrumental in preserving the Banteng in Australia, which has the world's only huntable population. Banteng are now targeted by breeding programs in Europe and North America. All specimens outside Asia belong to the Javan subspecies.

PHOTO CREDITS ♂: *Arthur Ramos*, White Oak Conservation Center, Yulee (USA). Head ♂: *Valerie Abbott*, Miami Zoo (USA). ♀: *Roel van der Hoorn*, Burger's Zoo (Netherlands). Head ♀: *Bev Armstrong*, Miami Zoo (USA). Young: *Steve Wilson*, Chester Zoo (UK).

Borneo Banteng
BOS JAVANICUS LOWI

BL: 190-225 cm. SH: 160 cm. TL: 65-70 cm. W: 600-800 kg (♂), 400 kg (♀). HL: 60-75 cm (♂). The smallest subspecies. Sexual dimorphism: mature males are black to dark brown in color, while females are pale brown. White color on all lower legs, rump, sides of upper lips, and a small but distinct patch just above the eyes. Males are larger and more muscularly built than females, with a raised dorsal ridge and a modest dewlap running posteriorly from the lower neck. Horns in males are larger at the base, and both horns are connected by a ridge of hard tissue; they grow sideways and later curve upward and inward, ending in sharp tips, less outcurved and with a smaller horn span than in other subspecies. Females are smaller, with much smaller horns that grow in a much narrower fashion.

♀

♂

Juvenile

♂

Bos javanicus lowi

OTHER NAMES Wild Cattle of Borneo. *French*: Tembadau. *German*: Ochse. *Spanish*: Banteng de Borneo. *Russian*: Борнейский бантенг.

SUBSPECIES *B. j. javanicus* (Java Banteng), *B. j. lowi* (Borneo Banteng), *B. j. birmanicus* (Burma Banteng).

REPRODUCTION *Gestation*: 285 days. *Young per Birth*: 1. *Weaning*: 6-9 months. *Sexual Maturity*: 2-3 years. *Life Span*: 20 years. No specific information for this subspecies is available, but probably similar to other subspecies.

BEHAVIOR *Family Group*: Alone or in small groups of up to 8 members. ♂ separate from their mothers at an age of 2-3 years. Sometimes ♀ calves continue living with their mother even beyond maturity. *Diet*: Mainly grass, but are fond of herbs, leaves, fruits, and blossoms, as well as the sprouts of trees, brush, and young bamboo. No specific information for this subspecies is available, but probably similar to other subspecies. Under favorable conditions they drink daily, preferring standing water. During droughts, they seem able to survive several days without water. In coastal areas where there are no mineral licks they can meet their need for salt by occasionally drinking seawater. *Main Predators*: Dhole. Very shy, hard to see in the wild. Within disturbed habitat, Banteng exhibit nocturnal behavior; however, where human activity is infrequent, Banteng will utilize forest edge grassland openly during the day.

DISTRIBUTION *Native:* Borneo. They were once widespread in Borneo but now they are confined to isolated forest reserves in Sabah and probably on the Sabah/Kalimantan border. In Sabah, they inhabits mainly two regions located in the middle to the E parts of the state; the largest area of habitat is the Deramakot-Malua-Maliau region in central Sabah; the second largest area is the Kulamba-Tabin region in NE Sabah.

HABITAT Remote tropical lowland mixed dipterocarp, swamp, or beach forest.

STATUS Endangered. Estimated population in Sabah was in the range of 300-550 in the 1980s. It is highly probable that Borneo's Banteng population has dramatically declined by >50% as a result of widespread deforestation and conversion to agricultural land, hunting, and disease transmission from Domestic Cattle. Hybridization with Domestic Cattle and inbreeding as a consequence of isolation are also likely threats.

PHOTO CREDITS ♂: *Richard Mittleman*, Lok Kawi Wildlife Park (Borneo). Head ♂: *Ian Rebbeck*, Lok Kawi Wildlife Park (Borneo). ♀: *Murphy Ng*, Sabah (Borneo). Head ♀: *Tino Dietsche*, Sabah (Borneo). Juvenile: *Nick Hadad*, Lok Kawi Wildlife Park (Borneo).

Indochinese Banteng
BOS JAVANICUS BIRMANICUS

BL: 190-225 cm. SH: 160 cm. TL: 65-70 cm. W: 600-800 kg. HL: 60-87 cm (♂). Adult males variable in color, from dark fawn to orange or chestnut or chocolate, shading into light brown below. Face usually lighter than the body, with the forehead and around the eyes whitish or tawny gray, darkening to light chestnut above the muzzle, and a whitish band separating this from the black muzzle. White rump patch, usually less developed than in Java Banteng. Legs are white from above the knees and hocks to the hooves. Forehead convex, and the ridge at the top of the skull is elevated in the middle, forming a gentle arch between the horns. Horns distinctly different from those of the Java and Borneo subspecies, growing out from the sides of the head, rather than the top, then curving sharply up, in, and slightly back, with the tips directed toward each other. Female's horns relatively long. Females are bright chestnut red, with rump patch, underparts, and lower legs whitish.

♀

♂
Juvenile

♂

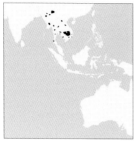

Bos javanicus birmanicus

OTHER NAMES Burma Banteng. *French*: Tsaine, banteng de l'Indochine, banteng de Birmanie. *German*: Hinterindischer Banteng. *Spanish*: Banteng de Indochina. *Russian*: Индокитайский бантенг. *Burmese*: Tsaine, Hsaine.

SUBSPECIES *B. j. javanicus* (Java Banteng), *B. j. lowi* (Borneo Banteng), *B. j. birmanicus* (Burma Banteng). Includes *porteri* (Thailand Banteng). Three varieties are usually recognized: the common light red bulls and cows (called tsaine bya), dark chocolate bulls and dark chestnut cows (tsaine nyo or tsaine mwe), and dark-faced bulls with red bodies (tsaine ni). All varieties may be found in the same forest, but a herd is said to consist of 1 variety only. The *porteri* race from Thailand has brownish hair marked by numerous small white flecks, and horns heavily ringed at the base. An unnamed form has been described from S Vietnam, in which bulls are bright orange with a paler dorsal streak, a fawn face with a white ring around the muzzle, a dark band above the knees and hocks, and a small white rump patch. Indochinese Banteng in Cambodia often carry the mitochondrial DNA of the Kouprey, which may indicate past interbreeding.

REPRODUCTION *Gestation*: 285 days. *Young per Birth*: 1. *Weaning*: 6-16 months. *Sexual Maturity*: 2-3 years. *Life Span*: 20 years. Although in captivity breeding has occurred throughout the year, wild Banteng in Thailand mate during May and June.

BEHAVIOR *Family Group*: Herds of 8-15 animals with a single mature ♂, though as many as 40-50 have been observed. Old ♂ are usually solitary or with 1 or 2 other ♂. *Diet*: Grasses, sedges. *Main Predators*: Dhole. With most activity in morning and evening, or at night when pressured by humans. During the heat of the day it retreats to dense forest among the paperbark trees. Sense of smell is excellent, hearing and eyesight are good. Very agile.

DISTRIBUTION Myanmar, S China (S Yunnan), Thailand, Cambodia, Laos, Vietnam, N peninsular Malaysia. *Regionally Extinct*: Bangladesh, Brunei Darussalam, India. Historically occurred from S China throughout mainland Southeast Asia, through peninsular Malaysia to the islands of Borneo, Java, and probably Bali. Wild Banteng currently occurs on Java and possibly Bali, in Kalimantan (Indonesian Borneo), Sabah (part of Malaysian Borneo), Myanmar, Thailand, Laos, Vietnam, and Cambodia. In Cambodia the species is still likely to be widespread in the N and E forests as well as in parts of the Cardamoms Mountains, with the bulk of the population remaining in the E forests, centered on Mondulkiri Province.

HABITAT Deciduous monsoon forest in SE Asia. Habitats vary between the extremes of dry wooded parkland with large grassy plains to tropical rainforest with small clearings. In W Thailand, they live in a belt of grass and bamboo thickets along upper slopes of dry mountains. They avoid large human settlements and plantations.

STATUS Endangered. The Burma Banteng is only kept in one or two Asian collections around Thailand, possibly Myanmar, Laos, and Vietnam.

PHOTO CREDITS ♂ and head ♀: *David Cabedo Cruz*, Salak Pra Wildlife Sanctuary (Thailand). Head ♂: *Sasil Sirivadhanakul* (Thailand). Juvenile: *Pierre de Chabannes*, Chiang Mai Zoo (Thailand).

Wild Yak
BOS MUTUS

BL: 306-385 cm. SH: 170-200 cm (♂), 137-156 cm (♀). TL: 60 cm. W: 535-1,000 kg (♂), 300-350 kg (♀). HL: 95 cm (♂), 51 cm (♀). Massive body with high and humped shoulders and a broad, drooping head. Jet-brown or jet-black coat, dense, woolly, and extremely shaggy. Golden Wild Yaks are also known, but are extremely rare. A fringe of long hairs extends around the lower part of the body, almost touching the ground. No dewlap. Gray-white hairs around the mouth. Short legs, with broad hooves and large dewclaws as an adaptation to mountainous environments. Tail fully haired and horse-like. Small ears. Smooth, cylindrical, gray to black horns, found in both sexes, though those of the females are considerably smaller and shorter. The curved horns grow out from the sides of the head and curve upward. Females can be one-third the size of males.

Bos mutus

OTHER NAMES *French*: Yak sauvage, vache de Tartarie. *German*: Wildyak, Jak, Grunzochse. *Spanish*: Yak. *Russian*: Дикий як. *Local name*: Dong, zhong, li, zuo.

SUBSPECIES Originally designated as *B. grunniens*, but this name is now only considered to refer to the domesticated form of the animal, with *B. mutus* being the preferred name for the wild species. Some authors still consider the Wild Yak to be a subspecies, *B. grunniens mutus*. No other subspecies are recognized.

SIMILAR SPECIES Domestic Yak are significantly smaller, have shorter legs, wider hooves, more variation in fur color, weaker horns, and usually lack gray-white hairs around the muzzle.

REPRODUCTION *Gestation*: 258 days. *Young per Birth*: 1 every other year. *Weaning*: 1 year. *Sexual Maturity*: 6 years. *Life Span*: 23 years. The mating season begins in September, lasting for several weeks in which ♂ fight each other for ♀. Young are born in June, the season of plenty on the Tibetan Plateau. ♂ Wild Yak can be seen mingling and mating with herds of ♀ Domestic Yak.

BEHAVIOR *Family Group*: Herds of 10-200 individuals consisting of ♀ and young, adult ♂ solitary or in bachelor groups with up to 12 members. *Diet*: Lichens, grasses, and tubers. *Main Predators*: Tibetan wolf. Due to the scarcity of vegetation in their habitat, they must travel great distances in order to obtain sufficient nourishment. In July, there is a general downward shift from the high plateaus to the lower plains, where mosses and swamp vegetation are at their peak. As the temperature rises in August, the herds head back up to the plateaus, even retiring to snowy regions to beat the heat. Although sensitive to warm temperatures, they can easily tolerate temperatures of -40° C. In severe cold, they have been seen bathing in lakes and streams. Generally distrustful, if a herd is disturbed they will flee for a long distance, galloping with their tails held erect. If something unexpected appears in their flight path, Yaks will bluff, attacking with a fast charge and normally stopping just 10-20 m away from the intruder. In spite of their bulky, awkward appearance, Yaks are excellent, sure-footed climbers. One of the few vocalizations is a loud grunt, made during the breeding season by Wild Yaks, while Domestic Yaks "grunt" throughout the year; hence the specific name *grunniens*.

DISTRIBUTION *Native*: China, India. *Regionally Extinct*: Bhutan, Nepal. Historically, this occurred throughout the Tibetan Plateau, including China, N India, and Nepal. In India, the species is currently known from the Ladakh region of Kashmir. In China, the species occurs in scattered populations on the Tibetan Plateau, with the main populations remaining in the Chang Tang Reserve, as well as in the Arjin Shan area of SE Xinjiang, and Kekexili Nature Reserve in Qinghai and adjacent areas of the Kunlun Mountains. Also isolated populations N and S of the main population, in W-central Tibet, S-central Qinghai, and W Gansu.

HABITAT Remote high-elevation alpine meadows and alpine steppe in rolling to mountainous terrain of the N Tibetan Plateau, at an altitude of 3,000-5,500 m.

CONSERVATION STATUS Vulnerable. It is estimated there are only 15,000 Wild Yaks. Poaching and interbreeding with Domestic Yaks are the most serious threats.

PHOTO CREDITS ♂: *Milo Burcham*, Yeniugou Wild Yak Valley, Qinghai (China).

Domestic Yak
BOS GRUNNIENS

BL: 145-218 cm. SH: 106-129 cm (♂), 112 cm (♀). TL: 60 cm. W: 197-593 kg (♂), 230 kg (♀). HL: 95 cm (♂), 51 cm (♀). Much smaller than the Wild Yak, with weaker horns and varied coloration, red, brown, black, or mottled. Humped shoulders, short legs, and rounded hooves. Forehead is wide and ears are small. Hair is thick, long, and shaggy, with a dense woolly undercoat over the chest, flanks, and thighs. The guard hairs are short on the back and much longer along the sides, forming a fringed cape or skirt that reaches almost to the ground and is more pronounced in males. The tail is long and very bushy, also with long guard hairs covering much of its length. Females smaller than males, with shorter horns.

♀

♂

Young

Bos grunniens

OTHER NAMES Grunting Ox. *French*: Yak, yack, vache de Tartarie. *German*: Yak, Jak, Grunzochse. *Spanish:* Yak doméstico. *Russian:* Домашний як. *Local name*: Dong.

SUBSPECIES *B. grunniens* is now generally only considered to refer to the domesticated form of the animal, with *B. mutus* being the preferred name for the wild species. They may interbreed with Domestic Cattle, producing fertile ♀ and normally sterile ♂ offspring.

REPRODUCTION *Gestation*: 258 days. *Young per Birth*: 1 every other year. *Weaning*: 1 year. *Sexual Maturity*: 6 years. *Life Span*: 23 years. During the mating season, ♂ leave their groups and join the ♀ herds. ♂ compete for access to receptive ♀, often violently. The mating season starts in September, with births usually occurring in June. Domesticated Yak may give birth to more than 1 calf per year. Most of the parental care is done by the ♀. Young are born able to stand and walk within several hours after birth.

BEHAVIOR *Family Group*: Herds of 10-200 individuals consisting of ♀ and young, adult ♂ solitary or in bachelor groups with up to 12 members. *Diet*: Lichens, grasses, and tubers; since they cannot digest grains, they often move to fresh pastures to feed. *Main Predators*: Tibetan wolf. Yaks have been domesticated for about 3,000 years and are found in association with people throughout the highlands of central Asia. They are used for riding, as pack animals, and for their meat, milk, and wool. Strong, docile, and sure footed, they are the most useful domestic animals at higher elevations. They graze in the early morning and evening and sleep during the rest of the day. They do not move very much, and may spend days in the same pasture, alternately grazing and lying down to ruminate. During severe blizzards they turn their broad bushy tail into the storm and remain motionless for hours. In contrast to the Wild Yak, Domestic Yak makes frequent grunting noises and is therefore called the "grunting ox." Wild Yaks may attack the domestic variety. Like Bison, but unlike cattle, ♂ wallow in dry soil during the rut, often while scent marking with urine or dung. The udder in ♀ and the scrotum in ♂ are small and hairy, as protection against the cold.

DISTRIBUTION Domestic and feral Yak are found extensively on the plateau of W China (from the S slopes of the Himalayas in the S to the Altai in the N and from the Pamir in the W to the Minshan mountains in the E) and N China (Hebei Province, Lingshan). The center of the Yak's distribution is the Qinghai-Tibetan Plateau. It is also found in W and N Mongolia (Hangay and Hovsgol mountains, Mongolian Altai), Russia (mountainous area on the borders with China and Mongolia, N Caucasus, Yakutia), Nepal, Bhutan, and India (northern provinces, Sikkim), Afghanistan, and Pakistan. Domestic Yak has been exported to parts of Europe, North America, and other parts of Asia.

HABITAT Alpine meadows, alpine steppes, and desert steppes.

CONSERVATION STATUS Domesticated. It is estimated there are as many as 12 million domestic and feral Yaks, 94% found in China. 15% are hybrids with *Bos taurus* and *B. indicus* cattle.

PHOTO CREDITS ♂: *Nivedita Ravishankar*, Himachal (India). ♀: *Alex Meyer,* Madrid Zoo (Spain). Head ♂: *Marie Hale,* Highland Wildlife Park (UK). Head ♀: *Molly Heng*, West Bengal Zoological Park (India). Young: *Sergey Chichagov*, Riga Zoo (Latvia).

European Cattle

BOS TAURUS VAR. TAURUS

BL: 150-250 cm. SH: 100-185 cm. W: 150-1,300 kg. HL: 20-100 cm. Large, sturdy animals. Due to the amount of variation present among breeds, specific morphological characteristics must be presented as approximations. Body covered in short hair, the color of which varies from black through white, reddish brown, and brown. May have a muscular complex very evident on the back, at the level of the withers. Short neck with dewlap hanging below the chin. Horns in both sexes, more marked in males. Thin tail, ending in a tuft. No cervico-thoracic hump. Males slightly larger than females, with stronger horns.

Young

♀

♂

Bos taurus

OTHER NAMES *French*: Vache. *German*: Hausrind, Rind, Buckelrind. *Spanish*: Res, vaca (♀), toro (♂). *Russian*: Домашний скот; корова (♀), бык (♂).

SUBSPECIES Cattle are usually identified as three separate species: *B. taurus* (European or Taurine cattle, including similar types from Africa and Asia), *B. indicus* (Zebu), and the extinct *B. primigenius* (Aurochs), which is ancestral to both Taurine cattle and Zebu. Some authors group the three as one species: *B. primigenius*, with *B. p. taurus*, *B. p. indicus,* and *B. p. primigenius* as the subspecies. *B. taurus* may be further subdivided into: European Cattle (*taurus* group) and Sanga Cattle (*africanus* group). Common European breeds include: Simmental, Gelbvieh, Maine, Anjou, Brown Swiss, Charolais, Romagnola, Chianina, Limousin, Blonde Aquitaine, Belgian Blue, Piedmontese, Angus, Hereford, Poll, Shorthorn, Galloway, Murray Gray, Devon. Cattle may interbreed with other closely related species. Hybrid individuals exist between some other members of the genus *Bos* (Yak, Banteng, Gaur and Bison). However, cattle cannot successfully be hybridized with more distantly related Bovids such as Water Buffalo or African Buffalo.

REPRODUCTION *Gestation*: 280 days. *Young per Birth*: 1. *Weaning*: 6 months. *Sexual Maturity*: 10-12 months (♀). 9-15 months (♂). *Life Span*: 20 years. In natural settings polygyny is observed, with dominant ♂ competing for chances to breed with available ♀. Mating may occur year-round, though more calves are born in spring months. Young are precocial; they learn to recognize their mother and are able to stand and walk soon after birth.

BEHAVIOR *Family Group*: Herds with 20-50 animals. *Diet*: Grasses, stems, and other herbaceous plant material. *Main Predators*: Wolf, lion, human, bear, tiger. Due to the process of domestication it is difficult to describe the natural behavior and ecology. Herds generally comprise ♀ and juveniles, with adult ♂ being separated and used primarily for stud purposes. This system produces a form of unnatural polygyny where access to the available ♂ is restricted, with only certain ♂ being allowed to breed with multiple ♀. This planned manipulation eliminates competition and fighting between ♂ and significantly alters the natural breeding behavior. Herds are structured according to a dominance hierarchy. ♀ are often protective of their young and chase anything that threatens them. ♀ also share parental care within the group. Bulk grazers with a focus on fresh grasses and other succulent vegetation. A herd will feed in a particular area until the preferred or available food sources are depleted, at which time it will move on in search of more vegetation. Cattle are used primarily for dairy products and meat. ♂ are used for pulling large loads or for plowing the soil because of their large size and strength.

DISTRIBUTION Currently found throughout much of the world.

HABITAT Domesticated.

STATUS Domesticated. The Aurochs originally ranged throughout Europe, N Africa, and much of Asia. In historical times, its range became restricted to Europe, and the last known individual died in Masovia, Poland, in about 1627.

PHOTO CREDITS ♂: Toro de Lidia Ibérico, Madrid (Spain). ♀: Raza Avileña-Negra Ibérico, AECRANI (Spain). Head ♀: *Pablo Murod*, Vlasin (Spain).

Sanga Cattle
BOS TAURUS VAR. AFRICANUS

BL: 150-250 cm. SH: 100-185 cm. W: 540-730 kg (♂), 430-540 kg (♀). HL: 20-100 cm. Due to the amount of variation present among breeds, specific morphological characteristics must be presented as approximations. Usually medium sized, with a cervico-thoracic hump, smaller than in Zebu. Body covered in short hair, the color of which varies from dark red to black, with a wide range of colors and patterns. Horns may be disproportionately large in both girth and length in some breeds. Relatively short neck and long face, with straight intercornual ridges, and a flat forehead. Long legs. Spreading horns, found in both sexes, oval in cross section, crescent shaped and thicker in males, lyre shaped in females. Males larger than females.

♂

Young

♀

Juvenile

Bos taurus

OTHER NAMES *French*: Vache. *German*: Hausrind, Rind, Buckelrind. *Spanish*: Res, vaca (♀), toro (♂). *Russian*: Африканский домашний скот (Ватусси).

SUBSPECIES Cattle are usually identified as three separate species: *B. taurus* (Taurine cattle), *B. indicus* (Zebu), and the extinct *B. primigenius* (Aurochs), which is ancestral to both Taurine cattle and Zebu. Some authors group the three as one species: *B. primigenius*, with *B. p. taurus*, *B. p. indicus,* and *B. p. primigenius* as the subspecies. *B. taurus* may be further subdivided into: European Cattle (*taurus* group) and Sanga Cattle (*africanus* group). Sanga cattle may have evolved from crosses between *B. indicus* and humpless Hamitic Longhorn and Shorthorn cattle in central and E Africa around 1600 BC. Breeds of Sanga Cattle include: Abigar, Afrikander (South Africa), Ankole-Watusi (Uganda, Rwanda, Burundi, Tanzania, DR Congo), Bonsmara (South Africa), Nguni (South Africa and Zambia), Red Fulani, Bapedi (Lesotho), Tuli, Nkone and Mashona (Zimbabwe), Landim (Mozambique), Sanga (Namibia), Tswana (Botswana).

REPRODUCTION *Gestation*: 274-308 days. *Young per Birth*: 1. *Weaning*: 6 months. *Sexual Maturity*: 10-12 months (♀). 9-15 months (♂). *Life Span*: 25 years. In natural settings polygyny is observed, with dominant ♂ competing for chances to breed with available ♀. Mating may occur year-round. Young are especially alert and are capable of running along with their mothers and the herd within a short time.

BEHAVIOR *Family Group*: Herds with 20-40 animals. *Diet*: Non-selective grazers and selective browsers. *Main Predators:* Lion, hyena. Sanga Cattle are able to utilize poor quality forage and limited quantities of food and water, being fully adapted to the region's climatic conditions. Their horns, which are hollow and extremely lightweight, disperse heat. These survival abilities have allowed them to not only survive in Africa but to become established in Europe, South America, Australia, and North America. Diurnal and highly social, much preferring to stay in a group for company and protection. At night they tend to form a circle with adults lying on the outside, horns out to protect the calves located in the inner circle. The calves will hang in groups; by day, always in close proximity to at least one adult, and when frightened will instinctively run in front of the horns of a retreating mother or under her belly for protection. Some animals may be quite aggressive and are known to charge strangers. Dominant animals within the herd will also charge other ♀, although they will more often just push the subordinate animals out of the way with their horns. Sanga Cattle have played a pivotal role in the lives of various African tribes, providing food, currency, and tribal status. Those animals with the largest and longest horns belonged to the king and were considered sacred.

DISTRIBUTION Originally, Nile Valley, Sudan, Egypt (Abyssinia, toward the upper Nile and Lake Chad). Currently found throughout much of the world.

HABITAT Domesticated. Savannas and open grasslands.

STATUS Domesticated. Thanks to the efforts of private breeders, zoos, and associations, this animal is no longer endangered.

PHOTO CREDITS ♂: *Patrick Braz*, La Barben Zoo (France). ♀: *Zoom Erlebniswelt* (Germany). Head ♂: *Cindi Darling*, Liar's Lake (USA). Juvenile: *Terri Wells*, Safari Wilderness Ranch (USA).

Zebu
BOS INDICUS

BL: 150-250 cm. SH: 86-106 cm. W: 150-200 kg. HL: 20-100 cm. Smaller than Taurine cattle, with a narrow body, a sloping rump, and rather long legs. Characteristic fatty hump over the shoulder, larger in males. Size and shape of the hump vary by breed and age of the animal. Drooping ears. Large dewlap, particularly in males. Abdominal skin fold. Thin tail, ending in a tuft. Males slightly larger than females. Body covered in short hair, the color of which varies from black to white, reddish brown, and brown. Horns in both sexes, more marked in males, although polled varieties exist.

♀

♂

Young

644

Bos indicus

OTHER NAMES Humped Cattle, Brahman Cattle, Indicus Cattle. *French*: Zébu. *German*: Buckelrind, Zebu. *Spanish*: Cebú. *Russian*: Зебу.

SUBSPECIES Sometimes classified within the species *B. primigenius*, together with Taurine cattle (*B. p. taurus*) and the ancestor of both of them, the extinct Aurochs (*B. p. primigenius*). European Cattle are descended from the Eurasian subspecies, while Zebu are descended from the Indian subspecies. Major Zebu cattle breeds include: Gir, Guzerat, Kankrej, Indo-Brazilian, Brahman, Nelore, Ongole, Sahiwal, Red Sindhi, Butana, Kenana, Boran, Baggara, Tharparkar, Kangayam, Chinese Southern Yellow, Philippine native, Kedah-Kelantan, and local Indian Dairy. Zebu may interbreed with other members of the genus *Bos*: European cattle, Yak (dzo, yattle), Banteng, and Gaur, but it cannot successfully be hybridized with more distantly related Bovid such as Water Buffalo or African Buffalo.

REPRODUCTION *Gestation*: 295 days. *Young per Birth*: 1. *Weaning*: 6 months. *Sexual Maturity*: 6-24 months (♀). 16-17 months (♂). *Life Span*: 16 years. Zebu cattle are known to be less fertile and have lower levels of milk production than Taurine cattle. Cows need to be stimulated by the presence of the calf for milk letdown. Although *B. indicus* breeds have a long gestation period, they are able to limit the birth weights of their calves, so they have practically no calving difficulties.

BEHAVIOR *Family Group*: Herds with 20-40 animals. *Diet*: Grass, seeds, flowers. *Main Predators*: Human, bear, wildcats. Due to the manageable size of the Zebu, and its ability to cope with tropical climates, it has been domesticated in both its native home in S Asia, and in Africa as the Zebu is predominantly used for lighter agricultural work. It also has its own particular behavior, being an affectionate animal. The Zebu is also farmed for meat in some areas and it is considered to be holy in India, where it is thought to have originated. Compared to Taurine cattle, Zebu herds show a high degree of social structure, and are based on matriarchal families interconnected by means of friendship and relationships between non-kin partners. In pastures, they tend to herd together in a very gregarious manner. Their bellowing call is very characteristic and distinct from that of *B. taurus*.

DISTRIBUTION There are thought to be nearly 4 million Zebu in farms around the world, with the highest number of these being found in India, Brazil, and the United States. The wild Zebu can still be found in small herds in S Asia.

HABITAT Domesticated. Tropical jungles and open plains.

STATUS Domesticated.

PHOTO CREDITS ♂: Based of photos from India. ♀: *Jean Marconi* (Brazil). Head ♀: *Katoosha* (India).

Kouprey

BOS SAUVELI

BL: 210-220 cm. SH: 170-190 cm. TL: 100-110 cm. W: 700-900 kg. HL: Up to 80 cm (♂), up to 40 cm (♀). Lighter in build than adult Gaurs or Bantengs. Tall, but narrow, body, long legs, and humped backs. Males gray to black pelage depending on their age, with grayish sides and white socks. Adult males have a pronounced dewlap growing 40 cm, which may touch the ground. Notched nostrils. Long tail. Horns found in both sexes; lyre shaped in females. The wide-spreading horns in males arch forward and upward in such a way that there is a splintered fringe of horn that cannot be rubbed off. Females grayish brown, with less marked socks but also a dark stripe on their forelegs. Calves distinctly reddish in color, turning gray when about 4-5 months old.

Bos sauveli

OTHER NAMES Southeast Asian Wild Ox, Gray Ox, Indochinese Forest Ox, Cambodian Forest Ox. *French*: Kouprey, boeuf gris Cambodgien. *German*: Kouprey. *Spanish*: Kuprey, toro cuprey. *Russian*: Купрей.

SUBSPECIES No subspecies are recognized. Considered as a hybrid between the Banteng (*B. javanicus*) and the Zebu (*B. indicus*) by some authors.

SIMILAR SPECIES Similar to Gaur and Banteng, but they have a very long dewlap hanging from the neck, reaching almost to the ground in old ♂, and horns are distinctly different. In ♂, horns have cores which are closer together, forming a convex curve for the basal half of the horns, dropping below the base, then rising upward and forward, extending slightly above the head with splitting at the tips. Horns in the ♀ are lyre shaped, corkscrewing upward, the tips are never shredded, and the cores are thinner and farther apart than in the ♂.

REPRODUCTION *Gestation*: 270 days. *Young per Birth*: 1. *Life Span*: 20 years. Mating takes place in April, with the births occurring from December to February. Mothers leave the herd to give birth, rejoining about 1 month after the calf is born.

BEHAVIOR *Family Group*: Small herds, primarily of ♀ and calves, of up to 20 animals, which commonly associate with Banteng. *Diet*: Grasses, sedges, and some browse. Very little is known about this rare species of cattle. Said to have become nocturnal to avoid contact with humans, the Kouprey moves into the depths of the forest during the day, emerging at night into nearby grassland to graze. Very active, traveling long distances, up to 15 km every night. While traveling, they often double back and wander to graze. During the dry season's hot days they rest in the dense forest, while during the rainy season this habit is reduced due to flies. In the early afternoon, herds bed down in tight circles, becoming active during the late afternoon. Herds divide and regroup constantly, often mixing with Banteng and feral Water Buffalo. They regularly use salt licks and water holes. Seasonal migration patterns have not been thoroughly studied, but there are indications that herds move to higher elevations during the rainy season. During the dry season, the sexes mix in herds of up to 20 animals.

DISTRIBUTION Cambodia, S Laos, SE Thailand, and W Vietnam. However, due to significant declines, this species is now thought to be possibly extinct.

HABITAT Open deciduous dipterocarp forests, especially those areas with extensive grasslands.

STATUS Critically Endangered (Possibly Extinct). The total population is unknown, and the species is most likely extinct. At most, there could only be a few individuals remaining, certainly many fewer than 250 mature individuals, and almost certainly fewer than 50 mature individuals.

PHOTO CREDITS Illustration by *José R. Castelló*.

Saola

PSEUDORYX NGHETINHENSIS

BL: 143-150 cm. SH: 84-95 cm. TL: 25 cm. W: 70-100 kg. HL: 35-55 cm. Medium-sized animal, with antelope-like appearance. Short coat dark brown in color, lighter on the neck and undersides, with a narrow black stripe which runs down the spine from the shoulders to the tail. Darker legs, with white dots just above the hooves. Face with white markings, including a stripe above each eye, resembling an eyebrow, and a variable pattern of spots and stripes on the cheeks beneath the eye. Chin and lips also white. White band crosses the rump, continuing onto the short tail, where it creates 3 distinct regions of color: brown at the base, a white strip, and then ending with a black tassel. Relatively long and heavy neck. Preorbital glands are very large and well developed. Slightly curved, black horns, found in both sexes, round in cross section, and usually smooth along their length.

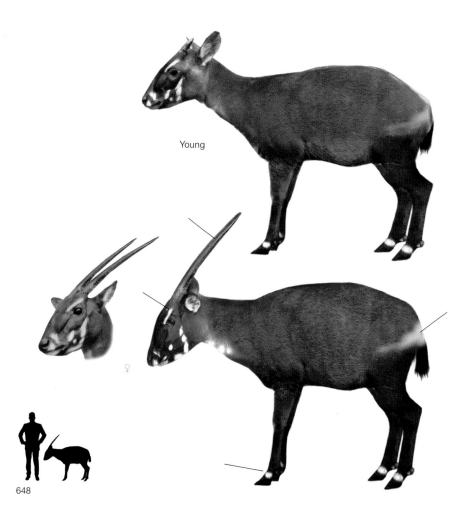

Young

♀

Pseudoryx nghetinhensis

OTHER NAMES Vu Quang Ox. *French*: Saola. *German:* Saola. *Spanish*: Saola. *Russian*: Саола. *Local names*: Sao la, vu quang-wildrindes, sun duong, yang, saht-supahp, lagiang, a ngao, xoong xor.

SUBSPECIES Monotypic.

SIMILAR SPECIES The Saola is a highly distinctive species: its dark color, bright white facial markings, and long, straight horns make it very unlikely to be confused with any other species.

REPRODUCTION *Gestation*: Estimated at 33 weeks (from similarly sized *Tragelaphus* antelope). *Young per Birth*: 1. *Weaning*: Unknown. *Sexual Maturity*: Unknown. *Life Span*: At least 8-9 years (based on a single animal). It is thought that, in Laos, the Saola breeds seasonally between the end of August and the middle of November. Births tend to occur between mid-April and late June (the very end of the dry season). The timing of the wet and dry seasons is different in Vietnam, so the Saola's breeding season may be different there.

BEHAVIOR *Family Group*: Solitary, sometimes in pairs, usually a mother and her offspring. *Diet*: Small leafy plants, especially fig leaves, and stems along rivers. The animal seems to have a browsing diet, considering its small incisors. *Main Predators*: Probably leopard, tiger, and dhole. Very few Saola have been studied alive, and most of our knowledge comes from observations of a single ♀ in a zoo. The species appears to be most active in the mornings and afternoons. The large facial gland can be opened to deposit scent on objects, which might be used in marking a territory. When threatened, they use their horns as weapons, standing (often in the middle of a stream) with the horns directed at the enemy. Saola are able to groom themselves using their long tongue. The only recorded noise is a soft, short bleat.

DISTRIBUTION *Native*: Vietnam, Laos. This species occurs only in the Annamite Mountains of Vietnam and Laos. Most records are from S of the Song Ca River in Vietnam, although a population to the N has also been found. In Laos, records come from as far W as central Bolikhamxay Province. Suitable habitat is, or was, probably more abundant in Vietnam than in Laos, but Vietnam's much higher human population density has severely reduced both habitat and Saola numbers in the habitat that remains. In Laos there is evidence of occurrence in Bolikhamxay, Khammouan, Savannakhet, and Xekong provinces; it probably also occurs in S Xieng Khouang Province. In Vietnam there is evidence of occurrence in Nghe An, Ha Tinh, Quang Binh, Quang Tri, Thua-Thien Hue, and Quang Nam provinces. It is suspected to occur in fewer than 15 forest blocks in the two countries.

HABITAT Broad-leaved rainforests. They favor the vicinity of small, deeply shaded streams.

STATUS Critically Endangered. Probably no more than a few hundred Saola remain, and possibly as few as a few tens. The Saola appears to be in grave danger of extinction only a couple of decades after its introduction to western science.

PHOTO CREDITS Based on photos by *William Robichaud, Toon Fey,* and *David Hulse.*

SKULLS OF BOVIDS

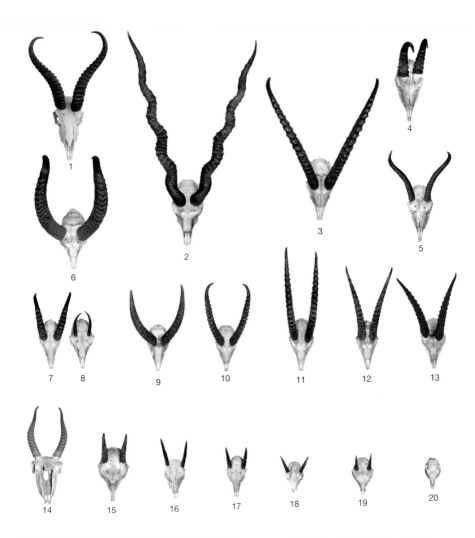

Tribe Antilopini: 1- **South African Springbok** *Antidorcas marsupialis* (231 cm). 2- **Blackbuck** *Antilope cervicapra* (228 cm). 3- **Grant's Gazelle** *Nanger granti* (239 cm). 4- **Dama Gazelle** *Nanger dama* (241 cm). 5- **Soemmerring's Gazelle** *Nanger soemmerringii* (237 cm). 6- **Southern Gerenuk** *Litocranius walleri* (225 cm). 7, 8- **Mountain Gazelle** ♂ ♀ *Gazella gazella* (185 cm). 9- **Goitered Gazelle** *Gazella subgutturosa* (183 cm). 10- **Dorcas Gazelle** *Gazella dorcas* (171 cm). 11- **Thomson's Gazelle** *Eudorcas thomsoni* (191 cm). 12- **Slender-horned Gazelle** *Gazella leptoceros* (194 cm). 13- **Chinkara** *Gazella bennettii* (198 cm). 14- **Saiga** *Saiga tatarica* (229 cm). 15- **Kirk's Dik-dik** *Madoqua kirkii* (208 cm). 16- **Steenbok** *Raphicerus campestris* (142 cm). 17- **Oribi** *Ourebia ourebi* (167 cm). 18- **Sharpe's Grysbok** *Raphicerus sharpei* (127 cm). Tribe Oreotragini: 19- **Klipspringer** *Oreotragus oreotragus* (138 cm). Tribe Neotragini: 20- **Pygmy Antelope** *Neotragus batesi* (121 cm). Photo credits: Atlantic Coral Enterprise, Inc. (1), Phil Myers, animaldiversity.org (2-4, 7-12, 15, 17, 20), Tennants Auctioneers, Ltd. (6, 13), Mikhail (14). To the same scale.

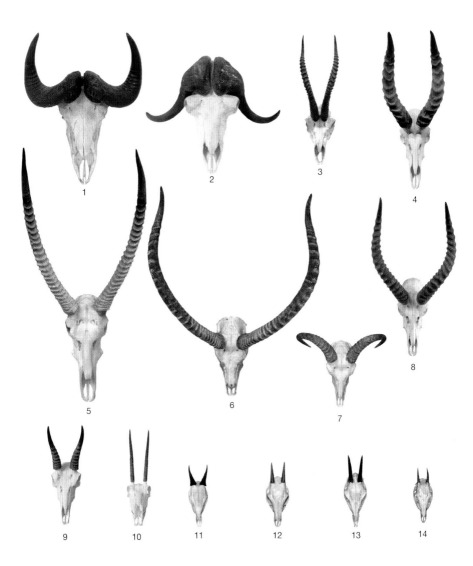

Tribe Caprini: 1- **Takin** *Budorcas taxicolor* (414 cm). 2- **Muskox** *Ovibos moschatus* (441 cm). 3- **Tibetan Antelope** *Pantholops hodgsonii* (191 cm). Tribe Reduncini: 4- **Puku** *Kobus vardonii* (298 cm). 5- **Ellipsen Waterbuck** *Kobus ellipsiprymnus* (394 cm). 6- **Red Lechwe** *Kobus leche* (298 cm). 7- **Southern Reedbuck** *Redunca arundinum* (225 cm). 8- **Kob** *Kobus kob* (291 cm). 9- **Mountain Reedbuck** *Redunca fulvorufula* (225 cm). 10- **Rhebok** *Pelea capreolus* (250 cm). Subfamily Cephalophini: 11- **Natal Red Duiker** *Cephalophus natalensis* (162 cm). 12- **Yellow-backed Duiker** *Cephalophus silvicultor* (175 cm). 13- **Bush Duiker** *Sylvicapra grimmia* (198 cm). 14- **Bay Duiker** *Cephalophus dorsalis* (163 cm). Photo credits: Tennants Auctioneers, Ltd. (1-3), Atlantic Coral Enterprise, Inc. (5), Skulls Unlimited International, Inc. (6, 7), Corepics (8), Blue duiker (9, 10), Phil Myers, animaldiversity.org (12-14). To the same scale.

Tribe Caprini: 1- **East Caucasian Tur** *Capra cylindricornis* (295 cm). 2- **West Caucasian Tur** *Capra caucasica* (294 cm). 3- **Markhor** *Capra falconeri* (285 cm). 4- **Iberian Ibex** *Capra pyrenaica* (233 cm). 5- **Alpine Ibex** *Capra ibex* (240 cm). 6- **Domestic Goat** *Capra hircus* (179 cm). 7- **Nubian Ibex** *Capra nubiana* (251 cm). 8- **Siberian Ibex** *Capra sibirica* (285 cm). 9- **Barbary Sheep** *Ammotragus lervia* (233 cm). Photo credits: Tennants Auctioneers, Ltd. (1, 3, 5, 8), Skulls Unlimited International, Inc. (6), Phil Myers, animaldiversity.org (7). To the same scale.

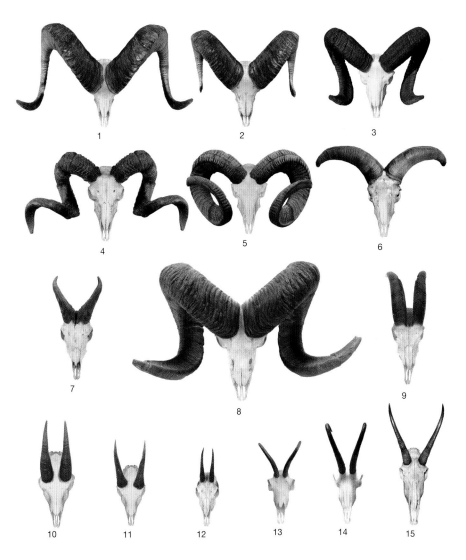

Tribe Caprini: 1- **Dall's Sheep** *Ovis dalli* (256 cm). 2- **Bighorn Sheep** *Ovis canadensis* (255 cm). 3- **European Mouflon** *Ovis aries* var. *musimon* (248 cm). 4- **Domestic Sheep** *Ovis aries* (285 cm). 5- **Transcaspian Urial** *Ovis arkal* (265 cm). 6- **Bharal** *Pseudois nayaur* (258 cm). 7- **Himalayan Tahr** *Hemitragus jemlahicus* (249 cm). 8- **Altai Argali** *Ovis ammon* (347 cm). 9- **Nilgiti Tahr** *Nilgiritragus hylocrius* (279 cm). 10- **Sumatran Serow** *Capicrornis sumatraensis* (294 cm). 11- **Japanese Serow** *Capricornis crispus* (221 cm). 12- **Himalayan Goral** *Nemorhaedus goral* (210 cm). 13- **Pyrenean Chamois** *Rupicapra pyrenaica* (197 cm). 14- **Alpine Chamois** *Rupicapra rupicapra* (212 cm). 15- **Mountain Goat** *Oreamnos americanus* (281 cm). Photo credits: Skulls Unlimited International, Inc. (1, 2, 4), Tennants Auctioneers, Ltd. (7-12), Beentree (3), Roan Serpentia (14), Phil Myers, animaldiversity.org (15). To the same scale.

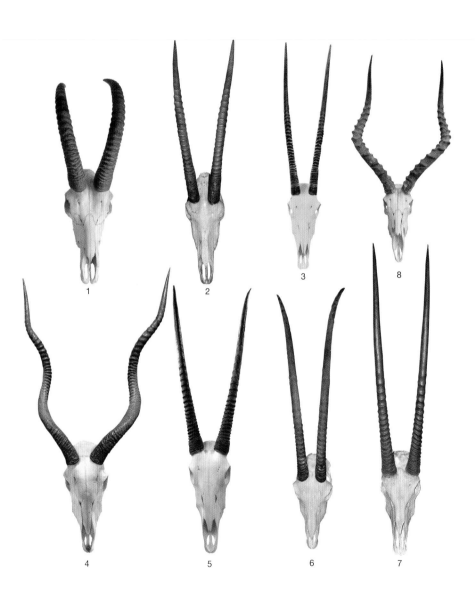

Tribe Hippotragini: 1- **Southern Roan Antelope** *Hippotragus equinus equinus* (435 cm). 2- **Sable Antelope** *Hippotragus niger* (408 cm). 3- **Arabian Oryx** *Oryx leucoryx* (311 cm). 4- **Addax** *Addax nasomaculatus* (420 cm). 5- **Gemsbok** *Oryx gazella* (409 cm). 6- **Scimitar-horned Oryx** *Oryx dammah* (364 cm). 7- **Beisa Oryx** *Oryx beisa* (376 cm). Tribe Aepycerotini: 8- **Common Impala** *Aepyceros melampus* (261 cm). Photo credits: Top Hat Taxidermy (1), Phil Myers, animaldiversity.org (2, 6, 7), Birute Vijeikiene (5). To the same scale.

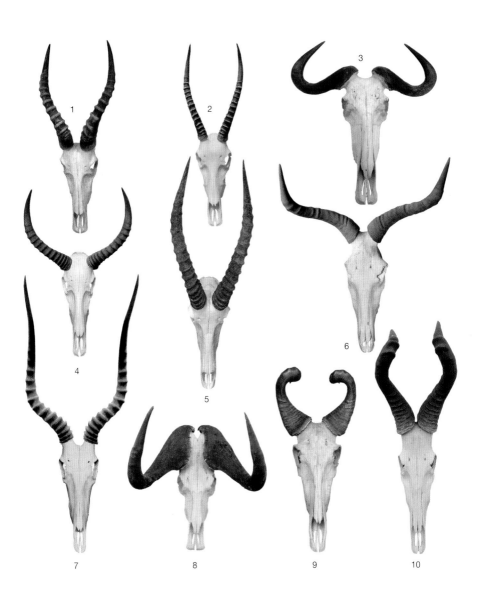

Tribe Alcelaphini: 1- **Bontebok** *Damaliscus pygarus* (313 cm). 2- **Blesbok** ♀ *Damaliscus phillipsi* (311 cm). 3- **Blue Wildebeest** *Connochaetes taurinus* (475 cm). 4- **Tsessebe** *Damaliscus lunatum* (407 cm). 5- **Topi** *Damaliscus jimela* (410 cm). 6- **Swayne's Hartebeest** *Alcelaphus swaynei* (435 cm). 7- **Hirola** *Beatragus hunteri* (468 cm). 8- **Black Wildebeest** *Connochaetes gnou* (410 cm). 9- **Lichtenstein's Hartebeest** *Alcelaphus lichtensteinii* (482 cm). 10- **Red Hartebeest** *Alcelaphus caama* (486 cm). Photo credits: Atlantic Coral Enterprise, Inc. (2, 8, 10), Jeff Banke (3), Skulls Unlimited International, Inc. (5). To the same scale.

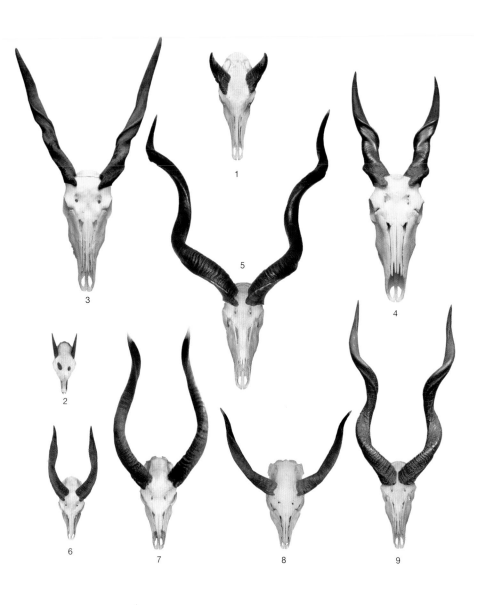

Tribe Boselaphini: 1- **Nilgai** *Boselaphus tragocamelus* (381 cm). 2- **Four-horned Antelope** *Tetracerus quadricornis* (192 cm). Tribe Tragelaphini: 3- **Giant Eland** *Taurotragus derbianus* (470 cm). 4- **Common Eland** *Taurotragus oryx* (490 cm). 5- **Greater Kudu** *Strepsiceros strepsiceros* (400 cm). 6- **Cape Bushbuck** *Tragelaphus sylvaticus* (238 cm). 7- **Lowland Nyala** *Nyala angasii* (300 cm). 8- **Western Sitatunga** *Tragelaphus gratus* (308 cm). 9- **Southern Lesser Kudu** *Ammelaphus australis* (310 cm). Photo credits: Skulls Unlimited International, Inc. (1, 2, 6), Atlantic Coral Enterprise, Inc. (3), Top Hat Taxidermy (4), Tennants Auctioneers, Ltd. (5). To the same scale.

Tribe Bovini: 1- **Indian Gaur** *Bos gaurus gaurus* (565 cm). 2- **Indochinese Banteng** *Bos javanicus birmanicus* (510 cm). 3- **Domestic Yak** *Bos grunniens* (593 cm). 4- **American Bison** *Bos bison* (560 cm). 5- **European Bison** *Bos bonasus* (481 cm). Photo credits: Tennants Auctioneers, Ltd. (1, 2), Skulls Unlimited International, Inc. (4). To the same scale.

Tribe Bovini: 1- **Cape Buffalo** *Syncerus caffer* (506 cm). 2- **Forest Buffalo** *Syncerus nanus* (451 cm). 3- **Cattle** *Bos taurus* (491 cm). 4- **Tamaraw** *Bubalus mindorensis* (295 cm). 5- **Domestic Swamp Buffalo** *Bubalus bubalis* var. *kerabau* (570 cm). 6- **Lowland Anoa** *Bubalus depressicornis* (305 cm). Photo credits: Tennants Auctioneers, Ltd. (1, 3, 4, 5), Tropenmuseum, Netherlands (6). To the same scale.

REFERENCES

The references listed below have been consulted during the work on this guide. Without them, this work would have been much more difficult and the end result less good. They can all be recommended.

Apps P. 2008. Smither's Mammals of Southern Africa: A Field Guide. 3rd ed. Cape Town, South Africa: Random House Struik.

Apps P. 2014. Wild Ways: Field Companion to the Behaviour of Southern African Mammals. 2nd ed. Cape Town, South Africa: Random House Struik.

Damm G, Franco N. 2014. CIC Caprinae Atlas of the World. Huntington Beach, CA: Safari Press.

Dorst J, Dandelot P. 1988. A Field Guide of Larger Mammals of Africa. Glasgow, UK: William Collins Sons & Co Ltd.

East R and IUCN/SCC Antelope Specialist Group. 1988. Antelopes: Global Survey and Regional Action Plans. Gland, Switzerland: IUCN.

East, R. 1999. African Antelope Database 1999. Gland, Switzerland: IUCN.

Estes RD. 1991. The Behaviour Guide to African Mammals. Including Hoofed Mammals, Carnivores, Primates. Berkeley, CA: University of California Press.

Estes RD. 1999. The Safari Companion: A Guide to Watching African Mammals. White River Junction, VT: Chelsea Green.

Foley C, Foley L, Lobora A, et al. 2014. A Field Guide to the Larger Mammals of Tanzania. Princeton, NJ: Princeton University Press.

Francis CM. 2008. A Field Guide to the Mammals of South-East Africa. London, UK: New Holland Publishers (UK) Ltd.

Frost W. 2014. The Antelope of Africa. Johannesburg, South Africa: Jacana Media (Pty) Ltd.

Gomez W, Patterson T, Swinton J, Berini J. 2011. Bovidae, Animal Diversity Web, ADW (accessed February 2013).

Groves C, Grubb P. 2011. Ungulate Taxonomy. Baltimore: Johns Hopkins University Press.

Haltenorth T, Diller H. 1988. A Field Guide to the Mammals of Africa Including Madagascar. Glasgow, UK: William Collins Sons & Co Ltd.

Hayssen V (Ed.). Mammalian Species. American Society of Mammalogists. Osford, UK: Oxford University Press.

Huffman B. UltimateUngulate.com. http://ultimateungulate.com (accessed August 2014).

Hutchins M, Kleiman DG, Geist V, McDade MC. 2004. Grzimek's Animal Life Encyclopedia, 2nd ed. Volume 16: Mammals V. Farmington Hills, MI: Gale Group.

IUCN. 2012. The IUCN Red List of Threatened Species. 2012.2. http://www.iucnredlist.org (accessed August 2014).

Kays RW, Wilson DE. 2009. Mammals of North America. 2nd ed. Princeton, NJ: Princeton University Press.

Kingdon J. 1982. East African Mammals. Volume IID. An Atlas of Evolution in Africa. Bovids. Chicago: University of Chicago Press.

Kingdom J. 1997. The Kingdom Guide to African Mammals. London, UK: A&C Black Ltd.

Kingdom J, Hoffman M. 2013. Mammals of Africa. Volume VI. London, UK: A&C Black Ltd.

Melleti M, Burton J. 2014. Ecology, Evolution and Behaviour of Wild Cattle: Implications for Conservation. Cambridge: Cambridge University Press.

Menon V. 2014. Indian Mammals: A Field Guide. Gurgaon, India: Hachette.

Mills G, Hes L. 1997. The Complete Book of Southern African Mammals. Cape Town, South Africa: Struik Publishers.

Nowak RM. 1999. Walker's Mammals of the World. 6th ed. Baltimore: Johns Hopkins University Press.

Safari Club International (SCI). Online Record Book. http://www.scirecordbook.org/ (accessed August 2012).

Shackleton DM (Ed.) and the IUCN/SSC Caprinae Specialist Group. 1997. Wild Sheep and Goats and their Relatives. Status Survey and Conservation Action Plan for Caprinae. Gland, Switzerland: IUCN.

Smith AT, Xie Y. 2008. A Guide to the Mammals of China. Princeton, NJ: Princeton University Press.

Stuart T, Stuart C. 2001. Field Guide to Mammals of South Africa. Cape Town, South Africa: Struik Publishers.

Wilson DE, Mittermeier. 2011. Handbook of Mammals of the World. Vol. 2. Hoofed Mammals. Barcelona: Lynx Edicions.

Wilson VJ. 2005. Duikers of Africa: Masters of the African Forest Floor: A Study of Duikers, People, Hunting and Bushmeat. Pretoria, South Africa: Zimbi Books.

Wilson DE, Reeder DM (Eds.). 2005. Mammal Species of the World. A Taxonomic and Geographic Reference. 3rd ed. Baltimore: Johns Hopkins University Press.

INDEX

The index includes the common English and scientific names. Scientific names are in italics.